J. M. Rockingham

Lord Byng

William Dillon Otter

Guy Simonds

Marching as to War

Marching

"The highest Christian conscience in the world today, when at all free from prejudice, most emphatically says that our Empire was not only justified in going to war, but that it was serving the high interests of the nations of the world in so doing."
— *The Christian Guardian, August 4, 1915*

"I could not have forced myself, had I wanted to, to prayer. . . . The idea of God disgusted me as much as the war, and I felt that only a weak-minded person could drag theology into this stark and meaningless room. . . . So, instead of taking God's name into my heart, I took it in vain again and again, silently, though others may have thought me praying."
— *Lieutenant Donald Pearce, under shellfire, Belgium, November 1944*

Pierre Berton

as to War

Canada's Turbulent Years 1899–1953

Doubleday Canada

Doubleday Canada and colophon are trademarks.

Canadian Cataloguing in Publication Data

Berton, Pierre, 1920–
    Marching as to war: Canada's turbulent years, 1899–1953

Includes bibliographical references and index.
ISBN 0-385-25725-2

1. Canada—History—20th Century. 2. South African War, 1899–1902—Canada.
3. World War, 1914–1918—Canada. 4. World War, 1939–1945—Canada.
5. Korean War, 1950-1953—Canada. I. Title.

FC540.B47 2001   971.06   C2001–901034–6
F1034.B46 2001

Jacket image: City of Toronto Archives, SC 266, Item 13157
Jacket design: CS Richardson
Maps: Malcolm Cullen
Illustrations: Tom McNeely
Printed and bound in Canada

Published in Canada by
Doubleday Canada, a division of
Random House of Canada Limited

Visit Random House of Canada Limited's website: www.randomhouse.ca

FRI   10   9   8   7   6   5   4   3   2   1

Maps

Drawn by Malcolm Cullen

Books by Pierre Berton

The Royal Family
The Mysterious North
Klondike
Just Add Water and Stir
Adventures of a Columnist
Fast Fast Fast Relief
The Big Sell
The Comfortable Pew
The Cool, Crazy, Committed World
  of the Sixties
The Smug Minority
The National Dream
The Last Spike
Drifting Home
Hollywood's Canada
My Country
The Dionne Years
The Wild Frontier
The Invasion of Canada
Flames Across the Border
Why We Act Like Canadians
The Promised Land
Vimy
Starting Out
The Arctic Grail
The Great Depression
Niagara: A History of the Falls
My Times: Living With History
1967, The Last Good Year
Marching as to War

PICTURE BOOKS
The New City (with Henri Rossier)
Remember Yesterday
The Great Railway
The Klondike Quest
Pierre Berton's Picture Book
  of Niagara Falls
Winter
The Great Lakes
Seacoasts
Pierre Berton's Canada

ANTHOLOGIES
Great Canadians
Pierre and Janet Berton's
  Canadian Food Guide
Historic Headlines
Farewell to the Twentieth Century
Worth Repeating
Welcome to the Twenty-first Century

FICTION
Masquerade
  (pseudonym Lisa Kroniuk)

BOOKS FOR YOUNG READERS
The Golden Trail
The Secret World of Og
Adventures in Canadian History
  (22 volumes)

Contents

The Uncertain Country

The last war fought on Canadian soil ended in August 1814 when an invading United States army—unpaid, mutinous, diseased, and dispirited—skulked out of Fort Erie and vanished across the Niagara frontier, never to return. For the remainder of the nineteenth century, Canada basked in its reputation as the Peaceable Kingdom: no Crimean adventure for her, no Caribbean crusade, no pitched battles save for a few skirmishes with the Fenians and the Métis.

That untroubled era ended with the Victorian Age, followed by half a century of turbulence—the most remarkable period in our past. Between the autumn of 1899 and the summer of 1953, young Canadians marched away, not once but four times to do battle in far-off fields, in wars that were not of our making. Only in this one period have we devoted nearly 30 percent of our time to war.

Turbulent years, indeed! And not only because of the battles we fought on the African veldt, the ravaged meadows of Flanders, the forbidding spine of Italy, and the conical hills of Korea: turbulent because these were Canada's formative years, when she resembled an adolescent groping with the problems of puberty, often at odds with her parents, craving to be treated as an adult, hungry for the acclaim of her peers, and wary of the dominating presence of a more sophisticated neighbour.

The change was spectacular. In half a century we were transformed from an agricultural nation, where the Masseys became quasi-aristocrats simply by getting rich selling farm machinery, to an industrial economy with a bedrock of natural resources. Canada, one of the least military nations in the West, was forced to cope—always at the last moment— with unexpected conflicts for which she was never properly prepared. In doing so, the nation grew up.

In the long tug of war between the forces of history and geography that marks those years, geography, in the end, won out. When the

1

Boer War broke out on the eve of the new century, we were a vassal state within the British realm, cheerfully rushing to the colours when the imperial trumpets sounded. Over the years the emphasis shifted. When the Korean War began in 1951, we found ourselves giving token support to American troops in what was essentially an American conflict.

In addition to war, two other tremors rattled the foundations of the emerging society. The first was the sudden, almost explosive creation of a new Western empire, stretching from the Shield to the Rockies, that would upset the political balance of power. The second was French Canada's burgeoning nationalism, which emerged at the outset of the South African conflict and reached its apogee in the conscription crises of the two world wars that followed.

As early as 1890, when the new province of Manitoba launched its plan to keep the French language out of its schools, the West had signalled its reluctance to accept the bilingual accord stitched together at Confederation. Thus the country found itself split down the middle— East versus West, French versus English, prairie farmers at odds with central Canadian capitalists. In war, it has been said, we found our maturity. It is equally true that in war we came close to tearing ourselves apart, creating a series of political crises that are still at the root of our national dilemma.

Our love-hate relationship with our neighbour mirrored our own international uncertainty in those early years. What, we asked, is a Canadian, anyway? British? American? French? Free trader? Protectionist? We couldn't be sure. The Great War victories symbolized by a single magical word, *Vimy*, made us cocky. But the wave of cultural nationalism that followed was diluted by a nineteenth-century literary mindset inherited from Mother England. Realism? We scorned the hard-boiled Yankee style. Four years of wartime propaganda had conditioned us to swallow the most preposterous lies and the most audacious masquerades. The Great War had helped transform the Age of Faith into the Age of Gullibility.

A giddy optimism pervaded those roller-coaster years of boom and bust, war and peace, dogma and doubt. In the days of the Last Best West,

Wilfrid Laurier claimed that the new century belonged to Canada and predicted five transcontinental railways and a population of 100 million people by the millennium. The Great War shattered the dreams of the railway builders. A generation later the Great Depression burst the bubble of the dizzy twenties. Ironically, it took a new war to get us out of the slump.

Peace at any price? That was the cautious view of the Depression politicians, alarmed at the appalling bloodletting of 1914–18 and also at the cost of a military buildup, not just in dollars but also in "national unity," the all-Canadian buzzword. To its shame, the Canadian government opted for appeasement at the very moment when its own man at the League of Nations was calling for tougher sanctions on the international bullies. Thus a new war—a sequel to the old one—became inevitable.

There is a paradox here. Canada has entered each of its four wars with hesitation and reluctance. We have produced only one first-rate general—Arthur Currie—and treated him shabbily. Yet at the outset of each conflict, Canadians have enlisted in astonishing numbers, drawn as much by the enthusiasm of youth as by a sense of duty. On each occasion our military leaders and politicians have misjudged the dimensions of the conflict. *Home by Christmas!* Young men eager to see action before the war's end have believed that flawed forecast. And Canadians, with their allies, have trusted the judgment of certain charismatic generals—Haig, McNaughton, Mountbatten, Montgomery, MacArthur—who let their own hubris cloud their vision with disastrous results.

Save for a few months at the ends of the two major wars, Canada's effort has been voluntary, making this country something of an international oddball. We have always started from scratch, unprepared, unoutfitted, and largely untrained. The miracle is that we have managed to turn a tiny peacetime army into a massive fighting force, far larger than could have been imagined when the first shots were fired. We sent green soldiers into battle and learned that, trained or not, Canadians will always fight fiercely and with courage.

Were these wars necessary? In three cases the answer is unequivocal:

certainly not! In 1900, Henri Bourassa was right. Why were we risking Canadian lives to support the ambitions of an empire determined to impose its will on a peaceful community of Dutch farmers? Why did we cross the ocean again, in the face of opposition from one-third of our people, to sacrifice our youth in an ill-considered war that solved nothing and led only to another? Why, again, did we ship our youth to the Orient to help the new American empire support a corrupt Korean regime?

One answer is that the majority of Canadians, encouraged by most of the press, clearly wanted Canada to take part. In all these cases, the Canadian government, from Laurier to St. Laurent, was reluctant to become involved but had to follow the will of the people and, equally important, bend to insistent international pressure. In the two world wars, Canada, the leading British dominion, could not shirk what was considered her duty. In the second, the Global War, she had no choice; nor was it necessary to demonize the enemy in order to create a popular cause. The enemy had demonized itself. And the slogans of one war made sense in its sequel.

In 1936, when the peace movement was at its height, I was assigned, with the other students in my high school class, to write an essay on war. It was assumed that we would all denounce the concept as disastrous, demeaning, wasteful, and immoral—a crime against humanity. I chose, instead, to be the odd man out and produced a trenchant defence of war as nature's method of slowing down what would later be called the population explosion. I didn't believe a word of it, of course, but I refused to run with the pack and write the usual clichés.

My English teacher was appalled. Caught up in the anti-war sentiment of those days, he wrote some scorching comments in my essay's margin and gave me an unflattering B minus. I was irked, not because he disagreed with my views, but because his disgust had apparently kept him from noting what I considered to be the high quality of my prose.

In trying to be different for the sake of being different, I had ignored a better solution. It would have been more effective to describe how the Great War had transformed my country (as an even greater war was about to transform it again). The evidence was there. The war had ended

4

the old Age of Faith and begun the slow, persistent decline of the established churches. A *just* war? A new generation had refused to accept that piece of pious hypocrisy from priests and pastors who ought to have known better.

I might also have written that the war had eroded the puritan ethic of the nineteenth century. After all, in my childhood the signs were all around me. My mother had bobbed her hair in 1925 and raised her skirts above the knee; my father had taken to serving something called a cocktail (gin and Mission Orange) to American guests at our summer picnics on the Yukon River. A gossipy peeping Tom of my acquaintance had actually seen Alice Samuelson, a member of the young set, with a cigarette in her mouth! My elders had traded in the two-step for the foxtrot, and I would always remember them capering about to the louder, faster music of groaning saxophones.

Another by-product of war, obvious even to a sixteen-year-old, was the emerging attitude to women. There was great irony here. In the old Age of Faith, Canadian women had fought for the right to vote because they were convinced that Christian temperance could be achieved only through political power. That continued to elude them until the echoes of distant cannons caused them to drop their politicking and rally round the flag. This tactic they accomplished with such energy that a grateful government gave them the vote as a kind of consolation prize for their efforts. It was, in a sense, a pyrrhic victory, for having achieved their goal of total prohibition, they discovered that the war itself had made the temperance movement obsolescent as a later war would make it obsolete.

The wars of the first half of the century have been all of a piece. In one way or another, each has led us to the next, and each has altered and transformed the nation. In my youth, with two wars in our immediate past and two more in our future, I could not write sensibly about war. Now, after fifty years of peace, it is possible to look back on those turbulent years and contemplate times of high courage and consummate folly when three generations of young Canadians were called upon to sacrifice themselves for their country. We can only pray that we have learned from that history and that we will never see its like again.

Kathleen "Kit" Coleman

The Age of Faith

Sunday, December 31, 1899. The New Year crept across the country as softly as a cat burglar and without the traditional bells and penny-whistles. The only bells that sounded were those that pealed from the steeples of the nation, for this New Year's Eve was also the Lord's Day, a pious pause in the week's worldly pursuits, inappropriate for high revels.

Was it really the last day of the old century? People argued, as they would one hundred years later about the date that would begin the new millennium. In those days the army had the deciding voice, for it had decreed that its military bands would not officially greet the new century until 1901, and in that fevered time the army was heeded. After all, there was a war on—the last of those colonial skirmishes in which the soldiers of the Queen did battle with the heathen of the Upper Nile or the hill tribes of India. But this was no skirmish; this was a bloody, bitter conflict in which white Christians fought other white Christians in the Transvaal and the Orange Free State of South Africa. "BOERS COMPLETELY ROUTED" was the Toronto *Evening Star*'s main headline that January 1. It was one of a number of enthusiastic but misleading newspaper banners that suggested all was going well on the veldt.

This foolish little war, fought for no reason other than national pride (as, indeed, most wars are), presaged a turbulent future. It would widen the cultural and language gap that was both the glory and the curse of the young dominion. Subsequent wars would increase it further. In the decade to come, the shrill arguments over free trade with the Americans would throw into sharp relief the opposing aspirations of the agricultural West and the industrial East. Meanwhile, the New Imperialism threatened to stifle the frail young flower of nationalism. Later, when nationalism flourished it would face an opposite threat: aggressive continentalism. As every prime minister was to discover, Canada's unique structure and its equally unique past made it a difficult, almost impossible nation to govern.

The new war, scarcely two months old and going very badly, marked the beginning of the end of an age in which people clung fiercely to the status quo and to the faith of their fathers, standards that two world wars would denature. In those credulous days, Canadians were a community of believers. They believed in the sanctity of the British Empire as they believed in the sanctity of the Lord's Day. The fat old queen ("the Widow at Windsor," Kipling had called her) still sat on the throne that she seemed to have occupied forever. Her people had long since forgotten the days when, reclusive and distant, she had been booed at Ascot. Now she was worshipped as a minor deity by her Canadian subjects, who saw in her the embodiment of Empire and the protector of those eternal verities they were loath to discard. They worshipped the Old Flag, on which the sun never set; they idolized the Land of Hope and Glory and prayed that God might make her mightier yet; they even made obeisance to that motley clique of blue-blooded twits in the upper tiers of the British class system who occupied positions of privilege.

The masses, upper and lower, harboured some bizarre beliefs. The telegraph and telephone were transforming the world, but many Canadians still clung to the fancy that spirits of the dead could be invoked by a kind of ghostly Morse code known as table rapping—clung to it even though the two adolescents who started the craze finally revealed that it was a fraud accomplished by cracking their double-jointed toes (a revelation that eluded the new deputy minister of labour, William Lyon Mackenzie King).

They believed in the wonders of science, including phrenology, the newest "science" of all, which had all the allure that Freudian analysis would enjoy a generation later. Even the medical world accepted, seemingly without reservation, the notion the bumps on one's head could reveal a person's inner qualities. No fewer than forty-two magazines dealt with the subject, and in Toronto alone nine practising phrenologists made a good living pawing people's craniums. Everybody, it seemed, wanted to have his or her head read (the phrase is still in use in a derisive context), and that included three British prime ministers, Queen Victoria's offspring, and the young Winston Churchill, whose stirring exploits reported from South Africa would soon transform a nasty conflict into a panorama of high adventure—a sporting event straight out of a dime novel.

The people believed in war as they believed in the Bible. War was seen as an extension of politics, a necessary tool in the advancement of civilization, a contest in which a few broken bones were forfeited in the interests of a higher cause. Every war in which the "Greatest Empire in the World" had ever been involved was considered to be a "just" war. That was the message broadcast from the Protestant pulpits in a country where religion was all pervasive. In Quebec the Catholics trooped to mass on Sunday morning, and apparently that was enough. But for any other young Canadian, fidgeting in the hard pews of the local church, Sunday was a day of endless prayer.

And not only Sunday: in well-to-do homes, such as that of Chester Massey, the Toronto implements manufacturer, the family prayed every day after breakfast and before work. The entire household attended as the ailing patriarch read passages from the family Bible, followed by prayers he had composed himself. His son Raymond remembered one phrase that kept recurring: "Make bare thine arms throughout all earth," which, as the future actor remarked, was the same as asking God to roll up his sleeves and do something.

A certain class of Canadians seemed to spend as much time on their knees as they did at their meals. On the Lord's Day, worship began as soon as they had rubbed the sleep from their eyes and continued, virtually non-stop, until they tumbled into bed with a final prayer on their lips. Hugh Keenleyside, a future diplomat raised in Vancouver, wrote that by nine o'clock on Sunday night, he had, between worship and Sunday School, walked his sixth church mile and returned from the fourth service of the day—and there was still more worship ahead before he laid him down to sleep.

How distant it all seems, this peaceful era when mothers did not need to fear that their sons would be taken from them by the call of war, and

Canadians talked aloud to their Maker and cheerfully contemplated the idea of a real Heaven. Chester Massey, who could not read without suffering severe headaches, apparently thought of the hereafter as a gigantic library. "When I go to Heaven," his son Vincent remembered his saying in a perfectly matter-of-fact tone, "I expect to spend the first thousand years reading."

In this typical well-to-do Methodist merchant family, there was little frivolity on the Lord's Day. Vincent was forbidden to ride his bicycle down Jarvis Street, nor could his cousin Dorothy put so much as a roll of Brahms on the self-playing organ. For these young people, dancing was evil and the stage a hotbed of sin. Vincent's patriarchal grandfather, Hart, never entered a theatre in his life, even to see a performance of Shakespeare.

Words—proclaimed from the stage or pulpit or published between hard covers—were the chief form of entertainment in those puritan days. It was a poor politician who could not talk on his feet non-stop for at least three hours in the Commons. It was an indifferent elocutionist who could not hold an audience in his palm for the same length of time. In the coming century a variety of visual diversions would diminish the power of words. But there was a time when a Canadian novel—*Beautiful Joe*, about a pet dog, of all things!—would sell 900,000 copies.

Something was stirring in Canada; suddenly there was a flourishing market for homegrown books. Between 1896 and 1911, a dozen new publishing houses opened in Toronto. In the words of Lorne Pierce, a long-time editor of the Ryerson Press (until 1919 the Methodist Book Room), "We were at the beginning of things as a nation." The whole country, Pierce recalled, "seemed outward bound, conscious of its emerging identity, and conscious also of its ability to speak for itself."

In those days, Canadian authors felt no need to conceal their heritage or Americanize their work. A Canadian setting was often an asset. The Klondike stampede, the Hudson's Bay Company, the opening of the New Northwest, and the Mounted Police—all these gave Canada a kind of glamour similar to that associated with Kipling's India. For foreign readers, even Canadian small towns and counties—Stephen Leacock's Mariposa, L.M. Montgomery's Cavendish, Ralph Connor's Glengarry—had a far-off, exotic flavour.

People devoured books hungrily. Nellie McClung's *Sowing Seeds in Danny*, based on her pioneer childhood in the West, sold 100,000 copies. Her next novel (she published sixteen in all) sold half as many again. Rarely afterwards would Canadian publishers enjoy such sales. Connor's first three novels sold a total of 5 million copies, after which his publishers never launched a Connor novel with a printing of fewer than 200,000.

Like so many other pious Canadians, these two literary icons would have their certitudes badly shaken by the coming world conflict. McClung, the fervent pacifist, would abandon her convictions once her son joined the fray. Connor—the Reverend Charles Gordon—would, as an army chaplain, modify his stringent temperance views when he realized that a daily ration of demon rum was essential to stiffen a man's resolve when he went over the top. The nation was on the cusp of change and the wars that followed would accelerate that change.

The old puritanism that damned Ontario's capital with the epithet "Toronto the Good" was grudgingly giving way to headier days as the nineteenth century faded and people began to glimpse the promise of a new era. For *new* was the magic word. The New Northwest was wide open for settlement. The New Imperialism was causing British hearts to beat faster. And the New Woman was making her appearance in the periodicals of the day. Change was in the air, but few Canadians contemplated the possibility of any future war. For more than eight decades the country had basked in an unparalleled period of peace. Not so the United States, whose own civil war had been among the goriest in history, and whose 1898 battle with Spain, stimulated by the Hearst press, was the product of another imperialism, one that happily did not involve Canada. But bloody or not, it still had an aura of glamour about it—enough to stop the Klondike stampede cold that spring as thousands of would-be gold seekers abandoned the chilly slopes of the

Chilkoot and rushed south to the new adventure. The spectacle of Theodore Roosevelt, leading his dauntless Rough Riders up the flanks of San Juan Hill to aid the embattled Cubans in their drive for independence, created an impression so indelible that it helped him in his subsequent quest for the White House.

Canada's contribution to the Spanish-American War was journalistic in the form of the redoubtable Kit Watkins (later Coleman) of the Toronto *Mail and Empire*, a New Woman, in the parlance of the time, and the most popular columnist in the country. Having covered most major international events, from the Chicago World's Fair of 1893 to Queen Victoria's Diamond Jubilee in 1897, she was determined to be in on the action. No woman had ever been accredited as a war correspondent, but Kit was unfazed. In Washington she buttonholed the secretary of war, General Russell Alger, who found her as fetching as she was determined. There was something about Kit that caused men to melt. She was so popular that after her second husband died, she received five proposals of marriage. She dressed dowdily, in the newsroom fashion, but she wore her auburn hair piled attractively high, and when she flashed her sherry-coloured eyes, men were captivated. She pestered Alger for days until he relented and hastily scribbled her credentials on the back of a telegraph form.

In Tampa, Florida, the army commander, General William Rufus Shafter, wouldn't let her sail for Cuba with the other correspondents. Off went wires to Washington, Ottawa, and Toronto. "I'm going through to Cuba," she told her readers, "and not all the old generals in the old army are going to stop me. I beat them in Washington and I'm going to beat them here." While she waited and fidgeted, the first wounded arrived at Key West and she scooped the other reporters who were still imprisoned aboard ship. Finally she wangled passage to Cuba on an old government boat and became one of the few correspondents to witness the surrender of the Spanish army to the Americans.

The *Mail and Empire* was unstinting in its coverage of Kit's adventures. After all, she was the only woman in a corps of 125 war correspondents. "KIT VISITS THE CAMP OF TEDDY'S TERRORS," the headlines screamed. "HOW KIT MOUNTED ON A MULE OF HIGH DEGREE, INSPECTED THE TROOPS."

Her exploits made "the intrepid lady from Toronto" (as one of her colleagues called her) internationally famous. But her own experiences affected her. She had earlier reported that green kids were being shipped to the war zone without proper training. On the transport ship returning to Florida, where wounded men lay moaning in rows on deck, without doctors or medicine, she tended them herself, sharing her own allotment of quinine with the malaria-ridden soldiers.

Back in the United States, General Alger, who had at first laughed at her request for accreditation, now wanted to sponsor her on a speaking tour of the country to tell American women about the war. She gave him a blunt answer that suggests the extent of her disillusionment. "Mr. Alger," she retorted hotly, "if I tell the women of the United States what I have seen, you'll have a riot on your hands." Having rejected further international publicity, Kit returned home, married the most patient of her several suitors (Dr. Theodore Coleman), and continued to turn out her hugely popular "Women's Kingdom" page in the *Mail and Empire*.

She did so as the country entered a period of unalloyed optimism. In little more than a decade Canada would lure a million immigrants to the empty prairies. Thus would be created a nation within a nation, an ebullient realm to act as a counterbalance to the stodgy, long-settled East.

A few popular songs of the day have lingered on to illuminate the era. Scott Joplin's "Maple Leaf Rag" reminds us that bordellos were active enough and competitive enough to have piano players; "My Wild Irish Rose" celebrates the twin immigration booms that brought the Catholic Irish to the United States and the Orangemen to Canada; "Hello! My Baby" is one of several Tin Pan Alley hits that help us to recall how newfangled the telephone was ("Send me a kiss by wire . . .").

We hear the music and sense the nostalgic attraction for the "good old days." The old songs and the yellowing photographs hint at a peaceful time—an era in which 95 percent of the population lived in single-family dwellings and the isolation of apartment existence was unknown.

We think of tree-shaded streets and mansions with big verandahs because few photographers bothered to point their bulky cameras at the wretched shacks of Montreal's lower town, where the population reached 300 an acre, where the air was redolent with the stench of 5,000 open-pit privies, and where one-quarter of all babies born did not live out their first year.

This was the age of the horse. At the annual Dominion Day parade in Queen's Park, Toronto, every kind of horse was on display, from heavy draft horses to cavalry steeds, from carriage pairs to fire department gallopers. Although Thomas Edison had predicted that "the horse is doomed," most people regarded the horseless carriage as a costly and unreliable nuisance. "Bicycles and automobiles are a fad," declared the *Bookman* magazine of New York. ". . . [They] will soon disappear, but the love of the horse will never die out of the human heart."

In 1900 only one gasoline-driven automobile—owned by Walter Massey, the most progressive member of that puritanical family—chugged down the leafy avenues of Toronto. Walter's nephew Raymond would remember his mother "sitting in a buggy which had small wheels and rubber tires. I am in her lap. There is a sort of box with a handle or crank coming out of it. Uncle Walter is throwing a rod that goes through the floor of the buggy. He too is sitting on the buggy seat. There is no horse!

". . . I remembered a man turning the crank. There is a lot of noise and the buggy is jerking forward by itself. Uncle Walter is cheering as he steers the buggy. My mother is laughing and cheering, too. There is a terrific bang. The buggy stops. . . ."

The terrific bang that startled young Raymond (who bravely copied his mother's laughter) presaged a future world in which not just change but the *acceleration* of change was to become the norm. But then new-fangled devices were still regarded with suspicion. The typewriter was acceptable for business correspondence, but the well-bred still wrote their personal letters by hand; anything mechanically produced might be considered insulting. The machine gun and the breech-loading rifle had already been developed, but, as a future war would demonstrate, the army commanders still thought in terms of the lance, sabre, and musket, and, of course, the horse. Yet the time was not far distant when the term "warhorse" would be an anachronism and that staple of nineteenth-century adventure fiction, the cavalry charge, would be as obsolete as those red-tabbed commanders who strove, stubbornly, to retain it. The best they could do was to cling to the nostalgia by inventing a new form of cavalry—the armoured brigade—that would retain some of the traditions of old.

Ingrained concepts were not easily rejected. *Outing* magazine was one of several publications that pooh-poohed the horseless carriage because "it needs a good hard road" at a cost of $4,000 a mile. That, the magazine claimed, would be prohibitive. In 1897, Canada's largest city, Montreal, had 3,000 horse stables and 500 cattle barns—but only 20 of its 178 miles of streets were paved. On these narrow lanes of cobbles and wooden blocks, stinking of fresh horse manure, women in long, voluminous dresses gingerly made their way, hoisting their skirts above the ordure, allowing the gawkers a surreptitious glance at what was then known as "a well-turned ankle," the accepted sexual symbol of the day.

As for women's legs, the word was taboo, considered not just indelicate but positively lewd. When it was necessary to mention them at all in polite society, the discreet word was "limbs"—a euphemism also applied equally to the legs of grand pianos.*

Canada remained a straitlaced world in which married women were cautioned not to engage in sexual intercourse more than once a month lest it affect their ability to bear children. Booze headed the long list of transgressions frowned on by the major Protestant churches, followed by masturbation, smoking, dancing, nude painting, certain styles of evening apparel, gambling, the theatre, prizefighting, and the employment of barmaids. When Robert Service was invited to recite some of his own work at a church concert in the so-called rip-roaring

---

* My mother, who was a child in the era of voluminous dresses, did not believe women had legs at all but was convinced their bodies were solid from ankle to hip.

gold-rush town of Whitehorse, he was forced to cancel "The Shooting of Dan McGrew" because, he was told, it was a little too raw for the parishioners.

In an era when a lady's ankle was considered erotic, all references to sex were taboo, and that included any suggestion of pregnancy. For the months that she showed her condition, no expectant mother dared appear in public. Young, unmarried women were confined, too, by the obligatory chaperone, and for some strict families, even a chaperone wasn't enough.

Such was the unfortunate situation of Hart Massey's daughter, Lillian. A comely if lonely girl, she was allowed no suitors at all. Mr. Barrett of Wimpole Street was no harder on his languid Elizabeth than the sombre, white-bearded old farm implements patriarch was on his own offspring. For Lillian there would be no Robert Browning. Once, just once, she had had the temerity to wave at a boy from her perch in an upstairs gable; her furious parent put her on bread and water. On a rare occasion when a young man dared to call, Massey went black with rage and, in a peculiarly Victorian gesture, advanced on the rubber plant in the hall and rent it limb from limb. In 1905, ten years after her father's death, Lillian, aged fifty, her beauty ravaged by time, was married to a much older man, the father of two grown children. She insisted on having a lavish, young girl's wedding. The groom's present to her was predictable. He gave her a Bible.

A Bible for a wedding gift! Only in the parlours of Toronto the Good could that have passed without ribaldry. Yet people did talk, and one of the topics discussed in those discreet confidences that passed between chatelaines of the nation's capital was the puzzle of the Prime Minister's private life. Was Wilfrid Laurier impotent, as some contended, or, as others whispered, had he fathered an illegitimate son?

His marriage was happy and long lasting, in spite of the later presence of another woman who may or may not have been his mistress. Emilie Lavergne was the wife of Laurier's law partner, and for a quarter of a century she and Laurier were virtually inseparable. She was no beauty (her teeth were bad); but she was vivacious and witty, and she dressed well. Theirs, to quote Sandra Gwyn, the chronicler of Ottawa's private world, was "perhaps the most remarkable romantic liaison in Canadian political history." Was it physical? Was the son that Emilie bore her husband in 1880 really Laurier's? There were those who claimed to see a family resemblance. But if there was, it was fleeting.

Wilfrid Laurier made no secret of his friendship with Emilie. It was his habit, every morning at eleven, to leave the office he shared with his partner in Arthabasca, Quebec, remarking as he went out the door, "Joseph, if you will permit it, I am going to chat with your wife." The two were certainly close friends and kindred spirits, but that kind of friendship was not unique in those decorous days between men and women of a certain class. (One has only to think of Mackenzie King and his close companionship with the happily married Joan Patteson.) There was propinquity but not much room for dalliance in the Laurier-Lavergne relationship. The two families were so inexorably linked that there was little opportunity for secrecy.

Yet it is impossible to contemplate the relationship between Emilie and her Wilfrid without considering the irony of Armand Lavergne's appearance on the scene. Whether or not Emilie's offspring was Laurier's bastard son, he was certainly his philosophical opponent. Not for him the reasoned federalism of his mother's intimate friend. The youth who grew up in the bosom of the two families developed into a fiery young nationalist, the bitter opponent of Canada's involvement in future wars, the comrade-in-arms of that quintessential Quebec nationalist, Henri Bourassa of *Le Devoir*, and his eventual successor as the political idol of a new generation of young Quebec extremists. As much as anyone, Armand Lavergne would help to sow the seeds of the separatist movement that would bedevil the century.

In the late nineties, as the alliance with Emilie began to fade, a change came over Laurier that baffled his contemporaries. The lackadaisical politician became an adroit and purposeful prime minister. A strong believer in national unity, he walked the political tightrope between the forces of the New Imperialism and the old French-Canadian nationalism. The issue was joined on the October day in 1899 when Britain declared war on the Boer farmers in the Transvaal and the Orange Free State. Suddenly, Laurier found himself pressed by most of English-speaking Canada to rush to Britain's side and pressed just as hard by French Canada to stay aloof.

As for Emilie, she made no secret of her own sentiments. Her son was firmly opposed to any imperialistic struggle and she herself apparently expressed her own anti-Boer War attitude at a dinner party for the young Winston Churchill. Even more revealing was her choice of a name for one of her favoured pets. She called him Kruger, after the Boer prime minister.

Maud Graham

1

Wilfrid Laurier did not want to send a single soldier to aid the mother country in the South African War. To him, the battle with the Boers was nothing more than "a petty tribal conflict," a conviction that reflected the majority opinion in his native province but not in the rest of Canada.

The war had surprised almost everybody. Who would have believed that a ragtag-and-bobtail crew of expatriate Dutch farmers would dare to challenge the might of the Empire? But they had done exactly that on October 11, 1899, and now half the country seemed to be chanting "Soldiers of the Queen," the theme song of the jingoists, while the other half maintained a glum and stubborn silence.

For Laurier, the war had come at an inopportune moment, just as the nation was enjoying an unprecedented unifying sense of optimism brought on by the end of the depression of the nineties, by the new immigration boom, and by the creation of a populous Northwest. A new kind of Canadian—the committed nationalist—was emerging as from a cocoon, and Laurier, the passionate Québécois, was himself part of that trend. For the first but certainly not the last time, a Canadian prime minister was faced with the almost insurmountable wartime problem of reconciling the simmering passions that threatened to undermine the shaky edifice of national unity.

As a French Canadian, Laurier understood and sympathized with his fellow Quebeckers who wanted nothing to do with imperialist adventures. His people had long since cut their ties with Europe; why should a single French Canadian shed his blood in a foreign cause? But Laurier had another concern. If Canada jumped every time the mother country crooked her finger, what hope was there of building an autonomous nation?

The war provided a foretaste of things to come and brought into focus the two political dilemmas that every future prime minister would be forced to acknowledge: how to keep the country from flying apart, and how to prevent it from being dominated by another.

The Boer War would stiffen Laurier's spine as a later war would stiffen that of his successor, Robert Borden. When hostilities broke out he had been in power for three years and would continue to hold office, uninterrupted, for another twelve, a record never surpassed before or since. An easygoing politician once known as "Lazy Laurier," he had, somewhat to his surprise, succeeded the weary Edward Blake as Liberal leader in 1887.

His colleagues had not expected him to last more than one term, nor had he. He was a politician of charm and grace, but there was a common notion that there was no iron in his constitution. As one backbencher put it, he didn't have enough of the devil in him. John Willison, editor of the *Globe*, noted that he had a reputation for indolence, which perhaps he could not overcome. "There was no energy in his deliverance," Williston wrote of Laurier's platform style. "It was thought that he was too gentle and too gentlemanly for the hard, rough, uncompromising aggressive warfare in which a politician must engage. . . ."

Yet by the time war was declared, something had changed him. Was it the influence of the spirited Emilie, as Sandra Gwyn has suggested? Was it the unwonted burden of office that can break some leaders and invigorate others? Or was it something more subtle, more elusive that put Lazy Laurier on his mettle? He was the first Canadian prime minister to comprehend and wrestle with the great Canadian quandary—the struggle between geography and history—and to grasp the need to seek an accommodation between the two. The new war would force Laurier to indulge in the kind of tightrope act that every successful prime minister would have to master.

Willison, who was to revise his original opinion, put his finger on Laurier's special position, a product of his dual heritage. He was, the influential editor wrote, neither an imperialist nor a federalist. He was not hostile to Great Britain; indeed, he had a reverence for British traditions and British institutions. "But he believed there was no advantage to Canadians in close connection with the Mother Country. . . . He was indeed a Canadian nationalist."

The four Tory leaders who succeeded John A. Macdonald after his death in 1891 were all English-speaking. In the election of 1896, the last of the lacklustre quartet, the aging Charles Tupper—all jowls and sidewhiskers—was a pushover. Laurier, who was fluently bilingual, became the first French-Canadian prime minister, but he was more than that. By clinging to power through four elections he established the Liberals as the dominant party in Canada. They would hold office for almost three-quarters of the twentieth century and do so by following the pattern of compromise between the nation's two language groups. In Canada, especially on language issues, inflexibility is a poor substitute for leadership, as Meighen, Bennett, and Diefenbaker were to discover. To both Mackenzie King and Pierre Elliott Trudeau, Laurier was a political deity.

Like most successful politicians, he was blessed with much more than a modicum of luck. He took office just as the severe depression of the nineties—the blackest the continent had yet known—was about to wind down, its demise accelerated by the Klondike discoveries that ended the stifling gold shortage and set the nation on a new economic path.

Lucky Laurier! How apt that his political fortunes should soar because of another extraordinary piece of luck—Siwash George Carmack's accidental discovery of a nugget on an obscure creek in an empty corner of the Far North. Again, like most successful politicians, Laurier knew how to make luck work for him. The North was crawling with high-spending gold seekers, and Laurier's Liberals rode to victory on a buoyant tide. It was Canada's century, he would keep telling his followers, and they believed him.

He had charisma before that overworked word entered everyday speech. When the war broke out he was turning fifty-eight, a tall, slender figure with a high, savant's forehead and a halo of chestnut hair, already streaked with silver. He was not above using his striking appearance for political advantage. "Follow my white plume!" was his rallying cry during the 1911 election, a phrase he borrowed from Henri of Navarre, though he lacked the French monarch's bold panache. Mackenzie King thought him "gentle as a child"; others have described him as debonair, romantic, passionate, urbane, Byronic, graceful, and enchanting—adjectives rarely used to describe your typical Canadian political leader.

Stylish, too. Laurier was fastidious about his attire. To the theatre critic Augustus Bridle he was "the best dressed man in Canada." He wore a silk hat as if he had been born in it, and when he affected a suit of pale grey (a novelty in those times), he made sure his topper matched. Not for him the rumpled wool jacket and baggy trousers favoured by so many of his predecessors. Laurier was a fashion plate.

Today, the popular press would call him sexy. His voice was sexy, too, mellifluent, almost musical. There was a languorous air about him that women could not resist; it matched his pallor, the result of a recurring fever, accompanied by a hacking cough, that on at least one occasion caused him to collapse at his desk, spitting blood. He was convinced that he had tuberculosis, which, being an affliction connected with romantic poets, was not without its attractions. Probably it was chronic bronchitis, a more plebeian malady.

Sick or not, he lived to the age of seventy-eight, far beyond the life expectancy of his contemporaries. Abstemious all his life, he drank only wine, and very little of that. Though he was to accept, a bit reluctantly, a knighthood from his queen, he invariably visited her representative at Rideau Hall not by carriage but always by the more democratic street-car, in whose confines he was sometimes forced to seek a far corner to avoid the importuning crowd.

The South African War caught him in a trap. If he knuckled under to the British, his own people would call him a traitor; at the same time, his instincts to maintain an arm's length relationship within the Empire would lose him the support of the rest of Canada. It was a matter of politics as well as principle. Whichever way he jumped, he could lose votes and even lose the country.

The imperialists in English Canada were howling for action, and Laurier could not ignore the cries. The New Imperialism, as it was called, had reached its apogee in the dying years of the nineteenth century with the Diamond Jubilee of Queen Victoria. Such a celebration had not been seen before. Streets were clogged with ceremonial arches bearing

23

patriotic slogans. Bands played at every corner, processions formed, fireworks dazzled in the skies, schoolchildren sang "Rule Britannia," and public speakers prattled in hushed tones about the Empire.

The Empire! The sacred Empire! Empire worship amounted to a religion. No school geography was complete without its map of the world showing all those countries upon which the sun never set, coloured an imperial crimson. The school readers were crammed with stirring accounts and even more stirring poems about British derring-do among the heathens. Empire building was equated with Christian manliness. The selfless adventures of British missionaries toting flag and Bible into the world's dark corners (David Livingstone was *the* schoolboy hero) enlivened the pages of *Chums* and the *Boys' Own Annual* that lay bulky beneath every Christmas tree.

The youth of Canada breathed in the spirit of imperialism with their breakfast porridge as they devoured the works of G.A. Henty, H. Rider Haggard, R.M. Ballantyne, and Rudyard Kipling—especially Kipling. As Arthur Lower, the shrewdest of our social historians, has remarked, "at the turn of the century, the Canadian public school was not making young Canadians, but young Englishmen."

The imperialist legacy has left its mark on Canadian cities, especially those in eastern and central Canada. Every small town in Ontario seems to have a Queen's Hotel, a Royal Café, and a King Street. The names of monarchs, their consorts, and their heirs are sprinkled about the country from Prince Edward Island to the Queen Charlottes.

In Laurier's day, the Empire was seen as a bulwark against the doctrine of manifest destiny being preached in neighbouring political circles. "The good Canadian nationalist first must be a good Imperialist," Charles G.D. Roberts, the poet and historian, declared in 1895. Stephen Leacock echoed that sentiment. "I am an Imperialist because I will not be a Colonial," he said. Only through clinging to the Empire could Canadians achieve full nationhood. The comforting knowledge that they were part of the Empire gave them a smug satisfaction, even an arrogance, over their neighbours—a whiff of anti-Americanism here that had lurked beneath the political surface since the days of 1812.

Canadians, especially the British-born, tended to be patronizing about Uncle Sam. In the periodicals, the stereotypic American was a cunning old codger who chewed gum and talked funny ("Wa'l, son, I reckon . . ."). At the turn of the century, the *Moon*, a satirical Toronto review, published six wicked full-page caricatures titled "The American Girl," none of which would be countenanced today. The first showed a coarsely attractive fortune-seeking parvenu, all hair and diamonds, labelled "The Society Girl," with the accompanying verse:

Sweet Sylvia, how your pa does slave
To trap with cash some noble knave—
      For son-in-law.
Sweet Sylvia with the winking eye
      And teeth just built for biting pie—
      And chewing gum.

In English-Canadian eyes, the British Empire was an institution second only to Christianity. The two, in fact, were interwoven. To evangelize the world in a single generation was the sacred aim of imperialists and churchmen alike. Newton Wesley Rowell, a leading Liberal and Methodist (and a future chief justice), had adopted Kipling's popular exhortation to "take up the White Man's burden" and worked out the cost to the last dollar. The task, as he saw it, was to convert 40 million backward people by recruiting 1,600 missionaries at an annual cost of $3.2 million.

For this was the age of the missionary hero who set out to conquer the world for Christ. "Conquer" was the operative word; the missionaries marched to martial music—"Onward, Christian Soldiers" and "Fight the Good Fight"—and in their fund-raising campaigns made use of military metaphors, as the Methodist Church did when it called for the conquest of "more territory for Christ's empire; more soldiers in His army; more ships in His white-winged navy of beneficence; more towers and fortresses thundering against sin; better enginery and better disciplined battalions. . . ." The church flung every warlike term into its promotional literature: ". . . storm and siege, standard and battle shout, rout and victory. . . ." As Carman Miller, the Canadian historian, has pointed out, "it was but a short step for churchmen to demand secular troops to defend a holy cause." War, in the words of one, was "the ploughshare to break up the fallow ground and prepare it for the gospel."

It is easy to be cynical about this apparent attempt to conceal British economic expansion under a cloak of missionary zeal. But it must be remembered that these were idealistic years—the same years that produced the social gospel, the campaign for women's suffrage, and the war against the demon rum. And English-speaking Canadians were convinced of the virtue and superiority of the Empire. There was something evangelical about the white-gowned ladies of the Imperial Order Daughters of the Empire marching down the aisles of the local theatres, lugging their oversized Union Jacks.

The New Imperialism took on the trappings of a campaign to Christianize the heathen in the spirit of sacrifice. Lord Wolseley, who had commanded the Red River expedition during the Riel uprising in 1870 and was commander-in-chief of the British Army during the South African War, declared that he had "but one great object in this world— that is to maintain the greatness of the British Empire." And not for reasons of selfish conquest! The issue was a moral one, or at least that was the imperialistic excuse. "I firmly believe," Wolseley stated, "that in doing so I work in the cause of Christianity, of peace, of civilization, and the happiness of the human race generally."

The imperialists were unshakeable in their belief that their cause was always just, no matter what the circumstances. The absolute certainty revealed in the *Canadian* magazine's snobbish Christmas message of 1899 that "the Anglo-Saxon race never errs, that it makes war only for the benefit of humanity" takes one's breath away. As Kipling put it, "Go, bind your sons to exile to serve your captives' need."

Nellie McClung remembered at the time of the Boer conflict that "The White Man's Burden" made a soaring climax to many an address. "It gave the whole business of war the high purpose of a Crusade and threw a glamour around the fighting man. We were not fighting for anything as cheap and corruptible as gold. We were paying our debt to the under-privileged, though perhaps the ungrateful people of the world."

This was the giddy atmosphere in which the South African adventure was launched. Somehow, though, the plight of the Uitlanders (Out-landers)—British newcomers in the Transvaal and Orange Free State, who were Christians, albeit difficult ones—didn't seem to fit in with the messianic zeal to succour the less fortunate people of the world. The Boers were god-fearing Dutch farmers whose forebears had first been settled at the Cape of Good Hope in the seventeenth century by the Dutch East India Company. The British took control of the Cape Colony during the Napoleonic war, but the Boers resented the imperial interference, especially the freeing of their slaves. Between 1835 and 1843 some 15,000 republican-minded Boers trekked north across the frontier and established the two semi-independent states. The war that followed half a century later was launched by the British to retain impe-rial supremacy over the two states to support the claims of the Uitlanders, who were mostly gold seekers, following the rich strikes in the Trans-vaal. The Boers, believing they would be overwhelmed by the fortune hunters, viewed Uitlanders as a threat to their independence and culture, and so denied them the franchise.

As usual, both sides believed in the righteousness of their cause. To the Boers, Great Britain was a greedy, imperialistic nation that had pushed the virtuous Boer farmers out of the Cape Colony. To the British, the policy of the Transvaal government was dictatorship—a brutal denial of basic freedoms to the Queen's subjects—which, incidentally, jeopardized British control over the largest gold-mining complex in the world.

There was the memory—galling to the British, glorious to the Boers—of the battle of Majuba Hill during the First Boer War, when a force of British redcoats had been decisively defeated on the Transvaal-Natal border in 1881. The British still thirsted for revenge; the Boers, on the other hand, were convinced by the victory that they were omni-potent. The war that resulted was, in effect, a civil war between two white nationalities seeking power following the major South African

27

gold discoveries. From this quarrel the black races stood aloof. So much for the white man's burden.

In spite of this murky background, much of it misunderstood, a majority in English-speaking Canada was solidly behind the British in the struggle. Hence it became essential to turn the new war into a crusade for freedom, a technique that foreshadowed the more sophisticated propaganda used in the Great War a decade and a half later.

Much of the English-language press was a willing partner in this deception, carefully playing down the extent of the British casualties in the face of the surprisingly effective Boer response. At the battle of Spion Kop, Natal, a staff blunder left British corpses piled three deep and more. But the photographs of this "acre of massacre" were not published because the British papers considered them "revolting Boer propaganda."

This was the last of the imperial adventures that marked the Victorian era and the first that involved Canadians. It differed from those earlier struggles in which British troops had maintained the Empire by subduing a heathen enemy in the name of Christian progress. In this war Christian battled Christian, each committed, if only in theory, to the greater glory of God. Hence the need to demonize the enemy, to divide the contestants (as Paul Fussell has pointed out in a later context) between Them and Us. The idea of good and evil, as sharply defined as black and white undiluted by any shade of grey, would mark future wars from that of Kaiser Wilhelm to Saddam Hussein's.

A string of newspaper stories detailed so-called Afrikaans atrocities. Boers were widely thought to murder the wounded, massacre civilians who showed sympathy for the British, flog natives, and execute their own people who tried to surrender. There was no hard evidence to support these stories, which were illustrated only by the grisly renderings of staff artists. One newsreel showed a Red Cross tent under fire from the evil Boers while brave British doctors and nurses strove to treat a wounded soldier. The film was a falsehood, shot in a London suburb using professional actors.

A piece of military doggerel popular at the time added to the call for vengeance:

28

To Arms, to Arms, for motherland and strike
　　the deadly blow!
Let crimson blood wash hill and dale and stain
　　the ocean's flow.

Vengeance for what? The English-language press in Canada, which swallowed the propaganda whole, abetted the purposeful demonization of the Boers. The Hamilton *Spectator* ran a completely false story that they had dynamited a train carrying women and children refugees out of the Transvaal. The Montreal *Star*, in a vicious campaign to force Laurier's hand and support an official Canadian contingent to South Africa, carried similar stories and reported, again wrongly, that the secretary of the South African League, a pro-imperialistic pressure group, had been kicked to death by a bunch of Boers.

Canadian progressives—social gospellers, educationalists, trade unionists, moral crusaders, and urban reformers—were persuaded that the Boers were a backward people.

The pro-war forces helped to personalize the conflict and transform it into a battle against "Krugerism." It wasn't easy to turn the plump, bewhiskered "Oom" (Uncle) Paul Kruger into the devil incarnate, but Kipling had a go at it. "Cruel in the shadow, crafty in the sun," the imperialist poet wrote of Kruger, whom cartoons showed as a poisonous mushroom, a slovenly peasant, or an uncontrolled tyrant. The avuncular Boer leader was depicted as a corrupt, beer-swilling (four gallons a day), ruthless despot. But, as Nellie McClung wrote, his pictures in the newspapers "showed him to be an honest, rugged old fellow, closely resembling, with his square face and chin whiskers, many of the faces in my father's ordination picture."

Thus was a minor imperial conflict in a far-off land transformed into a just war for freedom, democracy, and civilization. During a twilight service on New Year's Eve, 1899, a prominent cleric in Saint John, N.B., proclaimed that the year "had marked an epoch in the history of civilization." When war was declared, another banner headline announced triumphantly that "civilization advances."

In English Canada that summer and fall, the major Tory newspapers, led by Hugh Graham's fire-eating Montreal *Star*, were howling for war. In September the Victoria *Daily Colonist* claimed that what was needed was to have progressive ideas knocked into Kruger. "If it is to be done by bullets let us hope that after the Uitlanders become enfranchised it will be by ballots." The Fredericton *Reporter* declared that if ballots didn't solve matters "bayonets would." Although some Liberal papers loyal to Laurier adopted a wait-and-see attitude and some rural papers took an opposite view, most people thought that all of English-speaking Canada supported the pro-war enthusiasts.

This attitude was greatly reinforced by the arrival in Canada of J. Davis-Allen, an official of the South Africa Association, an English jingoist lobby that enjoyed the financial support of Cecil Rhodes himself. Davis-Allen helped influence public opinion by persuading Hugh Graham to dispatch some 6,000 telegrams to various politicians, military leaders, clergymen, and other notables across Canada asking for their opinions on Canada's role in the war. The prepaid (and often pre-written) answers appeared daily in Graham's newspaper, creating the illusion of a massive wave of support.

Significantly, not a single French-language newspaper favoured an armed conflict. If anything, French-Canadian sympathies lay with the Boers, who seemed about to suffer the ignominy of conquest by the big, bad Empire, just as the *habitants* had in 1759. Here was a war in which Canada was not in any sense threatened. Why send young men off to die for nothing—to slaughter people who had done them no wrong? In this they had the support of the most eloquent public figure in Canada, Laurier's former friend and protégé Henri Bourassa.

The arguments over Canada's participation in the South African War marked the beginning of a long quarrel that had been smouldering for decades between the two founding peoples. It was really a quarrel over history and geography, and the divided loyalties that resulted. In turning its back on Europe, French Canada had chosen geography over history; its roots were planted firmly in North American soil, and it saw no purpose in rallying to a foreign cause. But English Canada was bound to

Europe by historical and romantic ties that could not easily be broken. At this point, the quarrel could have been contained; memories of the cozy nation-building relationship between John A. Macdonald and his deputy, George-Étienne Cartier, were still green. But the problem would not go away. Through two future wars and their bitter legacies, it would return again and again to haunt nationalists and imperialists alike.

The imperialists wanted Canada to send a contingent to Africa to fight on Britain's side. And it was a *contingent* that Joseph Chamberlain, the colonial secretary, wanted—an *official* one, with CANADA written all over it, not offers from individual volunteers. At that point Britain didn't think a military contribution from Canada and the other colonies was necessary since the British regular army alone was expected to make short work of the Boers. Canada's contribution would be symbolic, an affirmation of Empire solidarity, a way of tying the restless colonial children to the apron strings of the mother country—a step, in short, toward Chamberlain's dream of imperial union.

Events were beginning to wriggle out of Laurier's control. Racist epithets were being tossed about like ping-pong balls. Bitter words like "traitor" and "treason" were being thrown into the bicultural stewpot. Laurier was attacked in English-speaking Canada as a weak-willed and weak-kneed fence-sitter. The extremes to which the pro-war campaign had gone were evident in one overheated Montreal *Star* story that claimed Laurier had been prevented from growing a beard only by fear of "betraying his sympathy for Kruger."

Lord Minto, the governor general, and the ambitious militia chief, General Edward Hutton, had apparently drafted a contingency plan for war, which was leaked to the *Canadian Military Gazette*. As a result, the British colonial office promptly wired its thanks to Ottawa for a contingent it had yet to offer and Laurier had no intention of dispatching.

Yet no prime minister could ignore a massive tidal wave of opinion from English Canada, however much of it was manufactured. The country—indeed, his own cabinet—was split down the middle. In the words of André Siegfried, the perceptive French commentator who studied the country in the late nineteenth century, "not since 1837 has the opposition between the two races been so bitterly manifested."

What to do? Laurier's only way out was the familiar Canadian solution of compromise. Young men, he decided, could offer to go to South Africa of their own free will to fight on the British side. They would be called volunteers, not recruits. The Canadian government would pay for their equipment and transportation, but on their arrival they would be incorporated into the British forces. The British were prepared to foot the entire bill, but Laurier wanted none of that. It would cost the Canadians almost $3 million, but in the interests of nationalism most were cheerfully prepared to pay up.

The decision was made without involving Parliament (then in recess), thus avoiding a damaging debate. With an eye to the future, Laurier was careful to make clear to the press that the announcement did not constitute a precedent. "This outlay . . . could not be regarded as an infringement of constitutional principles and Colonial usages nor as a binding precedent for the future." Thus the cry "When England is at war, Canada is at war" was relegated to the ash heap of out-of-date oratory.

Nonetheless, Laurier's compromise appalled Henri Bourassa, grandson of the French-Canadian reformer and near saint, Louis-Joseph Papineau. Bourassa was inflexible in his views, an unfortunate quality in a politician, especially a Canadian politician. "Is the British Empire in real danger?" he asked in an open letter to Laurier on October 18. "Does it ask the aid of our arms to save it? Or is this an attempt to involve us in a military federation, that cherished project of Mr. Chamberlain? . . . Is Canada prepared to renounce her prerogative as a constitutional colony, her parliamentary freedom, the understanding come to with the Mother Country after seventy-five years of contest? That is the question. . . . I, for one, will never consent to support this retrograde line of policy." And so saying, he resigned his parliamentary seat.

He was a handsome figure with his pointed black beard and stylish moustachios, and his quick wit did not sit well with the committed imperialists. A heckler attacked him during a Montreal meeting in which he tried to explain his opposition to war. "Ah, but the sun never sets on the glory of the British Empire!" he cried. To which Bourassa shot back, "This only goes to prove that not even God trusts the British in the dark," a response that, in a heated wartime climate, was seen as something close to blasphemy.

He would continue to be the real spokesman of his people, eventually founding *Le Devoir*, the most influential newspaper in the province. But he was not so popular within his own party. "Our French compatriots think with me," he declared during an argument with Laurier. To which the Prime Minister replied, "Yes, my dear friend, they think with you but vote with me!"

Bourassa's views were shared and his boldness admired, but his Liberal colleagues tended to blame him for putting principles before party. After all, one of their own occupied the prime minister's seat. Bourassa's uncompromising stand was seen as divisive because it effectively forced all French-Canadian Liberals to close ranks around Laurier. The Québécois might not approve of imperialism, but surely it was better to have one of their own in power than to play into the hands of their political enemies. Indeed, Bourassa's trenchant opposition to the war drove Laurier to such an extreme that, in the session of 1900, he made a most un-Laurier-like speech, defending Britain's policy. "Mr. Bourassa and I differ *in toto* on this question. He thinks this war was not just; I believe in my heart that England never fought a more just war than this." In a federal election later that year Laurier swept Quebec and won the country.

Bourassa always went to some pains to make clear that it was not just the British Empire that he opposed; it was *all* empires. History has been on his side. In little more than a generation the sun would set on every empire, including the British, and the only vestiges of imperialism would be the titles and trademarks retained by hundreds of Canadian companies. From the Royal Bank to Empire Pants and Boys Wear, they remind us vaguely of half-forgotten imperial glories, when every colonial war was, by definition, a just one.

2

When the Boers dared to take on the British in the autumn of 1899, the imperial attitude was one of contempt—a fly annoying a giant. The British had been through it all before: they were used to putting out fires in the dark corners of the globe; that was their God-given task. Whenever the natives grew restless, the British taught them a lesson. That was how it had been for half a century: brief, explosive encounters without much loss of life, especially on the British side; satisfactory victories to add to the roll of regimental battle honours; high adventure in the jungle and hill country with plenty of kudos to go around.

When the war started, the Dominion was convinced that hostilities would be over quickly. Some doubted whether the Canadians would see any action at all. How could a small band of lightly armed Dutch farmers stand up to the imperial might? In fact, they stood up very well.

Entrenched military leaders tend to have inflexible minds, fighting each war with the tactics of the previous one. In South Africa, the British thought in terms of the infantry and the thin red line that had worked so well in the Crimea almost half a century before. But in the rubbled kopjes of South Africa a different kind of war was developing—one in which Boer commandos and mounted guerrillas were adept. In the first two weeks of the conflict, the Boers had bottled up Mafeking, Kimberley, and Ladysmith. How unsporting of them! The wily Kruger wasn't playing according to the rules of the game.

British pigheadedness turned what should have been a brief struggle into a prolonged conflict. The British commanders had no understanding of the South African terrain and made no attempt to study it. Thus the Canadians were asked to send *dismounted* troops to South Africa, not the cavalry and artillery needed to battle the hard-riding Boers.

Joseph Chamberlain had told Canada that its contingent must embark for South Africa no later than October 31. That gave the militia department a scant sixteen days to recruit, organize, clothe, arm, and equip a thousand young infantry soldiers and dispatch them on a 7,000-mile ocean voyage to the war zone. This hasty "enrolment" of

34

volunteers was not confined to the eastern cities but took place amidst scenes of wild enthusiasm in every province, so that the contingent might reflect a cross-section of the nation. The tumultuous response, in the words of the Prince of Wales, "took England by surprise"—and the world as well. "They fancied," Lord Salisbury declared, "that the great British Empire, which looks so large on the map, was so separated by distant seas that its practical ability for co-operation was entirely destroyed, but they have learned their mistake."

The Boers, too, were baffled, as George Shepherd of Paris, Ontario, discovered later that year when he encountered an imprisoned Boer general in a military hospital. "Would you kindly tell me why it is that you have left a civil peaceful life to come here to fight a selfish war and endure all the hardships of the field?" the general asked him. "I am not surprised by the action of the English or the Cape volunteers, but it puzzles me why you identify yourself with the quarrel. I don't suppose it was the mere love of fighting that brought you here."

To which Private Shepherd replied, "It was not so much to actually assist England as to show the world the unity of the Empire, and to show that if one part of the Empire is touched, all are hurt."

"He did not say anything for a while," Shepherd wrote home, "but stroked his beard and appeared lost in thought."

Shepherd had responded to the call of the Empire; others simply answered the call of adventure. Indeed, the two were closely intertwined, as any reader of the *Boys' Own Paper* (and its yuletide *Annual*), with its accounts of epic British feats on foreign strands, would understand. "There was no great patriotism involved," one veteran of the war, Herbert Priestman, recalled. "I thought it would do me some good and I was searching for adventure."

Two-thirds of the volunteers in the newly formed Royal Canadian Regiment were young, urban, poorly paid white-collar workers or skilled blue-collar workers, many bent on escaping the strictures and stifling boredom of Canadian life. Some, like Priestman, were British-born, or their fathers were. Others enlisted for material benefits or because their employers had guaranteed their pay during their absence.

Few believed for an instant that they would face death or mutilation on the veldt. "Why was I not born a man?" mourned Mabel Anderson, whose husband cheerfully faced a reduction in militia rank so that he might be accepted. Young men were wild to join up—far more than could be accommodated. One, T.C. Wasson, a member of the 48th Highlanders, arrived in Victoria, B.C., from the Klondike only to find that he was too late to enlist and so headed off halfway around the world to Australia, paying his own way to South Africa. His family had no word of him until a letter arrived from the hospital at Kimberley where he was recovering from wounds in his left lung and arm.

All across the country bands were playing, crowds were cheering, flags were flying. An avalanche of gifts from private donors, organized charities, businesses, and commercial corporations was showered on the new troops: 6,000 pounds of tobacco, 20,000 cigarettes, 1,000 pipes from the Montreal Soldiers' Wives' League, 300 New Testaments from the Quebec Bible Society, a $1,000 insurance policy for every man from Sir Charles Tupper, the ex-prime minister—not to mention a monstrous accumulation of boxing gloves, punching bags, games, papers, books, and delicacies.

On October 20 the volunteers set off by railway from Ottawa to board the old cattle boat *Sardinian* at Quebec. As bands played outside on Wellington Street, 15,000 people surged through the barrier at the station to shake hands with the departing troops. The pressure of the crowd, fifty deep, forced one society matron into the ranks of the band. Off went the volunteers, admiring slogans ringing in their ears, "representatives of ideal Canadian manhood" . . . "the pick of the nation's sinew and brains" . . . "pure as the air of the sunlit north."

In truth, they looked like a contingent of pink-cheeked schoolboys. "Scarce was there ever a younger looking lot of soldiers recruited in a battalion," wrote the *Mail and Empire*'s correspondent, Stanley McKeown Brown. So great was the response that the militia had increased the height requirement by two inches, and so appealing was the eagerness of the new enrollees that age restrictions were often overlooked.

In Quebec City at the farewell ceremonies, a chorus of imperial slogans echoed off the granite walls of the ancient capital. Wilfrid Laurier called it "a unique occasion in the history of the world" and, casting previous doubts aside, went on to remind the troops that the scattered provinces of British North America had shown their willingness "to cement with their blood the unity of the Empire in its most distant part."

Before the ship embarked it was discovered that under the revised regulations twenty-nine new enrollees were too short to fight the Boers. Tears of disappointment flowed down the cheeks of the rejected ones until compassion triumphed and all but three were accepted. A crowd of 50,000 clambered up the citadel, blackened the Dufferin Terrace, perched on roofs and cliffs, and jammed the wharf as the *Sardinian* moved out into the St. Lawrence accompanied by hundreds of small boats, all whistling and firing salutes, and trailed for much of her river voyage by an exuberant procession of steam yachts. Only then was it discovered that twenty extra men were on board—enthusiastic stow-aways who had slipped on with the troops or hidden themselves in the overcrowded hold.

The hastily refitted *Sardinian* was ridiculously small for the 1,039 troops, who, in one description, "were literally falling over each other at every turn." Half would have bunks, the rest only hammocks, and on that first night there were neither bunks nor hammocks for fifty soldiers—nothing but the hard, cluttered decks. The *Sardinian* was only forty-six feet wide, and on this cockleshell the new soldiers of the Queen would be crammed together for the next thirty days.

The ship was in no sense fitted to convoy more than a thousand men across more than 7,000 miles of ocean. With no room for kit or equipment on the decks, everything had to be piled into each man's bunk, allowing little room for sleeping. There were not enough lifeboats for the number on board; no rules were posted at the outset to organize the troops in case of fire; and so little drinking water was available that a guard had to be placed over the tap.

In spite of this, the untried troops were subjected to an uncompromising regimental schedule better suited to the parade ground or rifle range. Their activities, which began when reveille sounded at 5 a.m. and did not end until early supper, reflected the zeal of the contingent's regimental commander, Lieutenant-Colonel William Dillon Otter, an austere professional with a fashionable soup-strainer moustache.

Otter's first experience in the field had been as adjutant of the Queen's Own Rifles in the battle of Ridgeway in 1866 against Fenian raiders from the United States who were waging guerrilla war against Britain for Irish independence. The battle was a disaster, with the regiment fleeing in panic from the battlefield. Otter, a fiercely ambitious militia officer, never forgot that embarrassing rout, which seemed to turn him into an aggressive commander and a stickler for military efficiency.

At Cut Knife Creek, during the second Riel uprising in 1885, Otter was eager to promote his career by launching an attack on Chief Poundmaker's Indians. As a result, going beyond the instructions of his more cautious commander, Major General Frederick Middleton, he provoked a fight he thought would result in an easy victory. It was nothing of the sort. Otter disguised his intentions by calling his foray against Poundmaker "a reconnaissance in force," the same weasel phrase used a few generations later to justify the tragedy at Dieppe. In fact, it was a victory for the Indians, and no amount of self-serving justification by Otter or journalistic glorification could change that. ("THE VICTORY!" cried the Toronto *World*. "HOW POUNDMAKER WAS WHIPPED.") Otter's force suffered twenty-two casualties to Poundmaker's nine. And evidence suggests that Poundmaker might easily have been won over without the Indians being goaded to further bloodshed if Otter had not moved so precipitately.

As the commander of the first Canadian contingent, Otter suffered from a sense of inferiority. He wanted desperately to be part of the Permanent Force of professional soldiers, but there were scarcely any P.F. men in Canada and there was no room for him. More than anything, Otter—a despised colonial—wanted to impress the British with his troops' efficiency and his own leadership. As Surgeon General George Ansel Ryerson was to declare, "It is an open secret that the majority of the British officers had a very hearty and healthy contempt for all

Colonials." Aware of this, the overly sensitive and ambitious Otter refused to relax under the straitened conditions.

His insistence that officers be saluted on every occasion caused confusion and resentment. As one sergeant, W. Hart-McHarg, recalled, "It seemed absurd that the hundreds of men, sitting, lying, and standing about the deck should come to attention every time an officer passed along. Sometimes officers would be passing backward and forward every few minutes. No wonder the men could not be got to carry out the order satisfactorily." Otter appeared innocent of the fact that compliments were not paid to officers aboard troop ships. In fact, very little saluting was done on active service; the officers in the fighting lines did not want to be bothered with it.

Equally ill-advised was Otter's order that in the tropics men should appear on parade with trousers rolled to the knee, leaving feet and lower legs bare, apparently to toughen them up for marching. In addition, neck and chest were exposed to the sun, shirt sleeves rolled to above the elbow, and cap folded to deny all shade to the face. "You will see at a glance that this was nonsense," Russell C. Hubly, a former school principal who travelled aboard the *Sardinian*, recalled, "besides being tormented by the heated decks, our feet had to avoid the many steam pipes. Many a foot was so burned by these as to require treatment; many arms were so sunburned that the wearing of the sleeves was painful; to see a chest with the epidermis peeling off was no uncommon sight." So many complaints resulted from this foolish order that the commandant finally reversed himself on the matter of bare feet. In a future war, Canadian soldiers would refer to the kind of hair-splitting order given under Otter's command as "chickenshit."

Sergeant Hart-McHarg wrote that the men "felt at times that there was a supercilious indifference on the part of the officer commanding and the majority of officers as to their welfare." Otter displayed this during the campaign by refusing to establish a dry canteen where the rank and file could spend their pay. That was an especial hardship because the ordinary soldiers' fare left much to be desired: the best cuts of beef went to the officers and the second best to the staff sergeants.

Instead of steaks, ordinary privates had to make do with greasy boiled meat. The YMCA representative with the troops asked Otter's permission to "establish a small coffee shop with eatables," but Otter turned him down, declaring that he did not think the men needed any more than they were getting and must get used to campaign fare.

The overbearing attitude of the militia officers was illustrated when the pretentious battalion adjutant slipped on the deck of the *Sardinian* and was saved from falling by a common soldier who reached out to steady him. He had no sooner regained his balance than he turned on the man and glowered, "How dare you lay hands on an officer?"

Thomas Guthrie Marquis, in his history entitled *Canada's Sons on Kopje and Veldt* written during the war, certainly followed what might be called the party line when he wrote that "the Government had made no mistake in choosing the commanding officer; his experience made the men glad to follow him. . . ." But among the men, who referred to him derisively as "the Old Woman," there were certainly dissenting voices. One was that of Corporal Hubly, the former New Brunswick school principal, who reached the heights of sarcasm when he described Otter: "Of course, he was beloved by all. Who could resist his powers of fascination, as he strode by, with a heavy scowl on his brow, and with head bowed, as though afraid to meet the eye of the regiment? Was he ever known to speak a kind word to those under him? Was he ever known to commend? Yes. I remember that when we lay at Belmont he was commissioned by a superior to convey words of praise to the R.C.R., and how gallantly he did it! How we adored him! He turned it in such a way that we wondered that we were permitted to wear the Queen's uniform. And if we overstepped the bounds of regimental propriety, and were paraded before the colonel, was he ever known to take an excuse? Did he ever bend from the rigid discipline that was so galling to his civilian soldiers?"

The ship docked at Cape Town on November 29, and here the Canadians enjoyed a welcome fling. Every man had received his month's pay in gold two days before arrival, and most had their own money as well. As one correspondent wired back: "The wild and reckless manner in which these men spent their money made the people fancy that Canada was a gold mine." In the expensive hotels, other guests gawked at private soldiers dining in style and drinking champagne. If the privates could live like millionaires, their officers must be incredibly wealthy! In Cape Town they learned that they would entrain on December 1 for the holding camp at De Aar, travelling lightly with only an overcoat, an extra shirt, a pair of socks, and a single blanket per man. All their kit bags and valises were piled up in rows and left in charge of a small party under a single officer. That was the last the men saw of their baggage, all of which was looted and stolen, an example of the slackness and confusion that marked the early days of the enterprise.

Otter continued to be uptight about his troops long after they disembarked. On the day after they reached Cape Town, when they entrained for holding camp crowds turned out along the right of way to cheer the RCRs, who cheered back, only to be reprimanded by the commander. He told them to remember that they were soldiers now and not to act like a lot of "damned fools." When Lord Roberts, the commander-in-chief, turned up at Kroonstad, the Canadians could hear the other troops cheering him. They were told that they too might cheer but on no account were they to accompany the cheer with a "tiger." According to Hart-McHarg, "'Tigers,' we were given to understand, were low-down things, only indulged in by people from wild and woolly regions and Lord Roberts would think we were wild and woolly instead of a barrack-square regiment if we let ourselves loose in such a manner."

As Hart-McHarg commented, the incident illustrated a fear that the Canadians would somehow "show a little independence or individuality." It also demonstrated Otter's sense of inferiority in the face of regular troops and his terror of departing for a single moment from the British way of doing things. "We were always made to copy any little 'wrinkles' of the British regiments, and our drill was changed half a dozen times to conform to something some of the other regiments did which took the adjutant's eye. . . ."

The news from the front was gloomy. The road to the embattled towns of Kimberley and Mafeking was blocked by Boer forces under sixty-five-year-old General Piet Cronje, the "Lion of the Transvaal." Ladysmith was under close siege. General Redvers Buller, known wickedly as "Reverse" Buller, was reorganizing his forces. Things were not going well.

At De Aar the Royal Canadians had their first encounter with the punishing South African climate. As they struggled to pitch their tents they were tormented by a violent sandstorm, the worst in seven years. Lifted by a stiff wind, the sand stung their cheeks and filled their eyes, ears, and nostrils, causing nosebleeds. It thickened the soup, turned the meat gritty, flavoured the butter and bread, ruined the tea, and invaded the tents. Worst of all, the young soldiers experienced the dreadful South African thirst that would plague them all through the campaign.

The Canadians had never known anything like it. "The ironstone radiated heat as though hot with internal flame," Corporal Hubly wrote. It shrivelled the corpses of the dead, who did not decompose but turned black. "It seemed too hot for the lizards to play over the face of the dead; so they hid themselves in the pockets of his coat or peeped at you from his shoe."

The merciless heat haunted the memories of those Canadians who survived the war. They had not reckoned on that in those cool autumn days when, with the maples scarlet in the Canadian forests and the lakes clear and misty, they had rushed to the colours. "Every letter from the front speaks of the insatiable thirst," T.G. Marquis wrote at the time. "On almost every hot night men have been struck down either while crossing the fire zone to acquire water for their comrades, or while exposing themselves to the enemy's fire in order to quench a thirst more agonizing than a wound." In the cruel marches—a feature of the war—men staggered forward, tongues swollen, lips cracked, and raw throats on fire. They drank gratefully from pools in which the rotting corpses of animals floated, from slimy ponds, putrid with decaying vegetable matter, from murky swamps in which a dozen mules were also submerged, and once, so it was claimed, from a river that had yielded the corpses of ninety dead Boers. The result was an outbreak of enteric fever that soon reached epidemic proportions. At its peak, 2,000 British soldiers died over a six-week period. Fifty-three succumbed in a single day, their bodies buried in long trenches by exhausted companions.

During one march, Corporal Hubly was given the unwelcome job of sentry duty at the water cart. "I have seen men almost fight for the small portion allowed," he remembered. "I have seen them surging around that cart with eyes like those of the demented and faces of a pale yellow tinge. I have heard them shout in thick, unnatural tones for one mouthful of water; and it was my duty to deny them when I would a hundred times rather have complied."

This was not the kind of war that the imperial publications had portrayed—gallant soldiers of the Queen driving all before them, standards unfurled, cavalry wheeling into action with hooves thundering, bayonets flashing in the sunlight. The Canadians had marched north from De Aar, hungering for action, to the little town of Belmont, and there they had sat on their behinds for two full months. Belmont, the scene of a minor but expensive British victory the previous week, was a charnel house, the railway station torn to pieces by bullets and the battlefield littered with the rotting corpses of stricken Boers and their horses intermingled with exploded shells and shards of shrapnel. Occasionally a human head, hand, or foot could be seen protruding from the misshapen boulders.

To the Canadians, the delay was insufferable. There were those who thought they were being kept out of the fight because the British regulars considered them inferior colonials; in fact, they were being used as garrison troops, defending the rail line and at the same time being trained for future action. Part of the delay, as well, could be attributed to the top-heavy organization of the regiment, which, in the interests of Canadian nationalism, was split into two battalions, each of four companies. The militia department was determined that the regiment should not be broken up and integrated into the British army. It would fight as an identifiable Canadian unit, with its own cap and shoulder badges and its own cadre of officers, many more of whom would be promoted to fill the needs of an expanded establishment that would also require an auxiliary staff and an administrative structure.

Ponderous though it might be, it would also bolster the regiment's image and make it self-sufficient.

At long last, on February 11, 1900, the Royal Canadians set out for the front, joining Brigadier Horace Smith-Dorrien's new British brigade—the Fighting 19th it would soon be called—at Graspan. The following day they left the railway line and with the thermometer at a temperature never experienced in Canada—114°F (46°C)—they staggered on for thirteen miles across the dry and dusty veldt to Ramdam, so consumed by a raging thirst that they flung themselves into the stinking waterhole along with the mules and the horses; no officer attempted to stop them. By then fifty-two of the marchers had fallen by the wayside, many dropping in a dead faint. Some attempted to strike up a song, but their throats would not respond.

The Canadians were now in enemy country. Ramdam, a battered Dutch homestead, smashed, stripped, and gutted by the advance troops of the British army, was the first stopping place within the Orange Free State. Here a massive counter-invasion was about to begin. The diminutive Lord Roberts—"Bobs," as he was universally dubbed—who had replaced Redvers Buller as commander, was assembling an army of more than 30,000 men, 5,000 native drivers, 20,000 mules and oxen, and 14,000 horses.

The Royal Canadians' ordeal had just begun. Weeks of weary, thirsty marching lay ahead, punctuated by short, stabbing engagements and crowned by one bloody but glorious victory, destined to go down in their country's annals as a defining moment along with Queenston Heights and Vimy: the vicious battle of Paardeberg Drift.

3

Marching
to
Pretoria
On November 7, 1900, with the first Canadian contingent still at sea, the Canadian government offered Great Britain a second contingent for service in South Africa. The British delayed their reply; they had what they wanted—a token force of colonials whose presence on the battlefield would go far to cement the Empire and fulfill

Joseph Chamberlain's dream of imperial union. The British were quite prepared to wrap up the war by themselves without the need for any more colonials.

That smug attitude had been summed up in October by Moberly Bell, manager of *The Times*, in a letter to Leopold Amery, the paper's chief correspondent: "My own plan is that about the 15th December we shall have in South Africa a nice little Army & all the materials for a respectable war except the enemy." That date was eerily significant, for it marked the climax of Black Week, the low point of the war. In just six days the British suffered three devastating defeats at the hands of the Boers: at Stormberg, on December 10 (696 British casualties); at Magersfontein, December 11 (902 casualties); and at Colenso on December 15 (1,138 casualties). It wasn't a token force that Britain needed to bind up the Empire; it was big guns and mounted men. That shortcoming, the result of British arrogance and blindness, had allowed the Boers to slip away time and again.

With the newspapers trumpeting "TERRIBLE REVERSE OF BRITISH TROOPS," Chamberlain hastily accepted the Canadian offer. On December 18, the day on which Redvers Buller was relieved, he asked for a second contingent of artillery and mounted sharpshooters. The Canadian militia responded with two battalions of mounted rifles, exactly the kind of men required to chase the galloping Boers over the sere veldt of the Transvaal. One battalion would be made up of Permanent Force cavalry. A second would be recruited under the direction of the commissioner of the North West Mounted Police, Lieutenant Lawrence Herchmer, an efficient if not too popular officer with thirteen years' experience in the force. Of the 325 roughriders in the battalion, 130 were Mountie veterans: the remainder came from western ranches. Thirteen of the nineteen officers were also Mounties. In addition, the contingent would include three batteries of trained gunners bearing the insignia of the Royal Canadian Artillery—the first Canadian artillery to fight in a foreign war. The contingent of 1,320 men left Canada on three ships in the first six weeks of 1900 and began arriving in South Africa at the end of February.

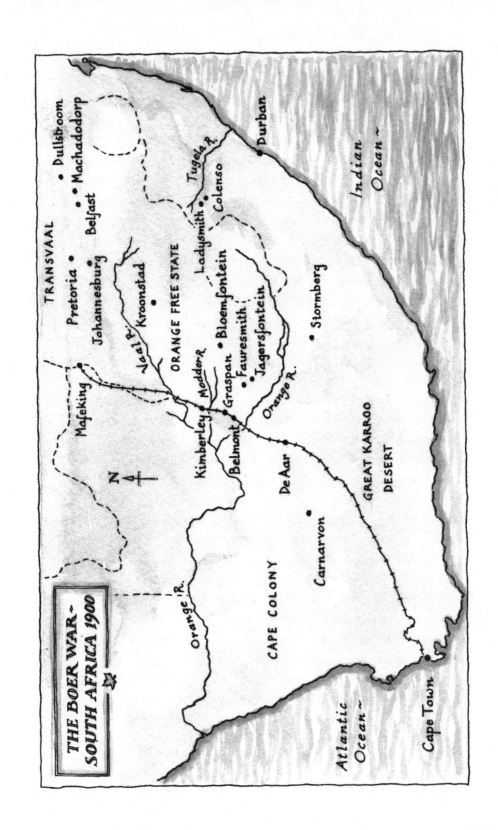

THE BOER WAR ~
SOUTH AFRICA 1900

TRANSVAAL

• Dullstroom
• Machadodorp
• Belfast

• Pretoria
• Johannesburg

Kroonstad •

Vaal R.

ORANGE FREE STATE

Tugela R.

• Durban

Indian
Ocean ~

• Colenso
Ladysmith •

• Bloemfontein
Fauresmith •
• Jagersfontein

Modder R.

Mafeking •

N

Kimberley •
Belmont •
Graspan •

Orange R.

• Stormberg

GREAT KARROO
DESERT

De Aar •

Carnarvon •

CAPE COLONY

Orange R.

Atlantic
Ocean ~

Cape Town •

Meanwhile, in England, Lord Strathcona, the weathered old fur trader now Canadian high commissioner to Great Britain, made a munificent offer to raise at his own expense a battalion of mounted men to fight in South Africa. Known to every Canadian schoolchild as the man who had driven the last spike on the Canadian Pacific Railway, Strathcona could easily afford the expense, having risen to the presidency of the Bank of Montreal and become its principal shareholder. It was said of this canny Scot that he had never sold so much as a single share of any stock that he had purchased during his lifetime. Laurier jumped at this windfall, whereupon Strathcona set about finding the right man to lead his personal cavalry. It was a short search. Twiddling his thumbs in Ottawa was Samuel Benfield Steele, the quintessential mounted policeman, smarting after his dismissal for political reasons from his job as the ruler of Dawson City. Strathcona, who knew a good man when he saw one, made him lieutenant-colonel of the newly formed Lord Strathcona Horse.

What a pair they were, these two great historical figures, united in a common enterprise and embarked upon a fresh adventure that would bring a whiff of the Canadian frontier to the South African veldt! Between them they had seen more of Canada and presided over more of her history than had any other Canadians of their time. Had they been Americans, Hollywood would certainly have exploited this pair as frontier heroes, for there is enough adventure, hardship, and sheer panache in their pasts to make them stars of a dozen films. They leap from the pages of history, their stories illuminated by a series of widescreen dramas that follow, one upon the other, like sequences edited on a movieola.

Strathcona, transmogrified from Donald A. Smith, was the longtime Labrador trader who, in a land devoid of financial institutions, had acted as banker for his fellows to nickel-and-dime his way to the very pinnacle of the Hudson's Bay Company, which had taken him on as an apprentice fifty years before. Now a grizzled octogenarian, he had saved the CPR from bankruptcy and amassed a fortune in the process.

Steele, a barrel of a man, "lithe as a pine tree and limber as a cat," had been a teenage soldier during the Fenian troubles, a private in Wolseley's famous expedition to thwart Louis Riel's uprising in 1870, and a sergeant-major in the memorable western odyssey of the Mounted Police. He had policed the CPR during its construction, chased the Cree Chief Big Bear across the prairies during the Saskatchewan Rebellion, and run the Klondike stampede like a military manoeuvre.

He built his cadre of officers and NCOs from the North West Mounted Police. He was besieged by would-be volunteers, some of whom arrived on snowshoes or by dogteam. It took a mere fortnight to bring the regiment up to its strength of 537, all ranks. Four times that number had come forward. "The men enlisted are the very pick of the cowboys, cowpunchers, rangers, policemen, and ex-policemen of the Territories and British Columbia," Steele reported.

This mixed bag of enthusiastic frontiersmen included the drunken son of the Duke of Hertford, a newspaper reporter, a fugitive from the law in the United States, and one man who had made a fortune in the Klondike. "There are men here who have travelled on foot 600 miles on the ice of the Yukon river to come here to volunteer," Steele told a civic luncheon in Montreal on March 12, just before embarkation. University graduates mingled with cowhands who could barely write their own names. One man who had been forced to resign his commission in the Essex regiment for conduct unbecoming an officer volunteered to serve as a sergeant. Hand-picked for their toughness, most were bachelors over the age of thirty. Coming from a territory of more than a million square miles, they were inclined to be rowdy—no problem for a tough disciplinarian of Steele's stripe.

The force was enrolled at twenty-three points between Victoria and Winnipeg, its members outfitted with western saddles, lassoes, revolvers, Stetson hats, and Lee-Enfield rifles. When Steele paraded his troops before Lord Minto in early March, the Governor General was appalled. This was not the kind of spit-and-polish regiment to which the titled Englishman was accustomed. He wrote of "the useless ruffians, the halt, the lame, and the blind that were piled into Strathcona's Horse."

But in South Africa, after days of hard training aboard the troop ship, they were to prove their mettle as shock troops and scouts, the advance guard for the main column under Lord Dundonald.

The second contingent of volunteers did not reach Cape Town until February 27, by which time the first contingent, as part of the 19th Brigade, was off on what has been called the greatest military march of modern times. Here began a full month of footslogging and skirmishing across the veldt from Belmont to Bloemfontein, the capital of the Orange Free State, marked by the ten-day battle of Paardeberg Drift on the Modder River, the bloodiest victory of the war.

The Royal Canadians, acting as rear guard for the brigade, reached the river on February 18 after a punishing 23-mile night march. They had landed at Cape Town 1,039 strong, but on this Sunday morning—Bloody Sunday it would soon be called—their strength was down to 872. Disease and exhaustion had put scores in the hospital; the incredible Boer sharpshooters accounted for others. One of the first Canadians to fall from a Mauser bullet was hit at a distance of no less than 1,500 yards.

This was, significantly, Majuba Day, the anniversary of the great defeat suffered by Empire troops in South Africa nineteen years before. At 8:30 on this morning, with very little sleep and only a biscuit, a canteen of coffee, and a ration of rum to warm their bellies, they were ordered into action at last against the troops of the Boer general Piet Cronje. As they struggled across the fast-flowing river, clinging to a rope strung between its banks, they felt a surge of excitement. A Prince Edward Island volunteer described the scene: "The water was up to our necks and running very swiftly. Horses were carried off their feet but as far as was known all reached the opposite side in safety. It was a wonderful sight, each man struggling against the waves, carrying his rifle ready for the fray. . . ."

Cronje had been outflanked by Roberts but now, caught in a tightening net, showed no sign of capitulating. The Royal Canadians moved up the river, advancing across open ground with scarcely any cover and not a living creature in sight. At last they reached the forward firing line held by the Black Watch and the Seaforth Highlanders. There, lying prone and firing into the trees ahead, they remained, hour after hour, through the fiery heat of the morning and a chill rain in the afternoon, with nothing to eat and their water bottles going empty. Only the incessant rattle of the Boer Mausers told the Canadians that the enemy was still entrenched behind the trees somewhere ahead.

Men died. Others, hungry and dehydrated, tortured by ants and flies, grew dizzy. The growing number of wounded lay where they had fallen as the Boers fired on the stretcher-bearers. The icy rain ended; the scorching sun emerged from the fleeing clouds; the stalemate continued. Otter, unsure of himself, hesitant to mount an attack, was put in mind of Cut Knife Creek during the Saskatchewan Rebellion: a similar terrain, an invisible opponent, the Métis' insidious tactics.

At four that afternoon, three companies of the Duke of Cornwall's Light Infantry arrived, a British unit commanded by the excitable Lieutenant-Colonel William Aldworth. He informed Otter, who was twelve years his senior, "I have orders to end this thing. I shall finish it in five minutes." Otter demurred. There were words. Aldworth was curt and peevish. Otter did not take kindly to his junior's insinuation that the Canadians were inexperienced, sluggish, and lacking courage.

One story has it that when Otter pointed out that the distance was too great and the enemy knew the range of every part, Aldworth declared, "If you don't like to, or don't know how to, the Cornwalls will show you." To which Otter replied, "The devil you will. We will lead and you can keep up if you can." However that may be, the facts are that at 5:15 p.m. it was Aldworth who gave the order to fix bayonets and charge, offering five pounds to the first man to reach the enemy trenches. On hearing the bugle sound, the Canadians, frustrated by their eight-hour wait, began to cheer and rushed forward with the Cornwalls into the face of the enemy. "Come on, boys!" cried John Todd, an American who had served in the Philippines, "this beats Manila hollow." A moment later he was felled by a Boer bullet. Aldworth, his body riddled with five bullets, died in the same fusillade and so did his adjutant.

50

This ill-advised assault was later compared to the more famous charge of the Light Brigade—magnificent, certainly, but not war. The popular Catholic chaplain Father O'Leary described it with more enthusiasm than might be expected from a man who would shortly be called upon to perform "the last sad, but consoling duty of committing them [the fallen] to the care of God's angels." He would never forget "that wild mad charge against an invisible enemy . . . nor shall I attempt to describe it. . . . Hell let loose would give but a faint idea of it. On, on we rushed through a hail of bullets, the air alive with deadly missile.

"On we rushed, madly, wildly, tearing through brambles, stumbling over prostrate comrades, eager in the delirium of bloodshed and destruction which had seized on us all to reach the enemy's trenches. And above the din of battle, oh, that wild soul-stirring cheer, or rather that savage yell! Like tigers our brave boys bounded over the open, but it was not to be; darkness closed on us ere the position was carried and the day won."

For the day was lost. None of the attackers got within three hundred yards of the enemy before they were mowed down or driven off. The charge was an unmitigated disaster, ordered, as it turned out, by Lord Kitchener himself, who had taken over temporarily from an ailing Roberts. Later recruiting posters depicted Kitchener as an aggressive leader, but here he was far too aggressive, charging a hidden enemy of Boer sharpshooters without artillery or cavalry. In this folly he was supported by the hubris of one vainglorious battalion commander who, like Kitchener himself, had not realized that the business of war had entered the twentieth century.

Thus ended Bloody Sunday. The Canadians had taken part in the charge largely through a misunderstanding brought on by the fact that some companies were cheek by jowl with Aldworth's Cornwalls. When they heard the order to the Cornwalls to fix bayonets, followed by the bugler blowing "Charge!" they could not contain themselves, nor did Otter make any attempt to stop them.

The whole affair was badly conceived. Kitchener himself had apparently given Aldworth his orders over the head of Brigadier Smith-Dorrien, who, from his command post a thousand yards away, watched the mad rush with horror and a sinking heart. Nobody made any attempt to estimate the Boers' position and strength or to look over the ground. The result was the bloodiest Canadian encounter since the War of 1812, and also the bloodiest Canadian engagement of the South African War. Three-quarters of the Canadian casualties endured that day were suffered during that one mad, senseless rush—twenty-one dead, sixty-three wounded.

The British, too, had reason to call it Bloody Sunday; for them it was the costliest day of the war, with 1,262 men killed or wounded. The chief contemporary historian of the war, T.G. Marquis, wrote that same year that "of all the blunders of this war this at Paardeberg is perhaps the most unpardonable." When Lord Roberts arrived, he issued a blunt order: *no more charges.* The charge was not needed, for it had become impossible for the Boers to win. The fighting continued for another nine days by which time the starving enemy, caught in Roberts's ever tightening net, were ready to give up.

On the morning of February 27, Brigadier Smith-Dorrien, from the safety of newly dug trenches only ninety yards from the Boer front line, called out to his opponents to surrender. After several similar calls he saw a white handkerchief tied to a rifle barrel waving from the nearest Boer trench. On his promise not to shoot, a head appeared, then another and another running the length of all the trenches until there were heads and white flags everywhere. "It's just like the resurrection!" Smith-Dorrien remarked.

As man after man came forward and threw his rifle on the ground, it dawned on the men of the Fighting 19th that the battle of Paardeberg was over. The tension snapped, "the fearful expectancy of death, the terrible, terrible sacrifice of life, were all past." They could draw a free breath without the fear of it being their last.

The Canadians began to shake hands with one another, to laugh and joke and sing, and to look forward to a good night's sleep. "We felt like school-boys," Corporal Hubly wrote, "although no one who saw us with gaunt, haggard faces and unkempt beards, with ragged clothes and worn out shoes, would have taken us for anything but tramps."

The Boers, too, appeared relieved that it was over. "Tall, thin, rakish looking men," Hubly described them, "with rope-coloured hair, and a thin beard of the same, dirty and unkempt, with clothes ill-fitting and ragged, out they scrambled. . . . As you watched the ragged, dirty motley mob shamble by, it burned unwillingly into the brain that this undisciplined horde, this miserable band, this crowd of hungry, gaunt, lean, lank, disreputable beings had defied for ten long days and nights the discipline of England. . . . For every life that left their ranks they took a life again. . . . We are forced to grant that they made a noble stand, and we have to acknowledge that they stood defeat with great fortitude."

Shortly afterward, Cronje officially surrendered to Roberts, who wore a plain khaki uniform without any badge of rank except his sword. The British commander waited until one of his generals rode up with an elderly man who was clad in a rough, short overcoat, a wide-brimmed hat, and ordinary tweed trousers. This was Cronje, the most redoubtable fighting general on the Boer side. His face was burned near black by the African sun; his curly beard was streaked with grey, his expression absolutely impassive. "You have made a gallant defence, Sir," Roberts told him after the two touched hats in salute. They breakfasted together as members of the opposing forces stood about, comparing notes. "We can stand the shooting of the average British soldier, but you Canadians are regular fire eaters and know no fear," one Boer was said to have commented—or so the press was to report.

The Boer commander and his wife and grandson were bundled aboard a train for Cape Town, where they were transferred to a ship that would take them to St. Helena, Napoleon's last place of exile, decreed as an appropriate prison by Roberts himself. Cronje and his wife sat silently together on deck, holding hands, until one of the officers produced a gramophone, which greatly intrigued them. Cronje, who had not even heard of Edison's recent invention, listened intently to the songs and music and asked if it was all the work of a ventriloquist. A British officer took the machine to pieces for him, and, as a result, Cronje was more astounded than ever. To his delight, his captors made him a present of the gramophone to alleviate his exile on St. Helena.

The news of his defeat was hailed in Canada with an outpouring of enthusiasm. The British press correspondents were widely quoted: "To Canadians we take off our hats. . ." (London *Daily News*); "The Canadian contingent played the principal part in the decisive moment which forced the stubborn leader to own he was beaten" (*The Times*). Similar tributes came from the British command. Roberts himself publicly praised them: "*Canadian* now stands for bravery, dash and courage. A gallant deed, worthy of our colonial comrades." An equally enthusiastic tribute came from the commander of the Gordon Highlanders. "The Canadians are wonders. Their charge toward the Boer trenches really took our breath away. We supported them but they sprang ahead like racehorses. Though beardless youths they fought like veterans."

On March 1, after more skirmishing on the Modder, the army of 40,000 set off on another trek to Bloemfontein. As one wounded private put it as he was invalided home, "It's not the fighting that kills, it's the marching." The Canadians had never known marches like these. The two-week march grew more arduous as men began to fall out with their boots in tatters. The ground was either rough and rocky or so swampy that the men tried to step high in order to get a sure footing and avoid the slime-covered stones, but the soles of their boots had been worn so smooth it was difficult to move forward without stumbling. By the time they reached Bloemfontein the Royal Canadians seemed an outlandish lot. Their clothes were in rags. Appearing on parade, in the description of one Canadian war correspondent, they wore anything "from the full dress uniform of the captain of a whaling vessel to blankets wrapped round their legs while their trousers were being put together piece by piece for the last time."

In spite of the merciless heat, some Canadians took to wearing overcoats in place of their ragged uniforms. In some cases their boots gave out entirely. Private Hatfield from New Brunswick, whose boots fell apart, wrapped puttees around his feet and limped stubbornly on, his toenails torn off and his soles clotted with blood blisters.

They finally staggered into the capital on March 13, so parched that they had even scooped up the mud from the swamps and gulped it down gratefully in an attempt to soothe their swollen lips. Here Arthur Conan Doyle observed them. "The Canadians are fine strapping fellows," he wrote in *The Times*, "broad-shouldered, clean-limbed and blue-eyed. They swung past with easy stride and free gait conscious of strength and pride brought with them from the lakes and mountains of Canada. Their boots were out at the toes, their stockings undarned, their breeches torn, then mended and torn again, but every stain was honour to these sons from over the sea, who have marched shoulder to shoulder with regiments of long and great tradition."

Bloemfontein, a community of 3,500, had been taken without a struggle, for the Boers had melted away before Roberts's army had arrived. Here, every public building in the town was transformed into a hospital for the scores of soldiers suffering from exhaustion and disease, especially enteric fever contracted from drinking water polluted by the corpses of men and animals. At one point, the Canadians had ninety-one men and four officers lying in various hospitals in the community.

Now, with the Boers fleeing before them in long wagon trains, they faced another gruelling march—300 miles from Bloemfontein to Pretoria, each man carrying 50 pounds on his back. The Boers had a habit of firing the long veldt grass, and as the Canadians advanced through the blinding smoke, Otter turned to Lieutenant C.F. Winter, one of his subalterns, and asked what it reminded him of. Winter replied at once, "The march across the ice in Jackfish Bay, Lake Superior, Sir, on Easter Day, 1885, when we were en route over one of the gaps in the then-new CPR to take part in the North West Canada Campaign of that year, only that instead of burning cinders it was sleet and ice that caused much of the same sensation. . . ." Otter replied that the same thought had occurred to him, but added, "I think I would prefer the cool freshness of our own land to this fiery furnace!"

In this eighty-four-day trek, the Fighting 19th Brigade lived up to its name by enduring more battles than any other unit in the army. On April 25, Otter himself was put temporarily out of action when a bullet grazed his neck and chin. By the time they reached Kroonstad, after marching and fighting for the first 130 miles, the regiment was down to 480 men of all ranks in spite of the addition of a new draft of 100 sent from Canada with the second contingent.

On May 26 the Canadians, crossing the Vaal River, became the first British troops in the Transvaal. When they marched through Johannesburg's deserted streets on May 31 it was "more like a funeral service than a triumphant entry." Pretoria, the capital, fell five days later, again vacated by the Boers. As far as the high command was concerned, this was the end of the war. But, of course, it wasn't.

Smith-Dorrien had a special word of commendation before the brigade was broken up. "The 19th Brigade has achieved a record which any infantry brigade might be proud of. Since the date it was formed, February 12, 1900, it has marched 620 miles, often on half rations, never on full. It has taken part in the capture of ten towns, fought in ten general engagements and on twenty-seven other days. In one period of thirty days it fought twenty-one of them and marched 327 miles. Casualties between 400 and 500. Defeats nil."

4

Dinky Morrison's war The second Canadian contingent arrived in South Africa early in February 1900—a much more practical force of mounted men and artillery batteries. Lieutenant E.W.B. "Dinky" Morrison, who would later make his name at Vimy, has given a graphic account in a series of letters home, describing D Battery's 500-mile trek from Cape Town to De Aar across the Karroo Desert, with the Second Battalion, Canadian Mounted Rifles.

This six-week march across the Karroo was, in Morrison's view, "the hardest march of the war, a most God forsaken region—a stony plain with here and there hills of khaki dust, their faces pock marked with bunches of blue-green sagebrush." Occasionally the column passed a huddle of desolate-looking corrugated iron houses or one-storey mud huts, encircled by large stone dikes. But there was no sign of agriculture except for herds of wild goats and sheep. The heat and the dust were maddening. Khaki-coloured storms circulated around the desert in blinding clouds. It was impossible to see a hundred yards to the front or rear of the long columns of ox, mule, and donkey teams that seemed to wind out of the mist and disappear into the dust ahead. Men and animals turned a yellowish green as the dust increased. There was no drinkable water; the column had to carry all its food and fuel. Oddly, the Karroo brought reminders of home, for it was perfectly flat to the horizon, "with here and there a blue kopje standing out like a rocky island on the bosom of Lake Huron."

On the morning of March 15 the column was assailed by a cloud of South African locusts, which covered several square miles so thickly it created a rusty fog lying thirty feet above the desert. The march was so trying, the men so exhausted (the column had moved sixteen miles in seven hours) that drivers fell asleep and tumbled from their horses, while gunners, falling unconscious beside their guns, were nearly run over. Soon the dust grew so deep in the trail that the wheels made no sound and "it was like moving with a ghostly procession in a dead land."

The field force reached the community of Carnarvon on April 7 and rested for twenty-four hours before setting out on another 150-mile trek to De Aar. The horses were in worse condition than the men, and there was no forage. Some animals were so stiffened that they could not move more than ten feet and were put in the middle of the gun or wagon team to be dragged along all day by the other five horses. So barren was the land that even in Carnarvon, a community of eight hundred, there was scarcely enough fuel available to cook supper.

"Day after day we rode along," Morrison wrote home, "sometimes in a seething cloud of dust, other times in deep sand or mud. . . . It is like moving along slowly at sea. You see a kopje ahead that does not seem to be far off, but you travel for hours before you get abreast of it, and hours more before it is out of sight. . . ."

The winding column reached De Aar on April 14, many of the surviving horses so weak that they could scarcely carry their harnesses and so ravenous that they devoured the little Karroo thorn bushes, roots and all.

At De Aar the force was refitted. The mounted infantry departed to join in the march from Bloemfontein to Pretoria. One Canadian artillery battery was dispatched to take part in the relief of Mafeking. But Morrison's D Battery was held at De Aar because of the condition of the horses, to the great disappointment of the gunners, who turned away from the bulletin boards with tears in their eyes at the thought of going home without having seen any action. With Pretoria occupied, it was accepted that the war was over. It wasn't. To this point it had been a nineteenth-century conflict; now it entered the new century. In the guerrilla war that followed, the Boers were adept but the British clumsy.

By early August, Morrison and his battery were at Pienaarspoort, sixteen miles from Pretoria, preparing to join Roberts's forces in pursuit of General Louis Botha, the Boer commander-in-chief, who was rapidly retreating north. The railway was being repaired to hasten the advance, and skirmishes were breaking out along the badly shattered line. Morrison took some leave and rode into Pretoria through country ravaged by the war. Here he found an empty city—nothing for sale in the stores, beer, matches, and tobacco unattainable (save the powerful Boer tobacco). At night, with the streets under curfew, it was a city of the dead. Where were the people? In the course of a 150-mile march to the Transvaal capital, Morrison had seen no more than a dozen houses that were occupied. In Pretoria, fully one-third of the houses were vacant or occupied by troops. Obviously, the citizens had trekked out into the countryside still held by Botha. But how were the women living? The horses had all been commandeered, there was no means of tilling the land, and the prices in the towns were all inflated because of the war.

On the way back to camp, Morrison stopped at the only inhabited farm to get a cup of coffee. The house was occupied by an old man and his two daughters who, though alarmed at a soldier's appearance, invited him in. "They were very intelligent people," Morrison noted; "in fact I have yet to make the acquaintance of the 'ignorant Boers.'" The elder daughter was the wife of a Boer farmer near Natal. She had left in February to visit her father and hadn't heard of her husband since but knew that her house had been burned and her farm ruined.

As the railway was repaired, the British moved gradually toward Belfast, the first objective point of Roberts's army. Here, in the mountains, Botha was expected to make his last stand. Morrison's battery marched to the Wilge River, skirmishing as they went. During the march, at one o'clock in the morning a bizarre incident occurred. The battery was awakened by a gunshot, followed by the trilling of an officer's whistle and much shouting. The infantry stood to arms; the battery manned the guns in the belief that a night attack was in progress. Then it turned out that the adjutant of the Royal Fusiliers had gone crazy, awakened, and fired his gun at one of the men. He was sent back to Pretoria in the morning. This was not an isolated case. "It is remarkable the number of officers and men who have been afflicted with brain troubles during this war," Morrison commented. "The severe strain tells."

By this time the army in South Africa was tormented by lice to the point of desperation. "To see a regiment or brigade or division 'delousing' itself is a sight for gods and men, but not women," Morrison wrote home. "The moment a corps halts, even on the line of march, thousands of men strip off their accoutrements, coats and shirts, and, sitting on the ground in the broiling sun or bitter wind, proceed to make the verb active. The whole army suffers dreadfully, pestered by day and kept awake by night. Luckily the officers escape this scourge, but the men who have to wear the same clothes for weeks at a time are never exempt," a comment that tells as much about the army class system as it does about the conditions.

Here, before the coming battle of Belfast, Lord Roberts was very much in evidence. The army idolized him. As Morrison put it, "he has such an unaffected friendly way with him and a total absence of 'side'. . . . Amid all the cares of handling a quarter million men he is never too busy to walk down from his private car to say a cheery word to a convoy of wounded . . . or to turn out with all his staff to inspect a Canadian field battery, because he knows it will give them pleasure." At Sunday morning service, the weather close and hot, he stood up for the entire affair though any number of men dropped in the ranks. He was sixty-seven years old at the time—a dapper little man, deceptively diminutive, his uniform fashionably cut—who lived upon the ordinary soldier's rations (what's good enough for them, he said, was good enough for him).

Kitchener, "the man of ice and iron," who towered over him, was cut from different cloth. "He gives one the impression of not feeling very much at home," Morrison commented. "I have never seen him chatting with anyone, even when the staff is 'standing easy'. . . . You instinctively think of something powerful and calmly ferocious under restraint. . . . Though so tall he is rather heavily built, and moves with a deliberateness that would be sluggish were it not for the impression of a tremendous physical strength. . . . He is the sort of man who would lyddite* sixteen thousand of the enemy, light a fresh cigar and lyddite sixteen thousand more with not a thought of anything but military exigency and the welfare of the state. He is, in a word, the very antithesis of his small, alert, benevolent-looking chief." It was Roberts, magnanimous in victory, who managed to ease the bitter tensions between the two sides. Kitchener, who replaced him, launched the vicious scorched-earth policy that turned so many Britons against the war.

The army was on the move again, strung out for ten miles like a huge khaki snake, undulating over the veldt, crawling around kopjes, squirming through passes, writhing over ridges and down through valleys, "its head of mobile mounted troops feeling this way and that in front. . . ." By this time the mounted Canadians had earned the admiration of other troops. On parade, as Morrison wrote, "they look like a regiment of cowboys, with their shaggy little ponies, prairie hats and rough-and-ready uniforms—for their original kit is worn out, and they wear any sort of clothes they can pick out."

Morrison noted a crucial difference between the Canadians and their British counterparts. He thought the Canadians' outpost work was the best he'd ever seen "for the simple reason that they know how to keep under cover." But the British soldier kept under cover only when he was being fired upon; otherwise, Morrison noted, he often chose a

* A high explosive consisting chiefly of picric acid.

conspicuous position on a ridge or hilltop where the Boers could spot him and take him out. "The Canadians keep under cover all the time, taking up their positions before daylight, and the Boers never know just where they will stumble on them or how many will be there." The captured Boers to whom Morrison spoke "were particularly intelligent men, and they bore the strongest possible testimony to the bravery of the British soldiers, especially the infantry; but they spoke with regret, rather than admiration, at the manner in which they threw away their lives."

"One keen-looking chap with gold eye glasses" told Morrison that the British would advance toward them to take a position, "and we just shot them down as quickly as we could load and fire. . . . We often spoke among ourselves how sorry we were to kill brave men like that. But what could we do? We always shot the officers in preference to the men. They were brave, too, but foolish. Why did they bring their men up like that?"

All along the route of march, Boers were surrendering. One morning an old man and his four sons gave themselves up, saying they were tired of living up in the rocks like monkeys. "A few thousand such as there are in the field now . . . cannot possibly fight two hundred thousand," one surrendering Boer explained. "The result is that the country is being ruined. Our troops in the field take what they want from the farms and what they leave your troops take."

Morrison was amused to note that so many Boer warriors carried parasols and umbrellas. "The Boer is a compound of all that is unsoldierly in style and soldierly in action. The appearance of a commando of Boers riding along in the sun on their shaggy, little unkempt ponies, or trudging placidly along on foot, every second man holding a gaily-striped parasol or an umbrella over his head, would not impress a representative from the war office as quite the thing. . . . Yet, when the firing commenced, these guileless rural militia folded up their umbrellas, and, no doubt carefully placed the elastic bands on them, and then sallied into the rocks where they put up a brand of fighting that earned them the respect of the best army in the world. And possibly they were far fresher and more fit because they carried this unsoldierly equipment than the British infantry man, staggering along in the heat under his brain-wracking helmet. . . ."

Meanwhile, Morrison noted, relations between imperial officers and colonial troops—never the best—were improving "for the simple reason that the imperial officers are gradually shifting their point of view." They now looked on the colonials "as tribes of shockingly hard-swearing, hard-fighting animals with whom it is neither fitting nor altogether safe to interfere." At Machadodorp, the provost marshal had gone into the Canadian lines and ordered lights out, "an order rarely enforced because fires burned all night as a rule." The Canadians told him to go to hell; they would put out the lights when they were good and ready or when one of their own officers gave the order. When the provost marshal insisted, one of the Canadians drew his revolver, shot out the provost marshal's own light and, with his cronies, threw a blanket over the officer's head, escorted him out of the lines, and fired several more shots to speed him on his way.

At Belfast, the Canadians fought one of the most spectacular actions of the war, a purely Canadian affair with the mounted troops pitted against five times their number of mounted Boers. To Morrison, the battle was "one of the finest military spectacles of the war," a hard fight against an enemy "whose dash and bravery exceeded anything yet done by the Boers in this war." The well-planned enemy attack was repulsed in spite of the long odds. "One Canadian trooper who was severely wounded . . . said he would not have missed being wounded for the privilege of being a spectator at the scene."

By November, with Roberts gone, Kitchener's scorched-earth policy was in full operation. All the men of Belfast were gone from the community, hidden in farmhouses and in small outlying villages that became depots for secret supplies of arms. What followed Morrison described as "the burning trek," with the column moving through the villages burning or blowing up the farmhouses in which the Boers were hiding and waiting. "Our progress was like the old time forays in the Highlands of Scotland two centuries ago. . . . We moved from valley to valley 'lifting' cattle and sheep, burning, looting and turning out the women

62

and children to sit and cry beside the ruins of their once beautiful farm-steads. It was the first touch of Kitchener's iron hand. And we were the knuckles. It was a terrible thing to see and I don't know that I want to see another trip of that sort, but we could not help approving the policy, though it rather revolted most of us to be the instruments."

The troops burned a track about six miles wide through these fertile valleys, leaving a trail of smoke that could be seen at Belfast. Many houses were surrounded by beautiful gardens abloom with roses, lilies, and hollyhocks and embowered by fruit trees. These too were reduced to ashes. From his artillery position on a nearby hill, Morrison could see a troop of mounted men heading for a farm and watched the women and children being bundled out, their bedding tossed out of the windows behind them. A moment later, smoke would begin curling up from the windows and doors, at first a pale blue mist, then a dense cloud as cavalry rode off leaving the women and children standing desolate in the yard.

Later, from a vantage point on a hill above the pretty little village of Witpoort, Morrison watched the mounted men ride in, looting and burning every house and shop except one belonging to a British sub-ject. Even the flour mill was blown up. When the mounted troops rode away, they "looked like a gang of dissolute pedlars." Their saddles were hung like Christmas trees with shawls, clocks, mandolins, tea-kettles, lamps—every imaginable article in addition to chickens, ducks, geese, suckling pigs, and vegetables.

On the fourth morning of the trek the column moved north to sack and burn the town of Dullstroom. "Nobody who was there will ever forget that day's work," Morrison commented. Here was a pretty little village, nestling in a valley, surrounded by flower gardens with the roses all in bloom. In rode the cavalry, and soon a dense cloud of smoke that could be seen for fifty miles rose up from the town.

"The main street was full of smoke and fiery cinders, and as the flames belched out in huge sheets from one side or the other our horses shied and plunged from side to side. The place was very quiet except for the roaring and crackle of flames. On the steps of the church were huddled a group of women and children. . . . The troops were systematically looting the place over, and as they got through with each house they burned it. Our Canadian boys helped the women to get their furniture out, much as they would do in a fire in a village at home. If they saw anything they fancied they would take it . . . but they had not the callous nerve to take people's stuff in front of their faces."

Morrison entered a little cottage standing in a rose garden on a side street. Members of the Canadian Mounted Rifles and Royal Canadian Dragoons were looting it but spending more time helping a woman out with her belongings than sacking the house. She was a "good looking, lady-like person" bustling about saving her valuables. "What would you want next, lady?" a big dragoon asked her, and she told him. Then she turned on Morrison: "Oh, how could you be so cruel?" she cried. She was the quintessential damsel in distress, and Morrison felt sorry for her until the house began to burn and a secret pile of ammunition exploded and nearly killed some of his men. "But all the same it was a sad sight to see the little houses burning and the rose bushes wither up in the pretty gardens and the pathetic groups of homeless women and children crying among the ruins as we rode away."

Like other Canadian troops, Morrison's gunners had signed on for a year, and the time to quit South Africa was fast approaching. The Royal Dragoons, Canadian Mounted Rifles, and Morrison's D Battery were leaving Smith-Dorrien's command after nineteen days as part of the Belfast Flying Column that had seen eight engagements with the Boers. In his farewell remarks, the general declared that "he would choose no other mounted men in the world before them." Morrison wrote home that he did not realize how popular the Canadians were until the time came for them to go. Even the Boers praised them. As one old woman said to him, "We like you Canadians. I hope you will get home safe to your friends." The Royal Irish Band played the colonials out to the tune of "Auld Lang Syne" while the officers and men of the Gordon Highlanders lined the track and cheered themselves hoarse as their old comrades in arms passed by.

In Pretoria the Canadians turned over their horses to the British

64

government. Out of a complement of 137 animals, 66 had survived. As their train pulled out there was a general expression of opinion that in the next war the Canadian troops should be formed into one division. Here were the first faint stirrings of Canadian nationalism that the war against the Boers had accelerated. "Judging from the credit each arm has gained in the force they have fought in, they would unitedly form a combination it would be hard to equal," Morrison wrote proudly. "That is the opinion that has been expressed by imperial officers. It is half the battle to be acting in concert with troops you can thoroughly depend upon. . . . It is everywhere admitted that many corps cannot adapt themselves to the work in hand the way Canadians do, and I suppose all colonials do."

On December 4, when all colonial troops at Pretoria tendered a banquet for the Canadians, the praise lavished upon them caused Morrison to feel his head "swelling as the truth gradually dawns . . . that the term 'colonial' instead of being the designation of a people 'a little lower than the angels' was in future to be synonymous in the military Valhalla with that of Mars himself." The Royal Canadians reached Halifax to cheering crowds and flag-bedecked streets on January 9, 1901, and were in Ottawa two days later, where a reception followed. When it was over Morrison climbed into a sleigh with a friend to make a run for home. As he did, a small boy he knew climbed in with him and snuggled down in the blankets as the sleigh dashed through the streets of the capital. "Mr. Morrison," he piped up, "did you have a nice time in the war?" Everybody laughed, but the more Dinky Morrison thought about it, the more he was sure that, in spite of everything, he *had* had a nice time.

5

The last Canadians to leave South Africa were the hard-riding members of the Strathcona Horse, whose voyage to the dark continent was marred by the death of 176 horses from pneumonia and another 44 when the regiment was under canvas at Green Park camp. These were replaced

The fruits of victory

by the smaller, rougher Argentine horses, more difficult to handle but no problem to the experienced frontiersmen who made up the unit.

In June the Strathconas were posted to the elite 3rd Mounted Brigade, commanded by the Earl of Dundonald. Steele told his men that they were brigaded with "one of the outstanding Corps in South Africa. You must show them that you can scout a country as well as they can; but damn the Strathcona that gets lost."

The physique of these Westerners impressed the British. "Why did you bring such big men as mounted troops?" General Buller asked Steele when they first met. "Well, sir," Steele responded, "I looked all over Canada and these were the smallest men I could find." Buller laughed at that. "I am something of a liar myself," he said, "but you beat me."

The Strathconas established their reputation when one of their sergeants, Arthur Herbert Richardson, won the first Canadian Victoria Cross of the war. The decoration came as a result of a close-quarters skirmish between thirty-eight Canadians and a party of eighty Boers. In the uneven battle, Corporal McArthur of the Strathconas was wounded twice and had his horse shot from under him. Richardson, whose own horse was wounded, galloped to within thirty yards of the Boer position, threw the wounded man across his saddle, and dashed back to camp with the enemy in pursuit, one bullet puncturing his Stetson and two more ripping into his tunic. A three-wire fence barred the way; Richardson's exhausted horse refused to cross it. The pursuing Boers were calling for Richardson to surrender when one of their bullets, missing the two Canadians, hit the horse in the shoulder, causing it to plunge forward, leap the wire, and gallop toward camp. The horse died an hour later, but by then Richardson and the wounded corporal were safe.

An extremely modest man, Richardson represented the North West Mounted Police at the coronation of Edward VII in 1902. Few of his friends knew he'd won the V.C. For several years an impostor passed himself off as the gallant sergeant. Richardson did nothing to expose the hoax.

When the regiment returned to Canada in March 1901, their reputation preceded them. Buller himself had snowed them under with plaudits. "I have never served with a nobler, braver or more serviceable body of men." Kitchener, in bidding them goodbye, had gone out of his way to reveal how many officers commanding regiments on the veldt had asked for the Strathconas. Steele, after a short leave, returned to South Africa to take command of a division of another military unit, the South African Constabulary. More significant, perhaps, was the accolade from the commission established after the war to investigate and assess the disappointing British performance. It went out of its way to make an exception of the Canadians and had nothing but praise for the former Mountie. "There is no better commander," its report declared, "than the rough-riding colonel from Canada."

By that time, with all the Canadians back home, the war had devolved into a series of guerrilla skirmishes, maddening the British who wanted the Boers to come out in the open and fight like men. Kitchener grew more ruthless. He increased the pressure on the Boer families that Morrison had witnessed during his battery's "burning trek" and set out to sweep the country clean of everything that could aid the guerrillas—horses, cattle, sheep, and yes, women and children, too.

But where to put these families whose houses and farms had been destroyed? Certainly they must not be allowed to aid their menfolk. The answer was to herd them into "relief" camps along the railway lines that were quickly given the name "concentration camps," a name that had the same grisly overtones it was to have fifty years later. In these camps, run on military lines, the diet was so poor that it abetted the spread of disease and ultimately led to death.

It is true that the non-combatants had been stuffed into the camps in a sense for their own protection. But that does not excuse the ghastly statistics that disturbed a liberal-minded section of the British public. At Bloemfontein, to take one hideous example, half the children and two-fifths of the adult internees died. The overall death toll in the camps was between 20,000 and 28,000, but no newspaperman dared jeopardize his career reporting those figures. When the great American correspondent Richard Harding Davis moved over to the Boer side of the war and began to record "enemy" casualties, he was expelled from his London club.

A dumpy, forty-one-year-old English spinster from Cornwall, Emily Hobhouse, was able to accomplish what the journalists neglected. She managed to wangle permission to sail to South Africa and observe the camps first-hand. The overcrowding appalled her—there were 60,000 already in the camps during her first visit and hundreds more arriving almost daily. But it was the death rate that sickened her: ". . . it was a death rate such as had never been known except in the time of the Great Plagues . . . the whole talk was of death—who died yesterday, who lay dying today, who would be dead tomorrow."

Back she went to England. There, her campaign against the camps created a tidal wave of shock. Others had serious concerns about the camps, *but she had been there.* And the death rates continued to rise: 34.4 percent per annum by October, and for children alone, about 60 percent. Near the end of 1901 Kitchener reversed his policy and ordered all column commanders to cease bringing women and children to the camps but to leave them with the guerrillas. At the same time schools were set up in the camps, and the death rate began to subside. By April 1902, with the death rate down to 3 percent and peace negotiations under way, Joseph Chamberlain, always alive to the need for Empire solidarity, hit upon a method of using the colonies to help in the education of the Boer children. He asked for volunteer teachers from all parts of the Empire to travel to South Africa at Britain's expense to take part in the plan. In Canada, a thousand applied; the colonial office wanted only fifty, and these young women became the first colonials to take advantage of the offer. Maud Graham of Owen Sound, Ontario (E. Maud Graham, she styled herself in the fashion of the day), has left a spirited account of her two-year adventure as a teacher among the Boers.

"Imagine, if you can," she wrote after her return to Canada, "forty girls of a hundred years ago being taken on a trip half around the world, feted *en route* like princesses, all expenses and comforts provided by their Government and paid £100 each for her services as teacher. Or imagine, if you can, forty men of the present day being treated in a like manner!"

They left even before peace was finally sealed, twenty aboard the *Corinthian* out of Halifax on April 12, the remainder aboard the *Lake Ontario* from Saint John a week later. In England they were treated as celebrities, wined and dined by various peers, and introduced at tea to Royalty before setting off on their adventure. "We Canadian teachers did not fancy our fellow passengers," the strait-laced Miss Graham recorded. "There was a party of English teachers aboard who found it amusing to sit about the decks on the subalterns' knees, until the officer commanding put a stop to it. We were rather pleased to hear that these called us 'the Canadian snobs.'"

They were curious about the Boers, of whom they had heard so much, most of it repulsive, some of it downright terrifying. When the ship reached St. Helena, where so many Boer prisoners were interned, they encountered a pleasantly helpful fair-haired young man, whereupon Gertrude Arbuckle of Summerside, P.E.I., asked if he would point out some Boers to the company. "Well, look at me, I'm one," he said, laughing at their surprise. He, too, was on army parole.

In Cape Town, a government lighter brought news that peace had finally been signed. But there were no signs of rejoicing, not so much as a flag flying. "We heard afterwards that the Cape people were not particularly elated, as they had made fortunes out of the war." The town itself was "very dirty and swarming with people, fashionable women, dusky Cape women with gay scarves on their heads, Kafirs, coolies, and khaki, khaki everywhere." The city was a jumble of handsome stone buildings and stuccoed native cottages, the roadways crammed with electric trams, donkey carts, carriages, cabs, ox-wagons, and troops of cavalry. In this hot and humid metropolis they tried to buy some ice cream only to find the shopkeepers amazed and hilarious. "Ices in the winter!" they fairly shouted in derision.

On the train trip north across the Great Karroo they passed a group of British Tommies on a siding. "You're going the wrong way," the soldiers yelled. Miss Graham noted the signs of war that were everywhere— a continuous entanglement of barbed wire surrounding every railway station, Kitchener's block houses of mud and stone fortified with sandbags, "and all uniformly desolate with a sign picked out in white-washed stones, 'Please throw us your old papers,' then a hospital hedged with white wooden crosses and more graves scattered along the route, bones bleaching in the sun, heaps of tin cans, and dead cattle."

At Norval's Point a peculiar smell assailed their nostrils as they moved into their tents. It was explained that this was the result of the weekly "smearing" of the floors with manure water to harden them. The doctors winked at the process, which had always been the custom in the poorer houses.

Here Miss Graham settled into her routine: a morning hymn first, generally a Moody and Sankey offering of which the Boer children were fond or "Dare to Be a Daniel," another favourite. Then she called the roll, examined feet, hands, necks, and ears, sending the dirtiest children back to their tents to wash. The girls she found cleaner than the boys—"odd wee men" who wore shapeless hats and clothes made of mud-covered corduroy. Children with veldt sores were sent to the line nurses for treatment. These sores, hard to heal, were caused by poor food; in many cases the only food the children had was the camp soup. Miss Graham then unlocked the big cupboard and distributed slates to her charges for the morning lesson.

One day at the end of June there was great excitement. A big Boer commando had surrendered and come into the camp, but the wives refused to believe peace had been signed and said they wouldn't believe it until they heard it from the Boer general, Christiaan De Wet, himself. They called their sons and husbands "hands-uppers" and proceeded to beat them with brooms and any other convenient weapon. As a result, the school superintendent telegraphed De Wet, who came two days later. For many it was a pathetic moment. "Before he finished," Miss Graham recalled, "everyone was in tears." The general said he had done his best in the war; no man could do more. They had fought bravely and had been fairly conquered. Now he advised them not to waste their energy in useless grumblings but to take advantage of the school, work their farms well, and show the world what good stuff was in them.

But the war was not forgotten when a little girl went up to shake the general's hand. He drew back. "Your uncle was a traitor who surrendered with Cronje, and I cannot shake hands with such people," he said shortly—a reprimand that caused the child to cry bitterly.

Miss Graham was posted to Maple Cottage, a school in the chief town, Fauresmith, reached by a "shocking road" out of the town of Jagersfontein. Most of the residents of Fauresmith had been wealthy before the war, but few had yet come home. The streets were littered with rubbish, broken furniture, wrecked pianos, empty tins, and dead animals. The shops were all shuttered, the fine homes broken into, and the big hotel in ruins. The eight-room schoolhouse had been sacked in turn by troops of Yeomanry, Highlanders, and colonials. Every bit of furniture was smashed, every mirror in fragments, every mattress ripped up and scattered, every dish broken. This indescribable mixture of debris lay six inches deep on all the floors. A good organ was in fragments; the cadaver of a horse lay in the yard; and next door was a heap of dead sheep.

The town library, too, had been sacked, all the silverware in the community looted, and, since there was no wood on the veldt, all the furniture used for firewood. Of sixty-two pianos in the town, only two escaped; three pipe organs had also been smashed. "It seemed," Miss Graham wrote, "as if the spirit of destruction had seized both sides equally, for Dutch and English agreed that what one side of the street had spared, the other had destroyed."

A number of families had taken and kept an oath of neutrality under Roberts and, as a result, had suffered severely at the hands of their neighbours. One elderly woman showed Miss Graham her dining room suite, from which the leather had all been stripped to mend the uniforms of Dutch commandos. When she asked an officer why they had smashed all the mirrors, he replied, "If you had been on *trek* for six months without a chance to shave or have a hair-cut you wouldn't ask that question." She and her fellow teacher, Miss Archibald, were not prepared for a cordial reception, but the townspeople were unexpectedly hospitable. They were greeted with presents of flowers, homemade bread, fresh butter, and even the occasional egg, none of which could be bought at any price.

"If those Fauresmith houses could have spoken, what a history they could have told of those vacant months," Miss Graham wrote, "of the repeated attacks on the town from the block-houses on the surrounding kopjes, with the Dutch making their last stand up in the big church tower; of the burning of the shopmen's goods in the market square; of the women grinding corn in the coffee mills to make coarse bread; of the long *trek* of the refugees to the various camps, or the East; of the endless succession of Highlanders, Dutch commandos, Yeomanry, more Dutch, Driscoll's Scouts, Remington's Constabulary, all looting and all destroying."

From the constabulary they were given the other side of the story: "How one of their sergeants, a quiet little Australian, had been imprisoned in a Boer laager, stripped naked, and sent back on foot across the burning veldt to his own camp, miles away, which he had reached almost dead; and how in one little village of Dopper Dutch, the women and children had mobbed the house of the only British residents, in the absence of the father, and told the wife and girls what the Dutch intended to do with them as soon as they had driven the English into the sea— and then fired on the house. . . ."

One day, when out for a stroll with Miss Archibald, Miss Graham heard the thunder of hooves behind them. The rider dismounted and cried out, "Excuse me! But I'm a Canadian and I was looking out of the mess window when you passed by, and I knew you were Canadians by the way you go up the street as if you owned the town. The fellows said you were the new teachers, and I just *had* to come and speak to you. I hope you'll pardon me but I haven't seen any but Dutch girls and Kafirs for three mortal years."

The two women were moved. "We felt a pride in our country swelling as he stood there, six feet of well-developed young Canada, with fair hair and blue eyes gleaming out of his brown skin. The unconventionality scarcely occurred to us; we were becoming accustomed to the friendly *veldt* fashion of greeting all strangers."

This lesson in nationalism, which all Canadians feel when they are far from home, was abetted when the two teachers encountered the members of an especially bitter and anti-British family on a nearby farm. One of the daughters, "a little fair woman with golden curls," had been a Boer ambulance nurse and later a spy. She was an excellent seamstress and did some work for the teachers, all the while railing at the English and calling them "white devils."

"Why do you talk like that?" Miss Graham asked her. "We are British, remember."

"Oh," she replied, "you may be British, but you are not English. You are Canadian, and we like Canadians—you come from a big free country and you are not stiff."

The teachers all spent two years in South Africa. As Maud Graham and her friend Margaret De Wolfe lolled against the rail of RMS *Gascon* in Cape Town harbour, preparing to leave for Canada, "a thousand uncertainties passed through our minds." The date was July 7, 1904, and now, watching Table Mountain looming dimly through the rain and mist—a counterpart to the scene that had greeted them two years before—they began to contrast their first and last impressions of the wartorn country. "In 1902 there had been curiosity mingled with hope; in 1904 there was hope mingled with anxiety, vague and formless, it is true, as the tablecloth of mist hanging over the mountains, but none the less depressing. It seemed as if those veiled mountains were typical of the hidden future of the vast, silent country to which they belonged."

The two talked about the ready adaptability of the South African temperament and agreed that "whenever there was a chance to be hopeful, everyone had the knack of shaking off trouble with the facility of children." The rains had arrived at last to banish the searing drought that had held the nation in thrall for almost three years. Some of the compensation promised after the war had been paid. The farms had regained a homelike appearance. Houses and fences were neatly repaired, and scarcely a trace of war remained. Not a yard of barbed-wire entanglement was to be seen, nor a blockhouse. The big camps had vanished "leaving immaculate neatness behind them; and no landmarks remained save the occasional grave."

They reached Southampton on July 31, spent three weeks visiting friends in England and Scotland, and were "agreeably surprised at the increased interest shown in Canadian affairs." On August 20 they sailed from Glasgow and reached Quebec City nine days later.

Back home in Owen Sound, Maud Graham was full of her experiences and found a willing audience. One friend, an old university acquaintance, listened to her story with enthusiasm and not a little longing.

"I wish I were a girl," he told her. "You girls have the best of everything nowadays." And, as she was to note in her reminiscences, "he was right."

By this time in Canada, the South African War was history. With the Orange Free State and the Transvaal firmly attached to the Empire, the cult of imperialism seemed a little threadbare. It was not easy to talk about a just and Christian war when, after the fall of Pretoria, things began to turn nasty—a harbinger of later wars. Canada's role had been minuscule, as Dinky Morrison noted when a package of two-month-old newspapers reached him at Belfast. "I notice," he wrote home ". . . that not a few newspapers and public men in Canada are talking about the sacrifices the Dominion has made for the empire in this war. It might be well to go softly on this line. Surely the speakers or writers are not aware that Australia has over ten thousand troops out here . . . and that New Zealand, with a population of half a million, has two thousand. The Dominion, with a population nearly twelve times that of New Zealand, sent out barely 3,500 troops,[*] all told, and one-seventh of that number were contributed by the private purse and patriotism of Lord Strathcona. . . . But regarded strictly as a national 'sacrifice' on the altar of our common country the chilly statistics should deter wise people from boasting."

In English Canada in the early months of the war, the victory at Paardeberg, the relief of Mafeking, and the fall of Pretoria had set off

[*] The actual figure was twice that.

paroxysms of celebration. (Towns like Kimberley and Ladysmith in British Columbia remind us of the intensity of the imperial sentiment.) When the news reached Toronto that Canadian troops had entered Pretoria the city went berserk with joy, mounting the greatest celebration in its history. As the *Toronto Star* headlined it, "A DELIRIUM OF GLEE SWEEPS OVER THE QUEEN CITY." Few Torontonians went to bed that night. Bonfires blazed at every corner. People poured into the street yelling, banging dinner pails and tin dishes, and sounding cowbells, trumpets, and kazoos. At King and Yonge the crowd was so dense it was impossible to cross the street. Processions of celebrants snaked through the city wearing or waving Union Jacks. One group broke into a store, seized all the fireworks, and set them off in the middle of the roadway. Men, women, and children danced in the streets, singing, shouting, and cheering. The following day the mayor declared a holiday, and more impromptu celebrations broke out with the news that Kruger had fled Africa for Holland.

Yet it was also impossible for the most virulent jingoist not to feel a grudging admiration for the Boers' stubborn stand. The British had put 500,000 troops in the field, the Boers a mere 70,000 and never more than 25,000 at any one time. Yet they had kept the Empire at bay for the best part of two years.

As the war dragged on, tempers had cooled and enthusiasm waned. In 1902, after the articles of surrender were signed, Toronto's Goldwin Smith, historian, journalist, and gadfly, published the kind of pamphlet he would not have dared to release at the height of the tumult. Titled *In the Court of History*, it had the subtitle *An Apology for Canadians Who Were Opposed to the South African War*. Smith wrote that since the end of the war, the minds of Canadians "must have been opened. They have all along been told, and have, no doubt, believed, that the Boer was a 'barbarian,' a 'perfidious savage,' a 'Marauder,' a 'Brigand,' a 'Buccaneer,' an 'assassin,' a 'Cateran,' a 'Dacoit'; that civilized war could not be made with him, that the only way was to treat him as a robber and shoot him down; and that, from this, sickly sentimentalism alone would recoil.

"They see now the Boer leaders hailed as gallant antagonists by our own generals, welcomed by Ministers, cheered by British crowds, honoured by Royalty itself. Is it not possible that they have been misled on other points by the same organs of information?"

Smith made the point that the position of the Boers, who left British rule to found two independent commonwealths, the Transvaal and the Orange Free State, in 1835, "somewhat resembled that of the founders of Canada," and "that these people were politically barbarians, needing to be civilized by the Anglo-Saxon sword, is the suggestion of our Anglo-Saxon self-esteem."

"In the course of this debate," Smith wrote, "it had more than once cropped up in certain quarters that 'equal rights,' the professed object of the war, is intended only for white men; an ominous insinuation for an Empire, five-sixths of the population of which are coloured, and whose ally is Japan. Such is the growing sentiment. England prides herself on having abolished slavery. Is it certain that she would do it now? In the craving of the mine-owners of Johannesburg for labour forced and cheap, we see, as far as they are concerned, the main object of war."

Smith listed other British war aims: "The suppression of Boer independence . . . the extension of British supremacy over the whole of South Africa . . . the possession of the mines, combined with revenge for Majuba Hill. . . ."

Again, Smith saw a Canadian parallel to the struggle of the Boers. Wilfrid Laurier "was the worthy representative of a race, the history of which resembled that of the Dutch in South Africa. Conquered, and politically depressed by the conquerors, it had been forced to strike for its rights, which, after a struggle, it had won. In the British loyalists at Cape Colony, pouring out their vengeance on the rebels, Sir Wilfrid Laurier might see the counterparts of the British loyalists in Canada, who, because they were not allowed to set their feet on the neck of the French-Canadians, stoned the Governor General and set fire to the Parliament House in Montreal."

Smith suggested another wicked little parallel. The British had treated the Transvaal as a "foreign state" until the Uitlanders began to pour in seeking gold. "What should we say," he asked, "if the American government were to claim for its citizens now pouring into British Columbia and the Northwest, participation in the government of Canada?"

"What are the fruits of the war?" Smith asked. "Who gains by it?" Later he answered that question, from the Canadian point of view: Laurier had vowed he would not allow Canada to be drawn into "the vortex of European militarism." But Smith predicted, with considerable prescience, that the prime minister "has only to look around him to see that Canada is on the very edge of that vortex, and in imminent danger of being sucked down."

Who gained by the war? Certainly Canada gained a new feeling of self-confidence. "A new power has risen in the West," Laurier boasted after Paardeberg. With the Western boom gathering momentum and the embattled Canadians earning the plaudits of the British, he could be forgiven such moments of buoyancy. But he, more than most, knew only too well what the war had done to national unity. For months some sections of the Francophone press had been taunting English-speaking Canadians over British defeats in South Africa. Then, on March 1, two days after the Paardeberg victory, a gang of McGill students, noticing an absence of flags above the Montreal offices of *La Presse*, *La Patrie,* and *Le Journal*, attacked their headquarters and then the Montreal branch of Laval University itself. The following day students from Laval responded, singing *La Marseillaise* and waving the French tricolour. They were stopped before they could reach McGill, but that evening an English-speaking mob of students, citizens, and town ruffians, fortified with free beer supplied by the jingoistic Montreal *Star*, prepared to attack Laval with frozen potatoes, sticks, and iron bars, only to be turned back when the police sprayed them with water hoses. In retaliation, the crowds broke every window in the Laval buildings. Thus did a foreign adventure serve to widen the split between Canada's two opposing cultures.

The war against the Boers had shown up the deficiencies in the Canadian militia, the "Saturday night" soldiers who would be called on to defend the country in case of need and would make up a manpower pool for the Permanent Force in the event of another war. Lord Dundonald, the British peer chosen by Lord Roberts to head the militia in Canada, discovered that these 35,000 men were either untrained or badly trained and that Canada itself seemed unworried by any prospect of invasion. He told a dinner at the Montreal Military Institute that there were in Canada "those who believed that in order to keep transgressors out . . . all Canadians had to do was to stick up a notice board: 'This is Canada.'" With those views, he said, he had no sympathy. He would very much prefer to see men with rifles in their hands behind the notice boards.

The real problem was political patronage. One of his predecessors, Major General Sir William Gascoigne, wrote to him in December: "You of all men will be little startled at the way military consideration outweighs everything—merit or good service." Dundonald had a practical lesson that same month when, while visiting a group of South African war veterans, he noticed a broken window in the drill hall, through which the rain was pouring. Why hadn't it been fixed? The colonel in charge told him that the problem had existed for some time; but the Liberal glazier was ill, and he had to wait for his recovery, as he was not allowed to get the work done by a Conservative.

The matter came to a head when Dundonald learned that the minister of agriculture, Sydney Fisher, had interfered in the appointment of an adjutant of the 13th Scottish Light Dragoons. In a speech to the Montreal Garrison of the Military Institute on June 4, 1904, he attacked "political interference on purely military matters." He went on to say, "I care not who the man is, if he advances one man or penalizes another on account of the political colour of his party, I say that man, whoever he may be, is not a friend of this country." He then mentioned Fisher by name and outlined the incident, which he described as "a gross instance of political interference."

That did it. Parliamentary debate followed, and ten days after Dundonald spoke he was fired by Frederick Borden, the minister of defence who was the Liberal cousin of the Conservative leader, Robert Borden. The public, apparently, was less concerned about political patronage, which, after all, was well known and accepted, than it was about the idea of a British peer interfering in Canadian politics—a sentiment that Mackenzie King would use to his advantage more than twenty years later.

Her successes in South Africa were beginning to work a subtle change on Canada's attitudes toward the mother country. After all, hadn't Britain bungled the war in the early months? Hadn't she called on Canadian roughriders to help her out of her difficulties? What business had a British blueblood, even a war hero like Dundonald, publicly spanking a Canadian cabinet minister?

The world was changing. In the new century, political patronage would become less blatant and the tools of battle more efficient. The South African War provided Canadians with a skewed vision of what war was all about. After all, they had known no other since 1814. It did not occur, apparently, to any military or political leader that war was about to change as a result of the magazine rifle and the machine gun. But it did occur to a Russian-Polish banker and railway magnate, Ivan S. Bloch, who, in 1898, produced a remarkable work, *Is War Now Impossible?* In it he made a series of prescient predictions:

> The day of the bayonet is over.
>
> The outward and visible sign of the end of war was the introduction of the magazine rifle.
>
> The rifle of tomorrow will be forty times as effective as the chassepot was in the Franco-Prussian War.
>
> The artillery of today is at least 116 times more deadly than the batteries that went into action in 1870.
>
> Everybody will be entrenched in the next war. It will be a great war of entrenchments. The spade will be as indispensable to the soldier as his rifle.
>
> Battles will last for days, and at the end it is very doubtful whether any decisive victory can be gained.
>
> The next war will be a long war.
>
> All wars will of necessity partake of the characteristic of siege operations.

Bloch, in effect, foresaw the battle of the Somme two decades before that bloodbath took place when he predicted that in front of any defended position "there would be formed a belt 110 yards wide over which will fly thousands and thousands of bullets and shells"—a belt in which no living thing could exist.

He was, of course, ignored by the military leaders in their myopia. One general referred to his work as "trash." For Bloch was an outsider— a civilian, a businessman, a foreigner, and, worst of all, a Jew.

The Boer War confirmed the military in its mindset in which armed conflict was seen as an acceptable device in international politics. It also convinced a generation of young Canadians that war was not terribly dangerous. Ivan Bloch had predicted that future conflicts would be long, exhausting wars of attrition that would drag on until one side was too exhausted and too depleted to continue. That is exactly what happened. But, especially for Canada, the Boer conflict had been, in army parlance, "a piece of cake." Of the 7,368 Canadians who went off to war in South Africa, a mere 224 were killed, and half of these succumbed to disease, not bullets. The Boers were beaten in the end, the Empire prevailed, and the international sabre rattling that provoked the next war continued.

The three wars that dominated the first half of the twentieth century can be seen as being as closely interlinked as an ivory puzzle. Each was launched in an atmosphere of sunny optimism. No red-tabbed general had the wit to absorb the chill mathematics of the despised Ivan Bloch. *Home by Christmas!* That hollow promise, regurgitated at the start of each new conflict, quickened the blood of the young men who could not bear to be left out of the next great adventure. And so each war led to the next. The South African adventure made war look glamorous, and relatively painless. It helped create an atmosphere of belligerence in which nations competed with one another for military supremacy in the belief that the next war would be a brief, successful skirmish in which Right would prevail. It was this posturing that led directly to the war that was supposed to end all wars. In fact, that one turned out to be so devastating that its survivors dreaded to do battle again, and so created an atmosphere of appeasement that brought on the worst war of all—a hot war that spawned a cold war, one that again saw Canadians locked in battle in a strange and distant land whose language they could not understand, all in the name of Empire solidarity— not the old Empire, but its successor, whose imperial masters pulled the strings from the new centre of the Western world, just south of the famous unfortified border.

Charles Saunders

1

A year after the Boer War ended, Canada came as close to armed conflict with the United States as she had since the rancorous days of 1812.
The Empire had lost some of its sheen in the face of the unexpected
Boer victories and the New Imperialists were hard put to defend it,
especially after the reports from the South African concentration camps.
In Sara Jeannette Duncan's *The Imperialist*, published in 1904, her protagonist, Lorne Murchison, tries to polish the tarnished creed by persuading his listeners that "the Empire is the real bulwark against
American culture and economic invasion.

"If we would preserve ourselves as a nation it has become our business not only to reject American overtures in favour of the overtures
of our own great England," he declares, "but to keep watch and actively
resist American influence. We often say that we fear no invasion from the
south, but the armies of the south have already crossed the border. . . ."

To any Canadian nationalist in the later years of the century, those
words would have a certain resonance; in the critical year of 1903,
when Duncan finished writing her novel, they hit home with all the
power of a truncheon. To Canada's great humiliation, the Alaska Boundary dispute was settled in favour of the United States, unleashing a
firestorm of resentment as much against the perfidious English as the
arrogant Yankees.

The border between Alaska and Canada had been in contention since
the Klondike stampede. The ravelled coastline—a series of deep fiords
and inlets—added to the confusion. The United States claimed a continuous section of unbroken coastline, while Canada wanted to control
the heads of certain fiords, especially the Lynn Canal that gave access
to the Yukon interior and would make Skagway a Canadian town.
Canada's position was already weak because during the Klondike rush
she had not protested American control of Skagway and its twin town,
Dyea. Indeed, she had tacitly accepted U.S. claims to the Alaskan territory by contemplating an "all-Canadian" railway or wagon road to
circumvent the U.S. customs barrier.

After a long wrangle, the two countries agreed to settle the matter through a tribunal of "six impartial jurists of repute," three to be appointed by the U.S. president, three by Great Britain. *Impartial?* The word stuck in the Canadian craw. The British took the conditions seriously. Sir Louis Jetté, the lieutenant-governor of Quebec, Allen B. Aylesworth, a distinguished Toronto lawyer, and Lord Alverstone, the chief justice of England, would make up the Canadian team. But the so-called jurists on the American side were anything but unbiased, having been carefully selected by President Theodore Roosevelt to make sure that the United States got exactly what it wanted.

Elihu Root could scarcely be called impartial, since he was Roosevelt's secretary of war. Nor could ex-Senator George Turner, who came from Washington, a state that had already shown its bias. Senator Henry Cabot Lodge, one of the leading professional Anglophobes in the country, was already committed publicly and before the fact against the Canadian position. The press reports of these appointments shook Canadians. Lord Minto saw them as "a breach of faith" and declared Canada a victim of "sharp practice."

The bellicose U.S. president made it clear to his nominees that should the verdict go to Canada, he would seize the disputed area by force. In March 1902, he ordered Root to have troops sent as unostentatiously as possible to southern Alaska. If necessary, the Big Stick methods for which he was known would solve the problem.

In London, it was an open secret that Canada was going to lose the dispute. "We are a small dog in a fight with a big dog," Laurier remarked as Canadians did their best to use the English press to demand British support. Cross-border insults became more frequent, and all pretense at impartiality vanished. To Lodge, the Canadians were "a collection of bumptious provincial bullies" bent on blackmailing the British into support.

Canadian opinion was blinded by over-optimism and a new confidence brought on by the war and the Western boom, by the success of the Liberal government's immigration program, by a resentful anti-Americanism, and by an enthusiasm for imperial unity. Canada had sent two contingents to South Africa at Britain's request, as well as the Strathcona Horse, partly expecting a quid pro quo in the border dispute. But Great Britain, while paying lip service to the Canadian claim, seemed remarkably indifferent to the outcome. With their diplomatic influence weakened by events in South Africa, the British had more serious concerns. If necessary, the foreign office was prepared to sacrifice British colonial relations with Canada in order to maintain her international relations with the United States. Roosevelt believed, with Lodge, that the Canadians "didn't have a leg to stand on."

Such was the political atmosphere when the tribunal met in London in October 1903. On the twentieth, the verdict was in—four votes to two in favour of the United States—and the deciding vote against Canada had been cast by Lord Alverstone! The Canadian members of the tribunal angrily refused to sign the resultant document.

The country was stunned, infuriated, and humiliated by the British peer's perfidy. It was generally assumed that he had knuckled under to the Americans in the interest of continuing good relations between the two countries. But, to be fair, the Canadian case was weak, and certainly Alverstone must have considered the consequences had he voted the other way. It could, in fact, have led to war.

These subtle considerations were not voiced by the Canadian press or public. "Canada seems to have been butchered by Alverstone to make a United States holiday," cried the Ottawa *Journal*. The Hamilton *Herald* was revolted that Lord Alverstone had "weakly and shamefully yielded" to the Americans. Clifford Sifton told his editor, John W. Dafoe, that the United States was "going to be the biggest bully the world has ever seen," and Dafoe responded in the Manitoba *Free Press* that the boundary award was "damning evidence of Great Britain's subservience to the United States when the latter's interest conflicts with those of Canada."

"Canada's ministers were tricked and deluded from the start," the Montreal *Herald* declared, adding a wicked little joke:

Teacher: Describe Canada.

Pupil: Canada is that proportion of North America the United States doesn't want.

A Montreal *Star* cartoon showed a vulture-like American eagle peering down at a slumbering John Bull and asking, "Let me see what else there is in sight now?"

Significantly, the full fury of press and public was directed not at the villainous Americans but at the mother country. Alexander Muir, author of "The Maple Leaf Forever," Canada's closest approximation to a national anthem, got permission to fly the Union Jack at half-mast at the Toronto school where he was principal. In British Columbia an audience booed the singing of "God Save the King." A group of Vancouver's leading citizens declared they would not sing it at all unless Great Britain justified herself.

In the heated reaction to the border dispute an awakening Canadian nationalism could be discerned. The *Globe*, for example, accused the British ambassador in Washington of acting as a "stool pigeon" for the United States in Canadian matters. People began to talk of the need for official Canadian representation in the American capital. There were even murmurs advocating separation from the mother country.

Undoubtedly this perceived betrayal contributed to the twilight of the New Imperialism. As *Le Canada* declared, "Mr. Chamberlain has given it to us in the neck. The decision is a rude blow to the cause of Imperial Canada." And also, one might add, a rude blow to the colonial secretary's dream of a centralized and unified Empire. "The tie binding Britain to Canada has been dangerously strained," one writer in *The Outlook* announced. And so it had.

Yet other ties were strengthened. For once, Canadians stood united against what they considered an injustice. All the little cracks and fissures that had disfigured the body politic were, for a time at least, papered over. The Alaska Boundary dispute marked a watershed in the relations between Canada and the mother country. Never again would the British connection seem so solid; never again would the imperial shield seem quite so comforting. The burgeoning dominion was reaching the point where it could ill afford to leave its international affairs in foreign hands. Five years after the Boundary Tribunal brought down its report, Laurier established the first department of external affairs.

By then the country was teeming with new arrivals who had no ties with the imperial past. The heady scent of independence was in the air.

To all this there was an unexpected but ironic corollary. In distancing the country from the embrace of the old empire, the squabble over the Alaska Panhandle had unwittingly nudged it into the arms of the new. Despite all the anti-American cries, the hand-wringing over Teddy Roosevelt's Big Stick, and the genuine suspicions of Yankee motives, Canada found herself more firmly than ever within the continental orbit.

2

The In the peaceful decade following the South African conflict, Canada,
Western enriched by her new Western empire, was close to becoming the bread-
delirium basket of the world. The Great War would tear Europe apart, but by its end Canada would zoom past her competitors to become the second largest exporter of wheat, next to the United States. Five years later she would be in first place, exporting as much wheat to feed the post-war world as her two closest rivals, the United States and Argentina, combined. This was a remarkable achievement for a small, developing country—by far the tiniest of the three—with a population that had not yet reached ten million.

It was no accident. In the continuing drama of Canadian wheat the leading actors were two remarkable but utterly dissimilar creatures. One was a frail and sickly scientist, Charles Saunders of the Dominion Experimental Farm, who would rather play the flute than scribble chemical equations. The other was Laurier's shrewd, hard-driving minister of the interior. Saunders supplied the product: Marquis wheat. Clifford Sifton supplied the producers: the immigrant hordes who tilled the rich loam of the land the tub-thumpers called the Last Best West.

Of this oddly assorted pair, who probably never encountered one another, it is the politician who gets the space in the history books but the scientist who deserves the greater accolade. Thin as a reed, docile as a puppy, he was overshadowed by his domineering father, William, who was his predecessor at what became the experimental farm and who summoned him to Ottawa like a drill sergeant rapping out an order. "I always go where I am pushed," the son once admitted, and off he went meekly, at the age of thirty-six, to become the new Dominion cerealist and change the wheat economy of Canada.

Charles Saunders was destined to perfect the most valuable plant in the world. Yet his years in Ottawa were so unhappy that he could never remember them "without pain, without a sick feeling." The elder Saunders, a demanding perfectionist, was never satisfied with his son's progress. Something of his formidable character can be divined from the knowledge that in a single year he sent out 11,406 letters, checking each personally, even licking the stamps on most of the envelopes.

Charles Saunders arrived in Ottawa in 1903, when the prairies were filling up with farmers to harvest the provender of the plains. Alas, the harsh autumn frosts could destroy crop after crop before the kernels of wheat ripened. A new, faster-maturing strain was needed; Saunders's task was to find it. Had his father not pushed him, Marquis wheat would probably never have been developed.

Where did it come from? That was the mystery. The standard crop since the 1880s was Red Fife, prized by millers and bakers alike. Its Canadian origins sprang from a handful of unusual kernels spotted on a Glasgow dock by a sharp-eyed Scot in a shipment of wheat from Poland and sent in 1842 to a friend, David Fife, at his Ontario farm. Thus did a chance observation help the wheat economy of Canada evolve.

The elder Saunders, in his search for a fast-maturing wheat, had already tried crossing several varieties with Red Fife, including one early-ripening seed from India, Hard Red Calcutta. Hard Red, however, was actually a mixture; in a few generations the cross had resulted in a bewildering number of varieties. Thus, when Charles Saunders went to work he was faced with a needle-in-a-haystack situation of almost one hundred varieties, each containing several strains. In this maddeningly complex family of kernels, surely there must be one early-maturing strain! But how to find it?

A less persevering man might have given up. Not Charles. Patiently, day after day, month after month, he examined one head after another, chewing each kernel, like a stick of Mr. Wrigley's Spearmint, into an elastic mass, using his teeth as grindstones to determine the milling qualities of those that seemed to mature most quickly and using his mouth as a kind of oven to substitute for the one he couldn't afford.

From the hundreds of grains he investigated, one emerged that seemed to have possibilities. These few kernels, twelve in all, he hoarded like gold, planting them in a single plot. He stored the yield from his tiny crop—a few ounces—over the winter in a paper packet, named the new strain Marquis, and after planting it the following year literally masticated his way into history.

As he chewed away he carefully examined the colour: was it too yellow? Or was it pale cream, the kind the bakers preferred? How would it behave in the baking process? The more rubber-like the result—the more gluten per kernel—the bigger the loaf that could be made from the flour. Chewing on Marquis kernels, he was elated to realize that the new wheat had all the qualities to make good, firm bread.

His jaws must have ached, for he had been chewing his way through hundreds of samples—chewing by day and presiding with his wife, a talented mezzo-soprano, over musical soirées by night. Music was a form of release from his dominating father.

By the autumn of 1906, after carefully husbanding the precious kernels, Charles Saunders had produced a bushel of Marquis wheat, which would soon overshadow Red Fife on the farms of the West. Tens of thousands of farmers working on millions of acres profited from his efforts. Marquis matured two weeks before Red Fife, pushing the Arctic back by two hundred miles and justifying the construction of new railway lines farther north. By the spring of 1918, farmers on both sides of the border had sown Marquis on 20 million acres, just fifteen years after the first single kernel had been planted and nourished in Ottawa.

For almost a century wheat has been one of Canada's staple products, the key not only to Western prosperity but also to the Western raison d'être. Without Marquis wheat, where would this country sit as a major trading nation? No wonder that historians consider Sir Charles Edward Saunders one of the great Canadians of the century—a man who preferred the concert hall to the laboratory, who once tried to escape to Germany to study with a celebrated flautist, but who was persuaded by his strong-willed parent to forsake a musical career.

While Saunders was munching away on wheat kernels in the early days of the century, Clifford Sifton was master-minding Wilfrid Laurier's massive immigration drive that transformed the nation in the years before the Great War. Sifton knew exactly what kind of people he wanted and also what kind he *didn't* want. In this he echoed the sentiments of the vast majority of Canadians; they wanted white people, not swarthy Mediter-raneans. Sifton made it clear that he didn't want "anything done to facilitate Italian immigration." Canada wanted farmers, not bricklayers. Laurier himself cancelled a plan to bring in a small number of Romanian-Jewish farmers. "I do not favour this movement," he said bluntly.

The contrast between the Canadian approach to immigration and the legendary American attitude as expressed on the pedestal of the Statue of Liberty ("Give me your tired, your poor, / Your huddled masses yearning to breathe free . . .") is striking. The message to the new Americans was *"What can we do for you?"* The message to the would-be Canadians was *"What can you do for us?"* In the United States the immigration boom of the nineteenth century was fuelled with genuine idealism. While the Americans saw their country as a haven for the downtrodden, the Canadian government welcomed only those who would contribute to the nation's wealth.

Sifton did not want "the wretched refuse of your teeming shores"; he wanted sturdy farmers, preferably of good British stock who would not dilute established bloodlines. To Canada's chagrin, he could not get them. What English yeoman wanted to leave the prosperous com-fort of his holdings to gamble his future on the cold prairie steppe? When an ecclesiastical con man, Isaac Barr, persuaded two thousand gullible Englishmen to set up an all-British colony in the Canadian West, it soon became apparent that these wide-eyed immigrants were white-collar workers from England's industrial hives with no farming experience and no understanding of Canadian conditions.

Unable to attract the right kind of English, Sifton had to settle for foreigners, but *northern* foreigners, since it was his belief that southern peoples would not make good farmers. Germans and Scandinavians were acceptable, and so were the sheepskin-clad serfs from northeastern Europe—Ukrainians, Poles, and Austro-Hungarian Slavs. All of these were lumped together under a single ethnic name, Galician, because so many—150,000—came from the old Austrian province of Galicia, where life had become unbearable and land impossible to obtain.

The Liberal half of the country endured them for political reasons, since they were Sifton's babies; the Conservative half wanted no part of them. To the Tories, the Galicians were "filth and vermin." The Galicians scrubbed themselves clean as soon as they climbed out of the crowded, stinking holds of the Atlantic steamers. But the Opposition press labelled them "a vile and shiftless people" (the Edmonton *Bulletin*) and "social sewage" (the Ottawa *Citizen*). Hugh John Macdonald, son of Canada's first prime minister, called them "a mongrel race." Rodmond Roblin, premier of Manitoba, considered them "foreign trash" and denied them the provincial vote. Since they already had the federal franchise, Roblin changed his tactics during the 1904 election campaign to praise their "diligence, their intelligence, their sobriety, and their generally estimable character."

The fear that the all-white Anglo-Celtic community north of the forty-ninth parallel would be diluted—"mongrelized"—by an influx of strangers was a very real one that still exists, watered down but ever-present, in the twenty-first century. The saintly J.S. Woodsworth succumbed to it in 1909 when he wrote that "people emerging from serfdom, accustomed to despotism, untrained in the principles of responsible government, without patriotism—such a people are totally unfit to be trusted with the ballot." It is strange to read those words, uttered by one of the country's greatest humanitarians, but Woodsworth was very much a product of his time—a time when it was universally accepted that only the "civilized" white race could control its destiny and that lesser peoples would not only take jobs from good Canadians but would also be a burden on the taxpayers.

Having given up on English farmers, Sifton began to turn his attention to the American Midwest. It was slowly dawning on Canadians that Americans were everything the British were not. They weren't paupers. They actually arrived in Canada with money, for they had sold their original farms in the United States for fancy sums and could buy more Canadian land for less. They were quiet, they spoke English, and most were of Anglo-Celtic extraction. They were go-getters who wanted to work. They mixed cheerfully with their neighbours, adapted easily to the orderly Canadian lifestyle, and would not dilute the ethnic and religious base that the older generation of Canadians prized so highly.

The Americans contributed to the loosening of imperial ties unwittingly fostered by Canada's immigration policy. They became enthusiastic Canadians whose aggressive presence in their adopted country helped pave the way for the decline of imperialism and the creation of the British Commonwealth. By 1914, one-third of all the settlers in the West would have no sentimental attachment to the Empire. The British-born would storm the recruiting offices, but the newcomers, both the Americans and the Europeans (having rejected Europe), would, in large part, cling to the land and seek exemptions for their sons, thus widening a growing disaffection between the two Canadas that persists to this day.

Canadians are sometimes thought of as a quiet, self-effacing people, crouching in the shadow of their more effusive neighbour. But Canada in the early years of the twentieth century indulged in a hyperbolic outpouring of press agentry that would daunt the most aggressive Madison Avenue flack today—the political brainchild of Clifford Sifton in his unprecedented efforts to settle the Last Best West.

Unlike Charles Saunders, Sifton made his work his life. He had the reputation of staying at his desk all night, leaving behind a pile of work for his clerks at dawn and returning at ten o'clock looking as fresh as ever. A consummate politician, he drove himself time and again into a state of exhaustion marked by bouts of high blood pressure, insomnia, and nervous collapse. During the Manitoba provincial election in 1896 he had reached a point where he could neither eat, rest, nor sleep. Yet he always bounced back until his increasing deafness shut him off from the world and ended his political career. In spite of this, the sickly, nervous insomniac has retained his reputation as an iron man. It was not his constitution that drove him; it was his iron will.

As minister of the interior he was determined to saturate the world with propaganda about Canada. By 1900 the blizzard of pamphlets pouring from his office trumpeting the glories of this northern never-never-land (where words such as "cold," "snow," and even "frost" were taboo) had passed the million mark. Sifton, "the young Napoleon of the West," dispatched an army of proselytizers into the United States and across Europe, armed with samples of grain, photographs of prairie homesteads, and magic lanterns to spread the gospel. He even hired the United States' leading adventure novelist, James Oliver Curwood, to publicize the Canadian Northwest. Curwood, the author of 26 novels whose work inspired no fewer than 122 motion pictures, responded by inventing the slogan "God's Country" to combat the notion that Canada was a forbidding land of ice and snow.

"Mammon's Country" would have been an equally accurate description. Sifton's press agentry helped create the railway madness that infected the nation. Politicians and pioneers alike made their obeisance to the Great God Railway. Railway created new communities and enriched old ones. Railway turned minor Irish contractors into captains of industry. Railway hoisted ambitious politicians up the slippery ladder of advancement. Railway promised a glittering future of turreted hotels crowded with free-spending visitors. Railway not only meant wealth: railway *was* wealth. And soon, thanks to Charles Saunders's remarkable development of Marquis wheat, there would be room for more railways to the north of the entrenched and (to Westerners) much-despised Canadian Pacific—two more, in fact. It was insane. The two new lines often ran parallel to one another, sometimes on twin bridges through mountains and across plains. In the end they bled the country white.

The sensible solution would have been to amalgamate the two companies, but rivalries and personal jealousies and ambitions conspired against that. The West favoured the Canadian Northern, a jerry-built network of prairie lines built and stitched together on borrowed money by two railroad buccaneers: William Mackenzie, an ex-school teacher with aristocratic features, and his black-bearded, bull-like partner, Donald Mann. Easterners dismissed them as a pair of backwoods money-grubbers, and few believed they could actually build a transcontinental line. Laurier distrusted both as pushy entrepreneurs but warmed to the urbane and erudite Sir Charles Rivers-Wilson, a British diplomat who was president of the rival Grand Trunk and its subsidiary, the Grand Trunk Pacific—and who knew no more about railways than the Prime Minister himself. That preference reflected an ingrained Central Canadian snobbery that would prove costly to the nation.

In leaning toward the Grand Trunk, Laurier unwittingly committed himself to both railways. The Prairie provinces and British Columbia were eager to shore up the Canadian Northern's credit by guaranteeing its bonds. The pressure from the West was so great that the federal government found it must support the stubborn backwoods line, which managed to gobble up another $100 million in bond guarantees from Ottawa alone between 1903 and 1914.

In the end, Laurier, weary of the Byzantine negotiations between the two companies, proposed a compromise that turned out to be the worst possible solution. There would be *another* railway—the National Transcontinental—running from Moncton, N.B., to Port Simpson on the Pacific Coast. The Grand Trunk's subsidiary, Grand Trunk Pacific, would build the western half from Winnipeg to British Columbia. The Canadian government would pay for the rest, including the unprofitable line crossing the formidable Precambrian Shield. Once it was built, the Grand Trunk would lease the government line. For Rivers-Wilson it was a sweetheart deal: the government was to build the difficult half of the railway and, in fact, underwrite the cost of the rest. Laurier had to use all his eloquence to push it through the House in 1903.

This elaborate scheme cost twice as much as it should have, but in those starry-eyed days, who counted the cost? Laurier was convinced he was ushering in Canada's century, a point he made on two public occasions in 1904—the year his party won the federal election, largely because of its railway policy! Canada had been hornswoggled into supporting three transcontinental lines: the CPR, the Canadian Northern, and the Grand Trunk–National Transcontinental complex. But the nation believed, with Laurier, that the population would soar to one hundred million by the year 2000, by which time there would be room for no fewer than *five* railways.

In the heady days following the creation in 1905 of Saskatchewan and Alberta, anything seemed possible. The real estate market went crazy as paper communities sprang up magically on the realtors' doctored maps. The future seemed as golden as the fields of ripening wheat. Europe was in turmoil, but then Europe was always in turmoil. Canada was infected with a kind of goofy optimism—everybody expected the boom to last forever. No one considered the possibility of war—a few Balkan skirmishes, maybe, but nothing that couldn't be finished by Christmas.

Bur war came like a thunderclap, following hard on the equally sudden collapse of the real estate boom. If these crises had been avoided it is possible that at least one of the new intercontinental railways could have survived. But the war ended that pipe dream. The lines were being built with borrowed money, and the new conflict, when it came, dried up the market for real estate bonds.

The end was inevitable, but the inevitable had to wait until the war was won. Then the government, which owned them anyway, took over the two faltering lines, merged them into the Canadian National Railways system, and shouldered the crushing burden of debt. That debt was so large it exceeded the total amount spent on relief during the first four years of the Great Depression of the thirties. For years Canadian taxpayers had to pay for the cost of the delirium that seized the West in the glory days before the Great War.

3

In the century's first decade, two crosswinds blew across the new Canada, fuelled by the Western boom. One was almost entirely masculine—the drive for material progress that reached tornado-like proportions before the Great War and seized civic boosters, politicians, gamblers, and get-rich-quick promoters alike. The other was largely feminine—a gentle but insistent breeze that slowly extinguished the old Victorianism with a growing concern for women's rights, social progress, and the evils of the demon rum.

It began with the New Woman movement and was followed by the temperance movement that led in turn to the suffragist movement. The Great War, which changed so much, silenced the shrill feminist pleas for recognition in the interests of a more pressing cause—but only temporarily. In the end the women got what they wanted, confirming the predictions of Kit of the *Mail* that "the man who stands in the path of the New Woman can be compared to an idiot attempting to force back a tidal wave with a cricket bat."

It has been said that the New Woman rode into the twentieth century on a bicycle. The new mobility was at odds with morality. The chain-sprocket drive heralded the advent of the much-despised, pant-like bloomer and the demise of Victorian dress. The die-hards clung to the old myths and invented some new ones. The editor of the *Dominion Medicine Monthly* insisted that "bicycle riding produced in the female a distinct orgasm."

But even Kit, who was something of a New Woman herself, was aghast when one exponent of the fad, Rosa Burke, boldly challenged all and sundry in the female world to a boxing match. Worse, the challenge was taken up by "a gazelle with soft, dark eyes" who—horror of horrors—declared she was prepared to strip to the waist for the event. For Kit, things were moving a little too fast. "Now advances the Muscular Maiden . . . and throws a dynamite bomb into the heart of society," she wrote in dismay.

The New Woman had many guises. Pauline Johnson was very much in the spirit of the breed—the direct opposite of the cloistered chatelaine of the Victorian era. Spirited, passionate, uncompromising, she recited her own poetry in every kind of environment, from pool hall to undertaking parlour. An effervescent and emotional performer with an hour-glass figure, she kept her audience enthralled for three hours at a time and drew crowds wherever she went. "Brave men went weak when she smiled," one biographer wrote.

When occasion seemed to demand it, she was not above uttering a blood-curdling war whoop. As sophisticated as she was flamboyant, she had a good many love affairs and was engaged (but not married) several times. Her energy seemed inexhaustible. She once managed to cram performances in four different provinces into a single week, reciting her own verse, including the popular favourite "The Song My Paddle Sings." According to one biographer, Peter Unwin, she rode on trains that were wrecked, sailed on ships that sank, and slept in hotels that burned down around her.

As the daughter of a Mohawk chief and the shy, delicate sister of an Anglican missionary, she loved to play on her mixed heritage. For the first half of her recital she appeared in beaded buckskins, sash, moccasins, and feathered headdress. After the intermission she glided onto the stage, a beautiful and buxom young woman in a long white satin evening dress. This unexpected transformation never failed to bring gasps of surprise from the audience.

Pauline Johnson was not a reformer. She simply made her way into a man's world without apology and was quite prepared to give as good as she got. But reform was in the air in the years immediately following the Boer War, and at times it took on the trappings of a fad, like ragtime music. In Sarah Jeannette Duncan's novel *Social Departure*, a group of women sets off on a world tour—unchaperoned!—declaring that "life amounts to very little in this age if one cannot institute a reform of some sort." They are glad to identify themselves "with the spirit of the times" and are thankful that "we had thought of a reform before they were all used up."

To Emily Murphy, another New Woman, who was to become the

first female magistrate in the British Empire, reform was more than a game. By the time she reached the West as a parson's wife in 1903, she was already widely known by her pen-name, Janey Canuck. She had chosen that defiant pseudonym during a sea voyage among some snobbish English passengers who sniffed that Canada was "a small community of fourth-rate, half-educated people." Irked by such disdain, she decided to emphasize that she was neither a Yankee nor an Englishwoman but the proud female counterpart of Jack Canuck.

Murphy's determined crusade for social reform began to pay off when, in 1911, the Alberta government passed the law that made it illegal for a husband to will away his wife's third of their property. Ahead of her lay the famous case in which the British Privy Council made the final decision that women were persons too—a decision that seems inarguable to us today but was considered outrageous by many when it was first advanced. That ruling, however, would have to wait— as so many things had to wait—until the coming war was fought and won. Between 1914 and 1918 the country was on hold. The railway crisis, social reform, the women's movement would all have to be postponed while men struggled and died in the murderous Flanders muck.

In Emily Murphy's era, there was no shortage of social conditions waiting to be reformed. One had only to call as evidence an industrial quarter of old Montreal that Herbert Brown Ames in his 1897 sociological study called *The City Below the Hill*. Bisected by rue Notre Dame, this teeming semi-slum had a population of 38,000 working-class Montrealers equally divided among English, French, and Irish. "Water Closet Ames," as he was called, fought an eight-year war against this "unsanitary abomination." His revelations were devastating. The statistics showed that a quarter of all the children born in the area died in their first year. That was twice the infant mortality rate of New York and made Montreal the most dangerous city in the Western world in which to be born.

In these foul surroundings the meticulous Ames, a future member of Parliament, counted 105 licensed saloons and another 87 grocery stores selling liquor. Booze—cheap, raw, and easily available—was the anodyne of the working class. Toronto had fifty more saloons than Montreal. And in Winnipeg, twenty-four hotels on Main Street and twenty-four others crammed together on side streets all served liquor.

The prevalence of saloons launched the women into action. Founded in 1875, the Woman's Christian Temperance Union had by the turn of the century ten thousand paid-up members in Canada, all on the warpath against the sale and use of alcohol.

Demon rum! We use those words in jest today, but the reformers took it with deadly seriousness. As one catchphrase put it, "It turns men into demons and makes women an easy prey to lust." The quintessential tale of voluntary abstinence concerns two of Hart Massey's sons, Walter and Fred Victor, who, parched with thirst while crossing the Sahara, bluntly refused the only drink available because it was wine and struggled on to the next oasis.

Early temperance movements rallied round the driving force of the WCTU. We tend to patronize these earnest women in their stately black, chorusing like gospel singers such temperance ballads as "Cold Water Glee"—

> Cold water pure, cold water free
> The drink for you, the drink for me.
> O shun the cup, O shun the bowl,
> It kills the body, kills the soul.

In fact, their campaign was both sensible and righteous. The hotel bar and the corner saloon were the curses of the age. Those who signed pledge cards never to touch liquor again were determined to wipe them out. That would not be easy. The liquor trade was abetted by the mushroom growth of the awakening little prairie towns. In one demented decade, the population of Regina rose from 2,200 to 30,000, that of Calgary from 4,000 to 45,000.

For bachelor settlers, who outnumbered the married by two or three to one, the hotel was a social centre, and the bar, with its polished oaken counter, glass mirror, brass rail, and half-full spittoons, was the heart of the establishment. At the end of a long day men dropped in for a drink as casually as they do now for a cup of coffee. This was an exclusively male preserve. The women were forced to sit outside, shivering, in the family buggy while the breadwinner squandered his weekly paycheque, which the saloon was only too happy to cash.

Here, in an atmosphere redolent of the mingled odours of machine oil, wood shavings, street tar, draft beer, tobacco juice, and honest sweat, men stood three or four deep after work, treating each other to round after round. Unlike the British public house, with its dart board and piano, the Canadian saloon offered no entertainment save the nightly drunken brawls. The results were predictable. Families were driven to destitution; married women with children, facing unpaid bills, were forced to take menial jobs as chars or washerwomen or even, in an appalling number of cases, as prostitutes.

By 1900 every man over the age of fifteen was consuming an annual average of a gallon and a half of hard liquor a year. Boozing was one vice that had a public face. "It is easy to see why we concentrated on the liquor traffic," Nellie McClung, an early recruit to the temperance cause, remembered. "It walked our streets. It threw challenges in our faces."

The temperance movement became part of the social and cultural life of the Canadian small towns, sponsoring spelling bees, opening reading rooms, training members in oratory, and showing schoolchildren the effects of alcohol on the stomach and drilling them in such spirited marching songs as "Tremble King Alcohol! We Will Grow Up."

It was inevitable that the WCTU would plunge into politics. Its spirited temperance campaign forced plebiscites in Ontario, Manitoba, Nova Scotia, and Prince Edward Island. In all four provinces prohibition was overwhelmingly endorsed. It was a hollow victory. Because the women had no vote, the all-male legislatures did nothing.

Nonetheless, the drumbeat of the temperance forces had an effect. No sooner had Laurier taken office than he announced a national plebiscite on prohibition. When it was held in 1898, every province except Quebec voted for the drys, an indication that the majority of English-speaking males had accepted the WCTU arguments. It did no

101

good; the Liberal strength lay in Quebec. And so the entire country remained wet.

That was the turning point. Naively, the women had believed the battle was won. Now they realized it would never be won until they had a say in the government of the country. Thus was launched the struggle for women's suffrage.

The suffragist movement, as it was then called, was larger than the WCTU since it attracted members of both sexes. It was also elitist, catering especially to the Anglo-Saxon Protestant professional classes for whom women's suffrage was only one of a series of proposed reforms sweeping the country. These social activists were intent on imposing Protestant morality on society at large. The membership of the various suffrage organizations—twenty-two sprang into being between 1877 and 1918—overlapped other social causes, such as protection of the feeble-minded, parks and playgrounds associations, child welfare, health reform, direct democracy, educational and municipal reform.

But where were the Protestant churches? Stagnating, in the view of committed reformers. Church attendance was falling off in the expanding cities; clergy were hard to recruit; even the puritan Sunday was threatened as industry tried to override it for profit's sake. To J.S. Woodsworth, the church's influence was waning: "It is not today coping successfully with the great social problems which in their acutest form are found in the city. . . ."

In short, the church had to wake up or fade away. Never mind the angels-on-the-head-of-a-pin theology. Practical farmers wanted something less ethereal. They found it in the activist doctrine of the Social Gospel, whose support was growing throughout the continent, especially among the non-conformist Protestant churches. Woodsworth, a Methodist minister and head of the All People's Mission in Winnipeg's North End, was an adherent, as were Salem Bland, the radical theologian from Wesley College, and the Reverend Charles Gordon, better known as the best-selling author Ralph Connor. This trio represented the conscience of the West.

Into the All People's Mission as a parish worker came the redoubtable Nellie McClung, whose upbringing had made her a temperance advocate. As a child she had watched a group of drunken neighbours ruin a peaceful picnic. As an adult she never forgot her mother's warning that liquor was "one of the devil's devices for confounding mankind." As a successful author and a brilliant, witty, and forceful speaker, she became a major figure in the women's reform movement. In her vast, flowered hats and brightly coloured gowns, she shattered the cartoon image of the solemn do-gooders the anti-temperance forces had tried to create. She brought the same panache to the lecture platform. Prohibition? She never mentioned that "hard sounding word, worthless as a rallying cry." She talked instead of the need to replace the demon rum with something better—parks and playgrounds, handicrafts, orchestras, folk dances, decent housing. She was convinced that Westerners drank "because it answered something in the blood, some craving for excitement and change." The solution was to find a civilized substitute.

These lively lectures made the audiences light up. She could almost hear the atmosphere crackle, and that sound seduced her. From the moment of her first platform appearance at a WCTU convention in 1907, Nellie McClung became a political animal.

The McClungs moved to Winnipeg from Manitou in 1911 at the height of the boom. There, Nellie's work with Woodsworth and the visit of the fiery British suffragette Emmeline Pankhurst completed her political awakening. Her wit and her literary abilities were soon much in demand.

She reached histrionic heights after a meeting in the provincial legislature when she appeared before the Manitoba premier, Rodmond Roblin, with a delegation asking for votes for women. Roblin was both pompous and patronizing. He talked of the early training he'd received from his mother and how she had instilled in him a great respect for women "that places them on a much higher plane than men." Yet he declared himself "unequivocally opposed to the vote for women in Manitoba."

Nellie couldn't believe that the Premier had been so stupid as to leave himself wide open to ridicule. The suffragists had planned a mock parliament in the Walker Theatre for the following night. It would be a fantasy legislature in which the gender roles were reversed, with the women in charge and the men voteless. The premier, played by Nellie, would respond to a request for suffrage from a delegation of men.

During Roblin's speech she had observed every gesture and tried to absorb every tone of his voice, from the ingratiatingly friendly style, calculated to set his listeners at ease, to the loud, commanding tones that brooked no opposition. That night she practised before a mirror. The following evening she stood on the stage and told the overflow crowd that she and her colleagues would be depicting a one-sex parliament, like Manitoba's, yet set in a country where the men, not the women, were deprived of the vote. When the curtain rose, the stage was occupied by women members in evening gowns covered by black coats. The first petition put before the House protested against men's clothing, urging that six-inch collars and ties be outlawed; the second was a bill to confer dower rights on men. Members of the Opposition were seen knitting, reading newspapers, and taunting the speaker with such remarks as "You're just trying to get right with men."

Now it was Nellie's turn as premier. "If all men were so intelligent as these representatives of the downtrodden sex seem to me, it might not do any harm to give them the vote. But all men are not intelligent." The audience, who had heard similar sallies the day before, broke into applause.

Nellie adopted the Roblin stance—hands at her sides, palms up. "There is no use giving the men votes," she cried. "They wouldn't use them. They would let them spoil and waste. Then again, some men would vote too much." How could men have the audacity to demand the vote when seven-eighths of the court offenders were men? "Surely, you do not ask me to enfranchise an army of lawbreakers? . . . Giving men the vote would unsettle the home. . . ."

A final sally gives the full flavour of the speech: "The modesty of our men, which we revere, forbids us giving them the vote. Men's place is on the farm. . . . It may be that I am old-fashioned. I may be wrong. After all, men may be human. Perhaps the time may come when men may vote with women—but in the meantime be of good cheer. Advocate and Educate. We will try to the best of our abilities to conduct the affairs of the province and prove worthy standard bearers of the good old flag of the grand old party, which has often gone down in disgrace but never to defeat."

The mock parliament, which was repeated in Winnipeg and taken to Brandon, brought new supporters to the cause and funded the rest of the campaign. But it did not win votes for women. It would take their support in a long and bloody war to achieve that.

4

The tinpot navy

At the end of the century's first decade, Canadians were still at odds with one another. Out on the prairies, a land of rutted roads, lonely, isolated farms, and lonely, isolated women, the fields were lush with waving acres of Marquis wheat. The country had never been so prosperous, and yet there was one constituency in the great Western empire of grain that was seething with discontent. From Manitoba to the Rockies, the farming community was up in arms over the protection policies forced on them by the politicians who seemed to be in thrall to the manufacturing giants in the despised East.

The forces of geography and history were creating further tensions. In Quebec, the recently formed Ligue Nationale of Bourassa adherents was threatening the traditional power of both established political parties. Elsewhere, imperialism, which had been on the wane since the South African War, was still potent enough to divide the nation into two camps, those who believed in the indivisibility of the Empire and those who were convinced that Canada and its fellow Dominions should be autonomous entities within the British family.

The autonomists quoted Kipling: "Daughter am I in my mother's house, / But mistress in my own." The imperialists had their own slogan, a rallying cry used by every loyal Briton from the flag-carrying ladies of the IODE to the pugnacious brethren of the Loyal Orange Lodge: *One Flag, One Fleet, One Throne.* That tocsin made its way into the schoolbooks, notably the newly published Ontario readers.

At the height of the naval controversy that plagued the country in the days immediately before the Great War, many wondered why the British Navy should be revered along with the monarch and the Union Jack. Why a fleet at all, the Quebec nationalists asked. Why not a small fleet of our own to patrol our coastal waters, some Liberals demanded; hadn't Laurier promised that back in 1902? How could Canada afford to pledge future funds to augment a royal navy, the prairie politicians wondered, when we cannot afford another transcontinental railway?

In the eyes of the ultra-imperialists, the British fleet was sacrosanct. The small territorial army might subdue the hill tribes of India, but it was the fleet that patrolled the world, a water-borne police force to protect the far-flung colonies. The fleet had created the Empire; the fleet kept it intact and indivisible; the fleet ensured that the map would always be coloured red.

The Royal Navy was invincible—or was it? It is hard now to conjure up the shock wave that washed over Great Britain, and, indeed, the whole British world, when in 1909 the First Lord of the Admiralty stood up in Parliament to announce, in those resonant, Victorian tones so familiar to a later generation, that the Germans were on a ship-building spree. They were trying to match the British fleet, Winston Churchill declared, and in just three years might easily achieve their ambitions. The nation was stunned. The greatest fleet in the world was being threatened by a truculent nation that was blessed with very little coastline and had been cobbled together out of a gaggle of disparate principalities only a few decades before.

The words were scarcely out of Churchill's mouth before the race was on. The Germans were matching the British ship for ship, but to the man in the street only one vessel mattered: the great, ironclad behemoth known as the dreadnought. The British were laying down four of these monsters, and within three years would lay down another four. The generic name, taken from the first ironclad *Dreadnought* launched in 1906, said it all. With their foot-thick armour and gigantic twelve-inch guns, the dreadnoughts indeed feared nothing.

106

Whichever country produced the most would, in effect, be master of the seas.

To Wilhelm II, the posturing kaiser who scorned his British relatives, the dreadnought race was a personal matter. No red-blooded Briton could forget his insulting speech at Cowes, five years earlier, when the fiercely moustached monarch had tried to provoke his uncle, Edward VII, by boasting during a toast to the English king of the greatness of the German fleet. The King's unruffled and condescending response had delighted his subjects, though it had scarcely helped relations between the two countries. "The interest," he said, "which for years I have taken in [here he paused slightly] *yachting* exercised too great an attraction to allow me to miss the opportunity of convincing myself how successful Your Majesty has been in inducing so many to become interested in the sport in Germany."

The *sport*? One can almost hear the sabre-rattling German monarch grinding his teeth over that one. The sport would be costly, for dreadnoughts didn't come cheap. Keeping up with the Hohenzollerns would force the British to foot an enormous bill. The mother country would have to turn for help to her daughters across the seas.

In Canada, the imperialists, egged on by their British counterparts, were again out in full force. A cry arose that Canada must come to the old country's aid and either place at her disposal a dreadnought or two or else present her with the money to build them, and hang the expense! But how was that going to play in Quebec? Indeed, how was it going to play in the wheatlands of the new West? Once again Wilfrid Laurier was faced with a kind of dilemma dictated by the country's contorted geography and tangled past. In a letter to a correspondent in 1909 he mused, "I ask you to consider this. Our existence as a nation is the most anomalous that has yet existed. We are British subjects but we are an autonomous nation; we are divided into provinces, we are divided into races, and out of these confused elements, the man at the head of affairs has to sail the ship onwards. If you were in the position in which I am, you would have to think night and day of these different problems. . . ."

Now, confronted with the subtle importunings of the British naval establishment, he could not yield to the imperialist cry for regular contributions; that would be in the nature of a colonial tribute. He was prepared, if a real emergency arose, to make a single contribution in Canada's name. If he offered anything more, Quebeckers would accuse him of being under the imperialist thumb. He would lose support not only in Quebec but also in the West, which was cool to any sort of expensive overseas venture. Frank Oliver's Edmonton *Bulletin* had caught the sentiment accurately when it opposed any cash subsidy to the navy as no more than "a donation for the relief of distressed Dukes." Yet Laurier was well aware that the real political power lay in Central Canada. If he refused to go to the aid of Mother Britain, he could say goodbye to the voters of Ontario.

The way out of the dilemma would have to be the kind of compromise that had got him through the South African War. Sir George Foster, a Conservative stalwart who had been minister of finance under Tupper, helped him arrive at it when, two weeks after the dreadnought race was launched in 1909, he rose from the Opposition front bench to declare in a carefully worded speech that "Canada should no longer delay in assuming her proper share of the responsibility and financial burden incident to the suitable protection of her exposed coastline and great seaports."

Not a whisper from Foster about a cash subsidy to the British: the Tories were as concerned as the Liberals about voter reaction in Quebec. Foster's recommendation was for a limited, local, independent force, ostensibly to protect the seacoasts. Who could quarrel with that? Only if a real emergency existed would Canada be honour bound to make a contribution, and certainly not on a regular basis.

Laurier was not convinced that any emergency existed, but "if the day should come when the supremacy of Britain on the high seas will be challenged, it will be the duty of all daughter nations to close around the old motherland." In that event, he himself would stump the country to impress on the nation, "especially my compatriots in the province of Quebec, the conviction that the salvation of England is the salvation of our own country."

Foster's resolution passed unanimously. Canada was to have its own navy to work "in cooperation with and in close relation to the Imperial navy." The following January the House passed the Naval Service Bill calling for an autonomous force of five cruisers and six destroyers, all under Canadian control. This time the reaction was not unanimous. Was that the best Canada could do, the imperialists asked. Manitoba's Roblin called it a "tinpot navy," a memorable phrase that Laurier had difficulty shaking off.

Nor could he quite shake off the imperial connection. In case of war the tinpot navy could, by order-in-council, be placed under British control. Did that mean war anywhere the Empire was involved, or only when Canada was affected? Laurier did not equivocate: "War everywhere. When Britain is at war, Canada is at war; there is no distinction. If Great Britain, to which we are subject, is at war with any nation, Canada is exposed to invasion. Hence, Canada is at war."

If this was true, then Canada's options were limited. Was she to find herself spilling blood in every petty skirmish undertaken by the incautious British? Henri Bourassa was quick to sense the paradox. On January 10, 1910, two days before Laurier introduced the Naval Service Bill in the House, he launched his personal daily newspaper, *Le Devoir*, an independent, privately supported journal of small circulation but immense power and prestige.

His timing was impeccable. "At the very hour that we appear upon the scene," he wrote in the inaugural issue, "parliament is deliberating a question of the highest importance, which is only a new episode in the Imperialist movement: the construction of a Canadian navy."

He harked back to the long wrangle over the South African adventure: "Shall we watch a repetition of the comedy of 1899? Will the Canadian people be the dupes of the machinations and miserable intrigues of parties?"

On January 17, Bourassa pounced on Laurier's offhand remark that whenever Britain was at war, Canada was also. "Let the notion occur to a Chamberlain, a Rhodes, a Beers, to gold seekers or opium merchants, of causing a conflict in South Africa or India, in the

Mediterranean or the Persian Gulf, on the shores of the Baltic or the banks of the Black Sea, on the coasts of Japan or in the China Seas, we are involved, always and regardless, with our money and our blood. . . . It is the most complete backward step Canada has made in half a century. It is the gravest blow our autonomy has suffered since the origin of responsible government."

Bourassa had taken Laurier's thoughtless remark to ridiculous extremes, but it played well in Quebec.

The two had once been friends. It was Laurier who had got Bourassa into politics, and for a time the older politician had been something of a mentor to the fiery young man. Their views on matters of national-ism were not that far apart. Bourassa was both a French-Canadian nationalist—he wanted Quebeckers to preserve a culture separate from that of English Canada—and a Canadian nationalist. He didn't want Quebec to be a separate sovereign state, unable to resist the gravita-tional pull of her American neighbour. He wanted a truly bicultural nation and one free to choose her own foreign policies.

"I am loyal to the traditions of the race from which I have sprung," he declared, "but I am also loyal to the British flag, which we all love and admire . . . my desire for the disruption of the British Empire . . . is not because it is British but because it is Imperial. All Empires are hateful. . . . They serve nothing but brutal instincts and material objects. All that is good in British ideals . . . would be better served by the free action of several independent British communities. . . . British nations have to choose between British ideals and British domination. I stand for ideals against domination."

It has been said (by André Laurendeau) that the British Empire made a Canadian out of Bourassa and that he was indebted to Laurier for the idea of *l'unité nationale*. Laurier had his eye on him as a potential leader. The blood of Louis-Joseph Papineau ran in the younger man—his mother was the daughter of the great revolutionary—and he had shown polit-ical promise in his early twenties as mayor of Montebello. He was thirty when Laurier took office, but political leadership was not Bourassa's style. Now, in his early forties, proprietor and editor of the most respected

110

newspaper in the province, he was fast becoming Laurier's successor, not as party leader but as spokesman for his people.

By the time of the naval controversy there was more salt than pepper in his short-cropped hair and trim, pointed beard, but the kinetic energy that distinguished him on the lecture platform was always evident in the dark, piercing eyes. No other politician could electrify an audience as Bourassa could. He hypnotized his listeners with his oratory and sometimes hypnotized himself, starting out slowly and softly and then, as his voice grew stronger and more resonant, his whole being seemed transformed, his gestures became more frequent, his utterances more biting. Striding about the stage, now facing his audience directly, now leaning over the platform railing, silent and motionless, now raising an arm to make a point, now striking his breast as if exalted by his subject, his words falling like hammer blows, he would unleash a torrent of eloquence that would arouse his followers to fever heat and provoke an outburst of wild cheering.

Though he was done with federal politics, he had more political power than any backbencher. Yet he had a distaste for exercising power. "I am of such a temperament that I never feel like being a whip," he remarked. "I have enough trouble in keeping myself in line. I have no desire to keep others in line." He chose to be not a demagogue but an educator of public opinion with *Le Devoir* as his pulpit.

Bourassa was certainly one of the most unusual figures to occupy the spotlight during the turbulent early years of the century. To André Laurendeau, one of his successors as editor of *Le Devoir*, he was something of a paradox—a founder of Canadian nationalism who took the French-Canadian nationalist movement as one of his favourite targets. His contradictions sprang from "the type of double allegiance he had accepted from the outset—that is from the fact that he refused to be only a Canadian or only a French-Canadian. He had decided from the beginning to be both intensely."

As Laurendeau explained, Bourassa refused to be a colonial, "refused to let this country accept the destiny of colony, whether of Great Britain or the United States. . . . Having been convinced from his youth that separatism was a dream that had come too late or too early, and it was therefore a dangerous chimera . . . he took the view that the whole of Canada would be liberated on the condition that Canadians stopped fighting one another."

It is a condition that Canadians, then and now, have found it difficult to accept. The imperialists of English-speaking Canada and the would-be separatists of his native province both saw Bourassa as a threat. For he was that *rara avis*, a pan-Canadian nationalist, passionate and eloquent, outspoken and unswerving in his views, untainted by the narrow regionalism that is the curse of the nation. His hopes and expectations for a united country have never really been realized. That is his tragedy; it is also our own.

5

No truck with the Yankees That summer of 1910, with the dreadnought race gathering steam and with tension rising between Eastern and Western Canada, Sir Wilfrid Laurier embarked on a three-month journey to the prairies to listen first-hand to the voices from the soil.

Here were sprouting the seeds of a problem that would bedevil the nation for the rest of the century. In creating a new Western empire with a flourishing wheat economy and a population of newcomers, the Laurier government had divided the nation. The pioneer West and the settled East were cut off from one another by a thousand miles of Precambrian rock and muskeg. New political attitudes were forming that would see no fewer than six Western-based political parties rise and fall or change before the century's end—United Farmers of Alberta, Progressives, Co-operative Commonwealth Federation, Social Credit, Reconstruction, and Reform.

A new dichotomy based on geography was about to be superimposed on the traditional one based on language and history. The West had trouble understanding the original bilingual/bicultural nature of the old Canada—Manitoba had dispensed with French in her schools as early as 1889. Frederick Haultain, premier of the old North West

112

Territories before Alberta and Saskatchewan were formed in 1905, was bitterly opposed to the old two-party system in the West; to him, that was an Eastern concept. The last thing he wanted was the kind of political split that would break up the common front against the East. In a sense he had his way. Alberta, for most of the century, would be subject to one-party rule. The real opposition was always Ottawa. In presiding over the speedy settlement of the West, Laurier had created a monster that could—and would—bring about his downfall.

When Laurier went west, the hatred of the East—the word is not too extreme—had been simmering for a decade. Part of it was regional: Westerners were proud of their open, pioneer way of life and more than a little contemptuous of Central Canadians, whom they considered hidebound and effete. But most of it was economic. The farmers were being gouged by the elevator companies, by the Eastern manufacturers, by the railways, and by the land speculators. Mainly, however, they were being gouged by the National Policy that forced them to sell their wheat in the unprotected markets of the world while buying farm equipment and household necessities in the protected home markets of Central Canada. What the farmers wanted was some form of free trade with the United States and Great Britain, and, as Laurier realized, they were mobilizing to achieve that end.

He was well aware that Western representation in Parliament had risen after the 1904 election from twenty members to twenty-seven. Just as disturbing was the growing political power of the Grain Growers Associations, which now boasted 28,000 members in the three provinces, and, perhaps more important, the influential *Grain Growers Guide*, which they subsidized. For Laurier, now in his seventieth year, it must have been an exhausting experience. Day after day, for three months, he listened patiently as hundreds of farmers' delegations assailed him with speeches and memorials, urging that the tariff be reduced. The Western farmers were as far apart, philosophically, from the Eastern manufacturers as the French Canadians were from the Anglophones. Having teetered on one tightrope, the Prime Minister was faced with another, equally shaky. How could he appeal to the

113

prairie voters and still retain the loyalty of his traditional constituency?

The Western farmers were not alone in revolt. The cry for tariff reduction was nationwide. Laurier was scarcely back from his prairie odyssey when the *Farmers Sun* of Ontario began to urge a march on Ottawa. What followed was unprecedented. From Nova Scotia to the Rockies, farmer delegations began to assemble. The *Grain Growers Guide* took up the cause and sponsored a special train that left Winnipeg on the night of December 12 with some 300 delegates, all bound for Ottawa. Hundreds more were preparing for the annual meeting in Toronto the next day of the Dominion Grange, the leading farmers' movement in Ontario.

When the train reached North Bay, scores of newspaper correspondents climbed aboard and began to file dispatches to newspapers across the continent. By December 15 more than 800 farmers had descended on the capital—300 from Ontario, 500 from Western Canada, 7 from Quebec, and 2 each from Nova Scotia and New Brunswick. They jammed into the Grand Opera House and by six that evening had hammered out a platform to present to Parliament the following day.

George Fisher Chipman, the editor of the *Guide* and official historian of the "Siege of Ottawa," wrote that "no movement of the same magnitude and nature has ever before been seen in Canada. Never before have the farmers taken a firm and united stand for economic justice."

The following morning all of Ottawa seemed to have crowded onto the streets as the farmers marched four abreast from the opera house to Parliament Hill. The crowd was curious. Who were these Westerners, anyway? What would they look like? It was as if they had arrived from a foreign land. As Chipman wrote, "the majority of the East still expected to see a 'wild and woolly' gathering armed with all sorts of shooting irons and ready to fight at a moment's notice." The onlookers were surprised and a little disappointed to discover that the "sodbusters"—a new term that year—were very much like themselves.

In the dozen speeches that followed in the packed chamber and gallery, the delegates made their demands known. Laurier had heard them before. The farmers wanted a publicly owned railway to Hudson

Bay to speed the dispatch of grain to Europe, improved terminal elevators and facilities at the Lakehead, and changes in the bank and railway acts. But first and most important, they wanted reciprocal free trade with the United States and ultimately with Great Britain. In short, they wanted the foundation on which John A. Macdonald had built his National Policy dismantled and consigned to the dustbin of history.

The Prime Minister, in a mild response that disappointed almost everybody, promised little. But there were hints—and more than hints—that seduced, perhaps, by what he called "the Western spirit," he was preparing to make a political about-turn. "In the West," he said, "your ideas are far more advanced than those of the East." He hastened to voice his suspicions that the Easterners were not prepared "to go as far as you gentlemen of the West," but there was little doubt where his sympathies lay.

In fact, even as the Siege of Ottawa was inspiring the farmers to new heights of oratory, Canada and the United States, after months of negotiation, were concluding a reciprocity agreement that both Laurier and President William Howard Taft saw as a vote getter on both sides of the border. On January 26, 1911, less than five weeks after the farmers' siege, Laurier's minister of finance, William Stevens Fielding, introduced the agreement to the House, and in doing so ignited a national uproar that did not abate until the so-called Reciprocity Election the following September.

In the House, Robert Borden made it clear that his Conservative Opposition was against the agreement. The Tory policy was "reciprocity within the Empire." It wanted "no entangling treaties or alliances" that might interfere with any form of Empire free trade.

Again the country faced a familiar dilemma. Borden was answering the call of history, Laurier the call of geography. Not only was the country badly split; so was the Tory party. Borden called a caucus the following day and found an atmosphere of "deepest dejection." Many of his followers were convinced that Laurier had found a winning formula that would give the Liberals another term of office. George Foster said, gloomily, that when he had heard Laurier outline the reciprocity agreement "his heart had gone down into his boots." The Western members told Borden that they dared not vote against the government's proposals; any who opposed reciprocity would be doomed to certain defeat.

The East-West split was not confined to the Conservative Party. Laurier, like Borden, had been so overwhelmed by the fury of the farmers' protests and the trenchant arguments of his Western supporters that he had neglected to understand where his real strength lay. The votes were in the East.

In the long and bitter debate that followed and led to the September election, all the old shibboleths that had lain dormant during the euphoria of the boom days—the sacredness of the imperial connection, the acquisitive greed of the despised Yankees, the "Old Flag," imperialism over continentalism, memories of the Alaska Boundary dispute—were trundled out by the anti-reciprocity forces. Laurier had thought he had achieved an economic coup in coming to terms with his American neighbours, but the call of blood was stronger than the call of the pocketbook, as the Eastern business community quickly realized.

Laurier's position was further weakened by Taft's heavy-handed declaration, made in a remarkably inept speech designed to defend reciprocity and, at the same time, flatter his Canadian neighbours. "The Dominion has greatly prospered. It has an active, aggressive, and intelligent people. They are coming to a parting of the ways. They must soon decide whether they are to regard themselves as isolated by a perpetual wall or whether we are to be commercial friends."

A parting of the ways? That phrase would be used like a mantra against the Liberals. Laurier's arguments for reciprocity might be practical; but the case against it was emotional, and it was emotion that would win the day as anti-Americanism was again bubbling to the surface. To Canadians, the very fact that the Yankees wanted reciprocity was a powerful argument against it.

The rift in the Liberal ranks was made apparent as early as February 16 when Sir Edmund Walker, a powerful member of the party, told a board of trade protest meeting in Toronto that "although I am a Liberal I am a Canadian first of all." It was, he said, much more than a trade question. "Our alliance with the mother country must not be threatened." Then he made the point that would be used to defeat reciprocity: "We must assimilate our immigrants and make out of them good Canadians." Reciprocity, he indicated, was a deadly danger, making that assimilation more difficult. By "good Canadians," of course, Sir Edmund meant good *British* Canadians, untainted by the mongrel society of the American melting pot.

That week Walker and eighteen members of the Liberal Party broke ranks, announcing that Canadian nationality was threatened by reciprocity. The dissidents included the most powerful of the Western Liberals, Clifford Sifton, who now cast his lot with the industrial East. There is no more spectacular example of the geographical division in the Canada of 1911 than that of Sifton, the publisher of the *Free Press*, on one side of the argument, and John Dafoe, his shaggy editor, in direct opposition. To Sifton, reciprocity would turn Canada "towards the path that leads to Washington. I say, so far as I am concerned: Not for me." But Dafoe stuck with the West; he had no desire to see his newspaper commit suicide.

Eastern opposition to reciprocity now began to rise swiftly. In Montreal, the Anti-Reciprocity Club came into being, in Toronto, the Canadian National League. Everybody from the Governor General to Pauline Johnson had a say. To Lord Grey, "the feeling in Montreal and Toronto against the Agreement could hardly be stronger if the United States troops had already invaded our territory." The Mohawk poet, who put those feelings into verse, was widely quoted:

> The Yankee to the south of us
> Must south of us remain
> For not a man dare lift a hand
> Against the men who brag
> That they were born in Canada
> Beneath the British flag.

Henri Bourassa was solidly against the agreement, not just because he opposed Laurier but also because, as a nationalist, he wanted, in the phrase of the day, "no truck nor trade with the Yankees."

To the West, it was, of course, a battle against the Big Interests—banks and railways—but it was more. Over the next several months the country was treated to an outpouring of Canadian nationalism that transcended the pros and cons of the agreement itself. In March at an anti-reciprocity rally in Toronto's Massey Hall, the audience hissed the Stars and Stripes. In Montreal the same month, Laurier's car was trapped in a crowd and pelted with rocks. Even the Manitoba Legislature, in the heart of free trade country, defeated a resolution approving reciprocity. The Ontario Legislature was, of course, overwhelmingly opposed, 52 to 17. Meanwhile, in the House of Commons, the Conservatives were staging an exhausting twenty-five-day debate that did not end until Parliament adjourned on May 5.

Laurier was in London attending George V's coronation in July when the American Congress passed the Reciprocity Agreement. That session was notable for some incendiary remarks that sealed the fate of the agreement in Canada, for it confirmed the public suspicion, fuelled by the Tories, that the Yankees were about to take over the country.

One congressman, Charles Davis, trusted that "a divine Providence . . . may use this so-called reciprocity treaty, this entering wedge, to further amalgamate these two countries, and eventually make them one, with but one flag—the Stars and Stripes." Another from Illinois declared: "Be not deceived. When we go into a country and get control of it, we take it." But the clincher, widely quoted across Canada, was uttered by James Beauchamp Clark, the powerful Speaker of the House of Representatives, who declared himself for the agreement "because we hope to see the day when the American flag will float over every square foot of the British North American possessions clear to the North Pole."

If Champ Clark had led an armed sortie across the border he could scarcely have created a greater outburst of nationalistic fury. More than seven decades later, during the debate over the Mulroney free trade agreement, those threatening words were still being quoted.

118

It remained for Laurier on his return to dissolve the House and call an election, as he did on July 29. Stumping the country at an exhausting pace in the bitter seven-week campaign that followed, Laurier still had waning hopes, but even he must have sensed what was happening. He had lost Quebec to Bourassa over the navy; now he was losing the rest of Canada. In vain his followers tried to divert the debate to other issues: Canada had never been more prosperous; her potential had never been greater; her natural resources seemed inexhaustible. But how could he counter the clarion call of Rudyard Kipling, who wrote that "it is her own soul that Canada risks today"?

For all of his fifteen years as prime minister Laurier had felt himself beleaguered by the same problems that had propelled him into office in 1896: French versus English; West versus East; imperialism versus autonomism; Catholic versus Protestant. At the end of the campaign he uttered a cry from the heart: "I am branded in Quebec as a traitor to the French, and in Ontario as a traitor to the English. In Quebec I am branded as a Jingo and in Ontario as a Separatist. In Quebec I am attacked as an Imperialist and in Ontario as an anti-Imperialist.

"I am neither. I am a Canadian.

"Canada has been the inspiration of my life. I have had before me, as a pillar of fire by night and a pillar of cloud by day, a policy of true Canadianism, of moderation, of conciliation. I have followed it consistently since 1896, and now I appeal with confidence to the whole Canadian people to uphold me in this policy of sound Canadianism, which makes for the greatness of our country and of the Empire."

There it was: *moderation and conciliation*, the all-Canadian policy that would always be the key to national unity and that later political leaders would abandon at their peril. But would it save Laurier from defeat in that fractious autumn of 1911? In its last edition before voting day, Hugh Graham's imperialistic Montreal *Star* covered its entire front page with a hard-hitting editorial headed "Under One Flag." Canada, it argued, was faced (as it was so often faced) with two choices: to keep its flag "floating in the clear northern air over our heads" or to "turn aside toward absorption in the great and glorious republic to the south."

That extreme oversimplification, the essence of political rhetoric, nevertheless reflected the instincts of voters. In the election they made it clear that they were uneasy about the consequences of free trade and unsure of American designs on Canada. Laurier lost, 133 seats to 86. Nationalism won. Predictably, Alberta and Saskatchewan, the two new provinces in which voting patterns had yet to be established, voted for Laurier. British Columbia and Manitoba, which had been settled mainly by British and Canadian immigrants, did not. In Quebec, the Liberals lost twenty-seven seats, largely over the naval controversy; in Ontario they lost an overwhelming seventy-five out of eighty-nine. Eight Liberal cabinet ministers went down to defeat. The outcome was a debacle. Free trade was buried for three-quarters of a century.

Six days later, Robert Borden arrived in Ottawa like a triumphant Caesar, his carriage dragged for miles through the crowded, flag-bedecked streets by one hundred men. He wore the political uniform of the time—top hat, high starched collar, black suit. A one-time farm boy from King's County, Nova Scotia, a solid, stocky figure with a shock of white hair and a dark, bushy moustache, he had little of Laurier's suppleness and charm. The Calgary *Eye Opener*'s Bob Edwards called him "a well-meaning but torpid person," who "lacked the arts which most appeal to the popular imagination."

Borden took himself seriously. As a youth he had pondered "the meaning and purpose of existence" (his words) and had developed a genuine horror of wasting time, dividing the hours of the days and preparing charts setting out the amount of time he should devote to each particular study. He had read every single word in the Bible and most of the classics, from Horace (in the original Latin) to Macaulay, besides committing to memory long passages from such poets as Milton and Byron.

He kept himself under tight control, revealing little even to his wife, Laura. His letters to her were, in Heather Robertson's description, "frightening in their frigidity, flat, banal little notes about the weather, his dinner companions and his health." Concern for that health was the bond between them. Borden was a neurotic, though he never let it show.

120

His continual worry about his physical well-being stamped him as a hypochondriac, a not unusual malady in those days when doctors had few tools to work with and a variety of diseases carried such vague names as "catarrh of the stomach" and "nervous dyspepsia," both of which were applied to Borden. One cannot study the lives of Victorian and Edwardian politicians without reaching the conclusion that half were tottering about in a state of near collapse. There were times when Borden was clearly suffering from exhaustion brought on by his work habits and the stress that resulted from the political problems that confronted him.

At the age of forty-six, Borden had been advised by his doctor to slow down, lead a quiet life, and avoid excitement—scarcely a prescription for an active political future. A year later, he reluctantly took over the Conservative leadership on the understanding it would be a temporary post—no more than a year. Now, a decade later, he was prime minister of a divided nation and, indeed, a divided party whose members were not at all sure he had enough of the royal jelly to hold on to the job.

Twice there had been attempts to topple him, one a secret intrigue during the naval debate in 1909, the second during the reciprocity controversy. This told as much about the state of the party as about Borden himself. Although he believed himself to be "hovering between madness and death" (Robertson's phrase) he did not allow his supposed infirmities to interfere with his statesmanship. The coming war did not diminish him; on the contrary, he grew in stature. In the councils of the nations, his would be the voice of reason. David Lloyd George, the feisty little British prime minister in the later war years, found him "the quintessence of common sense"—"a clear-headed sensible man . . . courageous" who was "very good in council . . . essentially a safe man," qualities in short supply during those demented years.

In spite of his exhausting work schedule and his many supposed infirmities, he was, in the words of his close friend and doctor, Campbell Laidlaw, "very rugged." Actually, he was healthy as a horse. It is typical of Borden that he retired in 1920 because of ill health, then lived on for another seventeen years, dying at the age of eighty-two of heart failure.

To be fair, the growing concern over the European situation and Canada's role in it would have given the most phlegmatic leader the jitters. Was there really a chance that war would come? We look back now through the inverted telescope of history and ask ourselves how the country could have been so blind. Here were two great antagonists, both peacock proud, each seeking to be the dominant international force, hurling insults at one another and each committing sultan's ransoms to a naval building program whose only purpose was war. At that time war was still, in Clausewitz's dictum, an extension of politics, an acceptable and not terribly damaging form of international one-upmanship. War was in the air; both sides wanted it, at least subconsciously. Yet here were Canadian politicians arguing about whether or not a "national emergency" existed.

If it did, then Canada was duty bound to give aid to the British fleet, as the Laurier government's Naval Service Bill had made clear. In March 1912, as a sop to the Bourassa nationalists, Borden announced that the bill would be suspended pending a permanent policy that would be submitted to the voters.

One week later the naval race heated up. With the Germans plunging forward to build even more monstrous warships, Churchill announced an increase in Britain's own dreadnought program. It was all hugely expensive, and the British made it plain that they needed financial help from the dominions. Borden went to England to try to make one thing clear: if Canada made a contribution, then Canada wanted a voice in imperial foreign policy. Asquith, the British prime minister, wanted nothing of the sort but was prepared to toss Canada a small bone, disguised as a big bone. If the Canadian problem came under discussion, he promised, then Canada could send a representative to one of the meetings of the Committee on Imperial Defence. What was not made clear to Borden was that the CID had no clout: it was nothing more than an advisory committee. In effect, the British had rebuffed any attempt by its senior colony to have a say in future decisions.

The debate over Canada's new naval bill, introduced on December 5, 1912, was, in the new prime minister's words, "the most strenuous and remarkable that had ever occurred in Canadian parliamentary history." He himself, "greatly exhausted by the intense strain of the long debate, the night hours and the tumultuous scenes," suffered a carbuncle on his neck and sat in the House swathed in bandages with a physician by his side. Under the new proposal, Canada would advance Britain $35 million to help pay for three dreadnoughts to be placed at the navy's disposal "for the common defence of the Empire." No tinpot navy for Canada—only the satisfaction of being part of the greatest navy in the world, though without any say.

The acrimonious debate that followed dragged on until May 1913, by which time Borden was forced to introduce closure, thus touching off *another* debate that lasted a fortnight. The bill finally passed its third reading on May 15. Two weeks later the Senate killed it, leaving Canada, on the verge of war, without a naval policy of any kind. Nor were the two parties able to arrive at any form of compromise.

Borden blamed Laurier's "inflexible opposition" for the impasse, and his bitterness is reflected in his own memoirs: "Sir Wilfrid at the beginning of the next session was enabled triumphantly to announce six months before the most terrible conflict the world had ever known, that there was no emergency, no danger of war; that my declaration to the contrary was a mere sham and a pretension." In truth, the two parties had in effect cancelled each other out as far as preparedness for war was concerned. The Liberals had balked at subsidizing the Royal Navy; the Conservatives had frustrated any attempt for Canada to have a navy at all.

Armageddon beckoned.

Private Peat

1

The monument

The monument In the mid-twenties, when the victory of 1918 had made travel to far-off climes once again practical and popular and the Klondike stampede was far enough back in time to seem romantic, the Yukon tourist industry prospered. During those brief, bright summers, steamboat after steamboat puffed into Dawson City loaded with American tourists, each inspired by the verse of Robert Service and determined to visit the little log cabin where the poet had lived before the war and done some of his best work.

To reach it, they passed another shrine: a granite obelisk in the exact centre of little Minto Park that was itself in the exact centre of the town. It sounds incongruous; what on earth was an Egyptian obelisk doing in such a prominent spot in a subarctic village?

But every man, woman, and child who trudged up Harper Street knew exactly what it was and why it was there; for this was a *cenotaph*—a word that crept into common usage after the war—a monument to the Fallen, whose names, inscribed on the bronze plaque at the base, "would live forever." They had given their lives in the spirit of Christian sacrifice so that others might live in freedom, or so we were told when, each November, we gathered shivering around the monument and listened to a man in a surplice talk about martyrdom.

There are more than thirteen hundred of these war memorials in Canada, each situated in what was the most prominent spot in the community in those early post-war years: granite obelisks and marble monoliths, statues and stelae, pillars and shafts, cairns, arches, crosses, slabs, and pyramids, all dedicated to the memory of the Fallen. *The Fallen!* How serene they look in their graven images—beautiful young men in unsullied uniforms, some with eyes closed gently as if sleeping, others carried tenderly aloft by angels, and all appearing very much alive and unmarked by battle. Robert Shipley, who has made a careful study of Canadian war memorials, can find only one that depicts a soldier who is clearly dead.

The Fallen are immortal. They "sleep" in Flanders fields. There is no suggestion of violence on granite or marble. One of the men, a colleague of my father's whose name is inscribed on Dawson's obelisk, was torn apart by a burst of machine-gun bullets; others drowned, gurgling in the mud of Passchendaele; not a few coughed themselves to death in the gas attack at Ypres. But in Dawson's monument, as in all the others, the ugly truth was hidden from that other army of grieving mothers.

It was in the mothers' names that the lies were told, the propaganda machine was oiled up, the demonization of the enemy was carried to insane lengths, and the brutal facts about "the war that will end wars" (H.G. Wells's unfortunate phrase) were unrevealed in all their naked horror. The mothers who so proudly sent their boys abroad to be sacrificed must never know how their sons really lived and died in the wastes of no man's land, nor must they be exposed to an even more dreadful truth: that the Men Whose Names Will Live Forever died for no good reason in a futile and foolish war that solved nothing.

On either side of Dawson's war memorial the tourists could note two bulky German artillery pieces, captured by the Canadian Corps and dragged all the way from the mud of Flanders to the permafrost of this remote community. There are 3,450 of these heavy guns scattered across the country, standing sentinel for the hundreds of cenotaphs. If my hometown's monument pays tribute to noble sacrifice, the guns speak of total victory. The monument's message, in the parlance of the day, is: *They died that we might live*. The guns' is more triumphant. *We won*, the guns tell us; *we beat the bastards; we licked the beastly Hun; we bested the demon Kaiser.*

The effort and expense required to bring these guns to Minto Park is mind-boggling. Pulled out of the mud of battle, they had to be trundled to the French coast, loaded aboard an ocean freighter, taken across the North Atlantic to a Canadian maritime port, hauled off that vessel, loaded onto a CPR flatcar, transported the entire breadth of the Dominion, unloaded again, hoisted aboard another sea-going freighter to sail up the West Coast to the long, tidal dock at Skagway, then placed on a narrow-gauge rail car to go up and over the mountain summit to the little railhead town of Whitehorse, and finally loaded onto a Yukon River barge, pushed downstream for four hundred miles by a stern-wheeler, unloaded at Dawson, and hauled along the gravel road by Dan Coats's livery wagon to their final resting place. There, for years we children used them as gigantic toys, clambering over them, playing at war, turning the little wheels that actually worked and caused the barrels to be raised and lowered, as we fought mock battles.

Every community in Canada, it seemed, wanted a brace of these captured guns to prove to the world that we won the war—not the Americans, who arrived late, but we, the British, who carried on against the hated Boche when the Russians collapsed and the French mutinied. For when the monument was erected by the "returned men" of the town (my father among them), the emotion was still palpable. It was this fierce hatred—built up during the war years by a propaganda machine so efficient that Joseph Goebbels copied it for his own campaign of lies and deceit—that made any whisper of negotiated peace impossible. Inflamed by the press, by the writers and novelists, by the politicians and the generals themselves, no Allied nation would have countenanced it. The Kaiser was the devil incarnate, and so were his followers who boiled Belgian babies, crucified Canadians, and shot innocent nurses.

The hate continued long after hostilities ended and the Kaiser was exiled to Holland, where he was occasionally pictured in the press, a portly, disturbingly benign figure, sawing wood in his backyard, his once fierce moustachios drooping sadly. In 1924, the same year Dawson was building its monument, the city of Winnipeg mounted a competition to choose the best possible memorial to honour the Fallen. A panel of judges pored over forty-seven entries and chose one that they declared was not only the best but also the finest they had ever seen. It was the work of Emanuel Hahn, a Toronto sculptor who had lived most of his life in Canada. But the name *Hahn* sounded uncomfortably Teutonic. Then it was revealed that although Hahn had studied his art in Toronto, he had actually been born in Germany! That did it. The sculptor was paid off; the monument was not built.

128

There is an ironic coda to this bitter little tale. In 1927 the contest was remounted, this time with the proviso that the winner be either a Canadian or a national figure from one of the countries victorious in the Great War. The design that outshone all others was that of a woman— Elizabeth Wyn Wood. Only after she was awarded the prize was it discovered that Ms. Wood was married to the despised Hahn! There was worse. When it was revealed that the winning entry included a nude male figure representing the Spirit of the West, the public (or at least the most vocal part of it) was incensed. Again the prize money was paid, but the memorial, with its trouserless Spirit, was never built. In the end an inferior entry was chosen and Winnipeg got its cenotaph, which, in Robert Shipley's view, "can never be accused of striking originality."

These memorials were erected to remind us of the bloodiest and most degrading of all military conquests, although that was not the mindset of the time. We call it the Great War—great because it was the first world conflict and, from a military point of view, the most devastating; great because it changed the way people thought about war; great because it shattered the eternal verities of the Victorian Age; great because it changed the world, brought about the destruction of four royal dynasties, sounded the death knell of one empire—the British— and hastened the rise of another—the American.

When we speak about the Great War we mean that it was an all-encompassing war, the kind no general could have conjured up in his wildest nightmares when it began. The statistics are as appalling as they are meaningless. Ten *million* casualties? Who can conceive of such an army of ghosts? Ten million mothers, crying into their pillows. Ten million children, unborn or fatherless. Ten million young men, broken by battle, ground into the swamps of Flanders until they were one with the mud, or seared in the cauldron of Verdun, torn into fragments by cannon and grenade, or frozen lifeless on the Russian steppes.

I have written elsewhere that this was a very Canadian war. In those four dreadful years more than 60,000 Canadians were killed at a time when Canada's population was no more than 8 million. One man was slain for every eleven that enlisted. In the second world conflict (the

Global War), the odds were only twenty-six to one. So far as Canadians were concerned then, the Great War was more than twice as bloody as the one that followed. But none of that was apparent to the fevered multitudes who thronged the streets of every major Canadian city in the first week of August 1914.

2

The crowds of August It has been called "one of the most spectacular crowd formations in modern history." The crowds that choked the streets had been growing mysteriously since August 3, when, perhaps for the first time, Canadians were forced to admit that war was almost inevitable. It sounds ludicrous: an assassin's bullet in the Balkans had touched it off, but the causes go deeper. As Barbara Tuchman has made clear in *The Guns of August*, Europe was hungry for war, and the dreadnought race, played out like a sports contest, helped make it unavoidable.

On the day before war was declared, people began to gather in front of the newspaper offices where bulletins in large type were posted on the walls and windows. In Winnipeg, a *Free Press* representative brandishing a megaphone bellowed out the latest news; each announcement brought forth a full-throated roar from his audience. In Hamilton, when the *Spectator* projected stereopticon lantern slides of world leaders on its walls, pandemonium ensued. In Calgary, the *Herald* used a motion picture projector for the same purpose. In Halifax, a similar mob was treated to patriotic songs from a donated gramophone.

A revealing phenomenon of this patriotic festival was the solidarity demonstrated by members of both founding peoples and even the new immigrants. Cries of *"Vive le roi"* mingled with those of *"Vive la France."* Leading French-Canadian newspapers carried pictures of intertwined Union Jacks and fleurs-de-lys. The wildly enthusiastic crowds that surged through Montreal's main thoroughfares sang "God Save the King," "La Marseillaise," "Rule Britannia," and "O Canada" in both languages.

Albert Sévigny, a popular Member of Parliament and a future Quebec chief justice, pledged that French Canadians were "standing shoulder to

130

shoulder with their fellow countrymen of other races." Even more significant was the declaration of Armand Lavergne, Emilie's son, now a leading Quebec nationalist, that his followers were ready to offer their lives for the King of England.

Henri Bourassa, to the considerable surprise of Anglo-Canadians, also endorsed Britain's entry into the war. "Without a doubt," he wrote in *Le Devoir*, "it is natural for any French Canadian to wish ardently for the triumph of the Anglo-French arms." Another Montreal paper, *La Patrie*, put it more strongly: "There are no longer French Canadians and English Canadians. Only one race now exists, united by the closest bonds in a common cause." That wistful hope was echoed across the nation, but ironically, the war that Canadians thought would be the basis for a new détente would prove to be bitterly divisive, widening the schism between the two language groups.

By August 5 war fervour was breaking out in spontaneous parades. In Toronto that night, a little band turned up, seemingly from nowhere as the throngs in front of the *Star* building cheered themselves hoarse, then roared out a string of patriotic airs. Within a block, as the band moved west along King Street, the crowd had swelled to three thousand. In Winnipeg similar demonstrations led young men to fall in behind two regiments marching to their barracks and fight for the chance to enlist.

When the news appeared on the newspaper boards that Britain had declared war on Germany for invading neutral Belgium, the tension that had tightened during the previous days suddenly snapped and the crowds went crazy, flinging hats and umbrellas into the air with wild abandon. In those days every man wore a hat: silk toppers for the privileged, cloth caps for working men and country squires, straw boaters for the younger rakes. Now, on this August night, there came a perfect eruption of headgear. In the words of the Toronto *Telegram*, "above the shrill babble of the newsboys' clamour that turned the streets into pandemonium last night, suddenly rose a booming roar that rose and fell in the narrow canyon of streets, and which broke again and again in an ever-growing crescendo. . . . It was the voice of Toronto carried away with patriotic enthusiasm at the thought that Britain, longing for peace, had determined to give the bully of Europe a trouncing."

No one doubted that the trouncing would be swift and brutal and that Britain would win hands down. Britain had *always* been victorious. Editorialists invoked Agincourt, the Spanish Armada, Trafalgar, and Waterloo as proof of British invincibility. It was the fleet, more than the army, that brought reassurance, making "Rule Britannia" a second national anthem.

The coming conflict was seen as a power struggle between Germany and the Empire. If Germany won, what would become of the precious Empire? The appeals for imperial solidarity that characterized these frenzied days spoke entirely of the whole and less of the parts. In Montreal's Christ Church cathedral on the eve of the war, Bishop Farthing made that perfectly clear. "We must stand to defend ourselves, for our whole empire will be at stake. Our nation may go down if we should be defeated, and our power will be lost. We shall be stripped of power, and of the future, no man can tell."

These August crowds were remarkable in that they were not celebrating victory, as similar crowds in Toronto had celebrated the relief of Mafeking or Pretoria during the South African War. It was not past triumphs that they cheered but future ones. They were so certain that the Germans would go down to defeat in short order—probably before Christmas—that they marched through the streets singing and shouting exactly as they would during a spontaneous victory parade. As Eric Leed, the author of *No Man's Land*, has written: "War was greeted as a liberation because it was felt to signify the destruction of an economic order." Men rushed to the recruiting offices fearing that it would all be over before they could get into action. After all, what nation, no matter how economically blessed, could sustain for more than six months the appalling waste of men and materials that a modern war presaged?

Two-thirds of the young Canadians who sprang to the colours that August had been born in Great Britain, creatures of the New Imperialism, to whom war seemed little more than a schoolboy lark, right out of the *Boys' Own Paper*. There was adventure to be had and deathless renown, and, if the South African conflict was any indication, all at very little cost. Agar Adamson, a gentrified Toronto diarist who enlisted at the age of forty-eight and was one of the first to go overseas, applied for a commission in the Princess Patricia's Canadian Light Infantry (PPCLI), remarking that "one might reasonably hope to see a little service under such glorious conditions as the European war." The glorious conditions turned out to be three years spent in the hell of the Flanders trenches, which, miraculously, he survived.

Given the mood of the time, few would admit to any crass reason for joining up. John Diefenbaker, then a young university student, remembered that although "old countrymen rushed to the colours in a surge of patriotism [they] were encouraged in many instances, I am sure, by the thought that if they didn't hurry they would miss a free trip home."

The odds looked good to the Canadian-born, whose numbers made up one-quarter of the first contingent. Most were victims of the two-year depression that followed the collapse of the Western real estate boom. They, too, were getting a free ride: food, shelter, clothing, and pay at the rate of $1.10 a day, a better deal than that faced by the average working stiff, and all wrapped up in an approving aura of patriotism.

They would never regret it, or so the principal of University College in Toronto told those of his charges who volunteered. "When you return your romance will not vanish with your youth. You will have fought in the Great War, you will have joined in the liberation of the world." It was hard to believe, wrote Diefenbaker, looking back, "that we entered the holocaust that was the First World War, if not exactly in the spirit of light opera, at least as if it were no more than the natural course of events."

They did not know what they were in for. If the generals did not understand what modern war was all about, how could the young recruits who had joined the peacetime militia for purely social reasons? As Ivan Bloch had so presciently forecast, the breech-loading rifle, the rapid-firing machine gun, and the spade had changed the nature of warfare. The days of the thin red line, in which the soldiers of the Queen had stood shoulder to shoulder and peppered the enemy, were gone with the flintlocks. Yet one tactic remained in the military manuals. The cavalry charge, the prospect of which quickened the pulses of so many young men, was a thing of the past. Nonetheless, former cavalryman Douglas Haig, who would soon take over command of the British army, wanted even *more* cavalry, firm in his belief that bullets had "little stopping power against the horse." But those bullets would drive men to burrow underground like moles, into what that brilliant literary analyst, Paul Fussell, has called "a troglodyte world" of filthy, vermin-infested ditches filled with a foul gruel composed of Flanders clay, excrement, human fragments, and rotting sandbags, where the ear-splitting cacophony of shellfire was all but unbearable and the odds for survival shorter than anyone could yet contemplate.

No hint of these new realities intruded upon the cloud-cuckoo-land of those early wartime months. One looks back on that fevered fall as if reading a bad novel peopled by unbelievable characters. Of these, the most grotesque was the Honourable Sam Hughes, the megalomaniac minister of militia, the strangest, most maddening politician in all Canadian parliamentary history, and certainly the most disastrous—the wrong man in the wrong place at the wrong time.

The most astonishing aspect of Hughes's career was that he kept his job for two years of war even though many of his contemporaries were convinced he was demented. To the governor general, Lord Connaught, he was "off his base: . . . a conceited lunatic." The Prime Minister believed his mind was unbalanced. His deputy, George Foster, declared that there "is only one feeling about Sam, that he is crazy." Sir Joseph Flavelle, a leading Canadian financier, concluded that he was "mentally unbalanced with the low cunning and cleverness often associated with the insane."

Hughes broke every dictum in the political rule book and got away with it. A civilian, he acted like a general, wore a general's uniform, and galloped about on horseback issuing and countermanding orders to the troops and military staff. That was unprecedented: a minister of the crown overstepping his position with a giant leap, reaching down past the brass and acting like a company sergeant major. It was as if

Art Eggleton, say, the minister of defence at this writing, had donned a uniform, galloped into Camp Borden on horseback, and started giving orders in front of the troops on parade ("Pipe down, you little bugger, or get out of the service").

This was the man who, after the South African War, had shamelessly lobbied for at least one and perhaps *two* Victoria Crosses for non-existent acts of bravery and who now began handing out contracts by the dozen to favoured friends whom he created honorary colonels. One of his first acts was to scrap the time-honoured names of militia units (Seaforth Highlanders, Black Watch) and replace them with numbered battalions. Esprit de corps went into the ashcan. "A smashing of regimental spirit," one military man called it, "the most unpardonable sin in the whole of Canadian mobilization."

Instead of putting the newly mobilized troops into an established training centre at Petawawa, Ontario, Hughes insisted on transforming an empty piece of real estate at Valcartier, Quebec, into a bustling army camp. The result, after the tents went up and the raw recruits arrived, was chaos. "Military training was negligible," Sir Andrew Macphail, the official army medical historian, acknowledged. "The time was occupied in organizing and reorganizing, issuing clothing and equipment, examining and inoculating recruits, writing new attestation papers, and preparing for reviews"—all of which could have been completed with more efficiency and dispatch at their home units. Reviews there certainly were, with the pompous minister in full uniform astride a cavalry horse, like a Caesar of old, haranguing the troops in a rough, imperious voice.

The embarkation of the first contingent of more than thirty thousand Canadians on September 23 was a horror, and again the minister was to blame. He peremptorily rejected the services of a government professional and put one of his cronies, created an honorary colonel, in charge. In the words of a civilian assistant, "chaos reigned supreme." Some units that arrived at Quebec City from Valcartier were marched onto ships without room to hold them, then marched off again to wait for others. Cavalrymen were separated from their horses; baggage and vehicles intended for one vessel were stowed in the wrong one. One mounted battalion found its horses on one ship, its harnesses and wagons on a second, and its wheels on a third. When the last of the transport vessels got underway, it left behind a mountain of baggage piled on the dock—not to mention 863 horses and 90 motor vehicles. An extra vessel had to be scrounged to take care of the overflow. It managed to clear the harbour five days after the fleet had departed and steamed off independently.

Hughes was the worst kind of Canadian nationalist: an Orangeman of the deepest dye who had no use for the British, a militiaman who scorned the Permanent Force, and a bigot who treated new Canadians with contempt and acted as if French Canadians didn't exist. He infuriated the Québécois by putting a Baptist minister in charge of recruiting in that province, and at Valcartier he shuffled all French-Canadian recruits into English-speaking units since at that camp all orders and instructions were given in the one language. He resisted efforts to form a French-speaking battalion, which might have given recalcitrant French Canadians a reason and a purpose to enlist. Not until November was such a unit formed, the Royal 22nd—the famous "Van Doos"—following a personal appeal to Borden by Wilfrid Laurier. But that was the end of it; no similar regiment was ever recruited.

In the heady days of August, the camaraderie of the two founding language groups had caused some Canadians to believe that the presence of a common enemy might serve to heal any breach between them. Hughes destroyed those hopes with his bungling interference and set the scene for the bitterness that would mark the disastrous conscription crisis of 1917.

Against all evidence, Hughes insisted that Canadian-made equipment was superior to that manufactured by the despised British. The soldiers' leather Oliver harness was, in his view, the best of its kind, but to the rank and file it was the "Oliver torture." Much of the problem resulted from the minister's cozy relationship with political cronies who produced shoddy goods in the interests of easy profit. The troops were outfitted with boots that turned to mush in heavy rains, greatcoats that soaked up water, wagons too big for European roads, old-fashioned bandoliers that couldn't hold a modern rifle clip, tunics that were too tight, belts that half strangled the wearer, water tanks too heavy to be cleaned, and spavined horses that had to be destroyed by the hundreds. One of the quirkiest pieces of equipment was the MacAdam spade, an entrenching tool with a hole in it that Hughes believed a soldier could use to observe the enemy while shielded from his fire. Patented in the name of Hughes's secretary, it was never used. The army bought twenty-five thousand at $1.35 per spade; all were sold for scrap.

"How they ever expected an infantryman to pack such a heavy and unwieldy article around passes comprehension," Donald Fraser, a private in the 31st (Alberta) Battalion confided to his diary. "Nevertheless they were issued to us in England and might have been stacked up in little piles outside the tents. They were never used. Every morning they had to be straightened out and dressed correctly so the O.C. and his satellites could glance down the lines and with admiring looks give the password, 'O.K.'"

An even more blatant example of Hughes's misplaced nationalism was the all-Canadian rifle that he clung to with the tenacity of a child clutching a teddy bear. Patented by a Scottish sportsman, Sir Charles Ross, it seemed the answer to a marksman's prayer, being lighter, shorter, and cheaper than the British Lee-Enfield. There was a certain amount of pique involved in Hughes's championship of the Ross rifle. During the South African War Canada had called for 15,000 Lee-Enfields only to find that the British had ignored the request in order to fill their own requirements. Hughes's response was to scrap the British rifle in favour of the Ross. Its inventor was soon made one of Hughes's honorary colonels, and the minister himself became the Ross rifle's greatest advocate. It was, he insisted, "the most perfect rifle in every sense in the world today."

Hughes's grandiloquence, which would have done a Hollywood press agent proud, became the subject of considerable argument when the new rifle was tested against the British model. The Ross was certainly a better target weapon, and Canadian snipers would use it to considerable effect throughout the war; but it had serious defects that some eighty changes in design could not correct. Once Canadian troops got into action these became evident. The Ross jammed easily. As a result, the bolt had to be bashed with the heel of an army boot before it would work. Moreover, the bayonet kept falling off. A delicate piece of equipment, the Ross was hardly the soldier's friend—not the kind of weapon one would want to rely on in the Flanders mud.

By the time Canadian troops got into action, the new Mark III Ross—a product of scores of adaptations—bore no resemblance to its inventor's design. It was now eight inches longer and a pound heavier than the Lee-Enfield. The troops hated it. "To hell with the gun. I'll take a club," one frustrated army driver commented. When they had the chance, the men in action tossed the Canadian weapon aside and grabbed a better rifle from a British corpse.

At the top levels the rifle had some support, especially from friends of Hughes, such as the Second Division's Major General R.E.W. Turner, who threatened to punish any man found with a Lee-Enfield. But Sir Edwin Alderson, who commanded the First Division and later, in 1915, the new Canadian Corps, had little use for the Ross. He had incensed Hughes during training on Salisbury Plain in England by scrapping Canadian equipment for British. He infuriated the minister further by sending out a questionnaire asking his officers to comment on the new rifle. One colonel had written that it was "nothing short of murder to send our men against the enemy with such a weapon." Alderson agreed: "I would not be fit for command if I passed over anything which would endanger men's lives or the success of our arms." Alderson proceeded to equip his men with the British rifle, at which Hughes blew up, turning aside Alderson's complaints as "absolutely absurd and ridiculous."

The spectacle of a Canadian cabinet minister insulting his top general suggests that Alderson's fate was already sealed. Hughes had been conspiring with another of his honorary lieutenant-colonels, Sir Max Aitken (the future Lord Beaverbrook), to have Alderson fired. And fired he was after the Canadian-born Aitken, Canada's official "eye witness" in London, reported to cabinet his belief that Alderson was "incapable of holding the Canadian divisions together." But it was generally concluded that the paramount reason for Alderson's dismissal in the spring of 1916 was his refusal to support the Ross. Ironically, when the results of Alderson's questionnaire were laid before Haig, the British commander-in-chief in effect agreed with Alderson. By 1916, all Canadian troops, except snipers, carried the Lee-Enfield into battle.

3

The blood-letting

Like a diver leaping to the aid of a struggling swimmer, Canada had plunged thoughtlessly into the maelstrom of the Great War. The first contingent that steamed towards Europe in the fall of 1914 was a rabble of eager volunteers, untrained and badly equipped, with little leadership or understanding of what they faced. No arrangement had been made to support the Canadians in the field. It had not occurred to Hughes, or anybody else, apparently, that troops in action must be reinforced. Even in a peacetime army the wastage is considerable from illness, accident, sheer incompetence, transfer, and promotion. In action the wastage can be devastating, as the men who came forward so eagerly in August were to learn at Ypres the following spring. How many men would be needed to replace those who were killed, wounded, shell-shocked, or missing? Nobody knew. In battle, the infantry takes the heaviest blows. But because the volunteers had been allowed to choose their own units, the army was already oversupplied with cooks, clerks, and lorry drivers and was short of fighting soldiers.

In her eagerness to rally round the flag and to demonstrate to a breathless nation that she was "Ready, aye Ready" (Laurier's phrase) to serve the mother country, Canada had dispatched a disorganized, if enthusiastic, mob to England. "Soldiers!" Hughes had cried on the eve of their departure, "the world regards you as a marvel. . . ." The world, from the Prime Minister down, regarded that as a joke. "As fine a body of officers and men as ever faced a foe," Hughes had bragged. The country had become used to such superlatives as a result of the arrogance spawned by the great prairie boom. But the finest body of untrained, ill-equipped Canadians would have been slaughtered to a man within fifteen minutes had they taken the field.

After twelve days at sea and another nine enduring the dreadful snarl on the Plymouth docks, the contingent was finally released from the prison of the troopships and packed off to the sodden expanse of Salisbury Plain for training. Here, in the shadow of Stonehenge's monoliths, their commanders struggled with the problem of sorting out the units and equipment that had been thrown into such a jumble at Quebec. That took several more weeks. Over the winter of 1914-15, the shoddy Canadian equipment was slowly replaced with superior British boots, tunics, webbing, wagons, and trucks, and, of course, a better entrenching tool to replace Miss Ena MacAdam's ingeniously impractical shovel.

Training suffered partly because the raw recruits were plagued by the wettest winter in decades and felled by a variety of illnesses from pneumonia to meningitis, but also because of the patronage appointments of Sam Hughes. The old lion of the frontier, Sam Steele, who had lost one job because of Liberal patronage, had got another from the Tories. Back from South African service at the age of sixty-five, he had been put in charge of training the First Division. Hughes gave the job of training the Second Division to another crony, J.C. MacDougall. Between these two jealous old soldiers there was no co-operation, nor was the training program modernized to fit the kind of war developing in France. These flaws were magnified by the presence of inexperienced Canadian militia officers, too old and unfit for battle and too out-of-date to train the men in their charge.

The untried Canadians were an unruly bunch who rebelled at the idea of saluting officers who were just as green as they were. Since Hughes, a temperance advocate, had banned wet canteens, hundreds simply took their leave from the camp at night, pass or no pass, to return considerably the worse for wear. Agar Adamson's wife, Mabel, waiting for her husband in the Old George Hotel, wrote to her mother that "Salisbury looks as if it were in the hands of the Germans. A picket goes around every night dragging drunken Canadians out of the pubs." She had counted one hundred arrests that night, including those of twenty-two officers.

In spite of Hughes's orders, Major General Sir Edwin Alderson moved quickly to solve the problem. Alderson was no stranger to his new charges; he had served with mounted Canadian troops in South Africa and liked them. After he ordered the installation of wet canteens, beer soon replaced hard liquor as the tipple of choice, and the unruly young soldiers stayed in camp. Alas, the word had already gone out: these undisciplined and untrained colonials were wild men—scarcely a match for the British Tommies, let alone the Germans.

The Canadians got their real training in the trenches, which by February 1915 stretched in a wriggling, unbroken line from Switzerland to the North Sea. The war of movement that everybody expected and that so many looked forward to was ended. There would be no gallant charges here in the mud and filth of no man's land. In parts of Flanders the scars of war were not yet evident. But as the months moved on, the Canadians would soon face a black-and-grey world, stark and forbidding, where the limbless cadavers of broken trees rose out of the slime like skeletal fingers. Not a leaf here, not a blade of grass, and no hint of human presence save the bones of those who had gone before: the dead were one with the mud. The living cowered below the parapets waiting for the night.

The neat, sandbagged trenches that have been preserved for the curious visitors who tour France and Belgium bear no resemblance to those foul ditches, calf-deep in gumbo, redolent with the stink of rotting flesh, the stagnant water alive with frogs and beetles. The dugouts swarmed with rats that scuttled over the bodies of the living and fed off the corpses of the dead.

In March, after a week of indoctrination by older sweats, the Canadians took their place in the line north of Armentières. Here, the historians of the war tell us, very little happened in the month before the division was shipped farther north. Very little, perhaps, to British staff officers reclining at headquarters far behind the lines; very little, certainly, in comparison with later, bloodier engagements. But to Captain Agar

Adamson of the PPCLI, it was stunning in its ferocity. "It is beyond my description to describe what has happened in the last four days," he wrote to his wife, Mabel (who had described to her mother the drunkenness at Salisbury), "but I know if I read what I am going to write, I doubt if I would be able to believe it was not written by a liar or the ravings of a maniac." The regiment, which was under British command and separated from the Canadian division, had come under German attack and lost seventeen men killed and forty-six wounded, including Major Hamilton Gault, the wealthy Montrealer who had raised it using his own funds.

After a twenty-four-day stint in that front line sector, the Canadian troops of the First Division returned to rest billets. Here, boarding with French farm families, they began to get a sense of the civilian suffering. Private A.R.B. Duck was billeted with an old man of sixty-seven and his wife whose two sons and son-in-law were somewhere at the front. He would always remember how, in the evening, the two old people would sit on either side of the fire and gaze into it without a word. "Sometimes a tear would roll down their faces and they would commence to talk to you. Seemed as if they were pleased very much that we came all the way from cold, cold Canada to help them. . . ."

The Canadians' real baptism of fire occurred on April 22 after the division moved north to the Ypres salient, just inside the Belgian border. In the parlance of war, a salient was a bulge in the line, an angular projection poking into the heart of no man's land. From a tactical point of view, it was something to be shunned as surely as trench foot, since it was an open invitation to slaughter: "one huge artillery target," in the later words of Basil Liddell Hart, the *Times'* perceptive correspondent. The troops defending this killing ground were subject to withering enemy fire from all three sides—and for no real strategic purpose. The Allies insisted on clinging to the salient, not because it made any military sense but for purely sentimental reasons. This blood-drenched piece of real estate was the only hunk of Belgium that the Germans had not overrun. "Brave little Belgium" had held them back! An outrageously costly symbol, the salient must *never* be lost to the enemy.

142

North Sea

HOLLAND

English Channel

Ostend

Passchendaele

BELGIUM

Ypres

Neuve Chapelle

Armentières

Montreuil

Lens

Mons

Vimy

Douai Plain

Arras

Cambrai

Valenciennes

Somme R.

Amiens

Trench Line from North Sea ~

To Switzerland

Meuse R.

LUXEMBOURG

GERMANY

Verdun

FRANCE

N

THE WESTERN FRONT

SWITZERLAND

The British and the French fought three battles in order to hang on to it, each bloodier than the last. The Germans in their turn fought just as fiercely to seize it, again at fearful cost. It beggars the imagination to contemplate the ironies and idiocies of Ypres—hundreds of thousands of men enduring a perfect hell before battling to a stalemate, not once but three times. "Wipers," as the soldiers called it, has become a symbol for Canada, too, albeit a different one. The salient went into our history books because it was in this moonscape that the Canadians proved their mettle.

The first battle of Ypres was over before the Canadians went into the line. The second began on April 22, 1915, when the world seemed to turn a sickly olive green. Scarcely anybody at the general staff level, British or French, had seriously considered the possibility of a gas attack, in spite of all the evidence. If the Germans had put up a placard reading "DANGER! Gas Attack Coming!" the clues could not have been clearer. An Allied agent in Belgium had predicted it. Captured German prisoners had confirmed it. One German deserter had even displayed an issued gas mask as evidence. But nobody on the Allied side thought to issue gas masks. The attitude of the French was that "all this gas business need not be taken seriously." Nobody thought to use aerial photography to confirm what the prisoners were saying. Had they done so, they would have spotted more than five thousand huge cylinders of chlorine gas, turned out by German chemical factories, lined up along the northern face of the salient.

The cylinders represented an experiment. The Germans had used gas before—in Poland, where the temperatures were too low to make it effective, and in front of Neuve Chapelle the previous October, where it was so weak it wasn't even noticed. The German high command had little faith in this newest weapon of war but was willing to try it out if the wind was right as part of the big attack that signalled the renewed battle of Ypres. If it didn't work, they had nothing to lose; if it did, they could drive the Allies into the sea.

When the Canadians went into the line on April 15, a mild warning did come through to the brigade commanders: "Attack expected at night to be preceded by the sending of poisonous gases to our lines and

144

sending up of three red lights." The attack did not come; as usual, the prevailing wind was at the Canadians' backs. The lull in the fighting (if a constant barrage of shellfire can be described as a lull) continued for another week. The Canadians held the left of the British line next to Algerian and French Territorial units who should probably have been separated by disciplined regulars.

When the gas came at five o'clock on the morning of the twenty-second, it crept toward the Canadian and Algerian lines, hugging the shattered ground (being heavier than air), then spiralling upward for about six feet as it approached the forward trenches. The scenes that followed were climactic. Behind that malevolent wall of green could be seen, dimly, the ghostly forms of the enemy hordes, who, in their crude gas masks, seemed to have sprung from another world.

Then, out of the green fog, came the black troops from North Africa, "running as though Hell . . . was behind them" in the words of one Canadian private. "Their heels barely seemed to touch the ground. As they ran they covered their faces, noses and eyes with their hands, and through blackened lips, sometimes cracked and bleeding, they gasped 'Allemandes! Allemandes!', fell and died by the score."

"A man dies by gas in horrible torment," Harold Peat, a private in the Third Battalion, wrote in his published memoir. "He turns perfectly black, those men at any rate whom I saw that time. Black as black leather, eyes, even lips, teeth, nails. He foams at the mouth as a dog in hydrophobia; he lingers five or six minutes and then—goes West."

Though the Canadians on the French right stood firm, clutching urine-soaked handkerchiefs to their noses, the line had been badly broken. A four-mile-wide gap, big enough to let in an army, had been punched through it, with no one left to defend it in spite of the French officers' attempts to halt the rout. The road to Ypres, only four miles distant, lay open. Nothing now could stop the Germans save the Canadians and the enemy's own caution and rigidity of mind. Fifty thousand Allied troops stood in jeopardy, but, astonishingly, the Germans failed to exploit success. For one thing, they themselves feared the gas that lurked greenly in the shell holes and the bottoms of the trenches.

Ironically, since they had little faith in the new weapon, the enemy had made no provision for reinforcements following a possible break-through. More, they lacked the flexibility to throw carefully laid plans aside and press the attack past the objectives the general staff had laid down. And so, obediently, they halted to wait until morning and lost their momentum as the Canadians harassed them with counterattacks.

A second death cloud came two days later, this time aimed directly at the Canadians, who held the apex of the salient. By then they had been issued cotton bandoliers, which, when soaked in the tubs of water placed along the line and then held to the nostrils, provided a defence of sorts. A vicious bombardment accompanied the gas, but the Canadians held on at the expense of their lungs.

A British private, David Shand, of the Gordon Highlanders, who had not experienced the gas, came out of the line with his regiment, stopped at a ditch near a first-aid clearing station, and beheld a spectacle he could never forget. "There were about two hundred to three hundred men lying in that ditch. Some were clawing at their throats. Their brass buttons were green. Their bodies were swelled. Some of them were still alive. They were not wearing their belts or equipment and we thought they were Germans. One inquisitive fellow turned a dead man over. He saw a brass clip bearing the name CANADA on the corpse's shoulder and exclaimed, 'These are Canadians!' Some of us said, 'For the love of Mike! We never knew that!' Some of the Canadians were still writhing on the ground, their tongues hanging out. . . . We saw one Canadian down on his knees. His finger was on the trigger of his rifle. He was dead. He had apparently turned around and was firing on the Germans because they were in pursuit. There was a big bunch of empty cartridges lying beside him. Then we reached the front line Canadian trenches. There were no trenches left."

By the time they were relieved on April 26, the Canadians had lost some six thousand men, dead, wounded, or missing, mostly from the shellfire that could strike with devastating and unexpected suddenness, as when Joseph Monaghan of the PPCLI asked his best chum for a match to light his pipe. "He handed me the box and when I turned to give it back to him he was dead." The shelling was far worse than the gas, which was never a major factor in the war. But in the years that followed, old soldiers in military hospitals would cough themselves to death, a grim reminder of those desperate moments in the green hell of the Ypres salient.

In this, their first major battle, the untried Canadians had launched what would become a Great War legend. They had startled a world that, in spite of Hughes's bluster, had paid them little heed. They had impressed the British command that had seen them as upstart colonials, no match for the king's regulars—brash, untrained, not entirely dependable. But here, on the afternoon of May 6, was the commander of the British Second Army, Smith-Dorrien, paraphrasing the plaudits he had lavished on the Fighting 19th in the South African War and applying them to the new Canadian Corps. As one of his staff officers remarked that day, "the whole army realized that it was only the gallant actions of the Canadians that saved Ypres; otherwise one of the greatest disasters in the history of the British army might have occurred." An official communiqué confirmed it: "The Canadians had many casualties, but their gallantry and determination undoubtedly saved the situation."

In December the British made a major change. Douglas Haig, who succeeded Sir John French as commander-in-chief of the British Expeditionary Forces, was the very model of a nineteenth-century general. More than any other commander on the British side he looked the part: the chiselled features, the carefully clipped moustache, the cold, blue, penetrating eyes. His riding boots were polished to a high lustre, the envy of his military compatriots. No smear of grime stained the immaculate perfection of his beautifully tailored uniform, no crumb of clay discoloured the whipcord of his riding breeches. But then, there was little mud or clay to be found twelve miles back of the lines at the comfortable château near Montreuil where he made his headquarters. It is, of course, necessary that general officers and their staffs stay far enough from the hurly-burly of battle to assess the overall picture, but Haig and his entourage went to extremes. His chief of staff, Launcelot Kiggell, never went near the front and is said to have visited a battlefield only once in his Great War career—and long after the battle had been fought.

Lord Haldane, who had been secretary of war before the conflict, thought that Haig was "the most highly equipped thinker in the British army," an astounding comment on a dour, reserved leader who was almost inarticulate. He often omitted verbs, fumbled for words, and broke off sentences in the middle, leaving others to figure out what he was driving at. Lloyd George remarked cuttingly, "In my experience a confused talker is never a clear thinker." The British prime minister's attitude to Haig was one of contempt, as his oft-quoted remarks indicate: "Haig does not care how many men he loses. . . ." "We could certainly beat the Germans if only we could get Haig to join them. . . ." "I never met any man in a high position who seemed to me so utterly devoid of imagination. . . . " Lloyd George was more right than wrong in his assessment. He would have liked to sack his *bête noire*, but Haig had too many friends in high places, including the King himself.

A veteran cavalryman, he surrounded himself with fellow cavalrymen, members of the most conservative arm of the forces. Throughout the war he continued to be obsessed with the fantasy of a cavalry charge that would result in a breakthrough and lead to victory. As late as 1927 he was submitting to the war office a secret brief advocating the continued value of cavalry units and defending their role in the Great War. But the days of the cavalry were over; the tank was about to replace the horse.

Haig came from a prominent Edinburgh distillery family, whose dimpled bottles of whisky still bear the Haig name. As a former aide-de-camp to Edward VII he stood near the pinnacle of a rigid military caste system that made it all but impossible for gifted rankers to join the officer class while blue-blooded twits were granted the king's commission.

The social gap in Haig's army, a reflection of the British class system, was remarked on by the Canadians who fought beside the Tommies. The opinion of Wilfred Brenton Kerr, a young gunner from Toronto, would later appear in print: ". . . . above all, we noticed that there seemed to be a gulf between them and their officers, marked by apparent subservience on one side, and by aloofness, even arrogance on the other."

Haig's prejudices were those of his peers. He had little use for his French allies, whom he considered "a wretched lot," nor for politicians. "You can't trust anyone who has ever been in Parliament," he remarked to his sycophantic director of intelligence, Brigadier General John Charteris. Like his master, Charteris was a superoptimist "who conjured forth resounding victories from each bloody hundred yards' advance, like rabbits from a hat," in the sardonic assessment of J.F.C. Fuller, perhaps the shrewdest of the military commentators.

Charteris's sunny assessments misled the press, the public, and even Haig himself with false news of victories. But Haig did not need an enthusiastic subordinate to boost his morale, for he was a man who harboured no doubts; after all, was not God on his side? Did he not pray daily for aid? "I firmly believe," he declared, "that every step in my plans has been taken with Divine help." He was convinced that a "Great Unseen Power" was sustaining him, "otherwise I could not be standing the strain for very long." The strain, such as it was, might have felled a more imaginative commander, but Haig, secure in his château, was blinded by his distance from the battlefield, by the myopia of his yes-men, and by his own refusal to face reality.

When the great Somme offensives ended in November 1916, Haig claimed the campaign had been a success because it took so much pressure off the French, who were drowning in the blood bath of Verdun. But that was not the purpose of the much-heralded Big Push, which was supposed to drive a hole in the German entrenchments astride the Somme River and win the war.

The Great Fuck-Up, as the troops called it, was the largest military engagement ever fought. The battleground was chosen for no other reason than that it marked the point where the British and the French sectors happened to connect. It did not bother Haig that the German defences at that point were the strongest on the Western Front. Each of the three lines of German defences was protected by two thick belts of barbed wire, thirty feet deep.

This was not the kind of fencing strung on the perimeter of Canadian cattle ranches; the barbs here were hefty, razor sharp, and deadly— strong enough to impale a luckless soldier who, caught like a fly in a web, could neither advance nor retreat. Any man "hanging on the old barbed wire," to quote a line of gallows humour from one of the songs of the trenches, was a sitting target for enemy snipers and machine gunners.

It was absolutely imperative, then, that the wire be cut, shattered, rolled up, reduced to smithereens. The answer, the British thought, would be a week-long barrage that would not only destroy the barricades but also force the Germans to skulk in their dugouts. By the time they recovered, shaken, from the incessant bombardment, the advancing British would be upon them, bayonets at the ready, with the cavalry close behind, lances pointed, sabres shining in the sun.

Nobody, apparently, thought to test the effect of shrapnel on wire. The test came on July 1, 1916, with the British advancing in line, shoulder to shoulder, as in the days of musketry. The big guns—1,537 of them—had fired steadily day after day, expending nearly three million shells on the enemy. Tragically, the wire was still intact.

There was worse. Haig had made no attempt to conceal his preparations. The Germans, safe from the bombardment in prepared dugouts that had been dug thirty to forty feet deep in the chalk, were ready. The advancing troops moved sluggishly; the days of the wild charge were long gone. Each man was burdened with sixty-six pounds of equipment, much of it excess baggage. Stumbling over the uneven ground for a distance that averaged five hundred yards, hopping from shell hole to shell hole without the advantage of a covering screen of smoke (the optimistic British felt it wouldn't be needed because the enemy would have been wiped out), the ill-starred Tommies fell in droves long before they reached the undamaged wire. The British guns had stopped too soon. The Germans, unfazed by the barrage, sprang out of dugouts and trenches, waited until the attackers were within one hundred yards of their lines, and then proceeded methodically to mow them down.

Wave after wave of doomed men advanced in the morning sunlight; wave after wave was shattered—eight waves in all. Some were killed even before they managed to clamber out of their trenches, instant victims of the withering fire from German machine guns that spewed out bullets at the rate of 600 rounds per minute.

Such was the fate of the Newfoundland Regiment, a colonial unit within the British Twenty-ninth Division, torn to fragments by the enemy fire. The Newfoundlanders were support troops who suffered heavily from the cannons even before they reached their own front line. By the time they struggled through the gaps torn in that line, the German machine guns a few hundred yards distant were cutting them to pieces. When the roll was called the following morning it was found that of the 801 men who had formed themselves into line to advance against the enemy, only 68 had survived. No other unit on the Allied side suffered as greatly as these volunteers from the outports.

By early afternoon the attack had petered out; those of the living who could walk were back in their own lines. The dead lay on the battlefield in heaps—19,000 corpses sprawled and contorted in the mud. Close to 40,000 more men were wounded or "missing," meaning, in most cases, that they had been blown into unrecognizable bits. It was the blackest day in British history; no other army had suffered such a loss in one day's fighting. A force of 110,000 had been reduced to less than half—the heaviest toll in British records.

Over the years the Somme has come to be seen for what it was: one of the great debacles in the history of warfare. Today, its defenders are few. By the time John Diefenbaker published his memoirs, he could write that "the outpouring of blood on the Somme, when the Newfoundland Regiment went into action, was in my opinion one of the most disgraceful episodes in history." There was a time when he would not have dared to used those words. Back in Canada there was no hint of the *blutbad*, as the Germans called it. All that tortured week and beyond, the cries of victory continued in the Canadian press: "BRITISH SCYTHE OF DEATH CUTS NEW SWATH," "BRILLIANT SUCCESS FOR FRENCH ON SOMME," "BRITISH SMASH FOES ON SOMME. . . ."

Haig remained unmoved by that first day's slaughter. The following day he resumed the attack, still attempting to make the breakthrough that had been frustrated. Again he failed. The next ten days were the bloodiest of the war in spite of the triumphant headlines—ten thousand casualties a day and very little to show for it.

Was Haig ever tormented by the magnitude of the butchery? Did that ghostly army of the Fallen, rising wraithlike from the sodden clay, disturb his dreams or haunt his nightmares? One doubts it. His paucity of imagination acted as a kind of shield to cushion him from the unthinkable. He was more concerned with the grisly mathematics of attrition. The Big Push having failed, he convinced himself that this wearing down was the best policy. The war would become a ghastly contest—a demented sports event in which the victory would go to the side that could count the fewest corpses. The Germans, in Haig's contorted view, would lose so many men that they would eventually sue for peace.

The bloodletting on the Somme continued for some two and a half months, with little ground gained or lost. "BRITISH TAKE AREA 300 YARDS SQUARE," the Toronto *Star*'s big headlines shouted on August 17, as if the gain of that churned-up patch of sodden gumbo constituted a major victory.

Then, on September 3, the Canadians, who had been spared the worst of the series of battles that followed the opening act of the tragedy, took over the line for the first time. They went into action on the ninth and seized the town of Courcelette on the fifteenth, terrifying the surrendering Germans who held up their hands, calling "Mercy, *Kamerad*." The fight had gone out of them. "Whenever they see the Canadians they as a rule meet them with their hands up," Gordon Silliker, a young artilleryman with the 25th Battalion (Nova Scotia Rifles) remarked. The veterans of Ypres no longer saw the Germans as supermen. "Fritz is fairly cowed by the bayonet," Norman Lowther of the Canadian Mounted Rifles later declared. "He simply can't face it."

That evening, as the Germans bombarded the newly captured trenches, Lowther had a narrow and unexpected escape from death when a piece of shrapnel tore into his knee. Four of his comrades carried him across open country under the shelling to a rear dressing station, but before they reached it a big shell exploded close by. A chunk of

152

shrapnel gashed Lowther's right wrist, then headed directly toward his right breast, ripping right through his pay book and breaking his new fountain pen. By great good luck his cigarette case was also in the way. Its presence saved his life.

As Lowther discovered, life and death on the battlefield were often determined by fortune's wheel. A few days later Harold Huggan of the 26th (New Brunswick) Battalion was trying to dig himself in under a hail of machine gun bullets when one entered the inside of his leg, ripped through his hip, and shattered his thigh bone. As Huggan lay bleeding, a young English soldier tried to help him, but even as Huggan put an arm around his rescuer's neck he was hit again. The bullet went through his arm, killing the Englishman instantly. Huggan, who lay out on the field for three days and nights without food or water, survived.

Haig, who could not get it into his head that his tactics weren't working, had decided to gamble on yet another Big Push, hurling all available troops at the German defences, supported for the first time by the strange new armoured vehicles known as tanks. The British had built 150 of these, 49 of which had arrived in France. A mass assault by this new armour might easily have tipped the balance, but Haig, the veteran cavalryman, wouldn't wait for the bulk of the force to arrive. He distributed what he had among his forces piecemeal, like bonbons at a children's party. The Canadians received seven, one of which actually got through to its objective, but the final result was disappointing. The week-long battle cost the Canadians 7,230 casualties. The corps had added to its reputation by seizing its objective, the town of Courcelette, after a hard hand-to-hand struggle. Once again, however, Haig's Big Push had run out of steam, and the stubborn commander returned to his policy of attrition.

The battle of the Somme—actually eight separate battles—dragged on inconclusively for another two months. On October 17, the new Fourth Division, still unbloodied, took its place in the line while the other battered Canadian units moved north to the Vimy area. The division's objective was a filthy ditch known as the Regina Trench, which *had* to be captured if any semblance of victory could be wrung out of the debacle. It took a month of tough fighting against an enemy so determined that any German officer who surrendered so much as an inch of ground was faced with a court martial. In spite of the freezing rain that never seemed to let up, the Canadians did the job. They took a section of the Regina Trench on November 11. A week later the entire support system was in their hands.

After more than five months, the Somme offensive, supposed to be the decisive hammer blow that would bring swift victory, ground to a halt. The ordeal was over. It had cost the Canadians 25,000 casualties, of which two-thirds were suffered in the contest for the Regina Trench.

In the battle of attrition, the two opposing armies had slugged it out to a draw. At enormous cost the Allies had managed to seize 125 square miles of insignificant farmland from the enemy but had lost more than their opponents in the wearing-down process that Haig thought would win the war. The Allied casualties were eventually reckoned at 623,907, the German losses at 465,525. About a quarter of the Germans were so lightly wounded they were returned to their lines and so went unreported, allowing the pencil-pushers to claim that the casualties were close to being equal. So much for attrition.

Once again the great conflict had been reduced to a bloody stalemate, although Haig, with his usual optimism, claimed a kind of moral victory. "There is reason to believe," he announced, using the fuzzy Haigspeak that had become his trademark, that German casualties were far greater than those of the British and French. The enemy's morale had shown "marked signs" of deterioration, while the British Army was "confident in its proved superiority." The German civilians were demoralized, and all that was needed (weather permitting) was another campaign that would surely prove decisive.

That campaign, in the spring of 1917, would be the ineffective battle of Arras, another big push that failed to make its objective except in one brilliant instance—the capture of Vimy Ridge by the Canadian Corps. When the Regina Trench was firmly in Canadian hands, all four

154

divisions had arrived in the Vimy area, training under Alderson's replacement, Lieutenant General Julian Byng.

Astonishingly, Sam Hughes was still minister of militia when the Canadians arrived in the Vimy sector and still doing his best to interfere in matters outside his jurisdiction. His support of the Ross rifle had undoubtedly cost the lives of scores, perhaps hundreds, of Canadian soldiers, but now the Ross belonged to the past. Nor could Hughes bully Julian Byng, though he tried. When Hughes announced to the new commander that he would continue to make all appointments within the corps, Byng replied courteously that he would always make recommendations to the Minister, but if Hughes tried to override him, he would resign. That ended it. Hughes backed down.

It remained Hughes's ambition to command the Canadians in battle. "If the struggle is not over by spring," he had said that first winter, "I will take the field myself." The prospect of this half-mad amateur soldier blundering over the top and into the killing ground of no man's land dismayed those who took his words seriously. But that appalling prospect was still alive as late as 1916, when it was rumoured that he might be offered a command in France if only to get him out of the Canadian cabinet. To this possibility, the *Globe* responded with a vituperative editorial. "It would be a crime, the ghastliest and most murderous stroke of the war, no matter what the excuse or what the cause, were General Sir Sam Hughes given a real command of living soldiers in a genuine engagement on the war's battlefront. . . . The fortunes of any Government or of any political leader in Canada are as nothing compared with the fate of a Canadian army on the French or Belgian front, dependent on the strategy or judgement of Sam Hughes. To acquiese [*sic*] in such a crime, as a condition of his resignation from the Canadian Government would be to try to wash out the reminders of political blundering in the life-blood of Canadian regiments. It is bad enough to have to suffer his aping of Napoleon as the World's other military genius; but to allow him a chance to put his apings into practice with the flesh and blood of Canada's sons and men—No!"

Certainly Borden wanted him out. Why, then did Borden not fire him? It was not that easy. Hughes on the outside was, in the Prime Minister's view, more dangerous than Hughes on the inside. He was a loyal member of the party and commanded a considerable constituency. He had the full force of the Orange Lodge behind him—or thought he had. His dismissal could touch off a political crisis.

Moreover, the Prime Minister shrank from confrontation. He was, in Hughes's backhanded description, "a most lovely fellow" but "gentle hearted as a child." It is likely that Borden was scared silly of facing the emotional roller coaster that would result if he dropped his excitable minister. Hughes had the distressing habit of breaking down and bursting into tears at the mildest reprimand. After one of these outbursts—he had once cried into the telephone after a challenge—he invariably pledged that he would reform, but he never did.

These confrontations tell us as much about Borden as they do about Hughes. The Prime Minister—ponderous, introspective, nervous, and slow of speech—hid his sensitivity and his enthusiasms behind a mask of serenity. In the early days of his leadership his followers had found him too reasonable, too indecisive, perhaps, to command the ship of state. Yet these qualities—the direct opposite of the posturing braggadocio of the insufferable Hughes—were the very ones that have served more than one Canadian prime minister in moments of crisis, from John A. Macdonald, Old Tomorrow himself, on down through Mackenzie King and his successors. Hughes managed to survive for almost half the war while colleagues struggled to find a means of getting rid of him without precipitating the kind of explosion that in the midst of war could have torn the country apart, or at least—and this was a prime consideration—the Conservative Party itself.

"It is quite evident that Hughes cannot remain in the government," Borden confided to his diary on April 3, 1916. But it was another eight months before he finally called for the minister's resignation. He had no choice, for this time Hughes, then in London, had overstepped the mark once too often, not only ignoring an order from Borden but also responding with a letter that, in effect, called the Prime Minister a liar.

This firm, if tardy, action could be called Borden's epiphany. Since becoming leader of his party, he had been growing slowly with the job, a growth accelerated by the war. Hughes almost collapsed when he received Borden's letter demanding his resignation, for he had firmly believed the Prime Minister would never dare to dismiss him. Borden, who appears to have been waiting for Hughes to blunder, managed to get him off centre stage without the expected political furor. "I determined to let him continue until I was perfectly sure that his dismissal would not entail any serious danger to my administration," was the way Borden justified it in his memoirs. Hughes would continue to rant from his seat in the House of Commons, but Borden paid him little heed. The cat's claws had been pulled.

4

The home front

The sense of bubbling enthusiasm that was one of the distinguishing aspects of the Canadian character in the early days of the century is not a quality that springs immediately to mind today. Caution, yes; circumspection, certainly; but *enthusiasm?* Still, there was a time when Canadians firmly believed, with Wilfrid Laurier, that the century belonged to Canada and that anything was possible.

Sam Hughes's reckless promise to send twenty-one Canadian divisions to the front can be dismissed as the rantings of a demented politician. But what about the equally rash promise made by Robert Borden on New Year's Day 1916, apparently without consulting his colleagues or military authorities? At a time when the country's population was less than eight million, Borden wanted to raise the size of the Canadian army to a total of half a million men—a sacred pledge, he called it. He did not seem to realize that, given losses from enemy fire, illness, transfers, and discharges, Canada would have to supply an average of twenty-five thousand new recruits every month to honour his impulsive words.

Like most English Canadians, the imperturbable prime minister had been caught up in the tidal wave of patriotic fervour that marked the early years of the war. So many young men had rushed to the colours that the supply of recruits initially exceeded the demand. To be fair, Borden had no more conception of the bloodletting than ordinary Canadians. The growing casualty lists provided some hints, but the newspapers continued to trumpet Allied victories and fantastic enemy losses. The true dimensions of the conflict did not begin to sink in until the winter of 1916–17, by which time Canada, having mounted a fourth division, was already planning a fifth.

By the spring of 1916, the pace of recruiting had slowed alarmingly. The mass of English-born enthusiasts who had made up the bulk of the army in its formative months had been used up. The farms and the factories, both essential to the war effort, needed men as desperately as the armed forces, whose total strength by the end of the year was just under 300,000—not much more than half of Borden's fantasy.

Now, with the manpower situation reaching crisis proportions, every effort was being made to lure more recruits into the service, or, if that didn't work, to shame them into joining up. Would-be soldiers no longer needed their wives' permission to enlist. Medical standards were lowered. So-called undesirables—blacks, native people, Asians—found themselves courted. It was no longer a "white man's war," in the unfortunate phrase of a Cape Breton recruiting officer in 1915. Now every able-bodied man was needed and even some not originally considered able-bodied, such as a young McGill student named Dodge Rankine. Turned down in 1914 because he'd once had typhoid, he was now passed as fit by a doctor who merely stuck a stethoscope against his chest. Private Rankine was on a ship bound for overseas that very afternoon.

In their stepped-up campaign for new recruits, the army and the government had the willing co-operation of most English-speaking Canadians, especially women, who were encouraged to humiliate so-called slackers who had not come forward to volunteer. They sang Muriel Bruce's new song, "Why Aren't You in Khaki?" which swiftly became the official anthem of the recruiting leagues. Members of another militant organization, the Women's Home Guard, dressed in khaki skirts and Norfolk jackets, occupied themselves handing out so many white feathers that it became an ordeal for a man in civilian clothes to walk down a city street unmolested. Charles Haddlesey of St. Catharines remembered that "all the girls were going around with white feathers. They'd stick one of those feathers on you if you were not in uniform." Haddlesey found himself getting the white feather treatment—a clear intimation of cowardice—even though he'd been rejected for service. He complained to an officer who agreed to take him to another doctor who would pass him as healthy. The following evening Haddlesey, too, was on his way overseas.

As recruiting dwindled, demands began to be heard for national registration and even conscription. Recruiting leagues across the country started to protest the haphazard methods of filling military quotas and in April sent a large delegation to lobby the Prime Minister. "The present system is a failure," S.F. Washington of the Hamilton Recruiting League told Borden. The chief justice of Manitoba, T.G. Mathers, was equally forceful: ". . . we have under the present system compulsion in its most obnoxious form. It is absurd to speak of enlistment at the present day as voluntary. In the cities of the West the man who is not in uniform is made to feel that he is a sort of social outcast. No man who joins the ranks today does so voluntarily. He does so because he can no longer resist the pressure of public opinion."

This atmosphere was recalled by Pierre van Paassen, a young Dutch immigrant who would later become a foreign correspondent for the Toronto *Star.* Van Paassen was accosted on the rear platform of a Toronto streetcar by a woman in mourning for her three sons who had been killed at the front. "Why aren't you in khaki?" she demanded. "Why do you dare to stand there laughing at my misery? Why don't you go over and fight? Fight, avenge my boys!"

When van Paassen tried to explain that he was not a Canadian, she began to scream at the top of her voice that she, "the mother of three heroes who had died for their king and country, had been insulted by a foreigner, a slacker, a German spy, a Red . . ." When the beleaguered Dutchman managed to get off the streetcar at the King Edward Hotel, his tormentor followed, still screaming about spies and Germans. A crowd of businessmen gathered, surrounded van Paassen, and gallantly rushed to the woman's side, forcing him to submit as she pushed a white feather on a pin through his coat and into his flesh. The following day, Pierre van Paassen joined up.

This was no isolated incident. In Berlin, Ontario (soon to change its name to Kitchener), civilians were forcibly manhandled on the street by members of the 118th Battalion and hustled to the recruiting office. In St. Thomas, members of the 93rd Battalion stopped young men and demanded they enlist, threatening to molest them unless they had good reasons not to join up. The "Give Us His Name" campaign by several Ontario regiments allowed the recruiting officers to finger and publicly identify the "slackers."

The imperial theme, "the Empire needs you," was an important part of the recruiting drive. "Britain has given you freedom. . . . She has given you peaceful years. . . . Will you help her now? She is in the gravest peril she has ever known and only her men can save her." The posters and the advertisements also gave play to burgeoning Canadian nationalism: "This is Canada's War. If Germany wins, your freedom will be lost."

The other side of the coin of hatred and revenge bore the themes of adventure, comradeship, and good old-fashioned fun. "We've got a big job out there," one veteran told a Toronto audience, "but there's some fun, too. We've got lots of baseballs and we need pitchers." One Ottawa battalion declared, "It's a man's game, this soldiering." An accompanying illustration showed a young man in uniform—tall, smiling, straight-backed, confident—while a slacker was depicted as a skinny-legged, hunched, and cringing figure.

The ardent patriotism that drove the recruiting campaign and coloured the press reports of the war left a disagreeable taste in the mouths of the fighting men at the front. The psychological gap between civilians at home and soldiers in the trenches grew wider as the war dragged on. It was as if there were two kinds of Canadians, as different one from another as the Francophones were from the Anglophones. Words like "honour" and "sacrifice," still being tossed about back home, ceased to have any meaning in Flanders. Returned soldiers were fed up with demands from friends and relatives to recount stirring tales of heroism and gallantry overseas. As one put it, "You felt like vomiting when the subject was mentioned."

Even the idea of leave in England, as welcome as it was, had its problems, as the English poet Robert Graves told an interviewer. "The idea of being and staying at home was awful because you were with people who didn't understand . . . what this was all about." Nor was it possible to make them understand because "you can't communicate noise. Noise never stopped for one moment—ever." The Canadian poet and novelist Theodore Goodrich Roberts, who served with the 18th Battalion at the front, warned his fellow soldiers not to talk about the war "to people who weren't there. You will be misunderstood if you do. . . ." Philip Gibbs, a leading war correspondent, made no bones about how soldiers on leave felt about civilians: "They hated the smiling women in the streets. They loathed the old men. . . . They desired that profiteers should die by poison-gas. They prayed God to get the Germans to send Zeppelins to England—to make the people know what war meant."

The narrator of Charles Yale Harrison's landmark post-war Canadian novel, *Generals Die in Bed*, reflects the mood: ". . . I feel that people should not be sitting laughing at jokes about plum and apple jam while boys are dying out in France. They sit here in stiff shirts, their faces and jowls are smooth with daily shaving, and dainty cosmetics, their bellies are full, and out there we are being eaten by lice, we are sitting trembling in shivering dugouts."

In the post-war years, those of us who were schoolchildren in the twenties could not help noticing a common phenomenon: those of our fathers who had returned refused to talk to us about the war. It was as if they were somehow set apart from the generation that followed. As Robert Graves's fellow poet, the wounded Siegfried Sassoon, described his evacuation in a hospital train, "We were the survivors; few among us would ever tell the truth to our friends and relatives in England. We were carrying something in our heads which belonged to us alone . . . and to those we left behind us in the battle."

Graves, in his memoirs, wrote that "the civilians talked a foreign language; and it was a newspaper language." That was even truer in Canada, where the censorship was harsher than in England and the theatre of war more distant. The tireless chief censor, Lieutenant-Colonel Ernest J. Chambers, an ardent imperialist to his fingertips, justified his draconian measures by arguing that the British, being closer to the battleground (and, of course, being British), were better equipped than the colonials across the water to deal with disturbing truths. The result was a program of suppression that "still ranks as among the most brazen affronts to democracy in the country's history," to quote Jeffrey A. Keshen's careful study of Great War censorship in Canada.

Sustained by the War Measures Act, made retroactive to August 4, 1914, the chief censor had almost as much clout as the prime minister and, since breaches of the Act carried a $5,000 fine or five years in prison or both, emerged as one of the most powerful men in the country. Brazen the new regulations might be, but the newspapers and magazines scarcely uttered a peep of protest, even when stories that had been cleared by British censors were still banned in Canada. *Maclean's* was one that knuckled under to Chambers's threats and killed a story whose only flaw was that it quoted from a British news report dealing with a Canadian defeat at Cambrai.

The Sault Ste. Marie *Express* was reprimanded for publishing an editorial titled "No More Canadian Soldiers at the Front." British books and pamphlets advocating temperance were banned in Canada because Chambers believed their accounts of Canadian drinking habits in England might inhibit recruiting. Chambers was especially irked by the graphic reports of Robert W. Service. The bard of the Klondike, working as an ambulance driver in France, also wrote for the press, including the Ottawa *Journal*. "I cannot turn the car in that narrow road with the wounded lying under my very wheels," Service reported in 1916. "Two mangled heaps are lifted in. One has been wounded by a bursting gun. There seems to be no part of him that is not burned. . . . The skin of his breast is of a bluish color and cracked open in ridges. I am sorry I saw him." Such dispatches horrified Chambers, who forced the *Journal*'s editor, P.D. Ross, to pledge that Service's material would be expunged or at the very least sanitized. "The more I see of Robert W. Service's matter from the front," he wrote, "the more impressed I become that it is of a character to seriously interfere with recruiting in Canada."

The slightest admonition from Chambers caused newspaper editors to scuttle for cover. In July 1916, the Moncton *Times* published an account of Harry Ison's shrapnel wounds—a cut over the eye, another on the eyelid, a third on the cheek, and a fourth that took off a piece of his ear. Did the editor not think "that the publication of such blood-curdling material of this character is likely to do more harm than good?" Chambers asked. The editor replied meekly that the paper "shall be very much on our guard in future in publishing letters from soldiers."

One man who assisted the censor in his desire to depict a "clean" war was the Canadian-born Max Aitken. The soon-to-be Lord Beaverbrook saw the war as a romantic crusade and was not above writing, in the second volume of his *Canada in Flanders*, that the six thousand men who had died at Ypres "died the best way men can: full of vigour of life and inspired by the determination to succeed at all costs." But then Aitken wrote in the same volume that "the presence of wounded men in a crowded trench passes the limits of horror." The censor watered that down to "the presence of wounded men in the trench makes it far worse." That was too much for Aitken, who felt that a good deal of the drama and bite were being removed from his report. He had powerful friends in Canada and succeeded after intense lobbying in getting his book published in the original form. The resultant delay meant that the volume did not appear until January 1917, by which time its contents had been overshadowed by the Somme battles.

To Chambers, all foreign language papers were suspect and all foreigners a potential threat to the British way of life, an odd attitude in a country that had made a point of throwing the doors open to a variety of immigrants. He prohibited 253 publications from entering Canada from the United States. Of these, 164 were in a language other than French or English. He obtained prohibition orders against not only

German, Russian, and Ukrainian publications but also those in sixteen other languages including Yiddish, Dutch, Swedish, Italian, and Arabic. In November 1916 he suppressed all William Randolph Hearst's newspapers for the duration of the war. Rather than opposing this blatant attack on the freedom of the press, Canadian newspapers applauded; after all, Hearst's Sunday editions were encroaching on their business.

As the war dragged on, Chambers's powers increased. He had already managed to oversee telephone and telegraph messages; before war's end he had censorship powers over movies, photographs, and even gramophone records. He actually banned pieces of music—thirty-one tunes in all. As for photographs, those that showed smiling soldiers were more acceptable; others depicting corpses of men and horses in the wreckage of a French city were not. Any suggestion of grisly death was to be avoided, as the Montreal *Star* and Toronto *Star* discovered when they came under the censor's fire for running an advertisement showing a few skeletons used to publicize a British film, *War's Horrors*. In the chief censor's hypersensitive view, that would scare off prospective soldiers or their mothers. Allied soldiers must be depicted as unfailingly cheerful, the trenches must appear to be as clean and dry as a kitchen floor, and death had to seem as peaceful as an afternoon nap. An American film, *Peace at Any Price*, was kept out of Canadian theatres because it "emphasizes the gruesome side of war through depiction of ghastly heaps of dead. . . ." But then, in Chambers's jingoistic view, what could you expect from a motion picture industry controlled by "disloyal Germans, Poles, and Jews"?

In the censor's fantasy world, in which good invariably triumphed over evil, all Canadian "boys" were well scrubbed, firm jawed, and rugged, while the entire German race was made up of Neanderthals controlled by the Beast of Berlin. In perpetuating this illusion, the newspapermen and novelists were willing accomplices. As Siegfried Sassoon wrote in his memoirs, ". . . somehow the newspapermen always kept the horrifying realities of the war out of their articles, for it was unpatriotic to be bitter, and the dead were assumed to be gloriously happy."

It had not been easy during the Boer War to demonize the avuncular Paul Kruger, but the strutting German emperor, with his spiked helmet and his fierce moustachios, was a ready-made villain. Long before the war began, when Germany was a friendly neighbour and some members of the British royal family still sported Teutonic accents, he had succeeded in irking the English with his posturing. The press began vilifying him as soon as war was declared. Philip Knightly has noted that in one edition of the *Daily Mail* in September 1914, the Kaiser was called a lunatic, a madman, a monster, a Modern Judas, and a criminal monarch.

L.M. Montgomery's *Rilla of Ingleside*, the only Canadian wartime novel with a home-front setting, captures the civilian attitude of the time. Cousin Sophia, bewailing the so-called atrocities in Belgium, cries out: "I was stirring the soup at the time, as you know . . . and I just felt that if I could have lifted that saucepan full of hot boiling soup and thrown it at the Kaiser I would not have lived in vain." Again, later: "When I wake up in the night and cannot go to sleep again, I pass the moment by torturing the Kaiser to death. Last night I fried him in boiling oil. . . ."

The same kind of wrath comes through in Harry Wodson's *Private Warwick, Musings of a Canuck in Khaki*, published in 1915. "What a beast the Kaiser is," Warwick's fiancée, Fanny, writes to his mother. "*He is a demon*, and terrible as war is, I hope there will be no peace until that fiend is shrieking for mercy at the hands of the men who will settle his fate. He set out to destroy the world's liberties, and when the time comes, he must be destroyed."

This hymn of revenge increased during the war, inflamed by the propagandists and literary liars, making any sort of sensible and negotiated settlement impossible. In demanding total victory, the war enthusiasts had a powerful ally. In May 1915, as the Canadian First Division was emerging from the embattled Ypres salient, a Canadian doctor paused briefly in his work to ponder the loss of a friend killed by shellfire the previous day. He scribbled fifteen lines of verse on a scrap of paper, then tossed it aside and went back to work. Somebody picked up the paper and tried to get the verse published. After several rejections, it finally appeared in *Punch*, unsigned, on December 8, 1915.

John McCrae's "In Flanders Fields" contained only three short stanzas, but it was certainly the greatest rallying cry since "La Marseillaise"—and it wasn't even set to martial music. Its impact was enormous, and not just in Canada, where it held its position as a best-seller for two years, but throughout the English-speaking world. Memorized by thousands of schoolchildren in the intervening years, intoned on every November 11, it remains to this day the quintessential war poem. Nothing can touch it—no other song or ballad, no war novel or memoir, no patriotic speech or fervent prayer. Because of McCrae's poem, the little red poppy, sold in tens of thousands on Armistice Day and the later Remembrance Day, has become the visual symbol of the War to End All Wars.

But what does the poem really say? What is the main message of these sincere, simple, hugely effective stanzas? It is, in effect, nothing less than a call, not just for victory but for unconditional surrender. In the final verse the surviving warriors are exhorted by their fallen comrades to "take up our quarrel with the foe." There the author uses the kind of sporting metaphor that had appeal with those familiar with Henry Newbolt's schoolboy whose voice rallied the ranks of his shattered regiment with "Play up! play up! and play the game!" "In Flanders Fields" evokes a kind of macabre relay race, in which runners cut down in mid-flight throw the torch to a comrade "with failing hands." It is the torch of freedom, and they are implored to "hold it high" because if they "break faith with us who die," the dead will stir in their graves, unable to sleep beneath the blood-red poppies.

What the poem says, then, is that anything short of total victory is a betrayal of those who fought and bled to achieve it. McCrae probably did not intend it (he died of pneumonia at the end of the war), but his poem served to quicken the blood and strengthen the resolve of those who were being once again conditioned for another disastrous *blutbad*.

Hate, revenge, and disdain were the emotions that drove the war machine. "There are only two divisions in the world today," declared

Rudyard Kipling, "human beings and Germans." H.G. Wells referred to the "Frankenstein Germans" and sneered at their "intellectual inferiority." Ford Madox Ford insisted, against all evidence, that there had been no German art of any quality since 1870. "I wish Germany did not exist," he wrote, "and I hope it will not exist much longer. Burke said that you cannot indict a whole nation. But you can."

These three literary giants were part of a well-organized propaganda campaign conducted by the British, who recruited the country's leading novelists and essayists to vilify the enemy, beatify the Allies, and hide the truth about the war. As Hilaire Belloc, the frankest member of this gifted company, put it ruefully, he "found it necessary sometimes to lie damnably in the interests of the nation. . . ."

The most prolific of the literary liars was the novelist Arnold Bennett, who wrote more than four hundred pieces of propaganda and finished the war as head of the entire propaganda organization. For sheer blatant inventiveness, however, it is hard to top John Buchan, who, as Lord Tweedsmuir, was to become governor general of Canada in the next war. In his multi-volume history of the war, Buchan reported that the German casualties in 1914 amounted to 1,300,000 while the British lost only 100,000, of which a mere 10,000 were killed. "We can, therefore, regard the long-drawn-out battle in West Flanders as an Allied gain," Buchan claimed. He topped those incredible statistics with what Peter Buitenhuis, in his "Writers at War," has properly called "the worst lie of the war . . . the most fantastic piece of fiction that Buchan was ever to write."

In the first of two books about the battle of the Somme, Buchan managed to turn the daily slaughter into a series of Allied triumphs and concluded that "the first stage, which in strict terms we can call the Battle of the Somme, has ended in an Allied victory." Perhaps as a reward for what was a tissue of lies, Buchan was made director of intelligence in the ministry of information. A peerage followed and with it the vice-regal post in Canada.

Much of this early propaganda was directed at the United States as part of the campaign to induce that country to enter the war, as it did in the spring of 1917. The man in charge was a Canadian by birth, Sir Gilbert Parker, then a popular novelist. Parker persuaded a phalanx of British novelists to trumpet the war in articles that were carefully planted in American periodicals and also in press interviews. Parker's network in the United States consisted of 13,000 influential people who helped read and distribute British propaganda, much of which was fed to friendly reporters on the *New York Times* and Chicago *News*. Parker reported that "in the eyes of the American people the quiet and subterranean nature of our work has had the appearance of a purely private patriotism and enterprise."

Arthur Conan Doyle, revered as the creator of Sherlock Holmes, wrote in a 1916 novel of "the most wonderful spot in the world, the front firing trenches, the outer breakwater that holds back the German tide." In tandem, Charles G.D. Roberts, perhaps the best known of the popular Canadian writers, in his book *Canada in Flanders* exulted about the Canadians at the Somme "to whom the impregnable and the invincible had come to mean a challenge which they welcomed joyously."

One of the purposes of Allied propaganda, as Robert Graves remembered it, was "to make the English hate the Germans as they had never hated anyone before." The 1915 report of Lord Bryce's committee of prominent lawyers and historians, formed to investigate alleged German atrocities in Belgium, fuelled the campaign. Here were tales of "murder, lust and pillage" that the report claimed were "on a scale unparalleled in any war between civilized nations during the past three centuries." Bryce's team told of the public rape of twenty-two Belgian girls, of the bayonetting of a two-year-old child, of the slicing off of a peasant's breast, and other examples of "murder, outrage, and violation of the innocent."

To say that the Bryce committee's findings were flawed is far too mild: in fact, they appear to be fiction. The 1,200 witnesses who gave depositions were never interviewed or placed under oath nor were they identified, while hearsay evidence was accepted as gospel. Several years later, a Belgian commission of inquiry looked into the matter and failed to corroborate a single allegation.

168

It may well be that both sides cried wolf so often that by the thirties, newspaper readers, rendered cynical by the campaign of Great War falsehoods, were sceptical of reports of atrocities by the Nazis and the Soviet Communists. Certainly, censorship and propaganda were creating a myth about the war that was hard to allay after tempers cooled. And the chances of forging any kind of sensible peace that might in the long run have helped bank the fires of German nationalism were non-existent.

Long before those days, the image of the "Hun," to use the widespread jingoistic word, was firmly established in the Western mind. It was a word the men in the trenches avoided. To them, the enemy was "Fritz," a name that suggested a human being, not an ogre. The informal Christmas parleys that took place in the early years of the war, with German and Allied troops exchanging gifts out in no man's land, were anathema to the high command, and it put a stop to them.

But even the men at the front succumbed, in that eerie world, to some of the enduring myths of the war: to the stories of a strange band of deserters who lived out in the neutral zone between the trenches, existing on what they could pilfer from the corpses around them; or the troops of husky young soldiers selected and plucked from the line by the Germans to satisfy the sexual needs of their war widows; or the German "tallow factory," in which the Allied corpses were rendered down to provide glycerine for the enemy's explosives. "We half believed these things at the time," wrote James H. Pedley in *Only This*, his Great War retrospective, "for we were in a mood to believe anything that indicated our enemy was in hard straits."

It is not surprising, given the official fabrications of the war years, that the most bizarre fantasies should be accepted as truth, such as the tale of the crucified Canadian, supposedly condemned to a slow death by a group of German soldiers who impaled his body on a barn door with bayonets. As in the urban myths of our own time, somebody knew somebody who knew somebody who had seen it. The victim was almost always a Canadian, and the setting identifiable: the Maple Copse near Sanctuary Wood in the Ypres sector. This tale, used in

Canadian recruiting posters, was widely accepted as gospel in Canada.

Some of these persistent legends have been tracked to their sources. The angel of Mons, which soldiers claimed to have been seen in the sky in the early days of the war, was based on a piece of magazine fiction; the tallow factory was the unwitting invention of Haig's intelligence officer, Brigadier General Charteris, who mixed up some photographic captions; the tale of the mutilated Belgian babies was started by a *Times* war correspondent and refined by the French *Bureau de la Presse*, a propaganda unit. Allied officials kept such legends alive and made up others. A German saw-toothed bayonet designed for pioneer battalions to saw off tree branches was portrayed as a fiendish invention for tearing living flesh. All these myths were fodder for a press that had very little to report apart from a series of fictitious Allied victories. No one, including the men in the field, was aware of the horrifying reality of the Somme slaughter. In England, the procession of broken men being hauled off on stretchers from ambulance trains hinted that something had gone very wrong on the Western Front. But Canadians were insulated from that spectacle by the controlled press.

If members of the Fourth Estate were guilty of swallowing the government propaganda uncritically, the members of the First were equally culpable. As Siegfried Sassoon put it, "In July 1916, the man who could boast that he'd killed a German in the Battle of the Somme would have been patted on the back by a bishop in a hospital ward." It is not too much to say that the Protestant clergy revelled in the war. The leaders of the Methodist Church, which by 1918 had become in Michael Bliss's estimate "the most radical religious organization in Canada," had adopted "an unquestioning belief in the righteousness of the conflict and the church's duty to play a positive role in achieving victory." This was, of course, a "just war, the only kind any committed Christian could support," to quote Dwight Chown, the church's general superintendent, to whom khaki was "a sacred colour." As for pacifism, which the church had supported in the pre-war days, it could not be tolerated, in Chown's view, "no matter who teaches it."

The Roman Catholic clergy were divided by the war because so many French Canadians opposed it. Protestants had no qualms. The theme of Christian sacrifice pervades most of the thirty-odd books written at the time. The wartime novelists stressed that the war was a conflict between God and Satan. Of all the ecclesiastic tub-thumpers, the best known and most effective was the Reverend Charles Gordon—the novelist Ralph Connor—whose leading character in his 1917 novel, *The Sky Pilot in No Man's Land*, is a young chaplain, Barry Dunbar. Dunbar appeals to the male members of his congregation to "offer your bodies—these living bodies—these sacred bodies—offer them in a sacrifice to God." Connor, himself a chaplain, wrote: "It was the ancient sacrifice that the noblest of the race had always been called upon to make. In giving themselves to this cause they were giving themselves to their country. They were offering themselves to God."

Apart from Connor, who was sent by Robert Borden on a tour of the United States as part of the Allied attempts to get America into the war, none of the novelists and memoirists of the war period were part of the official propaganda machine, yet their work slavishly followed the party line. Nellie McClung, who had been an ardent pacifist before the war, performed an about-turn and joined the ranks of the unwitting propagandists shortly after her son donned khaki. "I knew," she wrote, "without a word being said, that my boy wanted to go. . . . One day he looked up quietly and said, 'I want to join—I want to help the British Empire—while there is a British Empire.'" McClung wrote in *Next of Kin* that the Germans "worship the God of force; they recognize no sin but weakness and inefficiency." One of her characters in this semi-autobiographical work, a woman who has already lost two sons, explains why she has changed her mind: "It was the *Lusitania* that brought me to see the whole truth. Then I saw that we were waging war on the very Prince of Darkness. . . . I knew then . . . that no man could die better than in defending civilization from this ghastly thing which threatened her!"

Like so many writers, McClung emphasized the glory of sacrificial death in the trenches. The Fallen were "the brave ones" who "pass through the gates of Heaven to receive their eternal reward." This kind of sentiment encouraged the propagandists in their campaign to convince the mothers of the nation to sacrifice their sons for the greater good. What if thousands of mothers, sickened by the struggle, suddenly banded together and refused to allow their boys to join up? It was not the tears of Canadian mothers that bothered the chief censor, it was the prospect that maternal affection might discourage enlistment.

He need not have worried. Only a few of the war novelists had actually seen war first-hand. They were willing, if unconscious, partners in the campaign to convince the women of Canada that their boys' sacrifice was Christ-like, that death when it came was gallant and painless, and that conditions in the trenches weren't much worse than could be experienced during a journey through the Canadian wilds. Thus Lieutenant Corningsby Dawson, in his significantly titled memoir *The Glory of the Trenches*, claimed that soldiers did not fear death but faced it with serenity, knowing that those who fell in a righteous cause earned the right to "hang beside Christ." McElvey Bell claimed, against all evidence, in his *First Canadians in France* that a large number of men shot through the brain recovered, and when men died in battle they went to their Maker with a smile on their lips, like Robert J.C. Stead's hero in the final pages of *The Cow Puncher.* It all sounds ludicrous to us, but, after all, what Canadian schoolboy exposed to the Canadian Reader series had not had to memorize Browning's poem *An Incident of the French Camp*, with its ringing last line: "Smiling the boy fell dead"?

In their letters home, the men at the front also did their best to relieve their mothers' anxieties by playing down the horrors and discomforts of the front (tales that were subject to censorship anyway), perpetuating the fiction that life in the rat-infested muck was positively Elysian. In his 1917 foreword to the U.S. edition of *Private Peat*, one of the most successful of the Canadian Great War memoirs, Harold Peat had a message for the American mothers whose sons would soon embark for France. He set out to write "a book of smiles," he wrote, "but the seriousness of it all . . . crept into my pages. . . . Yet I hope along with the grimness and the humour, I have been able to say some words of comfort to those in the United States who are sending their husbands, their sons and brothers into this mighty conflict."

The most revealing book of all is the significantly titled *Mainly for Mother*, a collection of letters home from Armine Norris, a lieutenant in the Canadian Machine Gun Corps. They are unfailingly cheerful, as the following excerpts show, and crammed with warnings that his mother must not take reports of bloody actions too seriously. Indeed, some of his letters sound a bit like those of a schoolboy coming home from the class picnic.

"Now mother," he wrote back in 1915, "you speak of the 'terrible danger' and 'awful horrors.' Leave that sort of talk to the newspaper correspondents. The danger is not terrible and I have not in my personal experience of over two months in the trenches seen any 'horrors'. . . . I really like it. All the details I write you are just so you can see the fun in them. . . . The soldiers are the most cheerful in the world today. . . . We are well fed, warmly clothed, over supplied . . . and life is fascinating. . . ."

To Norris, a gas attack was "a glorious scrap" and the battle for the Regina Trench "great sport." At one point he apologized for one letter he'd written from the Somme as "totally uncalled for. . . . It must be bad enough for you to be worrying about the risk I run, as it is, without making it worse . . . and, Mumsie, I don't want you to imagine that that letter was written in a normal state of mind."

By January 1917, Norris was still keeping a stiff upper lip in his letters home. "I won't have any more of that talk about my 'suffering' in France. . . . Where on earth did you get that idea? I'd rather be in France than in England simply because I have a better time. . . ."

On and on he went through the spring of 1918, making light of his ordeal: "Poor Mumsie—what a trouble I am to you. . . . Mother, honest Injun, you sometimes make me laugh in your letters enduring all sort of imaginary things. . . . Truly, Mumsie, you'll never realize how light and easy my share is compared to yours." In June: "Weather is glorious and I'm having a splendid time. . . ." In August: "Oh, I'm glad I've lasted to see open warfare. This *is* war not sewer construction. . . ."

Then, on October 3, about a month before the Armistice, a telegram came to his mother from the director of records: "Deeply regret inform you that Lieut. Armine Frank Norris, Machine Gun Corps, officially reported missing in action, September 28."

Supplement to the London Gazette, January 11, 1919,
MILITARY CROSS: Lt. Armine F. Norris, 1st Batt. C.M.G.C.
When his battery commander was severely wounded he took command, pushing his guns forward to the exposed left flank of the infantry which he was supporting. He made skilful dispositions under both machine guns and direct artillery fire, and, inflicting heavy casualties on the enemy, assured complete protection of the exposed flank.

His efforts to assist the infantry were untiring.

5

Canada comes of age
One would be hard put to find two general officers as different in background and personality as Sir Julian Byng, who commanded the Canadian Corps at the battle of Vimy Ridge in 1917, and Arthur Currie, who succeeded him shortly after that famous engagement was fought and won.

Byng was the bluest of the blue bloods with all the provenance of a stiff-necked aristocrat—the son of an earl, the grandson of a field marshal, a product of the playing fields of Eton, and an intimate of royalty, known familiarly to the King as "Bungo." His mother was a peer's daughter and a Cavendish to boot, a family whose members had breathed the rarefied air of the privileged classes for centuries.

Currie was a former real estate agent, teetering on the verge of bankruptcy in the obscure colonial background of Victoria, B.C. He had no education past high school, and the best he could do in his early years was to obtain a third-class teacher's certificate.

Byng had been a professional soldier all his life and an avid student of military tactics for thirty-four years. He had commanded a cavalry unit during the Boer War, was a major general in the Egyptian command, was knighted for his distinguished record at Ypres, and had been promoted to lieutenant general.

Currie had no professional military experience unless one counts his service in the non-permanent militia, an organization less interested in military affairs than social ones. Currie certainly had aspirations: he changed the spelling of his name from "Curry," quit the Methodist faith for the more fashionable Church of England, married an English-born woman with a socially acceptable double-barrelled name, became president of the young Liberals, and jumped at the chance of a militia commission, even though it was more than he could afford—the dress uniforms were hellishly expensive. But afford it he did by embezzling the funds intended to pay regimental contractors.

Currie, whose troops admired him but did not love him (they called him Old Guts and Garters) in the way Byng was loved, didn't fit the stereotyped image of the British officer. At forty-two he was flabby and dismayingly pear-shaped, with more than a suggestion of a double chin marking his bland, clean-shaven features. Byng, by contrast, was fit and muscular, a man of commanding presence with intense blue eyes (Currie's were watery blue), a large military moustache, and a strong jaw. He could easily have done duty, as Kitchener did, on a recruiting poster, but it is impossible to imagine Currie's features on any placard crying out "I WANT YOU!" It was hard enough to find a uniform to fit his paunchy body, which made it difficult for him to manoeuvre through the narrow trenches.

Yet this unlikely Canadian, who had been appointed commander of the 2nd Canadian Infantry Brigade in September 1914 (with Sam Hughes's help), had vaulted over officers senior to him in age and experience, including one who had actually taught him tactics during his militia days in Victoria. Now, in 1917, he was a major general in command of the First Canadian Division in the Vimy sector and would shortly be promoted to lieutenant general, the highest rank in the British forces apart from field marshal. Impressions can be deceptive and stereotypes dangerous. By 1918, the British prime minister, who despised Douglas Haig, was prepared to make Currie supreme commander of the British forces in France should the war continue another year.

For Currie had more in common with Byng than background and outward appearance suggested. Both were brilliant tacticians whose outlooks verged on the unorthodox. Byng had made his reputation as a daring and innovative leader in South Africa, where he commanded the South African Light Horse (the least traditional of the cavalry units, made up of tough, irreverent colonials, trained to think for themselves) and where the style of battle encouraged commanders to toss aside the rule book. For Currie, of course, there was no rule book. Not having been schooled in nineteenth-century musketry tactics, he was able to look at the art of battle with fresh eyes.

Those eyes rarely blinked, for Currie was not one to show emotion. He never betrayed his inner feelings, although the prospect of being charged with embezzlement haunted him for most of his war career until two wealthier comrades-in-arms paid off his debts with personal loans. He had a dry humour, but he rarely smiled; nor was he outwardly emotional about the carnage that swirled around him. In victory or setback, he remained impassive to the end.

Byng and Currie shared another quality: they trusted their men. This was not a typical approach among the aristocrats of the British high command, whose attitude to private soldiers was one of master to serf. As far as the British were concerned, the ordinary soldier was a bumpkin who was expected to take orders cheerfully and follow them slavishly but who could not be expected to understand the bigger picture. Byng, the aristocrat, would have none of that. Under him, every man must be told every detail of the plan of attack so that when NCOs were killed their places could be taken by those they had led. That too was Currie's dictum—"maps to section leaders"—unprecedented in the British army. But then, as Byng knew, this was an army of unabashed Canadian civilians, who, with their lives at stake, did not take kindly to battle by rote.

The two commanders had another quality in common: they cared about their men's comfort and, indeed, their lives. Byng roamed the front lines, chatting with the men on the firestep. At the start of every engagement he prayed to God not for victory, as Haig did, but for the safe return of his troops. His first action when posted to the sweltering heat of India had been to order that the soldiers' high collars be altered and loosened. Currie, far more aloof and austere than the affable Byng, "had an almost fanatical hatred of unnecessary casualties," as Jack Seeley of the Canadian cavalry remembered. "He made it clear to his junior officers that the care of the troops must take precedence over their personal comfort."

For this reason, Currie was cool to the idea of massive night raids across no man's land, a Canadian invention that allowed men a respite from the boredom of trench life. Currie was not averse to the small raiding parties that his own First Division mounted in order to get information from captured Germans. But that was their only purpose in his eyes. "I am not sacrificing one man unnecessarily," he explained after he cancelled one raid.

In the fortnight before the Vimy battle, Canadian casualties reached 1,653—the equivalent of two battalions. That was a high price to pay, as events were to prove. The biggest raid of all, by the Fourth Division on March 1, five weeks before the battle, was a ghastly failure—one in which the Canadians used a new gas, phosgene, only to find the wind blowing it back into their own lines. Of the 1,700 troops who took part in the raid, 687 failed to return, including two seasoned battalion commanders. When the corps launched the assault on Vimy Ridge on April 9, the weakened Fourth was the only one of the four divisions that failed to reach its objective. Thus, tragically, Currie was vindicated.

The capture of the ridge on that chill Easter Monday was the first British victory after two and a half years of hard fighting—a fact that escaped most Canadians, who had been led to believe that *every* attack was a "GREAT ALLIED VICTORY," to quote the Toronto *Mail and Empire*'s enormous headline the day after the Somme debacle.

The standard tactic before Vimy had been to hammer the German lines with an all-out artillery barrage and then advance in line to kill the supposedly stunned defenders. That had not worked at the Somme. So Byng had sent Currie to the Somme and later to Verdun to analyze and report on the lessons learned. Currie's findings provided the basis for the training that resulted in the Vimy victory.

The first lesson learned was that shrapnel would not cut wire; a new fuse was needed to allow the shells to burst on contact, ripping the wire to shreds. E.W.B. "Dinky" Morrison, now a major general in charge of the artillery, pressed for a suitable fuse and got it. Second, the old concept of advancing in line had to be scrapped. Men would be trained in platoon tactics—to move forward in self-sufficient "blobs," making use of perimeter defence, fire, and movement. Third, a new kind of "creeping barrage" would be adopted and the men drilled to move closely behind a moving curtain of shells, giving the enemy no respite. Fourth, the enemy gun positions must be identified in advance and neutralized, a job that was given to Andrew McNaughton, a young McGill scientist. McNaughton stole three brilliant physicists from the British, who had ignored their invention of flash-spotting and sound-ranging techniques—considered radical nonsense by old-time British gunners. With the trio's help, McNaughton was able to identify and silence 70 percent of the German guns before the attack began.

For Canadians, this was the defining moment not only of this war but of all the smaller wars in which their soldiers had prevailed. More than Crysler's Farm or Chateauguay, more than Cut Knife Creek or Batoche, more than Paardeberg or Ypres, Vimy provided the shining vision that still illuminates our folk memory. We carry it with us, for it has been drilled into our minds by constant repetition, a tale retold, like a looped movie—the heart-thumping spectacle of the entire Canadian Corps clambering up that whale-backed ridge, enduring the dreadful din, and hugging dangerously close to the creeping curtain of high explosives that stupefied the burrowed defenders.

I remember at Basic Training an older sergeant instructor who had been an officer at Vimy (he had re-enlisted in the ranks in the Second World War) describing the state of the enemy at the moment the barrage lifted. "They were stunned out of their minds," he said *Bewildered! They scarcely knew where they were. We were on them before they could get their bearings.*"

That murky spectacle of the legendary invincible Germans—super-men who had hurled back much larger forces of the British and French in the earlier months of the war—now cowering, dazed, in their dugouts or stumbling forward with hands held high, had remained with him for twenty-five years. This was not the Somme, where the enemy had enjoyed a respite from the shelling before the attackers reached their lines. Here there was no breathing space. The Canadians were right behind that deadly curtain, on and over the Germans before the defenders had time to take a breath. There was nothing impetuous about it. The troops who followed the barrage had been trained to the split second in practice assaults behind the lines. Here, on the shattered slopes of Vimy Ridge, amid the cacophony of shellfire and the smoke of conflict, the myth of German superiority was extinguished, and Canada had a new myth of her own.

To Captain Walter Moorhouse of the 4th Canadian Mounted Rifles, "the Vimy prisoners were the most dejected looking specimens of humanity I had ever seen. They stood ankle deep in mud, hungry, cold, wet, disarmed and defeated. One of them told me that they had hardly eaten for the past three days on account of our shelling holding up their ration transport. I feel guilty in saying this, but I must confess I was a little envious of these men in one regard: for them the fighting was over, for us the end was not in sight."

Moorhouse's attitude was the direct opposite of that being promoted by the novelists and propagandists: "There was not a trace of hate in the heart of any man I worked with that day, friend or foe. Oh the futility of war! Some of the Germans were killed or wounded by their own guns that day. Surveying the ground we covered I marvelled how a man could live through that utter devastation. . . ."

With three of the four Canadian divisions on the crest of the ridge, eating their lunch a few hours after the dawn attack began, Canada had an imperishable legend to signal its march to maturity. The twin pillars of the Vimy Memorial stand on the ridge today, a kind of super-cenotaph, visible for miles around, the largest monument of its kind in all of wartorn France, and a magnet for Canadian tourists.

The world applauded the victory, causing Canadian hearts to swell with pride, especially when so much praise came from below the border.

179

"Well done Canada," wrote the *New York Times*—that from a nation where, to Canadians, self-praise sometimes seemed *too* excessive. Byng wrote to his wife that "the Canucks . . . are grinning from ear to ear." No longer a corps of amateurs, they "behaved like real disciplined soldiers." As Claude Williams, a medical student turned machine gunner, wrote to his wife, "One feels proud to be a Canadian out here now."

That, perhaps, was the real point—won at a cost of some ten thousand dead or mangled men. Canada, it has been said, came of age at Vimy, a phrase that has become shorthand for the singular Canadian contribution to the war and for the wave of nationalism that the war touched off.

It has never mattered that Vimy was a minor victory virtually ignored by the British in a long and bloody conflict; that it was a part—the one positive part—of the inconclusive battle of Arras; that it could not by itself achieve the massive breakthrough for which Haig so desperately prayed. The great plain of Douai lay wide open on the far side of the ridge, a beckoning pathway to even greater victory, but no Canadian guns could be dragged across those torn and bloody fields, no Canadian tanks could rattle over that corpse-strewn rubble of buried craters and old bones. Ironically, the very artillery that had won the battle of Vimy Ridge made further advance impractical by churning the new no man's land into an impenetrable obstacle course, pockmarked by shell holes, some as wide as a small lake and deep enough to hold a cathedral. In this land of the dead, the only living creatures were the ubiquitous rats, plump, sleek, and well-fed—the real victors in that great and terrible war.

Byng and Currie were both promoted after Vimy, the former knighted and given command of the British Third Army, the latter given command of the Canadian Corps, which was really a miniature army within the British force. To the British, a corps wasn't much more than a head-quarters, a collection of divisions that came and went as opportunity required. But the Canadians, both politicians and generals, insisted that their corps remain a distinct unit—a band of brothers who had a common background and had learned to fight together. Its divisions were not to be dealt out from corps to corps like so many playing cards.

As corps commander, promoted to lieutenant general and knighted (KCMG) by his king, Currie deserves much of the credit for the Canadian victories that followed. He talked Haig out of an ill-advised attack on Lens ("I said that if we were to fight at all, let us fight for something worth having"), then added Hill 70 to the catalogue of Canadian battle honours. Henry Horne, commander of the British First Army, called Currie's former division "the pride and wonder of the British Army."

Currie's success irked Sam Hughes, who was still minister of militia that summer. He had tried and failed to block Currie's promotion, but now, supported by the mischievous Max Aitken, he was putting intense political pressure on the new commander to give the First Division to Sam's son, Garnet. "God help the man who goes against my father!" the younger Hughes burst out after a bitter, three-hour scene in which Currie, who felt that Hughes was inexperienced and not terribly competent, remained obdurate. The two had been friends; indeed, Garnet Hughes had helped to persuade his father that Currie should get the division. But neither his personal feelings nor political pressure could shake Currie. "I'll get you for this before I'm finished with you," Garnet snarled—a threat more suitable for a silent movie subtitle than an argument between two officers—but get him, in a manner of speaking, he eventually did.

The Vimy victory was the only bright spot in an otherwise depressing year. The general public had no idea that Great Britain was facing sure defeat because of the U-boat menace in the North Atlantic. We know now the details of a military secret kept long after the war, that German submarines managed to slip into the Gulf of St. Lawrence and the great river itself to sink scores of Canadian ships. Censorship or not, the rising casualty lists hinted at the crisis. But the extent of the problem—Germany's decision that spring to wage unrestricted war against merchant shipping in international waters—was not realized by the civilian population.

The chief of the German naval staff, Admiral Henning von Holtzendorff, had estimated that if the Germans sank 600,000 tons of Allied shipping each month, Britain would be brought to the brink of starvation.

By April 1917, as the Canadians prepared for the attack on Vimy Ridge, the monthly average reached more than 800,000 tons, exceeding the Admiral's target. It is probable that the prospect of defeat at sea caused the Allies to institute the convoy system that reversed the trend and helped reduce the average to just under 400,000 tons by December 1917.

The German U-boat campaign also helped drive Britain to undertake a new offensive in spite of Lloyd George's concerns over rising British casualties. At the end of July the eternally optimistic Field Marshal Haig launched another massive attack in the Ypres salient—one for which he had been pressing for more than a year. His purpose was to capture Passchendaele Ridge or wear down the enemy by returning to his policy of attrition, or both. He neglected two factors: first, attrition was wearing down the British as well as the Germans. Second, the delicate drainage pattern of the battlefield had long since been destroyed by the guns of earlier contests so that the two sides found themselves literally fighting each other in a swamp. The remorseless rains that fell without let-up added to the problem—double the average for the first month of the offensive and five times the amount recorded for the same period in 1915 and 1916.

Haig himself was later to describe the terrain: "The valleys of the choked and overflowing streams were speedily transformed into long stretches of bog, impassable except by a few well-defined tracks, which became marks for the enemy's artillery. To leave these tracks was to risk death by drowning."

The British commander, who felt himself on the eve of a great victory, blamed all his frustrations on the weather. But Haig himself cannot be absolved. He believed what he wanted to hear, and what he wanted to hear were the optimistic reports fed to him by his chief intelligence officer, Brigadier General Charteris. Charteris seemed to believe that his main duty was to cushion his chief from unpleasant or disturbing truths. When Major Fuller, a future general and respected military analyst, sent Charteris a map showing that the tanks would have to struggle through what was, in effect, a shallow lake, Charteris was peeved. "Pray do not send me any more of these ridiculous maps," he told Fuller. Later he confided to a staff officer, "I am certainly not going to show *this* to the Commander-in-chief. It would only depress him."

There were times when Haig's own optimism exceeded even that of his intelligence officer. In June, he astonished Charteris by observing that within six months Germany would be at the end of her manpower. The following months he reported that same opinion to the war office. By October 1917, with the battle of Passchendaele well underway, both men were convinced, wrongly, that Germany had reached the breaking point.

For four weeks that August the contending armies did battle in an ocean of mud churned up by an opening two-week barrage that had cost the British taxpayer one million dollars in shells alone. The British advanced less than two miles along a few thousand yards of front at a cost of 68,000 men. That was victory? Apparently most of the cabinet thought so. To Lloyd George, they "were under the spell of the synthetic victories distilled at G.H.Q." And in September, after a pause, Haig determined to continue the Big Push in what Fuller would later analyze as "practically an impossible battle . . . an inexcusable piece of pig-headedness on the part of Haig." After a few minor victories, Haig was convinced that "the enemy was teetering and that a good vigorous blow might lead to decisive results."

Lloyd George could not convince his cabinet that the Passchen-daele campaign should be stopped. "We are losing the flower of our army and to what purpose?" he asked angrily. Haig squandered three weeks of remarkably good weather in September by regrouping his armies. Then on October 4 the torrential rains began again. It took the exhausted reserves of General Plumer's Second Army (replacing General Hubert Gough's Fifth) most of the day to struggle through the mud in order to reach the forward lines, a journey that in dry weather would occupy less than an hour. Plumer's assault on October 9 caused 28,000 British casualties.

Haig surely knew what was in store, for his staff had done their homework and told him that the weather broke early each August "with the regularity of an Indian monsoon." The land below Passchendaele Ridge had been reclaimed from the sea, artificially drained, and kept above water by an intricate system of dikes and ditches. Haig was aware that his heavy guns would destroy this drainage system and that the thick clay would not absorb moisture. He could have abandoned the salient and shortened and strengthened the British line. Instead, against the advice of almost everybody—all his army commanders, General Foch of the French, Winston Churchill, and, of course, Lloyd George, who felt that Haig had completely lost his wits—he plunged ahead.

The field marshal was gobbling up reserves at a dismaying rate. At one time or another, every division available to him had been bloodied in this third battle of Ypres. But there was one corps that had yet to experience that porridge of mud. On October 13, Haig summoned the victors of Vimy to move immediately to Flanders. Arthur Currie was ordered to submit plans for the capture of Passchendaele Ridge as soon as possible.

The Canadian Corps commander was appalled. "Passchendaele! What's the good of it? Let the Germans have it—keep it—rot in the mud! It isn't worth a drop of blood." He appealed personally to Haig with such vehemence, as he wrote later, that he would have been sent home had he been other than commander of the Canadian Corps. Currie forecast to Haig the Canadian casualties would approach at least sixteen thousand. Would success warrant that sacrifice? Haig remained obdurate. "Some day I will tell you why," he said, "but Passchendaele must be taken." After the war, the British field marshal justified his action by explaining that British and French morale required a victory. France was close to collapse as the result of massive mutinies in fifty-four French divisions, some *poilus* going into battle crying "Baah! Baah!" like sheep to the slaughter. Haig did not explain how the predictably indecisive battle in the swamps of the Ypres sector could do other than lower morale.

Currie grudgingly went along with Haig but insisted on two conditions: his corps must fight intact as a united unit, and not under General Gough, whose abilities the Canadian commander distrusted. It is a

184

measure of the growing Canadian independence in the war and Currie's own reputation that he got his way; no other corps commander could have dared deliver such an ultimatum to the British field marshal. "Currie," said Haig, "do you realize this is insubordination?" To which the impassive Canadian replied, "Yes, sir. But I cannot help that."

By mid-October the ground on which the battle would be fought was punctured by thousands of shell holes, each filled to the brim with scummy water and often red with blood. Bloated corpses floated about in that thick stew of clay from which human fragments—arms, legs, torsoes—protruded. The detritus of battle—wire entanglements, battered tanks, half-buried locomotives, broken artillery limbers—lay in the morass. And over it all hung the sickly odour of decomposing bodies. Currie, who, as usual, insisted on inspecting everything himself, had never seen anything like it. "Battle field looks bad," he told his diary on October 17, "no salvage has been done and very few of the dead buried."

The torrential rains never let up. As Agar Adamson of the PPCLI reported to his wife on October 23, "The ground beggars description. The strongest and the youngest cannot navigate without falling down." The glue-like mud sucked at the boots and legs of the Canadians, who realized with horror that sometimes when the sodden clay yielded under their feet they had sunk their boots into a human body. Here the wounded died in record numbers, a good many by drowning.

By October 23, five days after he took command of the corps sector, a mile southwest of Passchendaele village, Currie had finalized his plans for taking the ridge. At luncheon that day at corps headquarters—the first time that Haig had deigned to go that far forward—the commander-in-chief was brimming over with optimism. That surprised one member of Currie's staff, Major Alan Brooke, a future field marshal. "I could hardly believe that my ears were not deceiving me!" Brooke recalled. "He spoke in the rosiest of terms of our chances of breaking through. I had been all over the ground and to my mind such an eventuality was impossible."

Currie found himself pounding his head against a stubborn wall of British intransigence. Because of the lack of serviceable roads in that gelatinous mass, the Canadians considered the use of plank pathways fashioned after Ontario's corduroy roads. The British pooh-poohed the idea but finally gave permission to go ahead. When they stalled again, claiming that no planks were available, the Canadians suggested they build a sawmill and be given permission to cut down trees in the battle area. At last they were given a grudging go-ahead, set up their sawmill, made their own planks, and established their own road system. In time the reluctant British copied the Canadian example all along the French and Belgian fronts.

Currie's plan called for three operations in late October and early November. On October 26, the Canadians found themselves struggling through what one member of the Canadian Mounted Rifles called "a ghastly dreadful porridge, thigh deep." Here, the most minor wound could mean death. "If you got it in the shoulder blade with a bullet that merely knocked you unconscious for two minutes you drowned."

To the 4th Canadian Mounted Rifles, October 26, 1917, was the bloodiest battle in the regiment's history. In the second assault, two days later, the 49th Battalion suffered a casualty rate of 75 percent, the worst in its history. In the third, the 5th CMR lost two-thirds of its attacking strength. It was not until November 6 that the Canadians took Passchendaele Ridge, to the applause of the British press and the astonishment of the Germans. As one captured enemy officer put it, "With an army of men like these I could go anywhere." *The Times* called it a "very fine and gallant operation"; to the London *Daily Chronicle* it was "as fine and thrilling as an act of persistent courage." But the cost was heavy. With uncanny accuracy Currie had projected a loss of 16,000 casualties; the actual toll was 15,654.

One who survived, miraculously, was William McDonald of Glenwilliam, P.E.I. As he went over the top in that last battle for the ridge, the man next to him crumpled over, shot in the stomach, his machine gun in his hands. McDonald seized the weapon from him, then dashed forward with the others for about a hundred yards, only to hear a "thung" ringing in his ears. A sniper's bullet had hit him below the right ear, passing under the ear's entrance and exiting about half an inch from

186

his right eye. He tumbled into a shell hole beside the corpse of another friend, shot at the same time through the head. The pain was dreadful. McDonald found himself hoping his end would come at any moment but then suddenly realized "how sweet life really was" and determined to hang on.

He lay in the shell hole for hours until a seventeen-year-old Canadian private arrived, bandaged him up, and started back with him to the dressing station. The entire battlefield was a swamp, with the slime up to McDonald's waist. He sank several times and would have drowned, as so many others did in the blood-soaked morass, if his comrade hadn't pulled him free.

He staggered on—two miles to the dressing station. To reach it he had somehow to pass through the enemy's barrage. Pieces of human bodies lay scattered about him "like leaves." Then, as he lurched forward, a big German shell landed a few yards away and a piece of shrapnel pierced his right shoulder, breaking the bone and knocking him out. His friend hoisted him up, and he found he could still toddle forward in spite of the pain. When he reached the dressing station he collapsed and was carried to the casualty clearing station three miles to the rear. For him it was the end of the war.

In what Lloyd George called "the bovine and brutal game of attrition," Haig had lost 300,000 men in the three and a half months of the Passchendaele offensive, the Germans considerably fewer. On November 15, the commander-in-chief called a halt. In the intervening years the campaign has come to symbolize all the useless carnage of the Great War. What had been accomplished? Since the battle had begun in early August, the Ypres salient had been extended no more than four and a half miles.

Currie himself was bitter and heartsick. The venture had not been worth the cost. In Currie's view, with which Lloyd George agreed, its only purpose was "to save the face of the British High Command who had undertaken all through the autumn most unsuccessful and highly disastrous attempts." How valuable was this little hump of ground? How significant? The bitter answer to that question came the following spring when the British gave it up to the Germans without firing a shot.

There is a distasteful coda to this sordid chronicle of misplaced optimism. A month after the battle ended, Haig's chief of staff, General Sir Launcelot Kiggell, finally paid a visit to what had been the forward zone. He arrived by comfortable staff car, but as he drew nearer the scene of the carnage his agitation grew to the point where he burst into tears. "Good God!" he blurted, "did we actually send men to fight in that?" To which his army guide responded, "It's worse farther up."

The same revealing tale is evident in every major account of the fruitless campaign. The man whose job it was to plan every detail of the battle never bothered to look over the ground, as Byng and Currie had done before Vimy. Here, where so many thousands would go to their death, Kiggell had no first-hand idea of what faced them. The shattered regiments were identified as mere pins on military maps that gave no hint of the seething morass in which they fought.

It was time to stop the war. One man who wanted to stop it was the distinguished peer Lord Lansdowne, a former governor general of Canada, a prominent Conservative, and a one-time secretary of state for war. At the end of 1916, with the horror of the Somme sinking in, Lansdowne, in a secret memorandum to the war cabinet, suggested that unconditional victory was now impossible. "Can we afford to go on paying the same sort of price for the same sort of gains?" he asked. "Let our naval, military, and economic advisers tell us frankly whether they are satisfied that the knock-out blow can and will be delivered."

Lansdowne was ignored but tried again in November 1917. It wasn't easy. He first sounded out Arthur Balfour, the foreign secretary. That proved fruitless. He then wrote a lengthy letter to *The Times*, urging a negotiated peace. In spite of his stature, the newspaper turned it down. At last he managed to get his ideas into the *Daily Telegraph*. "We are not going to lose this war," he wrote, "but its prolongation will spell ruin for the civilized world, and an infinite addition to the load of human suffering which already weighs upon it."

The letter aroused a storm of controversy in England, with most of the daily press in full cry attacking Lansdowne's proposal as craven and inept, and touching off a flood of invective and a mass of abusive correspondence that in the words of his biographer "was marked by a violence that was rare in English public life." Lansdowne, although socially ostracized, had some supporters and continued his campaign into the next year. He got no further than the German chancellor had when he tried to put out peace feelers at the end of 1916, or Woodrow Wilson, the U.S. president, who called, vainly, for "peace without victory." ("That ass, President Wilson, has barged in and asked all belligerents for their terms," General Sir Henry Wilson, later chief of the imperial general staff, wrote in his diary.)

In spite of Passchendaele, none of the leading political or military figures on the Allied side wanted anything less than unconditional surrender, while Ludendorff, by then the de facto leader of Germany, was planning on yet another all-or-nothing offensive to drive the opposing armies into the sea. In these views the belligerents had the active support of their own people who, though they felt the pinch of war, had no conception of the enormous cost.

If the civilians at home had known what horror was visited upon those who suffered and survived, Lansdowne's proposal might have borne some fruit. One of the best descriptions of the results of shellfire is contained in a letter written by Donald Fraser, the Calgary private who had cursed the MacAdam entrenching spade. Early in the war, in Belgium, Fraser found himself in a dugout when the German guns opened up. It was his first bombardment. When it began he threw himself flat behind a two-foot wall of sandbags. A shell exploded no more than a yard from where he lay. The report dazed him. A rain of debris poured down on his prostrate body. The concussion put a terrific strain on his tissues: "I felt as if I was being pulled apart, as if some unseen thing was tearing me asunder, particularly the top part, especially the head. I knew I could not have stood a fraction more without bursting, the outward pull on the tissue was so immense. Getting over the daze, I quickly pulled myself together and got out of range for the time being. The incident passed off, although the bursting effect on the body rankled in my mind. It was the greatest body strain I have ever experienced."

A second bombardment almost finished him at Vimy on the day of the famous battle. Fraser, now a lance corporal in a machine-gun section, was awaiting the signal to move forward to complete the final objective when a German gas shell burst on the parapet almost in his face. In a moment his breathing stopped. "There seemed to be no air to breathe in or out, my mouth was open and completely stuck. I could not even gasp or choke. In a trice I had my gas helmet on and was breathing freely shortly afterward. It was a peculiar experience and for a moment or two I thought I was finished."

Fraser endured another bombardment during the Passchendaele campaign. He was a gunner with a packhorse train, spread out some twenty-five feet apart, carrying water and ammunition to the line. As they proceeded up Grafenstafel Ridge, the enemy guns opened up. The first group of four men and horses passed safely out of range but the second—Fraser's group—was trapped in the shelling. The man and horse behind Fraser were killed; the man and horse in front were also killed; the leading man was terribly wounded and his horse, too, was killed.

The explosion of the next shell threw Fraser into the mud, face down, killing his horse, whose body fell on him and trapped him. Fraser squirmed and struggled to get free. His legs were not damaged, but he felt he'd been wounded. Where? "My face burned as if hot wires were jammed into it. I was peppered in the face and hands with small pieces of shrapnel. Another salvo came over. The bursts this time so disturbed the air I could hardly breathe. I quickly headed down the road. It was then I noticed for the first time that my right arm was shattered at the shoulder and was dangling in front of me and twisted around. There were other injuries. . . ."

That was the end of the war for Donald Fraser, whose wounds were so severe he could not go back to the front. He returned to Calgary where, as a civilian, he worked for Customs and Excise for twenty-six years before retiring to Victoria, where he died of cancer, aged sixty-five.

In a later era, television's all-seeing eye could have given aid and comfort to a Stop the War party, as it was to do during the Vietnam conflict. A few reasoned voices, such as that of Bertrand Russell (who was immediately fired by his university for his anti-war stand and later imprisoned), were drowned out in the near universal cry for victory at any price. The French, staggered by the 1917 mutinies, turned at last to that old warhorse Georges Clemenceau, a politician who had never forgotten or forgiven the Germans for the Franco-Prussian conflict. "You ask what our war aims are?" he asked the National Assembly, and replied with a single incisive word: "Victory!" In France, anyone who called for a compromise peace did so at his peril. When Joseph Caillaux, the ex-premier, and Louis Malvey, minister of the interior, tried, they were charged with treason and clapped into prison.

The caveat of the Fallen haunted the belligerents as it haunted the graveyards of Flanders: *If ye break faith . . . we shall not sleep.* The propagandists on both sides had done their work not wisely, but too well.

6

The manpower crisis

In December 1917, with the blood of thousands of Canadians still staining the quagmires of Passchendaele, Canada was rocked by a controversy over conscription that represented the greatest crisis in her history. The controversy began to grow after the government introduced the Military Service Bill in June and reached its climax with the general election of December 18. By that time the nation was split so badly that in the assessment of Elizabeth Armstrong, the leading historian of the conscription crisis, "it seemed likely that the Confederation would be divided into the two component parts of which it had been composed, wrecked on the jagged rocks of Nationalism."

"Passion and partisan spirit and racial and religious hatred walked the streets unchecked," Armstrong, an American, wrote twenty years after the event. "Appeals to reason went unheard. Men distrusted their neighbours' patriotism and their personal honour simply because they did not belong to the same race or religion. Old party loyalties went by the board. Old political allies called each other 'traitors' and 'criminals'

191

simply because they happened to differ as to the part Canada should play in the war."

Here were sown the seeds of a future separatist movement; here the political philosophies of the major parties were shaped and even distorted; here Canada's diffident military role in the Global War of 1939–45 had its historical roots. The nation was divided into two warring parties; English-speaking Canadians were determined to invoke military conscription overseas to fill the gaps left by Haig's devastating war of attrition, and French-speaking Canadians were equally determined to resist it to the end.

The glorious days of 1914, when the entire country had been united in a common cause, when milling throngs swept through the streets of Montreal cheering the French republic and the British monarchy, when leading Quebec nationalists urged their followers to defend the Empire, when the Roman Catholic hierarchy pledged allegiance to the Union Jack and newspapers in both languages cried out that Britain's cause was just—those heady days were gone forever. Why? What happened?

The French Canadians' bitterness, obscured by the euphoria of the early war months, arose from the conviction that they had been betrayed by their English-speaking compatriots, especially in Ontario, and by a federal government dominated by Anglophone politicians.

It harked back to 1912, when Ontario had, in Quebec eyes, broken the deal made at Confederation that gave French Canadians control over their own education. Under Ontario's Regulation 17, adopted in 1912 and amended the following year, English became the sole language of instruction in elementary schools, Roman Catholic schools were placed under English Protestant inspectors, and French instruction was reduced to one hour a day.

By 1917 the phrase "Regulation 17" became a rallying cry not only among the growing number of committed Quebec nationalists but also for the whole province. Ontario had broken a promise to its neighbour; equally insulting was a second broken promise—Borden's sacred pledge that conscription for overseas service would never be invoked in Canada. In December 1914 he had told a Halifax audience that "there has not been, there will not be, compulsion or conscription." Now, with the losses mounting in Europe, he was hedging, telling the Trades and Labour Congress that if conscription "should prove to be the only effective method to preserve the existence of the state and of the institutions and liberties we enjoy" he would not hesitate to impose compulsory military service.

Borden was trapped by the mindset of the time (promoted by the official propaganda), which held that Canada was in mortal danger, if the war was lost, of having a draconian dictatorship imposed on the prostrate nation by the victorious Germans. That, of course, was fantasy. The existence of the state was threatened not by an enemy thousands of miles across the Atlantic but by the blunders of Borden's own party and particularly by his vainglorious and demented minister of defence.

Hughes must bear a large share of the responsibility for the bitterly divisive controversy that exploded in 1917. In more sensible hands much of what followed might have been avoided. Hughes's resistance to the formation of a French-Canadian brigade—a military family in which French-speaking recruits could feel comfortable and in which the Quebec population could feel a sense of pride—was unconscionable. Hughes wouldn't even allow militia units to take part in religious processions. Initially, new recruits were persuaded to join up in the belief that they would go into action as French-Canadian units. As a result of Hughes's meddling, that did not happen; under his aegis, two hundred militia battalions were broken up and their members spread about without any concern as to language, race, or religion. In the second month of the war, when a group of prominent French Canadians had urged the formation of a French-speaking battalion, the government had permitted the creation of the Royal 22nd, but in spite of the resultant enthusiasm in Quebec, there was no follow-up. One brigade was finally organized at Valcartier in 1916 but was later broken up.

Hughes's bigotry helps explain the growing reluctance of French-Canadians to join up after the initial rush to the colours. That in turn led some English-speaking Canadians to see Quebec as a province of slackers. In Ontario and the new realm of the West, an inflamed populace could not understand why the Quebeckers would not answer the call of Empire. But to Quebec, imperial needs took second place to those of regional unity.

Henri Bourassa, who, at the outset of war had just come back from Europe enamoured of France's bold stand against tyranny, quickly returned to his original stance. He was not against the British, he reiterated, but against imperialism in any form; it was not just the British Empire, but *all* empires that he opposed. A good many Canadians, especially the British-born, could not get it into their heads that France had long since given up any claim it had to be the mother country of Quebec and were baffled by that province's apparent refusal to rally to its cause.

By the spring of 1917, it was clear that the most intensive recruiting methods were not going to meet Borden's impetuous promise of an army of half a million men. The nation's resources were being stretched to the snapping point. Industries had gobbled up 300,000 men, and that did not take into account the needs of the farmers. Stunned by a blunt statement from the CPR's Lord Shaughnessy that Borden's pledge represented an unbearable burden, the government launched a national service plan to take an inventory of available manpower. The plan was attacked immediately by Quebec nationalists as laying the groundwork for conscription.

The groundwork was already being laid by the horrifying casualty reports in the press. In the first five months of 1917—a period that included the Vimy victory—the country had lost more than 56,000 men, killed, wounded, or missing. Some had been wounded more than once—thrice in certain cases—and were still being called into action. There was no way recruiting could keep up with the bloodletting. In that same period, fewer than 36,000 signed on.

In mid-May, Borden returned from England where Canada had finally been given a seat in the Imperial War Cabinet as part of Lloyd George's endeavour to get more support from the Dominion. The British prime minister's efforts bore fruit. On May 18, Borden finally announced in Parliament that the government intended to introduce conscription. He had visited the front lines in France, where he was convinced that the battle for Canadian liberty was being fought. With German U-boats close to cutting the Atlantic lifeline and Britain's Russian allies embroiled in the first stages of a bloody revolution, could Canada shirk her responsibilities, especially when the commitment of the other dominions was greater? At least 50,000 new men—perhaps 100,000— would be needed to reinforce the four divisions at the front.

That touched off an outcry in French Canada. Anti-conscription meetings erupted in Quebec City, Montreal, and smaller Quebec communities. Borden's solution was a Union Government, a coalition of the two leading parties committed to prosecute the war without partisan discord; but Laurier would have none of it. The Liberal leader was convinced that Canada could not raise the number of men needed, conscription or no conscription. And, so like the nation itself, his party was split wide open, the majority joining Borden, the minority, largely French-Canadian, clinging to Laurier.

"Put your trust in Laurier!" the mayor of Montreal urged a crowd of 15,000 on May 24. Thus fired up, his listeners marched through the streets, breaking the windows of those newspapers that supported Borden and attacking any soldiers who dared show themselves in public. Henri Bourassa counselled calm: he was concerned that continuing violence would see all of French Canada discredited. However, his chief supporter among the Nationalists, Armand Lavergne, declared he would go to jail or be hanged or shot before he would accept conscription.

The Prime Minister introduced the Military Service Bill on June 11, touching off an acrimonious two-month debate in Parliament. Bitter accusations were hurled across the floor of the Commons, especially at Laurier. Arthur Meighen, Borden's solicitor general, snidely suggested that Laurier could sit comfortably in his parliamentary seat only because Allied troops were holding the line in France. Dr. John Wesley Edwards, a Tory from Frontenac County, Ontario, accused the former prime minister of promoting Quebec's anti-British bias and espousing Canadian independence. Another Tory, John A. Armstrong from York

North, charged that Quebec was solely responsible for conscription because she had failed to do her duty.

All these attacks, centring on Laurier, illustrated the continuing paradox that bedevilled the nation in the first half of the century: how much did Canada owe Britain? How much did Canada owe herself? To English Canadians, especially the Tories, a failure to support the mother country was close to treason. But to French Canadians, Canada herself was the mother country. What was wrong with a bilingual Canada opting for independence? That, essentially, was Laurier's position: he saw the whole conscription controversy and the Union Government as part of an imperialist plot to shore up the Empire and wreck Canadian unity.

"I oppose this bill," he said, "because it has in it the seeds of discord and disunion, because it is an obstacle and a bar to that union of heart and soul without which it is impossible to hope that this Confederation will attain the aims and ends that were had in view when Confederation was effected."

Here was a warning for the future, a clear statement of the great Canadian dilemma—the old conflict between history and geography. How could Canada hold together if she divided her loyalties? But again, how could she hold together if she abandoned the nurturing mother whose very stamp was on her social and political institutions? Was that the intention of the men of Confederation, whose memory Laurier invoked? On the far horizon loomed the shadow of a new American empire, with which Laurier had flirted and Canadians had rejected in 1911. Could the old Empire protect Canada from the new? Bourassa, who rejected both, had sensed the danger; that was why his nationalism did not stop at the boundaries of Quebec.

But these were not the quandaries of the moment. Passions were such in Quebec that shortly after Borden's bill was introduced in mid-June, the dreadful word "secession" appeared in the columns of an extremist Catholic newspaper, *La Croix*. The possibility that the province might actually separate from the rest of Canada was remote, but the archbishop himself felt it necessary to warn his followers against going too far. As the debate in Parliament continued in those hot summer months, Montreal came closer and closer to violence. Anti-conscriptionist mobs poured through the streets, breaking windows and shouting "Down with Borden!" and were harangued by speakers urging armed resistance. One even boasted he had five hundred followers ready for action.

"Long Live the Revolution!" they roared. At the end of August, when members of a crowd of seven thousand were urged to get their guns out of storage, police tried to break up the meeting. In the resultant melee, one man was killed and four policemen injured. Even as a collection was being taken up to buy arms, authorities uncovered a plot to bomb the house of Hugh Graham (now Lord Atholstan), the wealthy leading conscriptionist who owned the Montreal *Star*. After that, with conscription the law, the French-Canadian press, including Bourassa's *Le Devoir*, urged an end to a violence that could only further infuriate the English Canadians.

The government did its best to keep the word "conscription" hidden behind a veil of euphemisms. Officially, the conscription act was the Military Service Act: conscripts were to be known as "drafted men." Every male Canadian between the ages of twenty and forty-five who was medically fit could be conscripted, but so many exemptions were allowed that it quickly became clear the vast majority (86 percent, by November 2) wanted to be excused.

Surprisingly, a greater percentage of potential draftees came from Ontario than from Quebec. In fact, the government was aware of a strong undercurrent against forcible service among the farmers and new immigrants in Ontario and the West. The previous June the Liberals had swept into power in Alberta and Saskatchewan. It was obvious that the waves of newcomers brought in during the Laurier boom years were transforming the political structure of the nation. These naturalized Canadians, who held no allegiance to Empire or King, had the voting strength to tilt the scales in the election that Borden was planning for December.

He was determined to win that election, if not by hook, then by crook.

Like other political leaders before and since, he was so convinced of the rightness of his cause that he was quite prepared to toss ethical considerations aside and follow Meighen's advice that it would be "a splendid stroke" to take the vote away from the "disloyal" and award it to the "patriotic."

Meighen introduced the Wartime Elections Bill in September—a shameless piece of gerrymandering that when passed gave the vote to every soldier, whether in Canada or overseas, and also to the wives, mothers, sisters, and daughters of anyone in khaki. At the same time it disenfranchised all naturalized immigrants from enemy countries who had arrived in Canada after 1902, and all conscientious objectors. Under the Military Voters Act, soldiers were given the option of simply voting for or against the government, without recourse to individual constituencies. As one loyal Liberal put it during the election, "The government chose the voters instead of the voters choosing the government."

The soldiers at the front were deluged with what one private called a "regular flood of pamphlets," all from the Union Government. "It will ever be a sore spot with the troops that only Government literature was allowed to reach us," one soldier, John Harold Becker, wrote in his memoirs. In his diary he declared, "It seems to me too bad that, as a soldier on active service I or my fellows are not allowed to express opinions on this or any other election because it might be termed a political discussion—but at the same time we are expected to cast a vote and expected to vote in a certain way." Though the censor had tried to scratch out the phrase "in a certain way," it remained legible enough for his sister to quote it in the book of reminiscences that appeared after his death.

This unsavoury manoeuvring all but assured a victory for the Union Government of thirteen Conservatives and ten dissident Liberals that Borden, after months of negotiation, had at last cobbled together. The campaign that followed was unlike any other, deliberately planned as a racist attack on Laurier and Quebec. The Liberal leader was presented on the hustings and in the press as a quitter who would take Canada

198

out of the war and play into the hands of the Kaiser, while Quebec was portrayed as a province that wanted to dominate the rest of Canada.

A full-page advertisement in the Toronto *Mail and Empire* said as much just before the election, declaring that Quebec wanted to rule all Canada, get out of the war, establish bilingual schools throughout the nation, and weaken ties with Great Britain. The Toronto *News* published a map of Canada with Quebec outlined in black, entitled "The Foul Plot on Canada." A Unionist Liberal attacked the province as "a plague spot on the whole Dominion." Even John Dafoe, a lifelong Liberal and generally seen as the voice of reason, turned venomous in the Manitoba *Free Press*: the choice, the paper declared, was for war and union, or for Laurier and disunion.

By election day, the *Mail and Empire* pulled out all stops. A vote for Laurier, it cried, was a vote for Bourassa, a vote against Canada's fighting arm, a vote against the British connection, a vote against the Empire, and a vote for Germany, for the Kaiser, for Hindenburg and von Tirpitz, and for the German submarine officer who sank the *Lusitania*. In Quebec, the violence surrounding the election made the earlier attack seem mild by comparison. Anyone speaking there for the government could not avoid being howled down and pelted with rotten eggs, or worse.

Having disposed of the new Canadians by denying most of them the vote, the Union Government moved to mollify the disgruntled farmers who had helped defeat provincial Tories in Alberta and Saskatchewan the previous June. On November 24, the minister of militia, General Sydney Mewburn, pledged regarding "any farmer's sons who are honestly engaged in farm work and in the production of food stuffs—if they are not exempted by the Tribunals and are called up for military service—I will have them honourably discharged . . . provided they go back to the farms . . ."—a pledge that was confirmed by Order-in-Council on December 2.

To nobody's surprise, Borden's Union Government won the election. The real surprise was the size of his margin. The Unionists emerged with a thumping majority of seventy-one seats—a surplus of 300,000 votes.

Ontario gave them seventy-four, the Liberals, only eight. In the West, it was fifty-five to ten. In the Maritimes Laurier was almost wiped out. Only in Quebec were the results reversed; there the anti-conscriptionists gained sixty-two seats out of sixty-five, a stunning victory for the Liberals, whose popular vote soared to almost four times its 1911 level. Canada was now split politically as never before. Eight provinces were solidly for conscription; one province was wholeheartedly opposed.

The cumbersome but necessary machinery of parliamentary democracy meant that plans to impose the Military Service Act and reinforce the army in the field moved with glacial slowness. The Act became law on August 29; the first men were not called until October 13, nor, because of Borden's pledge to wait for the election, did they begin training until January 3, 1918. And then they would need three months' training before they were ready for active duty in France.

It became apparent that in spite of all the patriotic calls to serve the nation, in spite of the recruiting posters, the white feathers, the impassioned speeches and equally impassioned prose, young men between the ages of twenty and twenty-two didn't want to fight. Of the 401,882 who registered under the Act, 379,629 sought exemptions. All these cases had to be investigated by tribunals in each province. Borden thought that conscription would provide the additional 100,000 men he felt were needed to swell the ranks of the overseas army. But on January 3 only 22,000 men were available to report for training.

With the casualty lists in from Passchendaele, the situation was serious. Lloyd George himself was putting pressure on Canada to speed reinforcements, but public opinion in Quebec was on the side of those who refused to serve. Riots broke out in the province when troops tried to arrest defaulters; four civilians were killed, five soldiers were wounded, and the jails were filled with protesters.

If the Military Service Act had never been proclaimed, would it have made any difference in the long run? Perhaps it might have, if the war had continued for another year—into 1919, at least. That was the expectation of the Allied leadership, which was woefully ignorant of the real situation in Germany. It must have been apparent after Passchendaele, when the enemy's resources were so badly depleted, that she could not long continue. The Allies had fresh reserves in the form of General "Black Jack" Pershing's Americans; the Germans had children and old men. In a twisted sense, Haig's merciless policy of attrition had succeeded.

Was the conscription crisis worth the national agony? The statistics give the answer. By the end of the Great War, after all the recriminations, the racial bitterness, the long-drawn-out legal battles, the parliamentary squabbles, the crushing military coercion used to track down reluctant draftees, the riots, the injuries, and the deaths—after all this, no more than 24,132 draftees actually arrived in France, and Canadians of both races were left with a bitter taste in their mouths that no amount of subsequent soothing syrup could ever expunge.

Arthur Currie was not opposed to conscription, but his main concerns were to keep his Canadian Corps up to strength and fend off the politicians who wanted him to come out publicly for compulsory service during the election—something he declined to do. Currie was frustrated by continuing political interference. Sam Hughes was gone, but his legacy lingered on in the shape of the Fifth Division, sitting in England—a unit that Hughes had created without any thought of reinforcements. Hughes's ambition for a big army of many divisions, with himself as its commander and a raft of political appointments at his fingertips, had helped to wreck national unity. The situation in the winter of 1917–18 could have been considered comical were it not for the seriousness of the problem. Here was the Union Government, struggling with the divisive problem of conscription, going through a maddening series of convolutions, revising the Military Service Act, and lowering the enlistment age to get more men, really scraping the bottom of the barrel and rending the country in two, while all that time 21,000 trained men twiddled their military thumbs in England under Sam Hughes's ambitious but less than competent son, Garnet. This, too, was unconscionable, but no politician seemed to realize it.

Currie did. It was his belief that what was needed above all was not necessarily conscription but a reorganization of the army. Better to have four divisions up to strength than try to reinforce five. In the months following the Passchendaele campaign he found himself fighting two battles—one to keep his corps intact, the other to prevent its being blown up into an army. The latter plan was the product of the same kind of starry-eyed optimism that had sprung up during the Western railway boom and was fuelled by the victories at Ypres and Vimy. Canada would have its own army! What a boost to national pride! What an opportunity for advancement for those ambitious officers rotting away in England! What a chance for political patronage! And what a boon for Garnet Hughes, the Fifth Division's commander, who was at the centre of the pressure for expansion! Hughes and his fellow officers naively assumed that conscription would solve the manpower problem, allowing a two-corps army of six divisions. Hughes was so certain of success that he offered to bet Currie any sum that he would shortly take the Fifth Division to France.

It looked as if he would get his way. By the time a firm proposal was made to the chief of the imperial general staff on January 11, 1918, it was generally accepted that the change was a *fait accompli*. But Borden was not certain the new divisions could be reinforced, given the weak response to the draft. Currie was even less enthusiastic. The new army would not only need extra services, such as artillery, but would also be overburdened with staff: an army headquarters, two corps headquarters, two additional divisional headquarters, plus brigade headquarters— ten in all, a wonderful opportunity for promotion but a waste of fighting men and an expensive price to pay for Canadian pride and personal ambition. Garnet Hughes made one final attempt, persuading Lord Beaverbrook to appeal to Lloyd George. Back came the answer, in sporting terms: "Our cock won't fight." Currie had won. In February, when the Fifth Division was broken up to reinforce the existing corps, Hughes ended up in England without a command.

Currie had put aside personal ambition for the sake of efficiency. To belong to that favoured band of successful generals who commanded an army in battle was a prize indeed. Money, power, and prestige could be his in the post-war world, as the peacetime careers of some of his British contemporaries proved. A lesser man, prodded by an equally ambitious staff, might have seized the chance, but Currie was above that. He wanted a lean, mean corps, and to maintain it he rejected the inevitable promotion.

In mid-March Currie faced a second crisis when Douglas Haig had to counter an unexpected last-ditch German offensive, again in the Ypres sector. The British high command now tried to break up the Canadian Corps. Two of Currie's divisions—the First and Second—were removed from his command; the Third and Fourth followed. Currie was left with only a headquarters, now placed in reserve. It was the British style to shuffle divisions about under various corps as the need arose. But it was not the Canadian style. Haig had broken his pledge to Currie in order to gain more flexibility and plug the gaps in the salient created by the German advances. Divisions could be more easily and quickly moved about than the larger, more ponderous corps. But Currie would not have that. He was furious. The four divisions had always fought under a single command with "an intimacy and understanding . . . which led to a singleness of thought and a unity of action" that made the corps, in Currie's estimation, "the hardest hitting force on any battlefront." The decision to break up the Canadians was an indication of the growing breach between the British command and the colonial upstarts.

More than once Currie had expressed his disgust with the performance of British troops, especially in one instance at Passchendaele when he had reported that they had "retired in a very bad and pronounced disorder, amounting to a panic." Tension was growing between the two commands. Some British generals, as E.L.M. Burns, a future general himself, has noted, were irritated by Currie's "tactless remarks . . . to the effect that some British formations did not fight very tenaciously." But, to be fair, Britain's best troops had long since been wiped out by more than three years of war.

Currie protested to Haig directly and through Sir Edward Kemp, Canada's minister of overseas military forces in England. Faced with the full pressure of the Canadian government, Haig reluctantly gave in, and Currie got his corps back; but the field marshal was certainly piqued. Who were these Canadians who seemed to feel they could interfere with the progress of *his* war? "I could not help feeling that some people in Canada regard themselves rather as allies than as fellow citizens of the Empire," he remarked. But that was just the point. To Currie and to Borden, Canada was no longer a mere colony, subject to the whims of the British aristocracy.

Canadian uniforms, ranks, and organization might be identical to those of Britain (save for the "Canada" badge on the tunics), but Currie's corps was a miniature army separate and distinct from its British counterparts, a truth difficult to explain to the military upper crust. Lord Derby had warned Haig a few months before that the Canadians could not be pushed around like chessmen on a board but that "we must look upon them in the light in which they wish to be looked upon rather than in the light in which we would wish to do so." That the British commander Henry Horne could not understand. He thought Currie was suffering from a swollen head after the Canadian complained to him about the British troops. "Many are not fighting. . . . Many of them will not fight and do not fight."

But Currie would not keep quiet. He was proud of his corps and convinced that Canadians fought better together as an experienced team—as Vimy had proved—and were imbued with an esprit de corps that would have been dissipated had they been dispersed among the British. The British decision to abandon the bloody ridge at Passchendaele that spring was, to him, a betrayal. He vented his frustration to Pershing, the American commander, deploring the fact that the ridge, which the year before he had been told must be taken at all costs and "for which the Canadians made the tremendous sacrifice of 16,000 casualties," had been so easily given up.

In June he met with Borden and found a sympathetic listener. The prime minister had suffered his own frustrations at the hands of the British. On his earlier trip to England he had been treated almost as an intruder. The British told him nothing; he had to read the morning paper to get any idea of what was going on. He warned Andrew Bonar Law, the Conservative leader, that he would "not advise his countrymen to put further effort into winning the war" unless he got more information. The English response was grudging and evasive.

The following year Borden was still demanding information and consultation. As he wrote to Sir George Perley, Canadian high commissioner in London, ". . . plans of campaign have been made and unmade, measures adopted and apparently abandoned . . . steps of the most important and even vital character have been taken, postponed or rejected without the slightest consultation with the authorities of this Dominion." It wasn't good enough. How could Canada be expected to put as many as half a million men in the field, yet "willingly accept the position of having no more voice and receiving no more consideration than if we were toy automata."

Here was a paradox: Borden, the leader of the Conservative Party— the wholehearted supporters of the New Imperialism—was becoming an ardent Canadian nationalist, not just for reasons of pride but because the very mother country that the imperialist faction worshipped had managed to alienate him to the point where his whole outlook had changed. "Procrastination, indecision, inertia, doubt, hesitation, and many other undesirable qualities have made themselves entirely too conspicuous in this war." These damning words in Borden's letter to Perley suggest the weight of the about-face taken by the slow-spoken, apparently stodgy prime minister. D.J. Goodspeed, the Canadian military historian and analyst, has put his finger on the lack of flexibility and the capacity for self-delusion on the part of the British commanders who were prepared to sacrifice thousands of men rather than abandon their own particular fantasy. They were, he wrote, more concerned with appearance than with reality: "They were more worried about the moral effects of failure than about the decimation, and the more than decimation of their own forces." Haig's stubborn insistence on clinging to the Ypres salient is the prime example of this refusal to face reality.

Borden was in London attending a meeting of the Imperial War Cabinet when, after hearing Lloyd George railing against Haig, he decided to get Currie's view of the situation. What he heard shocked him. The Passchendaele campaign had had no useful result, Currie told him. "No advantage in position was gained and the effect was waste." The venture was by no means worth the cost and was won only "to save the face of the British High Command who had undertaken all through the autumn most unsuccessful and highly disastrous attempts."

As one example of British negligence and casual indifference on the part of certain corps commanders, Currie told Borden that while his corps had put out 375,000 yards of barbed wire the previous autumn and winter, thoroughly protecting every trench, the comparative British effort had been minuscule. One corps commander told Currie he'd put out only 36,000 yards of wire, a second that he'd put out 30,000 yards, a third that he'd put out no wire at all. One British officer remarked that his men had been mainly employed in laying out tennis courts. That underlined Currie's conviction that the British army was top-heavy with senior officers who were not equal to the responsibility of their ranks.

This was really an indictment of the British class system under which no ordinary soldier could aspire to being "granted" a King's commission. Currie himself could never have climbed high in the British army. A *real-estate salesman*, holding a command position in the regular British army? A sergeant, perhaps, but a general? It was unthinkable. Stories of stiff-necked British officers ignoring Canadian enlisted men, even when their lives depended on it, were rife among the Canadians. George Henry Hambly, a future United Church minister from Swan Lake, Manitoba, would always remember such an incident after the Canadians took Vimy Ridge. Along came an imperial officer with a group of British soldiers. He had lost his way, but "when he found out we were only privates he wouldn't talk to us." He was a mile off course, on the wrong road, and couldn't read his map in the dark. The Canadians tried to steer him in the right direction, but he ignored them. "The way he snorted at us as 'Caneydians' showed extreme contempt for us as colonial troops." He haughtily disdained Hambly's attempts to set him right and marched off right into the German lines, where he and all his men were killed or taken prisoner.

Now Currie was telling Borden similar stories, not about young officers, but about British commanders. Borden was shocked. He took

Currie's criticisms to the Imperial War Cabinet and, in an uncharacteristically forthright declaration, hammered home his bill of indictments. Three days before the German counteroffensive began that spring, British intelligence had assured the command that there would *be* no offensive. There had been "conspicuous failures to remove incompetent officers" in the British forces. Talented young leaders faced a wall of opposition from the professionals, who refused to promote them above the rank of brigadier general.

Looking directly at Lloyd George, Borden declared, "Prime Minister, I want to tell you that if there is a repetition of the Battle of Passchendaele, not a Canadian soldier will leave the shores of Canada so long as the Canadian people trust the government of their country to me."

Borden's blunt action was unprecedented; it is said that he strode across the floor, seized Lloyd George by the lapels of his frock coat, and shook him. This was a different prime minister from the ponderous and cautious Maritimer who had reluctantly accepted the Tory leadership a decade before. The war had made Borden into a belligerent and a nationalist. When peace finally came, the new Robert Borden would fight for Canada's place in the conference that followed and the League that resulted. This remarkable episode in June 1918, which, somewhat to Borden's surprise, delighted and impressed Lloyd George, would lead, in time, to the Balfour Declaration of 1925 and the Statute of Westminster in 1931 to ensure that Canada and the other original dominions were equals and "in no way subordinate" to Imperial Britain.

7

The Last Hundred Days

In May 1918, Haig took the Canadian Corps out of the line to rebuild for the coming Allied thrust planned for August 8 near Amiens. Erich Ludendorff's all-or-nothing breakthrough offensives between March and July had failed after five tries. The Germans had come within a whisper of smashing out of the Ypres salient, almost destroying General Gough's British Fifth Army but ignoring the section of the front held by the Canadian Corps, perhaps, as some argued, because they had too healthy a respect for the Canadian fighting forces. Now the new Allied supreme commander, General Foch, was planning a knockout blow against the badly weakened enemy. In this, the final chapter of the Great War, known to history as the Last Hundred Days, the Canadians would be chosen as the shock troops to lead the advance.

Foch had called the corps "an army second to none," causing some of the British to refer to the Canadians as "Foch's pets." But there is no doubt that these were the elite troops of the British Expeditionary Force. For two months they were trained in a new kind of warfare that suited the Canadian temperament and was really an old kind of warfare—the open style of fire and movement that the long years in the trenches seemed to have made obsolete. But the development of the tank and the new emphasis on the rifle as a platoon weapon, plus the increased mobility of the artillery, had changed the way men fought. As one Canadian gunner remarked, "it was a wild, thrilling moment to be careening over the countryside."

The assault was touched off in early August when Currie engineered the great surprise attack of the war, moving the entire corps more than seventy miles south from Flanders to Amiens in a single week under a cloak of absolute secrecy. This intricate and seemingly impossible move stunned the German defenders. "You Canadians have no business down here," one officer exclaimed after he was captured. "We were told you were in Flanders; how I would like to hang our fools of Intelligence officers." The surprise was so complete that when the 9th Battalion captured a German regimental headquarters, the breakfast porridge was still warm on the table.

The Canadians spearheading the attack raced forward for eight miles following the greatest barrage of the war with more than six hundred guns massed along the corps front. To Ludendorff, August 8 was "the blackest day of the German army in the history of the war . . . the worst experience that I had to go through. . . ." When the news was broken to the kaiser, he told Ludendorff privately that "the war could no longer be won."

In the battle of Amiens between August 8 and 11, the Allies suffered some forty thousand casualties, the enemy close to twice that number. The "war machine," Ludendorff admitted, was no longer effective, and "the war must be ended." His brother-in-law, who commanded the German Eighteenth Army, did his best to excuse the defeat, explaining that "we were up against the élite of the French army and the celebrated Canadian Corps."

Ahead lay the formidable Hindenburg Line, a twenty-mile labyrinth of trenches and strong points, defended villages, rivers, and sunken roads. To Currie it was "without doubt one of the strongest defences on the Western Front." Here, on three days' notice in August, the Canadian Corps faced one of the hardest battles in its history.

Haig had picked the Canadians to storm and smash the Drocourt-Quéant Line near Arras, a key section of the Hindenburg complex. That would be, Foch declared, "the ram with which we will break up the last line of resistance of the German army." But the D-Q Line was stubbornly defended, and Haig realized that for him it would be a do-or-die effort. "If my attack is successful," he said, "I will remain on as C-in-C. If we fail or our losses are excessive, I can hope for no mercy! . . . What a wretched lot of weaklings we have in high places at the present time!"

The Canadians saved Haig's job on September 2, smashing the D-Q Line to become the first Allied troops to break through the Hindenburg system. "The prisoners surrendered in shoals," the commander of the Canadian Scottish, Cy Peck, reported. His was one of seven Victoria Crosses won that day, a record for the war. When fifty Germans surrendered to him, James Logan of the 39th Battery, Canadian Field Artillery, came out to get some souvenirs. "I pointed my finger at them. Down they went, saying: 'Oh, Kamerade! Mercy, Kamerade!' I couldn't touch them, they were so excited. I did not get a darn thing off them."

Later, Logan sat down and chatted with another bunch of prisoners. "You fellows got white bread?" one asked. "Will we get fresh white bread? I haven't had any white bread for four years. I had six brothers and my Dad killed in this war. I'm the last boy of the family and my Mother told me when I got in front of the English to give myself up. This was my first time in front of the English. I didn't know you were Canadians. When you started to shell this morning I came on a dead run."

An older prisoner, "a nice distinguished-looking man," turned to Logan. "You don't know it, but the war's over," he said. Logan asked him how he was able to speak such good English.

"I'm an English professor at the University of Berlin."

"A university professor and you're in the war?"

"They're scraping the bottom of the barrel. There's nobody left. They're taking everybody! We've lost the war. We should have quit long ago."

Logan would have liked to continue this revealing conversation, but an officer arrived and stopped it: no fraternizing with the enemy.

Yet this kind of fraternization was exactly what was needed—a surefire method of assessing the Germans' capacity to continue the war. Ludendorff's failed last-ditch stand had petered out. Germany's growing manpower crisis should have been obvious from the presence of so many underage youths and overage draftees in her army. And conversations such as James Logan reported should have made it clear that the enemy had reached the end of its resources. Yet in spite of mounting evidence, the Allied military and political leaders were convinced that the war would continue well into 1919. All this tells us as much about the deficiencies of the British intelligence system as it does about the enemy.

In Berlin the kaiser was as demoralized as his soldiers. "Now we have lost the war!" he cried. "Poor Fatherland!" He suffered a nervous breakdown, took to his bed, and refused to get up for twenty-four hours.

Behind the D-Q Line another apparently impenetrable obstacle barred the way. This was the half-completed Canal du Nord, a monstrous ditch one hundred yards wide. Its banks, down which troops would have to clamber, were overflowing with slime, creating a vast, impassable marsh, a miniature Passchendaele—and a potentially costly one. Behind this barrier the withdrawing Germans had formed up to frustrate the Allied advance.

A frontal assault against this flooded bulwark could be devastating, and Currie wanted no part of it. Instead, he devised a daring alternative. To the south, at the extreme limit of the corps boundary, was a dry stretch 2,600 yards long. He proposed to move two divisions south and across this narrow front. There, with the remainder of the corps following, he would fan out east and north in a semi-circular movement to take the enemy garrison from the rear. It was an intricate plan demanding speed, timing, and the full co-operation of the engineers in bridging the crossing. Horne, the First Army commander, tried to talk Currie out of it. The operation, he insisted, was too complicated. When Currie stood firm, Horne turned to Julian Byng, Currie's old comrade-in-arms in the Vimy days.

"Currie," Byng told him, "I've read over your plans and know they are as good as can be made, but can you do it?"

The laconic Currie replied that he could.

Byng persisted: "Do you realize that you are attempting the most difficult operation of the war? If anybody can do it, you can do it, but if you fail, it means home for you."

Currie did it. With the help of the engineers, his troops got across the canal on September 27. But the enemy had no intention of withdrawing. The battle that followed was the most savage and sustained in the history of the corps. The enemy, Currie reported, "fought like cornered rats," convincing him that the war could not be ended that year. "The Germans would keep on until beaten absolutely and totally." The Canadians, in their turn, fought back so tenaciously that German intelligence thought they were facing at least twelve divisions rather than four.

The Canadians didn't know it, but this was the last major battle they would fight in the Great War. Even as they crossed the Canal du Nord, the enemy was suing for peace. The Canadians captured Cambrai on October 9 without a single casualty, and the German army began a general withdrawal along the entire front. Now the Canadians found themselves in the unaccustomed role of liberators. As one young subaltern put it, "the troops coming out of the line are absolutely bedecked with flowers, and the horses carry so many that the poor beasts don't know what to make of it."

One final assault remained—the fortifications on Mount Houey, a 150-foot hill near Valenciennes, which the British had assaulted but failed to retain. Currie had been ordered to conserve shells in case the war continued for another year, but he refused. Shells were expendable; men's lives were not. Currie told McNaughton that this would be the last barrage he would make in the war. "Well, by Jove," McNaughton replied, "it will be a good one."

The assault force would consist of a single infantry brigade, but McNaughton's 303 guns would deliver "the heaviest weight of fire ever to support a single infantry brigade in the whole war." On that single day, the Canadian gunners fired almost sixty times the number of shells that had been fired by both sides in the Battle of Waterloo— a total of 2,149 tons of high explosives and shrapnel, not leaving a square yard of ground untouched. Currie's insistence on conserving lives, not shells, had paid dividends. The Canadians suffered 80 casualties, the Germans 2,600.

Now the race was on. The Canadians took Valenciennes, a city of more than 30,000, the key to the new German defence line. The rout continued as rumours of an armistice increased. "It won't be long now, boys," Currie called out to the 49th Edmontons as he rode past the battalion on November 8. By dawn on the eleventh, the Canadians had seized Mons.

On the morning of November 11, just before the Armistice was signed, the news that the war was over caused immense rejoicing among the civilians. As Private James Doak of the 52nd Battalion recorded, "only those who were privileged to be in close touch with the French and Belgian troops and civilians can fully realize the tremendous hatred these people have for the Germans."

The battalion was billeted at Wasmuel, a few miles from Mons. The civilian population was wild with joy. Down a side street Doak noticed an unusually noisy mob. "Their cries seemed filled with anger. Out of curiosity we wandered down that way and saw a sight which

212

would be beyond the wildest dreams of even the most bloodthirsty moving picture.

"The victim was a woman; a resident who was also a war widow. She was suspected of giving information, which led to the arrest and imprisonment of several civilians. For the past year she had been living at Mons with a German officer. She had been immune to harm before, because in the event of any injury, the whole village would have suffered. But she was among them now. Her powerful German protector could protect her no more.

"Someone jostled her as she walked along. In an instant she was the target for all manner of abuse. Women tore at her hair and clothes. Men and boys threw sods and stones until the poor wretch begged for mercy. There is no doubt in my mind that she would have been torn to pieces, but some of our soldiers came along. Forcing their way through the mob they formed a guard around the woman, taking her to the guardroom for shelter. She had a little boy who sobbed bitterly. He, at least, had done no wrong, but suffered along with his mother."

When the Armistice was signed at eleven that morning, many of the men at the front line couldn't believe it. In the words of a young private from Saskatoon, "A strange and peaceful calm followed. Not a cheer went up from anyone." Another recalled, "I think most of us were in a kind of shock or something."

Andy McNaughton was furious. "Bloody fools!" he exclaimed. "We have them on the run. That means we shall have to do it all over again in another twenty-five years."

8

In Europe, the soldiers lived with danger and expected it. In Canada, *Beyond* the civilian population was unprepared for the two most devastat- *enduring* ing disasters in their country's history, both of which stemmed from the war.

The first occurred on December 6, 1917. While the casualty lists from Passchendaele were still appearing in the Canadian papers, the freighter *Mont Blanc*, en route to France and loaded with more than 2,500 tons of wartime explosives, blew sky high in Halifax harbour, devastating 325 acres of that city, killing 1,963 people, injuring 9,000 more, and leaving 20,000 homeless. The second was worse—the pandemic of "Spanish" influenza brought to Canada in 1918 by soldiers returning with the disease that was already ravaging Europe. By the following year the plague had killed between 30,000 and 50,000 Canadians, most of them in the prime of life.

The Great War finally shattered Canada's Age of Faith and complacency. After the explosion in Halifax harbour destroyed all four churches in the suburb of Richmond, a middle-aged woman put into writing what a good many others were thinking: "Lots of good people have lost their faith in God, they think he has turned against this old city. In Halifax, the last three or four years has been given over to pleasure and money making. She has been too prosperous and the Great Father has called a halt."

The explosion occurred about half an hour after the Norwegian relief ship *Imo* drove her prow deep into the French freighter *Mont Blanc*, whose hold was jammed with a devil's brew of wartime explosives— 2,300 tons of picric acid, 200 tons of TNT, 35 tons of benzol, and 10 tons of gun cotton. On that clear, calm December morning, with only the slightest of breezes, human error was at fault, "a confusion of intentions" as one writer has called it.

A small shower of sparks—the result of the collision—touched off the greatest man-made explosion in history, not to be exceeded until the nuclear destruction of Hiroshima. The hideous blast that followed was so powerful that it shook houses in Truro, fifty miles away. The *Mont Blanc* literally vanished. A lethal rain of debris—3,000 tons of hot metal, composed of flying bits of her hull and superstructure—poured down, killing one hundred people. The barrel of one of her big deck guns was discovered buried in the ground three and a half miles away; part of her anchor, weighing half a ton, was flung two miles. No other wartime convulsion—not the explosive power of the Germans' feared Big Bertha nor that of the big naval guns at Jutland—could equal the brute force of this accidental eruption. The war in all its fury had touched the shores of Canada.

Two square miles of neighbouring Dartmouth were levelled, and every inhabitant was killed or injured. A thirteen-foot tidal wave raced across the harbour, sucking up the water to a depth of fifty feet and flinging the hulls of battered vessels for a mile along the Dartmouth beach. The shattered *Imo* was hurled onto the far shore. Acres of dockland were laid waste. Mangled corpses littered the streets. Roads and tramlines were buckled, trees uprooted, freight and passenger trains hurled from the yards. Large ships lost their funnels and superstructures; smaller ones simply vanished. So powerful was the blast that the very nails were sucked from woodwork and turned into flying projectiles.

Every school in Halifax was damaged. Tragically, the explosion occurred five minutes after classes began. One elementary school in the settlement of Richmond in the city's north end lost fifty children; another lost one hundred. In the Protestant orphanage, two hundred children and the entire staff perished. Halifax suffered more casualties in that single day than did London in any of the Nazi air raids of the Second World War.

The hospitals weren't prepared for such devastation. In some cases it was impossible to tell the living from the dead. Patients arrived bathed in blood, their clothes and skin dyed a dark, dirty grey by the "black rain" of oily soot and dust. Archibald MacMechan, the official historian of the Halifax Disaster Record Office, described it graphically: "It blackened the clothing almost like liquid tar, ruining housewives' linen. It blackened the faces and bodies of all it fell on, in some cases making it impossible to distinguish white persons from negroes."

The ground in front of the Victoria General Hospital was jammed with automobiles, wagons, and every conceivable conveyance capable of carrying the wounded. In offices, every inch of floor space was littered with mangled men, women, and children, suffering every imaginable wound or injury. One doctor described the scene at Camp Hill Hospital: "Many of us had seen terrible sights of human tragedies and suffering but nothing like this in the intensity of the number, and the frightful

215

and various character of the injuries. Men, women, and children were packed in the wards like sardines in a box, the cots all occupied and the floors covered so it was difficult to step between them." One young medical man, a Dr. Shacknove, was so affected by the spectacle that he lost his mental balance, returned to his office that night, and hanged himself.

The Hinch family, who lived on Veith Street, less than a thousand feet from the centre of the explosion, was virtually wiped out. Mary Jackson Hinch was severely injured and buried under debris for twenty-four hours. When she was rescued she found that her husband, Joseph, and all of her ten children had been killed—the largest loss suffered by a single family. The Hinches belonged to the extended family of James Jackson and his wife, Elizabeth. Within five minutes of the explosion, forty-six members of this close-knit family group were dead, and most of the twenty who survived were seriously injured.

One hundred and ninety-nine people were permanently blinded by flying shards of glass. Several more lost one eye. Dr. G.H. Cox, who arrived on the first relief train from New Glasgow, described the scene as "going from one corner of hell to another." At Camp Hill Hospital he operated on a kitchen table under a single electric bulb, using only the handful of surgical tools he'd brought with him. He worked from 6:30 that evening non-stop until 7:30 the following morning, when he was relieved. By then his instruments had become so dull they could no longer cut. His patients "had faces torn to tatters, as if clawed by a tiger. The wounds were stuffed with plaster and dirt. Some eyes were literally bags of glass."

Nor was this the end of Halifax's ordeal. On Friday, December 7, snow began to fall. By afternoon, a ferocious blizzard hampered all rescue attempts. The streets were clogged with drifts while the high winds and turbulent waters began to loose the ships in the harbour from their moorings. Just as repairs to the telephone service had cleared eight hundred lines, the blizzard knocked them out again. It slowed relief trains, interrupted repair work, hampered deliveries of food, fuel, and blankets, prevented exhausted relief workers from struggling home to

216

rest, inhibited people seeking medical aid, and forced others to huddle together for warmth in their battered homes. By nightfall, sixteen inches had fallen on the city, nor did the storm let up for several days.

If Halifax's ordeal brought out the best in people, it also brought out the worst. Anti-German feeling reached a new peak almost immediately after the explosion. Thomas Raddall, the future novelist, was fourteen when the *Mont Blanc* blew up. He rushed from school to his shattered home to find his distraught mother bleeding from breast to forehead. "The Germans—those beasts—they're shelling the city," she cried. Others thought that the Zeppelin that had bombed London had somehow managed to cross the Atlantic and wreak havoc on the city. Many believed the tragedy was the work of enemy saboteurs. An angry mob descended on the home of one Herr Hobrecker, who was rumoured to have a concrete gun emplacement under his lawn. When they found the house empty, they tore it apart. On December 10 the chief of police arrested every German citizen in Halifax. All were later released.

The Halifax *Herald* fuelled the hysteria with a leading editorial on December 12 that for sheer venom exceeded any previous diatribe against the "beastly Hun." "WE NOW KNOW . . . THAT THE PRIME RESPONSIBILITY for this, rests with . . . that arch fiend, the Emperor of the Germans; neither are we disposed to hold the German people entirely free of direct responsibility for this catastrophe. . . .

"There are strange things afoot. There are rumours . . . of a ship sunk suddenly in the harbour for possibly dark design, and of signals from house tops at night, which are not calculated to make easier the sad hearts of the survivors of this disaster. So long as there are people in Halifax who remember this past week, or whose children will remember it, so long will the name of the German be a name for loathing and disgust. This is for no other reason, because we know now what war is. And Germany, alone among all the nations of the earth, makes war with DELIBERATE INTENT."

The virulent anti-German feeling quickly calmed down, but one sentence from the *Herald*'s editorial made a valid point: "We know now what war is." For the first time, in one corner of Canada, ordinary citizens who had never fired a shot in anger and who lived more than three thousand miles from the trenches of Flanders had been given the same grisly lesson in the horrors of modern war that had been visited upon the distressed of Europe for almost fifty months.

The following summer and fall, as Halifax was repairing and rebuilding and the Great War was winding down, the most deadly scourge in history since the Plague of Justinian in the sixth century and the Black Death in the fourteenth struck Canada with chilling ferocity, killing between 30,000 and 50,000 people and leaving others with heart and respiratory troubles. It was an indirect result of the war in Europe as troopships brought infected soldiers to Canadian shores and railways scattered them from Nova Scotia to British Columbia.

The pandemic struck in three waves. The first "three-day fever," as it was called in June 1918, was relatively mild. So was the third, in February and March of 1919. But the second wave reached disastrous proportions in October 1918, when it was known as the Spanish flu, although it actually had its origins in China.

It first appeared in Canada on the last day of September 1918 among troops stationed in the Toronto-Hamilton area. Medical authorities did not take it seriously; it was "just plain grippe," Toronto's medical officer of health said. His provincial counterpart advised that "the public has been unduly alarmed." A twelve-year-old Toronto girl complained of a slight cold after she left her home in the suburbs. On the way to the city she suffered chills and a severe headache. By the time she reached her destination, she was delirious. Three days later she was dead, and similar reports were pouring in from all over the province. By mid-October the disease was raging across the country. In Toronto alone 10,000 schoolchildren and 124 teachers were stricken.

The flu struck so quickly that people were sick before they realized it. Severe pain in the back and limbs was the first hint that something was wrong. That was followed by a high fever and more pain in the neck, eyes, and head, accompanied by prostration and then delirium. In the last stages the lips and other body parts turned blue.

A businessman who went to work one morning at eight was carried

218

home on a stretcher at ten. A carpenter was struck while sawing through a plank and could not complete the task. A woman was hit during a whist game and couldn't finish the hand. As Tom Caulfield, an Edmonton banker, explained, "You could be talking to a man on the street, turn around and walk down the street. You'd look back and he'd fallen over." A medical corps doctor in Saint John recalled that it was not unusual to attend twenty or thirty people in the morning and find half of them dead by nightfall.

Death struck swiftly and without warning. After attending a lecture together, two girls from Woodstock, Ontario, working in nearby Paris, returned to the hotel room they shared. In the morning Claire Hunter called out to her friend, "Vera, I'm going downstairs to breakfast." She returned after the morning meal and called again. There was no answer. She pulled down the sheets of the bed and found Vera "dead and cold." The flu had crept in early that morning and killed her in her sleep.

The entire country closed down. Schools, theatres, pool halls, bowling alleys, and churches shut their doors. Sports events, such as the McGill-Ottawa football game, were cancelled. Ten thousand railway workers in Eastern Canada booked off sick in October. It was impossible to place a telephone call because the operators were all stricken. Half the coal mines near Drumheller, Alberta, were shut. Native reserves were wiped out. With fifteen deaths a day, the town of Sherbrooke, Quebec, virtually closed down. Montreal, recording 3,025 deaths in a single month, was one of the hardest hit cities. On October 21, it reported an all-time high of 201 deaths in a single 24-hour period; the following day 1,058 new cases broke out.

Every effort was made to halt the spread of the disease. Judges refused to allow witnesses in court to kiss the Bible. In some jurisdictions, spitting in the street brought a $50 fine. People wore gauze masks and carried small bags of camphor around their necks. Drugstores were jammed with customers seeking every kind of panacea from cough syrup to quinine to plain aspirin. Nothing worked—neither prayers, nor drugs, nor quarantine. The disease cut a swath across the country, and then, even as the warring nations were concluding an armistice in France, it vanished as quickly as it had arrived, to return in milder form the following spring.

The most baffling aspect of the pandemic was that it struck hardest at the strongest and the healthiest. The majority of deaths occurred among those Canadians between the ages of twenty and forty. Children under ten, adults over forty or fifty—the groups most likely to succumb to respiratory diseases—generally survived. The victims belonged to the same doomed age group as those who went off to war.

At least 40,000 Canadians struck down in the prime of life! Take that mean figure, add the 60,000 war dead, and contemplate the account rendered. In a country of 8 million, we lost 100,000 of our most promising citizens, and hence much hope for the future. How many poets and playwrights died of influenza or shellfire? How many novelists? How many scientists, healers, philosophers were interred in that ghastly army of the dead? What happened to the dreamers without whom no civilized society is complete? How many future leaders died in delirium on a hospital cot or bled to death in the muck of Flanders? Was there a future prime minister in that ghostly band?

The immensity of that loss can be distilled in the potential of one young man, the tragic hero of Sandra Gwyn's *Tapestry of War*—an attractive French Canadian named Talbot Papineau, "brimming over with joie de vivre and clearly cut out for stardom."

A thirty-one-year-old Montreal lawyer when war broke out, "with a passion for politics and a professional sense of place," Papineau had all the proper credentials, not the least of which was his name. For he was the grandson of one of French Canada's historical heroes, the great Louis-Joseph Papineau, the rebel leader of 1837. His mother, a Philadelphia aristocrat, was descended from one of the signatories of the American Declaration of Independence. Fluently bilingual, a champion canoeist, a devoted horseman, and an expert dancer, Papineau oozed the kind of charm and intelligence that made him attractive to men as well as women.

One of the first Canadian Rhodes scholars, he was spotted as a comer by an earlier governor general, Lord Grey, who wrote: "Young

Papineau . . . is able with English ideas and a French temperament and wit. If he has ambition, he may go far." But when he returned from Oxford, Papineau was, before all else, a Canadian, and proud of it. "Especially," he wrote, "I want to see Canadian pride based on substantial achievements and not on the supercilious and fallacious sense of self-satisfaction we have borrowed from England."

He was in Vancouver attending the annual meeting of the Canadian Club (he was president of the Montreal branch) when war broke out. There he departed briefly from a speech on his favourite subject, "The Nationalist Idea in Quebec," to make an acerbic comment on Canada's subservient role in the pre-war policy. "Canada did not have one word to say in the diplomatic negotiations leading up to the war or in the declaration of war," he declared, unwittingly anticipating Robert Borden's later views on Canadian independence.

"My profession," he had remarked, "is speeching not fighting." Yet he wired to his old friend Hamilton Gault for a spot with Gault's privately supported regiment, the PPCLI. Gault shot back a favourable reply, and Papineau, who had no military training and had even been opposed to Boy Scout uniforms in the pre-war days, rushed off to Ottawa to enlist, partly for adventure and partly to further his own post-war career. The Pats, a separate regiment attached to a British division and not to the Canadian Corps, sailed for England the last week in August after a farewell dinner tendered by the Rideau Club. "I made a long speech," Papineau wrote to his mother, "and was much congratulated. Some men said I should be Premier one day."

Overseas, he wrote almost daily to his mother, remarkable letters that, Gwyn has noted, "revealed the touch of a poet," showed him at odds with the prevailing attitude, and might have marked him for greatness. "There should be no heroism in war. No glorification— no reward. For us it should be the simple execution of an abhorrent duty, a thing almost to be ashamed of since by reason of our human imperfections . . . we would rather be killed and tortured than accept conditions of life that we have not been taught to regard as good."

Papineau's years in France clearly had their effect on his vision of his native land—a vision he was more easily able to view from the vantage point of distance. After the war, he knew "the issue in Canada . . . is going to be between Imperialism and Nationalism. . . . This controversy must result because we cannot continue as we are, and there is no longer any other alternative, though opponents of sovereignty threaten us with a third—namely political absorption into the States. . . . My whole inclination is towards an independent Canada with all the attributes of sovereignty, including its responsibilities."

As a result of these remarkably prophetic musings, Papineau decided to take public issue with his cousin Henri Bourassa of *Le Devoir*, who opposed the war as an imperialist venture in which French Canadians should have no part. Papineau was convinced that this attitude had brought French-Canadian nationalists "into a dispute from which they may never recover."

In March 1916, in an open letter to Bourassa that ran to nearly ten thousand words, Papineau laid out what might have been his political program in the post-war years: "As I write, French and English are fighting and dying side by side. Is their sacrifice to go for nothing or will it not cement a foundation for a truly Canadian nation, a nation independent in thought, independent in action, independent even in its political organization—but in spirit united for high international and human purposes to the two Motherlands of England and France?"

Bourassa made a spirited reply, explaining his credo that he was opposed not just to British imperialism but to *all* imperialisms. The European nations, he pointed out, were "victims of their own mistakes, of the complacent servility with which they submitted to all imperialists." And he put his finger on the uncertainty that continued to bedevil English Canadians: "A heavy proportion of recruits, after all, were recent British immigrants and, under the sway of Imperialism, a fair number have not yet decided whether their allegiance is to Canada or to the Empire, whether the United Kingdom or the Canadian confederacy is their country.

"The backward and essentially Prussian policy of the rulers of Ontario and Manitoba gives us an additional argument against the intervention of Canada in the European conflict. To speak of fighting for the preservation of French civilization in Europe while endeavouring to destroy it in America appears as an absurd piece of inconsistency. To preach Holy War for the liberation of people overseas, and to oppress the national minorities in Canada is, in our opinion, nothing but odious hypocrisy."

Thus was the issue joined. In hindsight, Bourassa's contention makes some sense. French Canada had long ago turned its back on Europe. Why must it return to Europe to take part in somebody else's bloody quarrel in which it had no say? English Canada, of course, did not see it that way. The Huns were at the gate! Freedom was in jeopardy, including the freedom of French Canadians to run their own affairs. Or so the propagandists had tried to make clear: the Empire must stand together in a life-and-death crusade against evil. And here was a French Canadian castigating a compatriot for failing to understand that principle!

Papineau, of course, was not writing about Empire solidarity but about Canadian solidarity—quite a different argument. But in the wave of enthusiasm that followed the publication of his letter to Bourassa, and which made him a national hero in English Canada, that was glossed over. To the *Globe* of Toronto, he had "risen to rare heights of impassioned eloquence . . . as he scourged the men who have brought Quebec into disrepute." *The Times* of London called the letter a "remarkable declaration" from "someone who had been closely linked with the High Priests of Canadian Nationalism." Mackenzie King called Papineau "one of the finest and bravest of men" and declared that "the most brilliant men in the country would be proud to serve in Parliament with Papineau as Prime Minister."

For Papineau this could have been the launching pad for a political career that might have propelled him into the highest office. But that was not to be. In mid-November 1917, following the battle of Passchendaele, a number of PPCLI officers searching for bodies in the filth of that sodden moonscape came upon a water-filled shell hole from which protruded a pair of legs with reversed puttees. Somebody remembered one officer who had always worn his puttees that way. They pulled what was left of the corpse from the water; a shell had blown away its upper body, but it was possible to identify what remained from the contents of the pockets. It confirmed their suspicions: that truncated cadaver, rotting in the muck, was all that was left of Major Talbot Mercier Papineau.

INTERBELLUM II
The Gullible Years

James Sutherland "Buster" Brown

1

The general returned to Canada just after midnight, August 17, 1919, to a reception the next day that, as the Halifax *Chronicle* remarked, was more appropriate to a funeral than a homecoming. It was, of course, the Sabbath, and this being Canada, the crowds that might have cheered him as he made his way to a reception at the city hall were at prayer. A guard of honour met Currie along with a gaggle of city officials who received him in silence. A garrison band played; the lieutenant-governor and the mayor greeted him. Then he was off to the capital.

"OTTAWA FORGETS TO CHEER" was the *Globe*'s headline on Tuesday morning over a long dispatch from its correspondent, who wrote: "Ottawa is characteristically undemonstrative, but perhaps that characteristic was never more marked than in the welcome accorded to Canada's foremost soldier." There had been scattered applause at the station when Currie disembarked, while on the route to Parliament Hill "the crowd gaped but that is all the crowd did do."

A faint cheer went up when the General passed the Rideau Club, "then silence, broken only by the band, which strove nobly to put some semblance of heartiness in the welcome." Here and there a man or woman endeavoured to start a cheer but failed to arouse any enthusiasm.

The Prime Minister was not on hand to greet the country's most distinguished son. He had gone off to Saint John to welcome a lesser hero, albeit a more glamorous one—the young Prince of Wales, launched on a tour of his own to cement Empire relations. Imperial protocol, of course, dictated the pecking order. How ironic! The greatest soldier in Canada's history—the man who more than any other had put the country on the map and given her an enviable international reputation—upstaged by a callow youth whose only attribute was the circumstance of his birth.

They made Currie a full general that day, the first Canadian ever to reach the pinnacle, and in September, when he departed on a triumphal speaking tour of the West, the crowds did cheer him so fervently that Δit drove him to the point of exhaustion.

226

Plaudits are cheap, but where was the largesse that a grateful nation was wont to lavish upon its military heroes? The British had given Haig £100,000 and made him a peer of the realm. His two senior generals each received £30,000, and corps commanders were given £10,000 each. These sums were major fortunes in those days, and Currie, who was in effect broke, could have used the money. The government toyed with the idea; Borden specifically suggested a money grant, but both the cabinet and the caucus "did not in the least favour the proposal," so the Prime Minister abandoned it.

Why this skinflint attitude? Borden had no qualms about bailing those two railway buccaneers, Mackenzie and Mann, out of bankruptcy by laying out $25 million to buy the Canadian Northern and another ten million for its rolling stock. But for Currie: nothing. Why?

It is not possible to remove the influence of the unspeakable Sam Hughes from the equation. The sixty-five-year-old Hughes, though approaching senility, was a Conservative MP seeking revenge for the treatment of his son, Garnet, and poisoning the parliamentary air with anti-Currie diatribes. The previous October he had written to Borden that what he called "the massacres at Lens, Passchendaele, etc." had only one objective: "to glorify the General in command." In March, having no reply from the Prime Minister, he took his charges to the floor of the temporary House (following a damaging fire in 1916), where he was safe from a slander action, to charge that Currie had needlessly sacrificed the lives of Canadian soldiers shortly before the armistice had been signed.

"Were I in authority, the officer who four hours before the armistice was signed, although he had been notified beforehand that the armistice was to begin at eleven o'clock, ordered the attack on Mons, thus needlessly sacrificing the lives of Canadian soldiers, would be tried summarily by court-martial and punished so far as the law would allow. There was no glory to be gained and you cannot find one Canadian soldier returning from France who will not curse the name of the officer who ordered the attack on Mons," Hughes thundered.

That caused an uproar. Currie's former comrades-in-arms, Cy Peck,

VC, and Richard Cooper, MP for Vancouver South, sprang to his defence. The *Globe* added its voice to Currie's defenders. But the government remained silent until May 1920, nine months after the General's return, when Sir Edward Kemp, minister of overseas military forces, made a passing reference in his official report to Currie's "valour, patience and skill" and his consideration for the men under him. Hughes was not deterred, repeating his charges that the General had unnecessarily sacrificed lives. Hughes was careful not to repeat his charges outside of Parliament.

To Currie, Hughes was "a liar," "at times insane," and "a cur of the worst type." But a section of the Canadian public, not to mention Hughes's own supporters in Parliament, were confused. Currie went on to become a popular and highly respected principal of McGill University with nineteen honorary degrees to his credit. After that, and with Hughes's death in 1921, one might have expected the controversy to die out. But it flared up again in mid-June of 1927 when the *Evening Guide* of Port Hope, Ontario, in the heart of Hughes country, ran a front-page article reviving the charges. "It is doubtful," the paper wrote, "whether in any case there was a more deliberate or useless waste of human life than in the so-called capture of Mons."

In a bitterly ironic passage, the paper referred to Ottawa's apparent dereliction in ignoring the top general as evidence that Currie had "conceived the mad idea that it would be a fine thing to say that the Canadians had fired the last shot in the Great War. . . .

"It does not seem to be remembered that even Ottawa, neither by government or Parliament, gave Sir Arthur Currie any official vote of thanks or any special grant as evidence of the esteem or appreciation for his services. . . ."

The author of this tissue of lies was W.T.R. Preston, a slight, wiry man of seventy-seven, a malodorous Liberal Party hack and a master of political fakery, bribery, and ballot stuffing that was extreme even for those times. "Hug the Machine for me," Preston had wired to one Liberal candidate before a blatantly fraudulent by-election. From then on he was known in Tory circles as Hug the Machine Preston. Currie was outraged when Preston's article was brought to his attention and immediately decided to sue him and the *Evening Guide* for libel, claiming damages of $50,000.

Every effort was made to talk him out of it. After all, the paper was obscure and the resultant publicity could be damaging. Hughes's hometown of Lindsay wasn't far away, and there were still many Hughes supporters in the area. But Currie was adamant, and any attempts at an out-of-court settlement came to nothing. Thus was the stage set for one of the most sensational trials in Canadian history.

It opened in Cobourg on April 16, 1928, and lasted two weeks, with nineteen reporters on hand filing an average of 72,000 words a day. Seventy-one witnesses testified and fifty-three exhibits were entered as evidence. During the examination for discovery, the General had been faced with a barrage of 2,645 questions, 861 of them disallowed by the judge when the case came to trial. These questions went back as far as the battle of Ypres. As Currie put it, "Preston sought by his questions not only to fight the war again, but to bring in everything he ever knew or heard which might in any way reflect on me." This included inferences about Currie's competence, as "a real estate general," to fill such a high post. In Currie's opinion, "Someone has taken the trouble to coach him very well."

Who was that someone? And why were Frederick W. Wilson, the Port Hope editor, and Preston so willing to go to court when they really didn't have a leg to stand on? Currie concluded that "there was more behind this thing than appears on the surface." And so there was. The someone "behind this thing," it turned out, was Sam Hughes's vindictive son, Garnet, still carrying a grudge because Currie had denied him command of the First Division. "I'll get you for this," the younger Hughes had threatened. In the Currie libel suit he saw his chance, feeding information to Preston and pumping Currie's estranged partner from the old real estate days in Victoria.

Not just the battle of Mons but many other engagements of the war were fought again, yard by yard, while the whole country looked on during an April heat wave. With some of the actors in the drama confined to the sweltering courtroom and almost prostrate from the heat, it often seemed that Arthur Currie himself was on trial. The defence was making every attempt to humiliate the embattled general and to prove there had been a needless loss of life at Mons even as the armistice was being signed. But the best they could come up with was one casualty, a Private George Price of the 28th Battalion, shot by a sniper four and a half miles northeast of Mons at three minutes to eleven.

The trial was marked by an avalanche of irrelevancies on the part of the defence—matters that had nothing to do with the case, such as whether or not Currie cared about the comfort of his soldiers. The presiding judge, Hugh Rose, continually clashed with the lawyer for the defence, Frank Regan, "Mr. Regan, you put a witness in the box, and you cross-examine, and you lead, and you coax, and you do all the things that the book says you must not do."

"I think you should know that we have had great difficulty in getting witnesses," Regan explained.

"What in the world has that got to do with the manner in which you are going to examine the witness when you do call him?" the judge shot back.

Regan himself was under pressure and by the end of the first week admitted he was not well and at one point had almost collapsed. Wilson, too, was in a bad way, feeling so faint that he was given permission to sit during the testimony.

Wilson testified that the offending article had come about as a result of the unveiling of a bronze plaque commemorating the Canadian capture of Mons. The late minister's diatribes in the House with specific reference to Currie and Mons were well known in his old riding. Preston, who, the editor said, "knew more about the situation than I did," was assigned to write the article, which he knocked out in three or four hours and which ended up on the *Guide*'s front page. Wilson tried to enter Hughes's Commons attacks in the court record, but since they were privileged, the judge ruled against him, declaring that the court had no intention of going back to all of Wilson's sources or "we may be here for years."

230

Sir Edward Beatty, McGill's chancellor who was also president of the CPR, had offered Currie the services of the company's counsellor, William Norman Tilley of Toronto. On April 23, Tilley scored a telling point by introducing as witness the commander of the Third Division, Fred Loomis (now Sir Frederick), who testified that on the morning of November 10, Currie visited him "to impress on me the necessity . . . not to undertake any serious offensive in the way of a heavy attack on a set piece with artillery; in other words to avoid casualties and losses." Other military witnesses confirmed that there was no fighting on Mons in the last day of the war.

It was Currie's turn to take the stand. Already exhausted and humiliated by the trial in spite of hundreds of letters of support pouring in, he now faced a gruelling seven hours in the witness box. When Frank Regan asked what objection he had to the editorial, Currie responded that "it holds me up before the public as a murderer, a man who didn't exercise due regard for the lives of the men under him. If that is true I do not deserve to be General of Reserve; I do not deserve to be the principal of McGill University. In fact, I am charged with a crime which is punishable. But that article is not true. . . . Not only is my own reputation, my own honour, my known integrity at stake, but also the reputation of every officer and non-commissioned officer that commanded men in the Canadian Corps."

After Currie, through his lawyer, had outlined the tactics involved in the capture of Mons, he was subjected to a cross-examination by Regan that one eyewitness categorized as "grotesque"—a great military commander "subjected to the cross-examination of a man who knew nothing of war but nevertheless undertook to instruct him in the art of attack, in strategy, in the command of a Corps, in the conduct of a gentleman and, for full measure, on how to be a Principal of a University."

Regan quoted from Currie's interim report for 1918, dealing with the last hundred days, when the four Canadian divisions had defeated at least forty-seven enemy divisions. "Don't you think, Sir Arthur," Regan asked, "that in the dying hours of the war, you might have saved your men a trifle more than you did?"

Currie struck back. "No. You are the man who is suggesting that those men who died should lie down and quit within two days of the final victory."

"I didn't say that," Regan expostulated.

"Oh, yes," Currie shot back, "you say spare them, you say quit."

Regan, cornered, tried to wriggle free. "I don't mean to lie down and quit."

Currie wouldn't let him off the hook. "Well, that is what you are suggesting," he said.

"No, it isn't," Regan replied.

"Yes, it is," Currie said. "You would have them disobey orders; you would have them mutiny, practically; you would have them guilty of treason . . . and act in an unsoldierly way, right at the very last. Those were not the men who did that sort of thing."

The trial wore on, Regan quoting from a stack of books and arguing with Currie about their meaning until the judge interposed: "If a whole library is coming, I think it is pretty nearly time the rules should be applied." And he added, "It is not true because it is in a book, you know."

In his final argument on April 30, Regan spoke for two hours, urging the jury at the end "not to give him a cent. . . . He says he is not after money. It doesn't look like it to me. But you can take him at his word. Give him nothing. Give him a verdict for the defence. . . . Our only desire was to give justice to these dead soldiers at Mons."

Preston followed. "I believe what I wrote in this article . . . evidence has been adduced to support every word." The attack on Mons "was madness. Cursed—I will not say anything else, and it was greater madness to decide that the fighting must go on until eleven o'clock . . . therefore impeach Arthur Currie before this bar on behalf of the widows, who lost their husbands, the mothers, who lost their sons, the sons, who lost their fathers, and the fathers, who lost their support with heedless, reckless, needless waste of life in his attack on Mons."

Tilley, in his own summing up, pointed out that "this is a libel suit not an enquiry into the war." The defendants had not justified their claims. All that Wilson, the editor, had done was to explain how the article came into being; and its author, Preston, hadn't even gone into the witness box.

"Gentlemen of the jury," he said, to scattered applause, "you are entitled in considering your verdict to consider that the fact that someone says something gives nobody the right to repeat it."

The jury was out for more than three and a half hours and voted eleven to one that the defendants were guilty of libel but awarded only $500 to Currie, probably because the General had indicated that it was vindication he wanted, not cash. He returned to Montreal to a tumultuous welcome but looked pale and fatigued. A military band greeted him when he stepped off the train, and his progress from Windsor Station to Peel and Sherbrooke streets was such that traffic had to be stopped—"a triumphant march," the press called it. Thousands cheered, sang, and paraded behind his car; students from McGill leaped on the rear bumper and led the crowd in a college yell. On the steps of the United Services Club on Sherbrooke he made a short speech of thanks as more cheers resounded and the crowd sang "For He's a Jolly Good Fellow." At a military banquet at the Mount Royal Hotel he was toasted and cheered by four hundred former officers of his corps. Telegrams and letters of congratulation poured in. "All your friends have been delighted," the prime minister, Mackenzie King, wrote. Depleted by the extended court ordeal, he took a long vacation on his doctor's advice.

"I cannot tell you how ashamed I am of myself in letting this cursed trial get on my nerves," he wrote to a Canadian friend from London, "but for ten years I had suffered from that malicious lie and when I had a chance to fight my defamers, I had to do it. I wanted the people of Canada to know the truth."

The strain of the marathon trial and the mental anguish brought on by years of public criticism told on Currie. He suffered from overwork and for long periods lived on a diet of milk and orange juice. In November 1933, his pet terrier went missing, and Currie caught a chill walking through the streets seeking it. He was taken to hospital where his condition grew worse. The newspapers carried regular bulletins

233

about the state of his health, and King George V cabled a personal inquiry about his condition. But pneumonia set in, and the General died on November 30 at the age of fifty-seven.

The trial ruined the reputation of the defence lawyer, Frank Regan, as Currie's latest biographer, Daniel Dancocks, has pointed out. Regan faded into obscurity, never again handled a major case, and with his law practice in tatters tried his hand at politics, only to find that his courtroom tactics had made him a political pariah.

Currie has gone down in history as Canada's greatest general, not only in the Great War but in all wars; no other military leader—not Crerar, certainly not McNaughton, not even Simonds—had the uncanny sense of tactics that seemed to have been ingrained in him at birth and had lain dormant until the call came in 1914. Yet in a sense he was a tragic hero. Some of the mud that the vindictive Hughes threw at him from the safety of the House stuck to him. In my early years in the army during the Global War, I more than once heard veteran soldiers repeating the false slander that Currie had wasted men's lives unnecessarily when the Great War was won.

2

The royal jelly With the war over at last, it was apparent that the cult of imperialism was fading and that the Empire was at a crossroads. Borden had made it clear after Passchendaele that Canada would no longer languish under the imperial thumb. She had entered the war as a vassal; now she intended to go her own way. She saw neither purpose nor profit in sitting idly by while Great Britain called the tune at the coming peace conference. She had every intention of demanding an autonomous seat at the League of Nations in the face of spirited resistance from the United States, which still thought of her as a subject state.

Chamberlain's old dream of a united empire was dead, yet something could still be salvaged from the political carnage that war had wrought. A gesture was needed—something that would quicken the blood and stir the souls of those who still made obeisance to the Union

234

Jack. As the Duke of Windsor was to recall in his ghost-written memoir *A King's Story*, "everywhere the vaunted bonds of Empire showed signs of weakening. . . . India was seething. In Canada, the resistance of French Canadians to wartime conscription had left an ugly lesion among the people. Australia resounded with radical talk and labour troubles. South Africa had its racial differences. People were exhausted by war and troubled by new economic forces that threatened to upset the foundation of their lives."

To all this, David Lloyd George had a solution: why not a royal tour of the old empire! As he told the King's eldest son, the appearance of a popular Prince of Wales "might do more to calm the discord than half a dozen solemn Imperial Conferences," all of which explains why Robert Borden was compelled to upstage his most famous general in favour of a royal stripling.

The tour that followed produced a frenzy of adulation that no other royal visit to Canada had ever aroused, even greater than that occasioned by the Prince's grandfather in 1860. There were reasons for this. The smiling prince had little competition: the country was small; people who lived on farms outnumbered those who lived in cities; there were few cars, fewer roads, and not much entertainment for the masses. But there was more to it than that. Royal tours have always attracted enthusiasm in Canada because royalty is the one glamorous asset Canadians have that Americans lack. No movie star of that or any other day—neither Garbo nor Chaplin, Pickford nor Fairbanks, Valentino nor Swanson—could compete with the pink-cheeked twenty-five-year-old, so slight, so boyishly handsome, so flawlessly turned out.

The Prince had other qualities: like his grandfather Edward VII (but not his stolid father, George V), he could make an eloquent and attractive speech without a note at the drop of a homburg, a skill he had honed with the help of Winston Churchill. His smile was absolutely dazzling: he exuded an aura of good cheer and delight that won the hearts of all those who fought to see him. His purpose, it was stated, was to thank the nation for its wartime effort—an appeal, there, to Canadian pride, indeed to Canadian cockiness. And he was *ours*.

And so, on August 5, 1919, with 225 pieces of baggage and a retinue of 20, he steamed off from Portsmouth aboard the *Renown*, the biggest battleship in the world, to capture the hearts of Canadians.

Sir Joseph Pope, who had made all the arrangements for the Prince's father during a tour in 1901, seemed to believe that the world had not turned by so much as a degree since those late Victorian days. He foresaw a series of state drives in horse-drawn landaus, complete with mounted escort, military parades, civic lunches, official dinners, and carefully arranged sightseeing detours to notable landmarks. But gilded ceremonials did not fit in with the new mood of post-war Canada. As Lloyd George had surmised, the country wanted "if not a vaudeville show, then a first-class carnival in which the Prince of Wales would play a gay, many-sided role."

The carnival began in Saint John, N.B., where the Prime Minister greeted the Prince with a ponderous speech, and nine shapely girls, dressed to represent the nine provinces, advanced to greet him, sparking a gleam in the royal eye that did not escape the British correspondents. "There was no doubt about the Prince's pleasure," one exulted.

In Halifax the royal reception was opened to the general public, a startling departure that allowed stevedores and teamsters to approach, still wearing their overalls and pumping the Prince's hand so fervently that the right one became badly swollen and he was forced to switch to his left. His mother, Queen Mary, was not amused: the whole thing, she suggested in a letter to her son, was unprecedented and undignified.

In Quebec City, the press reported that the crowds were "curious rather than demonstrative" and that only two stores had pictures of the Prince in their windows. But Toronto, where he was scheduled to open the Canadian National Exhibition, was a different story. The crowds en route became uncontrolled, almost ferocious. "They snatched at my handkerchief; they tried to tear the buttons off my coat," the Prince recalled, "welcome proof that the Royal Family still possessed a sure claim upon the affections of overseas British communities. . . ."

Sir Joseph Pope was mortified. This was a new kind of Canada. "I simply cannot understand what has come over the Canadian people, Sir," he said. "This utter lack of control—it is not at all what I would have expected." The Prince was more concerned by Pope's dictum that he must ride on horseback down the ranks of some 27,000 veterans massed at the Exhibition grounds to celebrate Warriors' Day. He was a good horseman, but he knew that the veterans would break ranks when they saw him and "God knows what this horse will do." Why not use a car, he asked. But that was the way things had always been done, and Sir Joseph assured him that the horse was specially trained and the crowds would behave with proper restraint.

The Prince was right. A human mass engulfed him and his steed, and he felt the horse's body quiver. Fortunately it could not rear up and bolt because the dense crowd held it as in a vise. The Prince was rescued and was able to mount the platform, slightly dishevelled, and speak to the cheering mob.

Pope was shocked by what he called the Canadian people's utter lack of consideration. At a civic reception at Toronto's city hall two days before, he had been outraged because everybody had been allowed to shake the royal hand, including one very dirty little boy wearing nothing but a bathing suit. As a result, the Prince had been an hour and a half late for a visit to the Royal Canadian Yacht Club, where Sir Joseph had planned a good long visit with the cream of Toronto society. "This will never do," Pope kept muttering under his breath. It was all too much for him, and on the train to Ottawa he gathered up his baggage and slipped away without so much as a goodbye.

In Ottawa, Mackenzie King pulled out all the stops in a speech in which he compared the Prince to Sir Galahad. This sort of adulation was standard in the Prince's circle. Everybody showered praise on him. The American papers burbled that he could run for Congress and easily get elected. Bonar Law, who ought to have known better, praised his "sheer commercial brilliance." The author of one of several sycophantic books about him went so far as to declare he could easily head a large corporation, a fantasy accepted by thousands of his credulous admirers. That he actually came to believe some of this twaddle is understandable.

So is the sense of betrayal that swept over the British world when he succumbed to the wiles of the elegant Mrs. Simpson.

At a civic reception in Ottawa, an elderly woman clung to him, seizing his hand and refusing to let it go as she cackled that he must marry soon and produce a bevy of offspring as handsome as himself. At the Ottawa Country Club he made the mistake of revealing that he was partial to a tune called "Johnny's in Town." From that point on, every band in the country insisted on making it a kind of theme song until he was heartily sick of it. On an unofficial side trip to Montreal (the official one was scheduled for his return from the West), the former chief justice, Sir Alexandre Lacoste, insisted on following out-of-date protocol by backing away after shaking the Prince's hand in the railway station. Overwhelmed by the aura of obeisance, he continued backing until he toppled over the edge of the platform and fell onto the rails with a thud that knocked him cold for two minutes.

The tour rolled west. At the Winnipeg Grain Exchange, the Prince made a gesture of confidence by buying fifty thousand bushels of October oats. The price immediately went down, racking up a loss for him of $375. At the Saskatoon Stampede his eye settled on some pretty girls, and he sent an equerry to bring them over. He talked to them, in one newsman's breathless report, "as freely as if he were simply a no-account farmhand." In Calgary, Bob Edwards of the irreverent *Eye-Opener* urged that at least a modicum of decorum be observed at the grand ball in his honour: "Female souses should be kept out of this affair entirely. Calgary doesn't want any of her semi-society she-drunks hanging on the Prince's neck and calling him 'Duckie.'"

Perhaps as a result, the affair was a little too decorous; everybody behaved so quietly it was assumed that Calgarians weren't much interested. But the entire country basked in a glow of pride when the Prince bought a four-thousand-acre ranch in the valley of the Highwood River, forty miles south of the city. George V was concerned, warning that his son had set a dangerous precedent for himself. Now he'd have to buy a sheep station in Australia, or an ostrich farm in South Africa, otherwise the rest of the British world would feel slighted. But, as

Edward later wrote, his impulse was far removed from imperial politics. It was the only piece of property he had ever owned, and he had been overwhelmed by "an irresistible longing to immerse myself, if only momentarily, in the simple life of the western prairies. There, I was sure, I would find occasional escape from the sometimes too-confining, too-well-ordered island life of Great Britain." Sadly, for him such escapes were to be virtually non-existent.

In the light of later events it is not easy to recall the wave of adulation that the Prince inspired in Canada. No other visiting dignitary could have matched it. In the West, he dispelled the cartoon image of the titled Englishman and the do-nothing "remittance man." A wave of pro-British sentiment rolled over the country like a comforter. We children had it dinned into us at school, where we were taught to colour the map of the world an imperial red. At home we had it dinned into us again. My father, returning from overseas and on his way back to the Yukon with my mother, never ceased to talk about actually seeing the Prince, closeup, at Banff. He had snapped his picture—a smiling young man, framed by a throng of admirers, his grey homburg tilted rakishly. Again and again that Kodak moment was brought out as my parents basked in their wonderful encounter.

In the quiet backwater of Victoria, the only alarming incident of the entire royal tour occurred. The Empress Hotel, where the welcoming ball was to be held, was suddenly crawling with Mounted Police. Someone had overheard an American phoning a friend in Seattle: "Yes, yes, I realize it is essential for you to be as close to the Prince as possible at the ball." It sounded like an assassination plot but, it turned out, was simply a young man phoning his girlfriend who wanted to be sure to have a good look at the Prince.

The round of speeches, receptions, and gala balls continued from coast to coast and back again. At the balls he showed a signal lack of democracy by shamelessly playing favourites. His prime choices, according to one reporter, Lucy Doyle of the Toronto *Telegram*, seemed to be "small, fair girls with the freshness of a youthful simplicity." One of these, a Miss Blanche Wilkinson, so attracted the Prince's eye that

239

at one affair he danced with her no fewer than nine times while others sat expectantly but vainly waiting for the royal nod. Between dances he spirited her off for a rest in the royals' room off the ballroom. "With her bobbed fair hair and big brown eyes and simple unaffectedness," Miss Doyle enthused, "Miss Wilkinson had all the air of a charming child." A startling contrast, one might say, to the dark and brooding maturity of his future consort, Wallis Simpson.

In spite of these apparent lapses, the tour was an unqualified success—one that maintained the British connection while at the same time taking into account the changed relationship with Canada. As the Prince wrote to his father, "I'm rubbing it in that although not actually Canadian born I'm a Canadian in mind & spirit & come here as such & not as a stranger or a visitor & that goes down well!! The Dominions appreciate being put on the same level as the U.K. . . . they've done so much to pull the Empire out of the war victoriously that one must recognize their established status as self-governing states of the Empire. . . ."

3

War games When the Prince of Wales wrote to his father during the royal tour about the need to recognize the dominions as self-governing states within the Empire, he was reflecting the new spirit of confidence that the Great War had instilled in the Canadian psyche. By 1920 the Canadian stereotype had undergone a significant change, partly because of the wartime successes and partly because of the Western boom. In the eyes of the world the typical Canadian was a brawny, two-fisted frontiersman, independent in action and thought, tough, bold, inventive, and hard as the impermeable granite of the Precambrian Shield. He had rolled back the frontier, opened the West, and prevailed against the Hun through daring and ingenuity.

It was not only the civilian soldiers who enhanced Canada's international reputation; it was also the young knights who fought in the clouds as members of the Royal Flying Corps. They came from small, isolated towns, mostly in the West—free spirits, impatient of military

240

tradition, reckless of rules and discipline, contemptuous of spit and polish. They handled their flimsy aircraft like spirited steeds, not surprisingly since so many were also superb horsemen.

Of the twenty-seven super-aces in the RFC—those who had downed more than thirty aircraft—eleven were Canadians. Of the ten leading aces on the Allied side, five were Canadians; all survived the war, including Billy Bishop, who ended up as the greatest living Canadian ace of all, with seventy-two kills to his credit. The Americans made a hero of Eddie Rickenbacker, whose tally was a mere twenty-one enemy planes destroyed, not enough to make him an ace in British estimation. Donald MacLaren of Ottawa, who survived his first dogfight in February 1918 on the day that Rickenbacker entered the war, knocked down forty-eight aircraft before the conflict ended, more than twice Rickenbacker's tally.

It irritated Canadians to hear Rickenbacker praised as *the* ace of aces, an imbalance that was partially corrected when *Maclean's* published George Drew's series "Canada's Fighting Airmen" in the mid-thirties. Yet even as late as 1975, American magazines continued to cite Rickenbacker as the leading Allied ace. In January of that year the men's magazine *Argosy*, in a long article on the leading fighter pilots of the war, declared that "two names stand out from all the rest—Baron Manfred von Richthofen and Captain Eddie Rickenbacker." The article dealt with other fliers, French and German, and published a list of what it claimed were the greatest aces of the Great War. But Billy Bishop and Donald MacLaren were ignored.

The Canadians' reputation for aggressiveness in the Great War was enhanced, though sometimes deplored, because they fought not only their German enemies but also their own Australian allies until it became necessary to separate the two corps in battle. They fought again with their own officers after the war ended when a series of riots broke out in the English holding camps as thousands of war-weary veterans demanded to be sent home as swiftly as possible.

The stereotypical Canadian is to be found in the cartoons of the time, where he was always known as Jack Canuck. There, each national figure was personified in pen and ink: John Bull, plump and a little self-satisfied in his waistcoat and topper; Uncle Sam, a rangy, cigar-chewing foxy grandpa. Jack Canuck was his own man, a young, clean-shaven figure, ready for action, with rolled-up sleeves, breeches, high boots, and a Stetson hat.

What changed this forthright figure, whose exploits garnered international plaudits? The Canadian stereotype has undergone a transformation since the days of Jack Canuck. "Nice" is the adjective most often applied to present-day Canadians—a nice, polite, well-mannered people who are wary of taking chances and make excellent peacekeepers, since peace is an act of compromise between two belligerents.

So what happened to Jack Canuck? What happened was William Lyon Mackenzie King, a politician whose image imprinted itself on two generations of his fellow countrymen and became, for the rest of the world, a living symbol—the embodiment of the typical Canadian. That was a mistake. King was no more the typical Canadian than a hockey player, an infantry soldier, or a fighter pilot. He was a man of no charisma, in public the blandest of the bland, whose tedious speeches, in and out of Parliament, were hedged about with qualifications and parentheses that verged on the ponderous. This was intentional, for King set himself up as the mahatma of obfuscation. Any opponent who tried to counter him found himself enmeshed in a hedgerow of verbiage. Internationally, he became known for the wartime photograph taken at the Quebec Conference—a small, rotund figure squeezed between the two contemporary giants, the charismatic Roosevelt and the eloquent Churchill. Mackenzie King—always in the middle; no Jack Canuck he.

More than one panel of historians looking back over the century has elevated King to the second position among the great Canadian prime ministers, right behind the father of the country, John A. Macdonald. This was not always so. There was a time when Mackenzie King, between elections, was perhaps the most despised politician in Canada, booed by the troops during the Second World War, scorned by many of his contemporaries. I knew one officer in the war, Pete Hepburn (tragically killed in the last week of that conflict), who spent all his spare time raging about King, a man he was convinced had ruined the country. In that he was akin to King's Conservative rival in the twenties, Arthur Meighen, whose view of the Prime Minister was one of pure, unadulterated loathing.

Yet the historians are right. For all his faults, for all his fustiness, for all his equivocations (or perhaps because of them), for all his curious private life, replete with ghosts and Ouija boards, William Lyon Mackenzie King understood his country better than any senior statesman has before or since. In his often maddening circumspection, he did his best to save Canada from itself.

His political credo followed the basic Canadian government policy and harked back to the time of his hero, Laurier: first, somehow to keep the fractious country patched together; second, to prevent it from being dominated by another. To achieve this difficult feat, compromise was essential, and King was a master of compromise. He had learned it in his years as a deputy minister of labour under Laurier when he managed to settle some forty strikes. He had honed those skills when, in June 1914, the Rockefellers hired him to head their department of industrial relations. In that position the great compromiser managed to take the heat off John D. Rockefeller and his son following the infamous Ludlow massacre in their strikebound Colorado mines, for which they were blamed. King solved the problem and the strike by inventing the company union, another compromise and a thorn in the side of organized labour in the years that followed. But it pleased his employers, who were forever grateful because the compromise managed to keep the more effective United Mine Workers out of their hair for decades.

King got his break in post-war politics at the National Liberal Convention in Ottawa in August 1919, after the death of Laurier the previous February. He won the party leadership on the final ballot against W.S. Fielding, the veteran Nova Scotian who had been Laurier's minister of finance. Fred Griffin, the Toronto *Star*'s top reporter, remembered the scene: King on the platform during the final vote-taking, "his face agleam with perspiration, his collar wilted, his eyes tell-tale under the strain, as he fingered his chin before a barrage of eyes." When the final votes were counted, pandemonium broke out and, according to Griffin, King "proved historically splendid when his turn came to speak."

King came to power with a ready-made personal platform outlined in his ponderous tome *Industry and Humanity*, of which he was inordinately proud, but which most of his colleagues found unreadable. Had they read it, in Bruce Hutchison's view, they would never have nominated him for leader of the party, for the book established him as a small-l liberal and more than hinted at the social reforms of the future: old age pensions first, then unemployment insurance, and then, under King's successors, such radical departures from laissez-faire policies as medicare. In championing King as Liberal leader his supporters were unwittingly presiding at the birth of a social revolution, one that would underline the fundamental differences between social democracy in Canada and in the United States.

When King took over the leadership of the Liberal Party in 1919, Borden's political days were numbered. The Prime Minister resigned in 1920, leaving a considerable legacy: Canadian autonomy. He had abandoned Laurier's credo that "when Britain is at war, Canada is at war" and, by ensuring Canadian representation at the Peace Conference and in the League of Nations, paved the way for the creation of a new organization to replace the Empire. The dominions, he had said in 1917, deserved recognition as "autonomous nations of an Imperial commonwealth." He could not have succeeded, of course, had it not been for the record of the Canadian Corps in the war—a record that made it impossible for Great Britain, or, indeed, the United States, to frustrate Canada's determination to free herself from the mother country's domination.

Commonwealth! That was a new word, and Borden was one of the very first to make use of it. To many Canadians, especially the English-born, it was just another word for Empire—a handy euphemism, no more. The change to which Borden gave impetus would come only after he left office.

244

At the end of the Imperial Conference of 1926, the aging Lord Balfour, himself a former British prime minister, issued his report, famous in Canada, that declared the five dominions to be "autonomous communities within the British Empire, equal in status, subordinate in no way to one another in any aspect of their domestic or external affairs, though united by a common allegiance to the Crown, and freely associated as members of the British Commonwealth of Nations." Events moved slowly in those days; it was another five years before the Balfour Report led to the Statute of Westminster, and Canada, which had entered the war with no voice in imperial affairs, was at last autonomous.

By that time the bugle call of empire had become a reedy plaint. The so-called Chanak crisis of 1922 marked for Canada the nadir of imperialism and the humiliation of Arthur Meighen who, for one brief but not very shining tenure, had succeeded Borden as prime minister.

For sheer brilliance, this gaunt and brooding Westerner towered over his political colleagues and opponents. As a debater he had no peer; many members of the Liberal opposition were wary of taking him on in any verbal contest. His speeches, in which no word was ever wasted, were marvels of lucid argument; his memory for facts and figures, as well as people's names, was prodigious; his energy was phenomenal.

Nothing seemed to rattle Meighen. A voracious reader, he had little time for idle chatter. Aloof, austere, slightly forbidding, he had none of the easy camaraderie that is so often the key to political popularity. He is the most tragic figure in Canadian politics, though he himself would not have seen it in that light. He was twice prime minister but served for no more than twenty months, brought low by his own stubborn inflexibility and the wiles of his shrewder opponent. Compromise— the one quality essential to success in Canadian politics—was not in his makeup. He was forty-six years old when he succeeded Borden. A lawyer from Portage la Prairie, Manitoba, a cabinet minister and former secretary of state, he had been born in the nineteenth century and still seemed to be part of it. He believed in "the doctrine of work," which he held to be "the normal condition of man." As his biographer has written, "it was work more than politics that consumed his time."

One could scarcely describe Meighen as forward looking. The war had changed the way Canadians thought and acted; the so-called roar of the twenties might be no more than a distant drumbeat, especially in the small towns, but American jazz, American fashions, and American dance crazes had their effect, especially among the short-skirted, foxtrotting young who, after the painful war years, insisted on blowing off steam. Meighen could not get it into his head that the old days were gone forever. The great task of Canadians, he declared, was "to get back . . . to old time sanity of thought and action, to get back to our high standards of living and character—standards handed down to us by our forebears."

He was not very popular in his own party. Almost all of Meighen's colleagues in Cabinet were opposed to his selection as leader. Yet none could deny his brilliance, even though, ironically, that brilliance had got him into political hot water. In the election campaign of 1921 he—a Westerner—managed to alienate the West by making the protective tariff the central theme of his campaign. His opponent, the master of double-talk, had no intention of tying the Liberal Party to any cut-and-dried policy on this, the most controversial issue in Canadian politics. Mackenzie King promised "a tariff for the consumer and producer" that would also "take care of the needs of all the industries." What did that mean? The Liberal candidates could take it any way they wished.

So multi-talented that he was handed the toughest political jobs, Meighen had drafted the 1917 Military Service Bill that led to the searing debate in Parliament over conscription and cost the Tory party Quebec. In spite of his oratorical brilliance, Meighen tended to suffer from foot-in-mouth syndrome. In replying to Laurier's demands for a national referendum before conscription was invoked, he blurted out, "Is it any wonder that a great proportion of the red-blooded sons of this country say that the reason the Right Hon. Leader of the Opposition now wants to take a referendum is because the forward portion of our population is overseas. . . ." Meighen undoubtedly had no idea of the slur he had cast on French Canadians, but the words were there in

Hansard's cold type. Were the anti-conscriptionists somehow lacking in red-bloodedness? And that reference to the "forward portion of our population": did that imply that the French Canadians who opposed his bill were somehow backward?

Having delivered a body blow to his own party in Quebec, Meighen went on to antagonize organized labour. In 1919, he was sent off to Winnipeg along with Senator Gideon Robertson to try to end the general strike that had brought that city to a standstill. The Ottawa *Citizen* dubbed this foray "the government's strike-breaking expedition." What Meighen learned about the strike came exclusively from opinions and information tendered by the anti-strike faction. His solution was the "rapid deportation" of the strike leaders to their home countries, a draconian approach flawed by the fact that at least one of them had been born in Canada. The strike ended, but Meighen remained convinced that such a "usurpation of government authority" could lead to "the perfection of Bolshevism."

In the election of December 1921, Meighen was swamped not only by King's Liberals but also by the new Progressive movement that denied King a clear majority. The Liberals got 116 seats; the Progressives stormed out of the West to gain 65 (24 of these in Ontario); and Meighen's badly bruised Tory party was reduced to 50. With four other seats going to independent or labour members, King found it necessary to seek support from the Progressives in order to govern— a not too difficult task given the intensity of the Western feeling against Meighen.

In 1922 Meighen committed the greatest political gaffe of all during what came to be known as the Chanak affair, an episode that, it was feared, could lead to another European war. The infidel was at the gates, or so the British professed to believe. Chanak was a small seaport on the Dardanelles, the narrow strait that connects the Mediterranean with the Black Sea. The strait's neutrality had been guaranteed in 1920 by the Treaty of Sèvres, mainly to prevent the Turks from grabbing it. Two years later the Ottoman dynasty had given way to a new power in Turkey. Mustafa Kemal, head of the revolutionary government, having routed the invading Greek army, pointedly refused to retain the old treaty and was poised to seize the strait. Shades of Sulayman the Magnificent!

The British, whose small garrison at Chanak was bottled up by Turkish troops, dispatched warships to the scene to prevent any attempt to close the Dardanelles. Lloyd George urged that in this crisis Canada should stand by the Empire. Both Australia and New Zealand promised to send contingents. Mackenzie King wasn't so eager. A threatened show of force by a united Empire might bring Mustafa Kemal to heel, but what if it didn't? Was King prepared to wage another war? Meighen apparently was. To a cheering crowd of fellow Conservatives at Toronto's King Edward Hotel he cried, "Let there be no dispute as to where I stand. When Britain's message came, then Canada should have said: 'Ready, aye ready; we stand by you.'" The phrase was Laurier's, uttered before the Great War. But Laurier's day was done and the times had changed.

The crisis fizzled out, but Meighen's words were to haunt him for the rest of his career. He did his best to retrieve his position, explaining that he wasn't really talking about a force of arms—only seeking an expression of solidarity within the Empire. It did no good. To Canadians who had just gone through four bloody years of war, Meighen seemed to be calling for another expeditionary force. Did he really expect young Canadians to rally to that cause? A war-weary nation was in no mood to chance another imperial adventure in an obscure Mediterranean port. Meighen's words suggested how out of touch he was with reality. If this was the "old time sanity of thought and action" that Meighen longed for, the country wanted no part of it.

The Chanak crisis underlined the emerging change in imperial relations. To this point, Great Britain had expected the dominions to answer the call of the Empire. Unlike the others, Canada was not prepared to jump when the British lion roared. The government and the people made it clear that Canada had no intention of embarking on every two-bit foreign adventure in which the mother country might find itself enmeshed. Chanak was a milestone on the long road to autonomy.

Even as the imperial dreams began to fade and the concept of a looser association of British dominions took form, darker suspicions of another empire—the American—began to take shape in the overheated imagination of Canadian military leaders. It was obvious that the only possible threat to Canada, if one existed, would come from south of the border. But would it? The prospect was fanciful. More than ninety years had gone by since the last American soldier had been driven from the country. Public figures boasted about the longest undefended border in the world; Canada and the United States enjoyed the best of relations. Still—shouldn't the possibility of an American invasion at least be considered and planned for? And what was the best way to counter such an attack? Why, by a pre-emptive strike, surely. Catch the Yankees napping and forestall any attempt to capture Canada by turning the tables and seizing key communication centres, canals, and bridges in the border states. The best defence must be offence.

This madcap plan seems to have sprung full blown from the mind of Colonel (later Brigadier General) James Sutherland "Buster" Brown, an ardent imperialist and a decorated war veteran (DSO, CMG) who held the key post of director of military operations and intelligence in the Canadian Army. In the spring of 1921, Brown applied for permission to drive incognito to the United States "in order to make a personal reconnaissance of four roads to Portland (Maine)." Accordingly, he and four officers, all lieutenant-colonels, and each decorated with the DSO, set out in civilian clothes to make a clandestine tour of the northern parts of New York state. The result was a sixty-page foolscap report, complete with fifty-six photographs and enlivened by a military assessment of the character of the people together with some history of previous conflicts.

Brown and his fellow colonels were, quite simply, spies. He extended his investigation the following year, driving 1,088 miles and producing another secret report on the neighbouring state of Vermont, also sixty pages long and containing as many photographs. There were other similar investigations. In 1926, for instance, a fellow lieutenant-colonel made a reconnaissance of the Upper Michigan Peninsula, a journey of

2,664 miles that took thirteen days. All these secret reports made up Canada's official, but highly secret, Defence Scheme No. 1 through most of the twenties.

Though any modern reader perusing Brown's meticulous reports might be excused for thinking him a bit of a nut, he was, in fact, one of the most highly regarded staff officers in the Canadian Army. His spying expeditions were undertaken with the approval of his superiors and the support of many of his fellow officers. He was a handsome man, sporting a full and apparently waxed Victorian moustache. His proud Loyalist ancestry explains his affection for England, his suspicion of Americans, and his rigid, sometimes pugnacious, Toryism.

The spectacle of these five brass hats tooling along the gravel roads, snapping their Kodaks at bridges and everything else from canal locks to highway overpasses, has a zany flavour about it, reminiscent of the silent comedies of the day: Keystone Kops crowded into one of the popular touring cars—a rented McLaughlin Six in this case. A few sections from Brown's secret Vermont report more than hint at both his character and his detailed strategic observations:

> BURLINGTON. . . . The tradespeople and others we came in contact with seemed to be very affable and the whole city struck one as not being so "American" as other U.S. cities one has visited.

> WELLS RIVER is a place of strategical importance being a focus of highway and railway routes. . . .

> While we stopped here near North Duxbury a man employed on the state roads in repair patrol came up. He was characteristic of a large number of men of the state—fat and lazy but pleasant and congenial. By way of conversation I said—pointing at the Camel's Hump "that must be one of your highest." He answered—"The highest in the state, it's the Camel's Hump." I then said, "You people here are like the camel, you can go seven days without a drink." The "Green Mountain"

boy answered—"By God, guess you're right. Mor'n that. My God! I'd go for a glass of beer. I'm going to 'Canady' to get some more."

RAILWAY ROUTES: There are really only four good routes running north and south through the state to the Canadian frontier. The two better ones run respectively to the shore of Lake Champlain and up the valley of the Connecticut [River]. . . . From these north and south routes there are five entrances to Canada. . . .

I got a stationer in Burlington to take an interest in the question of getting out a map of Vermont to show the physical features. I put it up to him from the standpoint of tourists and engineers. . . . He, of course, had no idea who I was except that I was a Canadian. I am collecting various materials together which will be handed over to the Asst. Director of Military Surveys to see if we cannot piece together a useful strategical map of Vermont similar to the one we got out of Northern New York.

Throughout the rural districts, English, Scotch and Irish names prevail. The men appear to be of two types, all apparently averaging about 5 feet, 9 inches to 5 feet, 10 inches. The first type is rather a lean, severe looking man and the second type is a fleshy, round-faced, rather congenial individual. If they are not actually lazy they have a very deliberate way of working and apparently believe in frequent rests and gossip. The women throughout the rural districts appear to be a heavy and not very comely lot.

SUMMARY. . . . The military importance of Vermont consists of it being a buffer for protection of part of the Canadian frontier . . . and being an obstruction or barrier between the New England states and New York state for any military combination against Canada. . . .

Whatever remarks I may have made about the people of Vermont there is no doubt but that they would make good soldiers if aroused but I think that they would have to have a good cause to be enthusiastic. . . . There is a large and influential number of American citizens, who are not altogether pleased with democracy as it exists in the United States of America and . . . have a sneaking regard for Great Britain, British Law and Constitution and general civilization and . . . are proud and boastful of the British descent.

Had any American or, indeed, any Canadian newspaper gained access to the results of Brown's spy expeditions, one can imagine the international brouhaha that would have followed. Brown went to great lengths to make sure that only the commanding officers of each military district had access to the VERY SECRET report and that it not be discussed with anybody. He travelled across the country to sell the scheme to the commanders of each military district, one of whom, Major General George Pearkes, later described it as "a fantastic desperate plan [which] just might have worked." The quixotic colonel did not envisage a wholesale attack on the United States but thought that flying columns of cavalry, machine-gun units, cyclists, and mobile infantry might be able to divert U.S. forces to the flanks and, as Pearkes was to put it, "hold them out of central Canada until Britain intervened or second thoughts prevailed in Washington."

Brown continued to expand his scheme, coming up with a secret report on the defence of Quebec and the lower St. Lawrence. "The day may come when the United States may think she is strong enough to bluff the British with a threat of war," he declared in 1928. "It is necessary then for the Empire to be in a strong position to meet this threat."

But that same year Andrew McNaughton became chief of the general staff, and Brown's defence planning was doomed. The new CGS placed the emphasis on harmony between Britain and the United States: "Politically Canada's position vis-à-vis the United States has been immensely

252

stabilized," he wrote. Brown's assumptions were scrapped, and all the documents relating to Defence Scheme No. 1 were burned. Happily some of the raw material, such as the report on Vermont quoted above, was saved.

It was not until 1974 that a Canadian historian, Robert A. Preston, revealed that, just as Brown was planning an aggressive repulse of any possible attack from the United States, the Americans themselves were plotting their own invasion scenario. Like Brown and his colleagues, American field officers in civilian clothes were touring about Canada, snapping their own photos, envisaging possible attacks on Halifax, the Great Lakes, Winnipeg, and the Pacific coast. In short, they were posing the same potential threat to Canada that the eccentric Buster Brown and his zealous band of Colonel Blimps had gone to such pains to counter.

4

Having tasted the prime minister's life only to meet humiliating defeat *King's* in the 1921 election, Arthur Meighen hungered for the office again in *gambit* 1925, apparently at any cost. That would prove his final undoing. His own insistence on high tariffs to protect the hated Eastern manufacturers had helped bring the Conservative Party low, but there was more to it than that. The war had shattered the traditional two-party system, and a new political force—the Progressive movement—had pushed the Tories into third place in Parliament.

The West was in open revolt. Wartime inflation, a prairie drought, and continued Eastern insistence on protection had caught the farmers in a trap between fixed debt charges and higher costs on the one hand and falling agricultural prices on the other. The West could not forget the 1911 attacks by Eastern manufacturers on Laurier's reciprocity program. Nor could it forget how, in 1917, Borden's Union Government stripped the farmers of their labour force by revoking the exemption of their sons from military service.

Old-time party loyalties, which had never been strong in the prairies, were swept aside. Even in Ontario a farmer-labour group seized political power; in 1919 the United Farmers of Ontario took over the provincial legislature. In 1921, the United Farmers of Alberta won a provincial majority. The following year, the United Farmers of Manitoba prevailed. Only in Saskatchewan did the Liberal government survive and only by giving in to the farmers and severing its official ties with the federal party. When, in 1919, Thomas Crerar, the federal minister of agriculture, along with nine Western members of the Union Government left the party, the stage was set for the rise of the Progressive movement.

The Progressives considered themselves a movement rather than a party. Their phenomenal rise signalled the West's disgust with Eastern machine politics and the two old parties. The Progressives held the balance of power in the House; without their support the Liberals could not govern. But the Progressives refused to dirty their hands in what they saw as a political cesspool. Although they had beaten the Conservatives by fifteen seats, they rejected the opportunity to become the official Opposition and, in doing so, hastened their own demise.

The decline of the Progressives can be seen in the results of the 1925 election. The position of the two old parties was reversed. The Conservatives under Meighen garnered 116 seats, the Liberals only 99. King himself and eight cabinet ministers went down to defeat. The Progressives had won only 24—a catastrophic decline from 65. In addition, there were two Labour winners and four Independents.

I was only five years old at the time, but I can still remember the magic word "Meighen" cropping up again and again in the drawing-room conversations. Dawson City was a Tory town then, its hierarchies dominated by Anglophiles, returned soldiers, and Conservative political appointees. My father was all three, and so, although I didn't quite know who or what "Meighen" was, I sensed that he was a towering, if controversial, figure in the life of our family and the country.

Even though the Conservatives now held the most seats, the Liberals had the right to stay in office if they could muster a majority in Parliament. To remain the governing party they must depend on the support of almost all the Progressive and Independent members. Shocked by the loss of an election he had expected to win easily, King was determined to cling to power by maintaining this razor-thin majority. His first move was to confer with Viscount Byng of Vimy, who had been appointed governor general in 1921. Thus the stage was set for what became known as the King-Byng Affair.

That critical incident was muddied from the outset because the two men misunderstood one another in their initial meeting. Each subsequently gave a different version of what had been said. King asked Byng's approval of his plan to govern with the help of the Progressives; if he couldn't win a majority, he would resign. Byng took this to mean a simple trade; if King lost a vote of confidence, he would step down and Meighen would become prime minister. King, on the other hand, later insisted that Byng had given him the chance to show that he could govern the country for a reasonable (though unspecified) period of time. Having thus proved himself, he would then have the right to call a new election, which meant the dissolution of Parliament. Enmeshed in vagueness, King's so-called deal with the Governor General would lead to controversy if he lost a vote of confidence.

The Government barely survived its first test on January 12, 1926. When the Tory Opposition moved an amendment to the Speech from the Throne, seven Progressives indicated that they would vote in its favour, which would defeat the Liberals by two votes. Vincent Massey, an unelected member of King's cabinet, managed to talk some of them out of it. With the help of the Independents, the Liberals defeated the motion by three votes.

But a much more dangerous issue surfaced in February, when Conservative MP Harry Stevens rose in the House to deliver a scathing indictment of corruption in the customs department. Well aware of flagrant abuse in Customs, the Liberals had ignored it to keep it from becoming an issue in the 1925 election. Now Stevens had unearthed their long-buried secret at the worst possible time. Addressing the House from midnight until four in the morning, he revealed the dimensions of the worst scandal in parliamentary history since the Pacific Railway scandal forced John A. Macdonald's government to resign in 1873.

The Customs scandal stemmed from a dramatic change in Canadian drinking habits brought about by the Great War. The Woman's Christian Temperance Union, frustrated in its attempts to establish a form of prohibition in Canada, used the war to support legislation that helped switch the nation from wet to dry. Alcohol, the WCTU argued, was needed for the war effort; moreover, heavy drinking could erode morale. But after the war, indeed *because* of the war, attitudes began to change. Thousands of young men were introduced to the army's rum ration, which warmed their bellies and stiffened their resolve before a battle. The daily tot of rum was strong stuff—so strong that any man who could choke out a "thank you" after knocking it back was allowed a second tot—called a "door prize." Many went into action slightly tipsy; some were roaring drunk. One officer of the 4th Canadian Mounted Rifles was so intoxicated that he pointed his men the wrong way and tried to open fire on the church at Mont St. Eloi, several miles behind the lines. Yet even a temperance advocate as strict as Brigadier General Victor Odlum was finally forced to set aside his own stern principles in the interests of morale. The best known of the army padres, the Reverend Charles Gordon, shelved his principles, too, declaring that "rum is an absolute necessity to the soldier in the field. I would rather dispossess them of their rifles."

John Harold Becker wrote in his memoir of the war, "It is my firm conviction . . . that this was the only means of keeping us from complete exhaustion. . . . If we had not been supplied I fear that not many of us would have survived. While we were engaged in this way, an organization in Canada, the W.C.T.U., were going up and down the countryside crying the terrible effect of the rum ration on these Sunday school boys from Canadian farms and villages and did their best to have the ration discontinued."

The temperance movement had backed the suffragist movement when its followers realized that the only way to fight the demon rum was through political clout. Now they had the clout. By 1922 both Canada and every province save Quebec had extended the franchise to women, largely because of their unstinting support of the war effort.

But the war had an unexpected effect: after four years in the trenches, the youth of Canada had learned to drink, and a good many wanted to go on drinking when they returned. Women's vote or no, the temperance fever started to cool.

The legacy of those moralistic years was two appalling all-Canadian institutions: the government liquor store and the beverage room, better known as a beer parlour. The first was an austere and characterless shop where the booze was discreetly hidden and buyers had to sign a bureaucratic document. The second was a crowded but cheerless room, gloomy and malodorous, where all signs of levity were frowned on—no standing at the bar (there wasn't one), no singing, no talking in loud voices, no entertainment of any kind, and no mingling of the sexes. In some jurisdictions a man was prevented by a barrier from enjoying a glass with his wife. As a result, Canadians became a hard-drinking lot, swilling entire bottles of liquor in the absence of mixed drinks, swallowing their booze raw without a chaser, or brown-bagging their little-brown-jugs illegally under nightclub tables. It took a quarter of a century and another war before this masquerade was abandoned and the ineffective grip of the provincial control boards was finally loosened.

Canada never had the all-out prohibition that rocked the United States in the Roaring Twenties. As the whisky ads used to declare in the early nineteen-fifties, "Canadians are a moderate people." It was not in the Canadian makeup to go to extremes as the Americans often did, not only in the prohibition years but also during the campaign for "zero tolerance" in the drug-taking days of a later generation. There were other reasons: the soldiers' new attitudes, the presence of a large French and Irish Catholic population that used wine as a sacrament, and the fact that in Canada the sale of alcohol was a provincial, not a federal, responsibility. Quebec was wet and so was British Columbia. Manitoba and Alberta were dry but on the verge of change. Saskatchewan had just gone wet; New Brunswick and Prince Edward Island were dry, to the delight of the island doctors who made small fortunes peddling prescriptions that allowed topers to buy liquor "for health reasons." Nova Scotia was wet for a time while Ontario was

257

dry except for wine, which continued to be legal in strengths as high as 28 percent, thanks to the powerful grape-growers' lobby.

Canadians didn't need to make gin in bathtubs. Distilleries were perfectly legal if they sold their products to a foreign country, delivering a handsome profit to the government in the form of excise and customs duties. But these duties were evaded as trucks and boats loaded with Canadian rye whisky crossed the international border, performed miraculous about-turns, and deposited gallons of booze onto Canadian soil, free of any government charges. As a result the customs department was a hotbed of bribery while smuggling became a way of life for those who lived along the border. In the words of *Saturday Night*, "Smuggling into Canada . . . has increased with such startling rapidity that it has become a national menace."

To all this the government turned a blind eye. In 1925, with an election in the offing, King didn't want any whisper of scandal. When a delegation of prominent businessmen formed themselves into the Commercial Protective Association, which urged the laws be tightened, he threw them a small bone by offering the services of an investigator, Walter Duncan of the finance department. Duncan and his tiny staff spent four months gathering a mountain of damning information, which King virtually ignored. R.P. Sparks, president of the protective association, got nowhere when he wrote to the Prime Minister in February 1925 that "from the standpoint of loss of revenue I think the smuggling business is second only to the loss occasioned by the Canadian National Railways." Sparks's chief target was Jacques Bureau, the minister of customs, whose department reeked of corruption. King's solution was to promote Bureau to the Senate, a body that he had recently, in an unguarded moment, declared needed reforming.

Shaken by the results of the 1925 election, his own job as party leader in jeopardy, King had got himself a safe seat in Prince Albert. Counting on the corporal's guard of Progressives to bolster him, he hoped for the best. But those hopes were dashed when Sparks, fed up with the government's dalliance and the increasing evidence of corruption in the customs department, laid the facts on the desk of Harry Stevens.

Now, in the Green Chamber, King listened with mounting alarm as Stevens denounced Bureau, the former minister. "Already nine filing cabinets filled with records containing damaging evidence have been removed . . . taken away to the home of the ex-minister and there destroyed."

He castigated Bureau's successor, Georges Boivin. "No warehouse receipt was surrendered; no order was given; simply a jingle of the phone, a familiar voice, and $200,000 worth of alcohol was turned loose." In that deal alone, Stevens declared, the government was defrauded of more than $200,000 "either by gross incompetence or connivance."

He was pitiless with Joseph Bisaillon, chief preventive officer for the department of customs in Montreal. "The worst of the crooks, he is the intimate of ministers, the petty favourite of this government . . . [who] rolls in wealth and opulence, a typical debauched and debauching government official."

And he charged the government "with knowledge, with positive knowledge, with abundance of proof, that the grossest violations of the customs laws were being perpetrated in this country for a year." With that, Stevens demanded the government convene a parliamentary committee of inquiry. He got it—a nine-man committee to look into the affairs of the customs department in detail.

The committee reported back in June 1926 with a unanimous decision: the government was guilty as charged. It backed up everything Stevens had said and went further. Smuggling was a two-way street. Millions of dollars' worth of liquor was being smuggled back into Canada tax-free, with forged receipts that were seldom scrutinized closely by corrupt or inattentive customs officials. In one instance, the committee found that six million gallons of liquor that supposedly left Maritime ports under bond had stayed in Canada at a loss to the taxpayers of more than $52 million in excise duties. In another case, the customs department, either through incredible gullibility or pure chicanery, had accepted the word of a known bootlegger that a quantity of Scotch whisky had been off-loaded in Buffalo and therefore wasn't liable for duty—a loss estimated at between $420,000 and $700,000.

The catalogue of fraud and plunder continued. In New Brunswick, one bootlegger, Moses Aziz, sentenced to a year in jail after his third offence, had been released without imprisonment because a local Liberal candidate, J.G. Robichaud, swore that he had been "the highest help to us during this campaign and we cannot do without his services." Georges Boivin had sold an entire shipment of seized liquor to a friendly distiller, former Member of Parliament W.J. Hushion, for thirty-six cents a gallon, tax-free, because it was listed as denatured alcohol. Denatured or not, the minister allowed Hushion to export it to the United States at a fancy price as fit for consumption.

In the face of this damning mountain of evidence, King's political future looked black. He had been trying to muddle along with the help of the Progressives, but that simon-pure movement could scarcely be expected to support a party so deeply enmeshed in scandal.

Stevens rose on June 22 and in a hard-hitting speech moved to expand the committee's report into an outright vote of censure on a government that had yielded to "improper pressure from the underworld." If it carried, this would be a death blow to the government in the coming election. The Stevens motion had to be buried, and King was prepared to bury it as the result of a deal with J.S. Woodsworth, one of the two Labour members in the House. King had dangled a choice plum before the one-time Methodist parson: a promise to institute old-age pensions in the coming session. That was enough for the pious reformer, who didn't want Meighen in power anyway. He proposed an amendment to the Stevens motion—that a royal commission would continue the customs inquiry! It was not much, but it would give King some breathing space: royal commissions move deliberately. The move served also to signal the promise inherent in King's *Industry and Humanity*: the Liberal Party was being nudged to the left.

After a long wrangle, the Speaker declared Woodsworth's "whitewash motion" in order. But would it pass? The Progressives, King's only hope, seemed to be coming apart at the seams, and when the vote was taken, after a long and exhausting wrangle on Friday, June 25, the motion lost by 117 to 115. Ten minutes later the government suffered a second defeat when a Progressive motion to strengthen and expand Stevens's damning motion was ruled in order, 118 to 116. The debate continued all night and into Saturday's dawn. King tried to end it with a move to adjourn that was again lost, 115 to 114. At five that morning, the exhausted Prime Minister gave in and allowed the expanded amendment. The House, with a sigh of relief, passed a second adjournment vote, 115 to 114.

King knew that this was the end, not only of the Liberal government but also his own position as party leader. The best he could do was to ask the Governor General for dissolution and go into the next election as prime minister, a lame duck, perhaps, but better than being discredited in the Commons before the campaign began. Defeat at the polls was preferable to extinction in Parliament; after all, the Stevens motion had yet to be debated and could not be debated until the electorate chose a new parliament. As always, King played for time.

Now the crisis born of the original misunderstanding between the two men reached its climax. The Governor General was astounded at King's request. Hadn't King promised him that if he couldn't govern he would step aside for Meighen? Now, surely, Meighen deserved his turn. Byng couldn't believe that King was prepared to fling aside what he saw as a gentleman's agreement. But King saw it quite differently. He *had* governed successfully for five months; surely that was enough to seal the deal. Lord Byng couldn't agree; after three separate interviews with King over that weekend, he refused dissolution, accepted King's resignation, and called on Meighen to form a government.

An eager Meighen seized the opportunity. At last the prize was his! The House met on Monday afternoon. King explained that the public interest demanded a dissolution, but His Excellency "having declined to accept my advice to grant a dissolution, to which I believe under the British practice I was entitled, I immediately tendered my resignation, which His Excellency has been graciously pleased to accept." With that he moved the House adjourn.

What was Meighen hearing? Had he really won? "Mr. Speaker," he blurted, "if I caught the Prime Minister's words aright, they were that the House adjourn; that the Government has resigned. I wish to add only that I am . . ."

King would not let him finish. "I might say that this motion is not debatable," he pointed out.

Meighen tried again. There should be a conference between him and the Prime Minister to work out the business for the rest of the session. But King was obdurate: "At the present time there is no government. I am not Prime Minister; I cannot speak as Prime Minister. I can speak as only one member of this House and it is as a humble member of this House that I submit that inasmuch as His Excellency is without an adviser, I do not think it would be proper for this House to proceed to discuss anything. If the House is to continue its proceeding someone must assume, as His Excellency's adviser, *the responsibility for his Excellency's refusal to grant a dissolution in the existing circumstances. . . .*"

The emphasis here is mine. King had yet to grasp the true significance of what he was saying, while Meighen, impatient for office (he was sworn in that night), failed totally to understand it. Yet King would soon discern, at the end of that long constitutional tunnel, a faint flicker of light that would break into a fiery beacon when he at last realized the weapon the Governor General had unwittingly handed him.

Under the archaic parliamentary rules of that day (revised in 1931), no minister who accepted a salary from the Crown could hold office without a confirming by-election. Meighen, then, was forced to resign and sit on the sidelines while King, slowly realizing the significance of the Governor General's action, began to pursue his strategy.

He launched his attack on Wednesday. His first victim was John Drayton, Meighen's deputy, who had taken on the role of acting prime minister. But had he taken the requisite oath of office, King asked (or, as he put it in his roundabout fashion, had he "complied with the constitutional practice in assuming office?"). Drayton stumbled. He didn't think he needed to take any oath since he was receiving no salary as a member of Meighen's new cabinet. But, as King knew, in his reference to "constitutional practice," an oath of office was mandatory. New cabinet members had to be sworn in before they could vote to spend the taxpayers' money. One by one King polled this shadow cabinet, and one by one they admitted they had not taken the oath. Under the law they could not take it without resigning their seats as Meighen had done, thus destroying the Conservatives' majority. King bore in: the country was being governed without a single minister of the Crown and without a prime minister with a seat in the House!

Only in Canada would such a contretemps be possible. The United States would never face it because the United States had no royal personage to deal with nor did the president sit in Congress. England would never face it because it would be unthinkable for the King to act without the advice of his first minister. But Byng, the old soldier who spoke for the King, was a political tyro. A pseudo-regent, he was a victim of the awkward imperial fiction in which a colony was not a colony and a dominion, at least on paper, was a subject dominion. Now that dominion was politically rudderless, without a prime minister and without a cabinet.

All the actors in the bizarre customs affair—the incompetent Jacques Bureau, the corrupt Joseph Bisaillon, the wretched, unjailed bootlegger Moses Aziz—faded into the wings as Byng and King took centre stage. Scandals, after all, were part of the political texture. The great John A. had survived the Pacific scandal and gone on to be acknowledged as the father of the nation. Clifford Sifton and his deputy, James Allan Smart, had emerged unscathed from the mire of the immigration department's spoils system—Sifton as a revered elder statesman, Smart as lieutenant-governor of Manitoba. But this was different. This went to the very essence of responsible government: a British peer turning back the pages of history.

There had been a time when governors general had interfered in Canadian domestic affairs, but that time was past. Canada had won her independence on the battlefields of Flanders and in the conference rooms of Downing Street. Now, as King shouted at Parliament, "If, at the instance of one individual, a Prime Minister can be put into office and with a Ministry which is not yet formed, be permitted to vote all the supplies necessary to carry on the Government of Canada for a year, we have reached a condition in this country that threatens the constitutional liberty, freedom and right in all parts of the world!"

With that florid statement, King set the pattern for the election that followed. Who was the "individual" to whom he referred? King didn't want to say, but everybody knew. Byng had insisted that Meighen be given a chance to govern, as, indeed, King had been given a chance. Could Meighen govern? The question was put to a vote when James Robb, the former minister of finance, moved that Meighen's cabinet, if legal, had no right to sit in the House and, if illegal, no right to transact business. The vote came two hours after midnight on July 2, with the Dominion Day celebrations still echoing on Parliament Hill. As always the vote was close, but for Meighen it was devastating: Conservatives, 95; Liberals, 96.

Parliament had shown that Meighen could not govern. It had been, to paraphrase the Duke of Wellington at Waterloo, "a near run thing." Nearer, in fact, than anybody had a right to expect. King had been saved by an unexpected stroke of luck—the unwitting vote of a Progressive who, under parliamentary practice, had been paired with a sick colleague and agreed not to vote and then forgot about it when the division was called. But the vote could not be changed. The government was defeated. And Meighen must advise the Governor General to dissolve Parliament— ironically, the very action Byng had refused to take on Mackenzie King's advice a few days before.

Meighen, in his innocence, was convinced that he would win the coming election: the customs scandal and his party's strong support of protection, outlined on the hustings with his own undeniable eloquence—these would do the job. As Bruce Hutchison has written, "the campaign went against Meighen not by accident but by the sure logic of history." Day after day King hammered his thesis home, "that an English governor and a Tory minister were trying to reduce Canada to a colony." Byng was the most popular governor general in Canadian history—the hero of Vimy, the darling of the people, lauded by the press and by his contemporaries. He had emerged from the war as one of the few general officers known to have the human touch, and he

264

seemed the obvious choice to occupy the vice-regal mansion. But none of that mattered now. The voters were in no mood to see their hard-won independence challenged by a titled Englishman. Again and again King made the point that no British sovereign had refused a dissolution to a prime minister in more than a century. The results on the night of September 14 confirmed his strategy: Liberals, 116; Conservatives, 91. Who could have predicted that upset in June?

King could also count on the support of the United Farmers and Progressive candidates, twenty-four in all. It was the end of Arthur Meighen and the confirmation of Liberal power: in the next three decades, William Lyon Mackenzie King and his successors would run Canada save for a merciful five-year respite during the Great Depression.

5

When the Great War ended, a tidal wave of cultural nationalism washed over the country. The prevailing thesis held that Canada had come of age at Vimy, albeit at appalling cost. The strident Yankee boasts that *they* had won the war grated on the country's soul and contributed to the growing anti-Americanism that was the dark side of nationalism. It became fashionable to view certain aspects of American culture— the new realism of the novelists, for example—as vulgar and degenerate. As for Britain, the war had loosened the imperialistic ties and given Canadians a sense of themselves as an autonomous community. The arts flourished in the twenties as the painters and writers did their best to stamp their works as distinctively Canadian. There was, however, a disturbing difference between what the writers put on the printed page and what the artists put on the framed canvas. With one or two notable exceptions, the novelists who wrote about the country were still influenced by the literary styles of the Victorian Age and the breathless rhetoric of the wartime literary liars. If the writers looked back, the painters looked forward; if the novelists rejected the unadorned prose of the so-called lost generation, the painters abandoned the muddy and derivative hues of their predecessors and discovered a surprising

The Maple Leaf psychosis

brilliance in the silver birches and flaming maples of the Precambrian Shield and the Persian carpets of the Canadian wild.

The Impressionist movement had already influenced a number of Montreal painters, such as Maurice Cullen and Clarence Gagnon, but it was the Toronto school, with its subtle sense of press agentry and its insistence on creating a Canadian look on canvas, that caught the public's attention and held it until those painters became the icons of Canadian art. One of their strengths was their choice of a name, the Group of Seven—a suggestion there of common purpose, not to mention a certain exclusivity: all for one and one for all. Their patron saint was Tom Thomson, an outdoorsman and self-taught artist whose own work was verging on the abstract before his untimely death by drowning in 1917, before the Group was officially formed in 1920.

As J.E.H. MacDonald, the eldest and most revered member, described it, the Group was "a friendly alliance for defence." They all knew each other. Five—MacDonald, Fred Varley, Arthur Lismer, Franklin Carmichael, and Franz Johnston—had worked together as graphic artists before the war. Varley and Lismer were war artists, as was A.Y. Jackson, who became a kind of spokesman for the others. Lawren Harris, in whose home the Group first formed itself, was a scion of the family that was part of the famous farm implements firm, Massey-Harris. They differed one from another—the patrician Harris was independently wealthy, Varley was a Bohemian—but theirs was a common resolve. "The Group derived its purpose from the vast land itself," Harris declared.

The Great War that marked the nadir of so many institutions also presaged the end of colonialism in art. The country emerged from the trenches with a new vision. Individually and as a body, members of the Group managed to create two enduring myths about their work that helped to establish them in the public mind as all-Canadian iconoclasts. The first was that they had resolutely turned their backs on Europe. But European influences are evident in their early canvases: the hand of the Impressionists and the Post-Impressionists (Lismer, especially, was a Van Gogh fan), the decorative art nouveau style that dominated so many of their wilderness sketches, and the paintings of the Scandinavian school that

266

had a powerful effect on both Harris and MacDonald. Their visit to the exhibition of modern Scandinavian art at Buffalo's Albright Museum in 1913 was, in Harris's words, "one of the most exciting and rewarding experiences either of us had." To the sensitive and poetic MacDonald, the pictures "might all have been Canadian and we felt 'This is what we want to do with Canada.'"

The second myth, perpetuated by all seven but especially by Harris and Jackson in their autobiographies, presented the painters not only as iconoclasts but also as underdogs, sneered at by the public and the art establishment. Although there were some adverse reviews and a number of angry letters, it is difficult to sustain Harris's statement that "the painters and their works were attacked from all sides. Whole pages in the newspapers and periodicals were devoted to it. Such a display of anger, outrage, and cheap wit had never occurred in Canada before." If this was true, it applied mainly to their earlier work. The Great War was opening up people's minds and changing their tastes, from women's fashions to modern architecture. By the time the Group was formed, post-war Canada was ready for something new, especially when it celebrated the very texture of the nation.

In fact, the members of the Group enjoyed and exploited the controversy, thus maintaining their image as young radicals battling the establishment. They weren't so young by the time the Group was formed. The oldest at forty-seven, J.E.H. MacDonald, a shy man who had none of the woodcraft abilities of the others, was considered the most radical of all by the public owing to his spirited defence in 1916 of the new art movement. But the real radical was Frederick Horsman Varley, predominantly a portraitist and a former Yorkshire schoolmate of Arthur Lismer.

In 1918, Varley, as a war artist, broke all the unspoken rules: no cheerful soldier boys manning the guns or marching to victory with a song on their lips for him. He was the one war artist to actually depict the dead not as fallen heroes expiring gracefully but as a heap of corpses thrown into a cart and dragged to the burial grounds. His cynical title *For What?* summed up his own attitude to war.

267

"I tell you, Arthur," Varley wrote to his former classmate, "our wildest nightmares pale before reality. How the devil can one paint anything to express such is beyond me. The Story of War is told in the thousand-and-one things that mingle with the earth—equipment, bits of clothing unrecognizable, an old boot stuck up from a mound of filth, a remnant of a sock inside, and inside that—well, I slightly released the boot, it came away in my hand and the bones sifted out of the sodden rags like fine sand. Ashes to ashes, dust to dust. I find myself marvelling over the metamorphosis from chrysalis to butterfly, but I never get beyond marvelling. . . ."

Varley, who had seen more of the war than his fellow artists, continued to be a rule breaker. As with his bitter canvas *For What?*, he insisted on painting what he saw and not what others wanted him to see. That was certainly true of his commission to paint Alice Massey's portrait. Varley refused to change the expression he had given her and when she demurred, seized a palette knife, forgot about his fee, and slashed the canvas to ribbons. On another occasion, when her husband, Vincent, arrived an hour late for his portrait session, Varley sat him down, prepared him for the sitting, then set aside his brushes and announced, "You wait here. Now *I'm* going out for an hour."

By the time the Wembley exhibition of Canadian art was mounted in London in 1924, and again in 1925, contemporary Canadian painting and that of the Group in particular had come into its own. The National Gallery of Canada, thanks to its perceptive director, Eric Brown, acquired so many of their canvases that academic artists protested and tried, vainly, to get Brown fired. The time would soon come when every schoolchild in the country was experiencing the Group's work through those silkscreen prints that have become part of the folk memory of the period between the wars.

Meanwhile, the post-war wave of nationalism had engulfed the literary world, partly as a result of the formation of the Canadian Authors Association in 1921, a year after the official birth of the Group. Six new periodicals sprang up during the decade, the most significant being the *Canadian Forum*, pledged to "foster, trace, and value those

268

developments of arts and letters which are distinctively Canadian." The most shameless was the *Canadian Bookman*—taken over by the CAA—a magazine that never encountered a Canadian novel it didn't like. A group of rising young McGill poets could not abide the CAA's fawning boosterism; "a pillar of flim flam" in the words of one of them, Leo Kennedy. Another emerging poet, E.J. Pratt, coined a phrase to describe the uncritical attitude to Canadian writing. He called it "the Maple Leaf psychosis." The CAA was so desperate for members that, as Madge Macbeth recalled, it was prepared to accept "practically anyone who had an interest in literature and whose cheque was honoured by a bank."*

Nevertheless, something was happening in those post-war years. In 1923, *Bookseller and Stationer* reported "a wave of reading spreading across the country." The University of Toronto's librarian, W.S. Wallace, declared that a new spirit had risen among the undergraduates since the war, "a thirst for knowledge . . . such as was unknown before." Wallace wrote that the evolution of a national consciousness was "the central fact in Canadian history," an evolution that had culminated with the Great War.

Yet the balance was shifting. *Maclean's* magazine pledged to print only Canadian non-fiction and to reduce fiction by foreign authors to a minimum. The *Canadian* promised to emphasize Canadian content rather than quality. Book publishers fell into step. The Ryerson Press initiated a gold medal to be awarded to an outstanding Canadian literary figure. McClelland & Stewart began to reprint nineteenth-century Canadian classics. Graphic Publishers, an Ottawa firm, was founded in 1924 with the express purpose of "producing and marketing all-Canadian books by Canadian writers."

In this "Canadian revival," as it was called, the emphasis was nationalistic. Most of the fiction produced in Canada in the twenties is highly

---

* In the thirties, when my mother was president of the Victoria and Island branch of the CAA, anybody who had written a letter to the editor of the *Times* or *Colonist* and seen it published was enthusiastically signed up.

forgettable. The editor of *Maclean's*, Napier Moore, an unalloyed Eng-lishman, told the CAA that the magazine did not want gloomy pieces but "short stories of romance, adventure, and love stories in a lighter vein." In *Canadian Bookman*, a British Columbia novelist, Hilda Glynn-Ward, railed against literary realism as "a pandering to the morbidly unwhole-some in human nature."

Why were Canadian writers ignoring the most powerful literary movement of the post-war period? In 1928, the poet A.J.M. Smith pro-vided a theory: blind optimism and Canadian nationalism forced a writer to express himself "in the prevailing spirit of pep and optimism" if he wished to hold his audience.

"Of realism we are afraid—apparently because there is an impres-sion that it wishes to discredit the picture of our great dominion as a country where all the women are chaste and the men too pure to touch them if they weren't. Irony is not understood. Cynicism is felt to be disrespectful, unmanly. The idea that any subject whatever is suscep-tible of artistic treatment . . . is a proposition that will take years to knock into the heads of our people. . . ."

The boosterism of the Western boom, followed by the accolades of the world after the stunning success in France, had convinced the credulous that the century really did belong to Canada. Having crept out from under the English coverlet, Canadians were in no mood to have their clean, outdoor dominion sullied. There was more than a hint of snobbism in the condescending attitudes to the new realism, for this was an *American* realism, the work of hard-boiled and hard-bitten Yankees—members of the same upstart and vulgar nation whose leading lights kept crowing that the Germans had been defeated by the likes of Eddie Rickenbacker and Black Jack Pershing. So many American novels seemed to be set in the cities, the domain of sky-scrapers and huddled masses. Canadian novelists clung to the pure atmosphere of the hinterland of which they were inordinately proud— the great sweep of the prairies, the pine-scented northern woods, the romantic realm of stalwart farmers, bold trappers, bush pilots, *coureurs de bois*, and explorers. In short, Group of Seven country.

Jessie G. Sime's *Our Little Life*, set in the Montreal of 1917–18, was the only realistic novel to make its appearance in the immediate post-war period. It was almost entirely ignored by Canadian critics and readers. Sime was an early feminist whose novel depicted the life of a middle-aged Montreal seamstress, "Miss McGee," who survived poverty and failure in the city through her courage and endurance. One of the few reviewers of this realistic novel that deals extensively with the immigrant experience in Canada was B.K. Sandwell in *Canadian Bookman*. It was headed "A Good Novel about Your Dressmaker."

Apart from Sime, the young Morley Callaghan, whose first novel was published in 1928, was the only Canadian novelist of quality to choose urban settings. Montreal and Toronto, ignored by the tub-thumpers of the CAA, formed the background of his best-known works. Nor could the critics turn their backs on him, as they had with Sime. For Callaghan had achieved the kind of nirvana to which every Canadian writer, be they hack or heavyweight, aspires. *His stories were being published in American magazines*—and not just any magazine but the influential *Scribner's* and *The New Yorker*, whose standards were notably high. At last a Canadian fiction writer had blessed the new realism with the ultimate imprimatur.

Until this time, Canadian writing had revealed a strong British strain. Callaghan changed that; his influences were more American than European. In a sense it can be said that he was to literature what the members of the Group of Seven were to painting, but though his settings were Canadian, he was never overtly nationalistic. In a brief time in Paris he had brushed shoulders with an old Toronto *Star* colleague, Ernest Hemingway, and other members of the so-called lost generation. With Hemingway's help he honed his own spare style and returned to his home in Canada. His unadorned prose was a reaction to the florid dishonesty of the wartime novelists. "Tell the truth cleanly"—that was his credo. "Weren't the consequences of the fraudulent pretending plain to anyone who would look around? Hadn't the great slogans of the first World War become ridiculous to me before I left high school. . . ?"

Callaghan remained in Canada and was never part of the highly publicized New York literary scene, perhaps to his own detriment. His novels were well received in the United States but were never raging best-sellers. In the sixties the American critic Edmund Wilson visited Canada and "discovered" Callaghan, whom he described as "perhaps the most unjustly neglected novelist in the English-speaking world," a remarkably provincial remark to describe a novelist who in his own country received more of the leading prizes, awards, medals, and honours than any other writer of his time.

6

The *masked* *writers* The Great War had transformed the Age of Faith into the Age of Gullibility. The newspapers believed what they were told—had they not heralded the Battle of the Somme as a glorious victory?—and the public believed what the newspapers printed. The wartime propagandists had encouraged the credulous, and the malady lingered on. Canadians had been conditioned to accept the most unlikely fantasies and to swallow the most outrageous hogwash. Anybody who accepted the myth about the Angel of Mons, or the German tallow factory, or the crucified Canadian—let alone the carefully contrived image of the demonic Kaiser who sanctioned the amputation of Belgian babies' hands— was prepared to gobble up the wildest fiction. The gullibility did not end with the armistice; it continued on through the Roaring Twenties and into the Dirty Thirties.

Thousands still believed that the anti-Catholic garbage in *The Awful Disclosures of Maria Monk* was the gospel truth. Like marks in a shell game, thousands more gloated over paper profits in stocks bought with money advanced by their brokers because they believed the optimistic messages from established business leaders (the president of the CPR declared he'd never seen the country looking better; the president of the Bank of Nova Scotia predicted "an unprecedented period of prosperity"). When the stock market collapsed, as the Western real estate boom had collapsed, Canadians believed the new wave of political medicine men who offered panaceas for their financial ills.

In British Columbia, they believed Duff Pattullo's election promise of "work and wages" for all and swept the florid premier into office. What they got instead were strikes and riots in the relief camps—one hundred in 1934 alone—and bloody violence outside the post office in Vancouver.

In Alberta, they believed Bible Bill Aberhart's election promise of $25 for every voter who supported his cause—believed it to the point where one typical Albertan actually had his wife return from Chicago to claim her cheque. But Bible Bill could not and did not deliver.

In Ontario, they believed Mitch Hepburn when he promised the voters to "swing to the left," soak the rich, and fire the lieutenant-governor. What they got was the new premier's quasi-private police force, an army of strikebreakers charged with keeping the American labour movement out of Ontario. "Hepburn's Hussars" had the backing of the Premier's new cronies, a body of mining promoters and wealthy industrialists devoted to preserving the status quo.

In Quebec, they believed Maurice Duplessis and his new-broom Union Nationale. He won the premiership by promising a series of reforms designed to smash the trusts; but the trusts prevailed, and what the voters got was the infamous Padlock Law, which a squeamish federal government declined to declare ultra vires.

They believed in a spectacular range of commercial nostrums that, according to the patent medicine ads, nine out of ten doctors were convinced would banish forever a formidable array of deadly, if improbable, disorders—halitosis, B.O., pink toothbrush, athlete's foot, and tired blood, not to mention those two dreadful affronts to good grooming and purity, five o'clock shadow and tattle-tale grey.

They believed, as well, in more dangerous mythologies. They believed the Prime Minister when he described Adolf Hitler as "a simple peasant." They believed that Mussolini was the answer to Italy's chaos because he made the trains run on time, even though he force-fed his enemies castor oil, a so-called children's laxative that, in large doses, savaged their stomachs and tore at their guts. And they believed, some of them, that Joseph Stalin was an avuncular, pipe-smoking leader whose distorted Marxist theories made sense—not only for untutored Russian serfs but also for Canadian unionists and tradesmen.

The press of Canada remained remarkably passive in these inter-war years. The tabloid-inspired age of ballyhoo south of the border scarcely influenced the media in Canada. The cult of the personality had little impact. Our popular icons were the traditional ones: hockey stars, military heroes, titled Brits, maverick politicians. American-style hype did not really begin in Canada until the birth of the Dionne quintuplets in 1934. Canadian magazines and newspapers lacked both the resources and the inclination to exploit such pop culture as existed. Two hot stories that might have provided scoops for any eager young reporter lurked dormant under the noses of the press. The most popular series of boys' books in the world, *The Hardy Boys*, was written under the pseudonym of a Canadian journalist, Leslie MacFarlane, but nobody knew it. The most famous suspense serial in cinematic history, *The Perils of Pauline*, was the work of a Canadian novelist, Arthur Stringer, but nobody knew that, either; it was assumed that both works were by Americans. This blindness owed something to the British connection— a contempt for the vulgar and a disdain for Yankee-style popularization that did not fade until the end of the Global War and the arrival of television.

Remarkably, in this climate of wide-eyed innocence, the same magazines and newspapers that had not twigged to MacFarlane and Stringer fell all over themselves to carol the fake achievements of three magnificent frauds who flourished at the same time. All were immigrants fleeing stultifying environments and lured by the promise of the Canadian frontier. All were impostors who reinvented themselves as entirely new characters, each a product of his own colourful imagination. And all three managed to fool the country. In the inter-war years, Archibald Stansfeld Belaney, Sylvester Long, and Felix Paul Greve donned their masks and achieved fame in their adopted country.

Belaney was the first to arrive, in 1906 at the age of eighteen. He was dazzled by tales of "Red Indians," thirsted for adventure in the

274

Canadian northwoods, and was weary of a stagnant, middle-class existence in Hastings, England, in the company of the two genteel maiden aunts who were his guardians. Belaney may have been a drunk, a bigamist, and a ne'er-do-well as well as a monumental liar, but he transformed himself after the Great War into an aboriginal saint known as Grey Owl, hailed by small boys and doting women—not to mention his ecstatic publishers—as the first Canadian conservationist.

The Great War helped him hone his special talents. When he enlisted in 1915, he claimed previous military experience with "Mexican Scouts and 28th Dragoons." That helped him get promoted to lance corporal, a rank he forfeited when he went AWL for six weeks after reaching England. Aloof and reticent, he served as a sniper-observer partnered with a Métis private in the Canadian Black Watch. His fellow soldiers believed him to be Métis, too. He hated the army and did his best to get discharged. He tried to fake a bout of influenza and complained of terrible pains in his stomach. That didn't work—but a slight wound in one foot gave him what he needed. He began to hobble grotesquely and to complain of a terrible agony. He also took to wearing glasses, suggesting his eyesight was too poor to snipe at anyone. He was shuttled from hospital to hospital, but nobody could find anything wrong. Finally he was given a medical discharge and in 1918 returned to Canada, where he threw away both the limp and the glasses. His eyesight was actually so good that in later lectures he was able to read ordinary print at arm's length. As for the limp, it became, in newspaper parlance, his "long, loping stride."

Back in Biscotasing in Northern Ontario, he never mentioned his war service. Among the trappers and hunters in the area, he was thought of as a boaster and a kind of backwoods Munchausen. The public never twigged to his secret, which was no secret at all to those who knew him before he became famous. It did not occur to them to blow his cover, nor did the North Bay *Nugget*, which had the story but didn't use it. Canada in those days had no tabloid press, nor was there a long tradition of investigative reporting. The newspapers had not yet shaken themselves free of the servility they had shown during the war when they had slavishly accepted the most arbitrary and indefensible of the censor's strictures. By the time Belaney had turned himself into an Indian, any such revelation would have been considered as sacrilegious as Robert Service's brutal wartime accounts of mangled men, subsequently toned down by an apologetic editor. Grey Owl was a Canadian celebrity; he had befriended Canada's national symbol, the beaver; he had fought against the exploitation of the wilderness. Any suggestion that he was a charlatan would have been seen as a form of *lèse-majesté*.

There was another reason for Grey Owl's success. He was a living scourge to the whites' underlying sense of guilt about the native peoples, who, to many Canadians, were little more than drunken illiterates whose children had to be dragged off to residential or religious schools to "save" them from the aboriginal life. Now here was a "full-blooded" Indian, to use the accepted expression, who could read, write, publish books, make speeches, and help produce movies that were shown in every schoolroom.

An actor who never left the stage, he dyed his hair, braided it, darkened his skin, wore buckskins, even changed his style of penmanship to help preserve the illusion. He explained his blue eyes by saying he was the son of a Scotsman named O'Neill and an Apache woman—"Kitty Cochise," he called her, invoking the memory of another native hero.

He did not look like an Apache and certainly not like an Ojibwa, the tribe he adopted as his own. He looked like what he was: a handsome Englishman with sensitive, aquiline features and a good profile. He got away with it because few Canadians actually looked at native people; they looked *through* them—human furniture, indistinguishable one from another, part of the background.

Lloyd Roberts, the eldest son of the poet Charles G.D. Roberts, was a freelance writer who visited Grey Owl in the bush country and found him "the first Indian that really looked like an Indian from the thrilling Wild West days of covered wagons, buffaloes and Sitting Bulls. The stamp of his fierce Apache ancestors showed in his tall, giant physique, his angular features, his keen eyes, even in his two braids dangling down his fringed buckskin shirt." What Roberts was describing, in his naive fashion, was a Hollywood Indian, the stereotyped "red man" played by any actor prepared to darken his features and say "*How!*"— from William S. Hart to Richard Dix, from Wallace Reid to Wallace Beery—all of whom wore two braids dangling down their buckskin shirts as part of what the authors of *The Only Good Indian* have dubbed the Instant Indian Kit.

Belaney reached the climax of his charade when, on a tour of England, he was commanded to appear before the two young princesses, Elizabeth and Margaret Rose. So great was his fame that their parents, King George VI and Queen Elizabeth, wished to come too, with a platoon of bluebloods, to ogle the sainted Native. At this point in Grey Owl's counterfeit career, his British publisher, Lovat Dickson, realized that his author was behaving "more like a successful dramatic impresario than a man with a mission." How would he act in the presence of royalty? Would he say something indelicate? Dickson was worried, and Vincent Massey, Canada's very proper high commissioner, was visibly nervous at the prospect of an Indian in Buckingham Palace.

Protocol required that the audience, including Grey Owl himself, be assembled dutifully in their seats. Then the doors to the drawing-room would be thrown open by two liveried footmen and the royal couple would enter with their two daughters. Grey Owl would have none of this. He made it clear that the entire retinue must be seated— King, Queen, equerries, titled hangers-on. When the doors were opened, he and he alone, dramatic in buckskins and leather, would make his appearance.

Consternation in court! "You should have thought," Dickson remarked, "we were suggesting something that outraged decency." But Grey Owl had his way. When the moment arrived, he raised his right arm in salute, looked directly at the King, greeted him with the phrase *How Kola!* which he informed Their Majesties meant "I come in peace, Brother," then uttered a few words in Ojibwa and began his lecture.

The princesses were enchanted. "Oh, do go on!" Elizabeth cried, and so he continued for another ten minutes. When it came time to leave he extended one hand to the King and placed the other on his shoulder. "Goodbye, Brother," he said. "I'll be seeing you."

Dismay! *He has touched the King!* That just wasn't done. But the Noble Savage could get away with anything. How shocked that glittering assemblage would have been had they known that the man in buckskins was, in reality, a former English schoolboy from the backwater of Hastings!

The man who called himself Grey Owl died on the morning of April 13, 1938, in his fiftieth year. The following day, the Toronto *Star* broke the story of his masquerade, but so strong was the myth he had contrived that his publishers, Hugh Eayrs of Macmillan in Toronto and Lovat Dickson in London, refused to believe the revelations. Dickson spent eighteen months investigating Grey Owl's past, a search that finally convinced him of the truth. The result was a biography, *Wilderness Man.*

One of Grey Owl's heroes was Chief Buffalo Child Long Lance, whose name conjured up an image of stalwart horsemen pursuing the thundering herds of the old West. Grey Owl read his so-called autobiography in 1931 and hailed Long Lance as "a splendid savage" (a strange remark from one supposed Indian to another), never realizing that he, too, was an impostor. One fake Indian had duped another fake Indian.

Maclean's, to which Long Lance contributed several articles, described him in 1923 as "a full blooded Indian chief of the Blood tribe" who had been "appointed to West Point by then President Wilson in 1915." None of that was true. He was born Sylvester Clark Long in 1890 in Winston-Salem, North Carolina, to a family designated as "coloured." His mother and his grandmother had been slaves—Indian slaves, the family insisted. Sylvester was part Cherokee and part Croatan, a mixed race of white, Indian, and black ancestry. Winston-Salem was no place for an ambitious young man with even a fraction of black blood. Sylvester Long lost no time getting admitted to an Indian residential school in Pennsylvania. Later he obtained a band scholarship to the exclusive St. John's Military Academy in New York state and used that as a springboard to try to get into West Point.

278

The fact that he had actually written to Woodrow Wilson asking for an appointment to the Point was too good a story for the gullible press to ignore. "FULL-BLOODED CHEROKEE TO ENTER WEST POINT," one newspaper declared. The headline was premature; he failed three of the six entrance examinations and ended up instead in the Canadian army, boldly listing West Point as his military background. He fought at Vimy, was wounded a month later, and was eventually discharged in Calgary in the summer of 1919. As his biographer, Donald B. Smith, has shown in his detailed investigation into Long Lance's astonishing masquerade, he was able to extend his military background in the years that followed to ridiculously implausible but remarkably undetected heights.

The Calgary *Herald* hired him on the strength of his invented background. He claimed that he'd been an intelligence officer in Italy, was educated at West Point, had received the Croix de Guerre for bravery, had risen to the rank of captain, and had been wounded twice. None of that was true, but nobody checked. The *Herald* was eager to publish this phony provenance to enhance his byline.

During his three-year stint in Calgary, he converted himself from a Cherokee to a Plains Indian and even got himself installed as an honorary member of the Blood tribe. Henceforth he always called himself Chief, although, of course, he wasn't one.

In 1922 he moved to Vancouver in his new role of Chief Buffalo Child Long Lance, and sold the Vancouver *Sun* a series of articles on local Indians. The *Sun* was delighted to publish "a regular story from a regular Indian, one of the few outstanding figures of his race . . . the only Indian appointed by . . . the President of the United States."

Long moved east again and had himself photographed in a curious costume that included a Blackfoot vest, a Blood tobacco pouch, Crow Indian pants worn backwards, and a headdress used in the native chicken dance. The Winnipeg *Tribune* illustrated his articles with that photograph: "Arrayed in full regalia of his tribe, Chief Buffalo Child Long Lance . . . presents a picturesque and striking appearance."

By the mid-twenties, the pseudo-Indian was a successful writer, even a sports writer (he covered the Dempsey-Firpo fight in 1923), albeit an inaccurate one. His specialty was the origins, customs, religions, and languages of the Indian tribes. He got a good deal of it wrong since he knew little Canadian history and less about native lore. It didn't matter. He lectured to universities, to business groups, and to Canadian Clubs. His byline appeared in the leading North American periodicals. He was hot copy for a press eager to interview him and publish his story—a careful blend of fact and fiction—without further investigation. "To the Plains Indians, Chief Buffalo Child Long Lance is 'Big Boss,'" the Minneapolis *Sunday Tribune* declared. "All their tribes, in addition to the Blackfoot Indians of Alberta, are said to look upon him as leader." The Bloods knew better. Shocked by the appearance of his photograph in "tribal dress," some felt they were being used for commercial advantage. But they didn't blow the whistle; in the white man's eyes, Long Lance made their people look good.

In 1925 he published his "autobiography," titled *Long Lance*. "The first thing in my life that I can remember," the opening sentence reads, "is the exciting aftermath of an Indian fight in northern Montana." The critics raved. The Philadelphia *Ledger* called it "a gorgeous saga on the Indian race." To the New Orleans *Times-Picayune* it was "by all odds the most important Americana offered this year." The book sold well in Europe as well as America. "This book rings true," carolled the *New Statesman*; "no outsider could explain so clearly how the Indians felt. . . ."

In what Donald B. Smith has called this "era of wonderful nonsense," Long Lance became the toast of Broadway, dubbed "the social lion of the season" by the widely read columnist O.O. McIntyre. A dapper figure in a well-cut tuxedo, he squired Broadway stars and light-opera songstresses with such success that Irvin S. Cobb, the journalist and wit, referred to him in his New York *World* column as "the Beau Brummel of Broadway."

By the end of the twenties, Long Lance was calling himself "the spokesman for the Indians of North America" and claiming that he had not only been decorated by three governments for gallantry under fire but that he had also been wounded, not once, but *eight* times in battle.

The *Star Weekly*, among others, accepted his unverified account of a thirty-day dog sled trek north of The Pas, Manitoba, and an equally fictional 4,800-mile airplane journey northwest of Nome, Alaska. Goodrich Rubber came on the market with a Chief Long Lance Shoe, and the firm commissioned him to write a thirty-four-page pamphlet entitled *How to Talk Indian Sign Language.**

In September 1929, just before the stock market crash, when the Age of Gullibility was entering its second decade, Long Lance was made a member of the exclusive Explorers' Club in New York and again cited as "a full-blooded chief," this time of the Blackfoot Indian tribe. At the club's annual dinner the following January he was chosen as guest speaker, his topic: "Indian Sign Language." A film, *The Silent Enemy*, in which he and four native Indians were given leading roles, was released to critical acclaim. Long Lance got most of the attention. To *Variety*, he was "an ideal picture Indian, because he is a full-blooded one. . . . An author of note in Indian lore and now an actor in fact."

Clearly, Sylvester Long could not continue his increasingly reckless masquerade. Chauncey Yellow Robe, an authentic Sioux chief who had starred in *The Silent Enemy*, was making inquiries that confirmed his suspicions of Long Lance's ancestry. Further investigation suggested that the so-called Plains Indian was, by southern racial standards, a Negro. The producers were aghast; their whole promotion had been based on a lie. But with Yellow Robe's death they had no choice but to send Long Lance on a Hollywood promotion tour.

That was the beginning of Sylvester Long's slide from Broadway celebrity to paid companion of a wealthy California heiress, Anita Baldwin, who fell under his spell in Hollywood. She took him overseas and through five European countries, where the great chief of all the tribes was reduced to the humiliating position of a "secretary-bodyguard" who drank too much and whose behaviour was becoming increasingly bizarre.

---

* Long Lance knew little about sign language but had no trouble cribbing from the work of others.

Back in New York he began to suffer from the increased tension of knowing that he faced being unmasked. He fell in love with an eighteen-year-old dancer who, in spite of a wealthy background, lived a Bohemian life in Greenwich Village. When she wed another his despondency increased. The end came on the night of March 18, 1932, when, in the library of the Baldwin house, he took out his .45 revolver and shot himself. He was just forty-two years old.

Felix Paul Greve's masquerade was of quite a different order from that of Archie Belaney or Sylvester Long. Greve, a part-time poet and translator, was born in Prussia but raised in Hamburg. With big dreams and mounting debts he evaded his creditors by faking his own suicide in 1909 and fleeing to the United States and later to Canada at the height of the immigration boom. He promptly turned himself into a Swedish writer named Frederick Philip Grove. His novels, which dealt realistically with prairie life, won the respect of the critics and elevated him to the uncrowded pantheon of serious Canadian novelists. His best works, including *Over Prairie Trails*, *Settlers of the Marsh,* and *The Master of the Mill*, written between 1920 and his death in 1948, have become Canadian classics and are still studied in university courses. Like almost everything written in the interwar years except Callaghan's novels, they are relentlessly rural.

Through his writing Grove became a public figure, introduced to a larger audience by three transcontinental tours for the Canadian Clubs, awarded the Lorne Pierce Medal in 1934, and elected to the Royal Society of Canada in 1941. Yet there was something odd about Grove. His two major autobiographical works, designated as non-fiction— *A Search for America*, published in 1927, and *In Search of Myself* in 1946—contained so many maddening inconsistencies and vague references that the academic world was baffled by his background.

Grove came to admit that his first autobiographical work, an account of his wanderings in the United States before coming to Manitoba about 1912, was "in a sense fiction." And so it was. The second was almost entirely fabricated but taken so seriously that Grove actually won the Governor General's Award for *non*-fiction in 1947. Even the dean of

Canadian literary critics, Desmond Pacey, was hornswoggled by Grove's highly dramatic account of his European years. During his lifetime his admirers were intimidated by his cold and haughty personality. As one academic fan, Arthur Phelps, put it, a little ruefully, "it was a measure of our naiveté in those early days that we never would have dreamed of questioning him. And Grove wouldn't have stood for it if we had."

From the very first paragraphs, *In Search of Myself* reveals a flair for the melodramatic that in a more cynical decade might have aroused a modicum of doubt: "The first few hours on this planet seemed to mark me for a life of adventure. . . . I was born prematurely, in a Russian manor house while my parents were trying to reach their Swedish home. . . . Incredibly, within an hour or so of the event, the hospitable house, belonging to friends of my parents, was struck by lightning and burned to the ground. . . ." Incredibly, indeed; good stuff for an award-winning memoir, if true, but there wasn't a tittle of verity in it.

The "castle Thurlow" on the Danish coast, where Grove claimed to have been raised in luxury with hundreds of servants responding to his will and a stable of highly bred horses awaiting his family's pleasure, was also pure fiction. He could not resist further melodramatic fictions. While in Egypt (Egypt?—he was never in Egypt), he claimed he heard of a terrible accident suffered by his father when the cable of an elevator snapped and the cage plunged five or six storeys. His mother was "an accomplished graduate of the Vienna Conservatory" who took him on a nomadic tour of European capitals, apparently to seek out musical events, from Edinburgh to Munich (his list was endless: "and later, Constantinople, Smyrna, Cairo and Fez"), where he rubbed shoulders with the great composers and concert artists of Europe, such as Mahler and Brahms.

All this was pure invention, as was his long trek across Northern Asia on a scientific expedition with his great-uncle "Rutherford," a shadowy relative who existed only in Grove's imagination but "had had the most amazing adventures." Across Siberia the two intrepid explorers traipsed—the great-uncle and the teenaged youth—even spending three months within the Arctic Circle and, later, travelling with a clan of Kirghiz herdsmen on the steppe. They returned home to Europe by a roundabout route, so Grove wrote—Java, the Malay ports, India, and the Mediterranean. He had, he claimed, visited all the seven seas.

The effect of the Siberian experience, Grove wrote, "was enormous and enduring . . . the steppe changed my whole view of life; the steppe got under my skin and into my blood . . . only when I stuck my roots into the west of Canada did I feel at home again. . . . When stranded in America, I remained in Canada and clung to it with my soul till it replaced Siberia as the central fact in my adult mentality."

That, of course, was hokum. Grove had never gone near the steppe nor any of the exotic places he listed in his so-called autobiography— South Africa, New Zealand, Australia. His accounts of his student life and his connections with the European literary world were equally inventive. One reads this unbelievable book with growing dismay. How could any literate reader be bamboozled by such a weird pastiche? How could it have won the nation's top award for non-fiction— or for fiction, for that matter? Only in an uncritical age when academics and casual readers alike had been taught not to question what they were told.

One of these was Pacey, a respectable if gullible critic, whose supposedly definitive biography of the author, based on Grove's original typescript of his "autobiography," was published in 1945 to the usual huzzahs. Following that, a series of scholars accepted the award-winning book and Pacey's summary of it as fact. Then, in 1969, a Queen's professor of English, Douglas O. Spettigue, published the first of two works that challenged Grove's story and would finally set the record straight—or all of the record that exists. Pacey continued to cling to his belief that although Grove may have exaggerated a little here and there, his basic story was true. In the course of a CBC symposium in 1962, he dismissed some critical comments as "sour grapes."

Spettigue, however, continued his relentless research, following Grove's trail across Europe and through North America, checking every document he could find, interviewing former acquaintances, and tracking down the inconsistencies in Grove's own story. It took him two years to establish that Grove was German, not Swedish. Later, he arrived at a startling revelation. During the time Grove claimed to have been in the United States—between 1902 and 1903—he, as Felix Paul Greve, had served a year in prison in Bonn for fraud, having cheated his best friend out of large sums of money to support a recklessly extravagant lifestyle.

Though Greve promised to repay his friend, he was not able to free himself of debt. On a trip to Sweden in 1909, he simply vanished, to reappear in the United States as Grove—"a fugitive from his own past" and also "a man of new beginnings" in Spettigue's estimate.

He tried farming, worked as a labourer, moved to Manitoba, and in 1914 married a woman who had no knowledge of his European background. The two taught school in the province for almost a dozen years and were, by all accounts, remarkable teachers. Greve retired in 1923 after his first book, *Over Prairie Trails*, received critical applause. That left him free to write full time and to continue the long masquerade that persisted for a quarter-century after his death.

What followed, after Spettigue's first sceptical work, had some of the qualities of a boxing match between two literary heavyweights, except that as academics, Pacey and Spettigue went out of their way to record their mutual respect and admiration for each other. Pacey, who could not believe that Grove was not what he claimed to be, went to considerable trouble to counter Spettigue's scepticism. In a literary sense, Pacey "owned" Grove, who was the subject not only of his first major book but also of his collections of critical essays and the Grove short stories in 1970 and 1971. Then in 1972, Spettigue, in the *Queen's Quarterly*, was able at last to reveal Grove's real identity following his researches in Europe. That was a body blow to Pacey, who at the same time had published a long but inconclusive article, "In Search of Grove in Sweden," that attempted to cast doubt on Spettigue's earlier findings. The contest ended the next year when Spettigue weighed in by following up his *Quarterly* article with a carefully researched book, *F.P.G.: The European Years*.

That was it. The last of the masked writers had finally been stripped of his disguise and the Age of Gullibility was no more than a rueful memory.

7

Hard times More than most politicians, William Lyon Mackenzie King understood the importance of luck in a political career and also the importance of recognizing it and using it to his advantage. Good luck, in the shape of the Governor General, had saved him from humiliation and defeat in 1926. How was it, then, that King, in the election of 1930, failed to recognize that luck had handed him another present, gift-wrapped and disguised as a political defeat? King had every expectation of winning a handsome majority and so rested on his laurels while his opponent, Richard Bedford Bennett, stumped the country, crossing it twice, racking up 14,000 miles of hard travel, visiting every province, and delivering 103 speeches in his rapid-fire style. Bennett did not recognize the joker in the pack that fate had dealt him. He had achieved a smashing majority, taking 137 seats to the Liberals' 91, but the victory was pyrrhic. King won out in the long run because it was not he but his voluble opponent who took the blame for five years of black depression.

Bennett hung on to power as long as the constitution allowed, clinging to the forlorn hope that the economy would improve to the point where he could win a second term. The gravity of the Depression escaped him, as it escaped so many of his ilk. More than a year after his election he remained convinced that those federal MPs in the West who insisted on talking about "hard times" were "blackening Canada's character." That fancy was supported by his minister of labour, the aging but foolishly optimistic Senator Gideon Robertson, who told him that the Depression was only temporary and that "perhaps next year we may be out of it." But the country was not out of it and wouldn't be until a new war forced the government penny-pinchers to perform what had been considered impossible—to feed, clothe, house, and pay close to 700,000 young men and women to do battle for their country.

Bennett was in office for the first five years of the decade. Those were not just the worst five years of the Depression but were also the worst five years in Canadian history.* They doomed him politically, as they would have doomed Mackenzie King had he won the election.

Some Liberals liked to suggest, with their leader's support, that King had foreseen and welcomed his own debacle, leaving Bennett to take the blame for the dreary years ahead. That, of course, was nonsense. King was convinced he would win. "There may be a real Liberal sweep," he told his diary on election day. "I look to the Govt. coming back stronger than it was." The spirits had got it wrong again. His Kingston seer, Mrs. Bleaney, the confidante of ghosts, had told him in 1927 that he would be married within a year. In 1930, having again examined her crystal ball, she predicted that Bennett would never last as leader. But neither of these flawed forecasts shook King's unswerving faith in the powers of his ancestral shades.

King had no more idea than Bennett of what lay ahead. The financial prophets, who were just as far off the mark as the spooks of his Kingsmere estate, kept insisting that the economy was "fundamentally sound," a phrase that was disinterred during later slumps. VOTE CONSERVATIVE FOR BETTER TIMES, the Tory campaign slogans had carolled, as Bennett stumped the hustings, announcing that his party was "going to find work for all who are willing to work, or perish in the attempt." In the Age of Gullibility, that was heady stuff.

Thus began the shameful decade of drought and despair we now call the Dirty Thirties, tucked in neatly between the stock market crash and the Second World War. Memories are a little blurred now, but the symbols remain: the wan men standing shapeless in the doorways of the corner stores, wistfully holding out their tin cups; the hot winds tearing at the rich loam of the prairies; the hobo jungles on the rims of the cities; the freight trains overflowing with shabby men taking their protests to Ottawa; newspaper photographs of mounted police attacking

---

* The economic situation brightened in the next five years except in 1937, which was another disaster year.

the mob and being attacked; Steve Brodie, prone on the pavement, trying to protect his head as the police truncheons rained down during the Vancouver post office melee.

The idea that it was disgraceful to accept the dole trickled down from the top, all the way from R.B. Bennett himself—who in one shockingly insensitive statement declared he would "never subsidize idleness"—to the man in the street doing his best to ignore the outstretched hands of the tin-canners. The victims became part of the landscape in the thirties, as Irene Baird, in her much underrated novel *Waste Heritage*, affirmed in her description of the look in the eyes of the passersby. "It was a mixture, very obscure, of conscience and evaded responsibility over a long period, together with consternation that the jobless scourge had come right out on their own streets, after having rattled around vaguely in the political cupboard for the past eight years."

Baird's novel is the only one written at the time that dares to deal with the specifics of the Depression when most Canadian authors confined themselves to pastoral romances, small-town existence, and historical narratives. Nobody wanted to read about the Depression; it was too close, too all-encompassing. That was also true of the drought. Only Anne Marriott dealt with it in her poem *The Wind, Our Enemy*, published at the end of the decade.

The country was at a standstill. People with families couldn't move if they needed relief, which was doled out locally. Single men could hop a passing freight and take a chance, but no family could pull up stakes. They were rooted to the spot where they lived. For two decades the population had shifted about restlessly and purposefully, supplying the country with the kind of kinetic energy that comes with human interaction. Now, tens of thousands on relief were rendered immobile, caught like flies in amber, their lives stultified, their horizons limited.

Tens of thousands more, living on subsistence, not relief, were caught in a similar trap. Like my own family, they didn't have the fare to pay for as much as a mile of travel. Vancouver, a glittering metropolis to us, lay just across the water from our new home in Victoria. For seven years, from 1932 to 1939, it remained unreachable.

To those of us who eked out those dark days, personal memories come back like yellowing engravings in an old, tattered book: my father's strained, expressionless face when he told us that after twenty years of government service, he, a Great War veteran, had been "superannuated" on a pension of forty-eight dollars a month. . . . My Sunday School teacher, a former business executive, digging in a ditch for a relief pittance, and I, passing by, averting my eyes and stifling my greeting to mask the sense of shame I felt for him. . . . My father and I scrabbling in an end-of-season berry field on Vancouver Island to garner enough fruit for our dinner.

How luxurious that seemed to a thirteen-year-old boy whose allowance was one cent a week! A Saturday morning movie was a nickel; a milkshake without ice cream was a nickel; a hamburger at Wimpy's, cut in half, was a nickel—all beyond my own finances. We hauled our firewood for stove and furnace up from the beach, along with kelp to fertilize the garden. We ate day-old bread at a nickel a loaf and made mulligan out of scraps for a non-existent dog, thanks to an accommodating butcher—stewing beef, at fifteen cents a pound, was a luxury; sirloin steak at a quarter was beyond our resources. My mother bargained for Jersey milk by paying the milkman a month or so in advance. He'd give it to her at seven or eight cents a quart—until he decamped with the money.

Bennett's personality is stamped as firmly on that era as a crown on a dime. The Bennett Buggy—a car drawn by a horse because the owner couldn't afford gasoline—is one of the symbols of the thirties. So, too, are the Bennett Boroughs—shacktowns for the jobless—and the Bennett Barnyards—abandoned prairie farms. King escaped this dubious form of immortality not only because he wasn't in power during those harsh years but also because Bennett's combative personality was a target for epithets.

The contrast between the two was such that they seemed to have been raised on separate planets. No two prime ministers have differed so sharply in character, speech, and outlook. King, outwardly bland but inwardly complex, approached every problem by moving sideways like a crab. The pugnacious Bennett, outwardly forthright but inwardly shy, was a bull in the political china shop, a practitioner of the frontal attack. He would end the Depression, he cried during the election campaign, "or perish in the attempt," an unwise pledge that King regarded as "demagoguery, declamation, and ranting."

In those early days before television introduced the thirty-second clip, every public figure was an orator, prepared to devote at least three hours to a political speech. King fussed and fiddled with his ponderous pronouncements. Bennett's platform style was that of a human bulldozer, smashing out a torrent of words that in his young days had earned him the nickname of Bonfire Bennett.

Bennett was a nineteenth-century Canadian who revered the British connection, brought back the titles that had been abolished in 1919, and revelled in patriotic imperial airs. King, who disdained the aristocratic British style, was the quintessence of caution. He weighed every course he took while Bennett plunged ahead, regardless of consequence.

Both men were openly religious, but they worshipped at different altars. If Bennett, the strict Methodist, spoke directly to God—he read six verses of the Bible every day of his life—King's communications with the All High were filtered through the shades of the deceased.

They were both wealthy, King because of the Rockefeller connection and his own parsimony, Bennett by virtue of a handsome legacy from an old school friend, the widow of E.B. Eddy, the match king, who left him a controlling interest in the Eddy company. That made him one of the richest men in Canada. King, who cried poor, was worth half a million dollars in 1940—more than four million today—half of it raised from wealthy Liberals. In those deflationary times, when income tax was minimal, he was taking home the modern equivalent of a quarter of a million dollars annually.

Both leaders remained unmarried: Bennett because, as his crony Beaverbrook remarked, he feared a woman's domination; King because no woman on earth could possibly replace his sainted mother. Both

290

were lonely men, denied the softening influence of a wife who might have made them more human, perhaps more compassionate.

King and the Liberals were so far removed from the realities of the day that when the 1930 election campaign opened, the party's newspaper advertisements scarcely mentioned unemployment. They emphasized instead taxation and trade to solve the country's economic problems. The Great Depression crept up on these innocents like a cold front, unnoticed and unremarked. Once again, as in the old pre-war days, the expectation was that good times would go on forever, that the slump was no more than a brief interruption in the triumphant march of prosperity. In Victoria, in 1932, I made a new friend, Phil Ballem, whose father, a plumber, painted a big sign on the side of his truck: WASN'T THE DEPRESSION TERRIBLE? But his customers soon realized that the optimism was flawed, and the sign came down.

Bennett relied on political promises that he could never fulfill, invoking the old shibboleth of the protective tariff. "I will use tariffs to blast a way into the markets that have been closed to you," he told a Winnipeg audience. *Blast?* That was *Bennettspeak*. The conviction that he could cope with hard times by raising the duty on everything from butter and eggs to textiles and kitchenware (which he did after he took office) suggests the extent to which Bennett's assumptions had been mired in nineteenth-century nostrums.

In spite of his lusty imperialism Bennett managed to widen the gap that had grown up between Canada and Britain since the days of Robert Borden's disillusionment over the Passchendaele campaign. The Imperial Economic Conference of 1932 was held in Canada at his suggestion and under his enthusiastic chairmanship. It was a failure, not just because Bennett had so little to offer the British but also because of his own abrasive personality. It was to make him a lifelong enemy of Neville Chamberlain, the British chancellor of the exchequer, who declared that "most of our difficulties centred around the personality of Bennett" who "strained our patience to the limit."

The new prime minister was isolated from the real world by his work habits, by his lifestyle, and by his outdated political philosophy.

He had no home of his own but spent most of his life in hotels. A workaholic, he lived on the job, remote from the public, confined within a narrow geographical circle—Chateau Laurier, Rideau Club, East Block, Parliament. His callous statement that he would never subsidize idleness suggests a conviction that the multitudes of jobless were wastrels who really didn't *want* to work; nor did they need charity, which he identified with any form of relief. "I will not permit this country with my voice or vote to ever become committed to the dole system," he thundered.

He was forced, of course, to change his tune after he took office. The Unemployment Relief Act of 1930 provided $20 million for aid to the jobless—an enormous sum at the time but only a fraction of what would be needed. There would be no handouts; people would have to work to pay for relief through a form of "workfare," to use a modern appellation. Work, when there was no work? It was a naive assumption. By 1933, 30 percent of the labour force couldn't find jobs.

Bennett didn't trust the people. He was fearful of violent revolution and of the small band of Communists, some of them Moscow-trained, who did everything to confirm his fears. The politicians and the police, invoking "British institutions, British traditions, and British principles," responded with draconian measures. The result was riot, violence, and bloodshed that led, in turn, to the trampling of the very principles the politicians were pledged to uphold.

The Communist Party claimed four thousand members. The idea that they could somehow take over the nation looks ludicrous today. But Bennett took it seriously, announcing that he would crush the Reds "under the iron heel of ruthlessness." The real revolutionaries, of course, were the young idealists who in 1932 formed the CCF (Co-operative Commonwealth Federation) in Regina—non-violent Fabian socialists whom the establishment did its best to equate with the shriller Marxists.

Bennett's response to the farcical prospect of an armed, coast-to-coast uprising was to get the troublemakers out of the cities and scatter them through the hinterland. The scheme sprang full blown from the inventive mind of the chief of the general staff, A.G.L. "Andy" McNaughton,

292

one of the heroes of Vimy. McNaughton was appalled at the waste of manpower evident during his cross-Canada tour of military establishments in the summer of 1932—thousands of homeless men living in hobo jungles, begging in the streets, swarming aboard freight cars. Tens of thousands of potential soldiers who would be needed in any coming war were not only deteriorating but becoming susceptible to what the General considered subversive propaganda. In McNaughton's view, the situation had all the makings of serious trouble. His solution, which Bennett enthusiastically adopted, was to get them all conveniently out of sight in more than two hundred and twenty "relief camps" run by the military.

In reality, the camps were prisons. Any man who left would be denied all further relief. He either stayed or he starved. How could anyone find work in the isolated areas where these compounds had been purposely situated? Food was barely adequate, conditions often filthy, and no entertainment was provided—not even on Christmas. The inmates were forced to toil eight hours daily for the "gift" of twenty cents. Small wonder the relief camps became known as "slave camps," a phrase the Communists, who were supposed to be outwitted by the plan, used to telling effect. The official pretence was that the camp workers would help to build the country. That was camouflage. Most of the jobs were make-work, designed to keep the presumed agitators as busy as possible, so that men toiled with picks and shovels while earth-moving devices stood idly by.

The plan was self-defeating. McNaughton had merely shifted the potential for disorder from the cities to the camps, and the camps were seething with discontent. The climax came in the summer of 1935, when more than one thousand disgruntled relief camp workers quit and staged a march on Ottawa, riding freight cars out of Vancouver in a vain attempt to take their complaints to the capital. It was the last thing Bennett wanted, although it would have been politically preferable to the violent and bloody riot that ensued in Regina after he ordered the authorities to stop the trek. A less pugnacious prime minister might have recognized the possibility of dangerous political fallout in an election year and evaded it by welcoming the trekkers to the nation's capital with flags flying and trumpets sounding, but that was not Bonfire Bennett's style.

The Prime Minister didn't have that kind of flair, nor did King, who succeeded him and closed the camps. In the United States, Roosevelt's New Deal had an opposite approach. The Civilian Conservation Corps enrolled a quarter of a million young men, a number that rose to three million by the end of the decade. The American camps were designed as part of a crusade to save the nation's heritage. There were few complaints because the volunteers realized they were working for a cause. In Calvinist Canada, the jobless must never be led to think that they were getting something for nothing. In the United States, camp workers were given money, entertainment, playing fields, radios, and sports equipment. They were paid a dollar a day, not twenty cents, worked a thirty-hour week, and were given weekends off. In Canada, as the defence department boasted, "not one cent of money has been spent . . . on reading material and recreational equipment."

Nor did the Canadian government spend money on the arts. Any attempt to support writers, painters, dancers, or performers—the human fabric that gives a community its rich texture—would have been considered wasteful and, indeed, treasonable by the politicians, the press, and the public. Today Americans boast of a private-enterprise culture. Seventy years ago under Roosevelt, however, the U.S. government (but not the Canadian) supported the work of artists of every kind through the Works Progress Administration.

Roosevelt gave America a revitalized culture and a sense of hope, but his vigorous attempts to deal with the Depression were viewed with suspicion, even horror, by a section of the Canadian establishment. King, the cautious penny-pincher, was aghast at FDR's radical medicine (as, indeed, were many middle- and upper-class Americans). "I am beginning to thoroughly dislike the man as a dictator whose policies are absolutely wrong," he wrote in 1933, "amateurish, half-baked, downright mistaken." How strange it all sounds now—King attacking "state control and interference," the very attitudes for which he himself would eventually be castigated.

By the end of 1934, even R.B. Bennett, whose interest in the arts was confined to Elgar's hymn to imperialism, realized that something drastic would be required if the Tories were to hold on to power. Could they hope to win the election that must be held in the fall of 1935? Like an oracle of old, Bennett examined the political entrails and found the omens disturbing. The traditional two-party system that had held since Confederation was in shreds. Provincial politics were in chaos. The established parties were falling like ripe fruit. By 1936, eight premiers would be out of office; only John Bracken's leftist Progressive Manitoba government would survive.

In British Columbia and Saskatchewan, the new CCF had shaken up the establishment by forming the Opposition. In Ontario, an onion farmer, Mitchell Hepburn, had ousted the discredited provincial Tories. In Alberta, a radio evangelist, William Aberhart, was steamrollering his way to almost certain victory with a goofy economic cure-all, Social Credit, that he himself did not fully understand. In Quebec, Maurice Duplessis's newly minted Union Nationale was threatening the shaky, graft-ridden rule of the Liberal satraps. In Ottawa, Harry Stevens, King's scourge during the customs scandal, had left the Bennett cabinet to create havoc in the business world by his aggressive investigation of economic abuse as chairman of the Price Spreads Committee. He, too, was about to form a new political movement— the Reconstruction Party.

The country was moving to the left; even a political innocent could see that. Bennett was stubborn; but he was no innocent, and he had his brother-in-law, William Herridge, to stiffen his backbone. Herridge, Ottawa's minister in Washington, was an enthusiastic New Deal fan. For some months he had been doing his best to soften Bennett up, urging him to shake himself free of old assumptions and launch a New Deal of his own. Old-fashioned Toryism was dead, Herridge told his brother-in-law in the summer of 1934. The policies of laissez-faire had to be abandoned. The party must keep on the move and seek a remedy for the economic malady. "This is your job and no one can take your place."

The result was the greatest political turnabout in Canadian history. On January 2, 1935, Bennett surprised the country and shocked many of the old guard with a program that seemed to many a carbon copy of the New Deal. Typically, he had given no hint of his intentions—not to the cabinet, not to the Conservative caucus, not to anybody save Herridge.

In keeping with his new approach, Bennett dispensed with the outdated forum of Parliament and chose radio to bring his platform directly to the people—five half-hours in prime time between January 2 and 11 on a network of thirty-eight stations. The party did not foot the bill for air time. How could it? Like a Mississippi riverboat gambler, the poker-faced prime minister had kept all his cards concealed. He picked up the tab himself.

This was the heyday of radio, and Bennett, to his credit, had fought hard in Parliament for a national publicly owned radio network. In introducing the government's broadcasting bill in December 1932 he had declared that "the country must be assured of complete Canadian control . . . from Canadian sources, free from foreign interference or influence." This was Richard Bedford Bennett's shining legacy to the nation, equivalent to his Tory predecessor's vision of a railway from sea to sea. It stands out like a bright star in an otherwise murky firmament.

Now, half a century after the last spike was driven, he was addressing the nation at his own expense, and not on the CBC—for that would have been a political intrusion into the network whose independence he had fought for and guaranteed. These were the days when national hockey broadcasts drew Canadians together, making Foster Hewitt even more popular than the stars of the fifteen-minute American serials with the double names—"Amos 'n' Andy," "Lum and Abner," "Vic and Sade." But Bennett's stunning political reversal, almost an atonement, outdrew them all. By the third broadcast, 8 million people—almost the entire adult population—were hanging on every astonishing word:

- The old order has gone; it will not return.
- In my mind, reform means government intervention. It means government control and legislation.

296

- Free competition and the open market place . . . have lost their place in the system . . .
- . . . faults in the system have been seized upon by the unscrupulous and greedy as vantage points in the battle for self-advancement.

Was this really Iron-Heel Bennett speaking—the man who had opposed the dole, who had implied that the jobless were idlers, who had treated the relief workers with disdain, who had insisted that the Depression was receding and that the government was not responsible for unemployment?

He sounded more like Tim Buck, the Moscow-trained Communist leader, than a dyed-in-the-wool Tory. Indeed, Bennett's broadcasts give the impression that he, a man who never seemed to panic, had indeed panicked. He hadn't waited for his cabinet colleagues but rushed pell-mell to the microphone with Bill Herridge's words burned into his brain—words that, in his haste, he had apparently studied carelessly and understood imperfectly, his nerves showing as he stumbled and fumbled through that first speech.

Nonetheless, the general attitude of Canadians was favourable. That of the cabinet was less so. The darling of the Tory party seemed to have gone mad and was promising to wipe out "corporate evils"—such as the right to issue shares at no par value!

Mackenzie King was outraged—not so much by Bennett's New Deal as by a more personal insolence: the Prime Minister had stolen his stuff! He had blatantly filched King's ideas from his personal Bible, *Industry and Humanity*—"the most gigantic plagiarism that has been made at any time anywhere by one man." King could not contain himself: ". . . the effrontery of it all!" The suggestion that Bennett had somehow managed to struggle through that dense tome says more about King's ego than his opponent's reading habits.

King also realized that he was in danger of being caught in a trap. With the Tories on one side moving leftward and the CCF on the other, the Liberals were being boxed in. Bennett had seized the initiative; the

297

notorious broadcasts would be his political platform in the coming election. His supporters gloated; King's Liberals had been demanding exactly the same kind of reforms that Bennett was now espousing. In this Looking-Glass world, the Tories saw their chance. Robert Manion, himself a future Tory leader, was beside himself with glee. "If King backs Bennett, he is merely trailing and if he abuses him he's reactionary. I really think Bennett has scooped him rather badly."

But the wily Liberal had no intention of being outmanoeuvred. Bennett had plunged recklessly into his New Deal without making any plans to implement it. The details, he indicated, would be outlined in the forthcoming Speech from the Throne. Election first, legislation later—that was his cart-before-the-horse approach.

King was delighted. The Conservative program could be debated in the House of Commons long before it reached the hustings. Thanks to Bennett he knew what was coming and how to meet it. When King rose on January 21, Bennett expected him to move the traditional no-confidence motion, but in this topsy-turvy political circus, King had no such intention. To the Tories' consternation, the Uriah Heep of Canadian politics sweetly and humbly offered his party's co-operation. He would not move no-confidence. Instead he urged that specific legislation be placed before the Commons where it could be debated and passed. *What* legislation? Apart from a bill calling for unemployment insurance, there wasn't any. Bennett had been cold decked.

In the election that followed in October, King made few promises, the main one being to get rid of the relief camps. By this time the Tories were in disarray; the defection of Harry Stevens, once a loyal supporter, had "crucified the party," in Bennett's bitter words. One minister had died; eight had declined to run. The Conservative campaign slogans had all the appeal of a traffic summons: STAND BY CANADA (what did that mean?); A CHANCE FOR YOUTH (had Bennett given youth a chance in Regina that summer?); VOTE BENNETT (his name was no longer a vote-getter). The public had come to the realization that the Bennett broadcasts were no more than a cynical device to curry favour. The Liberals had a more telling slogan: KING OR CHAOS.

298

With war clouds gathering over Europe, the result was a decisive majority for King: Liberals, 171; Conservatives, 39; Social Credit, 17; CCF, 7; Reconstruction, 1; and 10 others. Twenty-two years would pass and Canadians would fight in two more wars before the party of Borden and Bennett regained power.

8

Peace at any price

The hangover that followed the Great War was being felt worldwide about a decade after the armistice. A sense of disillusionment began to creep in, abetted by the post-war memoirists and novelists—the British poets, the American realists, and Germans such as Erich Maria Remarque. His anti-war novel *All Quiet on the Western Front*, published in 1929 and filmed by Hollywood the following year, had an enormous international influence, especially on the burgeoning peace movement.

In Canada, the first of the anti-war books appeared in 1926 over the name of Harold Peat, a veteran of the First Infantry Division. That book, bearing the title *The Inexcusable Lie*, represented a shocking contrast to Peat's first book, *Private Peat*, published in 1917. The earlier book, a jaunty account of his days in the line that played down the horrors and realities of the war, had been a thumping international success. Peat's promotional tour, in *Maclean's* words, "electrified audiences . . . from one end of America to the other." In 1918, the magazine had published an article called "a message of good cheer" by Peat suggesting that army life wasn't as bad as new recruits thought it would be. "I am glad I went to fight," Peat wrote. "Personally I believe that every man who goes will be glad of it before he comes back . . . *all* of Canada will see the good that comes out of evil . . . I tell you, Comrades, in going to this fight, no matter what comes to you from it, *you will yet be glad*."

Nine years after the first book, *The Inexcusable Lie* appeared. The two books might have been written by different authors. The first was full of what Peat called the "keep cool and crack a joke spirit that is so splendidly Anglo-Saxon." He had revelled in Canadian victories, such as the Ypres gas attack. ("It was wonderful. I shall never forget it . . .

with a spirit such as these men showed even against desperate odds, nothing but victory could result.")

The second book is sombre and far more passionate. In war, Peat learned that his "visions of something gallant, glorious, chivalrous and heroic were the veriest mirage. . . . I learned that War is none of these things . . . that War is a thing of horror, filth, degeneration, bestial obscenities. . . . It is a hideous thing. . . . We went to War because War was injected into our systems, because War is a part of the curriculum of schools. . . . We fought thoughtlessly until hate came."

Peat's book was published at the height of the craze for war memorials, which he loathed. "Can any artist—dare any sculptor design and execute in stone, in bronze, the ghastly truth of the soldiers' fate in War? Will any town decorate its parkway, the city hall square, with that thing that truly visualizes War, truly commemorates with eternal greenness what War means?"

The year 1926 when *The Inexcusable Lie* appeared was a watershed marking the literary boundary between what might be called the Holy War school of authorship and the Obscene War school that followed. Now more and more writers waxed bitter about the conflict that had engulfed them and that they had experienced as combatants, unlike the literary liars of the Great War years. Wilfred Brenton Kerr, a gunner who enlisted in March 1916 and fought at Vimy and Passchendaele, published his *Shrieks and Crashes* in 1929. After describing the Passchendaele tragedy Kerr asked, "Was this the best plan the generals could devise, to sacrifice us in battalions in a useless attack under conditions where we could not possibly make any gain at all commensurate with our loss? . . . Could our generals not see how hopeless it was? Did not the whole Flanders battle, from beginning to end, reflect serious doubt on their competence?"

The filth and horror of the trenches had become a pervasive theme in Canadian post-war novels by the end of the twenties, as in Peregrine Acland's 1929 novel, *All Else Is Folly*. His protagonist, Alex Falcon, describes a captured enemy trench: "The smell of the earth, too, would have been pleasant, if it hadn't had another odor mingled with it . . .

the scent of human decay. And it wasn't so pleasant to find, in that trench every three or four yards, a dead man . . . with blackened face and outstretched, stiffened hands. Big green flies buzzing busily above the eyes, nose, mouth. Nothing in that trench but dead men. . . . Through bay after bay, nobody but the dead. . . . So silently rotting beneath the blue sky. . . . Just dead Germans of course. . . . As if *that* made a difference."

The Canadian anti-war novels interred forever the clichés of the Great War. Passages that would not have been written—*could* not have been written—for fear of hindering recruiting and causing grief among the nation's mothers began to appear in print. Here is a Victoria Cross winner speaking to a bunch of prospective recruits in Philip Child's *God's Sparrows*: "I once heard a man say on a recruiting platform that the uniform is attractive and will undoubtedly fetch the ladies. Maybe he was right, but I knew at once he was trying to fool young fellows with dirty, lying half-truths. I'll tell you what you're in for if you take the uniform. You're in for mud and lice and foul stenches and disgust and fear till you wonder if you're going mad. You're in for killing men you've never seen before, and wounds maybe, and maybe death hanging out on the barbed wire till you're blue in the face and the flies and the rats get you—that's what you're in for."

George Godwin's bitter novel, *Why Stay We Here*, published in 1930, contains passages that wartime censorship would never have allowed, such as his description of a military hospital where surgeons struggled to repair the mutilated faces of their soldier patients: "How many facial cases! Noseless men, and men with gaps for mouths, and men with mutilated cheeks, criss-crossed with scars, faces moulded laboriously by the patient hands of plastic surgeons, built up as a modeller of clay builds up his model. But modelling, this in human flesh. And sometimes bones. Ribs for noses. . . . And men . . . with hardly any features left at all; men whose faces had been blown away. . . ."

The Christian principle that one should love one's enemies had been given short shrift even by the wartime clergy. As Siegfried Sassoon had made clear: "The man who could boast that he'd killed a German in the Battle of the Somme would have been patted on the back by a bishop in a hospital ward." The cynicism that the established churches unwittingly created was reflected in many post-war books published in Canada. In *The Towers of Mount St. Eloi* (1933), Archie Murray writes of the Easter Monday attack on Vimy Ridge and recalls the chanting of the French priests the previous day: "Praise the Lord! What irony! Praise the Lord! What for? For the whistling shrieking shells that would soon take their toll of living, quivering flesh and blood! For the snapping, cracking machine guns before whose flame of death hundreds of us would fall and die in the mud and filth! . . . For the snow, freezing our wet clothes to our shivering bodies! For the cursing, dying cries of men who would soon be struggling in their death agonies! Truly, it was the very essence of irony!"

In the most cynical novel of the era, *Generals Die in Bed*, Charles Yale Harrison sounded the same acrid note: "How will we ever be able to look back to peaceful ways again and hear pallid preachers whimper of their puny little gods who can only torment sinners with sulphur, we, who have seen a hell that no god, however cruel, would fashion for his most deadly enemies?"

Harrison's novel was published in 1929, although excerpts appeared in magazines in 1927 and 1928. The American-born author had gone to work for the Montreal *Star* at the age of sixteen when the war broke out. He enlisted in the Royal Montreal Regiment and served as a machine gunner in France and Belgium until he was wounded at Amiens in 1918. Back in Canada, he wrote his book, which was too savage for many Canadian sensibilities. It contains what is probably the most brutal passage of all, written in the blunt style of short, stabbing sentences that heralded the tardy arrival of the new realism to Canadian fiction. In the following passage, which deserves to be quoted at length, Harrison's nameless narrator describes a gut-wrenching encounter with an enemy soldier.

> I run down the trench looking for prisoners. Each man is for himself.
>
> I am alone.

I turn the corner of a bay. My bayonet points forward—on guard.

I proceed cautiously.

Something moves in the corner of the bay. It is a German. I recognize the pot-shaped helmet. In that second he twists and reaches for his revolver.

I lunge forward, aiming at his stomach. It is a lightning, instinctive movement.

The thrust jerks my body. Something heavy collides with the point of my weapon.

I become insane.

I want to strike again and again. My bayonet does not come clear. I pull, tug, jerk. It does not come out.

I have caught him between his ribs. The bones grip my blade. I cannot withdraw.

Of a sudden I hear him shriek. It sounds far-off as though heard in the moment of waking from a dream.

I have a man at the end of my bayonet, I say to myself.

His shrieks become louder and louder.

We are facing each other—four feet of space separates us.

His eyes are distended; they seem all whites, and look as though they will leap out of their sockets.

There is froth in the corners of his mouth which opens and shuts like that of a fish out of water.

His hands grasp the barrel of my rifle and he joins me in the effort to withdraw. I do not know what to do.

He looks at me piteously.

I put my foot up against his body and try to kick him off. He shrieks into my face.

He will not come off.

I kick him again and again. No use.

His howling unnerves me. I feel I will go insane if I stay in this hole much longer. . . .

Suddenly I remember what I must do.

I turn around and pull my breech-lock back. The click sounds sharp and clear.

He stops his screaming. He looks at me, silently now.

He knows what I am going to do.

I see his boyish face. He looks like a Saxon; he is fair and under the light I see white down against green cheeks.

I pull my trigger. There is a loud report. The blade at the end of my rifle snaps in two. He falls into the corner of the bay and rolls over. He lies still.

I am free.

Too crude for many Canadian sensitivities, Harrison's novel was largely ignored by the book-buying public, and its author was attacked for inventing scenes that the reviewers, forgetting that this was fiction, claimed had never occurred. A *Saturday Night* critic said it was a book of "very dubious literary merit . . . very ugly reading indeed." The Montreal *Gazette* review accused the author of doing a disservice to his fellow soldiers by concentrating on the evils of war to the exclusion of the good. In some military quarters Harrison found himself vilified. Cy Peck, a Victoria Cross winner, called it "pure obscenity, totally unrelieved by the slightest flash of genius . . . a gross and shameful slander on the Canadian soldier by a degenerate-minded fool." Veterans' groups demanded the book be banned. General Sir Archibald Macdonnell lived up to his nickname of Batty Mac when he cried that he hoped to live long enough to have the opportunity to shove his fist "into that s— of a b—— Harrison's tummy until his guts hang out of his mouth." Currie, who was incensed by the title (two of his generals had died in action, not in bed), said he'd never read "a meaner, nastier, more foul book." Will Bird, himself a veteran and noted war memoirist, declared that such books were "putrid with so-called 'realism.'"

Oddly enough, Will Bird's memoir *And We Go On*, which appeared in 1930, contains similar incidents, as Jonathan Vance reminds us in *Death So Noble*, his eloquent study of memory and meaning in the

Great War. Unarmed prisoners are bayonetted by some Canadian soldiers (one because he doesn't want to go home without having "killed a Heinie"), officers are threatened, and the protagonists end the war bitter, sullen, and confused. Yet Bird received stunning reviews while Harrison was excoriated. Why? The answer, Vance suggests, lies in a single word that occurs in the reviews of Bird's book: *clean*. It is used in a metaphorical sense: "The souls and spirits of Bird's soldiers remain pure." To *Saturday Night* it was a "clean, fine book, unusually temperate." The Moncton *Transcript* praised the fact that "there was no filth in it." To the Halifax *Chronicle*, it was a book "without filth or favour." Bird was praised as "the man who went through the awfulness of it all and came through clean, like thousands of his fellows and other thousands of clean heroes."

By filth, the reviewers did not mean the filth of the battlefield. They meant "filthy" in an amoral or sexual sense. As one critic wrote, "it has no profanity nor does it feature loose women," or, in the words of the Moncton paper, "it lacks the amourous [*sic*] experiences which have been played up by other writers in an attempt to increase sales by pandering to depraved minds"—a backhanded slap, surely, at Hemingway realism.

The image of the Canadian soldier as a fine, upstanding young man, pure in thought and action, dedicated to treating women as he would his own sister, was hard to eradicate. In spite of the Roaring Twenties (largely an American phenomenon), Canada was still in thrall to nineteenth-century morality.

The harsh attacks on Harrison's blunt narrative underline the doublethink that Canadians harboured about the war. Many would agree, in retrospect, that the war was obscene. But to *portray* it as obscene, as Harrison had done—did that not constitute an uncalled-for swipe at the men who had fought at such cost and sacrifice? The growing peace movement was attacking the whole concept of militarism. Yet there were few Canadians, at least in English-speaking Canada, who could resist the thrill of pride in the much-heralded victories of their famous corps. Foreign newspapers had praised it to the skies; statesmen and generals had echoed those plaudits. *Vimy*—that shining, unifying moment when old quarrels were forgotten, had given the country a sense of purpose and confidence. Even the *New York Times*, the Bible of America, had gone overboard in a paean of flattery. It would be, the paper declared, "in Canada's history, one of the great days, a day of glory to furnish inspiration to her sons for generations."

All across the country cenotaphs were sprouting like the poppies of Flanders to remind Canadians of the purity of their cause—a purity reflected in the prettification of the trench system, scoured free of grime, the walls rendered neatly geometrical with fresh sandbags, the old battlefields scrubbed clean of all taint of war save for the odd fragment of human bone unearthed by a farmer's plough.

In the architectural draughting rooms of Toronto's Walter Allward, plans for an even greater monument were taking shape. It would become the most massive war memorial in all of France, its twin pillars of flawless Adriatic marble rising from a vast concrete plinth, 40,000 square feet in size, above the crosses, row on row. To Canadian politicians, the Vimy Memorial was a shrine, and they spoke of it in a religious context. To Mackenzie King it was "one of the world's greatest altars." To his Quebec deputy, Ernest Lapointe, it was "sacred." To the Speaker of the House, it was "hallowed ground."

The biggest monument for the smallest battle! The Vimy Memorial was more than a shrine; it was also a boast. As Will Bird wrote in *Maclean's* in 1930 when the monument was under construction, "Europe, when viewing the finished work, will change her impressions of the Canadians as a people," a hint—and more than a hint—of the country's continuing insecurity.

The work on the memorial didn't stop during the Depression. Other national projects were postponed, downsized, cancelled, or abandoned, but Allward's artisans continued to raise the spires, polish the marble, and shape the twenty carved figures that adorn the structure. No government would have dared to halt the work. King was defeated; R.B. Bennett came and went; Mackenzie King took over again, until at last in 1936 the memorial was complete and Vimy fever gripped the country.

Now was unleashed the greatest outpouring of patriotic fervour since the relief of Pretoria. In the very heart of the Depression—its worst year, 1937, was just around the corner—6,400 Canadian veterans and their wives paid their own way across the Atlantic in five ocean liners to be present when Edward VIII unveiled the great monument. In the spirit of the time it was rightly called a pilgrimage, with the Vimy monument as its Mecca. It was also a celebration, not of war, for "war" had become a dirty word in the thirties, but of wartime comradeship forged in a crisis, of victory, of remembrance, and of reaffirmation.

But what of peace? Everybody was talking wistfully of peace in the year of the Vimy pilgrimage. "The world is athirst for peace," Ernest Lapointe told the Vimy pilgrims. ". . . Canada is ready on its part to do all it can to maintain peace." In the light of what was happening—or what *wasn't* happening—those words sounded hollow. Canada, clinging to the security blanket of its isolation policy, was doing precious little. All the omens pointed not to peace but to war.

While Canada vacillated, Benito Mussolini had marched into Ethiopia. Three months before the memorial's unveiling, Adolf Hitler's troops reoccupied the Rhineland in defiance of the Treaty of Versailles and with scarcely a murmur of protest. Three months after the pilgrimage, the two dictators established the Rome–Berlin Axis.

Like most of the rest of the Western world, Canada was isolationist. The gut-wrenching memory of the conscription crisis of 1917 hung over the country like a pall. The leading isolationist was Mackenzie King himself, whose policy was to keep Canada at arm's length from both Britain and the United States while healing the breach between the two founding cultures. And, of course, to win elections. "National Unity" was the key phrase then as it is today.

King opposed war on moral as well as political grounds, and his opposition was in tune with the general attitudes of his countrymen. The peace movement that had sprung up after the war had the support of the major Protestant churches. In 1924, Dr. William Creighton, editor of the *Christian Century*, executed a remarkable contortion in which he managed to twist himself about on the subject of war and peace until he was facing in the opposite direction. As late as 1918, Creighton had declared that pacifism could not be tolerated "no matter who may teach it." That same year his trenchant editorial "The Voice of Pacifism" had driven some committed pacifists out of the Methodist Church. Now here he was, just six years later, declaring that "we must learn to think peace, to talk peace, to insist on peace, because anything else is a horrible achievement."

In 1926, W.A. Gifford, a prominent theologian, with the help of several Montreal clergymen produced *The Christian and the War*, in which he wrote: "We who make this appeal cannot conceive any future war in which Christian men can participate."

In 1930, at the Lambeth Conference in England, the Anglican Church, while stopping short of an out-and-out pacifist approach, accepted the general declaration that war was "incompatible with the teachings of Jesus." The United Church followed suit with a series of resolutions condemning war as contrary "to the mind of Christ."

In 1933, the Christian Commonwealth Youth Movement endorsed the position of the War Resisters International that "war is a crime against humanity." They were "determined not to support any kind of war and to strive for the removal of all causes of war."

This climate of anti-militarism affected officers' training courses on some university campuses and cadet training in schools. In this the Student Christian Movement took the lead. The SCM's Dalhousie branch, for example, resolved in February 1929 that "it is not in the best interests of international peace, good will and equity, to harbour a militaristic movement in their midst." At the same time the SCM removed from its songbook any hymn with wartime symbolism, such as "Onward, Christian Soldiers" or "Fight the Good Fight."

Even the Boy Scouts were not immune from the anti-militarism attitude, as I well remember. My best friend wasn't allowed to join the St. Mary's troop in Victoria because his mother did not want him to be wearing *any* kind of uniform. As for cadet training, it was, in Agnes Macphail's words, "the most vicious part of our national defence scheme. . . . Military training in the schools thrives on toy soldierism."

With the Germans routed and the Kaiser exiled, the anti-militarists found a new adversary: the armament makers—the "Salesmen of Death" as *Maclean's* called them in an August 1931 article by George Drew. The chief villain was Sir Basil Zaharoff, known as the Mystery Man of Europe, who "built himself a fortune . . . by selling the machinery of death to all comers." According to Drew, "This sinister figure has wandered through Europe during the past fifty years surrounded sometimes by romance, cloaked always in mystery, which, in the name of national security, brings rich contracts to the armament countries. It is their business, their very bread and butter, and they will do all they can to see that their business does not languish."

The new attitude made it politically possible for a financially pressed government to cut back drastically on its military budget. For most of the years between the two wars, the navy, army, and air force were bled white. So much time and effort was spent battling for a slice of the budget that training suffered, as it also did when Permanent Force soldiers were called out to aid civil authorities as policemen in various Depression-bred disturbances. McNaughton's relief camps used up an excessive amount of training time. The chief of the general staff was so busy with this pet project that he hardly had time to see his director of military training, whose job was to put an efficient army in the field in the event of war. His severest critic, Brigadier General J.S. "Buster" Brown, contended that McNaughton used the controversial camps as a ploy to keep the spotlight off the poor state of the militia.

The government consistently shaved the military estimates during the interwar period—and got away with it. In the mid-twenties, when everybody was riding high economically, Canadians spent far less on defence than any other Western democracy—$1.46 per capita compared to Australia's $3.30, the United States' $6.51, and Great Britain's $23.04. When the Depression came, it would have been political suicide to give the army what it asked. Money for relief camps to protect the country from its own citizens—that was politically popular—but money for guns or even for uniforms? That wouldn't buy votes. It is unfair to blame either the Bennett or the King government for putting a squeeze on military spending. The nation was in an anti-war mood, the people still aghast at the continuing revelations about the horrors and stupidities of 1914–18. In spite of the ominous sabre-rattling in Europe, the entire country was indulging in a mass fantasy of wishful thinking. There wouldn't be—there *couldn't* be—another world conflict.

Canada's soldiers were not prepared for war. Money was so tight that only officers and NCOs were able to attend training camp; the non-permanent artillery had no funds for firing practice. By 1931, all militia training at camp was done away with. Pay was virtually non-existent. A captain with the Camerons recalled that instead of individual pay his men got streetcar tickets, coffee, and sandwiches. "Those who held the unit together did so at great personal cost . . . in the face of much public jeering at Saturday soldiering."

An officer in charge of supply wrote: "We had a Horse Transport Company. We had harness [but] never did have a horse. We never did have a wagon. We had a Mechanical Transport Unit. . . . They had no equipment whatever—absolutely none. From 1926 until the outbreak of war we never had one item of mechanical transport issued to us. Not a motorcycle, not a van, not a truck. . . ."

The artillery, too, was badly shortchanged. An officer of the Midland Regiment remembered that the total ammunition allotted a battery for shooting practice was exactly ten shells. "So generous was Canada to its citizens who were trying to make ready to defend her. It can be imagined with what grave responsibility I called the fire orders for battery when my shell was to be fired. Of course, we only used one shell for each set of fire orders. So we trained to meet the German army."

The desperate state of the artillery concerned McNaughton, the consummate gunner of the Great War. In April 1931, he wrote optimistically to a friend that "the cuts are temporary only." Two months later the government chopped off another quarter of a million dollars. By the spring of 1935 there wasn't a single anti-aircraft gun of any sort in Canada and only enough ammunition for field guns to sustain a ninety-minute

310

barrage. On the Pacific coast, the defences were so deficient that many guns couldn't fire more than a dozen rounds. The air force suffered as well. Canada had only twenty-five service aircraft available—all obsolescent—and not a single bomb.

As a result, the army was totally unprepared for the coming war and was forced to make do with the equipment of 1918. Those of us who donned the uniform in the early years came up against the problem. In January 1942, when I found myself in the infantry basic training centre at Vernon, B.C., the Bren gun—the most efficient light machine gun in the Allied forces—was only just coming into use, replacing the old Lewis gun with which the first recruits had been trained.

The lack of up-to-date equipment sprang, in part, from a curious doublethink on the part of Canadian politicians, who believed that any preparatory measures taken against a potential enemy would somehow fan the flames of European conflict. The politics of timidity was not confined to Canada; appeasement was in everybody's subconscious. That was manifest early in 1935 when Mussolini launched his African adventure, intent on seizing and subjugating Ethiopia. The reputation of the League of Nations would stand or fall on the actions of its fifty members. Collective security, especially the enforcement of oil sanctions, would have brought Italy to her knees in three months. But as a result of what came to be known as the Riddell incident, the League was reduced to little more than a high school debating society. For that, Canada must bear the greatest share of the blame.

Walter Riddell was a long-time Canadian diplomat, a former deputy minister of labour and since 1924 a permanent representative accredited to the League of Nations with the title of Canadian Advisory Officer. He had been concerned about German militarism as far back as 1912 when, as a young graduate student, he had first visited Europe—"a rude awakening," as he described it in his memoirs. Now, more than twenty years later, he had little doubt about Hitler's aggressive intentions following Germany's withdrawal from an abortive disarmament conference to which he was the Canadian delegate. As Riddell noted, the European nations were all talking peace and all spending more and more on guns and armies. Nor was the League giving any of them the security they craved.

Where did Canada stand on the issue of Italian aggression? Unfortunately for Riddell, the country was in the throes of the 1935 federal election campaign, and the politicians were away on the hustings. He asked three times for instructions and finally received an evasive answer: Canada was to abstain from the League vote on Italian aggression; nothing could be settled until the new parliament met. The issue was further complicated by Mackenzie King's victory on October 15. A subcommittee of the League was already considering the question of oil sanctions against Italy. What was Canada's position?

On October 28 the Canadian government, in a tortuous memorandum to Riddell, made an attempt at an answer that discussed "the difficulty of making general commitments in advance to apply either economic or military sanctions." That was followed with what appeared to be a gesture of support. "In the present instance where an earnest effort is being made to test the feasibility of preventing or at least terminating war by the use of economic sanctions, and when there is no room for doubt as to where the responsibility rests for the outbreak of war, and having regard also to the position taken by Canada at the recent Assembly, the Canadian government is prepared to co-operate fully in the endeavour. . . ."

Riddell took this remarkable example of bureaucratic double talk as a firm go-ahead. When he appeared before the League's subcommittee he learned that one of the proposals under consideration—the prohibition of certain products to the offending country—might be amplified: the French wanted to add oil, coal, iron, and steel to the prohibited list. The addition of oil alone, Riddell wrote later, "would do more to defeat Italy than all the other sanctions together."

Riddell realized that the situation was urgent; no other country wanted to take the initiative. "It seemed a moment when an immediate decision had to be taken if sanctions were to become really effective and if we were to safeguard Canada's interests." With that opinion, and with the advice of his fellow diplomat Lester Pearson, he went ahead.

If Riddell had demanded the immediate bombing of the Eternal City, the reaction to his speech before the subcommittee could not have been more alarming. Mackenzie King read it with "amazement." With the help of his fellow isolationist, O.D. Skelton, deputy minister of external affairs, he drafted a tough reprimand to Riddell. To his dismay, the incident did not blow over but was amplified. To the press and in the chancelleries of the world, it became known as "the Canadian proposal" or "the Canadian initiative." As the Canadian Press reported, "League of Nations circles believed tonight an oil embargo against Italy will go into effect early in December in conformity with Canada's proposal to the League sanctions committee."

Here was a paradox. Canada was being applauded around the world for taking a bold action against the Italian dictator—but Canada didn't want any part of it! The government scrambled to issue a press release repudiating everything Riddell had proposed. The speech "represented only his personal opinion and not the views of the Canadian government." The whole matter was due to "a misunderstanding." It was not our finest hour.

The repudiation of sanctions—for that was how the government's move was interpreted—brought world headlines and international embarrassment. As the Italian ministry stated (seizing an opportunity that had been handed to it on a platter), "As the oil embargo has just been repudiated by the Government supposed to have made it, we believe it must now be discarded." Fortunately for Canada, the furor was overshadowed by an even greater outcry when it was learned that Britain's Sir Samuel Hoare had conspired with France's slippery Pierre Laval to buy peace by offering Mussolini practically everything he wanted.

Mackenzie King was set on firing Riddell, who, he thought, needed "a good spanking," but was talked out of it. The prime minister managed to persuade himself that if he had not disavowed the diplomat, "the whole of Europe might have been aflame today." The League continued to procrastinate until Mussolini had seized most of Ethiopia and Hitler marched his troops into the Rhineland. Would he have done so had the

League shown its stiffening opposition by accepting the so-called Canadian proposal? Riddell certainly thought not. In his memoirs he suggested that it would have given Hitler pause and could have averted the Second World War.

Neville Chamberlain expressed the prevailing diplomatic opinion, however, when he described sanctions as "midsummer madness." King agreed: ". . . my action . . . in exposing Riddell's action and thereby restraining the application of sanctions against Italy at the time we did, saved European war for which Canada would be blamed." The ghostly shadow of the Great War haunted King as it haunted almost everybody. Any option was acceptable in the interests of peace—that was the accepted creed: peace at any price.

For King, there was another factor to be considered: the position of Quebec. Ernest Lapointe spoke for his province when he said bluntly that "no interest in Ethiopia, of any nature whatsoever, is worth the life of a single Canadian."

To King, in the fall of 1936, the League of Nations wasn't much more than "a Tower of Babel." The man who had restored the Rockefellers' reputation after the bloody Colorado massacre by inventing the company union remained firm in the belief, as he told the League Assembly in September, that "emphasis should be placed upon conciliation rather than coercion."

With that sentiment he had the support of the Canadian people, with the exception of John Dafoe, the tough-minded *Free Press* editor, who used the word "discreditable" to describe "the rejection by Canada of the League." With that phrase Mackenzie King could not quarrel. "I wish the League of Nations could be gotten out of the way altogether," he told the Governor General.

King was convinced that personal discussion between national leaders could result in a better understanding. To support this naive assumption, he set off for Berlin in June 1937 for a face-to-face talk with Adolf Hitler, whose unopposed occupation of the Rhineland had caused dismay in the capitals of Europe. Hitler, who had an almost hypnotic ability to charm his guests, impressed the Canadian prime minister as "a man of deep sincerity and a genuine patriot." King was perfectly certain, as he wrote to the Governor General, "that the Germans are not contemplating the possibility of war." That would be a catastrophe for Canada; for King understood that if Britain went to war, Canada must surely follow, and the country would again be torn asunder by Quebec's traditional intransigence regarding any European adventure.

Appeasement was, then, the only way to prevent such a debacle. When Neville Chamberlain announced in the fall of 1938 that he too would initiate a personal interview in Berlin with the German dictator, King's enthusiasm knew no bounds. "I am sure the Canadian people will warmly approve this farseeing and truly noble action," he told the press. In that his instinct was sure. The public and the press, always excepting the forthright John Dafoe, stood behind him.

"I believe it will be found that Chamberlain has saved the day," King predicted when the British prime minister announced that he would deal directly with Hitler in Berlin. After the 1938 Munich settlement he wrote to Chamberlain: ". . . the heart of Canada is rejoicing tonight at the success which has crowned your unremitting efforts for peace. . . . Reason has found a way out of conflict. . . ." Not a whisper there about the military occupation and final dismemberment of Czechoslovakia. Appeasement was not yet a stench in the nostrils of the British or Canadians.

One must, however, be fair to the Prime Minister. The public relief after Munich was overwhelming. Did it really make sense for Canada to go to war over an obscure Slavic nation? Politically, it would have been all but impossible for King to adopt any other stance, though his bubbling enthusiasm might have cooled down. The memory of one brutal war affected Canadian policy on the eve of the next. In the words of one observer, "The Great War brought Canadians to Europe, but left Europeans remote to Canadians."

Six months after Munich, when Germany seized what was left of the Czech republic, Chamberlain was dumbfounded. Appeasement had failed, and he abandoned it. King, however, remained a true believer, and relations between the two prime ministers turned cool. As Lester Pearson put it, "King prefers Chamberlain the appeaser to Chamberlain the avenger." King's alter ego, O.D. Skelton, the other disciple of that worn-out policy, moved to stiffen his master's resolve. In Skelton's view, the British prime minister was "self confident to the point of arrogance, intolerant of criticism, and at the moment sore because he thinks in the eyes of the world Hitler made a fool of him. . . . Born and bred in a Tory Imperialist school [he] cannot imagine that any part of the British Empire has any chance but to halt when he says halt and march when he says march. . . ." Shadows of the old contest between colonialism and autonomy!

In March 1939, King told Parliament that his government would refuse to say whether or not Canada would support Britain if war came. Besides, he argued, the country could not afford it: "We have tremendous tasks to do at home, in housing the people, in caring for the aged and helpless, in meeting our heavy burden of debt, in making provisions for Canada's defence, and in bringing our standard of living and civilization to the level our knowledge now makes possible."

Why should Canada be called upon "to save periodically a continent that cannot run itself, and, to this end, risk the lives of its people, risk bankruptcy and political disunion?" To King, that prospect "seems to many a nightmare and sheer madness." Once again the people were with him, especially in Quebec, whose former premier, Louis-Alexandre Taschereau, sent a note of congratulation. "You have no idea of the wonderful effect it had to clarify the situation," he wrote. For King, this was vindication; national unity was secure.

King's stubborn isolationism, however, was alarming the British Foreign office, which conveyed its concern to Chamberlain that spring. War with Germany seemed imminent, yet here was the leader of the Commonwealth's senior dominion hinting that his country would do well to stay out of any future conflict. Something spectacular was needed to cement the British connection, and fortunately that something was already in the cards. The idea of a royal visit to Canada had been hinted at more than a year earlier; both Mackenzie King and Lord

Tweedsmuir, the governor general, would take credit for the idea. After Chamberlain's historic meeting with Hitler at Munich in the autumn of 1938, tensions had relaxed to the point where such a tour seemed feasible, if not advisable. The announcement was made from Balmoral Castle on October 8, disguised as an acceptance by Their Majesties of Mackenzie King's invitation.

The decision delighted King, who felt that such an event would help unite a country fractured by hard times and bitter regional disputes. And it would also, in his words, "add much to the history of the Liberal party." Canadian party politics, however, were far from Chamberlain's mind when he had persuaded a reluctant British cabinet and a diffident monarch to go along with the idea. His ministers were wholly preoccupied with the European situation and were concerned about their frail sovereign, who didn't feel it proper to leave the country in the midst of a crisis. George VI changed his mind when it was made clear where his duty lay: his presence in Canada would help firm up commonwealth relations. He insisted, however, on travelling by a Canadian Pacific liner, the *Empress of Australia*, rather than the battleship *Repulse*, which, he pointed out, could hardly be spared with war threatening.

Equally important—perhaps more important—was the need for a side trip to the United States, which would add another week to what would have been a three-week tour. Many Americans had viewed the British refusal to accept one of their own—Wallis Simpson—as the royal consort in the light of a snub. With the isolationist mood in the United States far more alarming than feeling in Canada, the royal visit would provide a convenient opportunity to show off the shy new king and his charismatic queen like Hollywood stars.

The tour that followed, from May 17 to June 14, was a thumping success, and far more spectacular than its organizers had foreseen. It was one of those joyous, ritualistic occasions—like Christmas—that involved the entire nation. Everybody, it seemed, turned out to see the royal pair, and everybody harboured a memory, an anecdote, a memento, or a photograph that would remain with them through the turbulent years to come. Vincent Massey, Canada's high commissioner to Britain, estimated that 8.5 million Canadians had viewed the royal couple—an optimistic assessment that nobody was prepared to challenge. It was the first time a reigning monarch had set foot on Canadian soil, and there was little doubt, in that last peacetime summer, where the nation's heart lay. From sea to sea, Canadians felt a glow of pride in their heritage. An ecstatic Mackenzie King went overboard in his appraisal of the tour's impact. "I feel increasingly certain," he told his diary on May 21, "that this visit of the King and Queen is going to be the dust in the balance which will save a European, and if so a world war."

The tour also underlined the changed relationship between Prime Minister and Governor General that had flared up during the King–Byng incident. Lord Tweedsmuir was packed off to New Brunswick on a fishing trip while Mackenzie King, who had always harboured a deep suspicion of vice-regal appointees, moved to the front and centre. He made all the major decisions regarding the tour and insisted on staying at the royal couple's side for the entire visit in spite of opposition from members of the royal entourage. King got his way, convincing himself that it was his duty to watch over the royal visitors: "There might be riots. There might be anything. If I had allowed the King and Queen to travel without my being there to protect them, the country would never forgive me," he told his diary in justification.

The touchy prime minister was ever on the alert to the slightest suggestion of colonial subservience. The monarch's private secretary, the popular Alan "Tommy" Lascelles, had made a passionate reference in the course of a dinner at Laurier House to Mackenzie King about handing over his "charge" to George VI on the monarch's arrival at Quebec City. That rankled. Why didn't he call Canada a "colony" and be done with it, the Prime Minister asked the Governor General.

Even more grating were the attempts to keep him from appearing with the royal pair during their visit to the United States at the end of the Canadian tour. Canadian prime ministers have always tended to see their role as that of an honest broker between Great Britain and the United States. To King that fancy was close to being an obsession. He got his way, of course, in spite of attempts to keep him on the side-lines—seated at too far a distance from the royal guests in one instance. Seating arrangements, indeed, were always a delicate problem during the cross-Canada tour, as public figures vied for precedence. In Quebec, Premier Maurice Duplessis felt himself insulted over his inferior position at the head table during a welcoming luncheon and refused to attend, to the consternation of officials who held up the meal in a vain attempt to locate him.

In spite of this rebuke, French Canada had gone wild over the royal party, thanks in part to Cardinal Villeneuve, who made sure that every parish greeted the royal visitors with cheers and bell ringing. But the enthusiasm of the Quebeckers was genuine. The 114-mile route from Montreal to Ottawa was jammed with a million fervent well-wishers, the largest turnout of the entire tour.

By the end of the royal visit on June 14, it became evident that the celebration had more than achieved its goal. "That tour made us!" the radiant queen, now the most popular public figure on the continent, told Mackenzie King. "It came at just the right time, particularly for us." It also marked the nadir of isolationist sentiment in Canada. "You can go home and tell the Old Country that any talk they may hear of Canada being isolationist . . . is just nonsense," Henry Willis-O'Connor, the Governor General's senior aide, emphasized to Lascelles.

Even as the 42,000-ton *Empress of Britain* steamed back to England with the royal entourage, events were now moving at a pace that no statesman, certainly not King, could hope to control. Relations between Britain and Germany were deteriorating so fast that rumours spread: both Winston Churchill and Anthony Eden, so it was whispered, would be included in the British cabinet. King was horrified. For years this maverick pair had fought appeasement with bulldog ferocity. Yet King would not give up, and it is impossible not to admire his stubborn insistence on clinging to the idea of a negotiated peace. War would wreck his entire political program of massive social services to conquer the Depression and to prevent Quebec from dismantling the shaky edifice of national unity.

But war was coming, and no plaintive pleas from Canada could slow the momentum. On August 25, King tried one last time to reason with the unreasonable by sending dual messages to Hitler and to the president of Poland. "The people of Canada . . . believe that force is no substitute for reason." Surely Hitler's "great power and authority will be used to prevent impending catastrophe. . . ." It was a vain hope. Hitler did not bother to reply.

Six days later, as Canadians sang "There'll Always Be an England" and danced the Lambeth Walk, German tanks rolled over Poland. Britain and France declared war on September 3, but Canada registered her independence by waiting a week before accepting the inevitable.

The war had six years to run—much more a world conflict than its predecessor, for it sucked in Africa, Asia, India, Australia, and New Zealand as well as Europe and North America. When it was finally over, Mackenzie King would still be in power, an international statesman by that time, not quite the equal of Roosevelt, Churchill, or Stalin, but close enough to bask in the verdict of history.

BOOK THREE

The Global War

"Buzz" Beurling

1

"When Britain is at war, Canada is at war," Wilfrid Laurier declared in ringing tones during the naval debate that preceded the Great War. Thirty years later, Mackenzie King said just the opposite. He refused to admit that Canada was necessarily at war when Great Britain sounded the tocsin.

Both prime ministers knew that they were talking nonsense. As the Chanak crisis made clear, no Canadian government was prepared to send its citizens to some insignificant foreign strand where the mother country found itself entangled. King, for all his vacillating, knew quite well that when Britain went to war with Germany, Canada would follow. Public opinion demanded that he simulate his country's independence. But public opinion also demanded that when Hitler rejected the British ultimatum and plunged the world into a new global conflict on September 3, 1939, Canada would be part of it.

Stephen Leacock caught the sentiment exactly in an article in the *Atlantic Monthly* in June: "If you were to ask any Canadian, 'Do you have to go to war if England does?' he'd answer at once, 'oh no.' If you then said, 'Would you go to war if England does?' he'd answer, 'oh, yes.' And if you asked, 'Why?' he would say, reflectively, 'Well, you see, we'd *have* to.'"

To maintain the fiction that she was a totally independent state, "subordinate in no way" to Britain, Canada waited a week while Parliament indulged in a ritual debate on a matter that was foreordained. This was no ringing, clarion call to arms. To Bruce Hutchison, King's biographer, the Prime Minister's lengthy speech was "bumbling and lamentable," marked by an "endless recitation of documents" and "the fussy recital of details that no one cared to hear."

There was a major dissenting voice in the chorus of ayes that day—that of J.S. Woodsworth, urging the country to stay out of the conflict. There he stood in his place, a slender wisp of a man, with the House deathly silent as he clung to the creed from which he would never vary.

"I have boys of my own," the CCF leader said, "and I hope they are not cowards. But if any of these boys, not from cowardice but through belief, is willing to take his stand on this matter and if necessary to face a concentration camp or a firing squad, I shall be more proud of that boy than if he enlisted for the war."

Canada had declared war at last! But the mood of the country was markedly different from that in 1914. In Ottawa, Hugh Keenleyside, walking along Sparks Street toward his office in the East Block on the day Britain entered the war, had noted the strange silence, "a silence one could almost feel" that seemed to brood over the city. The few people he met were depressed, grim, almost monosyllabic, and when they spoke it was with anger and revulsion. "Memories of 1914–18 were in everyone's mind, and we were now convinced that it was all going to happen again. Yet, strangely, there was mixed with the dejection and wrath a curious and almost universal sense of relief." That attitude was reflected in the words of a colleague: "Well, we knew it was coming and now it has. We'll *have* to go through the whole bloody thing again."

British Columbia's great painter Emily Carr sensed the same mood in an outing in a Victoria park. "Nobody was smiling," she told her diary. "Everybody spending Labour Day guiltily, in a melancholy peace."

The low-key reaction of the public was reflected in the equally low-key announcement of Canada's declaration broadcast by the CBC— a news report that allowed the *Financial Post* to indulge in an early example of CBC-bashing:

"No sense of the sober gravity of the moment seized the CBC. Raucous swing band music continued. Suddenly, the music stopped. The blare of the clarinets and saxophones were stilled while the news announced that Canada had formally declared war. And then without a second's silence came the announcer's voice: molten, mellow tones poured into a mould . . . while the government's radio swung back into the utterly inappropriate Broadway dance tune, 'I Poured My Heart into a Song.'"

The point, of course, was that the official declaration was scarcely news. Everybody knew what was coming. Newfoundland, then a colony, had been officially at war for a week. Most newspapers didn't bother to give the new war the main headline but placed it beneath the real news that was coming out of the German blitzkrieg in Poland. The week-long delay did have one advantage. Because Canada was still officially neutral, President Roosevelt was able to dispatch a number of obsolete aircraft to bolster the thin resources of the RCAF. The old planes were trundled up to the border and lassoed by Canadians on the other side who hauled them into Canadian territory.

It was the season of the fall fair in Canada, a harvest ceremony so entrenched that the biggest of all, the Canadian National Exhibition, could easily out-do its major American rivals, the two 1939 World's Fairs in San Francisco and New York, which pretended to look cheerfully forward into an unclouded future. But the future looked gloomy to the throngs that surged through the Princes' Gates in Toronto on the day following Parliament's decision. They bore little relation to the crowds of August that greeted the start of the Great War. The country had as yet no sense of the truly staggering dimensions of the sacrifice that would be required.

The prime minister's plan—it seems naive in retrospect—was to fight a war of limited liability in which Canada would suffer as few casualties as possible and thus escape the devastating results of another searing conscription crisis. The emphasis would be on air training. The future was in the clouds, where adventure was still to be found. George Drew's recent *Maclean's* series had taken some of the sting out of the Great War by reintroducing Canadians to the deeds of Bishop, Barker, Collishaw, and others—a pantheon of heroes in a country desperately yearning for role models. The RCAF had already been given priority in the parliamentary estimates; that was where the future lay, or so King believed. He saw the nation as the arsenal of democracy, its farms turning out food and its factories armaments for the Allied cause, with bloodshed kept to a minimum.

In March of that year the Opposition had agreed with his wistful belief that "the days of great expeditionary forces of infantry crossing the ocean are not likely to recur." The Commonwealth Air Training

324

Plan in Canada that the British government was urging would be a politically appealing alternative. It would reduce the pressure on manpower that a huge army would create and would keep a good portion of the air force at home, training other pilots and therefore out of danger. It would be costly, but, as Charles Stacey, the official historian of the war, has written, it "seemed an answer to any Canadian politician's prayer; and King embraced it accordingly."

Yet King's policy of keeping as many young Canadians as possible at home and out of danger, though laudable to some, probably cost as many lives as it might have saved. The neglect of the military during the Depression, coupled with the disinclination to give it the kind of battle experience that every soldier needs to survive, was to have its effect on the untested Canadian army when it finally departed from its garrison duties in England and found itself up against Hitler's hardened veterans.

The legacy of the Great War obsessed Mackenzie King as it obsessed so many who had survived that ordeal. It was not so much the spectres of the 60,000 dead that disturbed his dreams and haunted his nightmares; it was the memory of the 1917 conscription crisis that had torn the country apart, creating a schism that had not yet healed.

When the war broke out—a war that many thought would be over by Christmas—the Prime Minister had reiterated a firm pledge to Parliament: "I wish now to repeat the undertaking I gave . . . on March 30 last," he said on September 8. "The present government believes that conscription of men for overseas service will not be a necessary or effective step. No such measure will be introduced by the present administration."

In those early months, King was caught in a crossfire. In Quebec, Maurice Duplessis was sniping at the King ministry on the grounds that its war measures infringed on provincial rights. In Ontario, Premier Mitchell Hepburn fired a broadside in the form of a resolution denouncing the government's lacklustre war effort.

Duplessis called a snap election for October 25, 1939. King countered by throwing his Quebec ministers into the fray, led by Ernest Lapointe, his right-hand man and minister of justice, who swore that if Duplessis won, he and all the Quebec ministers would resign. In the government's view, Duplessis was waging an anti-war campaign that could easily weaken King's anti-conscription ministers in Quebec, making them less effective than their pro-conscription colleagues in English Canada. In this convoluted argument, a Duplessis victory was seen, in the words of Professor Frank Scott, as "more likely to bring on conscription than to retard it." Fortunately for King, the Quebec premier was soundly trounced and his Liberal opponent, Adélard Godbout, took over.

No sooner was Duplessis out of the way than Hepburn, the maverick Ontario onion farmer, launched his own attack in the legislature on January 18, regretting that the King government "has made so little effort to prosecute Canada's duty in the war in the vigorous manner the people of Canada desire to see."

The wily prime minister responded by calling his own snap election, calculated to deflate Hepburn and to catch the Tory opposition in the House unprepared. As in Quebec, conscription was the issue. No matter how forcefully Dr. Robert Manion, the Conservative leader, tried to emphasize his opposition to compulsory overseas service, he continued to be plagued by the memory of his party's past sins. The public feared the Tories would bring in conscription.

The Liberal strategy was to seize the middle ground in the election and to be all things to all voters. Norman Lambert, president of the National Liberal Federation, spelled it out in a February 1 memo: "We shall blow both hot and cold on the subject of preparedness for war, showing that the Government in its wisdom and foresight did actually make great strides in the matter of preparedness while, at the same time, the Government had to fight against a Canadian public opinion, which was definitely antagonistic to anything approaching military preparedness."

This policy won for Mackenzie King the largest majority in the country's history: 178 seats for the Liberals out of 245, with a solid mandate of 58 seats in Quebec and the Tories clinging to no more than 39. King was now in complete control of the electorate for the duration of the European conflict. It was not just luck; his own political canniness had led him to call the election during the period of the phony war when a policy of limited liability was acceptable and even popular. His belief that expeditionary forces were things of the past was as unrealistic as his earlier conviction that he could reason with Hitler. Conscription may have been unpopular in some quarters, but English Canadians certainly wanted Canadian volunteers to join the fray, not so much for imperialistic reasons or sentimental patriotism, though these were present, but simply because *it was the thing to do.* In spite of the tragic memories of the Great War, in spite of the isolationism of the thirties, in spite of a bloody and dismaying future, they wanted their country involved. In this they differed profoundly from their neighbours across the border. Significantly, Canada was the only major country in all the Americas that had not separated itself violently from Europe. Now it was answering the call of history.

In 1939, a million Canadians were still on relief. Hunger as much as patriotism drove them to the recruiting stations. The lure of $1.30 a day and three square meals was hard for the "breadliners" to resist. A few days before the war began, the commanding officers of militia regiments across the country had received a one-word telegram: *Mobilize.* They needed little more to fill their ranks. So great was the influx that recruiting officers could afford the luxury of accepting only perfect specimens. Medical officers rejected more than they accepted, most of whom were turned down, apparently, because few had been able to afford to pay dental bills during the Depression.

The volunteers were in no better shape than the army itself, which, until 1938, hadn't possessed a single tank. The uniforms were as obsolete as the Lewis guns, so old and moth-eaten that Farley Mowat, the historian of the Hastings and Prince Edward Regiment, described the new troops on parade as resembling "a motley collection of comic opera soldiers from a third-rate vaudeville production." Tip Top Tailors, the nation's first war industry, moved into high gear, producing new uniforms at the rate of 25,000 a week. Women war workers stuffed encouraging messages, such as "God Bless You," into some of the pockets, only to have them removed by government inspectors who

327

thought these might be coded spy messages. Here, in these uniforms, could be glimpsed the last, wistful gasp of imperialism. All dominion soldiers would be garbed identically in the British battledress.

The vanguard of the Canadian First Division arrived in England that December. By January, 23,000 Canadians had crossed the ocean, most of them to be hived in the Aldershot area. Half were raw recruits with no military training. Many would not see their wives or families for almost six years. Of these men and those who followed—five divisions, close to half a million soldiers—some 41,000 would leave their bones on the battlefields of Europe. It was a substantial loss, but given the population increase not nearly as great as that suffered in the Great War. The figures bear repeating: in the 1914–18 war, one man in eleven was killed; in the Second World War, the number would be one in twenty-six.

Following his smashing victory in March, Mackenzie King began to assemble what is universally acknowledged as the greatest and most powerful cabinet in Canadian history. Prodigious workers, hard driving, innovative, scornful of red tape, the elite ministers became the stars of the day, their photographs in the press, their pronouncements in the headlines, their exploits and backgrounds fodder for the periodicals, their names familiar to virtually every adult Canadian. With the exception of the flawed general Andrew McNaughton, whose own star would burn fiercely and then fizzle out, they managed to outshine the dour and colourless military leaders who sat on the sidelines for more than half the war. This was a complete reversal from the Great War days when Arthur Currie, "Batty Mac" Macdonnell, Victor Odlum, yes, and Andy McNaughton too, had basked in whatever limelight the censors allowed.

King put his cabinet together between the end of the phony war and the fall of France. In March he put the tough-minded, American-born Clarence Decatur Howe (already in cabinet) in charge of a new department, Munitions and Supply, where Howe swiftly established himself as "minister of everything." Next to King's burly, slow-spoken Quebec deputy, Ernest Lapointe, Howe was the most influential man in the

328

cabinet—in Lord Beaverbrook's words, "one of a handful of men of whom it can be said 'But for him the war would have been lost.'"

The all-powerful minister revolutionized Canadian industry, let contracts for staggering sums, and, with near dictatorial powers, put Canada on a wartime planned economy. He grabbed top business executives from industry and public service, "men of experience, men who know values, men of absolute integrity"—men such as Donald Gordon, the future president of the CNR, and E.P. Taylor, who founded Argus Corporation—paid them a dollar a year, and set an example by working fourteen hours a day, with lunch at his desk. Howe had little understanding of the heritage of his adopted country. At one point he wanted to tear down the venerable East Block of the Parliament Buildings—John A. Macdonald's office and all—and replace it with a modern office building. From that he was dissuaded, but as a benevolent wartime despot he had no peer.

By July 1940, King's powerhouse cabinet was in place. James Layton Ralston, a decorated veteran from the Great War with a pugnacious profile to match, became minister of defence. Another tough nut, especially when it came to money, he had, as minister of finance, brought in a record $1.1 million budget, slapped an excess profits tax on business, and taxed everybody, from automobile importers to single men.

When Ralston moved to defence, he was succeeded by James Lorimer Ilsley, a red-headed Nova Scotian who had little use for King but served faithfully under him. Ilsley, who dealt in millions, was so parsimonious he used the streetcar to save gasoline and so hard-working he ruined his health trying to fight inflation and solve the intricate problem of wartime finance. Ilsley avoided the backslapping techniques of the run-of-the-mill politician, although, as Grant Dexter, the veteran Winnipeg *Free Press* journalist, wrote, he had "great aptitude for coating bitter pills." He couldn't be wheedled, had no ambition for place, power, or money, and was immune to flattery. But the public admired him for his courage, common sense, and honesty.

Maclean's described the new air minister, Charles Gavin "Chubby" Power, as the "surprise of Ottawa." The antithesis of his colleague,

Ralston, and a one-time playboy, he had become "a brilliant, driving minister, resourceful and innovating, decisive and masterful in cabinet, a cutter of red tape, irreverent of military formula." The third man responsible for the armed forces, the minister of national defence for naval services, was the "poetic Gael" Angus Macdonald, the orator of the cabinet. His wife had warned him to stay out of the cabinet and told him not to trust Mackenzie King. "He will use you all," she told an informal meeting of her husband, Ralston, and Ilsley, "and when he is finished with you will hurl you from the battlements." As Colonel Richard Malone, a Canadian liaison officer, put it in his memoirs, "her warning proved entirely accurate . . . in the end he betrayed them and discarded them ruthlessly."

The phony war ended in the late spring and early summer of 1940 with the German blitzkrieg across the Low Countries, the British retreat from Dunkirk, the replacement of Neville Chamberlain by Winston Churchill, and, on June 22, the fall of France.

André Laurendeau, the young editor of *L'Action Nationale*, recalled those days: "The thing that most surprised me was the dull pain you could read on the faces of the Montreal crowds. I didn't think France represented that kind of reality for them. But for several days, for several weeks even, it was as if the city was in mourning. People were wounded personally; they felt pained, deceived, perhaps a little ashamed, for their pride in the name 'français,' which they bore and loved, had been roughly shaken."

To King, the German victories put Canada in mortal danger. All her efforts, he told himself, must be concentrated on repulsing a potential invader: "My heart aches for the people in the British Isles. However I see wherein now that there is a real possibility of invasion of our shores, an effort will be made to seize this country as a prize of war. We have, therefore, changed now to the stage where defence of this land becomes our most important duty." In short, the possibility of overseas service was out of the question, and that avoided the disagreeable necessity of conscription beyond the nation's borders.

King, of course, was grasping at the weakest of straws. The Germans had not shown they could cross the English Channel, let alone the Atlantic. But the vision of a nation united in diversity, its sons and daughters standing shoulder to shoulder in a common cause, determined to repulse the Nazis in Churchillian fashion on the beaches, was as enchanting as it was unlikely.

Meanwhile, the Canadian Legion was demanding conscription and King's own cabinet colleagues were pressing for a wartime measure that would allow the government to call out every young man in Canada for military training. That resulted in the National Resources Mobilization Act, enacted on June 21, just one day before the fall of France, that allowed the government to requisition the property and services of male Canadians for home defence. King made it clear that this bill would relate solely to the defence of Canada. Recruiting would continue on a voluntary basis, he told Parliament, and no measure for overseas conscription would be introduced by his administration. The Prime Minister also promised that national registration would follow but again found it necessary to declare that "the registration will have nothing to do with the recruitment of men for overseas service." Chubby Power followed with details: "Every able-bodied man in Canada will be given the opportunity of training in the use of arms, so as to come to the defence of the homeland if necessary." The period of service, required of unmarried men only, was fixed at thirty days.

That was a gesture of sorts, but only a gesture, "very costly and completely useless" in the assessment of the chief of the general staff, Harry Crerar. "Of what possible utility could it be to train men for thirty days?" Crerar asked in a private interview with Grant Dexter. "None. We now have in Canada a direct conflict in policy—compulsion at home, voluntary enlistment for overseas. These were mutually destructive."

Crerar's criticism was echoed by Arthur Meighen, who attacked the NRMA program in the Senate as a "colossal waste that would produce nothing but half-trained, hothouse soldiers." On the other hand, Crerar admitted, thirty days' training was all the army could handle because of the lamentable lack of equipment—obsolete American rifles of Great War vintage and no ammunition.

National registration began across the country on August 1. The next day the ebullient and popular mayor of Montreal, Camillien Houde, issued a press statement attacking the entire concept as a step toward conscription. He announced he would have nothing to do with it, revoked the city's permits allowing municipal buildings to be used for the registration, and asked the populace as a whole not to conform to the law.

Houde was the most colourful chief magistrate in the country, known from Victoria to Charlottetown for his wit, his charm, and his vast bulk. Standing at five foot seven, he weighed 267 pounds—a French Canadian with a huge head, black, snapping eyes, and a monstrous clown's nose. Four times mayor of Montreal, he inspired a host of anecdotes, the best known being that he had actually managed to make the King laugh during the 1939 royal tour. In the great banquet hall of the Windsor Hotel, the assembled VIPs were suddenly amazed to see the reticent monarch burst into gay, spontaneous laughter and invite the Queen, on Houde's left, to share in the joke—an action that caused a marked lessening of tension among the nervous brass hats who had feared the impetuous mayor would spoil everything with an offhand remark.

Houde later explained how he had managed to break the ice after a quarter of an hour of painful silence at the head table when he pulled a piece of paper from his pocket and, frowning at it, spoke to himself: "Now I have been told that I must not address my King unless he speaks to me himself. However, were he to speak to me, I would certainly tell him many things, remembering not to mention these subjects I was told to steer clear from." The King reached for Houde's memo, laughed heartily, and from that point on enjoyed himself.

One year later Houde became a guest of His Majesty's government, behind barbed wire in an internment camp for the next four years. When somebody remarked later that this was a curious turn of events, Houde replied, "Not curious at all. Return of courtesies."

Houde's swift internment, which came just two days after his statement regarding national registration, touched off a controversy across the country, not so much because of what had been done to Houde but

332

because of the actions of the official censor. All newspapers, as well as the Canadian Press, were warned by the censor that any publicity on the incident would probably constitute an offence under the Defence of Canada regulations. However, the early editions of both the Toronto *Globe and Mail* and the Montreal *Gazette* had already quoted Houde. The *Gazette*, indeed, had run an eight-column headline and a lengthy front-page editorial on the incident. In the next edition both had vanished from the paper to be replaced by a small report that they had been removed "by order of the censor at Ottawa."

There followed a struggle between the press and the censor. Irish-born John Bassett, president of the *Gazette* and an old press gallery hand, knew exactly what to do. He phoned R.B. Hanson, the Conservative leader in the House, and gave him the full text of the Houde statement. Hanson read it into Hansard, over which the censor had no authority. But newspapers were forbidden to comment or report on any other aspect of the incident. They could publish the text of the Hansard report, nothing more. In a confidential report to the press, the censor asked that editors "refrain from material likely to aggravate harmful controversy between groups in Canada." As a result, every major newspaper in the country recorded its opposition—"devastating in near unanimity," to quote the *Globe and Mail*—to the suppression of public statements by men of prominence.

The censor had clearly bungled in trying to hush up an incident that could not be concealed. For the King government, the whole matter was an embarrassment. As the Toronto *Telegram* asked, were the censors mere yes-men for the government? Were they only rubber stamps for the ministers? "Does the attempt to suppress the news of the Houde incident reflect the policy of the Government in such matters?"

Yet the censors deserve some sympathy. They were in the tricky position of trying to stop news reports or subversive statements when they had no power to do so and, as Gillis Purcell, the chairman of Canadian Press, put it, "no sound reason for feeling that they should." Finally, in August 1942, the censorship regulations were loosened. The department of justice ruled that irrespective of the law, no newspaper could be prosecuted for reporting in good faith a publicly made subversive statement, providing it was not supported or exploited. Newspapers no longer had to submit such matter to the censors; if they did, in borderline cases, it was automatically cleared. As Purcell reported, "The censor's worst bugbear—rulings on opinion—had been all but eliminated."

Houde, however, remained behind barbed wire. He took his incarceration philosophically, the most even-tempered of all the prisoners, according to a fellow inmate, and certainly the most popular. At one camp, Petawawa, he was the champion woodcutter, at another, Fredericton, the champion long-distance skater, the champion long-distance walker, and also the Chinese checkers champion. When he was released on August 18, 1944, to the cheers of fifty thousand Montrealers, he had lost one hundred pounds, all of which he rapidly put back on. He had no difficulty winning a smashing majority when, shortly after his release, he ran a fifth time for mayor.

2

Hong Kong Late in 1941, Canada squandered two untrained battalions in the futile defence of Hong Kong, touching off a public outcry and parliamentary wrangle that the most feverish attempts at a cover-up could not long contain.

The travesty began in July when Major General A.E. Grasett, having just retired as commander-in-chief of the Hong Kong garrison, passed through Ottawa and looked up his old friend Harry Crerar, then Canadian CGS. Grasett was Canadian-born, though his accent and his Wodehouse habit of ejaculating "What! What!" on every occasion made him sound like a pukka sahib. With the goofy optimism that bore the stamp of a British colonial mind, Grasett assured Crerar informally that reinforcement of the Hong Kong garrison by an additional regiment or two would enable them to hold the colony for an extended period of time against any force the Japanese could bring to bear against it.

That, of course, was the same kind of military nonsense being preached about Singapore. In truth, the British military didn't believe that the Crown Colony could be defended. Earlier that year Winston Churchill had declared that it would be the height of foolishness to send reinforcements to Hong Kong: "This is all wrong. If Japan goes to war there is not the slightest chance of holding Hong Kong or relieving it. It is most unwise to increase the loss we shall suffer there. Instead of increasing the garrison, it ought to be reduced to a symbolic scale. . . . I wish we had fewer troops there. . . ." Now, with Grasett in England pressing his case at the war office and insisting there was little danger of a Japanese attack, the British prime minister allowed himself to be persuaded by the naive argument that if war did come, this show of force might scare the Japanese off! It was an attitude that he later "regretted deeply."

In retrospect this passes all understanding. It can be explained only by the mindset of a time when the Japanese were looked down on as an ineffectual, almost comic people. This attitude seems to have been based on such witty, fifteen-minute radio sitcoms as "Frank Watanabe and the Honourable Archie." Even though they were making inroads in China against another "inferior yellow race," the idea that they could somehow thwart the British masters of colonial Asia was scoffed at.

In Canada the Japanese were thought of as copycats, good at producing cheap windup toys and shoddy cameras, in effect stealing the designs but certainly not the workmanship from their European betters. It was generally held that all the Japanese sabre-rattling was pure bluff. That was the attitude of the British military planners on whom Canada depended, since there was no Canadian intelligence service. In the language of the time, white troops or white-led troops could easily prevail against the "little brown men," as they had prevailed against the "wogs" and the "fuzzy-wuzzies" of the colonial world. Why, the "Japs" were even afraid of the dark—or so it was suggested by those military experts who claimed they were no good at night attacks—a flawed assessment of monumental proportions.

As a result of this remarkable misconception, the British on September 19 asked the Canadian government to send "one or two" battalions to Hong Kong to support the four British battalions garrisoned there.

In spite of her vaunted independence from Mother Britain, Canada cheerfully fell into step and on October 2 agreed to dispatch *two*. Because it would be necessarily disruptive to send two trained battalions already destined for the European theatre to Hong Kong, and since the Canadians would be involved in nothing more strenuous than garrison duty, why not take a couple of regiments just back from similar duties in Newfoundland and the West Indies? The geographical balance—the Royal Rifles from French Canada and the Winnipeg Grenadiers from the West—was also politically appealing.

Not all of these troops had been trained for combat, Ralston admitted, putting the best possible face on the decision, but then nobody in Ottawa was expecting combat. Mackenzie King's only concern was that sending the troops might lead to another call for conscription: ". . . it must be clearly understood that the troops were available and that this further commitment would not contribute to the creation of conditions which would make conscription for overseas service necessary in order to meet all of our obligations." Seven years later, King claimed that he had "strenuously opposed sending troops to cross the Pacific Ocean." There is no evidence that he had.

Because of the international situation it was held necessary to organize the expeditionary force at top speed and under a cloak of secrecy. The kind of panic that generally leads to sloppiness is evident in the breakneck pace with which the force was mounted. There is irony here: if the military organizers and their political masters had planned more methodically and with less confusion, the growing certainty of impending tragedy might have caused cooler heads to prevail and call off a blatantly foolish enterprise.

If, as the Canadian government believed, war with Japan was only a distant prospect, why rush madly about dispatching an untrained force to the Orient? On the other hand, if war was a probability, as it certainly was, what possible use could two green battalions be in staving off a Japanese onslaught? In an obvious, but belated, attempt to justify his own role in the tragedy, Mackenzie King in February 1948 confided to his diary that he had "never been able to understand why the people of the Defence Department were so anxious to send the men they did in such a hurry except to make a name for themselves and the Dept."

Canadian headquarters itself had classified the men of the two battalions as either "in need of refresher training or insufficiently trained and not recommended for operations"—a clear contradiction of General Crerar's later assurance that they were adequately trained men of "proven efficiency." At the end of the war, Major General C.M. Maltby, in command at Hong Kong in 1941, sent an official report on the battle to the British war office in which he declared that the Canadians with their lack of training should never have been sent to the Crown Colony when it was obvious that war was about to break out. The Canadian high commissioner in London received a token copy of the draft, which was toned down considerably as a result of negotiations between Canadian and British military and political officials. Even in its amended form it was not made public for another eighteen months and then only after a parliamentary outcry.

The army cobbled together its Hong Kong force, which included 1,975 infantry soldiers, in just two weeks in an atmosphere of incredible confusion, the result of lamentable staff work. Canada was now paying in blood for its neglect of the armed forces in the pre-war Depression years. Staff officers are the backbone of any military cadre. No commander can operate without them. But they cannot be trained overnight, and the rapidly expanding Canadian army had very few competent staff men in 1941. Those who worked on the hurried embarkation of the Hong Kong force managed to bungle affairs badly. When it sailed on October 27, barely six weeks before Pearl Harbor, it was discovered that fifty-one soldiers weren't on board; they had deserted some time before. Twenty-three *were* on board who shouldn't have been. They had been added to the expedition as reinforcements, even though another battalion had discarded them as medically unfit.

Nobody, apparently, had examined the converted passenger ship *Awatea* that was to take the force to Hong Kong. As it turned out, it was too small to handle the full complement. Some 150 men had to be crammed aboard the *Awatea*'s escort, the CNR's merchant cruiser

Prince Robert. Worse, there was no way the *Awatea* could carry the expedition's transport—212 vehicles. The quartermaster general, E.J.C. Schmidlin, didn't even bother to check what was transpiring. The arrangements to purchase and ship the vehicles to Vancouver from the East were made by minor army officials and a civilian transport controller based in Montreal. No senior officer was involved in planning the expedition. When the controller finally learned that the *Awatea* could handle no more than twenty vehicles, he cancelled the shipment but did not bother to tell the army, apparently hoping that a larger carrier could eventually be found.

The junior officers in charge of planning decided, after considerable discussion, to ship twenty "priority vehicles" by rail to Vancouver in the hope that they could be crammed aboard the *Awatea*. These arrived the day *after* the expedition sailed to the surprise of the local ordnance officers, who hadn't been told they were coming. Eventually, all the support equipment was loaded onto an American freighter that sailed for Hong Kong on November 4 but never arrived, having been diverted to the Philippines after the attack on Pearl Harbor. At the time, none of this was known to the politicians, and certainly not to the general public. The senior planners didn't know that the vehicles hadn't accompanied the troops until some time after the ships sailed. Ralston didn't learn of it until December 15. The troops themselves had no idea of their destination until they reached Hawaii.

When some of the sorry story of the Hong Kong debacle finally emerged after the hearings held by Chief Justice Lyman Duff, Grant Dexter put his finger on the problem in a letter to his boss, John Dafoe: "The truth is that the Army is in the hands of permanent force incompetents. On the one occasion when we had to organize an expeditionary force—Hong Kong—the General Staff, the Quartermaster and the Adjutant General made a mess of it. . . . If we are ever invaded it will be a disaster. The only word for them is incompetent!"

There are times when military ventures take on a momentum of their own. That was certainly true of the Hong Kong tragedy as it would be the next summer when the Dieppe raid was allowed to continue in the face of obvious defects. On October 16, 1941, nine days before the troops embarked, the situation in the Far East changed for the worse. The Japanese government was replaced by a war party under the leadership of the bellicose Hideki Tojo. The United States put its Pacific forces on an immediate alert, but Canada took no action.

On that very day the Japanese were mounting a festival at which every Japanese soldier volunteered to die for his country in battle, his name to be emblazoned in perpetuity at the Yasukuni shrine. That was no secret. A senior Canadian intelligence officer had been alerted by the Americans, who were so concerned that they rushed the news through uncoded. The various intelligence agencies in Canada failed to absorb its significance. Nobody at any senior level paid any attention to this clear indication that trouble was brewing.

On October 24, two more cables from the Canadian office in London mirrored the growing concern over events in the Pacific. One provided a pessimistic view of the Allied position; the other quoted the admiralty's instructions to the British naval commander in China to provide an armed cruiser escort for the *Awatea*, "in view of the altered circumstances." On October 26, with the troops preparing to embark, another cable made it clear that Japan would go to war; the only question was when.

The following day the *Awatea* slipped her cable and steamed away. That same day, Mackenzie King, speaking in Ottawa, remarked that "any day we may see the Pacific Ocean as well as the Atlantic the scene of conflict." But he took no action. Some 1,900 green troops, many of whom didn't even know how to use a rifle, were being propelled into a maelstrom from which 555 would never return and many others would be broken in spirit and in body.

William Allister, a signalman with the Royal Rifles who was one of the survivors, remembered that "a sense of doom seemed to creep through our ranks" and that "the soldiers unwittingly began to echo Churchill's prophetic words that this was 'all wrong.'" But nobody in Canada had the common sense to recall the ship from mid-ocean and avoid the disaster that followed.

When the troops were finally told of their destination, the news was dismaying. "My God," one corporal said, "another Dunkirk!" To which someone answered, "No, fella, at Dunkirk they had somewhere to go."

The *Awatea* docked at Hong Kong on November 16. Although the Canadians would be positioned on the island, their barracks were on the neighbouring peninsula of Kowloon. Allister, who later wrote a novel about his experiences as a Japanese prisoner of war, was astonished to find that life in Hong Kong seemed to be business as usual. The prices were dirt cheap. "Hired a valet at 28 cents a week. He shines our shoes and buttons, presses our uniforms, gets an *amah* to do our laundry, makes our beds, runs errands, serves tea in bed. U.S. fags ten cents a deck. Beer ten cents a bottle—we get shaved in our bed while we sleep—for ten cents a week! What a time!"

For the Canadians there was a dreamlike aspect to these Elysian days. As Allister remembered, "There was a kind of hysteria in the air." Who could believe that there were some 50,000 seasoned Japanese troops only 30 miles away? Spies were everywhere in this colony of a million and a half, disguised as barbers, as tailors, as dentists. Their intelligence headquarters was the very hotel that numbered the top British brass among its clientele.

The idyll came to an abrupt end on December 8 (December 7 in North America), the same day that Allister sent an airmail letter home on the China Clipper. "Nothing to worry about," he reassured his family. "You can rest easy, Mother dear, the war is thousands of miles from your darlin' boy." The letter never reached its destination; the Japanese shot the Clipper down.

Allister and his comrades were shaving when they heard the air-raid sirens. They paid no heed, figuring it was only artillery practice, until one of them walked out onto the balcony and saw Japanese planes swooping. "They're dropping bombs," he said, and, as Allister recalled, "we nearly died laughing." The hilarity died, too, when all the windows blew in and the shrapnel began to fly. As they watched, a Chinese coolie's head was blown off. Some fifty Chinese corpses already lay at the main gate. As the future novelist put it dryly, "We had the distinct impression there was a war on."

In the murderous and unequal struggle that followed, the Canadians fought fiercely, but they were no match for the hordes of hardened veterans, who overran Kowloon by December 13 and then concentrated on the twenty-nine square miles of Hong Kong Island. Here the lack of training made itself felt. One corporal remembered that he had to teach a member of his platoon how to load and discharge his rifle. Alas, "he was killed before he even got to fire it." Another Canadian remembered that he'd had exactly thirty days' training. "I learned how to left turn, how to right turn, how to salute—all the usual things. But I never fired a shot until I got to Hong Kong." In one instance during the Japanese attack, the raw Canadians were lobbing hand grenades without realizing they had to pull out the pins. An angry British sergeant yelled at them, "What are y' tryin' to do: 'it 'im on the 'ead with it?"

On Hong Kong Island the troops dug in, refusing Japanese demands to surrender. On December 15 a landing party was beaten off by the Royal Rifles. Again the Japanese demanded surrender; again the British and Canadians refused. The orders were to fight to the last man. On December 18 the enemy launched a devastating barrage at point-blank range across the harbour. That night 7,500 Japanese again tried a landing, this time in pitch-dark conditions. Over they came, in small boats, ferries, homemade rafts, and sampans, some even swimming—the so-called little brown men who were supposed to be afraid of the dark. Onto the shore they came in waves—a fifth column had already cut the barbed wire—firing from the hip, dying in the face of the defenders' artillery and machine-gun fire, but still coming, wave after wave, in the confusing darkness.

The week-long battle for the island could have only one outcome. The snafu over the missing transport didn't help. As one private in the Winnipeg Grenadiers put it, "The whole thing was disorganized confusion. Nobody was prepared for it. There was no communication. We didn't have transportation. You carried everything on your back."

The uneven contest was illuminated by signal acts of stubborn bravery. As the Grenadiers' ammunition began to run out, they did what they could with a few Bren guns and half a dozen submachine guns. When Japanese grenades landed among them, they did their best to catch them and throw them back to explode among the attackers. One landed in a huddle of men next to the company sergeant major, John Osborne. Since there was no time to hurl it back, Osborne sacrificed himself and saved the others from mutilation by throwing himself on top of the grenade and taking the full charge. For that he was awarded a posthumous Victoria Cross.

The day following the amphibious assault on the island, the Japanese overran the headquarters of the Canadian brigadier, J.K. Lawson, at the critical Wong Nei Chong gap in the heart of the island. An ever-tightening ring of Japanese surrounded Lawson and his staff. Before the ring closed, a small group of reinforcements reached him, but the situation was clearly hopeless. Lawson informed the British commander, Maltby, at his headquarters by phone that the enemy was now firing into his position at point-blank range. He and the others would go outside and fight it out, he told Maltby, "rather than be killed like rats." After destroying the telephone exchange, Lawson, in a scene reminiscent of a John Wayne movie, charged out with a pistol blazing from each hand and crumpled in the face of enemy machine-gun fire before reaching cover. The rest of the staff died with him, surrounded by a line of enemy corpses.

The worst was yet to come. The colony officially surrendered on Christmas Day; by then the horror had begun. Half of the Canadian forces had been killed or wounded—a total of 783 men and 59 officers. In St. Stephen's hospital at Stanley, some 70 Allied wounded were bayonetted in their beds and the nurses repeatedly raped, often to death. Captain James Barnett, padre of the Royals, had to watch helplessly as five Japanese bayonetted some 15 or more wounded soldiers. There were no sanitary arrangements, no water, no food; close to 90 men were jammed into the padre's room, so tightly packed they could not sit down. Barnett watched as one of the hospital patients, E.J. Handerson, was escorted from the room; a moment later he heard his dying screams from the corridor. A second rifleman was taken out, and again his screams echoed through the beleaguered hospital.

Osler Thomas, a second lieutenant serving at the Royals' first-aid post after the surrender, escaped by jumping into a deep water drain (or *mullah*) and feigning death. "Suddenly," he testified later, "three Japanese soldiers started to bayonet our unsuspecting men from the rear amidst cheers from enemy onlookers. Some of our men had to be bayoneted three times before they would fall and then their bodies were kicked into the *mullah*."

Corporal N.J. Leach of the medical corps was at the same post when it surrendered. About one hundred Japanese troops poured in, stripped the Canadians of most of their clothing, and removed their jewellery, rings, and watches. The prisoners were being herded down a slight slope facing away from their captors when a loud moan was heard, and Leach saw Sergeant Watt bayonetted and then stabbed several times as he lay on the ground. At that point Leach felt a sharp blow on the back of his neck; it shot him into the air and spun him around as he fell face downward onto the ground. Blood was pouring from his eyes, ears, and mouth, and all around him he could hear the moans of dying men. As the Japanese moved away he heard several shots fired at intervals, and after each shot the moaning lessened. After lying prone for some time he pushed himself clear of the corpse that shielded his body and rolled down the slope into the *mullah*, where other fresh corpses lay in the trickle of water. There he stayed till morning when he climbed back to a block of smashed houses and hid again in one of the basements. When a group of Japanese arrived he escaped again, hiding out in a clump of bushes, suffering terribly from hunger and thirst. When the Japanese left he returned to his former hiding place and slept until the next morning. The following day, on the way upstairs he encountered three Chinese civilians who attempted to rob him. He fought them off with a piece of broken chair but was eventually stabbed with a fork. The Chinese departed, leaving him bleeding. He remained in the house for the best part of a week, until he finally made it to the North Point internment camp. He spent the next three months in hospital.

Private L.M. Cavinet of the Royal Canadian Ordnance Corps was another who survived. The Japanese stormed the house in which he was stationed on the early morning of December 23. "The wounded men were literally murdered in cold blood," he testified later. "One white flag was torn down, and our interpreter was bayonetted and pinned on the door to die." The Japanese then sprayed the room in which Cavinet was stationed with a barrage of machine-gun fire and grenades. Cavinet received a chunk of shrapnel in his jaw; others were more seriously wounded or killed.

At this point the Japanese poured kerosene on the ground floor and set fire to the house. The survivors got as many of the wounded out as possible, then jumped out themselves. In the face of more machine-gun fire, eight started to swim across Repulse Bay. Cavinet was one of the four who made it. By that time he was almost completely exhausted through loss of blood and the hard job of swimming two miles. The wound in his jaw had left him dazed. He set off for Stanley but got lost. Shortly afterward, a party of six Japanese captured him and his three comrades. "They tied us together, and when eventually we were made to crawl into a ditch, we knew that the end had arrived for us," Cavinet testified.

"Then the shooting started. I was hit four times and I lay very quiet, waiting and hoping that the next shot would be a clean one and have it finished. I had heard my comrades die miserable deaths." A group of Chinese arrived, looted them of their last belongings, and untied Cavinet, who struggled up the hill toward Stanley. Many Chinese refugees were heading for Victoria with all their belongings. "After one look at me they started to scream and run away. The maggots were falling freely from the hole in my jaw by this time and the sight was not pretty." But Cavinet survived. He was picked up by a truck and taken to hospital, where his wounds eventually healed.

These appear to have been spur-of-the-moment incidents on the part of individual Japanese soldiers and their commanders, enraged at the stubborn refusal of the defenders to quit until the last bullet was spent. They were protected because the Japanese government had declined to ratify the 1929 Geneva Convention regarding the treatment of prisoners of war. Moreover, to the Japanese, a soldier was not an official prisoner of war until he reached a POW camp. In fact, as the luckless

Canadians were to discover, there were no regulations regarding the treatment of prisoners until 1943. By Canadian standards, conditions in the Japanese camps, two of which held the Canadians, were appalling. Treatment was harsh, accommodation inadequate, and rations so meagre that they led to semi-starvation or worse. By the end of the war, 195 Canadians had suffered miserable deaths in the camps. An unknown number of the survivors died prematurely after their return to Canada.

The Hong Kong debacle touched off a storm of protest in Canada, spearheaded by George Drew, who was launching a campaign for conscription with the backing of the *Globe and Mail.* Drew, leader of the Ontario Conservative Party, had some details on how badly the Hong Kong expedition had been planned. In January he made headlines when he accused the government of dispatching untrained troops into an area where it was known war was imminent. Ralston, in a measured speech in Parliament, revealed for the first time what the general public had not known—that the troops had been dispatched without their motorized vehicles.

In the long controversy that followed, Drew was always front and centre. A strong Tory who had his eye on the federal leadership, he had made his name first as the mayor of Guelph—at thirty-one, the youngest mayor in Canada. A chesty six-footer, bayonet straight, who kept his weight at 185 pounds, he had the well-scrubbed look of a barrack room. Neatness and efficiency were his watchwords. His 1937 assessment of Russia ("Stalin's home front is hopelessly weak") was based partially on the fact that he had found Moscow citizens dressing sloppily and Soviet soldiers slouching and smoking on duty. The handsomest man in Canadian politics, Drew was not helped by his good looks. Mitch Hepburn taunted him as "the Miss Canada of the Legislature." As one early political organizer remarked ruefully, it was "too bad George hadn't been kicked in the face by a horse when he was young."

Britain, to Drew, had a stature similar to that of God in an evangelical sermon. The quintessential imperialist, he was suspicious of the Americans and almost slavishly pro-British. When he wanted to be really vicious, he attacked his political enemies on imperialistic grounds.

He called Hepburn "anti-British," the worst epithet he could bestow, and Hepburn's leading supporter, Arthur Roebuck, "an insult to the British flag."

Badly injured in the Great War as a subaltern, he had become a lieutenant-colonel in the militia, but now he was plain Mr. Drew to everybody but the Toronto *Star* ("a vile sheet"), thanks to some shrewd advice from the *Globe*'s George McCullagh, who realized that in the thirties a military title was no political asset.

Long before Drew climbed the political ladder, his byline was familiar to *Maclean's* readers. In 1928, irked by the "we won the war" attitude of some Americans, he answered the chest-beating in the American magazines with a tough article, "The Truth about the War." It sold out the magazine, which followed with half a million reprints, all snapped up in the months that followed. His book *Canada's Fighting Airmen*, serialized in the magazine, was written as part of a crusade to counter the anti-war movement and rekindle some pride in Canada's Great War accomplishments. In 1938, he created a national uproar when he analyzed the contract between the government and the John Inglis Company to produce seven thousand Bren guns. Drew found the contract wanting. All payments were to be made on a cost-plus basis, and no other tenders had been called for. As a result, the government created a new department of munitions and supply, and Ian Mackenzie, the defence minister, was booted into pensions.

A rising tide of public and political pressure against the Hong Kong fiasco forced Mackenzie King to establish a commission of investigation under the Public Inquiries Act. In doing so he followed a practice that went as far back as John A. Macdonald and the royal commission that investigated the Pacific Scandal. He selected as chairman a prominent Liberal supporter who could be depended upon to produce a friendly result. This was the chief justice himself, Lyman Duff, no stranger to commissions of inquiry, a good friend of King, a foe of conscription, and a jurist who had no use for Drew, whom he considered a "damned cad," "a blackguard and a fool."

Duff later told his friend the prime minister that, in King's words, it was "all he could do to restrain himself from throwing Drew out of the courtroom altogether." He said Drew's behaviour was "intolerable." King replied that it was "an intimation of present day politics to gain popularity by being subversive of institutions." Duff remarked, in turn, that "it is a terrible thing the way in which all institutions are being undermined; how few sane men there are left to manage affairs."

Drew dominated the twenty-two-day hearing. Duff was instructed to determine (a) whether the government knew that war was imminent, (b) how the troops for Hong Kong were selected, (c) how well they were trained, and (d) why their transport was sent separately. The evidence from a long list of military and political witnesses was a tissue of obfuscation, self-serving, suppression, and omissions. The Chief Justice ignored much of this. As he told King in one of their cozy conversations—this one at a dinner for an Australian diplomat—he had "his mind made up on the Hong Kong matter," an indiscreet remark that convinced the prime minister his government would be absolved. Although the last witness—General Crerar, in England—had not yet replied to a series of written questions from counsel, and the lawyers had not made their final summations, Duff knew where he stood. His report, when it was issued, was a clear whitewash. Both the government and the military were cleared of any wrongdoing, although Duff recommended mildly that "more energy and initiative" might have been shown in the case of the missing vehicles.

King was delighted. The report "really made me rejoice." He sent a note of congratulations to Duff, who, on hearing of the favourable reaction in the House, remarked, "Well, I think this occasion calls for a visit at the Country Club," which, in those days of wartime temperance, was, as a private organization, legally able to serve him a congratulatory drink.

Drew, however, would not keep quiet. Most of the evidence at the inquiry had been given secretly under wartime conditions, which Duff himself had enforced. His report was no sooner tabled in the Commons than Drew, in an interview with the accommodating *Globe and Mail*, charged that the "actual facts brought out in the evidence were so blood-curdling that the public have a right to know what did take place," and that the "evidence of inexcusable blundering, confusions and incompetence had been hidden from the public."

On July 11, Drew followed up with a long letter to King accusing Duff of countenancing a whitewash and charging that he had not only failed to discuss critical evidence but had also misinterpreted what evidence he did disclose. In the bitter, two-day debate that followed in Parliament, King continued to refuse to table Drew's letter because, he said, it contained a copy of Drew's own written argument to the commission and therefore breached the rules of secrecy. The hatred and indeed fear of George Drew on the part of the Liberals was such that a group of King's backbench supporters, all Great War veterans, wanted Ralston to smear Drew as a "5th columnist, pro-German, anti-Russian, with Italian family connections"—a veiled reference to Drew's vivacious wife, Fiorenza.

Drew's letter was not tabled, and the Hong Kong cover-up—a word specifically used by Duff's biographer, David Ricardo Williams—continued. It flared up again, as Williams's careful analysis recounts, when General Maltby's official watered-down report on the battle, completed in 1946, was finally released in January 1948. Maltby's original report had contradicted Duff's conclusions. Brooke Claxton, then minister of national defence, sought the advice of General Charles Foulkes, chief of the general staff. Foulkes indicated that Drew had his facts right and told the minister that if he'd been in command at the time of the transport bungle, he would have had the responsible officers court-martialled. Still, in Mackenzie King's phrase, Foulkes didn't believe in "opening old wounds."

The furor over the Maltby report, even in its amended form, again brought demands in Parliament to table the evidence of the Duff commission and also Drew's letter of 1942. King consulted with his old friend. Duff was so irked by a CBC commentator who had declared that "Drew had been right" that he urged that "CBC should be spoken to about matters of that kind." King was too wise to venture down that slippery path, but he did take Duff's advice that the evidence should be tabled lest the public think the government had something to hide.

King tabled the evidence but not the Drew letter, which Drew himself released to the press. King saw this as "a Tory plan to make me the scapegoat. . . ." Now at last the public knew most of the details of the Hong Kong tragedy. In Parliament, the Prime Minister put the best possible face on it, praising Duff, attacking the Opposition, refusing on the convenient grounds of security to release the two telegrams from London that detailed the "altered circumstances" of the Japanese threat in the Pacific. Nor did he reveal that the Maltby report had been diluted for political reasons.

The Speaker was powerless to control the debate that followed, with speakers on both sides jumping to their feet and interrupting each other until his cries for order were drowned out. The *Globe and Mail*, Drew's personal organ thanks to his friendship with publisher George McCullagh, had the last word. The evidence at last available to the public was "directly contrary to the findings of the Commissioner, Lyman Duff," the paper concluded, adding that all the facts brought up before the inquiry "were disregarded by the Commissioner in his report, and his findings were false on the four points at issue."

Thus ended the lengthy and demeaning squabble over the Hong Kong affair with the country's leading newspaper proclaiming that the chief justice was guilty of a falsehood, with a triumphant George Drew poised to accept the leadership of the Conservative Party, and with the bitter memories of valour, defeat, and a horror that could have been avoided undimmed in the minds of the survivors.

3

In Vancouver on that misty December morning in 1941, with the radios blaring the shocking tale of dive-bombing Zeros shattering the American fleet at Pearl Harbor, a young Nisei girl, Toshiko Kurita, gained an ugly insight into what was to come. An old man came up to her as she was walking home and spat full in her face. She ran all the way to

The displaced people

her house in Vancouver's East End, went up to her room, fell on her knees and prayed, "Oh, God, we didn't want this war. We aren't part of Japan now. We are Canadians. Please help us, God." That afternoon, when Toshiko's mother boarded a streetcar, a white passenger tore off her hat and stamped on it.

It was this sort of racism that caused the uprooting of 23,000 people from their homes and forced the sale of their property. Originally, the government had intended to move only enemy aliens (about one-fifth of the total population of Japanese origin) from the coastal area. But its hand was forced by the intense racist outburst from British Columbia. G. Ernest Trueman, an official of the department of labour who was on the scene, made no bones about it: "The reason for the mass evacuation is not because of the Japanese but because of the whites. The problem was one of mass hysteria and racial prejudice."

To the majority white world in British Columbia, the Japanese, whether Canadian-born or immigrants, were pariahs and always had been, political outcasts held hostage by a government that was more interested in Western votes than in human rights. They were victims of the Yellow Peril myth that denied them the franchise, entrance to the professions, and even admission to the prime sections of the theatres and sports grounds.

When the CCF, at its first national convention in 1932, declared that it would seek equal treatment before the law for all residents of Canada, irrespective of race, nationality, and religious or political beliefs, B.C. Liberals used the pledge as an election ploy in the 1935 provincial campaign. "A vote for the Liberal candidate in your riding is a vote against the Oriental enfranchisement," their advertisements read. "The Liberal party is opposed to giving Orientals the vote."

On December 7, 1941, Roosevelt's "Day of Infamy," British Columbia's Oriental problem became simply the Japanese problem. After all, the Chinese were fighting on the Allied side, and the Chinese dictator, Chiang Kai-shek, and his steely, American-schooled wife were being inflated by the American press into larger-than-life freedom fighters, their portraits on the cover of *Time* and their political ruthlessness transformed into a benevolent form of democracy by Henry Luce's China lobby.

The virus of prejudice flourished in British Columbia because of a series of myths about the Japanese. They were supposed to have taken over the fishing industry, yet when war broke out they held no more than 14 percent of the commercial fishing licences, and supplied only 10 percent of the labour and 5 percent of the capital. Their birth rate was allegedly sky-high, yet the 1941 census showed the average number of children born to a Japanese Canadian woman was 2.75, higher than that of the national average but lower than that of any other single ethnic group. The Japanese were said to be lawless, yet a survey of thirty-three B.C. correctional institutions showed only half as many Japanese in custody as British. In the Fraser Valley they received longer credit from white companies because their credit rating was better. It was true that they concentrated in certain economic fields, such as farming. What choice did they have when their fellow citizens made it impossible to go into the professional world?

The Pacific war put British Columbia in a panic, much of it fuelled by racist attacks on the Canadian-born Japanese, or Nisei. The major cities were blacked out, adding to the alarm. Those of us who lived in Vancouver at the time will remember groping our way through the Stygian gloom and losing all sense of direction as volunteers from the Junior Board of Trade acted as wardens to make sure all windows were shuttered while the radio mourned the sinking of two of Britain's largest battleships. The lieutenant-governor, W.C. Woodward, predicted that British Columbia would be bombed within six months. In Parliament, the member for Vancouver South, Howard Green, warned of Japanese invaders bayonetting prisoners and raping and murdering women. The MLA for Point Grey, J.A. Paton, foresaw British Columbia becoming the "meat in a Japanese sandwich, with landing parties in front and 'quisling, fifth columnists and enemy aliens' in the rear." Few made any distinction between the Japanese-born and the Canadian-born. The attorney general himself, Gordon Wismer, declared that all Japanese were dangerous and advocated their removal from strategic areas.

Ottawa was urged to move all people of Japanese ancestry away from the Pacific Coast. With the inflammatory alderman Halford Wilson leading the pack, the Vancouver city council moved that they were "a potential reservoir of volunteer aid to our enemy, Japan, in the event of raids or an invasion." Mackenzie King, in his diary of February 19, admitted that "public prejudice is so strong in British Columbia that it is going to be difficult to control the situation." Service clubs, veterans' associations, boards of trade, women's organizations all howled for action. The reeve of Maple Ridge, in the heart of the Japanese farming area in the Fraser Valley, warned of "riot and bloodshed." The premier, John Hart, warned Ian Mackenzie, British Columbia's spokesman in the cabinet, that feeling in the province was "simply aflame."

King and his new justice minister, Louis St. Laurent, were worried by the prospect of moving Canadian nationals out of their homes and transporting them hundreds of miles without their consent. After all, Canada was a democracy. But King was even more concerned about the volatile political situation on the Pacific Coast. The solution was an amendment to the Defence of Canada regulations that would give the minister of justice power to "take any required security measure with regard to any person in the protected area." This carte blanche would be excused on the grounds that the Japanese needed to be protected from mayhem at the hands of a murderous mob. Such violence, it was suggested, might lead Japan to take action against Canadian prisoners of war.

The first move came in the spring of 1942 when the government sent all able-bodied Japanese men—about 1,200—to work camps in the Rockies. These men were reunited eventually with their families, who were being evacuated to a series of abandoned mining towns in the Kootenay region and desperately needed male help to re-establish themselves. The Suzuki family, for instance, shut their cleaning shop in Vancouver and shared a four-room apartment above a fish-freezing plant in the Kootenays with four other families. They were among the most fortunate. Those who didn't find accommodation in old buildings moved into tiny government-built tarpaper shacks with two families crowded into a three-room hut. They paid their own board or if they couldn't afford it received government relief, which was deducted from money received by the Custodian of Enemy Property as a result of the forced sale of their belongings.

These forced sales embittered many of the Nisei, who saw their life savings frittered away by a government order over which they had no control. Seven hundred farms, mainly in the Fraser Valley, were sold for a fraction of their real value to the Soldier Settlement Board. Not all of these went to war veterans but were turned over at a profit that in some instances was as high as 700 percent. One 100-acre farm on Saltspring Island that the government sold to itself for $245 went for $2,000.

People living in isolated coastal villages were especially hard hit, for many had as little as twenty-four hours' notice to pack up and get out. A storekeeper in the Skeena district was forced to leave his entire stock behind. The custodian's representative did not arrive to inventory it until a year later, by which time the sugar had spoiled, the tins were rusted, and the rice bags were eaten by rats.

Fishing boats were corralled by the navy after Pearl Harbor and sold at once by a special committee. Their owners never saw their craft again after December 7. Bill Okada's trim white *Violet S.*, his pride and joy, was one of these. He had bought it three years earlier for $2,000 and had converted it at some expense into a deep-sea trawler. After the navy took over, a floating log sank it. It was dredged out of the Fraser, repaired, and sold for $1,000. Okada, who had gone into the fishing business to earn enough to go to university, got $800. The rest was charged to expenses that included, ironically, a night watchman.

The move to the ghost towns in the Kootenays was at first seen as a temporary measure. The internees were blackmailed into staying permanently away from the coast; if they wished to remain in Canada after the war they must accept resettlement. Evacuation farther east did not really begin until 1943, but a good many families, such as the Saitos—Mrs. Saito and seven children—volunteered to do farm work in Alberta. The Saitos left their home on Vancouver Island in April 1942 in order to keep the family together; otherwise the women would have been sent to one of the ghost towns and the men and boys to work in road camps. They left their trim, white-and-green seven-room house for a three-room unpainted shack with no wallpaper or floor covering, no plumbing, no toilet facilities, and only a stove for furniture. Because there was no room, the boys slept in a nearby granary.

The Saitos had no way of knowing their property would be sold. Since they fully expected to return within a year, they left their beds, stove, chinaware, furniture, and linoleum behind. In 1946 they finally received the proceeds from the sale of their home: $50 for the house, $8.50 for the furniture. The entire process had taken place without any kind of hearing.

The seven children toiled in the sugar beet fields while their mother did the cooking. From May to October they worked, thinning, hoeing, and harvesting the 48 acres of sugar beets allotted to them. For the season's work they were paid $27 an acre. In the winter, the girls worked as domestics at $27 a month; the boys went to lumber camps in Northern Alberta. That continued to the end of the war. In the end they moved to Ontario, selecting York Township after being refused permission to buy a home in Toronto.

All across Canada, from Lethbridge to Ottawa, city councils were prejudiced against the Japanese. The mayor of Saskatoon declared that they should be put into concentration camps. Lethbridge banned Nisei girls who had obtained work as domestics and also launched a move to ban all Japanese from beer parlours and liquor outlets in the province.

The mayor of Calgary wanted all Japanese removed from Alberta, and the Edmonton city council went so far as to reject one Nisei who wanted to stay long enough to take a six-week automotive engineering course. Allowing even one Japanese in the city, the council felt, would establish "a dangerous precedent." Only in Manitoba, where the Winnipeg *Free Press* took a strong stand against racism, and in Montreal did the Japanese receive a more friendly reception, though not from the Montreal *Star*, which published a blistering editorial entitled

"Clear the Japanese out of Canada," depicting all as "secret agents of Tokyo."

In the B.C. interior, prejudice was rampant. "WE DON'T WANT JAPS," the Grand Forks *Gazette* headlined. When an Okanagan farmer hired two Japanese as gardeners, a similar bold-face sign was posted on his gate. Kelowna, in the heart of the Okanagan, was a hotbed of racism, spearheaded by the weekly *Courier*, which declared that "their presence is an insult and a stench in our nostrils and no technical, legal, or economic considerations should be allowed to stand in the way of complete expulsion." British Columbia's own federal cabinet minister, Ian Mackenzie, continued to make political hay out of the situation when he declared that he would "not remain 24 hours as a member of any Government or a supporter of any party that ever allows them back to these British Columbia shores."

The King government faced a dilemma. British Columbia did not want a single Japanese within its boundaries. Ottawa's aim, then, was to disperse these people as thinly as possible across the rest of Canada. But the rest of Canada had made it clear that it didn't want them either; a Gallup poll published in December 1943 showed that 54 percent of all Canadians favoured sending back all residents of Japanese race to Japan, whether or not they were born in Canada. To complicate matters further, most Japanese wanted to return to their homes on the West Coast.

In 1944 the government laid down its policy. The Japanese must either disperse east of British Columbia or face the prospect of deportation. A notice placed in the Interior camps signed by the commissioner of Japanese placement carried more than a whiff of blackmail: "Japanese Canadians who want to remain in Canada should now re-establish themselves east of the Rockies as best evidence of their intentions to co-operate with the government's policy of dispersal. Failure to accept employment east of the Rockies may be regarded at a later date as lack of co-operation with the Canadian Government in carrying out the policy of dispersal."

Canadian-born Japanese who agreed to be sent to Japan had to give up their citizenship. The Nisei, many of whom had lived a pillar-to-post existence since 1941, didn't want to go to Japan, which they saw as a foreign country, but most Canadian provinces had made it clear that they wouldn't be welcomed after the war ended. As a result, by August 1945, 10,397, including 3,484 dependent children, had signed repatriation papers. When it became apparent that many had been forced to sign under pressure, the tide of public resentment began to turn, except in British Columbia. With the war over, civil liberties advocates and church groups protested the deportation of Canadian-born Japanese and the revocation of their citizenship. M.J. Coldwell, the CCF's parliamentary leader, announced he would seek a suspension of the plans "in the interests of Canada's reputation among the nations of the world."

The press split. The Halifax *Herald* ignored the considerations of birth and declared the problems faced by the Japanese in Canada were "the fault of the Barbarians of the East who have committed the foulest and most monstrous crimes against humanity and civilization." The *Telegram* of Toronto proclaimed that "any Japanese man who wanted to forsake Canada when he thought Hirohito and Tojo were going to win cannot be trusted to be loyal to this country and he certainly should be thrown out." The Toronto *Star* took an opposite view, pointing out that one of the crimes charged against the Nazis was the deportation of civilians on racial and religious grounds. "That is precisely what Canada is doing in respect to her Japanese citizens." British Columbia's largest newspaper, the Vancouver *Daily Province*, which had never followed the shrill invective of the rival *Sun,* wrote that "we cannot deport Canadian citizens without dishonouring Canada and casting doubt on the value of Canadian citizenship."

A flood of letters disputing the forcible deportation of Canadian citizens, much of it organized by the Nisei newspaper the *New Canadian*, helped convince the government in 1947 to cancel the entire program. Even in British Columbia public opinion by that time was changing. The fact that the great majority had been dispersed across Canada contributed to the change of mood.

Still, there were political considerations, and in Canada political considerations took precedence over human concerns. Early in 1948, just as General Maltby's watered-down Hong Kong report was finally made public, the Canadian cabinet considered removing all wartime restrictions. But British Columbia remained a problem. The CCF was in the ascendant, having forced the two established parties to form a coalition government. This was still clinging shakily to power under a new leader, Byron "Boss" Johnson, who feared that any indication of condoning the Yellow Peril would lose votes in two upcoming by-elections and in the general election of 1949.

And so the restrictions remained in force after the war was over. Canada continued to have two laws for its native born; no matter what their allegiance or birth, persons of Japanese ancestry could not live within 100 miles of the Pacific Ocean. Some 4,000 still living in the interior of British Columbia were banned from moving 50 miles without a permit. Persons of Japanese origin were not allowed to take out commercial fishing licences, nor could they work in British Columbia on Crown lands, roads, and mines or take up a series of professions such as optometry or law. They couldn't vote in a federal election or in a provincial election in British Columbia or Alberta, both of which also refused to pay for their education, hospital benefits, or old-age pensions.

These draconian strictures, which made a mockery of the war for peace and democracy, were allowed to continue until April 1949, almost four years after the war in the Pacific had ended. Then at last Canadian-born citizens were allowed to travel freely in their own country and, if they wished, return to the province in which most of them had been born. Given the shameful history of their long ordeal, it's not surprising to note that the great majority wanted no part of it.

4

The war stopped the Depression cold and brought unprecedented prosperity to Canada. Everybody was working. The shipyards that had employed 3,500 in 1939 now had jobs for 80,000 workers, both male and female.

Don't you know there's a war on?

After ten dreary years of economic slump, the desire to rush out and indulge in a kind of post-Depression buying spree had to be quelled or inflation would create the kind of chaos that had occurred after the Great War. The answer was economic dictatorship—a program of rent and price controls, severe taxes, rationing, and a forced savings plan that could work only in a wartime emergency. As Donald Gordon, the bull-like chairman of the new Wartime Prices and Trade Board, warned, "If it doesn't work the whole economy is going down the drain." Gordon threw himself into the fray with an enthusiasm approaching glee. "Gentlemen," he told one group of protesting trade unionists, "where I come from, black-hearted bastard is a term of endearment."

The propagandists' task was to make any form of extravagance seem traitorous. "Use it Up. Wear it Out. Make it Do," the prices board's advertisements urged. A woman executive who sported an orchid at a public luncheon was vilified for "running around the country at the taxpayers' expense." When one Ottawa businessman sent a special-delivery airmail letter, he was attacked in the press because the missive required special handling at the airport and took up unnecessary space. The common phrase "Don't you know there's a war on?" was universally used to dampen enthusiasm. Negligees and lounging pyjamas vanished from the store windows. Pleats and cuffs were banned from men's trousers. Women cheerfully wore "victory stockings" made from artificial silk in the knowledge that the real silk was needed to manufacture parachutes. A good many simply painted their legs.

Automobile factories turned out tanks, not cars. Nobody was allowed to destroy a usable tire, let alone buy one. To publicize conservation, the president of General Motors of Canada, R.S. McLaughlin, drove to work in a horse-drawn buggy. Some people rode bicycles powered by washing-machine engines. Hard liquor was rationed to the point where, in some provinces, all you could buy was a mickey a month, a stricture blamed as much on the WCTU as on the war.

Canadian manufacturers who were still dependent on domestic sales countered government anti-inflation messages with advertisements that adroitly turned an appeal to patriotism into a sales pitch, especially after the United States entered the war. Borrowing Madison Avenue techniques, advertising agencies used army parlance to push their clients' products, such as one well-known toothpaste: "HEARTS GO A.W.L. When Smiles Get Ipana's Special Care." Others tried to tie their product to military success: "VICTORY WON'T WAIT FOR THE NATION THAT'S LATE: BIG BEN Keeps Canada on Time." Others offered their product as a cure-all for unexpected irritants: "Sometimes army boots cause blisters. After proper treatment cover with a ready-made BAND-AID. No fussing with awkward home-made bandages."

Supporting the war effort was a constant theme: "No time out for headaches. So War-Time seamstresses sewing tanks with blow torches, take Aspirin for almost instant relief." And if certain products weren't available or were in short supply or rationed, well—"Don't you know there's a war on?" Peace, the consumer was told, would bring plenty: "Masonite has indeed gone to war . . . but when Masonite is mustered out . . . it will be available once again and as popular as ever with the Canadian public."

A companion theme was the exhortation to use the advertised product to help service morale: "I'VE JOINED THE ARMY: No more rosy-red nail polishes, no more glamorous hair-dos, no more jewelry, as I'm in the army now. And I love it . . . And on those days when being a member of the fair sex doesn't seem so fair, I sure am thankful for the extra softness of Modess . . ."; "Entertain Service Men and Women in Your Home: TARGET FOR TONIGHT—THE RITZ! When the Air Force comes to tea there's no need to make it 'fancy' . . . just put down a big plateful of Ritz and watch them hover over the target! Ritz is a favourite with men and women in the Services. . . ."

Ads also targeted civilians at home who had sons or daughters overseas:

"'Do You Blame Me for Wanting Snapshots from Home?' Keep your Kodak busy. Send him snapshots every week."

Even lipstick advertisements carried a wartime theme: "In Defence of Glamour—Patriot Red—the bright new shade for warm, pulsating lips . . . Today patriotism is in the air . . . and the new spring clothes have military dash that's very young and vital. If you'll do justice to your new trim outfit, you must get a new shade in lipstick, too! You'll love Patriot Red. . . . as brilliant as St. George's Cross . . ."

But the award for the longest stretch in wartime advertising must go to Constance Luft Huhn, head of the House of Tangee, who personally signed this remarkable paean to lipstick as a wartime morale builder:

WAR, WOMEN and LIPSTICK—

For the first time in history, woman-power is a factor in war.

Billions of you are fighting and working side by side with men. In fact, you are doing double duty—for you are still carrying out traditional "woman's work" of cooking, and cleaning, and home-making. . . . It's a symbol of the free, democratic way of life that you have succeeded in keeping your femininity—even though you are doing a man's work! If a symbol were needed of this fine, independent spirit . . . I would choose a lipstick. . . . A woman's lipstick is an instrument of personal morale that helps her conceal heartbreak or sorrow; gives her self-confidence when it's badly needed . . . it symbolizes one of the reasons why we are fighting . . . the precious right of women to be feminine and lovely—under any circumstances.

Meanwhile, even before the advertisements began to trumpet patriotism, the government had at last faced up to the problem posed by the National Resources Mobilization Act of June 1940 and the subsequent registration of young single men for the defence of Canada. As General Crerar had noted, a thirty-day training period for prospective soldiers was laughable. In February 1941, training was extended to four months, then to six months, and finally to full time for the duration of the war. The men conscripted for home defence would train together with the volunteers, working side by side in the same platoons, taking both basic and advanced training together and receiving the same pay and allowances.

The volunteers would be known as "A" troops and were given the privilege of wearing the word "Canada" on their shoulders—the only mark that distinguished them from the conscripts, or "R" men. The first of the "R" men reported for duty on March 24, 1941, but nobody called them "R" men. To the entire country they were identified by the pejorative "Zombies," the so-called walking dead characters featured in the B-class horror movies so popular at the time.

Remarkably few novels were written in Canada in the immediate post-war period—fewer than half a dozen compared to the outpouring of some thirty during and just following the Great War—but those that did appear were far closer to reality than their predecessors. In his novel *Home Made Banners*, Ralph Allen, a seasoned war correspondent, wrote tellingly of life in a basic training centre after the Zombies appeared:

> Strange business, having two different armies in the same hut, one pledged to fight and the other pledged to do nothing at all but march around a parade ground, learn a little bit about weapons and map reading and gas and then go away to some other camp to learn the same things all over again. Strange the way the people who ran the camp seemed to be trying to make you feel it was all the same thing and at the same time trying to remind you that it was not the same thing at all. The way the bunks were arranged, for instance. An Active man below and a Reserve man above and then on the next tier, an R man below and an A man above, all the way down the hut, forty-five A men and forty-five R men spaced and mingled in an exact geometric pattern. Kennebec, the man who knew everything, claimed this studied arrangement was based on the theory that each set of bunk-mates would become inseparable and that when the two months' basic training period ended, the R man would go active in order to remain with the A man. Kennebec said the reasoning was ridiculous, like almost all the army's reasoning, and so far he seemed to be right. There was no hostility between the R men and the A men, not even anything that could be called coolness.
>
> But it was pretty obvious that two R men and two A men had more in common than one R man and one A man, and

during the ten-minute breaks in the training syllabus, the two
kinds tended to split into two groups. . . .

The Zombies were given special privileges at the outset—marched
to the drill hall or to a warm lecture room for special talks while, as
Allen described it, "the A men kept slogging across the frozen parade
square with a full corporal howling orders at a mile a minute. . . ."

The idea, of course, was to make everything so easy for the Zombies
that they would "go active," to use the phrase of the day. Only in Canada,
a nation with a split personality, could such an awkward arrangement
have been countenanced, but from the point of view of national unity,
the problem was a very real one. Nor did it go away. As the war progressed, the number of "A" volunteers available began to decrease, and
no amount of patriotic tub-thumping produced enough enlistments to
meet the army's overseas requirements. There were speeches, Victory
parades, a national tour by the Prime Minister, a nationwide address by
Ralston, another in Quebec by Ernest Lapointe, and a massive advertising campaign using press, radio, and billboards urging service in
"Canada's mechanized army" (no suggestion of foot slogging there).
The campaign met its quota of recruits, but after it ended in July 1941,
enlistments again began to lag. The overseas army would need
37,000 new recruits over the next four months; only 24,000 enlisted.

If the nation was lukewarm, one reason was that the soldiers sitting
in England had seen no action. The lack of fighting experience, Ralston
told the Cabinet War Committee, "accounted for the degree of apathy
evidenced by the public as regards the war effort and prevented enthusiasm being aroused. . . ." That did not sit well with Mackenzie King,
who abhorred the idea of men fighting and dying simply for the sake
of recruiting publicity.

If civilians at home were frustrated by the lack of action overseas,
so apparently, were the troops. To the first arrivals, England was a foreign country and a more permissive one. The temperance movement
had ensured that Canada was relatively dry, although that barbaric, all-
Canadian institution, the beverage room, was permitted in Ontario and

some other provinces. But the typical Canadian beer parlour, its tables awash with spilled brew, bore no relation to the venerable British public house. The freedom to buy a real drink across the counter from a jolly barmaid was hard to resist, even among the apple-cheeked farm boys, a large number of whom had never had a real drink before. A quarter-century after the first Canadian Expeditionary Force arrived in England to sample the mild-and-bitter, history was repeating itself. Peter Howard, a member of the editorial staff of the *Daily Express* and a leader of the Moral Rearmament movement, described the results in a letter to his paper's general manager: "The best story from Oxford is the conduct of the Canadians who are there in force. They are becoming really disliked by the population as well as by the British soldiers and the military police. From personal observation I can testify that they are really a little extreme in their pleasures. There were hundreds of them around the streets last evening, and without exaggeration half of them were drunk. They were yelling like redskins, breaking a certain amount of glass, etc., and grabbing hold of the women. They were driving their military vans fast and recklessly and I was told they have had several accidents. . . ."

Their superiors in Canada were already concerned. In October 1940, General McNaughton wrote to all units and formations in the composite 7th Corps: "The many complaints that are reaching me regarding drunkenness and disorderly behaviour, damage to private property, dangerous driving and loss of equipment . . . are evidence of a grave failure in the discharge of their duties on the part of officers, warrant officers, and N.C.O.s."

That same October, the chief constable of Croydon complained about drunkenness and rowdiness, mentioning that Canadian soldiers were "interfering with property left exposed by the smashing of windows," a clear euphemism for looting.

Within a few months, Canadian officials were worrying about a corollary problem. A study by the air ministry of letters sent home from February to April 1941 noted that a large number of Canadians in Britain seemed unhappy in the dark days that followed Christmas. "The damp, to which they were unaccustomed, made them miserable. Inactivity and a feeling of being unwanted lowered the morale of many and made them disconsolate and homesick. They did not understand the English, and the English did not always understand them."

The censors had expected that the Canadians' gloomy mood would dissipate with the coming of spring, but that didn't happen. "The Canadian does not appear to be adapting himself at all willingly into wartime conditions and restrictions," their report stated. "He grumbles repeatedly about the food; and he does not really submit to discipline." But, the censors concluded, the problem was not one-sided: ". . . on the other hand, his suggestion that the Englishman cold-shouldered him may not be without foundation."

This report quoted one air force sergeant, who wrote: "I've been in England for eight weeks now and yet I've never been inside the door of an English house. . . . They don't know what hospitality means." Another wrote: "People over here are not the friendly type, and also I suppose it is impossible for them to ask anyone to their house on account of rations. But they will not give one a lift in their cars. Oh! Well! C'est la guerre." The airmen found the Scots more hospitable, a fact attested to in scores of letters. "The people in Scotland are different altogether," one wrote. "They don't like the English either and think the Canadian boys are tops."

It may well be that these were exceptional cases, although the fact that the censors singled them out for comment suggests otherwise. One contributing factor was surely the difference in pay. A Canadian private soldier made fifty cents a day more than his English counterpart, and that gave him a head start in the contest for female companionship. As General George Pearkes, commander of the First Division, wrote, "The men of the Div are inclined to consider, with some justification, that the English chaps are inferior to them in intelligence, physique, training and discipline." But Pearkes, who had won the Victoria Cross at Passchendaele in 1917, failed to note that the flower of the British army had already been badly bruised by war.

Still, as Pearkes wrote, "One seldom sees Canadians and English soldiers fraternizing in the public houses and places of amusement. . . .

English soldiers appear to be jealous of our Canadian soldiers, who on account of their better education, intelligence and more life, appeal to the female elements of society more than the slower witted English. I can hardly say that English officers, N.C.O.s or men are popular with the Canadians. These remarks do not apply to Scottish units where relations are all of the best."

These remarks by a distinguished Canadian, snobbish as they sound, suggest the ever-widening gap between the two cultures that had been growing since John A. Macdonald had cried, to great applause, "A British subject I was born; a British subject I shall die." For better or worse, Canadians were becoming more North American. The Second World War can be seen as a historical dividing line, marking the slow decline of the British Empire and the ascension of the American. The new order was taking over; geography was winning out over history.

Relations between the British and Canadian troops began to change for the better, however, as the censors themselves reported in 1943. The worst troublemakers in Aldershot were not the old hands but the men fresh from Canada. The arrival of American soldiers in England also changed attitudes. After Pearl Harbor the Canadians began to tell the English, "If you think we're funny, just wait; there are funnier people coming up." To the surprise and, indeed, the consternation of the English, the newcomers appeared to be an entirely different breed of North American. As Charles P. Stacey, the official historian of the Canadian Army, wrote in *The Half-Million*, "One thing is amply clear, and every Canadian who was there will testify to it: the Canadians in Britain did not identify with the Americans. Their wartime experience in general made them more consciously Canadian than they had been before; but their particular experience in England, as the years passed, brought them closer to the British people and gave a new reality to the Commonwealth connection."

Just as the Great War had stirred the simmering pot of nationalism, so did its sequel. Thousands of young Canadians were now seeing their country whole, as through a telescope, and were discovering what every traveller discovers—that familiar landmarks look brighter from the far side of the street. The estrangements of the early war years began to fade. The statistics make that clear: by the time the war ended, close to 45,000 Canadians had married British women and, by the end of 1946, had produced more than 21,000 children.

In Canada, meanwhile, the military establishment was demanding a larger army of five divisions, a prospect Mackenzie King was reluctant to contemplate unless he could be assured that the goal could be achieved without conscription. The new chief of the general staff, Kenneth Stuart, under direct questioning from the prime minister, assured him that it could. "The program has been worked out so as to fit into the government policy of voluntary enlistment for overseas." What would happen after the army got into the fight? Would there be enough reinforcements? Yes, Stuart told him, enough to cover "foreseeable circumstances." To this hazy assurance, which required the same kind of crystal gazing with which King himself was familiar (after all, nothing is foreseeable in a shooting war), the prime minister responded favourably and Stuart got the army he wanted: ". . . the kind of army a soldier dreams of commanding—hard hitting, beautifully balanced, incredibly powerful." And one, it might be added, that would bring plaudits and promotion to the military higher-ups.

The program Stuart proposed was approved in January 1942, and Canada, which had initially planned to send no more than one division to Europe, now would have a full-sized army there—five divisions and thousands of ancillary troops—as well as a substantial air force and navy.

Half a million men for a country of 10 million people! That optimistic figure took no account of the need for labour on the farms or in the war industries. The country was being stretched to the limit. When the war began, close to one million Canadians were jobless. Now everybody worked and the nation faced a manpower shortage. It became acceptable—indeed, positively patriotic—to hire women to perform industrial tasks that society had once denied them. Rosie the Riveter was a popular cult figure, albeit a lonely one, given the increasing absence of eligible men. So many of the wartime songs are hauntingly sad: "Saturday Night Is the Loneliest Night of the Week" . . . "I'll Walk

366

Alone"... and the huge, Canadian-written hit, "I'll Never Smile Again."

By the time the troops got into action in Europe, the number of women in the labour force would double to more than a million, and that did not include the 800,000 women doing part-time work on the farms. To free physically fit servicemen from such tasks as cooks, clerks, or drivers, the government began to recruit women. The number of women in uniform eventually reached 50,000 in spite of strong opposition from military leaders, a whispering campaign that suggested servicewomen were somehow immoral, and the fear of many women, as well as men, that they would lose their femininity if they donned a uniform.

Old injustices die hard. The hierarchical peacetime structure continued. Members of the Canadian Women's Army Corps, for example, were paid less than their male counterparts, and potential women recruits could not sign up before the age of twenty-one while men were being accepted at eighteen. The general feeling was that once the war ended, women would return to their traditional occupations as mothers and housewives.

The government drive to recruit women used advertising techniques like those employed to peddle soft drinks and lipstick. Glamour shots of attractive women in khaki or Air Force and Navy blue began to turn up in the periodicals. Slogans such as "We Serve That Men May Fight" appealed to patriotism while reinforcing the accepted attitude that women were still the second sex.

Meanwhile, the general recruiting for the army was falling; no patriotic campaign could supply the quotas needed, especially when the bloodletting began. There was only one source: the Zombies. The R men would have to be talked to, cajoled, pressured, shamed, bribed, even threatened to go active.

In the training camps where R men and A men had been bunked together in the hope that the resultant camaraderie would persuade the Zombies to enlist, the atmosphere changed. Ralph Allen caught the mood accurately in his novel: "No one was really aware how or even when the almost invisible line ... grew and thickened into a wall of suspicion and hostility. . . ." The Zombies, he wrote, "lived in a little society of their own. They drew more fatigue duty than the active men. If one made a blunder, he was singled out and named by the NCO in charge, in contrast to the treatment given the Active men. During an inspection, if a Zombie turned up with muddy gaiters or an unpolished cap badge, the entire platoon was penalized—confined to barracks for two nights."

In Allen's novel, the platoon is offered a two-day leave at the end of basic training, but only if every man signs up for active service. "I know that no man in Number Nine would want to deprive his entire platoon of the last leave they'll be getteen [*sic*] for a long time," the officer in charge tells them. "So talk it over among yourselves, and that's the British way, the way that means so much to all of us."

Anyone who served in a basic training centre, as I did in February 1942, will understand how close to the truth that scene is. In Allen's book, one Zombie who won't go active is beaten up by his fellows. But the pressure worked two ways. It got the Zombies' backs up to the point where those who thought of going active were themselves treated as pariahs by their fellow draftees. I was one of ninety "R" men sent to take basic training at Vernon, B.C. We all shared the same army hut, without the presence of A men. Three of us decided at once to join the active army, walked down to the orderly room, and received the distinguishing "Canada" shoulder badges. Back we went to the hut to face our comrades who, with a single voice, shouted "Suckers!" It was a good-natured catcall, but it suggested the depth of the Zombies' stubborn refusal to be coerced. The general attitude at the time was, "If they really want us to go overseas, why the hell don't they bring in conscription? Then we'll go willingly." It is significant that none of the men in that hut were French Canadians, who were being vilified at the time for their refusal to be drafted. They were all Westerners, Canadian-born, long since scrubbed free of the patriotic call to arms that had marked the Great War generation.

A good number of men registered under the NRMA succeeded in evading service. By the summer of 1943, a total of 1,351 had been prosecuted for non-compliance. By March 31, 1944, the number reached

5,227. By D-Day some 20,000 had failed to respond for the medical examination for military training. Some of them, it turned out, had enlisted voluntarily. Others had changed the addresses they gave to the authorities. Still, it was a substantial number, enough to reinforce a division in the field. Equally alarming was the fact that of the 1,800,000 men in age classes liable for service, some 608,000—almost exactly one-third—had been found medically unfit, a clear reflection of the debilitating effects of the Great Depression.

Back in December 1941, when the war was transformed into a global conflict and newspapers like the powerful *Globe and Mail* demanded conscription, Mackenzie King had maintained his opposition to compulsory military service. His cabinet supported him, though Ralston, Ilsley, and Macdonald were lukewarm. In November, to replace Robert Manion, who had lost his seat in the 1940 election, the Tories had finally chosen a new leader (actually an old one). But Arthur Meighen, still in the Senate, could not sit in Parliament unless he won a by-election in February. His mild-mannered predecessor had been opposed to conscription, but everybody knew where Meighen stood. He had taken the conscription side in the disastrous 1917 debate that continued to haunt King. Now, it seemed, history was about to repeat itself.

Meighen was no sooner chosen Conservative Party leader than he let loose a familiar blast demanding compulsory overseas service. The Manitoba legislature followed suit with a unanimous resolution, and the Liberal premier of New Brunswick, J.B. McNair, added his voice to the rising cry. In January 1942, two hundred leading citizens—the "Toronto 200," they were called—placed full-page ads in every Ontario newspaper demanding both conscription and a coalition government, which might easily destroy the King administration.

What to do? If Meighen was unleashed, the country could be ripped asunder in a tempest of emotional oratory so reminiscent of 1917. There was one way out, and the pragmatic prime minister seized it. Why not put the question of conscription to the people—not directly, but in a cautious, middle-of-the-road way that could not unduly antagonize the conscriptionists but would give the government room to manoeuvre?

Why not a plebiscite in which the voters could decide whether or not to release the government from its no-conscription pledge? That was the democratic way; that was the Canadian way; that was, above all, the way to mute the inflammatory oratory of the new Conservative leader.

The King government was in the position of being all things to all people. To English-speaking Canadians, the plebiscite, if it passed, could be seen as a giant step toward conscription; to Quebeckers it was nothing of the sort. The voters weren't being asked to vote directly for compulsory overseas service, only for a little breathing space, and King had no intention of moving a single step further.

Arthur Meighen immediately swallowed the bait that King dangled before him and made conscription the key issue in the by-election in Toronto's York South. King's policy, he exclaimed, left him "shamed and humiliated by our Government's despicable evasion." It was "a base and cowardly insult." But with the conscription issue more or less settled for the moment and his CCF opponent hammering on doors and stressing social welfare issues, Meighen again sounded like a voice from the past. The Liberals did not contest the by-election, and Meighen was trounced by a vote of 18,500 to 9,500. One cannot help feeling compassion for Meighen, the long-time loser, the upright citizen who had all the Boy Scout qualities save one: the man with the nineteenth-century mind lacked the political shrewdness to understand his own people.

In Quebec, meanwhile, the anti-conscription campaign organized by Maxime Raymond and André Laurendeau's Ligue pour la défense du Canada was bearing fruit. Quebec voters were urged to vote No in the plebiscite scheduled for April 27, since it was obvious (so La Ligue argued) that the government intended to break its pledge. Otherwise why bother to ask for a release from that pledge?

The result contained few surprises: 2,945,514 Canadians voted Yes; 1,643,006 voted No. In Quebec, the No votes reached 72.9 percent. French-speaking Canadians in other parts of the country followed suit. Significantly, ethnic voters on the western prairies also voted No. These cold statistics emphasized once again the continuing Canadian dilemma that stretched back to the oratory of Henry Bourassa. The prospect of

370

losing support in Quebec and the West confirmed Mackenzie King in his conviction that the government must do all in its power to prevent the nation "from reaching the point where necessity for conscription overseas would arise."

Canada had been at war for more than two years and, save for the tragedy of Hong Kong, no blood had been spilled in battle. For the prime minister this was a matter of some satisfaction. Andy McNaughton was continuing to insist that the five Canadian divisions must stay together as a fighting force, a band of brothers not unlike the corps that had assaulted the slopes of Vimy on that memorable Easter Monday so many years before. Canada's soldiers would remain in England as garrison troops until the big moment arrived—"a dagger pointed at the heart of Berlin," in McNaughton's colourful phrase.

For the moment, then, there would be no more bloodletting, no Somme-like casualties. With that King was content. Yet he could not still the growing restiveness on the part of those Canadians, in and out of khaki, who felt that some gesture was needed. Why couldn't some Canadian troops join one of the British raiding parties that were being mooted for attacks on the French coast? Why not, indeed? The army commanders were enthusiastic, and the British were already planning an attack on one of the French coastal towns. The code name for this foray was "Rutter." But those in the know were well aware that the target would be the holiday resort known as Dieppe.

5

How ironic it is that for Canadians the defining battle of the Great War *Dieppe* was a glorious victory while its counterpart, twenty-five years later, was a bitter defeat.

Vimy and *Dieppe*. They each conjure up a mosaic of conflicting impressions: for the first, glory, heroism, panache, comradeship; for its successor, frustration, calamity, disaster, yes, and even betrayal.

The Vimy triumph, one must remember, was far more costly than the Dieppe tragedy: 10,602 casualties, of whom 2, 598 were killed. At Dieppe the loss was 3,367, most of whom were prisoners of war. The Dieppe force was much smaller—a single division compared to the four that stormed the famous ridge. The Dieppe battle lasted just four hours; capturing the entire ridge had taken four days.

Why did Dieppe fail when Vimy succeeded? The answer to this question is complicated, as more than a score of books make clear. But certain conclusions stand out.

The reason for attacking Vimy Ridge was clear cut. It was part—the only really successful part—of the battle of Arras, and the objective was simple: to take and hold the ridge. The reason for the assault on Dieppe remained obscure. Was it "a reconnaissance in force," as the apologists insisted after the fact? Was it designed to counter Stalin's insistence on a second front in Europe? Was it fought because of Canadian politicians and generals who demanded some kind of action for troops who had not yet been bloodied?

The chain of command at Vimy was simple and direct. It went from Haig to the army commander to the corps commander, Byng, and then down to the divisional commanders—Currie, Burstall, and the others. But the chain of command at Dieppe was muddled by the confusion over who was in charge of the Canadians. Was it the British, under General Sir Bernard Paget, or McNaughton, the Canadian general? Interservice rivalries and personal ambitions caused Dieppe to be postponed and then remounted. Why? And by whom? To this day the argument continues over who made the final decision to launch the attack.

Much of the success of Vimy resulted from the opening artillery barrage—at that time the greatest in history—that demoralized the Germans and made a frontal attack possible. But at Dieppe the planned softening up by aerial bombardment and by a massive naval barrage was watered down—again as the result of interservice rivalries and personal ambitions, and also because of more pressing priorities.

At Vimy the Canadian troops knew exactly what they were up against, thanks to intelligence from observation balloons, night patrols, and captured prisoners. They also knew every square foot of the ground from personal reconnaissance. At Dieppe the intelligence on both sides—Canadian and German—was execrable. The Canadians thought they would be facing a small force of second-rate troops. In fact, the force against them was far larger and tougher than they expected.

Even under ideal conditions—and the conditions were far from ideal—a frontal assault on the most impregnable fortress on the French coast by green troops under a commander with no divisional experience would have been an unjustified gamble. Significantly, Lord Lovat, whose commandos achieved the only real victory at Dieppe, called it "a bad plan [that] had no chance of success." In Lovat's words, "only a foolhardy commander launches a frontal attack with untried troops, unsupported, in daylight against veterans . . . dug in and prepared behind concrete, wired and mined approaches—an enemy with every psychological advantage." John Keegan, the leading British military analyst, has written that Dieppe "in retrospect looks so recklessly hare-brained an enterprise that it is difficult to reconstruct the official state of mind which gave it birth and drove it forward."

Politicians, military leaders, and war correspondents later did their best to keep Canadians unaware of the futility of the assault, portraying it as a "reconnaissance in force," a curtain raiser providing valuable information that would be used in the coming invasion of Europe. But a reconnaissance suggests an effective search for information, a probing of the enemy strength, the capture of prisoners, and, perhaps more important, the seizure of valuable enemy documents. The phrase was not used by those who planned the raid. No revealing documents were captured; no prisoners were taken to be debriefed. Nothing of this kind had been contemplated, nor was there time—a mere four hours—to carry out any kind of reconnaissance. Few valuable lessons were learned that weren't already known or that couldn't have been learned more cheaply and more easily by other means.

The town of Dieppe lay within an encircling horseshoe of dizzy cliffs on either wing of which the steep slopes were bristling with guns. The beach itself was composed of shale and small pebbles over which tracked vehicles could move only with great difficulty. That beach had been a pre-war tourist Mecca; any vacationing Englishman could have described it to the most junior intelligence officer. Why then did no one seem to realize that it would be an impediment to tanks?

Why Dieppe? John Hughes-Hallett, the chief naval planner, explained the reasons for the selection in negative terms: "Dieppe was chosen for no particular reason originally except it was a small seaport and we thought it would be interesting to do—to capture—a small seaport for a short time and then withdraw. . . . It was not thought to be of any particular military importance. . . . And it appeared . . . that it would be about the scale of objective that would be suitable for a divisional attack. . . . But I must impress that we were raiding for the sake of raiding. . . . There was no particular significance attachable to the places that were chosen." Boulogne and Calais, the two closest ports within range of air cover, were too large for a divisional attack and packed with French civilians. That left Dieppe.

Who was ultimately responsible for the Dieppe debacle? Should the British politicians and military leaders shoulder the blame, as Denis and Shelagh Whitaker argue in *Dieppe, Tragedy to Triumph*? Should the main responsibility rest on Vice-Admiral Louis Mountbatten, the ambitious new head of combined operations, who remounted the flawed plan and pushed it through, apparently without authority, as Brian Loring Villa argues in *Unauthorized Action: Mountbatten and the Dieppe Raid*? Or were the chief culprits the Canadians themselves who could have stopped the attack but didn't, as Peter T. Henshaw insists in his article "A Product of Misplaced Nationalism" in the *Canadian Historical Review*?

All these arguments are plausible because in each one there is more than a grain of truth. All the chief participants—Churchill, Mountbatten, McNaughton, and Crerar—had something to gain by the raid, which was really a political excursion billed as a military attack. In retrospect, the conception and planning—or lack of it—seem like madness. But as J.L. Granatstein and Desmond Morton, the authors of *A Nation Forged in Fire*, have written, it was "just one more example of the human inability to foresee the obvious."

It must be remembered that 1942 was a bad year for the Allies.

Sinking of Allied shipping by German U-boats was mounting alarmingly. After a failed attempt to take Moscow, Hitler's armies were still attacking the USSR on the Eastern Front. In Libya, Erwin Rommel's panzers were driving across the desert to El Alamein. In the spring and early summer of that year, Winston Churchill was under intense pressure from the Soviet Union and his own people, as well as the Americans, to *do* something. He himself was angered and disappointed by the lack of aggressive spirit shown by the British in the African campaign, culminating in the unexpected fall of Tobruk on June 21. A civilian Second Front Now campaign had been mounted in England while the Americans were clamouring for some sort of gesture to prove to Stalin that the West cared. Churchill, who had managed to survive a motion of censure in Parliament, knew that something had to be done to appease these critics if he was to stay in power. On June 10, unable to promise an immediate second front, the British chiefs of staff, with Churchill's approval, promised to "continue our policy of raids against selected points on the continent. These raids will increase in scope and size as the summer goes on." During this period, several massive raids on the French coast (with such names as "Sledgehammer" and "Imperator") were planned but for various reasons rejected.

Meanwhile, a frustrated Canadian public (exclusive of Quebec, as usual) was demanding action. Canadian troops had been garrisoned in England for as long as two years. Canada was spending money on tanks and aircraft, but her sons had not yet seen action. As far as Mackenzie King was concerned, that was all to the good. A serious conflict with serious casualties would bring a renewal of calls for conscription and another divisive conflict with French Canada.

Yet a series of smash-and-grab raids such as the chiefs of staff were proposing would not only assuage public opinion but also bolster General McNaughton's refusal to break up the Canadian army. McNaughton and his corps commander, Harry Crerar, both highly ambitious officers, had been irked when the British resisted giving untried troops the lead in raiding operations. Crerar insisted that "a very high proportion of these prospective raids should be undertaken by detachments from the Canadian Corps" and warned that enforced inactivity in Britain would have a serious effect on morale.

Did Crerar really believe that? The idea that ordinary soldiers are absolutely itching to get into action is one that has been promulgated by their superiors, especially generals with an eye on their careers, and by the press. The Canadian military historian Desmond Morton has given the lie to that myth: "No one in touch with Canadian army morale ever believed that soldiers demanded blood-letting at Dieppe as a curb on their frustrations. . . ." Denis Whitaker, who fought at Dieppe, is especially bitter about "the myth that Canadian soldiers were howling for a fight" or that the Canadian people "were demanding the blood of volunteer soldiers overseas"—action for action's sake. It was "a lie propagated by a sensationalist press and manipulative politicians."

The war committee, not entirely convinced, grudgingly yielded to the hard lobbying of the two Canadian generals and at the end of October 1941 gave McNaughton limited authority to conduct "minor raids." Crerar soothed King's worries about casualties by implying that the raids were inconsequential; indeed, he used the adjective "trivial" to describe them.

King's reservations were further mollified by the memory of an early Canadian raid on Spitsbergen during the phony war—a mild effort carried out without any loss of blood. King was no strategist. If Spitsbergen had been bloodless, why not future raids? Thus was the stage set, built up plank by plank, girder by girder, for the greatest raid in history to date, the attack on Dieppe.

The British commanders opposed the raid because the Canadians had seen no earlier action and because they doubted the quality of their training. Earlier in 1942, General Bernard Law Montgomery, then in charge of the South-East Command, had visited all the forces in southern England to assess the state of their training and the effectiveness of their leadership. His report on the Canadians was not encouraging: much of the training was inadequate and many of the leaders, starting with divisional command, were found wanting.

376

Less than three months before the Dieppe raid, Montgomery had observed the Canadians in Exercise Beaver IV—one of the many mock battles designed to measure training efficiency. At the time he wrote: "The weak point in the Canadian Corps at present is the knowledge of commanders in the stage management of battle operations, and in the technique of battle fighting, generally on their own level." Two of the four divisional commanders, George Pearkes of the First and C. Basil Price of the Third, were, in Montgomery's cutting phrase, "no good." Montgomery reported that "Pearkes would fight his Division bravely until the last man was killed; but he has no brains and the last man would be killed all too soon." As for Price, he not only had "no military ability, but he is not a fighter by nature and has no 'drive.'" Both commanders lost their jobs as a result. Major General J. Hamilton Roberts, who would be in command at Dieppe, was found acceptable.

This disturbing assessment helps explain the British reluctance to use Canadians on a major raid. These soldiers and their commanders had been in England for more than two years, presumably training for the kind of battle that would shortly ensue. Yet here was a top-ranking commander, who supporters and detractors alike agreed was a superb trainer of men, casting doubt on the efficiency of the troops and their leaders. On the other hand, Montgomery softened up the importunate Crerar in a letter, remarking that "your men should be quite first class at raiding," a suggestion that Canada might have some kind of role in the prospective coastal attacks.

Crerar's spirited lobbying eventually wore the British down. It was galling, he told General Sir Alan Brooke, chief of the imperial general staff, that the Canadians had been denied any chance to meet the enemy, adding that their enforced inactivity would have a serious effect on morale. Brooke, who had planned to use commandos, finally agreed, and as a result Montgomery promised that a way would be found to include Canada in the next big raid. That, as it developed, would be Dieppe. On April 30, the Canadians were officially invited to take a role in the attack.

Crerar now had to wangle permission from a reluctant Mackenzie King. Dieppe certainly did not come under the Cabinet War Committee's classification of a "minor" raid, nor could it be called trivial. In asking for special authorization, however, Crerar did not indicate its scope. Operation Rutter "*might* involve three brigades, that *might* all be Canadian" (italics mine). This vague briefing carefully omitted the word "division," which also meant three brigades but sounded larger. King, unschooled in military terminology, gave his reluctant approval.

As Lord Lovat well knew it is an axiom of war that a frontal assault on a prepared position is the most hazardous of all manoeuvres. If the defenders are resolute it is doomed to failure unless a preliminary and massive softening up of the enemy's position (as at Vimy) is plotted. The combined operation called for just such a tactic. A massive bombardment of the Dieppe defences by heavy bombers of the Royal Air Force would be, to quote Montgomery's liaison officer, Goronwy Rees, "so devastating in its effect that any opposition would be merely nominal." This was "an integral and essential element of the plan." Additional fire support from the long guns of two battleships would wreak further destruction on the enemy defence.

None of this came off because the Allied services could not or would not co-operate. The RAF needed every bomber it could get for its projected thousand-plane raids on German cities and was lukewarm to the prospect of detaching any of these for the Dieppe operation. Besides, Air Marshal Arthur "Bomber" Harris had insisted that his aircraft could not be used later than thirty minutes before dawn because of the danger from the Luftwaffe's daylight fighters.

The British navy was already under heavy criticism for the loss of two capital ships, *Repulse* and *Prince of Wales*, to the Japanese, and was still smarting over the daring escape from Norway of two German cruisers, *Scharnhorst* and *Gneisenau.* The First Sea Lord, Admiral Sir Dudley Pound, was unwilling to inflame public opinion by risking the loss of another battleship to U-boats skulking in the narrow English Channel. As Mountbatten put it, ". . . should the battleship be sunk, we could never claim Dieppe as a victory; it was highly important at this period to be able to report a victory (Russia, our own morale, etc.)." But how could a victory be achieved if the means of obtaining it were removed?

The raid was to be launched during the first week in July, when the tides were right. The troops climbed aboard the ships in an atmosphere that can only be described, in hindsight, as goofy optimism. The German defence force was estimated at about 3,000 troops, some of whom were said to be labour battalion troops and not of the best quality. The Canadian and commando forces numbered 6,000. With the German 10th Panzer Division as much as 60 miles away, the task didn't seem too difficult. Roberts, in outlining the complete plan to his officers, was not yet aware of the RAF's reluctance to co-operate. Inexplicably, he laid great stress on the heavy air bombardment that would precede the attack. The officers were impressed. Ross Munro, the Canadian Press correspondent who would cover the raid, heard one exclaim, "This will be a piece of cake!" Casualties were estimated at no more than 500, killed, wounded, or missing. "Everyone left that room with a feeling of high elation," Munro wrote. "Here was the job at last; all this training was now to be put to use as the real thing on a daring operation."

The troops boarded the ships on July 2 and 3. Five frustrating days followed as the crossing was postponed again and again because of weather. On July 6, after the fourth postponement, the troops went ashore for a route march and returned in a better mood after the physical exercise. But the following morning the heartbreaking news came: "The operation has been cancelled repeat cancelled because of unfavourable weather conditions." Munro wrote that some men broke down and cried on the troop decks while the officers drank "innumerable double Scotches (at eight cents a glass). I have never been so depressed in my life." By July 8, some 6,000 men were back in their barracks or in the pubs, and within a fortnight scores of civilians knew about the aborted plan. Montgomery recommended that Rutter be cancelled, but Mountbatten, as head of combined operations, kept open the possibility of reviving it. The chiefs agreed; the Rutter forces would be held in reserve under Mountbatten's control until a decision was taken. Montgomery, who wanted nothing more to do with the plan, was cut out of the chain of responsibility, and so was the naval force commander, Rear Admiral H.Y. Baillie-Grohman, who was equally cool to the idea. But the Canadians continued to be assigned to Montgomery's South-East England command.

Direct responsibility for the remounted raid on August 19 rests with Mountbatten. Combined operations issued preliminary orders for the operation, renamed Jubilee, on July 31. On the evening of August 17 the troops began embarking on the ships that would leave the following day. Mountbatten undoubtedly needed Dieppe. The raids planned for the spring of 1942 had, for various reasons, been cancelled. Morale was at a low ebb and would not be improved if Dieppe was cancelled permanently. Mountbatten had his eye on a top job: chief of staff to the supreme commander in the coming invasion. A raid would be his last chance to prove himself to his colleagues and to the public. He had been built up as a glamorous and brilliant wartime leader by army public relations and the press at a desperate time when Britain needed a charismatic hero to keep up morale. His ambition was unbounded; he had already vaulted past several of his contemporaries in the chain of command. It did not hurt that he was related to royalty and was Churchill's protege. During the original planning for Dieppe he seems to have spent much of his time as an adviser on the film *In Which We Serve*, in which Noel Coward starred as a fictional Lord Louis.

He was not quite the paragon whose tall, commanding figure appeared on the British front pages. His official biographer, Philip Ziegler, painted him warts and all: "His vanity, though child-like, was monstrous, his ambition unbridled. The truth, in his hands, was swiftly converted from what it was, to what it should have been. He sought to re-write history with cavalier indifference to the facts to magnify his own achievements." Nigel Hamilton, Montgomery's own official biographer, who had even less of an axe to grind, came to a similar, indeed harsher conclusion. Mountbatten, he wrote, "was a master of intrigue, jealousy, and ineptitude. Like a spoilt child he toyed with men's lives with an indifference to casualties that can only be explained by his insatiable, even psychopathic ambition."

Mountbatten, then, must bear a major share of the responsibility for the disaster. But what about McNaughton? Save for the two British commando units, it was a Canadian operation. All the evidence suggests that this was a harum-scarum production; we know that both Montgomery and the ranking naval commander, Baillie-Grohman, were opposed, and it swiftly developed that the Second Division's General Roberts, too, had his doubts. In May 1942, McNaughton was at last given full powers by the Canadian war cabinet to commit Canadian forces to any raid as long as the British government approved. Because McNaughton and his corps commander, Crerar, did not need to give the Canadian government particulars of the plan, Operation Jubilee went ahead without the King government's knowing any of the details.

The ambitious Crerar, too, bears his share of responsibility. Lieutenant General Guy Simonds in 1969 wrote that "there has never been any doubt in my mind that Crerar was primarily responsible for the revival of Dieppe as a Canadian operation, as he had been in the original initiation." As Crerar remarked to Simonds at the time, "It will be a tragic humiliation if American troops get into action on this side of the Atlantic, before Canadians, who have been waiting in England for three years."

There is also no doubt that Canadian pressure was largely instrumental in mounting the raid, ensuring that Canada had a major role in it, and in remounting Rutter again as Jubilee. In his zeal for Jubilee, McNaughton brushed aside the British military worries about security and backed Mountbatten. He could have stopped the raid dead had he wanted to, but that was far from his mind. If he and his Canadians were going to spearhead the attack on Berlin, as he had planned and hoped, Dieppe would provide a stepping stone to that leadership. McNaughton's insistence on keeping the Canadian forces together would, of course, be bolstered by such a victory. Otherwise, the pressure to attach some Canadian units elsewhere to give them battle experience would be hard to resist. If Dieppe were a success—and McNaughton's wishful thinking assumed it would be—then his dream of a united Canadian army with himself at its head, driving relentlessly to Berlin as Currie and his Canadian Corps had driven to Mons, would be complete.

When the original raid, Rutter, was in the late planning stages and it was learned that heavy bombers would not be available to clear the way for the assault, success would have to depend on secrecy and split-second timing. *Secrecy?* With thousands of men in the know traipsing about southern England? Every authoritative account of the Dieppe raid insists that the Germans did *not* know. If so, it presupposes a glaring defect in German intelligence that can be only partly explained by the fact that, under the Double-Cross system, the British had captured every German spy in England and turned them into double agents. But surely the Germans were aware that *something* was up, although when and where they could not be sure. On the final day of Rutter, German planes had bombed some of the assembled vessels destined for Dieppe. Whether or not they knew the specifics of the attack, they certainly strengthened their forces along the French coast in the Dieppe area.

If German intelligence was ineffective, so was the British. All the optimistic talk about a small enemy force of second-rate troops, many from labour battalions, was given the lie as soon as the landing craft approached the beaches and came up against hardbitten defenders.

Split-second timing? On an intricate manoeuvre of the Dieppe scale, that was scarcely possible. As it was, everything that could have gone wrong went wrong. First, a small German convoy happened upon the left flank of the flotilla approaching Dieppe, precipitating a short sea battle, the sound of which alerted the Germans on shore. Its force scattered the boatloads of commandos who were supposed to scale the cliffs and destroy the Germans' big guns on one flank of the city. Of twenty-seven landing craft, only seven got ashore. Unfortunately, knowledge of this could not be transmitted because of damage to the commandos' radio equipment.

Faulty communications also helped doom the Royal Regiment of Canada at Puys, one and a half miles east of the town. Here, surprise and split-second timing were indeed essential, but the Royals were late, dawn was breaking, and the Germans were fully alert, opening fire on the first wave before the troops climbed out of the landing craft. With the sea full of corpses and the beach strewn with more, it was time to call off the remaining two waves. But once again the radio equipment was damaged; of the 550 Royals, only 65 returned to Britain.

This catastrophe was one of the keys to the defeat that followed. The shattered Royals were unable to fulfill their task of clearing the headlands that overlooked Dieppe from the east. As a result, the Germans were able to continue to pour fire on the Canadians as they hit the beach. The tanks should have landed at the same time, but the landing craft that carried them were delayed by navigational errors. Most were hit even as they tried to land. None of the tanks got into the town.

It was clear that the timing required for victory wasn't working. One regiment, the South Saskatchewan, was landed more than a mile to the east of their objective and found it impossible to get back to climb the high ground and attack the radar station at Pourville. Another, the Cameron Highlanders, landed late and managed to push inland but were stopped before they could reach their ultimate objective—the airfield—and were forced to fall back on the beach. The only real success was that of the No. 5 Commando, which got ashore on time and took out one of the two coastal batteries overlooking the town.

Aboard the command ship HMS *Calpe*, "Ham" Roberts, the force commander, had no real idea of what was going on. The radios weren't working and the heavy fire was putting the operators out of action. When Roberts heard that the Essex Scottish had made it across the beaches and into the buildings, he decided to send in his reserves, little knowing that the message was inaccurate. Off across the churning bay went the Fusiliers Mont-Royal, their purpose to back up the Essex. Instead they were propelled into a hurricane of fire. Their boats were blown out of the sea or shattered, and those men who did not die or drown failed to get over the headland and onto the main beach.

The Dieppe adventure lasted a brief four hours. The flotilla limped back to England carrying less than half the men who had set out. The casualty rate—killed or captured—was 2,700, more than five times the comfortable figure of 500 that the planners, in their giddy optimism, had predicted. The men fought bravely, even fiercely. Two won VCs: Lieutenant-Colonel Cecil Merritt, for his example in leading his men nonchalantly across a bridge under heavy fire, and Major John Foote, padre of the Royal Hamilton Light Infantry, who talked himself into the raid as a stretcher bearer, refused to be evacuated, and tramped for two days on bare feet to a German prisoner of war camp.

Dieppe stands as Canada's greatest disaster in the Second World War. Any statistical summary is a litany of grisly superlatives. More Canadians were captured at Dieppe than in all the rest of the campaign in northwestern Europe. In that half day, more died than in any other day of fighting in the war. The Second Division was all but obliterated; it would take more than a year to create what would be, in effect, a different fighting force. And, after D-Day, it was statistically the weakest.

The decision to remount the battle in which victory was such a forlorn hope was the product of two monumental egos—Mountbatten's and McNaughton's. Either one could have stepped in and cancelled Jubilee. The hard truth is that in spite of the heavy odds against them, they didn't want to. Like riverboat gamblers, they took long chances, bluffed their way through the play, and, when the chips were finally on the table, concealed the weaknesses of their hands. Mountbatten made sure that as few people as possible knew that Rutter had been remounted as Jubilee. He kept his own staff in the dark, including his deputy, Major General Charles Haydon, who quit mainly for that reason. The service intelligence chiefs weren't told, either, nor was the Inter-service Security Board.

McNaughton in his turn told the Cabinet War Committee no more than he needed to, and he didn't need to tell them anything; back in May he had engineered his own appointment as the man in charge, given freedom by the Canadian cabinet to commit forces to large-scale raids. Roberts, who had misgivings about mounting the raid after Rutter was cancelled, reviewed the situation with McNaughton in Mountbatten's presence. He had signed a letter, along with Baillie-Grohman of the navy and Trafford Leigh-Mallory of the air force, asking for a military appreciation—a careful appraisal—of a situation that would involve all three services. They didn't get it. On July 16 at his meeting with McNaughton, Roberts told his chief that if he was instructed to carry out the operation he would do so. That was one of the turning points in the long, sad story of the Dieppe disaster. Although Montgomery had opposed Rutter, as had the navy, McNaughton, who could have stopped it with a single word, chose not to do so and instructed Roberts to go ahead.

The Dieppe raid was clearly a public relations attempt to grab headlines that would help the demands for a second front by the hard-pressed Soviets and also appease the frustrated Canadian public who wanted to see their boys in action. After it failed, every attempt was bent to make it appear a success—costly, yes, and not without its problems, but a worthwhile and necessary curtain raiser for the D-Day invasion. As Churchill ruefully remarked in a letter to Lord Ismay after the fact: ". . . for many reasons everyone was concerned to make this business look as good as possible."

The comforting notion that this was a "reconnaissance in force" was now bandied about. The war correspondents, who were on the spot, rushed into print to emphasize in books and magazine articles that valuable lessons were learned on Dieppe's bloody beaches—lessons that made the D-Day invasion possible.

Thus Wallace Reyburn in *Maclean's*, October 1, 1942: "If we had gone into France cold with our full force but without the experience of Dieppe, we would have been like a boxer who runs out of his corner, takes a wild slug at his opponent without sizing him up through some sparring. That is the first thing that Dieppe taught us."

Thus Ross Munro in *Gauntlet to Overlord*, published in 1945: "I'm convinced that if the raid had not been carried out as a prelude to the North African landings, the combined operations in the Mediterranean and the Normandy invasion, these might have been so badly bungled that the war could have been prolonged for years."

Thus Ralph Allen in *Ordeal by Fire*, published in 1961: "Dieppe . . . provided many of the lessons which made a full-scale invasion of

Normandy in 1944 a decisive and unexpectedly inexpensive success."

These bold and unequivocal assessments served to soothe Canadian public sentiment and assuage the grief of those whose sons had died or been imprisoned as a result of the battle. As the Great War monuments had trumpeted, *they did not die in vain.* That was Mountbatten's post-war alibi and one that the much-publicized admiral made sure was actively promoted among his contacts in the press. In Mountbatten's view, Dieppe would "prove to have been the essential prelude to our forthcoming and final success." He was still preaching that gospel as late as 1973 when he wrote to the retired Canadian general Churchill Mann, "I do hope that the Dieppe boys will have at last understood that without their brilliant efforts we could never have had Overlord" (the code word for the D-Day invasion).

Even before that time, however, as historians and military analysts were able to examine the documentary evidence, early assumptions about the value of the Dieppe raid began to crumble.

The Germans' own assessment of the Dieppe raid, in captured documents that came to light two years after the event, was highly critical of the Allies' planning. Though the raiders had very good maps of the Dieppe fortifications, the German 81st Corps reported, "Corroboration by secret agents was evidently not carried out (e.g., the strength of the tank barriers in Dieppe was not known)." The Canadians "completely miscalculated the strength of the German defence and tried 'to grab the bull by the horns' in landing the main body of their invasion forces, particularly the tanks, right in front of Dieppe. They persisted with this plan although they were aware of the strength of the Dieppe street defences. . . ." The Germans were baffled that "contrary to all expectations" no effort was made to employ parachutists or airborne troops, who might have made a difference at Puys. "It is astonishing that the British [Canadians] should have underestimated our defences, as they had details of most of it from air photos; equally striking is the short time in which they expected to carry out the operation." The rigidity of the plan also struck the Germans. "The operational order fixed every detail of the action for each unit. This method of planning made the failure of the whole raid inevitable in the event of unexpected difficulties."

The German appraisal also seemed to support the early British reluctance to use untried troops rather than commandos in such a complicated battle: "The Canadians on the whole fought badly and surrendered afterward in swarms. On the other hand the combat efficiency of the Commandos was very high. They were well trained and fought with real spirit . . . [and] showed great skill in climbing the steep coastal cliffs."

In 1967, on the twenty-fifth anniversary of Dieppe, Wallace Reyburn in a letter to London's *Sunday Telegraph* revoked his earlier assessment of the raid in his book *Rehearsal for Invasion* and called it "a criminal farce." It was, he said, "wonderful on paper, but a fiasco in practice." Reyburn was commenting on Mountbatten's contention in a speech that weekend that the raid had proved that "a strongly defended port cannot profitably be seized by direct assault." As Reyburn commented, "Why, to use a Canadian expression, did we have to learn it the hard way? . . . All these 'valuable lessons' were lessons that Earl Mountbatten's planners could have figured out for themselves without the sacrifice of 1,137 lives."

Since then a good many books and articles have analyzed the entire Dieppe tragedy. Brian Loring Villa's *Unauthorized Action* (1989) and John S. Campbell's *Dieppe Revisited* (1993) are perhaps the most critical. Campbell demolishes, point by point, the "lessons learned" excuse. His key argument can be reduced to a few lines: ". . . no mere raid could in any literal sense have been a rehearsal for an operation of such magnitude and complexity as the cross-Channel invasion of 1944. . . . It would have taken a raid on a far greater scale than any attempted to yield lessons about marshalling, embarkation and sailing of an invasion force."

It is hard to dispute Villa's contention that Mountbatten plunged into Jubilee without authorization. As he makes clear, there isn't a shred of evidence that the chiefs of staff, who held the ultimate responsibility, knew what the admiral was up to. Long before Villa launched his investigation, Mountbatten grew uneasy. It would create a major scandal and be an end to his ambitions if it became known that he had broken a cardinal military rule and launched, on his own initiative, a hazardous operation that turned into a disaster.

Churchill, in an earlier draft of *The Hinge of Fate*, had written that the Dieppe raid was revived "on the initiative of Admiral Mountbatten." Mountbatten, who was one of Churchill's many collaborators on that magisterial history of the war, was sent a copy and read it with dismay. Churchill, obviously, was praising Mountbatten, not knowing that the chiefs were totally in the dark.

Churchill himself was puzzled by the absence of any documentation regarding the remounting of the raid. He tried to find out but was thwarted time and again. As he wrote in that early draft: "From the time when the enterprise was revived by Admiral Mountbatten, there is no record of the revised plan being further examined, nor of any decision to launch it being taken by the Chief of Staff or by the Defence Committee or by the War Cabinet."

This was an incredible state of affairs. Here was an operation involving the lives of thousands of men that had been cancelled apparently forever, inexplicably and mysteriously revived. If Dieppe had been a howling success, one can be sure that the handsome admiral would have stepped forward to accept the plaudits of the nation. Brave, bold Louis Mountbatten, plunging ahead regardless, putting the naysayers in their place! So what if he acted on his own?

But the raid was a tragic bungle. The last thing that Mountbatten wanted was any suggestion, especially by Churchill, that it had never been authorized. When Churchill asked him to comment on the draft, Mountbatten—who, according to Villa, had written the Dieppe section—simply crossed out the offending paragraph, which does not appear in the final version of *The Hinge of Fate*. There it has been replaced by a paragraph suggesting that Mountbatten had Churchill's blessing for the Dieppe raid: "In discussion with Admiral Mountbatten, it became clear that time did not permit a new large-scale operation to be mounted during the summer, but that Dieppe could be remounted . . . within a month, provided extraordinary steps were taken to ensure secrecy. For this reason no records were kept." What also appears in the final draft is Churchill's statement that Dieppe was "a costly but not unfruitful reconnaissance in force. Tactically it was a mine of experience. It shed revealing light on many shortcomings in our outlook. . . ."

Mountbatten liked to support his version of the Dieppe affair by using Churchill's words. And well he might, for they were his own.

One newspaperman who was not bamboozled by Mountbatten's campaign for self-justification was the puckish proprietor of the London *Daily Express*, who confronted Mountbatten at a dinner party. Beaverbrook did not mince words. "You have murdered thousands of my countrymen," he told him. "You took those unfortunate Canadian soldiers. . . . They have been mown down in their thousands and the blood is on your hands."

6

On November 20, 1942, some three months after the Dieppe raid and a third of the way around the world from those murderous beaches, 200 American and Canadian officials presided at the opening of the 1,500-mile highway that would change forever the face of the Canadian Northwest and establish a foreign presence on Canadian soil. The location, to be called Soldiers' Summit, marked the highest point on the Alaska Highway, a twisting ribbon of gravel hacked out of rock and forest to join Dawson Creek in the Peace River country of British Columbia to Fairbanks, Alaska.

The American occupation

Its purpose was to service the daisy chain of new airfields that made up the Northwest Staging Route, a lifeline linking North America to the embattled armies of the Soviet Union. It wasn't much of a highway, no more than a narrow tote road, a crude trail bulldozed through country much of which had never known the imprint of a moccasin. The task had been accomplished in just over eight months by a workforce of 16,000 soldiers and civilians who cut corners, spent lavishly, and, with the Japanese occupying two Aleutian islands, toiled without rest to push the road through. One typical company of engineers

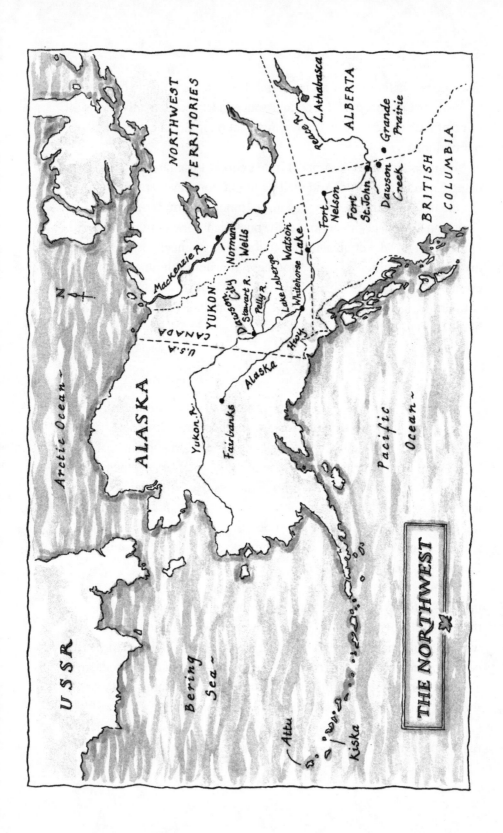

THE NORTHWEST

worked 69 days, from June 14 to August 22, without a break.

The highway project was only part of a gigantic military enterprise that included a string of airfields, a producing oil field at Norman Wells, a 600-mile pipeline through the unexplored Pelly and Mackenzie mountains, a newly built oil refinery at Whitehorse, and another 1,000-mile network of pipelines through northwestern Canada and Alaska to deliver refined gasoline. At an overall cost of more than $500 million, it was the most expensive construction project of the war. In the words of the American army engineer Colonel Heath Twichell, who worked on the project and whose son wrote *Northwest Epic*, the definitive account of those construction days, it was "the biggest and hardest job since the Panama Canal."

It was also the most controversial. Would the highway have any post-war value? Did the military payoff justify the enormous expense? And how about the waste and mismanagement revealed by a U.S. Senate investigating committee?

The project was largely an American effort, conceived and paid for by the United States with the reluctant agreement of Canada. As Ian Mackenzie, the cabinet minister who represented Canada at the ribbon-cutting ceremony, said, "Canada provided the soil; the United States provided the toil." Over a two-year period some 40,000 American soldiers and civilian contractors were involved, the largest number to invade this corner of Canada—an area four times the size of Texas—since the days of the Klondike stampede. "Invade" is the appropriate verb. In Whitehorse at the height of the war, telephone calls to the Northwest Service Command were answered with a cheerful "Army of Occupation. What office are you calling?" It was treated as a good-natured jest by the Americans, but it grated on the nerves of old-time Yukoners. The Americans had had their eye on the Canadian North for some time; now with Alaska vulnerable to Japanese attack the time seemed ripe, in the words of the U.S. War Plans Division, to "take advantage of the present war to secure the necessary agreements from Canada to start work now and finish perhaps many years to come."

The idea of a transportation corridor through British Columbia and the Yukon was not new. The premier of British Columbia, T. Dufferin Pattullo, himself a former Klondiker, had pushed the concept in the 1930s as an imaginative scheme to fulfill his election promise of "work and wages" and to spend his way out of the Depression. Since the Canadian government was not in a spending mood in those lean years, Pattullo put forward the idea of an American loan. Nationalism forestalled him. The B.C. premier got a chilly response from Ottawa. A flabbergasted O.D. Skelton, King's adviser as undersecretary of state for external affairs, told the prime minister in a stiff memo the plan amounted to "regarding Canada or British Columbia as a subdivision of the United States." To accept the money "would be mortgaging our financial independence." King scribbled a note on the memo that the B.C. proposal would be nothing less than a "financial penetration if not a financial invasion of a foreign power."

A highway was one thing, but a great circle air route to the Orient was another. In 1935 the Canadian department of transport had commenced a survey for just such a route from Edmonton to Alaska, with emergency landing strips planned at Grande Prairie, Fort St. John, Fort Nelson, Watson Lake, and Whitehorse. In September 1939, these sites were still being surveyed. The outbreak of war soon underlined their value. They became the nucleus of the Northwest Staging Route, which was ready for use by the autumn of 1941, soon after Hitler invaded Russia in June of that year.

This chain of airstrips dictated the route any future highway would take. It would run through a sullen land, known colloquially as the "Graveyard of Lost Planes," a relic of the pre-radar bush-flying days, when men like Grant McConachie and Russ Baker used the tips of mountains as signposts to find their way through the fog-shrouded peaks. Those days were not yet over, as more than one green pilot, ferrying planes to Alaska and unused to the strange terrain, learned to his discomfort.

When the first contingent of American war planes destined for Russia headed out over the route early in January 1942, twenty-seven crashed on the way to Fairbanks. It took a month to repair ten to the point where they managed to limp into Alaska. The rest never made it. Inexperienced pilots, bad weather, and lack of navigational aids in an unfamiliar and rumpled mountain terrain contributed to the hazards.

Bizarre tales of navigational blunders along the staging route emerged after the war:

- The pilot of a U.S. army transport setting his wheels on the runway at Prince George, looking about him, and remarking in a bewildered voice: "My God, this doesn't look like Seattle!"
- A pilot flying south from Fairbanks, trapped by weather, making an emergency landing and reporting to the White-horse tower that he'd set down on the shore of a large lake. "Taste the water," Whitehorse control suggested. Only when it was found to be salt did he realize he'd flown directly across the peaks of the St. Elias Mountains, some of the highest on the continent, and come out, unscathed, on the Pacific.
- A big plane circling over Whitehorse in the fog and mistaking the town's street lights for a runway. Ordered off by the tower, it was never seen again until months later U.S. army pilots, fly-ing over Lake Laberge, saw its silhouette beneath the surface.
- A DC-3 lumbering into Watson Lake, only dimly visible through the curtain of snow, making a stab at the runway, falling, rising into the air and vanishing, thus touching off a ten-day search by ground parties whose members, brewing tea over a makeshift fire, found the outline of a body beneath the snow—that of a crew member of the plane that had crashed so close to the airfield that nobody had thought to look there.

In the winter of 1947, I saw from the air the weirdest sight of all: three Martin B-26 bombers, apparently intact but belly down in the snow in a direct line about two miles apart. This was the notorious Million Dollar Valley in the southeast corner of the Yukon. Here, in the early days of the staging route, the lead pilot ferrying the trio of bombers to Alaska had lost his way and brought his plane down into the first valley he saw. The others followed like so many sheep—a million dollars' worth of aircraft trapped between a cliff and a rock face, unable to take off, their crews saved by Russ Baker, who brought them out in shifts in his vintage Junkers monoplane. When the highway was built, the army bulldozed a road into Million Dollar Valley to salvage from the stranded aircraft the valuable Norden bombsights that were top secret at the time.

Canada was pushed into building the road by the Americans early in 1942. They feared that the Japanese might cut sea communication to Alaska. If an interior air route, far from the ocean, was to be used, then the road would be needed to supply the necessary airstrips. On February 25, the Permanent Joint Board on Defence advised the United States to accept the route the American army had chosen from the Peace River to Alaska and that construction start at once.

Canada had reservations. Hugh Keenleyside, Canadian secretary of the board, thought the strategic justifications for the road were questionable but noted that, on the other hand, Canada "cannot possibly allow itself to be put in the position of barring the United States from land access to Alaska." The road "would be a monument to our friendship for the United States," he told Norman Robertson, his chief at external affairs, "but would otherwise be pretty much of a 'white elephant.'" By the time the road was ready, he emphasized, the United States' ambitious program of planned ship construction would make a sea attack impossible.

Franklin Roosevelt had already told Fiorello LaGuardia, mayor of New York and U.S. chairman of the PJBD, that "there was good cause for timidity on the part of Canadians. They fear a political backlash." The new route bore no relation to the one that Pattullo of British Columbia envisaged. But if the Canadians wouldn't build it, the U.S. army would. On March 6, Mackenzie King did his best to mollify critics by making it clear that the route had been selected on "purely military considerations" and that it would become part of the Canadian highway system at no cost to Canada.

The Americans didn't wait. The U.S. army was prepared to push a no-frills road through with all possible speed. Later on, the U.S.

civilian Public Roads Administration would bring it up to a standard two-lane gravel highway, maintained by the army for the duration of the war and then turned over to Canada without strings. The Americans didn't stand on diplomatic ceremony. On February 14, before the PJBD met, the U.S. war department ordered its chief engineer to begin construction.

This was no easy task, given the chilling temperatures and conditions along the rutted trail that led from Fort St. John to Fort Nelson on the first leg of the proposed highway. Army truck drivers, working at an exhausting pace to move equipment north, became drowsy and disoriented from the bone-chilling cold that reached -72° Fahrenheit. With the men's reflexes and judgment dulled from lack of sleep, accidents became endemic; the wrecked and broken vehicles accumulating so fast they couldn't be towed to the base camp for repairs.

Heath Twichell, Jr., using his father's notes, has given a graphic description of the collection of battered vehicles at the Fort Nelson Pool that March: "Lined up on the damp, raw earth stood ninety-three half-ton dump trucks, forty-four heavy and medium bulldozers, twenty-five jeeps, sixteen heavy and medium cargo trucks, twelve three-quarter-yard pick-up trucks, ten command cars, nine road graders, six twelve-yard carrying scrapers, six rooter plows, two half-yard power shovels, several pile drivers, a truck-mounted crane, a six-ton flatbed, a concrete mixer—and one sedan. Off to one side were enough pontoon boats and decking timbers to cross a good-sized river." The army had to set up a training school on the spot to teach heavy equipment operators how to do more than start, stop, and steer their machines. There had not been time for more in Fort St. John.

But how were these machines to be fuelled? How were the big warplanes being ferried to Alaska and hence to Soviet Russia to be serviced? The problem the U.S. army faced suggests the helter-skelter speed with which events were accelerating. American panic, provoked by the once-despised Japanese, spurred the politicians and military leaders. Nobody had any real idea of how to keep traffic moving or the aircraft supplied. Oil and gasoline could be trucked north once the pioneer trail was finished, but the cost was daunting, even in a wartime mood when a hang-the-expense attitude prevailed. A truck would need three gallons just to keep rolling for every four it carried to Alaska on a round trip.

The army's requirements, estimated at between three thousand and four thousand barrels of crude oil a day, were beyond anything the resources of the North could supply or even prophesy. The closest source was Norman Wells, a lonely huddle of whitewashed buildings on the high bank of the Mackenzie River. It was managing to produce 450 barrels a day for Imperial Oil. If more wells were drilled, that amount might be increased threefold; but that would require a four-inch pipe to ship the crude to Whitehorse, the mid-point on the highway, and a new refinery there to turn it into gasoline. That called for yet another engineering project—a 620-mile pipeline (CANOL) through totally unexplored and unmapped country, devoid of so much as a footpath, over the serrated peaks of the Continental Divide.

Nonetheless, in April 1942 the Americans plunged ahead, and on May 16 the Cabinet War Committee approved Project CANOL. The Canadians didn't believe that Norman Wells could increase its output more than sixfold to three thousand barrels of oil a day. The Americans ignored these reservations, and Canada didn't protest; after all, it was getting everything for free. The U.S. secretary of the interior, the pugnacious Harold Ickes, *did* protest; he thought the whole scheme unpromising and impractical. At the end of May he tried to reason with the president, but Roosevelt too was caught up in the growing sense of alarm. That very week Japan invaded the two Aleutian islands of Kiska and Attu and bombed Dutch Harbor. FDR agreed that there was no positive assurance that CANOL would succeed, "but we are daily taking greater chances and, in view of the military needs of Alaska, the project has my full approval."

Ickes was right. In January 1944, an investigation committee under Senator Harry Truman damned the entire project as "inexcusable," "unsound," "impossible of accomplishment," and "a drain on our resources in 1942 and 1943." The project, which in the end cost more than the highway itself, was an example of military folly that closed

396

soon after it opened. But in 1942, with FDR's blessing, the army went ahead. African-American soldiers of the 388th Engineers, slaving at loading cargo and cutting firewood, were soon joined by thousands of American civilian workers in the pay of the Bechtel Corporation, CANOL's largest employer. Bechtel posted this warning in its employment office:

THIS IS NO PICNIC
WORKING AND LIVING CONDITIONS ON THIS JOB ARE AS DIFFICULT AS THOSE ENCOUNTERED ON ANY CONSTRUCTION JOB EVER DONE IN THE UNITED STATES OR FOREIGN TERRITORY. MEN HIRED FOR THIS JOB WILL BE REQUIRED TO WORK AND LIVE UNDER THE MOST EXTREME CONDITIONS IMAGINABLE. TEMPERATURES WILL RANGE FROM 90 DEGREES ABOVE ZERO TO SEVENTY DEGREES BELOW ZERO. MEN WILL HAVE TO FIGHT SWAMPS, RIVERS, AND COLD. MOSQUITOES, FLIES AND GNATS WILL NOT ONLY BE ANNOYING BUT WILL CAUSE BODILY HARM. IF YOU ARE NOT PREPARED TO WORK UNDER THESE AND SIMILAR CONDITIONS
DO NOT APPLY

The warning did not exaggerate. Small wonder, then, that in spite of extra pay and a great deal of overtime, few workers could stick it out. The annual turnover on the CANOL project exceeded 100 percent! Yet new workers kept pouring in. By the summer of 1943, the Canadian frontier was crawling with men and the Northwest would never be the same again. I remember standing on a dusty street in Whitehorse on the day war was declared. It was then a tiny hamlet of fewer than five hundred people at the headwaters of the Yukon River, so quiet that husky dogs stretched out and slept in the middle of the gravelled main street. By 1943 it had mushroomed into an open-all-night northern metropolis of twenty thousand, a stopover for the miles of trucks travelling the long, dusty road to Fairbanks. Five thousand trucks were suddenly arriving in a region where there were scarcely that many people: the American invasion was proceeding, full speed ahead.

In the spring of that year, the author and poet Edna Jaques wrote in *Maclean's* that she had counted no fewer than one hundred brown-hooded vehicles "rolling northward through the silent hills." To her, the sight resembled "a great brown snake crawling along the right of way." The whole country, she reported, had gone truck crazy. "All you hear from morning to night is people talking about trucks. . . . One company has 1,000 trucks on the road day and night and wishes it had 1,000 more, men who were begging for jobs a couple of years ago are now kings of the highway. . . . A good truck driver can just about name his price. One trip alone will clear up to $700. . . ."

Ms. Jaques described Dawson Creek, at the start of the highway, as "a hundred boom towns rolled into one, a hundred army camps, a stampede, a madhouse where human emotions run amuck and the devil lurks behind every hitching post."

In February, war came to Dawson Creek in an unexpected manner. A fire in a business block spread to a livery stable where dynamite used in highway construction was stored. As a result, a large section of the town was blown sky-high, five people were killed and one hundred and fifty injured. The cost was estimated at half a million dollars, a large sum when the going wage was only $1.50 an hour.

To all this hustle and bustle on Canada's northern frontier Ottawa remained strangely passive, preoccupied with the problems of the army garrisoned in England, the Hong Kong debacle, and the abortive Dieppe raid. This attitude alarmed an informal group of influential civil servants who cared about the Canadian North and were disturbed that the Americans had been given carte blanche to make plans that might jeopardize Canada's control of its own future.

Dubbed the Northern Nationalists, the group attracted the new British high commissioner, the Right Honourable Malcolm Mac-Donald, himself the son of a former British prime minister, to their cause. MacDonald toured the North in August 1942, and again in March 1943. The massive changes that had taken place in that brief six-month period alarmed him. He went immediately to Mackenzie King, who was already concerned about post-war American domination of the Northwest. The road, in King's early view, "was less intended for protection against Japanese than as one of the fingers for the hand which America is placing more or less over the whole of the Western Hemisphere."

Now, with hundreds of Americans toiling to bring the original tote road up to U.S. highway standards, King agreed with MacDonald that his government "was going to have a hard time after the war to prevent the U.S. attempting control of some Canadian situations." A few days later MacDonald submitted a "personal informal and frank note" to the Cabinet War Committee, which he admitted was out of bounds diplomatically, but "the situation in the North-West is so disturbing that I felt something had to be done. . . ."

In the note, which he "set down as tactfully as I could" (a copy went to Clement Attlee, the minister responsible for the Dominions office), MacDonald commented on the "serious deterioration" of conditions since his previous visit. "It is surely unfortunate," he wrote, "that the Canadian authorities have no real say as to, for example, the placing of these airfields, and the exact route of these roads on Canadian soil. The Americans decided these according to what they consider American interests. Responsible American officials will tell you frankly in confidence that in addition to building works to be of value in this war, they are designing these works also to be of particular value for (a) commercial aviation and transport and (b) waging war against the Russians in the next world crisis. . . . The Canadian counterparts of the Americans who swarm through the country are conspicuous by their absence. The inhabitants of those regions are beginning to say that it seems that the Americans are more awake to the importance of the Canadian North-West than are the Canadian authorities."

This was a significant appreciation and an ironic one, coming from a highly placed Briton. Canada, which had done its best to shake off the grip of British imperialism in the first great war, was now finding itself caught in a similar grip of American imperialism in the second.

MacDonald's report sparked similar comments from those officials who understood the North. J.R. Baldwin in the Privy Council office bemoaned the fact that "the United States had undertaken the economic development of one of Canada's largest and most strategically important areas without any measure of Canadian participation or control in the development." Bob Beattie, director of northern research for the Bank of Canada, returned from the North and agreed that "as far as Canada is concerned the Northwest is today in many respects a foreign country."

In April the Cabinet War Committee, on MacDonald's recommendation, appointed a special commissioner, Major General W.F. Foster, to go to Edmonton in a gesture to reassert Canada's sovereignty over its own Northwest. Foster's presence brought about a substantial change of attitude, but progress was still slow. As one visiting British official, Sir Patrick Duff, reported, "Canadians on the Northwest Staging Route are only caretakers in their own homes." Most of all, Duff declared, "Canadians see perpetually the United States rolling up the Highway or steaming through the air to war along the Aleutians, while neither they themselves nor a single Canadian vehicle nor a single Canadian aircraft are on a similar mission. The men along the route feel themselves just hewers of wood and drawers of water."

Duff went so far as to suggest that this ignoring of Canadian interests was causing a number of officers "to apprehend the intention of the United States to make the Northwest Staging Route a Polish corridor" (a symbol named for the disputed right-of-way that separated East Prussia from Germany).

The real victims of the American invasion, however, were the native people. Far from relieving the long-term problems of infectious disease and alcoholism, the sudden influx of cash and the availability of short-term jobs increased them. Liquor-related offences soared tenfold during the construction period. Young people began to take to drink. In every native community along the highway the massive white encroachment produced a litany of affliction: One community alone—Teslin—in the winter of 1942–43 suffered outbreaks of measles, dysentery, jaundice, whooping cough, mumps, and meningitis. Almost equally serious was the problem of overfishing and overhunting. Workmen shot moose for sport, then left the carcasses to rot—an appalling waste of resources in native eyes, and totally contrary to their social ethic.

But then, the entire Alaska Highway project was a memorial to sudden, extravagant waste. Twichell quotes an old-time Indian trapper, Norman Harlin, who told him that "we missed too many meals in the bush, livin' on bannock and moose meat, to waste anything." But when he took a job surveying the CANOL line, "they brought a reefer of meat up there . . . probably twenty tons and the medics—their refrigerator had gone on the hog—the medics opened it up and took a look at it, and the meat . . . on the top had started to lose the frost. It hadn't thawed much. The frost had gone off . . . and they took a look at it and said: 'Dump 'er!' Twenty tons! Mostly big, choice pork loins and sides o' choice beef. And they dumped 'er."

When I travelled the highway in 1948, before it was officially opened to the public, and again in 1962, when hundreds of tourists were rolling north, old-timers were still reminiscing about the mountains of supplies left behind in garbage dumps by the departing Americans, and the vast array of abandoned machinery and mechanical equipment that they didn't consider worth shipping back to the United States. But the greatest waste of all was the immense CANOL pipeline, which was never able to deliver more than a comparative trickle of oil and was left to rot and rust in the wilderness once the danger of Japanese invasion was over. Today no vehicle can manage to navigate the wilderness road that once linked Watson Lake to Norman Wells' oil field.

Alerted at last to the danger to its sovereignty created by the American invasion, Canada bought its way out of the problem at a cost of $130 million, of which $88 million went to purchase American equipment along the highway. The big road itself had never been brought up to standard as the Americans promised, but there is no way it could have been abandoned to the fate of the CANOL line; the enthusiastic buildup in magazines and newspapers had been a source of Canadian pride. It was turned over first to the Canadian army and later to the highway departments of British Columbia and Yukon Territory.

Since those wartime days, the Alaska Highway has been re-routed, straightened out, maintained, and for most of its length, hard-surfaced. In the summer an unending stream of tourist vehicles makes its way into Alaska and the Yukon, providing a sheen of prosperity for the communities along the route. In the half-century since those demented construction days, for better and sometimes for worse, the highway has opened up and modernized a huge chunk of the Canadian North. Feeder lines now stretch out to once dying communities such as Haines, Alaska, and Dawson City, Yukon. How odd that for Canada, the long, lonely road across the Northwest should be one of the lasting trophies of an expensive and exhausting war.

7

The lonely sea and the sky Apart from the ill-fated Dieppe raid, the Canadian troops hived in England for more than three years saw no action. During all that time, however, Canadian airmen and seamen were fighting in the far corners of the world, from Murmansk to the Mediterranean, from the North Atlantic to the South Pacific. To some the statistics may seem surprising. The total number of men and women serving in the navy and air force was greater by 20,000 than those who served in the army. The death toll was greater for the air force, which lost 17,000 men out of 280,000, compared with the army, which also lost 17,000 out of a total enlistment of 330,000. (Of the 106,000 who served in the navy, only 2,024 were fatal casualties.) With one or two notable exceptions, their remarkable exploits went unsung for two reasons: one was wartime censorship; the other was the hard truth that the Canadians' presence was often obscured because they were combined with other British or Commonwealth forces.

The latter was one reason why Mackenzie King insisted that the RCAF create its own distinctive bomber group made up of Canadian squadrons. The memory of Vimy still haunted the political and military leaders. Arthur Currie's insistence on keeping Canadian soldiers together in the Great War was not forgotten. In spite of spirited opposition from Air Vice Marshal "Bomber" Harris, Canada finally got its own unit, No. 6 (RCAF) Group, in 1943, the only non-British group in the history of Harris's bomber command. By war's end, the RCAF had forty-eight squadrons of bombers and fighters operating in Europe, almost entirely manned by Canadian officers and men.

Spencer Dunmore, who trained as a Royal Air Force pilot in the Commonwealth Air Training scheme, was surprised to discover that the Canadians he met in England were part of something called 6 Group. "It consisted of a dozen or more heavy bomber squadrons—manned by Canadians, administered by Canadians, and paid for by Canadians." Why, he asked, had he and his fellow Britons never heard of it? "Not a whisper in any newspaper or BBC broadcast that we were aware of. Did the Canadians prefer to be anonymous participants in democracy's battle? It seemed unlikely, particularly when we heard them telling us that fully one in four of the airmen in the air force were Canadians."

Dunmore liked the Canadian pilots because "they were possessed of a healthy lack of respect for military claptrap, including ranks, grades, and traditions." They believed, he wrote, that "the fastest most efficient way was the only way anything should be done. It mattered not a whit how the Duke of Wellington did it." Half a century later Dunmore decided to write a book "as a long overdue tribute" to his new-found friends. In that work, *Above and Beyond*, Dunmore provides chapter and verse detailing the Canadians' early difficulties with their British Allies.

- When the first bunch of Canadian-trained sergeant wireless operators and gunners arrived at Camwell, Lincolnshire, they were treated as recruits and sent on endless route marches in the rain. When they refused to march, an apoplectic air vice-marshal was dispatched from the air ministry to deal with these "mutinous colonials." It took all of Vincent Massey's diplomatic expertise to stave off a minor international incident.
- In 1941, Herb Hallett of Windsor, Ontario, one of the first pilots to graduate from the Commonwealth Air Training Plan, was irked that the captain aboard the troopship taking him overseas referred to the Canadian airmen as "a bunch of

colonial pigs" and warned that anyone who disobeyed his ship's rules would be clapped in irons.

• A Canadian navigator, John Harding of London, Ontario, was censured by an RAF officer for not wearing gloves. "You Canadians will never know how to wear the King's uniform. You're improperly dressed," he said. To which Harding shot back: "You bloody RAF types, you blow your nose on your hanky, then tuck it up your sleeve."

The strict and often callous discipline grated on the young Canadians. The RAF accepted no excuse from men who, after long stretches, suffered from battle fatigue and found they could not fly. The attitude seemed to be, Dunmore wrote, "that if the slightest leniency was shown to aircrew who refused to fly, squadrons would soon be emptied of personnel." Formed up in hollow square, his fellow airmen would watch while the offender was humiliated by having his stripes torn off—a treatment that infuriated the Canadians. "I felt we were like cardboard pawns in the hands of these unfeeling, la-de-dah upper-class Englishmen who seemed to run the RAF. At times I felt that war was a game to them," one RCAF navigator remembered. "They would brook no battle fatigue, everything was blatantly labelled 'cowardice.'"

The British class system extended to the air force, where a gulf existed even between trained pilots, separating those who were commissioned officers from those who were mere sergeants. Flight sergeants stuck to the public bars, avoiding the saloon bars and lounges frequented by officers because it just wasn't done for flight sergeants to drink with commissioned airmen, even if they were performing the same tasks. Once, when a squadron was moved north to a station under construction, the new arrivals discovered there was as yet no sergeants' mess. They ate their dinner standing in the falling snow, while the officers enjoyed the private dining room.

The Canadians found themselves largely forgotten when it came to publicity, promotion, and decorations. When Vernon Woodward, known as "Imperturbable Woody," received the Distinguished Service Cross for "gallantry and devotion to duty in the execution of an air operation," the *London Gazette* made no mention of the fact that he had secured the first kill in the western desert and that his aerial victories now topped twenty.

All this had changed by the time George "Buzz" Beurling was shipped back to Canada for a war bond drive early in November 1942. Beurling was the country's greatest war hero, one of the top ten aces in the Allied air forces, holder of the DSO, the DFC, and the DCM with bar, and known to the breathless press as the "Falcon of Malta." On that beleaguered island he had managed to shoot down twenty-seven enemy aircraft in just fourteen days—and all this by the time he was twenty-one years old.

He was just what Canada needed—a tall, handsome, rangy hero with chilling eyes of china blue. Everyone wanted to meet him, especially Mackenzie King, for at this moment, with Tobruk lost and the Japanese seemingly in control of the Pacific, spirits were at a low ebb. No wonder the nation went wild over Beurling. In Montreal, cheering crowds surged forward en masse to catch a glimpse of him behind the windows of his limousine. In his native Verdun, ten thousand squeezed into the local arena to deafen him with applause. Good taste was tossed aside that evening as twenty-eight Girl Guides and a Brownie stepped forward one at a time to present him with a blood-red rose, one for each of his kills. Everybody knew him; everybody wanted to seize his hand and beg his autograph. Women went crazy over him, lining up to meet him and whispering shameless invitations in his ear.

Beurling obviously loved his celebrity, but toward the end of the Canadian tour, having shaken thousands of hands, listened to hundreds of sycophantic greetings, and eaten far too much overcooked chicken, it began to pall. He loved flying more—loved it to the exclusion of everything else. To him it was more than a passion; it was an obsession. He seemed to have been fashioned specifically for aerial combat, and it is pertinent to wonder what he would have done with himself had there been no war. A soldier of fortune, possibly? There is no doubt that, in a narrow sense, he was a certifiable genius—the Mozart of the art of deflection shooting. No other pilot had quite mastered that difficult, often maddening skill to the extent that Beurling had. It required a computer-like brain and the eyes of an eagle to estimate correctly the exact speed of an enemy aircraft and to aim ahead of the target so that a single burst of fire destroyed it at the right moment— and all this while executing quick and violent turns. That was Beurling's forte and one that he honed to a high polish. His eyesight was uncanny. He could pick out a girl across a broad and crowded avenue and remark, correctly, on the colour of her eyes. He could look into a empty sky, as he once did, spot a squadron of thirty-eight Flying Fortresses that no one else could see, and give out the exact number.

While others relaxed in the mess, Beurling spent his time studying every aspect of his most recent combat, jotting down columns of figures, making diagrams in his notebook, going over his rapidly accumulating data on speeds and heights. His marksmanship was phenomenal. On Malta, he practised shooting the eyes out of distant, fast-moving lizards with his .38 revolver.

"I am always thinking of angles of fire," he told an interviewer. "Even when I walk down the street, I look at the angle at which telephone wires cross the line of a building. I calculate angles as I walk along and sometimes stop and go back to check an angle. The way pianists can enjoy music by hearing a note in their heads, that's the way I am about angles."

Early in the war he had tried to join the RCAF, which turned him down, partly, no doubt, because of his lack of education. In those days the air force was so small that it could not handle the rush of volunteers and so could afford to discriminate. That rankled. In May of 1940 Beurling worked his way to England and joined the RAF. He never forgave the RCAF in his later public statements.

The public sensed that Beurling was a loner. He purposely avoided making close friends because of the stress of losing so many comrades. In one week in Malta, half of the pilots in his squadron became casualties. What the public did not know was that Beurling was unpopular with the RAF brass and with his fellow flyers because he was temperamentally unable to be part of a team. The old, individualistic Great War days of Bishop and Barker were gone. Teamwork was essential in the

406

squadrons that crossed the English Channel and tangled with the Luftwaffe. But time and again in his first sorties with the RAF, Beurling broke formation to single out an enemy aircraft. His kills began to mount, but so did his reputation as a difficult, even insubordinate, pilot. The RAF shipped him off to Malta to get rid of him. There he stubbornly refused a commission, and when it was finally forced upon him, he continued to dine in the sergeants' mess.

The air battles over Malta, however, suited his penchant for individual engagements. He loved the six months he spent on that besieged island. After the war he told an interviewer that he would give up ten years of his life to live those days over again. "The food was lousy," he remembered, "and we were bombed all the time. My weight dropped from 177 to 128 pounds. But the flying weather was good and every time you went flying the sky was full of Germans." To Beurling, who came from a family of evangelical Christians and didn't drink, that was all that mattered. His flight commander, Laddie Lucas, realized within a month of Beurling's arrival "that he was made for this rarefied form of island warfare, whereas he was likely to be unsuitable for the large set-piece wing operations with which we were so familiar at home."

After the Canadian war bond drive, Beurling yearned to return to the island. But the RAF insisted on bringing him to England as an instructor. "You're the best deflection shot we've got," he was told, "so you've got to teach the others how to do it." Meanwhile, the RCAF wanted him: it was insufferable that the greatest Canadian ace of the war was not in the Canadian air force. Bored with his instructor's job and with the RAF giving no indication of returning him to air combat, Beurling forgave the RCAF, and on September 1, 1943, signed up.

It was a sensitive relationship from the beginning. Would Beurling grab all the headlines? Not if Air Marshal H. "Gus" Edwards knew anything about it. He told his public relations staff that "further publicity concerning this officer is to be withheld." Beurling was posted to 403 Squadron, part of the famous 127 Wing with its Canadian squadrons. The wing's commander, Johnny Johnson, one of Britain's most famous fighter pilots, warned him: "There is one rule and it is not to be broken. We always fight as a team." Beurling smiled. "Okay, boss," he said.

But it wasn't okay. "We couldn't make a team player out of him," Johnson admitted. "The Wing would take off, but over France he would do a half-roll, disappear, come back and say he'd shot this and that down—which he had, he wasn't a liar. . . . I could do nothing with him. . . . We should have given him a long-range Mustang and said, 'Okay, go off and fight your own private war.'"

The climax came when Beurling disobeyed a standing order to refrain from stunt flying over the squadron's airfield. For Hugh Godefroy, a Torontonian and squadron CO, that was the last straw. He called Beurling on the carpet, only to have Beurling tell him, "You can't tell me what to do." Godefroy placed him under arrest preparatory to facing a court martial for refusing a direct order.

To the RCAF's high command, that posed the worst sort of dilemma. How could they court-martial Canada's greatest ace? But what choice did he have, Godefroy asked the Air Marshal.

"No choice?" Edwards cried. "Don't you know the prime minister has just crowned him king of Canada?"

Though Godefroy held his ground, Beurling had his sentence reduced from open arrest to grounding, thanks to the intervention of air minister Chubby Power. On November 7, 1943, the stubborn ace was levered out of his old unit and reassigned to 412 Squadron. Back in the air in December, he managed one more kill, shooting down a German PW-190. But the tactics were changing. The RCAF's job seemed mundane—operating en masse as escorts for the big American bombers in their ceaseless raids across the Channel. A frustrated Beurling dismissed them as "taxi rides"; for him the freewheeling Malta days were over. In the end, he resigned his commission and a relieved RCAF let him go. He tried to rejoin the RAF; they didn't want him. The Americans didn't want him, either. The invasion of Europe took place without him. He just didn't fit in.

He had borne a charmed life in the hurly-burly of air combat. Brian Nolan, his biographer, figured out that he had exactly as many lives as the proverbial cat—a total of nine escapes from a variety of serious accidents. He was hurled into the sea, swam toward shore, and reached it just before he collapsed from exhaustion. He crash-landed more than once and walked away. He leaped out of a burning plane and waited until the last possible moment before pulling the rip cord on his parachute. Once, as he struggled to bring his Spitfire back to level flight, his eyeballs began to hemorrhage from the pull of gravity, and he blacked out, to awake just in time to save himself. On his Canadian tour, he limped from shrapnel wounds in his foot and ankle.

Civilian life in post-war Canada was not for him. In the fall of 1947 he tried to make a living selling rides in a Tiger Moth to locals from a farmer's field near Montreal. The following year he finally had a chance to get back into action when he was smuggled overseas to fight for Israel in its war with five Arab nations. But he never reached the new state. At Urbe airfield outside of Rome, he found himself checking out a Canadian Norseman on a routine practice flight. Suddenly, to the horror of those on the ground, a thin sheet of flame flickered on the bottom of the fuselage. At three hundred feet the plane headed for the runway only to explode just as the wheels touched the ground. How did it happen? What was the cause? To this day there is no answer. Buzz Beurling, for mysterious reasons, had used up his nine lives. This was his tenth accident, and his last.

Unexpected deaths, miraculous escapes, bizarre accidents, improbable twists of fate of the kind that might have made headlines on pre-war front pages were commonplace among those who flew those unfriendly skies. Unlike the "returned men" who tried to banish the Great War's horrors from their minds, the survivors of its sequel talked freely, if sometimes ruefully, of their escapades. It is doubtful, however, that any other airman, not even Beurling, lived through as many miraculous escapes as a young Toronto navigator named Ray Silver.

Silver was so accident-prone (if that is the proper term) that half of his squadron mates would, in his words, have "preferred court-martial to travelling in the same aircraft with me." The other half "figured I was the luckiest guy in the world." They called him "Lucky Silver," and he agreed. "I figure I'm the most fortunate guy alive," he declared when he resumed his career as a freelance writer after the war and summed up his most spectacular experiences in print:

> As a flyer I have been thrown for 600 feet over a mountain top by the impact of a crash—literally knocked into the next country.
>
> I have smashed, at 80 miles an hour, through a fence and two tin huts in a bomb-and-fuel-laden aircraft and walked away from it.
>
> I have hung in a parachute harness over burning Cologne with the sound of an aircraft out of control whistling in my ears and another coming at me in the dark. They missed me.
>
> I have waited breathless over Mannheim while a crewman battled a high explosive fire. He got it out.
>
> I sat as a navigator over Hamburg while the Germans pumped 38 holes in our Whitley and brought it screaming down over the rooftops.
>
> I fought to get aboard an aircraft once and they wouldn't let me go. The aircraft went missing.

Silver flew with the RAF bomber command after training with Duke Schiller, one of the best-known Canadian bush pilots. On August 10, 1941, he arrived at his squadron and was called for his "nursery trip," a night operation over Le Havre. Twenty-four hours later, two of the crew were dead and the rest in hospital. On its return trip, travelling at 160 miles an hour, the big plane had crashed into a 2,012-foot peak that sent it hurtling to the earth with such force that Silver was thrown through the roof, to land some 600 feet farther on, face down in a bog. That saved his life, and thus began the legend of his jinx.

The average member of a flight crew survived no more than eight trips. Silver survived two crashes, three tricky landings, four "written-off" aircraft, a night fighter encounter over the island of Sylt, and finally, "a lethal hosing near Hamburg." But, like Beurling, Silver finally ran out of luck. As part of the first thousand-bomber raid on Cologne, he leaped

410

from his shattered four-engine Halifax, hung in his parachute three miles above enemy territory, and watched the city burn in the distance. As he recalled, "A German camp was a peaceful place to ponder my memories."

Although members of a Dutch family risked their lives to provide him with civilian clothing, he was captured two days later. The Gestapo grilled him for three days and told him he would be shot as a saboteur. But Silver glibly lied his way through the ordeal without giving away his Dutch Samaritans and finally convinced his inquisitors that he was an airman. He spent the rest of the war in a German POW camp. After his release, en route to Antwerp, Lucky Silver survived a head-on train wreck and another close shave when he boarded a Dakota transport for England. The plane ahead blew a tire as it hurtled down the takeoff strip and burned at the end of the runway, just as Silver's Dakota was revving up for takeoff. Fortunately, it blew a tire, too, and rolled to a safe, but bumpy, stop.

"That sure was lucky," a crew member told him as they climbed out. "If that had happened a few seconds later down the runway we'd have ground looped like that other kite."

"I know," Silver told him. "It's always like that."

Silver's years in Stalag Luft III with other air force prisoners were comparatively mild when set against the ordeal suffered by airmen who ended up under sentence of death in the infamous Buchenwald slave camp. That was the fate of John Harvie, a twenty-one-year-old RCAF navigator who bailed out of a stricken Halifax bomber over France a month after D-Day. Harvie fell in with a group who claimed to be members of French resistance and who smuggled him into a Paris secure house to wait for help to get him across the Spanish border. But his new friends were actually Gestapo agents.

In Gestapo headquarters, when Harvie invoked the Geneva Convention regarding prisoners of war, he was struck across the face. "It doesn't matter anyway," the German interrogator told him. "You will be shot within a week." Harvie and several other Canadians were moved to the largest and most famous French prison at Fresnes where French civilians charged with attempted sabotage and other crimes against the occupation forces were held.

In his month at Fresnes, Harvie was never allowed to wash or change his clothes. Toilet paper was a single sheet torn from a book. The food was execrable; lunch was "a piece of cheese-like substance that smelled like rotting fish." At first he could not swallow it, but he soon became so ravenous that on the next occasion he ate it all.

In mid-August, 1,650 dishevelled prisoners were shipped off to an unidentified destination by boxcar and dumped at the gates of a vast prison camp. Harvie now realized he was standing on German soil, deep inside enemy territory; this was Buchenwald, then virtually unknown to the outside world. It was surrounded by a ten-foot-high fence built of closely laced barbed wire and supported by concrete posts stretching off into the distance from both sides of the main gate. Thick rolls of barbed wire had been laid on the ground against the inside, making escape from this huge compound all but impossible. Solidly built guard towers loomed up at hundred-yard intervals along the fence line from which sentinels posted ten feet above it enjoyed an unobstructed view.

Here no blade of glass nor any other plant life was visible. Within the enclosure Harvie noted clutches of prisoners in grey-striped clothing, moving about against a backdrop of grey, single-storey structures, bleak as the tomb. In the distance a column of dense, black smoke issued from a thirty-foot chimney atop another building. That eerie sight, Harvie later discovered, marked the crematorium, which operated day and night without a break. Six ovens consumed the corpses from the multiple hangings that took place during evening roll call, from the garrottings by piano wire in the basement, and from victims murdered by being thrown down a chute to the crematorium floor. In one of the buildings—Block 50, euphemistically called the Hygiene Institute—experiments were carried out on human guinea pigs, who rarely survived.

Harvie did not know this when he and the others were herded into the compound, but he quickly learned how crowded Buchenwald was. Built before the war, it was intended to house 18,000 prisoners. At this point, 84,505 were jammed into the camp.

At last he was given the opportunity to scrub off six weeks of grime.

He was shaved bald and then, to his surprise, found the brown suit in which he had made his escape returned to him—but without the shoes. He and his fellow flyers found themselves part of a mixed group of some eighty Americans and ninety British. It occurred to him then that nobody had asked him for his name, rank, or serial number. That deliberate lack of interest was disturbing. Did the camp authorities consider them all nameless bodies who could die or disappear without a trace?

A stripe-suited inmate, who Harvie later learned was a *Kapo*—a prisoner assigned to a position of authority over other prisoners—led them stumbling on their bare feet to the barrack room that would be their sleeping quarters. On the way, other prisoners watched their slow and painful progress with lustreless, sunken eyes. Harvie looked at them curiously. Many had taken off their shirts and were picking at the seams, apparently for lice. "These hollow-cheeked wretches were painfully underfed—they were nothing but skin and bones. I was shocked. I had never seen anyone so thin."

Even though thousands died from starvation, disease, beatings, random shootings, and executions, the camp was so crowded that there was no space in any barrack room for the new arrivals. They would sleep on the hard ground of the prison yard, with no covering and no shelter from the weather. There they would receive their rations and be counted, one by one, during the two daily roll calls.

Surely, Harvie told himself, this place cannot be real. He must be in the middle of a bad dream. But it *was* real. Every prisoner was identified by a coloured triangle of cloth that defined his status: red for political crimes, grey for murderers, pink for homosexuals, and the Star of David for Jews, who occupied the bottom of the pecking order.

The meticulous Germans had given every prisoner a number, though Harvie did not know what his was. The prisoners came from every country in Europe; Harvie even spotted a few Asians. The senior Allied officers in charge of his group were as baffled by their fate as he was. They had not been able to meet with German authorities; no arrangements had been made for the new arrivals to go to a proper prison;

nor had they been able to find other Allied prisoners of war with whom they could compare treatment. They did, however, meet with several Allied civilians, including one Canadian who had been convicted of spying and sent to Buchenwald to be executed.

Within a few days Harvie realized that he was becoming so hardened to camp life that he scarcely noticed the dead carted off to the crematorium. (There were no gas chambers in Buchenwald, which had been built before the last chapter of the "Final Solution" was written.) So far his group had lost none of its members, but how long would that last? His own health was deteriorating; half his comrades were limping from festering sores on their bare feet. Only a few were fit enough to carry the wooden food tubs from the kitchen. The grim thought that the SS might slaughter them all before the Allied troops could liberate Buchenwald obsessed them. If that didn't happen, they might easily be killed by the Allied aircraft that dropped bombs in the area one dreadful day. *"No! No! No!"* Harvie cried out in impotent despair. "Can't you see we are fellow airmen! Stay away, you fools, you'll kill us by mistake!" There were no bomb shelters in Buchenwald, no ditches in which to cower. That day, 315 prisoners were killed and 525 wounded in the air raid.

Harvie did his best to keep his eyes and ears open among the foreign prisoners. He was nauseated by one story that came from those who were fighting a fire in a barrack room set up as a museum. Here they were horrified to find lampshades and book covers made of human skin and displayed as interesting examples of the art of tattooing.

After two weeks of living without cover, the Allied group was given space in one of the cell blocks, and Harvie, whose morale had reached a low point, felt a feeling of hope surge through him. The hut was desperately overcrowded. They slept on tiers of deep wooden shelves and were forced to lie at night with only a few inches of space between each man—so little, in fact, that no one could lie on his back or stomach. Everyone had to turn at once during the night—like "bundlers" in pioneer Canada. Nonetheless, with the rain beating down on the roof, Harvie felt as though he were in heaven.

414

He found the roll calls, morning and night, increasingly exhausting. Each seemed to take forever, as the Germans completed their head count. Harvie soon found there was a grisly reason for these delays. The SS needed extra time to hang prisoners in front of the roll call assembly. Permanent gallows had been erected especially for this purpose.

The only acceptable diversion was the cinema. There, the Allied prisoners were treated to propaganda films showing German forces slaughtering the Normandy invaders. "If I hadn't known better," Harvie wrote, "I might have thought Germany was winning the war."

He liked the Russian prisoners, some of whom cheerfully offered primitive first aid to those with foot ailments. Thousands of the Russians in Buchenwald were treated almost as badly as the Jews—assigned to the worst jobs, beaten, kicked, abused, and "considered to be ignorant savages best used as slaves." The Russians told Harvie that should they live long enough to be liberated, they could never return home because they would be shot by their own troops for having surrendered.

One day the entire Danish police force showed up. Their obvious sympathy for the Allied cause had been too much for the Gestapo, who arrested all 1,900 and sent them under guard to be interned. They brought a supply of food that they shared with the Allied prisoners, and this, along with their high morale, was a tonic to the others. So was the unexpected return of the footwear that had been taken from Harvie and his fellows. "It was such a wonderful feeling to wear civilized shoes again! What a break! And just when snow could be expected any day!"

Morale dropped again, however, when the senior officers in the Allied group announced that the civilians who had been convicted of spying had all been hanged in a fortified bunker near the parade ground. This shocking news stunned Harvie and his comrades, who were themselves in limbo, not knowing whether the Germans recognized them as proper prisoners of war. How long would the war last? Would they ever be moved up to a proper camp? Was it worthwhile trying to stay alive in all this misery? Even night brought no rest. "There was never room to lie on my back or stomach. The unshielded lights burned continuously overhead. The hut was never quiet because we all groaned or talked in our sleep, or yelled out with the torment of nightmares. We all had diarrhea and there was the continual disturbance of men struggling in and out of their bunks two or three times a night.

"We were all wasting away and looking more and more like the wretches around us. Dysentery was rampant. All of us had festering sores, cuts, or fleabites. Should we be liberated, most of us would immediately be hospitalized. Everything seemed so futile, with our armies apparently still far away and the weather getting colder."

No one knew that their camp documents bore the admonition in German: "Not to be transferred to any other camp"—in short, they were not to leave Buchenwald alive. Nor did they know that their disciplined military behaviour had convinced a secret underground of prisoners that they actually were Allied airmen. The word was filtered through to the Luftwaffe, which hated the SS and was officially responsible for guarding their captured counterparts.

As a result, some officials arrived from Berlin to investigate the story that Allied airmen had been interned at Buchenwald. They wore civilian clothes, spoke fluent English, asked only a few questions, and departed, leaving an open question: would the group be moved to a proper prisoner of war camp or left in Buchenwald to die?

The answer came on October 18, literally at the eleventh hour. Harvie learned that the SS had just received orders that all were to be hanged. Instead they were told they would leave for a POW camp the next day— all but a dozen men too sick to travel. Harvie was able to limp to the parade ground where, standing in the cold October rain in his summer clothing, he waited for six hours with the others, all shivering and stamping their feet, while every man's name was checked against various lists. Then, at last, the massive gates of Buchenwald swung open and they moved to a string of boxcars waiting to transport them to the comparative luxury of Stalag Luft III. The order for their release did not come a minute too soon. Only the intervention of enemy airmen had saved their lives.

If prison camp was an occupational hazard for members of Canadian bomber crews such as Ray Silver and John Harvie, it was scarcely a consideration for those who joined the navy. Many of the 100,000 men who joined the senior service did so because they felt that life on the ocean would be preferable to life in the trenches—or their equivalent. As one of them, Hal Lawrence, put it, "Is there such a thing as a *good war*? We in the Royal Canadian Navy think so. . . . We had a hammock or a bunk to sleep in; hot food, usually; the man directing the battle was, if not on board, at least within a mile and not in headquarters behind the lines—he *led* us, he didn't merely direct. We had fewer maimed than the pongos, and if our small ship was hit and we were hurt we usually sank, drowned—a 'clean' death—and as a consequence we were not sweating out the soldier's prayer on going into battle, 'Not in the gut, please Lord.'"

A good war? Lawrence's boast is difficult to swallow, especially in the light of conditions aboard the corvettes that escorted convoys across the Atlantic and on the icebound Murmansk run from Iceland to the USSR.

The corvettes were a new kind of craft, designed especially for the Global War to fill the need for small, manoeuvrable escort vessels that could be thrown together cheaply by private firms, thus reducing the pressure on the overworked naval dockyards. In the description of Edward O'Connor, a crewman aboard HMCS *Morden,* the corvette was "one of the toughest ship types ever built." The name sprang from the fertile mind of Winston Churchill, who remembered such a warship from the days of sail. Patterned after a similar craft designed in 1935 for whaling, it was halfway between a destroyer and a gunboat in size with a powerful engine that allowed a speed up to sixteen knots.

The first corvette was the 1,200-ton HMS *Gladiolus.* Like those that followed, she was 205 feet long, 33 feet in the beam, and designed to catch German E-boats, not whales. After she was launched on April 6, 1940, close to 300 others were rushed into service.

In spite of cramped quarters, corvettes often picked up survivors from torpedoed vessels and managed to cram them aboard. The champion survivor-carrier in the entire Allied naval forces was the *Morden.* Between August 1942 and June 1943, she plucked a total of 357 men, women, and children from the cold Atlantic waters. At one point in October, the tiny craft had 260 aboard, with the crew sleeping on deck and so little food available that there was no more than a single spoonful of stew-mix per person. Some crew members gave up their own rations for those who needed food more, while at the same time cutting up towels for baby diapers, making baby bottles out of Coke bottles, and fashioning the fingers of rubber gloves into nipples.

On that occasion, *Morden* was given permission to leave the convoy and head for St. John's, Newfoundland, at all speed. Speed, alas, was not possible when a gale moved in from the west and, in the words of one crew member, "turned life into a living hell." Vomit lay inches deep in the messes as the seamen worked tirelessly, taking care of babies for mothers who were too weak or sick to do it. Four days later the corvette limped into port with only two pounds of meat left for food. The ship was back in service a week later, having been steam-cleaned and fumigated. With the grateful survivors in local hospitals, this was not a journey that could be kept quiet by censorship.

Service was no pleasure aboard these strange new vessels that rolled and pitched so alarmingly in heavy seas. It required remarkable ingenuity to stow enough provisions to last a month into every bit of available space. One seaman, Lorne Power, who served aboard HMCS *Moncton*, recalled that after twelve days at sea in a raging storm in the winter of 1942–43—one of the worst in years—the food supply was down to hardtack, a little tinned butter, and tinned sausage.

When the storm blew up, the *Moncton* was escorting a large convoy from the eastern seaboard to mid-point in the Atlantic, where another set of escorts would pick it up. But the storm was so violent the convoy could not be kept together, some ships making it to Iceland, others to New York, and some getting back to Halifax. *Moncton* was so damaged that the water rose a foot above the deck in the stokers' mess, leaving all types of gear, including hammocks, floating about. Ice built up so quickly that the corvette was at risk of capsizing until the captain did a 180-degree turn and steamed downwind to give the seamen a chance to chip the ice off the forward part of the vessel. But once the *Moncton* returned to her original course, the ice built up again. With the water too deep for the pumps to handle, and a thick layer of ice on the decks and superstructure, the ship would roll almost to the point of no return until the heavy seas flipped her back to the other side.

Every time the corvette wallowed the starboard lifeboat was plunged into the sea, and the water quickly froze on it until it looked like "a huge rounded lump of ice." It was Power's job, with the help of Don Ash, the vessel's sick-berth attendant, to chip it free. Since the only place to start work seemed to be the starboard side of the lifeboat, the two concocted a plan: holding the fire axe, Ash would place himself face down and head first toward the outside of the lifeboat, while Power would brace himself, holding on for dear life to the tail of his partner's duffel coat. Ash was then able to make three or four chops at the far edge of the ice before the ship rolled again, taking him under. "The next sea rolled the ship back up and Don came to his feet spouting sea water." Half a century later in O'Connor's *The Corvette Years*, Power recalled this incident as a hilarious joke. The passage of time edited out the misery and the terror. "How interesting," Power remarked, "that this humorous aspect of an overall dreadful experience comes more readily to mind than the fearful parts."

Convoy work was no laughing matter, as the voyage of the ill-fated Convoy PQ17 demonstrates. Here were thirty-four merchant vessels heading out of Iceland for Russia in the summer of 1942, escorted by a covey of corvettes and destroyers. By that time, Canada's naval personnel had risen to 40,000—two-fifths of the Allied naval forces patrolling the Atlantic convoy routes. By the end of the summer, 60 million tons of cargo had been moved, but at a horrendous cost in lives and materials. German U-boats were sinking Allied ships faster than they could be replaced—losses that would reach a total of 306 ships by the end of 1942. The German admiral, Erich Raeder, badly wanted Convoy 17, whose ships were loaded with $700 million worth of tanks, trucks, gun carriers, and general cargo, enough to equip an army of 50,000 in the field. The British wanted the German battleship *Tirpitz*, and its destroyer escorts lurking then in a Norwegian fjord, just as badly.

A desperate battle between the opposing naval forces was looming—an encounter that the British might have won that could have shortened the war. It did not take place because the British admiral, Sir Dudley Pound, decided not to stand and fight. The Admiral cabled to the escorting vessels: "Owing to threat from surface ships, convoy is to disperse and proceed to Russian ports."

About the same time the Germans, too, got the wind up. When Pound's order was dispatched, the *Tirpitz* and two destroyers were still in their Norwegian fjord, nor did they sail until the following morning. The next evening Raeder called them off, fearing an imminent attack by the Royal Navy.

Years later, Hal Lawrence of the RCN wrote in *Victory at Sea* that Pound's order—dispatched over the heads of the officers on the spot—caused "incredulity and a sense of guilt . . . that has not been mitigated over the years." To the navy, it was a missed opportunity with a tragic result. Of the thirty-four merchant ships in the convoy that left Iceland, scattered, unescorted, and undefended, twenty-three were sunk by U-boats; only eleven reached their destination. As Lawrence ruefully noted, "It was not our finest hour."

Yet for Lawrence, and those who commanded the small, fast motor torpedo boats (MTBs) or gunboats (MGBs), it *was* a good war, for much of the time. "Did you ever try Devon cider?" Lawrence was once asked. "I must have," he replied. "I tried everything else!"

After a stint on corvettes, Lawrence served with the so-called Champagne Navy of small coastal raiders that attracted so many young amateur sailors whose families were well enough off in the Depression years to afford a motorboat, a launch, or a sailing craft. "Have you been sailing all your life?" an admiral asked Jack McClelland as he was applying for a commission. "No," the future publisher responded, "only since I was five."

They were young, dauntless, and devil-may-care, these erstwhile skippers, few of whom were older than twenty-five. A substantial number of MTBs and MGBs were captained by Canadians, perhaps, it has been suggested, because the wide open water, like the wide open spaces of their native country, appealed to them, and also because the dash and freedom that this new kind of warfare required fitted their temperament. The 56th Flotilla, which operated in the Mediterranean in 1943 and 1944, was known as the Canadian Flotilla because it was commanded by a Canadian, and so were each of its six MGBs.

Lawrence has suggested that "the Big Ship Lords disapproved of these strange little boats. The larger ships were a *career* with a past that went back with previous ships of the same name to the Spanish Armada and before. They were *pusser*; they were *home*; and one dressed for dinner. . . . Who were these unruly youngsters careening over the ocean at forty knots, in hare-brained actions, fought at ranges that had gone out with the age of sail—fifty yards, twenty yards, even less! And how did they comport themselves away from the hand of properly ordained authority? And who could tell what abhorrent deviations of discipline were perpetrated?"

The commander of the Canadian Flotilla in the Mediterranean in early 1944 was Douglas Maitland, one of a legendary trio of close friends from Vancouver nicknamed the Three Musketeers. They had gone to a private school for boys, had sailed together on English Bay, and had enlisted together in the Royal Canadian Naval Volunteer Reserve the moment war broke out. Maitland was taking part in a regatta in Cowichan Bay on Vancouver Island when he heard the news. He and his crew stopped racing, toasted the King in gin and orange juice, and headed off to the mainland to enlist. At the same time, his two closest friends, Cornelius Burke and Tom Ladner, got the news on a portable radio at their neighbouring summer homes on Paisley Island. Both came from well-known British Columbia pioneer families. Burke was the son of the president of Boeing Aircraft and affianced to Wendy Bell-Irving, whose brother would later become lieutenant-governor of the province. Ladner's family name was enshrined in a thriving Fraser Delta community.

The two cronies joined up at once with Maitland and began their training in Vancouver. Much of it was routine parade ground drill, scarcely the forte of saltwater enthusiasts. Burke was so fearful he

421

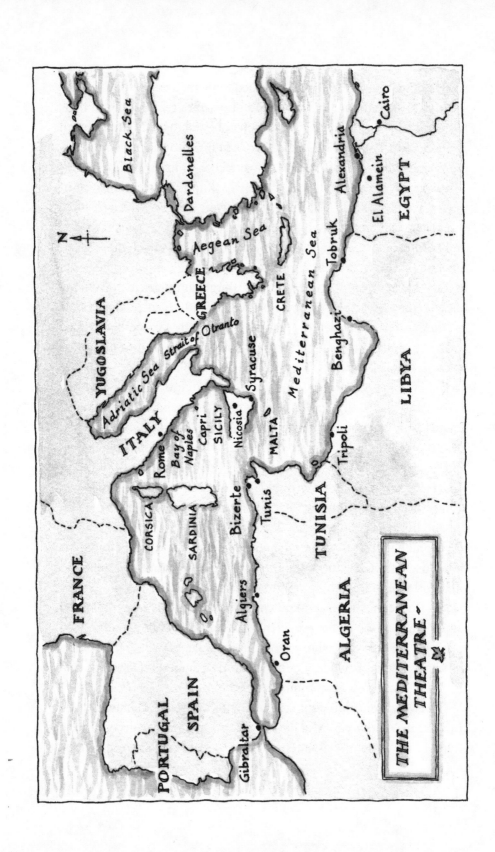

THE MEDITERRANEAN THEATRE

would fail his examinations that he armed his new bride, Wendy, with a broomstick, and marched her around their bed-sitting room on Vancouver's Robson Street. Burke's attention to duty, together with his natural flair for the unorthodox, paid off when he was sent on loan to the Royal Navy in March 1940 and managed, with the help of several bottles of Scotch, to smuggle Wendy aboard the troopship for England. There, in the course of time, he met up with his old schoolmates.

This legendary trio of recreational sailors served in one another's company for most of the war. Each commanded an MGB in the English Channel and later in the Mediterranean, emerging with a chest full of decorations: *seven* Distinguished Service Crosses, four Mentioned in Dispatches, and one Croix de Guerre. The miracle is that all survived the war.

The Three Musketeers were soon accepted into the elite coastal force where each rose to command one of the long, sleek, Fairmile Class D gunboats, universally known as Dog Boats—high-speed attack craft powered by massive Packard engines. The Dog Boats were created especially for the Global War to disrupt German convoys in the English Channel and elsewhere. They usually fought at night and at close range in encounters described as "the equivalent of a shotgun duel in a pitch black room."

With other Canadians the Musketeers helped develop new tactics for these small boat raids. They learned how to clear out enemy minefields by deliberately speeding over them just ahead of the triggered explosion. They learned to pursue their quarry at top speed, slow down at the last possible moment, make the final hundred-yard approach by stealth, and then hit the enemy with everything they had. They learned to run parallel to their main targets—the bigger and better-armed German E-boats—then pull a high-speed ninety-degree turn at the bow and dump a couple of depth charges to break their keels.

By the time the trio left for Gibraltar in April 1943 to join the Mediterranean command they were seasoned veterans who had led charmed lives. Burke had survived when an acoustic mine blew the stern of his boat to smithereens off the Bristol Channel. Maitland had also lost the stern end of his boat when 500-ton bombs from enemy Dorniers rained down on the flotilla. Ladner had been aboard the armed merchant cruiser *Farfare* when it was torpedoed 350 miles off Iceland, probably by the German U-boat commander Otto Kretschmer, known as the Tonnage King because he had sunk more Allied ships in the first eighteen months of the Battle of the Atlantic than any other captain— 44 ships, 266,629 tons. Flung into the sea and clinging to a float, Ladner lay out in the frigid air for most of a day until he was finally picked up by another ship, which was itself on fire. Of the 190 souls aboard the *Farfare*, Ladner was among only eighteen who survived.

The Musketeers roamed the Mediterranean like pirates, from Gibraltar to Malta, from Algiers to Syracuse, from the Dalmatian coast to the Aegean Sea, from the Strait of Messina to the Strait of Otranto, carousing between battles. When the Allies invaded Sicily in May 1943 with half a million soldiers and 3,700 aircraft, they were there guarding the coastal waters. When the Americans invaded Anzio on the west coast of Italy in the following January, they were there, too.

What stories they could tell! And what stories they did tell in later years when they gathered for lunch at the Vancouver Club, solid citizens at the heads of their own firms, sipping their scotches and reliving the days of their youth, from the English Channel to the Adriatic:

The time when, en route to Gibraltar from England, one of the fuel tanks exploded, turning Maitland's boat into a torch. As the flames leapt fifty feet, Maitland instinctively turned the power to full throttle, grabbed the wheel, spun it around, and drove headlong back into the raging sea, which rushed over the craft, extinguishing the flames. "All right, now," Maitland imperturbably signalled. "Slight casualties only, one petrol tank burned out and considerable experience gained in fire fighting."

The time when Burke, during a thick fog, mistook Ladner's boat for the enemy and fired a burst, which happily missed. When Ladner demanded to know what Burke was doing, his old schoolmate replied over the loud hailer: "That's for getting me caned when I was a fag and you were a prefect."

424

The time when Maitland sank an enemy flak trawler (something small boats weren't equipped to do) by bumping up against her, dropping a fifty-foot depth charge, and dashing off at full throttle as it exploded under the vessel, springing her plates and starting a roaring fire—"ammunition streaking up, steam hissing, a lovely sight."

The time when Burke went to his base commander in England and tried to resign his commission because he wasn't satisfied that his senior officer was being aggressive enough. Burke kept his commission; the officer was transferred to bigger craft.

The time when Maitland, disgusted because the Germans were disguising their troop trains as hospital trains, led a small flotilla of Dog Boats within five hundred yards of the Sicilian coast, lined them up in line astern, and with that combined firepower blasted an entire train off the tracks.

The time when Burke, finding life at sea too damned routine, crept up on the sleepy seaside resort of Avola on the Sicilian shore and, having no other target, shot up the unmanned lighthouse to let the enemy know he'd been there. Said the Admiral, poker faced, severely, "Burke, in the Royal Navy we leave the killing of women and children to the RAF."

The time in a Malta nightclub, when a kilted Scot danced a jig on Maitland's table and challenged, "I bet ya canna do that!"

"No," Maitland replied, "but I wonder if you can do this?" Whereupon he ordered a sherry in a long-stemmed glass, drank it, and proceeded to eat the bowl. "Now, sir," he told the Scot, "I've left the greatest delicacy for you. What about it?" and handed him the stem. Before the night was over the military police had to be called.

The night they "liberated" the Isle of Capri, three days after the Germans left, moved into the magnificent villa of Mussolini's son-in-law, Count Ciano, where the fittings included a mink-lined toilet seat cover.

The night they invaded Ischia opposite Capri in the Bay of Naples, only to find U.S. Rangers on the spot, with 2,500 people on the dock singing, wearing flowers, and waiting for the mayor in a carefully planned ceremony to surrender the island not to them, but to Lieutenant-Commander Douglas Fairbanks, Jr., of the U.S. Navy.

A *good war?* For them, yes.

8

The soft underbelly It is a military axiom that generals tend to fight the current war tainted by the tactics and memories of the past. So it was with Andrew McNaughton, who could never forget the days when his old corps had won the plaudits of the world and his old commander, Arthur Currie, had refused to allow the British to break up his fighting force. McNaughton was determined to follow Currie's example.

Yet this was a different kind of war, and it required a different approach. McNaughton was lauded as a passionate nationalist—a new Canadian breed emerging from the imperialistic umbrella—but those commendable convictions, larded as they were with more than a smattering of personal vanity, were outweighing military considerations. How could the Great War hero lead his army to victory if it were split into pieces? It had been easy enough to keep the old corps united and the troops bonded together in the static warfare of 1914–18. This, however, was a mobile war that did not fit easily into old soldiers' mental horizons, shaped in the trenches.

Because of McNaughton's unbending doctrine, abetted by Mackenzie King's phobia about conscription, the newly arrived Americans gained battle experience in the invasion of North Africa while the Canadians grew stale in England. Richard Malone, a Canadian on Montgomery's staff, has pointed out that the country was lucky not to have faced an additional three months of warfare, for in that event the army would have had to be broken up for lack of reinforcements. "It was a close call," he wrote in *Missing from the Record*. An army in the field requires an enormous number of men to support the fighting infantry—clerks, headquarters staffs, engineers, work battalions, and more. When the battle was joined at last and the casualties began to soar, would Canada have the manpower to fill the gap?

In the eyes of the Canadian public, McNaughton could do no wrong. In Malone's words, he was "revered almost as a God." To the Governor General he was "an idol in the eyes of his countrymen." He certainly looked the part. In his photographs he did not smile, he *glowered*. His piercing grey eyes, deep-set beneath his shaggy brows, burned fiercely into the camera. Yousuf Karsh, the Ottawa photographer who had gained some fame by removing the cigar from Churchill's mouth, giving him a bulldog look, performed the same service for the general when he draped an oversized army greatcoat over his thin shoulders, providing the press with its most memorable portrait.

McNaughton was the centre of a vast publicity build-up in which Malone took part and later regretted. The country needed a symbol— a Canadian Kitchener to boost morale and aid recruiting, and McNaughton was the only candidate. Certainly, the fusty, roly-poly prime minister did not fit the stereotype. Nor did the other Canadian general, Harry Crerar, the ambitious 1st Corps leader and later McNaughton's successor, who was too flabby to act as a symbol— prosy and stodgy, in Montgomery's assessment. E.L.M. Burns, Crerar's successor as commander of 1st Corps, was cold and austere, devoid of outward personality (though known privately for his sexual adventures), almost totally humourless, with no time for small talk and no aptitude for personal relations. The troops called him Laughing Boy. The Second Division's dour and unapproachable Charles Foulkes had no more charisma than a newt, "a cold fish" in the words of C.P. Stacey. The brilliant Guy Simonds, who would command the 2nd Corps in action in northwest Europe, undoubtedly the best tactician in the Canadian forces, maintained an icy exterior. Cold and ruthless, he was respected but unloved. The exception was Chris Vokes, who would command the First Division in Italy, rough, rowdy, even hot-headed, a two-fisted drinker but a mediocre leader and a little too off-centre to serve as a Canadian symbol. After all, he had once tried to establish a brothel in Italy for his troops and had come within an ace of succeeding!

Only McNaughton fitted the desired pattern. He loved the press and the press loved him. He made himself available at all times to war

427

correspondents while his staff worked hard to build him up, especially in the Luce publications. His portrait appeared on the cover of *Time*. He was the subject of an article in *Fortune* and a leading personality in the *March of Time* documentaries, "an almost legendary figure," in the words of Guy Simonds's brother Peter, "a symbol of the indomitable spirit of the Anglo-Saxon peoples. . . ."

"He is the answer to a photographer's prayer," Wallace Reyburn wrote of McNaughton in a major article in *Maclean's* early in 1943. "As a man McNaughton may definitely be rated as great. Anybody who has been in contact with him cannot help but feel he has a mind, an outstanding mind, one of the greatest Canada has produced. One comes away from seeing him at work among his troops or from a conversation with him, saying to one's self: 'That man's a genius.'"

Both *Time* and *Fortune* in their laudatory articles reported hints that McNaughton might indeed become supreme Allied commander in Europe. The general himself was always ready with colourful and belligerent quotations, such as the famous description of the Canadian army as a "dagger pointed at the heart of Berlin." He had another one for the press when he visited Roosevelt in Washington: "I have never done anything else but talk of offensive in Europe. We intend to give it to the Hun—right in the belly."

McNaughton's prestige was so high that he was able to have his way with the Canadian cabinet. When it was suggested that part of the Canadian force in England be used in the coming invasion of North Africa, it was he who blocked the idea. Here was a chance for Canadian soldiers and, more importantly, their leaders to gain experience in a comparatively easy campaign. Instead, the new American troops, with much less training than the Canadians, did the job. That was what bothered the Canadian defence minister, J.L. Ralston, himself a Great War commander with a record as enviable as McNaughton's. Ralston was concerned that no Canadian leader had yet been tried in battle, that younger officers had been given no chance to show their abilities, and that no future commanders were being developed. The Americans got the experience.

428

Although the public and the press did not know it, McNaughton himself was being found wanting. He was, in the words of a recent critic, "an insatiable dabbler," who wanted to "put his finger in every pie." His scientific preoccupation with new military gadgetry conspired against his real task—to train those under his command to a high peak of efficiency. In C.P. Stacey's opinion, the Canadian Army got "rather less than it might have" from its training period in Britain owing to the "casual and haphazard attitude" of its officers. General Kenneth Stuart, chief of the Canadian general staff, concluded late in 1943 that McNaughton "lacked most of the attributes of high command." According to Stuart, he "neglected his chief responsibilities as commander, was interested largely in the mechanical, rather than the human side of command, was excitable and very highly strung. . . ."

It was not McNaughton's fault that years of appeasement had contributed to the neglect of Canada's military forces and the paucity of trained commanders and staff officers without whom an efficient modern army cannot prevail. But his own inattention to training in England was a different matter. War correspondents were fond of echoing his declaration that the Canadians were the best-trained force in the world, "thoroughly prepared for battle." Indeed, McNaughton held to the conviction that they were overtrained and might become stale from too much emphasis on training. That was fiction, as the great military manoeuvre known as Exercise Spartan in March 1943 was to prove.

Spartan was the largest exercise ever to be mounted in England, a massive war game involving a quarter of a million men and 72,000 vehicles spread out for a fortnight across a large area of southern England. It was designed to simulate real battle conditions and to test the problems that might arise when invading troops made an assault landing, broke out of their bridgehead, and set off in hot pursuit of the defenders. Unlike the Dieppe raid it was a proper rehearsal for D-Day in Normandy.

It was also, for McNaughton, an unmitigated disaster. Here his capacity as a commander was tested, for he was in charge of the attacking army. His advance was slowed by a dreadful traffic snarl, there was a problem of gasoline supply, and a fifteen-hour loss of wireless communication blacked out the connection between corps and army headquarters. At one point McNaughton lost all control of the battle and did not even know where some of his divisions were. Spartan not only showed up flaws in training but also emphasized the inadequacy and incompetence of some Canadian staff officers. McNaughton's lack of professional knowledge was shocking. One example was his attempt to move 2nd Corps in a single night; apparently he had no idea that an army corps required a minimum of twenty-four hours to execute any major task.

Sir James Gregg, British secretary of state for war, who was a witness, was "appalled at McNaughton's indecision" as "he stood in front of the situation map hesitating what to do and what orders to issue." Brooke, the CIGS, who also watched McNaughton in action with a sinking feeling, wrote in his diary that his worst fears had been proven true, ". . . that he is quite incompetent to command an Army! He does not know how to begin to cope with the job and he was tying his force up into an awful muddle! . . . I felt that I could not accept the responsibility of allowing the Canadian Army to go into action under his orders." Brooke was critical of McNaughton's dithering, of his weak handling of operations, and his lack of confidence that, in the report of General Sir Bernard Paget, "resulted in missed opportunities, delayed decisions, changes of orders and frequent and conflicting short moves of units and formations."

Guy Simonds noted another failure—a lack of energy on the part of the forward brigades in coming to grips with the enemy in comparison with that displayed on a previous exercise, Tiger. There was also the continuing problem of road movement that would turn up again in the Normandy campaign. The Canadians were reluctant to leave the roads, partly for fear of damaging crops and civilian property but also because of poor staff planning at the corps level. The congestion on the roads suggested that too many vehicles were being used, a defect noted by Montgomery on a previous exercise but still not rectified.

Brooke's tough report was watered down for Canadian cabinet consumption, and the details were kept from Canadians for months to come. Nevertheless, McNaughton's reputation with the cabinet began to decline. On more than one occasion he had been able to bypass cabinet because of his high profile, a breach of protocol that irked Ralston and resulted in an open break between the two. The defence minister was haunted by the prospect of Canadian troops going into battle with no experience of actual warfare and was further annoyed by McNaughton's breezy inattention to detail. Early in the war, the general had announced publicly that the Canadian Army was to be totally mechanized, with all armoured divisions, artillery, and infantry operating on wheels. That was all very well; Ralston was indeed trying at the same time to convince the cabinet that, costly though it was, the mechanization would have to be accepted. But who was going to man those vehicles, and who was going to maintain them? McNaughton plunged ahead into what Richard Malone called "a fantasy world" without giving any serious thought to the task of recruiting and training thousands of motor mechanics.

Malone was present at McNaughton's first encounter with Ralston at which the general, with scarcely a nod to the minister, spent an hour delivering "a rather condescending report on our overseas forces." As an afterthought, McNaughton outlined various new agreements that he had made with the British over the use of reinforcements, the reorganization of existing units, and the creation of new ones. Ralston, who was confined to a wheelchair by sciatica, listened carefully and then, very slowly and precisely, told him, "'Those decisions which you have just reported, General, are all matters which will be properly decided by the Canadian government, not independently by yourself.'

"There was a complete and icy silence in the room for the next few minutes. McNaughton stared into Ralston's steady gaze and then slowly sat down. There was no doubt left in anyone's mind as to where authority rested or who could exercise it."

After Spartan it was quietly understood that McNaughton was not the man to lead the Canadian army into battle. The general, who was not yet aware of the British high command's attitude (nobody, apparently, was prepared to bell the cat), was still insisting that his army be kept together. Ralston, however, having been rebuffed on the North African landings, was determined that some Canadian units would be given a chance to experience actual warfare during the planned attack on Sicily. McNaughton opposed this with what Brooke called "fanatic antagonism" but reluctantly gave in with the assurance that once Sicily was captured, the Canadians would be sent back to England, bringing with them the benefit of their battle experience. That did not happen. Instead, Canadians remained in the Italian campaign that followed, and Canada insisted that an armoured division, the Fifth, be added. A Canadian corps was thus created, not for tactical reasons—a tank division wasn't useful in that spine of mountains—but because of the fear that without this kind of gesture Canadian influence in the post-war world would suffer. Again the shadow of the Great War hung over these decisions. Canada's brilliant record had contributed to its post-war prestige, especially in giving it an independent seat at the League of Nations.

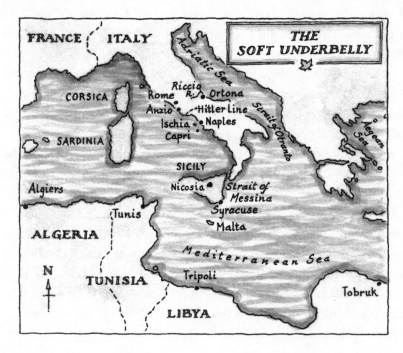

432

Operation Husky, the joint invasion of Sicily by American, Canadian, and British troops, began on July 10, 1940, with Guy Simonds in charge of the First Canadian Division. American and Canadian troops took the town of Nicosia in central Sicily, but the Americans were temporarily stalled, and Simonds was faced with a critical decision. Should he press on against the retreating enemy, allowing them no respite, or should he follow the book and wait for the Americans to move up beside him on the left flank? Simonds tossed the book aside and decided to maintain momentum. With the Canadians driving a narrow wedge into the enemy centre, the Germans began to fall back before the Americans arrived.

Sicily was conquered in thirty-eight days at a cost of 2,300 Canadian casualties—fewer than expected. It was here that the First Division— "the Old Red Patch"— began to gain its reputation. It was noticed that the Germans were building up their forces against the Canadian sector. As one prisoner of war exclaimed, "We see the Red Patch coming and we fire our mortars hard. But the Red Patch just keeps running through the fire. I can't understand it. Other troops we fought lay down and took shelter when the mortars fired right on top of them. The Red Patch are devils. They just keep coming." Montgomery's assessment was equally glowing. He told the Canadians, "I regard you as one of the veteran divisions of the Eighth Army. Just as good as any, if not better."

These were good days for army morale, but not good days for McNaughton. He had been told that the Canadian involvement in Husky was temporary; now both Ralston and Stuart were demanding a corps effort in Italy. When the General tried to visit the troops in Sicily, he suffered another blow to his ego. Montgomery didn't want visitors to his headquarters when he was occupied with battle, and he especially didn't want this visitor. According to Malone, he was prepared to place McNaughton under arrest if he set foot in Sicily. This ticklish contretemps threatened to become a political issue. McNaughton was infuriated, "livid with rage," according to Alan Brooke, who later declared that the Canadian general "would sooner have risked losing the war than agree to splitting the Canadian forces." But McNaughton's position was already weakened and, for better or for worse, the Canadian Army was split in two, no longer the dagger pointed at the heart of Berlin. Two divisions—the First and later the Fifth Armoured—would fight for most of the rest of the war in what Churchill had called, with characteristic but flawed panache, "the soft underbelly of Europe." Canada's other three divisions—Second, Third, and Fourth— would stay in England until the Normandy invasion.

McNaughton faced another problem, reminiscent of Sam Hughes's skewed nationalism in the Great War. He had publicly supported the concept of a totally mechanized army, and every effort had been made to give him one. But Sicily revealed major flaws in Canadian-designed equipment. It turned out that the large lorries expressly made for the campaign to carry troops and equipment could not fit between the decks of any merchant ship. They would have to be dismantled before the convoys sailed for Sicily and reassembled on shore—an impossible situation during an assault landing. The lorries had to be discarded and replaced by British vehicles at a time when Britain needed every bit of equipment it could get. Shades of Miss MacAdam's patented shovel and Charles Ross's notorious rifle! This error cost Canada hundreds of thousands of dollars, and McNaughton could not escape the blame because in such matters he had near-dictatorial powers and had promoted the use of Canadian design and development for the army.

As the summer and the fall wore on and the Allies attacked the not-so-soft underbelly, causing the Italian government to sue for peace, McNaughton began to demonstrate an increasing paranoia. In his distorted fancy, everybody—Montgomery, Ralston, the British and Canadian cabinets—was involved in a conspiracy to stab him in the back. The Canadian decision to change course and increase its presence in the Italian campaign to corps level infuriated him. He seemed to go along with the idea when it was first broached, but two days later he changed his mind and threatened to resign if the army was broken up. It was at this point that Ralston was given the distasteful job of telling the general what he didn't know and refused to accept: that the British (and later, as it developed, the Americans) had no confidence in him. To Ralston, McNaughton "took it like a soldier," but in fact he was seething inwardly. He was sure the minister was acting out of spite and stormed up to London to have it out with CGS Stuart and later with Brooke and also Montgomery's successor, General Sir Bernard Paget, as chief of the South-East England Command, who tried to placate him. Their sympathy was enough to confirm him in his mistaken belief that he had their confidence and that he was the victim of a political cabal with Ralston at its centre.

Off went a coded message to Mackenzie King in which McNaughton twisted Paget's soothing diplomacy, claiming that he "welcomed me remaining in command of the Canadian Army both now and later in N.W. Europe. . . ." As for Ralston, "I can no longer remain in command of the First Canadian Army responsible to any government of which he is a member." Ralston's action, McNaughton declared, was "the meanest and most despicable of my own experience."

King was now thoroughly alarmed. Here was his army commander telling him that the British had total confidence in him and that Ralston was out to get him. Here was his minister of defence telling him the exact opposite. If the controversy became public it would have a terrible effect on army morale and, it went without saying, be politically disastrous. In discussions that followed in London between Ralston and an outraged Paget, McNaughton was forced to back down completely and apologize. Now a way had to be found to save the embattled general from himself, ease him out of command with the least possible fuss, and find a new Canadian army commander.

Not surprisingly, McNaughton was suffering from fatigue and tension, which an army medical board confirmed after the respiratory infection that had plagued him the previous year returned. The board recommended a three-month leave of absence with the general freed of all military responsibilities. McNaughton at last agreed to retire for health reasons, but on his return to Canada he muddied the waters by insisting that he had never been in better health. Then he applied, in writing, for extended sick leave.

Now, as the Canadians moved up the boot of Italy and attacked the

Adriatic port of Ortona, the problem of McNaughton's replacement continued to bedevil his political masters. The army was doing battle, in effect, without a commander-in-chief, and facing the toughest battle yet.

To Canadians of that era, Ortona became the symbol of the "spaghetti campaign"—the slow, stubborn push up Europe's underbelly. To more than one writer it was "a miniature Stalingrad." To its definitive historian, Mark Zuehlke, it was "Canada's epic World War II battle." Epic it certainly was for the exhausted and unshaven troops of the First Division, who fought a week-long, house-to-house battle in the rubbled streets of the town, blasting their way foot by foot through the walls of booby-trapped buildings, where even the family Bible could be wired to blow up in their faces.

It was an expensive victory—almost 4,000 troops killed, wounded, or incapacitated—but not a very significant one, virtually ignored by most historians except the Canadians. One, David Bercuson, has wondered why nobody thought of sealing off the town and bypassing it, as was done later with Dunkirk during the Normandy campaign. The answer seems to be that both sides were trapped by their own publicity-mongers. Albert Kesselring, the German commander, told his troops he didn't want to defend the town, but "the English have made it as important as Rome . . . you can do nothing when things develop in this manner." The idea of fighting in built-up areas was one that the tacticians on both sides rejected. But Ortona became a symbol, with the help of war correspondents and the press. By December 11 it had become "the chief obstacle facing the Canadians," in the view of the *New York Times*, while the Ottawa *Citizen* declared that "the whole current Eighth Army thrust hinges on success of the Canadians in capturing Ortona." In the words of one military analyst, Major D.H. Cunningham, the press "played a large part in turning a tactical fight into a prestige battle with the consequent unnecessary loss of many lives." On both sides national pride and prestige were at stake. Hitler himself reacted when, on Christmas Eve, he ordered that Ortona be held at all costs—something the German army had never contemplated.

Since the days of the halberd and the pikestaff, the great variable in battle has been that provided by the human equation. Military commanders are not machines. Vanity, ambition, rivalry, ego, jealousy, dogma—these characteristics, along with the usual Boy Scout virtues, are present in soldiers who wear what John Keegan calls "the mask of command." As it was in the days of Xerxes and Hannibal, so it was on the riven approaches to Ortona.

Montgomery, commander of the famous Eighth Army of which the Canadians were a part, had believed that the Germans were all but finished in Italy. He had outfought them, or so he fancied, and all it would take to finish them off would be to hit them "a colossal crack." That vainglorious prediction, read out to the troops in his November 25 order of the day, turned out to be hollow. The Eighth, in support of General Mark Clark's U.S. Fifth Army, would drive on to Rome. Montgomery seems to have seen the fighting as a kind of Olympic event—a race between the Yanks and the British toward the Italian capital. He had not forgotten the humiliating fact that General George Patton had won a similar race in Sicily when Simonds was transferred to the Fifth Armoured Division. The new commander of the Canadian First Division was the blunt and profane Chris Vokes, a strapping six-footer with a fierce moustache and a bluff manner that contrasted sharply with Montgomery's.

The key to Ortona's defence lay in a trench-like natural depression, three miles long and two hundred yards wide, bristling with German armour. Known colloquially as the Gully, it barred the way to the battered town. Its presence stopped the Canadians and frustrated Montgomery's clear intention to try to beat the Yanks to Rome. Montgomery sent Malone, his liaison officer, to hurry Vokes up in his attempts to cross the Gully. "Old Monty wants to know what the problem is, why you're getting along so slowly," Malone reported. Vokes blew up. "You tell Monty," he roared, "if he would get the hell up here and see the bloody mud he has stuck us in, he'd know damned well why we can't move faster."

Vokes was new to command. He had been given charge of the division just two months before. Now, spurred on by Montgomery's impatient demands, he persisted in a series of failed frontal attacks in which he introduced his weary and depleted battalions piecemeal instead of combining his forces for a single powerful blow. As Zuehlke has noted, Vokes apparently "could not think on a divisional scale." He allowed each regiment "to be chewed up before withdrawing it and sending another into the fray." It took seven days and a new plan before the Gully was finally breached and the Canadians were able to fight their way into the town.

Commonwealth forces had not been trained in the techniques of street fighting that marked the battle for Ortona. The German snipers controlled every lane, every avenue, every alleyway; to venture into the open was to die. It wasn't mere privates the snipers were after: it was officers, NCOs, and radio signallers. Like the British and the other Commonwealth forces, the Canadians had neglected the use of snipers, but to the Germans these crack shots formed an elite. Each enemy division had a large number who operated on their own and couldn't be used for other purposes, and the First Parachute Division—tough veterans of the Russian front—had more than most German divisions.

The buildings in which men crouched as they worked their way up the narrow streets were equally dangerous because of booby traps. Jock Gibson, a Seaforth Highlanders company sergeant major, watched in horror as an officer moved to bash a door in with his rifle butt. Gibson shouted a warning, but it was too late. The officer swung his rifle and the resultant explosion knocked him into the street, his ankle all but ripped from his body.

The solution to the snipers and the booby traps was "mouse-holing," a technique perfected by Captain Bill Longhurst of the Loyal Edmonton Regiment. Blasting holes through the walls of the upper storeys, Canadians moved from house to house, working their way up the street hidden from the enemy—but also from their own commanders, who often had no idea where they were.

The German First Parachute Division, relatively fresh and up to strength, had relieved the exhausted 90th Panzer Grenadiers on December 12–13 during the struggle for the Gully, a clear indication

438

that the Germans meant to hold Ortona as long as possible. The Canadian units were badly depleted. The West Nova Scotia Regiment, for one, was virtually destroyed in the last battle for the Gully, with 194 casualties, 18 of them officers including the battalion commander. The Seaforths and Loyal Edmontons—the two regiments that fought the street battle in Ortona—were badly under strength, and the reinforcements they did receive were inexperienced and untested. One group sent up to relieve the Seaforths' badly battered "D" company arrived without any grenades. "What's this?" one man asked the company sergeant major. ". . . I've never had one of these before." These green troops didn't even know how to fire a Bren gun or clean a rifle— "lambs to the slaughter," as the sergeant major told himself.

The attack on Ortona, launched on December 20, 1943, was still raging on Christmas Day when the forward company of the Seaforths (but not the Edmontons) was rotated from the front to enjoy a festive dinner—a public relations dream that made the front pages in Canada from Halifax to Victoria. The dinner was served at the Seaforths' battalion headquarters in the Church of Santa Maria di Costantinopoli, just south of the town. "Well, at last I've got you all in church," the battalion's padre, Roy Durnford, told the dirty and unshaven men who came directly from the battle. As more men arrived in a series of company rotations, the plates were cleared from the tables and piled high above the altar. "I might once have thought it a desecration of the Lord's Table," Durnford wrote in his diary, "but it did not strike me this way today." To many a soldier it seemed bizarre to quit the table and travel, with their bellies full of pork, mashed potatoes, Christmas pudding, and mince pie, twenty blocks back to the firing line and often to death. Not all the Seaforths attended. Private Ernest "Smoky" Smith, a one-time construction worker, told his six-man section, ". . . people are going to get killed going to that dinner and others are going to die coming back from it. So you're all staying right here."

After seven days and nights of savage and unremitting struggle, a quiet fell over the city: the Germans had pulled out. On the last night— December 27—in the midst of one final enemy bombardment a young woman was found buried alive in the rubble of a shattered building. Troops from both regiments worked to free her only to discover she was pregnant and in labour. A sergeant from Vancouver helped with the delivery, and the baby and mother survived, both in good health. She promised her rescuers that the baby's middle name would be Canadese.

After the hard-fought battle for Ortona, the Canadian troops entered what one military writer, Fred Gaffen, called "a rather static period." And so it was for the exhausted men of the First Division, but for the new and untried troops, now experiencing their initial baptism of fire a few miles north of the shattered city, life was anything but static. The Canadian Fifth Armoured Division now entered the line against the veteran paratroopers. The green troops exulted at the news. As Stanley Scislowski, a private in the Perth Regiment, part of the 11th Infantry Brigade, remembered, ". . . there was probably not a man in the entire regiment who wasn't excited over the prospect of action."

Scislowski would never forget the feeling of elation that surged through the ranks—and its aftermath when the reality of battle changed their lives and their attitudes. Half a century later, in his eloquent memoir, the events of that first day of battle, January 17, 1944, were as sharp as if they had occurred the previous day. "Bravado had nothing to do with the way we felt," he wrote. "What it really boiled down to was that we were ignorant, not in the sense of crass stupidity, just the ignorance that comes with youth seeking adventure and perhaps fame. We had somehow been led to believe, perhaps through the movies, books on war, and our own government propaganda that battle was the ultimate adventure, the most glorious and heroic undertaking a man could take on."

This was Everyman speaking—every man in every war since the beginning of history. "I don't think there were many that looked to the fact that men die, often in droves, and in the most brutal and gruesome ways. And very few of us dwelled on the possibility of our own death in battle. . . . No, not me. I was indestructible. . . ."

The regiment got its first whiff of reality when, en route to the front, a clutch of mortar bombs missed them and exploded a hundred yards

440

away. Every muscle in Scislowski's body began to twitch uncontrollably. He couldn't stop shaking and thought at first it might be an epileptic seizure. "I was scared, but I didn't think I was that scared that I should lose all control of my muscles." Once the danger was over the twitching stopped; later experience told him that this was only his adrenal glands kicking into high gear.

The day before the attack, the Perths were assured that no opposition was expected. The planners were confident the enemy would be in no condition to put up a stiff resistance because of the massive artillery barrage that would precede the battle. "It all sounded so easy—not a thing to worry about. Our first battle would be history by noon. . . ."

But sleep did not come easily that night. "Visions of heroic acts dominated most of my thoughts. I saw myself as a one-man-army charging into the heart of the enemy positions, bludgeoning and bayoneting my way through a swarm of defenders. I also saw myself standing before the King at Buckingham Palace as he pinned the coveted Victoria Cross on my tunic."

How exhilarating these thoughts were! "How was I to imagine that the battle would not go the way the planners painted it to go, that instead it would turn out to be the grimmest, most heartbreaking, most spirit-draining day in my life and everyone else's who was there for the baptism?" It was just as well he didn't know, as he drifted off to sleep, that he was no better and no different than anyone else—"just another frightened and disillusioned kid wishing to hell he'd never joined the infantry."

In the final hour before the battle he suffered an acute attack of incontinence; so did everyone else. A steady procession of men lined up at the latrine. "We learned for the first time the powerful diuretic and laxative effect pre-battle nerves can have on a man." And then at half-past five, "the gray light of approaching dawn flashed into brightness as if someone had just flipped a light switch" and the barrage opened up. "What was happening around us was both fascinating and frightening. It stunned the senses. Who could not be afraid at a moment like this?"

After fifteen minutes the guns were turned off as suddenly as they had been turned on and "an unnatural stillness descended on the battle-field, a stillness almost as unnerving as the din that made our ears ache and turned our stomachs into knots." Scislowski's unit—Dog Company—was in reserve. Up ahead Charlie Company was moving forward down the slope into the Riccio River valley under long bursts of machine-gun fire.

With dawn breaking at seven and Charlie Company pinned down, Dog Company was ordered into battle to free Charlie Company for the final rush. They had just started moving out of the protection of a ditch when mortar bombs began to explode all around them, catching them in the open with no place to hide. As Scislowski hugged the ground, chunks of half-frozen earth pelted his face. "Here we were only minutes into the battle and already I thought I was going to die!" He thought he'd better start praying, "even though I didn't know how to address God." Probably, he thought, a lot of young Germans opposite were also praying. "So whose prayers would He answer, ours or theirs?

"I was so terrified now, I forgot what I was babbling about as I uttered my crude prayer." Then, as he raised his head momentarily, he spotted some tank tracks five yards away, only about three inches deep "but better than nothing." He crawled over to the tracks between mortar blasts and there came face to face "with a guy whose face showed an even greater fear than mine." In training he'd been as tough as nails and "wasn't shy about throwing his weight around when he felt the need to. But the mortars had done something to take the fight out of him. His eyes were the size of two half-dollar coins, his lower lip flapped like a flag in a March gale. He couldn't talk." Scislowski couldn't help laughing, perhaps "because I suddenly realized I wasn't the only one almost out of his mind with fear."

Suddenly the mortaring stopped, and Dog Company moved forward again, approaching the valley of the Riccio where the two forward companies, Charlie and Able, were locked in a losing battle with the enemy. They passed two corpses—Seaforth Highlanders—not "mangled or twisted in any way, but beside one lay an upturned helmet with the red, pulpy remains of the man's brain pooled inside." The sight etched itself into Scislowski's memory. He could not shake the gruesome image. "It bothered me for the balance of that long, terrible, heart-breaking day."

Halfway to the Riccio they came under mortar and machine-gun fire again and hurled themselves into a number of well-dug trenches. "For the next fifteen minutes the enemy threw everything at us but the kitchen sink." He began to wonder if any of his fellows had been hit. Was he the only man left alive? Peering briefly over the trench he saw some of his comrades dashing for cover with bullets snapping at their feet. He hesitated for five minutes, trying to screw up his courage, and then he too tore ahead for seventy-five yards and hurtled into the protection of the embankment. Gasping for air, his heart pumping wildly, he realized what he'd gone through and felt proud of himself. ". . . in a small way I'd conquered the fear that had been growing by the hour . . . I began asking myself what it was that had drove me to taking such a risk in making that run." But he already knew the answer: "It was unwillingness to let the others in my platoon show me up. . . ."

Here, instinctively, Private Stanley Scislowski, recently of Windsor, Ontario, had put his finger on the reason why men fight. They do not fight for reasons of patriotism or for king and country, or for the leaders who spur them on, but for each other—for those whose friendship has been thrust upon them through the roulette wheel of war. Like football players, they cannot let the side down.

Something had gone wrong on that crisp January morning. The opening artillery barrage hadn't destroyed the enemy's capacity to fight back. "Here it was, past three in the afternoon . . . and we'd done nothing yet worth bragging about. . . . Here we were, not even a full day into the battle and already it felt like we'd been fighting forever. . . . I could see no way out of this war for me. Somewhere down the line I had to die." Then, having plumbed the depths of despair and self-pity, he got hold of himself. "To hell with it! Moping and worrying . . . isn't going to do me one damn bit of good. If I die, I die."

At half-past three, Dog Company got new orders. Another fifteen-minute artillery barrage was planned to soften up the Germans. Ten minutes after it ended, the attack would continue. At four o'clock sharp the guns opened up. "The sky above us was a crowded highway of shells all going in one direction. . . ."

After the mandatory ten minutes, their ears deafened by the cacophony above them, the men of Dog Company "ran resolutely on towards the valley of decision. Although we were all as 'green as grass' when it came to combat and our nerves rubbed raw from prolonged exposure to instant death, not a single man hung back."

As they plunged closer to the valley, the din grew louder with every step. Scislowski caught a glimpse of a small group of Charlie Company men "stumbling back from the slaughterhouse of the valley, two of them with wounded draped over their shoulders." The far slope was a boiling mass of shell bursts, the valley was thick with smoke and reeking from the stink of high explosive shells. A line of machine-gun bullets kicked up the dirt past his boots, so close he could feel the vibration through the double soles. A second burst followed and he hit the ground, believing his whole section had been killed until one "snapped out at me sharply, to get my goddamned boot out of the crack of his ass and I knew they were still with it."

For those at the bottom of the slope, to move was to die. They were pinned down, "glued to the ground." Then the killing began. When the forward platoon, No. 16, splashed across the shallow river, a mortar barrage all but destroyed the lead section in a matter of seconds. One man lived for an hour, crying out in agony "for help that was not to come," then died. It tore Scislowski apart to realize that nothing could be done for him. A dozen men from the wiped-out section lay writhing in pain from wounds. At this point the attack died.

Dog Company could go no farther. They stayed, clumped together, at the bottom of the east slope. "As I lay there with face pressed tight against the ground, my heart racing like a runaway engine, twinges of guilt came over me."

In early evening the firing slackened off, and the members of the pinned-down platoon chanced another dash to join some of the others. It was a gamble. The enemy could easily have cut them down. "I like to think that not all of the enemy were the evil people we'd been conditioned to believe, that there were some decent types amongst them. I had to believe it was these types that held their fire and let us get away. Maybe they felt we'd had more than enough for one day.

"We were all in a state of shock . . . besides losing the battle, we'd also lost a hell of a lot of our buddies. The battle ended with nothing to show for the heavy expenditure of shells, and more so, the more grievous expenditure of human resources, young men in the prime of life whom we'd sorely miss."

It was pitch black by the time the company reached members of the Hastings and Prince Edward Regiment, holed up in a tight group of houses just back from the lip of the valley. There they spent the night. Shortly before daybreak they set off across country in the direction of Ortona, whose rooftops they could see in the distance above the lunar landscape. There, on the northern limit of the shattered town, they saw the remnants of Dog Company climbing into trucks. "Our spirits took a giant leap. The company had not been wiped out after all." But the toll was daunting: forty-seven dead, sixty-two wounded, twenty-seven taken prisoner—about one-fifth of the battalion. Half an hour after getting into the trucks they were off-loaded in the same soggy field below San Vito from which they had departed six days before to march to the front for their first action.

An hour later as the roll was being called, Chris Vokes rolled up in a jeep. The 11th Brigade, including the Perths, had gone into action under Vokes's temporary command. "He gave us a short address, with backhanded praise for our efforts, but in the same breath let us know in no uncertain terms there was no excuse for being pinned down."

Vokes did not endear himself to the Perths with that reproof. As Scislowski said, dead men accomplish nothing, and to stand, under that fire, was to die. "In fact, hardly had the words left his lips when someone directly behind me said loud enough for the bewhiskered general to hear, 'Give me a fuckin' Bren and I'll show you, you bastard,

445

what it's like to be pinned down!'" Did those words recall Vokes's own recent undisciplined outburst to Malone about Montgomery? Certainly his face turned several shades of pink, and with those words ringing in his ears, he tapped his driver on the shoulder and moved off to continue the fight up the soft underbelly of Europe.*

9

The Andy McNaughton had gone down in flames, but as D-Day approached,
untried the Canadian cabinet continued to face the dilemma of finding a
army replacement. The Great War had cast a long shadow. The paucity of
field commanders in the Second World War was directly attributable to the bloodletting in Flanders that had horrified so many Canadians in the First. In the intervening years, it had become fashionable to sneer at the military and politically attractive to starve the armed forces. The 1917 conscription crisis haunted King while the golden memory of Vimy inspired McNaughton. Both visions combined to keep the ill-prepared and untested Canadians out of action, denying their leaders the battle experience essential for the coming struggle in northwestern Europe.

More than any other troops in Britain, the Canadian forces were subject to the tug of history and the gradual metamorphosis of Empire into Commonwealth. Tactically they were under the command of Montgomery and his successor, General Paget. Politically they were controlled by the Canadian cabinet. The British had not yet grasped the implications of the Statute of Westminster of 1930. To them, the Canadians were ultrasensitive about their status as equals within the Commonwealth.

* Stanley Scislowski survived the war. In January 1945 he was hospitalized for what he later discovered was post-battle traumatic stress syndrome, a delayed psychological condition that may affect a man who has seen too much battle, once he's removed from the dangers. He returned to Canada in 1946, married his sweetheart, fathered six children, and became a partner in an electroplating business. In 1997 he published his memoir, *Not All of Us Were Brave*, from which I have quoted, with the permission of his publisher, Dundurn Press, Toronto.

McNaughton had been called a whiner because he insisted on keeping his troops together.

To dyed-in-the-wool careerists, such as Alan Brooke, winning the war was the only priority. It was difficult to stomach an attitude that seemed to put nationalism ahead of strategic priorities. Added to that was the baffling problem of Canada's dual identity, which had split the Canadian cabinet into two factions: those who preferred a volunteer army and those who felt that conscription was the only sensible answer. To observers on the sidelines, it must have seemed comically complicated—a country half British and half French that wasn't sure it wanted to be British at all, and an army that was also divided between committed volunteers and others in uniform who were not volunteers at all: an army within an army, serving a land that was itself a nation of two nations.

Mackenzie King was a McNaughton man from the start; after all, the General had managed to save his political hide by keeping the forces unbloodied for four years. On the other hand, Ralston and Macdonald were pro-conscriptionists, and only King's manoeuvring had prevented them from resigning. Within the army, the same dichotomy prevailed. McNaughton's corps commander, Harry Crerar, was critical of his senior not only on the conscription issue but also because he disagreed with the general's lax view of training. Crerar was fiercely ambitious, had lobbied hard for promotion to lieutenant general, and was a proponent of the big army, with at least two corps of five or six divisions each.

Crerar was also a skilled political infighter with powerful friends in high places. While proclaiming his allegiance to McNaughton he had done his best privately to undermine him in the eyes of such men as Ralston and High Commissioner Vincent Massey. The idea of a big army was politically attractive in Canada because it would provide a much-needed injection of the kind of national prestige that Canadians had always craved.

Hong Kong, Dieppe, and the long wait in England had not done much for the national ego. But now, at last, Canada was in the fight, and the public mood demanded a strong presence in Europe—much stronger than King had intended. Not only had the First Division been kept on after Sicily to fight in Italy but the ambitious Crerar had also forced the Fifth Armoured Division (not to mention an entire corps headquarters) on Montgomery, who didn't want or need it and, indeed, didn't know about it until the troops had set out from England. "Why would they send them out without asking if they were needed first?" the nettled general expostulated. Crerar established his corps head-quarters in Sicily, top-heavy with ancillary troops and with himself as its commander—a lieutenant general at last!

Crerar's ambitions went further. His full army of two or three corps would have himself at its head, leading the Canadians to victory as Currie had in 1918—McNaughton's shattered dream writ large. Mont-gomery would have preferred an experienced British commander such as Major General Miles Dempsey to lead the Canadians after the D-Day invasion, but that was unthinkable. At Vimy, a British general—Byng— had commanded the Canadians. But twenty-five years had passed. The Canadian Army—a polyglot force with more British units under its banner than Montgomery's famous Eighth and an entire Polish division added—could scarcely be a source of national pride without a son of Canada at its head. The small two-division corps in Italy, top-heavy with non-fighting troops, would, in the months before the invasion, serve to salve Canada's hunger for a place in the international sun.

The cabinet was faced with a difficult choice for an army commander because the field was so narrow. The ablest commander was Guy Granville Simonds, a career officer who since his graduation from the Royal Military College had lived and breathed the army. A major when war broke out, Simonds was a brigadier in the Italian campaign and would shortly be recalled to England as a major general in charge of the Second Division, badly mauled at Dieppe and now being readied for the Normandy invasion. Ruthless in battle and also with his own staff when he found them wanting, he was, in the words of a fellow brigadier, "a tough baby [who] brooked no sentiment and demanded results . . . an admirable battle commander but not a man one could love." But at thirty-nine, Simonds was judged too young to shoulder the heavy responsibilities of command. Others, such as Ken Stuart, the current CGS and a temporary commander after McNaughton's resignation, were veterans of the Great War, seen as too old and too set in their ways to fight a different kind of battle. Some, such as Chris Vokes, had risen to the level of their capabilities. Vokes, in Montgomery's assessment, "was not in the same parish" as Simonds. "I am trying hard to teach him but he will never be anything more than a good plain cook."

It took the cabinet three months to appoint a successor to McNaughton. It settled on Crerar, aged fifty-five, a gunner, like most of the Canadian high command, and also a Great War veteran who had no field experience in the new war. He had been sent to Italy to acquire some, but his own vanity worked against him. Montgomery tried to give him a chance by offering him temporary control of the First Division. But that would have meant a step down in rank from corps commander, and the new lieutenant general, to Montgomery's dismay, refused the offer. He would be following in the footsteps of Simonds of whom he was already jealous, and that he could not stomach. As a result he spent no more than a month in Italy and returned to England to take charge of the 2nd Corps without having commanded troops in action.

Ralston had had some early reservations about Crerar. He finally came to the conclusion that Crerar was the best man available for the job but also had "very grave weaknesses in character. He is immensely ambitious and is constantly seeking to arrogate to himself the whole business of the department."

Crerar had lobbied for the job from the outset of the war. In 1942, during McNaughton's absence through illness, he had pushed hard for the Dieppe raid and Canada's major role in it. When the raid turned into a fiasco he popularized the excuse that it had been worthwhile because of the "lessons learned." His refusal in 1943 to relinquish, albeit temporarily, command of the Canadian Corps in Italy had riled Montgomery, who reported to Brooke on December 23, "The more I think of Harry Crerar the more I am convinced that he is quite unfit to command an army in the field at present. . . . He has already (in Sicily) started to have rows with Canadian generals under me: he wants a lot of teaching."

At this point Crerar and Simonds were like two alley cats snarling at each other on a backyard fence. If we are to believe Richard Malone, each man thought the other insane. The contretemps was triggered, apparently, after Simonds, on entering his caravan, found one of Crerar's underlings taking notes and measuring it for size. The Corps commander wanted to have one like it built for himself, but Simonds, enraged at finding a stranger in his private quarters, gave the junior officer a tongue-lashing.

To Crerar, this was a "personal discourtesy" that suggested Simonds's nerves were overstretched and that his impulsive action might affect his decisions in battle. He urged that Simonds undertake a self-examination and diagnosis of his mental and physical condition. Crerar then went on to advise Montgomery that he had "serious cause to doubt" Simonds's suitability for high command. Simonds, he suggested, with his tense mentality under strain through increased rank and responsibility, might go "off the deep end very disastrously indeed."

Malone, flying into Crerar's headquarters then in Sicily, was astonished to find that the chief psychiatric adviser to the Canadian forces had just arrived from London, summoned by Crerar "to come out and certify that Guy Simonds was insane." At dinner, Crerar explained to him that Simonds, who had been ill, had been released from hospital too soon and was mentally unfit. The following day, having flown to Simonds's Fifth Division headquarters in Italy, Malone heard the other side, again at dinner, when Simonds brought up the subject of Crerar. "The man was 'quite bonkers', he assured us . . . had gone off his rocker . . . should be in an institution . . . was sending insane signals all over the place." Fred van Nostrand, the psychiatric adviser, threw up his hands. "I am going back to London as fast as I can get there," he confided to Malone. "This isn't a problem for me."

It all blew over in time, but Crerar's jealousy of his subordinate did not abate, nor did Montgomery's reservations about the man who would be chosen to lead the Canadian army into battle in northwestern Europe. As a tyro commander in the veteran Eighth Army, he didn't quite fit in.

The young Simonds, with his chiselled features, his bayonet-straight stance, and his impeccable battledress, looked every centimetre the soldier. The middle-aged and paunchier Crerar was flabby by comparison.

A long-time Permanent Force staffer—and a good one, by peace time standards—he was also a stickler for the superficialities of military etiquette and discipline. But now, with the parade ground supplanted by the battleground, commanders in the field had neither time nor inclination to fight the kind of paper war that was popular in the pre-war army bureaucracy. The Canadian Corps in Italy under Crerar was smothered in an avalanche of paper because its commander believed that everything should be written down. Crerar "had a passion for formal orders and would not leave the paper war alone"; through years of soldiering in the regular army it had become a disease with him. Montgomery, on the other hand, had virtually eliminated paperwork after he took over the Eighth in the desert. He believed, as did his protege Simonds, in giving clear verbal orders that could be discussed on the spot. The First Division was proud of the fact that since the landing in Sicily it had not issued a single written order. The same was true of the landing in Italy under Simonds. But when the new corps moved it did so in a blizzard of paper.

In the matter of dress the Desert Rats of the Eighth were refreshingly informal. Montgomery was far more interested in the fighting abilities of his men. His own costume—loose sweater, baggy trousers, black beret with two cap badges—set the tone and also, it must be acknowledged, gave the General a distinctive public relations image. When Crerar arrived, however, a new set of dress regulations, to be followed to the letter, were invoked, and all informality was banned. Montgomery had boasted that on only one occasion had he issued an order on dress to his Eighth Army headquarters: a naked Canadian soldier had leaned out of his truck and raised a top hat—his only item of clothing—in mock salute as he passed the General. To that Montgomery replied in kind: "Top hats will not be worn in Eighth Army."

Crerar also balked at the common practice of adorning army vehicles with the names or pictures of girlfriends. He put a stop to that and relented only slightly when one of his divisional commanders protested. He would allow the practice, he declared, provided the name was no more than one inch high and on the dashboard where only the driver could see it. There was no humour in him, no sense of fun, and no understanding of the importance of army morale. After the hard-won Normandy invasion, when the Canadians launched the miserable battle of the Scheldt estuary, fought largely in silt and slime, Montgomery paid the Third Division a visit and told the troops they had earned the title of Water Rats. The officers and men liked the idea so much—it was, after all, reminiscent of Monty's famous Desert Rats—that the engineers began to paint rats on the bridges and road signs. Crerar's reaction was predictable: "Take that lousy rodent down!" he ordered.

This was the man destined to lead the first army Canada had ever sent into battle—the only general in the Allied invasion with no field experience. Crerar had a bare three months to organize the new force before the June 6 invasion. The army, as such, which was not yet operational for seven weeks after D-Day, would consist of two corps: the 1st, still fighting in Italy, and the 2nd, under Guy Simonds, stationed in England preparing for the invasion.

The Canadian forces, however, entered the Normandy campaign piecemeal. Those who stormed the beaches on June 6—the Third Division and the 2nd Armoured Brigade—were attached to the British Second Army under Miles Dempsey's control, not Crerar's. Montgomery didn't want a new and untried headquarters cluttering up the crowded beaches during the initial phases of the operation. He was no respecter of national aspirations and a little baffled by the Canadian insistence on flaunting its independence. "I have grave fears," Montgomery wrote to Brooke on June 23, "that Harry Crerar will not be too good; however I am keeping him out of the party as long as possible." None of that, of course, was known to the newspaper-reading public, who were excited, even euphoric, that Canadian troops were part of the D-Day triumph. The Third Division, indeed, advanced farther, albeit at greater cost, than the British at Juno Beach.

452

One of the 156,000 soldiers who stormed the beaches on that day was Charles Cromwell Martin, a company sergeant major with the Queen's Own Rifles of Canada. The Queen's Own, indeed, was the first Canadian battalion to set foot on Juno Beach. It would be a long day. Martin's "A" Company had risen before dawn and climbed aboard the landing craft at five. Their objective: the village of Bernière-sur-Mer.

As soon as they climbed down the loading nets and into the landing craft they realized that this was nothing like the training exercise they had been given in England. Here, in a stiff gale, Martin's boat was tossed about like a cork, yawing and swaying on its rope ten or fifteen feet from the mother ship. Each man was carrying at least fifty pounds and often more; if one made a mistake he would drop like a stone into the furious waters and could be crushed by the landing craft as it slammed against the ship.

When ten landing boats had been loaded with two companies of the Queen's Own there was a frustrating one-hour delay, which meant the assault would take place in daylight instead of just before dawn. They had five miles to go to reach the beach, and as they finally got underway, they were shocked to realize that they had lost contact with the rest of the assault fleet. "We had never felt so alone in our lives," Martin wrote in his memoirs. As their objective loomed out of the mist, a quiet fell on the enemy beach. "It could have been a picture postcard of any one of a hundred tiny French beaches with a village behind—not the real thing." But they knew the entire beach was open to murderous fire from the enemy machine guns, positioned for a full 180-degree sweep.

Suddenly a nervous gunner in one of the German pillboxes opened up prematurely, cutting a rifleman, Cy Hardin, on the cheek. The naval rating operating the craft bandaged the wound quickly. "If that's the worst you get, you'll be lucky," he said. Martin ordered him to take the boat in as fast as possible until the prow grated on the gravel. Down came the ramp and the Germans opened up with mortar and machine-gun fire. "Move! Fast!" Martin shouted to his friend Sergeant Jack Sampson, who sat across from him. "Don't stop for anything," he

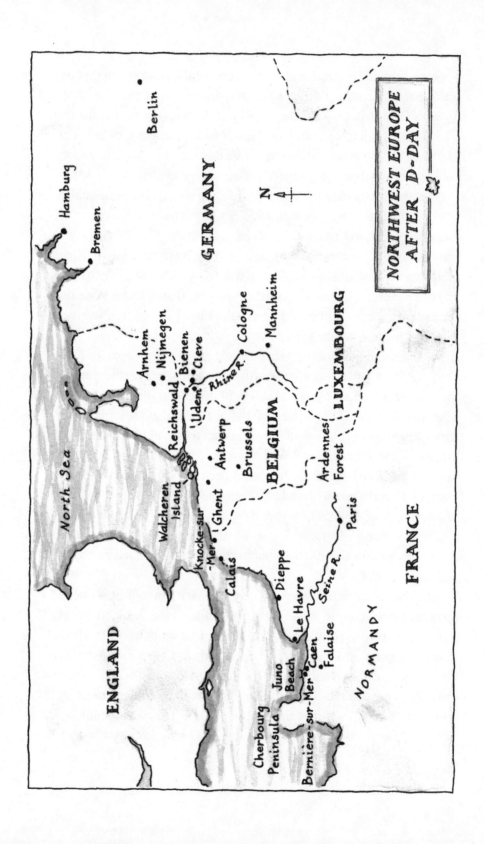

shouted to the men, "Go! Go! Go!" as they raced down the ramp and headed for the seawall.

Men began to die. The leaders—section and platoon commanders—were the prime targets. Sampson was one of several from Martin's boat cut down on the beach.

The seawall, one hundred yards away, was masked by six-foot sand dunes. "We had no time to think much. Our training did that for us. We were men who could run sixty miles with a twenty-five-pound pack, first-class marksmen . . . and all of us drilled in the credo: 'don't stop for anything.' "

To the left Martin spotted a small gap in the wall manned by a two-man, belt-fed machine gun whose single operator was gesturing furiously for someone to feed the belt as he did the firing. Bert Shepherd stopped for a second and took the gunner out as they raced on. Machine-gun and mortar fire seemed to come from everywhere. Minefields lay on both sides. As they crossed the railway tracks, barbed wire blocked the way. Martin, as CSM, pulled rank and insisted on cutting the strands himself, bending them back "just wide enough for a man to belly through." By this time others had joined his group, and fifteen men prepared to cross the minefield. Martin advanced ten paces and then unwittingly stepped on a jumping mine, the kind that spreads its contents—old nails, buckshot, and the like—over a broad area. Martin held his foot in place so the mine wouldn't go off. Then he got every-one else to the far side over a fence and into some gardens by the houses. A bullet grazed his helmet, which spun round and round and took off. Martin released his foot, flattening himself on the ground as he'd been taught in training. The mine exploded and jumped five feet in the air, but caused no damage.

On they ran, entering the village of Bernière-sur-Mer where they split into two sections, each using the techniques of fire and movement they'd learned during battle drill. As the heavy fire increased, Martin's unit stopped for a moment in a doorway. Shepherd stepped up and sliced off the part of Martin's sleeve that identified him as a CSM. "He said they were concentrating fire because of me."

At a quarter to nine, less than half an hour since they had hit the beach, Martin's section took its objective—a road through the village at its southwest point. The other section joined them, having made it through without a loss. But they saw no one else from any of the three companies of the Queen's Own that had been aboard the assault craft. "Our small group, holding to the objective, had at that time no notion at all of what was going on with any of the others."

Martin's "A" Company had, by this time, been badly mauled. Nevertheless, they formed up as best they could into two groups and moved on to the next objective, the village of Anguerny, seven miles distant. "We followed the fields, picking out draws, sloughs, and low ground when we could. We needed to locate the enemy's machine gun fire in order to pin point our own fire and this was done in erratic bursts of running and flopping, stops and starts that—while in the end effective—made that kind of advance worse than the beach itself."

Early that afternoon, the Queen's Own captured Anguerny. One company had actually managed to move half a mile forward of the objective, while the battalion set up an all-round defence. "We were the only regiment to capture and hold the assigned D-Day objective," Martin wrote. But that evening "a moment came when some reality sank in about things that had happened that day. It hurt. We had reached only the edge of Bernière-sur-Mer when we learned that half our original company—those that I had joined up with in June 1940—had been killed or wounded. And we'd taken still more casualties as we'd gone on to Anguerny.

"The tears came. I went behind a wall. So many had been lost, I found myself questioning—idiotically—why war was conducted this way. Four years of training and living together, a common purpose, friends who had become brothers—then more than half of us gone. Why didn't they just round up any collection of men in uniform and throw them into this killing machine? Why these, when anyone— somebody else but not these—could have paid this price in human life? In grief there is not always good sense. It was one of those times. Gradually though, in asking helplessly what we could do, we would find an answer—we could carry on and do our best, that's what."

As the war progressed, the press continued to hail Allied victories in Normandy. It looked as if the Germans were on the run and that the war itself might be over in a few months or even weeks. Yet an underlying, though never stated, sense of growing frustration can be discerned in the reports from Normandy. The key city of Caen was supposed to drop into British and Canadian hands like a piece of ripe fruit immediately after D-Day. It was not secured until July 9, a month later than planned. The entrapment of the main German force at Falaise was hailed as a consummate victory, but the blunt truth is that the Canadians failed to encircle the enemy and close the thirty-mile gap in the line that was the German escape route.

In recent years a number of military historians have commented on what Max Hastings has called "the feeble performance" of the First Canadian Army. Two Canadian general officers, Charles Foulkes and Harry Foster, have both admitted that the Canadians were no match for the Germans. A lack of drive on the part of commanding officers, a failure to exploit success, an inability to follow through after an attack, the habit of committing forces piecemeal, a continuing inclination to use the main roads, thus creating the kind of traffic jam that the lessons of Exercise Spartan warned against—all these were parts of the problem. The experience of the Great War could not be erased from the minds of many of the senior commanders, who were often chosen because they were artillery men, like McNaughton and Crerar. In the static war of 1914–18, the artillery had been the key element on the road to victory. After all, Vimy was won by history's then greatest bombardment and the subsequent creeping barrage. But in this new war of fire and movement, the infantry was the core of the army. For troops to pause to consolidate and wait for the guns to come up gave the enemy breathing space that he exploited brilliantly.

In an official pamphlet written in 1942, a German military analyst wrote that while the Canadian troops were probably as good as the British, their high command "has shown itself to be particularly inflexible and ponderous." David Bercuson made a similar comment in his

1995 study of Canada's role in the war. In failing to close the Falaise gap, he wrote, the armoured brigade of the Canadian Fourth Division was especially to blame for having been "ponderous and indecisive in its operations."

The most detailed study of the Canadian army in the Normandy campaign, which he subtitled *A Study of Failure in High Command*, is that of John A. English. In his view, "had the Canadian Army achieved its objectives along the road to Falaise it would undoubtedly have attained a military renown equal to Lieutenant-General George Patton's more famous Third U.S. Army." Indeed, English suggests, the Canadians might have been the spearhead of Montgomery's subsequent advance—a dagger, indeed, pointed at Berlin's heart. The contrast between the hell-for-leather Patton and the circumspect Crerar served to reinforce national stereotypes.

In Normandy, young Canadians were paying with their lives for the sins of their forebears. Not only had the armed forces suffered from neglect during the Bennett period, but they had also been badly misused as a kind of national police force to keep the jobless under control at the expense of their training—the legacy of Bennett's unwarranted fear of an armed revolution. In the penny-pinching Depression days, the military had been denied weapons, uniforms, and tactical expertise. The most vocal sections of the Canadian public, who scorned the military and shared Mackenzie King's isolationism, applauded. No wonder there was a paucity of military leaders! As English wrote, "The Canadian high command proved incapable of conducting worthwhile training in Britain. The overseas army thus wasted its time and had to be taught by others the business of war, which truly professional armies had long recognized was more profitably studied in peace."

English also noted that Canada's sudden, frenzied rush into training activity was such that the need for co-operation by all branches was de-emphasized, with the result that "some higher commanders in Normandy unknowingly and unnecessarily cast the lives of their soldiers away." That is a serious indictment, largely ignored by earlier military writers but subjected to a more searching scrutiny in the final years of the century by historians who had Colonel Stacey's official history to lean on. Stacey wrote that "Canadian formations failed to make the most of their opportunities"—particularly at Falaise—and suggested that an early closing of the gap "might, even considerably, have enabled us to end the war some months sooner than was actually the case."

The First Canadian Army became operational on July 23, well before the fall of Falaise. At last Canada had an army of sorts in the field. It was not quite the brotherly Canadian band that the Vimy veterans, McNaughton and Crerar, had dreamed of. The 1st Corps was still in Italy, a part of the Eighth Army. Simonds's 2nd Corps, astride the Caen–Falaise Road, remained, for the time, under Dempsey. Lieutenant-General John Crocker's British 1st Corps was now part of Crerar's command. Crocker was an experienced commander, and Montgomery, now in command of the 21st Army Group in Europe, had clearly hoped that Crerar would learn from him.

Crerar didn't learn. He was in the party at last, and Montgomery, in order to break him in, had given him a minor task: to make a small advance, cover Caen's port of Ouistreham, and deny it to the enemy. The Canadian commander's operational order turned out to be an unnecessarily detailed tactical plan, set down in writing in the Crerar style. It did not sit well with Crocker, who argued that it would result in "purposeless losses" and that he was not prepared to be responsible for carrying it out. When the British general suggested an alternative plan, Crerar exploded, accused him of insubordination, and appealed to Montgomery that Crocker resented him, either for personal reasons or "because of the fact that I am a Canadian."

Montgomery was not impressed. He could not forget that the touchy Canadian general had turned down his chance to gain a little experience in Italy for reasons of personal pride. As he wrote to Brooke on July 26, "Harry Crerar has started off his career as an Army Comd by thoroughly upsetting everyone; he had a row with Crocker the first day, and asked me to remove Crocker. I have spent two days trying to restore peace. . . ." The basic fault, in Montgomery's opinion, was Crerar's. "I fear he thinks he is a great soldier and he was determined to show it the very moment he took over command at 1200 hrs on 23 July. He made his first mistake at 1205 hrs; and his second after lunch."

In spite of Montgomery's reservations, the Canadians were handed the most important task of the Normandy campaign. On August 4, with Simonds's corps back in the Canadian line and a Polish division also under Canadian command, Crerar was told to punch through the German defences on the Caen–Falaise road, drive eighteen miles to Falaise, and trap the enemy forces retreating before Dempsey's Second British Army. The attack was launched on the night of August 7, and what followed was an unmitigated disaster. The Canadians had air and military superiority—five divisions and two armoured brigades with six hundred tanks. The Germans had two battered divisions and sixty tanks, yet they stopped the Canadian army dead. They had better equipment (their tanks were far superior), better trained leaders (hardened veterans in contrast to the Canadian and Polish rookies), and a superior understanding of the use of ground.

The Canadians had their share of bad luck. On two occasions they suffered heavy casualties when the supporting air bombardment got too close. They also suffered, in the opinion of their German opponent General Kurt Meyer, from too *much* planning. In Sicily, Simonds had thrown the book away in order to press on. But here his inflexible plan calling for an eight-hour pause to regroup his forces denied him the advantage of hot pursuit. The Canadians did not yet appreciate that speed was "the most powerful weapon of armoured warfare." The Fourth Armoured Division's commander, Major General George Kitching, lost his job because of his sluggish attack during the battle for Falaise. Another high-level casualty was Major General Rod Keller of the Third Division, who was wounded but also slated for replacement. Thus, in the first months of the operation, the Canadian Army lost two of its three Canadian divisional commanders.

This leadership vacuum was felt at the lower levels as the casualties mounted. In Normandy, more than a dozen Canadian commanding officers were killed, wounded, or replaced. As Denis Whitaker has noted, "In battle, it is the leaders who inspire men to fight. . . . This

460

turnover of command upset the continuity of leadership style and rocked the solid confidence of the battalions."

The Canadians finally took the town of Falaise on August 16; but the gap between the attacking forces was still eleven miles wide, and the Germans were escaping through it. More than half got away, though without their weapons and equipment. The carnage was dreadful—Allied aircraft had taken a fearful toll on the enemy. The roads were littered with thousands of German corpses, wagons, tanks, and the rotting cadavers of animals, swarming with maggots and bluebottles—"a miasma of putrefaction and decay," in the words of one visitor. "The unburied Germans, swollen to elephantine grossness in the hot sun . . . lay with blackened faces in grotesque positions. . . . Fragments of bodies festooned the trees." It was, in the description of the supreme commander, Dwight Eisenhower, a killing ground, "unquestionably one of greatest of the war, the evidence of an inferno that could be described only by Dante."

The Lincoln and Welland Regiment had taken a terrible beating—162 casualties in less than a fortnight. On August 18 as they rested briefly near the neighbouring town of Trun they were ordered forward again. As Corporal Charles D. Kipp remembered, "We were told that when the Gap was closed, the war would all be over and we would be sent home. . . . By now, most of us had seen all the war we wanted."

But the war had more than eight months to go. The gap was not yet closed and the Germans were using it to escape by the thousands. Kipp and his platoon surprised one group of them as they fled. They shot and wounded four and captured the rest. Stretcher-bearers arrived to take care of three of the wounded. The fourth had two bullet holes in his chest; one bullet had just missed his heart and had lodged in his lungs. It was clear that he was dying. Kipp stayed with him as the others were taken away.

"I sat down beside him. He had a few words of English, and I had a few of German and French. He got it across to me that he was twenty-two years old. He was a very good-looking boy. He showed me pictures of his parents and his girlfriend. He gave me his parents' address and

461

asked me to go and see them when we got to Germany. He knew he was dying. He began to cry, and clasping my hands tight with his, he pulled them down to his chest. I would have given anything to have saved his life, but I was helpless. And to make matters worse, I was the one who had shot him. He did not have much more time to live. A few minutes later, he started to choke and cough. He was weakening fast and there was red froth coming out of his mouth and nose when he breathed. He held both of my hands in his and cried. Then, pulling them both up tight under his chin, he coughed up blood all over my hands; and died. I had killed him. I threw the things he had given me away, went back to my men, and washed the blood from my hands. I can truthfully say, that was one of the hardest things I did in all the war. It is something you do not forget. There is not a day of my life I do not think of him."

Kipp himself had a bad shrapnel wound in his back. He would be wounded eight more times before his war ended. But no scene haunted his memory as much as the one that briefly unfolded there in the shadow of a hedgerow on the bloody Falaise road.

At last, in the late afternoon of August 21, Canadian troops were able to reach the Polish division, which had been cut off by the retreating Germans. Thus was the gap finally closed and the Normandy campaign concluded. But thousands of the enemy lived to fight another day, and these survivors included a large number of divisional and corps commanders and army staff who would rebuild the German army and prolong a war that might have ended on the killing grounds of Normandy.

10

Not necessarily conscription During the month of September 1944, as the Canadians fought their way slowly but steadily along the hide of northwestern Europe, the minister of national defence grew increasingly nervous about the reinforcement situation. True, General Stuart, in England, had told Ottawa that the situation was "very satisfactory," indicating that enough reinforcements would be available for the next three months and thus reassuring the Prime Minister that conscription would not be necessary. Stuart was making sure that Ralston and King were hearing what they wanted to hear. Indeed, he had gone so far as to ensure that communications he considered "alarmist" should not be forwarded to Ottawa. The only reports the minister received from Stuart were on the sunny side. But there were gaping flaws in his optimism. The army had too few fighting men and was top-heavy with tradesmen, clerks, gunners, engineers, military police, cooks and bottle washers. This was not surprising; the new recruits were loath to join the "poor bloody infantry" when other arms of the service beckoned.

Using British statistics based on experience in North Africa, the Canadian high command reckoned that 48 percent of all casualties would be suffered by the infantry. The actual figures in northwestern Europe, however, turned out to be 77 percent. Again, although statistics showed that half the wounded would be recoverable for active duty, there was no all-inclusive definition of what active duty meant. A cook could be put on active duty when his wounds healed, but a recuperating rifleman, carrying a forty-pound pack and marching at 120 paces to the minute? That defied all logic.

Ralston was not aware of these discrepancies, though he would have been had the overseas commanders curtailed their optimism and levelled with him. Why didn't they? Was it because confidence was politically attractive? Was it because they did not want to admit to mistakes? Was it because of the general feeling that the war would be over in three months? In the Great War the Allies had overestimated the capacity of the Germans to continue past 1918; now the opposite was true. This war would not be over by Christmas. In September 1944, it had eight more months to run.

Ralston could read the newspaper stories of poorly trained reinforcements and convalescents returned to duty before they were fairly recovered. On September 18, Major Conn Smythe, the hockey entrepreneur, recovering in Toronto from a wound received in France, issued a press release from his hospital bed that the officers with whom he

463

had talked across the country "agreed that reinforcements received are now green, inexperienced and poorly trained." Smythe quoted specific instances of men who had never thrown a grenade, had little knowledge of the Bren gun, and, in most cases, had never seen a PIAT Infantry Anti-Tank Projector, much less fired one. "These officers were unanimous in stating that large numbers of unnecessary casualties result from this greenness." Such casualties were borne not only by rookies but also by more mature soldiers who had to look after them.

The answer, Smythe insisted, was to send well-trained soldiers to the battleground. That, of course, meant NRMA men—Zombies. In the light of U.S. victories in the Pacific they were no longer needed to defend the Pacific Coast. The government had widened the age regulations, expanded the theatres in which they could serve, and employed every means, from bribery to blackmail, to force them into the active army. But there they sat, a frustrating statistic—some 60,000 men, protecting every corner of the North American hemisphere from Alaska to British Guyana—from what? From an enemy army that couldn't even cross the English Channel?

Besides the increasingly critical newspaper reports, Ralston was getting cables from overseas suggesting that efforts were being made to remuster men from other services to join the infantry. What was going on? Tradesmen who were being urged to leave their jobs in order to pick up a rifle were promised that they would not lose their extra pay. If the reinforcement situation was "very satisfactory," as Stuart claimed, why was this expensive and time-consuming reorganization necessary? Ralston had only one choice. He would go overseas to find out for himself.

What he learned in Italy and France that September alarmed him. Did he want the official story or the truth, one officer asked. The truth was worse than he feared: the reinforcement problem was building up to crisis stage. As far as the infantry was concerned, the pool was exhausted. In spite of an overall surplus of 13,000 men, the infantry was short by 2,000. The French-Canadian battalions, especially, were in trouble. Soldiers with French names who did not speak a word of

464

English were being transferred to fill the gaps in English-speaking regiments, a situation headed toward chaos. As a result, the Canadian army had the worst leave record among the Allies. Soldiers who deserved to be given a break and allowed to go home for rest and recuperation after four years' service couldn't be spared. Morale plummeted; dissatisfaction was rife. In Italy, General Burns indicated that the troops would feel the government was letting them down if it didn't send NRMA men overseas.

The sad truth is that in the autumn of 1944 untrained men remustered from other branches of the service were sent into action against a battle-hardened enemy during the crucial struggle for the Scheldt estuary. During the bloody contest for the key objective of Woensdrecht in mid-October, the Royal Hamilton Light Infantry took such a beating that after the first day of the battle "we had not enough bodies on the ground to probe forward against the German line of defence or even control our position." The words are those of the CO, Denis Whitaker, who in his history of the Scheldt campaign does not conceal his outrage at Mackenzie King's refusal to invoke conscription. Reinforcements were rushed forward to fill the gaps in the battalion, a "travesty" in Whitaker's account, because most of the men had been remustered—"shunted over to infantry units without the most rudimentary training. Tragically, they did not know how to look after their weapons—or themselves. They did not, for example, know how to load or fire their weapons. . . . It was then that we first fully realized that as soldiers we were being placed in jeopardy by our own Canadian military and government leaders. . . ."

The high casualty figures made a mockery of Stuart's optimistic and self-serving reports. In the battle of the Breskens Pocket on the south bank of the estuary, the Stormont, Dundas and Glengarry Highlanders were so badly depleted that their CO, Lieutenant-Colonel Roger Rowley, had no option but to accept raw recruits in mid-battle. It was, he said later, "inexplicable and inexcusable." These men had been trained as anti-aircraft gunners but knew nothing of the infantry. "They just came in, went out on the line and zap—they were either wounded or killed. They were nice guys but they weren't much use to me wounded or dead."

In England, Ralston was told that the infantry pool would be empty by December 31 unless 15,000 reinforcements could be found. He cut short his visit and returned to Canada, depressed and suffering from a heavy head cold. In his absence, George Drew, by then premier of Ontario, had attacked him personally over Conn Smythe's revelations, which had yet to be answered. That hurt. In the Great War, Ralston had risen to command a brigade; he was admired by his colleagues in and out of the army as a fearless, honest, and forthright man. He saw himself as the spokesman for the ordinary soldier. He was convinced he knew where his duty lay: he was prepared to advise his government that the terms of duty for NRMA men be extended to service in any theatre.

The minister's return to Ottawa touched off the most serious crisis the Canadian cabinet had suffered since its counterpart in 1917. It split the cabinet, split the Liberal Party, split the country, and turned that much-used phrase "national unity" into a bitter joke.

Ralston's blunt advocacy of conscription shook the Prime Minister and stunned first the war committee and later the full cabinet when he revealed that the summer's forecast of three months to victory had been badly skewed. Instead of an estimated 11,000 casualties, the army had suffered just under 18,000. Worse, the estimate of casualties for the last three months of the year was even greater: more than 22,000. There was no alternative, Ralston declared, "but for me to recommend the extension of the service of NRMA personnel overseas."

In his diary, an overwhelmed prime minister wrote that "when Ralston had concluded there was an intense silence. . . . The men who had not heard anything before looked intensely surprised, amazed and concerned. . . ." In his response, King did his best to split hairs: the need for conscription had not yet reached a crisis point, he indicated. He had promised in 1942 to impose conscription *only if it was necessary to win the war*. It was not necessary; the war was almost over; the addition of a few thousand conscripts could hardly make a difference. If the government was driven to the extreme that Ralston suggested, the Liberal Party would be destroyed "for indefinite time to come," and, in the inevitable election, the CCF would be handed complete control of the government. *That* could mean, he said, stretching the point still further, that Canada would be removed "as a steadying force" between Britain and the United States, which might adversely affect any future plans for a world organization.

Over the next days King struggled to find some method, no matter how far-fetched, to escape the gathering political storm. Maybe the army, which was obviously too large, could be reduced in size; maybe the Zombies could be attracted by "financial inducements"; maybe the fitness standards could be lowered; maybe Charles DeGaulle's provisional government, now that it had been recognized in Canada, could supply one or two of its units to fight with the French Canadians—an extraordinary suggestion.

As these increasingly impractical fancies suggest, the situation was desperate. To pull himself out of the political pitfall in which he was trapped, King grasped at the flimsiest of straws. On October 22, through Malcolm MacDonald, he approached Winston Churchill himself, advising him of "the most critical situation which has arisen since Canada's entry into the war." He foresaw "appalling consequences if a course could not be found which will avoid the risks involved in raising in Canada an overseas conscription issue at this time. . . ." What King wanted, though he did not put it in so many words, was to have Churchill use his clout to keep the First Canadian Army out of any major operation that would bring heavy casualties and intensify the growing cry for conscription.

We cannot know what Churchill's gut reaction was to King's extraordinary suggestion, but one may be allowed to suspect that it bordered on distaste. Ever since Dunkirk the flower of his country's youth had been sacrificed in Europe, North Africa, and Asia, while for much of that time Canada had been spared. Now he was being asked, in King's circumlocutory fashion, to keep Canadian soldiers out of further danger for political reasons. Five days went by before Churchill responded as diplomatically as the circumstances allowed and answered the two transparent questions that King had asked. First, he expected the war

467

to go on until the summer of 1945; second, he anticipated that the Canadian army would be involved in a large-scale operation during the final defeat of Germany. Yes, he cabled, he was concerned about the situation as King had outlined it, but "no comment is called for from me at this juncture." Having deftly stepped aside from the political and practical consequences inherent in King's broad hint, he engaged in an obligatory bit of buttering-up: "Whatever you decide you may be sure that it would in no way prevent His Majesty's government and myself from continuing to pay the warmest tribute to the brilliant and massive help which the Canadian Army has given to the whole of our war effort, for which the British nation will ever remain profoundly grateful."

King was badly disappointed that Churchill had, in effect, given him the brush-off and, worse, had failed to offer him any ammunition to support his own devout desire that the war would end soon and more Canadian troops would not, in the circumstances, be needed. He was careful not to mention any of this when the cabinet met that afternoon. That would give the pro-conscriptionists all the ammunition they needed.

One may be inclined to ridicule King's spirited, even fevered efforts to save the country (by his definition, the Liberal Party) from itself. Yet one must also sympathize. For all of his political career his dream had been to see the country whole—to find a compromise for Lord Durham's famous remark about "two nations warring in the bosom of a single state." He knew only too well what some of his colleagues seemed to have forgotten and what his adversaries—Meighen, certainly, and Drew—could not comprehend: a massive imposition of conscription could dismember the nation and even cause riots, violence, and civil war. How ironic if the bloodshed in Europe should be the cause of more bloodshed in Canada! Was the nation to be transformed into a Carpathian demesne, rent by bitter memories and old conflicts and balkanized by racial minorities?

These were extreme possibilities, but the times were extreme. King felt himself prodded and pressed by the more ambitious commanders of an army that had grown too big, too fast. It was not something he had contemplated in the early days of the war when he felt the air force would do the job and only one or perhaps two infantry divisions would be needed. But he had grudgingly gone along with it. He was not a military man, and he harboured the civilian's suspicions of the army, especially the generals, that had marked the pessimistic post-war years of the Depression when a uniform—*any* uniform—was the object of calumny. Ralston, the Great War veteran, while loyal to his political master, was on the army's side. To King, the firm-minded minister was bent on frustrating his every attempt to find his way out of the dilemma. "What annoys me about the Defence Dept.," he complained to his diary, "is that any proposal made short of conscription of NRMA men, meets with instant rejection."

The revelation that there were 120,000 Active service men still in Canada and 90,000 more in the United Kingdom did nothing to alleviate King's frustration. Couldn't 15,000 men be found from this enormous pool? Probably they could have been, but only at the cost of disrupting the inflexible military machine that had been constructed from scratch in the fleeting months since the fall of France. Thousands of apparently available men, still being trained or remustered, were physically unfit, too old, underage, on course, on leave, or in the hospital. Thousands more were members of various non-infantry services, such as the forestry corps, or were part of the key personnel who staffed the huge administrative organization needed for a modern army. By the time these men were pried out of their jobs and the army reorganized, the January 1 deadline for reinforcements would have long passed.

That left 68,000 Zombies, only 16,000 of whom were fully trained. Another 26,000 with the proper age and medical requirements were available to serve as reinforcements. To a large number of Canadians, this imbalance seemed ridiculous, as one piece of doggerel suggested:

Seventy thousand Zombies, isn't it a farce?
Seventy thousand Zombies, sitting on their arse,
Eating up the rations, morning, noon and night,

Squatting here in Canada while others go to fight.
Seventy thousand Zombies, hear the buzzards sing:
Here's our thanks to you, Quebec, and old Mackenzie King;
Never mind our comrades, let them be the goats,
As long as politicians protect their slimy votes.

The country was divided not only along racial and language lines but also by age, as one poll taken in November showed. Half of those polled between twenty-one and twenty-nine years of age did not support conscription. The figures changed among older respondents. When those up to thirty-five were polled, support for conscription rose to 58 percent; among those over fifty, support for conscription grew to 61 percent. In short, the men who would have to fight didn't want it; the men who wouldn't have to fight were for it.

The crisis into which the nation was now plunged confirms history's view that Mackenzie King was the canniest of all first ministers, one who knew, as John A. Macdonald had known, the inestimable value of delay. Fusty he may have seemed to that section of the populace that was baying for action. By and large that estimate was accurate. In King's long reign caution had become a secondary Canadian characteristic, made necessary by the structure of the country and by its perilous racial schism. It can be argued that the latter-day charges made against Canadian troops in Normandy—that they moved too slowly—were as much the result of it as was lack of experience. Even our best general, Guy Simonds, suffered from it when he chose to consolidate rather than press on. King, however, turned caution into an asset. His cabinet was being riven by dissension, with conscriptionist ministers—Ralston, Ilsley, Macdonald, even Howe—on one side and others like Power and Pierre Cardin on the other. King reckoned the score at 13 to 8 in his favour, but this was not a hockey game. The resignation of two or three front-benchers would have a devastating effect on the country, the party, and the war effort.

Since Ralston's return from Europe on October 18, King had acted as a political juggler, keeping several balls in the air—his attempts to

470

find means other than conscription to secure overseas reinforcements, his marathon series of cabinet and war committee meetings, his cable to Churchill and its delayed response—to make sure the situation remained fluid enough to forestall any precipitate action by Ralston and his colleagues. During this period he talked to the chief "conspirators"—for the paranoid prime minister was convinced that a real conspiracy was being mounted against him—to keep them on side.

He had done his best to talk Macdonald and Ilsley out of resigning, but Ralston was a different matter. He was admired for his iron integrity. If he quit the cabinet over the conscription issue, it could touch off a political storm, with some of his colleagues following his lead.

In the final days of October King did his best to persuade Ralston to stay at least long enough to give voluntary enlistment a chance. By the time the cabinet met at three o'clock on the afternoon of November 1, the prime minister's appeals seemed to be working. Ralston, apparently, was prepared to accommodate King and continue working to prevent an ugly cabinet split. Did the prime minister respond with a sigh of relief? Quite the opposite. Like a conjurer pulling a silk scarf out of thin air, he reached into his pocket and took out a piece of paper, three years old. It was Ralston's resignation, offered during the 1942 crisis and rejected at that time by the prime minister but hoarded carefully for just such an emergency. It was a stunning coup, perhaps the most dramatic and certainly the most brutal in parliamentary history. King had, in effect, fired his minister of defence, not precipitately, as it must have seemed, but only after careful preparation.

Who could replace the irreplaceable? There was only one public figure who could step into Ralston's boots and reassure the nation that all was well. That was General Andrew George Latta McNaughton, the country's most popular soldier and a firm proponent of voluntary enlistment. McNaughton had returned to Canada with an unblemished public record, who had swallowed the story of his illness. King had him tabbed as the governor general; now, after some days of negotiation, the old soldier had agreed to join the cabinet, if necessary. That meant the end for Ralston, who could not be moved to another ministry because McNaughton, still bitter over what he considered back-stabbing by the former defence minister, refused to join any cabinet of which he was a member.

King allowed himself a few crocodile tears. It was, he told his diary, "one of the hardest things I had to do in my life," but he was confident that the general could accomplish what Ralston could not. The prime minister's faith in McNaughton's magical appeal was little more than wishful thinking, for he already had plenty of evidence that the 60,000 stubborn NRMA men represented a hard core that could not be shaken.

Every effort had been expended to get them to "go active," but nothing worked. The previous April the army had indulged in a "gloves-off" recruiting campaign designed to shame them into signing up. Prospective recruits were paraded before an officer to be told that "no man should wear that khaki uniform unless he is willing to wear it anywhere." The pressure was turned up: more speeches, more interviews, more urgent appeals to patriotism by officers and even padres. There followed a massive selling campaign aimed not only at the Zombies but also at their parents and friends. Advertisements from coast to coast referred to the CANADA patch, stitched on the sleeves of General Service soldiers, as "a badge of honour." Recalcitrant recruits were told: "The fight is OVERSEAS in the face of the enemy . . . and you must be an OVERSEAS soldier to get into it . . . you can't share the victory unless you are ready and willing to take your place with the boys who are earning it."

Well-worn devices that had once been used to peddle soft drinks and cosmetics were hauled out and refurbished. One advertisement showed a pretty girl in a Canadian Women's Army Corps uniform declaring, "Gee, there's something about a G.S. man!" Another had a group of children gawking at a soldier wearing a CANADA badge and saying, "Gee, he's a G.S. soldier!" If this patronizing huckstering had any effect it was the opposite of that intended. The Zombies were not stupid; they knew a con game when they saw one. They had long since been desensitized by the Madison Avenue-type appeals promoting everything from toothpaste to floor coverings ("Congoleum

472

is doing a great morale job!") in the name of patriotism. It was not just ludicrous; it was insulting.

Now McNaughton faced the same problem. On November 6 he chaired a new committee on recruiting. The following day it presented a report based on talks the general had had with various officers and officials about the attitude of the NRMA men. They had, the report said, a group loyalty to their comrades and the pressures on them had given them "a sense of importance, even martyrdom." The report advised that since the need for home defence had largely passed, the Zombies should reassess their responsibilities and join "the great comradeship of volunteers." The prime minister, it continued, should speak to the nation to minimize the importance of the Zombies issue "by lifting people's sights beyond the NRMA People are shirking their duty if they do not take the long view." His speech "should put forth the voluntary effort as the best method to do the job in the light of all the circumstances" and should contain "an appeal to young men to volunteer and to the general public to do what they can to encourage volunteers among the NRMA personnel and others. . . ."

An enormous bureaucracy was contemplated, all for the purpose of changing men's minds—and their mothers' minds, too. "The men should not be talked to in large formations, but should be canvassed individually or in small groups. A card should be prepared for each man and the result of each interview entered and reported to the person holding the next of kin card. If a young man says 'I will go if my mother agrees' the man canvassing the mother should know this."

Did McNaughton really believe that these proposals would work where everything else had failed? Apparently he did. He was a super-optimist with an immense ego, well aware of his Karsh-reinforced image, and superbly confident of his ability to arouse the nation. King, too, was seduced by McNaughton's aura. He could not match it and didn't try to. In his radio address on November 8 he confined himself to insisting that "the voluntary system has not broken down," urging an intensified effort on the home front to get more trained soldiers for overseas service, and warning of "genuine difficulties" that "might be very grave" if conscription was applied—a guarded reference to the situation in Quebec.

In his appeal to friends and families to encourage overseas enlistment, King laid the groundwork for the recruiting committee's plan to raise yet another subcommittee to canvass *individually* the next of kin of all NRMA soldiers who were up to infantry standard, urging them to encourage their young men to enlist. This absurd proposal conjured up a vision of army officers knocking on the doors of the mothers and fathers of 42,000 Zombies, not to mention their sisters and their cousins and their aunts. It suggests the cloud-cuckoo-land that McNaughton and his desperate team inhabited.

General Pearkes, the officer in charge of Pacific Command, in a speech that almost got him court-martialled, had already made it bluntly clear that "the reason men do not go active is because they do not want to go Overseas. They do not want to leave Canada and will invent a hundred and one excuses. They are not interested, they are narrow, they have been miseducated for twenty-five years and have no feeling of patriotism whatsoever. . . . The fundamental thing is that men do not want to go. For all you say about them not going back to civil life until others are disbanded, the men do not believe it. . . ."

Significantly, the recalcitrant NRMA men were divided between Quebec and the rest of Canada in about the same ratio. They were young men, but old enough to remember that during the Depression the government had lied to them repeatedly that good times were just around the corner. The war was not of their making; what, really, did they owe their country?

Pearkes had made his statement at a conference in Ottawa that McNaughton had called with senior officers from across the country. But the new minister had allowed his overoptimism to blind him to reality. He issued an astonishing public statement that the conference had only confirmed his view that the voluntary system would work. The conference had confirmed nothing of the sort; indeed, McNaughton's statement was a direct contradiction of what had been said. It produced a storm of protest from the military: Brigadier F.M.W. Harvey, commander of the Calgary district, complained at once to the chief of staff that McNaughton had placed those present "in an entirely wrong position," reminding him "at the very least we asked you to inform him that our opinions were quite to the contrary." McNaughton, under pressure, did his best to waffle his way out of the blunder in his exculpatory response. The officers, he admitted, had been frank to note "serious difficulties," but all had assured him of their full support "in another endeavour to solve the problem," which he was sure could be solved.

It was becoming clear, however, that it could not be solved. In the first three weeks of McNaughton's term as minister, scarcely more than five hundred Zombies had gone active. T.A. Crerar, minister of mines and resources and a pro-conscriptionist, wrote to King on November 17 about "the storm of indignation arising across Canada" and intimated that he would have to resign if by month's end it was shown that voluntary enlistment wouldn't work. An embattled McNaughton told King "that he was the most hated man of Canada today." His desk, he said, was showered with anonymous letters of protest. "I told him I still thought I could do him one better on that score," King told his diary.

At a full cabinet meeting on November 21, King himself talked of resigning and letting the pro-conscriptionists carry on. That statement was followed by "a period of intense silence" (King's description), but the threat had its intended effect. A number of speeches assured the prime minister of support, but then both Angus Macdonald, the naval minister, and Ilsley spoke of resigning. The explosive situation was rapidly approaching a critical point. King saw his major support dwindling, with six ministers on the verge of quitting. The government was about to break up.

The House was recalled into session for the following day—an alarming prospect. Could the government survive? King realized that some change of policy was essential. He had delayed, delayed, delayed, trying to keep the crisis in abeyance, trying to prevent the whole shaky edifice of national unity that he had struggled so hard to preserve from toppling, and toppling himself as well.

Then, at the last moment, even as the members were making ready to troop up Parliament Hill, King was saved by the kind of last-minute reprieve that turns up in the final reel of an old Saturday morning movie serial. It came in the form of a gloomy telephone call from a devastated McNaughton. He had been advised by the CGS and the entire headquarters staff, he told the prime minister, that the voluntary system of recruiting could not meet the immediate problem. The news, McNaughton said, had hit him like a blow to the stomach. One district commander had already resigned; others would follow suit until "the whole military machine would run down, begin to disintegrate and there would be no controlling the situation."

What was a blow to McNaughton was like a shot of adrenalin to King. He had done his best to support the voluntary system, and he had been *seen* to do his best. "Conscription if necessary but not necessarily conscription"—that had been his slogan. Now, the very man he had appointed to save the situation, with the unanimous backing of the military establishment, had declared that it *was* necessary. It was King's clear duty to introduce the necessary Order-in-Council bringing in a limited form of conscription for 16,000 reinforcements, and to ask for the confidence of the House.

Of course, he got it. There was one cabinet resignation only, that of Power from Quebec. There were repercussions on the Pacific Coast—a major Zombie revolt at Terrace, B.C., and minor disorders in six other camps, but no bloodshed. When the new draftees were given embarkation leave in January and again in March it was discovered that large numbers had gone absent. That produced a reaction, such as the one at Drummondville, Quebec, where a strong detachment of mounted police and members of the Provost Corps seeking defaulters were attacked by a mob in a skirmish that lasted several hours.

But the crisis was over, and King, in his usual roundabout fashion, had got his way. Laying the responsibility on McNaughton, while it did nothing to enhance the General's reputation (he lost his attempt to win the necessary by-election), helped to cool the passions of both sides in the great conscription crisis. One shrinks to contemplate the

476

devastating effect a sudden arbitrary imposition of compulsory service would have had on national unity. There were some who believed that conscription should have been brought in at the outset of the war, as in other countries—the only just way in which Canadians from all walks of life could make their contribution and their sacrifice. But Canada was not like other countries; she was a captive of her own history. None of the other belligerents were plagued with the impossible paradox that Lord Durham had identified in that single memorable phrase a century before. The newcomers who poured into the promised land had difficulty absorbing this reality. Why was Canada so fragmented? Why wasn't the prime minister commander-in-chief of the army, as the American president was? Wouldn't that make matters simpler?

But, again, Canada was not the United States, nor was she wholly united. Perhaps more than any other political leader, Mackenzie King understood the Canadian dilemma. He had learned, as others had not, the lessons of 1917. The general public failed to understand him. To them he was stodgy, he was boring, he never seemed to make up his mind. When he went to England to review the troops, they booed him, though to be fair the army brass had kept them waiting on the parade ground an unconscionable length of time. The next time round, the same brass and King's own staff were so terrified of a second incident of catcalls that they kept his presence a secret and didn't spring it on the troops until the very last minute—a curious, but very Canadian, piece of political legerdemain.

King's fustiness masked an inner subtlety that served him well as a politician. We did not understand, during those puritanical war years, that behind that bland exterior lurked a passionate and practising mystic, a relic of the Age of Faith; a man who hungered for feminine companionship and got it in spite of his sexual inhibitions; who, in his younger days, walked the Ottawa streets at night, too cautious, one suspects (in spite of historian Charles Stacey's prurient suggestion), to sample the forbidden fruit that was ripe for him to pick; who ogled the naked limbs of the women bathers disporting themselves on a Manitoba beach; who feared and struggled with what he thought of as the terrible

477

sin of masturbation; who kept up a lifetime flirtation, much of it by mail, with several women whom he admired but to whom he could not pledge his troth because they could never measure up to the memory of his sainted mother.

We didn't know, as we listened to his flat, unaccented tones on the radio, that this bland little man rejoiced in the company of ghosts— wraiths from the past, old, dead cronies, and long-gone relatives— including that same mother whose immaculate character he had fabricated to his own subconscious satisfaction and with whom he was in regular communication, thanks to the psychic talent of the lady mediums who acted as long-distance operators to the hereafter.

It was just as well. King understood that in Canada blandness is a political virtue and the middle of the road leads to the top. Would he have survived had the voters believed he was in thrall to a certain Mrs. Bleaney, a crystal gazer from Kingston? The press, which in those tactful times shrank from invading a politician's privacy, kept his secrets and indulged his masquerade. And so we saw him as an unpretentious and ultimately boring leader. He droned his way through his dry speeches, never uttering anything resembling a rallying cry, hedging his bets as always with endless qualifying clauses and circumlocutory passages dressed up in such a fashion that they could never be used against him by political opponents. And in any case, French Canada would scarcely have responded to any call for blood, toil, tears, and sweat.

It is surely significant that in the country to the south, military aphorisms abound: *We have met the enemy and they are ours. . . . Damn the torpedoes—full speed ahead. . . . I have not yet begun to fight.* But Mackenzie King's only memorable phrase is scarcely unequivocal: *Conscription if necessary, but not necessarily conscription.* When his ministers threw that one back at him, King had his justification prepared. *Necessary* was the operative word, by which he meant *necessary to win the war*, not *necessary to support the army*. When the real necessity arose and there was no way out, King felt his conscience was clear.

11

The Canadians were not destined to lead the Allied troops in the final *The*
drive toward Berlin as so many politicians and military leaders had wist- *drowned*
fully hoped. Undoubtedly, their comparatively sluggish performance in *land*
the Normandy campaign was a factor. Instead, they found themselves
out in left field—given one of the most thankless and dispiriting tasks
of all. The baseball metaphor fits. They would occupy the left flank of
the invading forces, charged with seizing the channel ports from Le Havre
to Calais to Ostend, and then clear the tangled and sodden estuary of the
Scheldt River just inside the Dutch border.

Between Le Havre and Calais lay Dieppe, a port that brought back
bitter memories. The German defenders, who were well aware that the
Second Division troops had fought there, bombarded them with pamphlets in both French and English.

Hello Boys of 2nd Canadian Division!

Here you are again, after those nasty hours at Dieppe where
out of 5,000 brave lads of the Royal Regt., the Essex Scottish,
the Mont Royal Fusiliers, the Camerons, the South Sasks, the
Black Watch and the tank gunners of the Calgary Regt., only
1,500 escaped death or capture.

Now your division is in for the second time.

First your pals—and now you.

It was a lousy trick they played on you that time, wasn't it?

Why exactly were you forced to do it?

Every child knows now that the whole Dieppe affair was
nothing but a big bluff.

First the Bolshies had to have their Second Front for which
they so urgently clamoured.

Secondly the Brass Hats needed "Invasion-Experience" and
quite naturally they wouldn't think of sacrificing any Limeys in
a job like that.

Surely you understand. . . .

Now joking aside—this thing is much too serious. We

haven't the slightest intention of poking our noses in your affairs. *But we Germans honestly despise the idea of having to fight against decent fellows like you,* inasmuch as we know you're not fighting for yours truly or for Canada.

You know that only a few old scraps of paper bind you to England, an England that in its entire history has never done a damn thing for Canada that would help its future. Canada's sole purpose has always been to fight and bleed for England.

In the next few days this God damn slaughter will start again. WE can't help it, since we are, after all is said and done, fighting for our very existence.

But WE WARN YOU Hitler didn't give up France for the fun of it.

Let those who gain fight their own bloody battles.

To the Canadians, Dieppe had taken on an importance far beyond its strategic value. Montgomery, newly promoted to field marshal and in charge of the 21st Army Group, which included the First Canadian Army, could not comprehend the national fervour that the very mention of the word *Dieppe* implied. This led to "what may be called a tiff" between Montgomery and Crerar as Colonel Stacey, in his scrupulously careful way, reported it. It certainly was that.

On September 3, the Second Division held a series of ceremonies at Dieppe to remember the fateful day. The previous afternoon Crerar had received an order from Montgomery to meet him at his tactical headquarters on the same day and at almost the same time as the Dieppe ceremony. Crerar asked for a brief postponement so that he could take part at Dieppe. Receiving no answer, he assumed the request was acceptable and flew to Dieppe to attend the official march past.

Montgomery was furious. He didn't want to hear Crerar's explanation. The Canadian aspect of the Dieppe ceremonial, he said, was of no importance compared to getting on with the war. Crerar responded that he had a definite responsibility to his government and to his country that at times might run contrary to the commander's wishes. One can sense Montgomery's frustration. Why were these sensitive Canadians being so bullheaded? To him, Dieppe was a small blunder, best forgotten. He himself had been opposed to it. He was blind to the reality that the Canadian army was in no sense an imperial army. Crerar might take his tactical orders from the field marshal, but politically he was bound to Ottawa.

As Crerar recorded, Montgomery stubbornly reiterated "that I had failed to comply with an instruction written by him and that such a situation could only result in his decision that our ways must part." Now the simmering discord between the two officers was out in the open. Montgomery was clearly indicating that he would have Crerar's head over the matter. Crerar held his ground. He told the field marshal that he could, of course, take the matter up "through higher channels," but he himself would have to report the situation to his own government.

Thus did a "tiff" threaten to become a political *cause célèbre*. Montgomery could envisage the headlines in Canada as easily as he could spot the coastline: MONTY FIRES CRERAR FOR HOMAGE TO DIEPPE FALLEN. He quickly backed down. "I am sorry I was a bit rude the other day," he wrote to Crerar, "and somewhat outspoken. I was annoyed that no one came to a very important conference. But forget about it—and let's get on with the war. It was my fault."

That, for the moment, was that. But Crerar was convinced that Montgomery "was out to eliminate, forcefully, from my mind that I had any other responsibility than to him." He would, he told Ottawa, do his part to ease these strained relations though without departing from "what I consider it my duty to do, or not do, in my capacity as a Canadian."

Montgomery at the time was occupied with the plans for Operation Market Garden, his failed attempt to leapfrog across Holland in mid-September toward Germany and seize the bridge over the Rhine at Arnhem. He gave this venture, which actually prolonged the war, priority over the job of seizing the channel ports and clearing the Scheldt estuary, even though he knew from intelligence sources that the Germans were intent on making a stubborn fight for the ports.

For weeks the German defence of the unholy tangle of channels and islands that formed the Scheldt estuary prevented the Allies from taking a key objective, the Belgian city of Antwerp. That port, the second largest in Europe, lay just south of the Belgian–Dutch border at the lower end of one of the narrow, twisting arms of the North Sea. Captured intact, Antwerp would be the only port sizeable enough to supply and sustain the four million men who would form the massive Allied invasion force by the time the Rhine was reached. But before that last barrier was attained, the Scheldt estuary had to be cleared of the enemy.

The failure to clear it swiftly and thus allow cross-Channel supply ships to reach Antwerp was, in John Keegan's estimation, "the most calamitous flaw in the post-Normandy campaign," inexcusable because Montgomery knew that the Germans intended to hold out as long as possible astride the approaches to the city. Colonel Stacey commented, "Could we have struck immediately after 4 September, we might have opened the Scheldt much more rapidly and cheaply than we were able to do in October." If that had been done, Germany might have been defeated before winter set in.

In the unglamorous Scheldt campaign, the now seasoned Canadians made their name and earned the undying gratitude of the Dutch, whose queen had found refuge in Ottawa. In that drowned and desolate land, the troops of the First Canadian Army struggled, fought, and sometimes died in a drawn-out battle that lasted from October 2 until November 28, when, thanks to their efforts, the first convoy of supply ships reached Antwerp.

The conditions in the estuary beggar description. One is reminded of two champion wrestlers trying to score a fall while up to their thighs in mush. The long, dispiriting battle was fought on land that had been reclaimed from the sea and was sometimes only a few feet above sea level, sometimes a few feet below it. This was not the glutinous mud of the Flanders campaigns in the Great War. This was slush and filth, impossible to fight in, an uninviting network of polders (half-drowned acreage) protected by dikes, many now broken, with no distinguishing

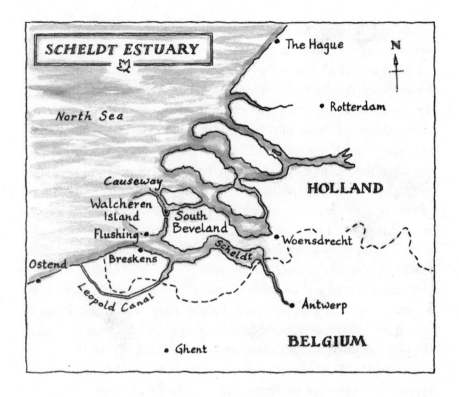

SCHELDT ESTUARY

North Sea

The Hague

N

Rotterdam

HOLLAND

Causeway

Walcheren
Island

South
Beveland

Woensdrecht

Flushing

Scheldt

Ostend

Breskens

Leopold Canal

Antwerp

BELGIUM

Ghent

features—no hillocks, not even a rise in the ground that might offer protection. It was an easy country to defend, an almost impossible country to attack. "The whole fucking country is just one dike after another," one company commander said. "It's not a country at all." The Dutch had created it themselves, secure in the fancy that no enemy would ever breach it—a sodden land, gloomy under a drab sky from which a pitiless downpour never seemed to let up. It was, as R.W. Thompson wrote in his history, "the grimmest piece of 'ground' for which men have ever been called upon to fight."

Again, one is tempted to involve national stereotypes. It seems ironically appropriate that while the Canadians were slogging their way through the death trap of the drowned land, General Patton's Americans were dashing lickety-split toward Germany. This is unfair in that Antwerp was the key to victory, and the Scheldt was the key to Antwerp.

"Dash" was not possible here in this wilderness of water. But stubborn patience was—a Canadian trait?

On September 25, Crerar was felled by a devastating attack of enteric dysentery that hospitalized him for the duration of the Scheldt campaign. Guy Simonds took over as acting commander of the army. He was, in Montgomery's estimation, "the best straight tactical and operational commander the Canadians had." History has confirmed that assessment. Ruthless, cold-eyed, and aloof, he had the lean good looks and bearing of a Hollywood military idol—the type sent over from Central Casting to play the role of a steadfast British commander, stiff upper lip and all. When I met him after the war in the offices of *Maclean's*, he still looked every inch the soldier with his carefully clipped mustache and his impeccably tailored pinstripes.

An imaginative and unorthodox tactician, he had more than once shown his ingenuity on the Caen–Falaise road, where he created a beacon for an armoured night attack (compasses being useless), setting up a stream of phosphorescent tracer fire to lead the tanks to their objectives. Had Simonds rather than the obedient Crerar been in charge during the ponderous movement to capture the channel ports, it is possible the Scheldt campaign would have ended sooner. But Crerar's orders were to take the ports—rather than bottle up and bypass them, which might have worked better—and Crerar was not about to challenge Montgomery when their relations were already strained. Simonds, as Lieutenant-Colonel G.A.B. Anderson, the leading Canadian army staff officer, said, "had a pipeline to Montgomery." Chafing under the impossibility of pursuing the enemy, he might have used it. As it was, the Germans had time to prepare a stubborn defence of the estuary, turning it into a fortress.

Montgomery and, indeed, Eisenhower, his superior, must share much of the responsibility for neglecting this key to the invasion of Germany. The estuary was, in effect, virtually surrounded—threatened on the east by the Canadian Second Division and on the south by the Third. But the Second was held back to protect Antwerp after Montgomery drained it of British troops needed for Market Garden, while the Third was preoccupied with the channel ports. That gave the Germans the opportunity to protect the south bank of the estuary by turning the parallel Leopold Canal into an impregnable barrier.

As soon as he took command of the army, Simonds began to push hard for his pet project, a bold and inventive master stroke that Crerar had rejected out of hand. It involved the capture of Walcheren Island, whose vast, featureless bulk, much of it reclaimed from the sea, constituted an unbreachable barrier squatting at the mouth of the estuary. This half-flooded farmland was a death trap. Mines and barbed wire lurked just below the surface and extended out into the channels. A formidable array of coastal installations protected its defenders. Until it was captured, no Allied supply ship could dare approach the channel that led to Antwerp.

But how could the island be captured? Simonds had a daring solution: *Sink it!* Sink an entire island? The idea was labelled crazy, half-baked, impossible. But, as Simonds kept pointing out, the island was actually several feet below sea level. It was connected to the waterlogged land by a single causeway that the Second Division would have to cross before it could be attacked. That seemed like suicide. The only possibility was to destroy the German defences by bombing huge gaps in the dikes and letting in the sea—a solution that Crerar had insisted was "NOT practical." But Crerar was no longer in charge. Simonds's plan began to make sense. The Germans were using the existing beaches to defend the island. But under Simonds's innovative scheme, a whole new series of beaches would be formed, bewildering the enemy and forcing them to spread out their defences more thinly. Simonds's plan was to follow the bombardment by landing airborne infantry and also sea-borne infantry forces on the flooded areas to destroy the defences and break the morale of those Germans holding the "unsinkable" portions of the saucer-shaped island.

There were problems. The airborne attack was ordered cancelled "because of terrain factors and types of targets" and also because the paratroopers were needed elsewhere. Political considerations loomed large. This was a rich piece of farmland; if the Allies allowed the salt sea to creep over those fields and orchards that farmers had tended for generations, could they ever be used again? If the Germans had broken the dikes out of spite, it would have been seen "as a calamity equal to an earthquake or a volcanic eruption." It took ten days of hard lobbying before Simonds got approval from Eisenhower to flood the island.

The bombing attack that followed—274 bombers unleashing 1,270 tons of explosives—was, as Montgomery put it, "an operation of truly magnificent accuracy." By the end of October, the island "resembled a saucer filled with water." The Germans were mesmerized, their communications destroyed, their morale sapped to the point where they were reduced to inactivity. Captured prisoners cried out in despair and frustration: "The water! Without that terrible water you would never have beaten us!"

For all that month the Canadians had struggled and died in the estuary's flooded checkerboard of polders, dikes, causeways, and channels. The infantry had two choices, neither of them inviting. They could push their way along the narrow banks of the dikes and causeways, leaving themselves wide open to enemy fire, or they could flounder through the drenched farmland up to their armpits in brackish water.

This was ideal country for the defenders, and they made the most of it. For the Canadians it was sheer horror. The German commander had told his troops that they must stand and if necessary die. Anyone who surrendered would be regarded as a deserter: "In cases where the names of deserters are ascertained these will be made known to the civilian population at home and their next of kin will be looked on as enemies of the German people."

For the Canadian troops, crawling, crouching, and stumbling through the polders, the carnage was dreadful. They had underestimated the German strength and the German will to fight to the death. In one battle when the Canadians fought to seal off South Beveland (literally "drowned lands") and capture the German strong point at Woensdrecht, the fighting raged for three days without a yard of sodden real estate gained. In the attack that followed on October 13, every rifle company

486

commander of the Black Watch was killed attempting to lead his men, clambering up the slippery dikes and squishing through the polders.

The Black Watch that day had only 379 officers and men in its rifle companies. Of these, only 159 had more than three months' infantry training. The remainder had very little: a total of 174 had one month or less; 14 had no infantry training at all. In the assessment of the battalion's second-in-command, the "one month probably represented considerably less time actually training. That assumption was borne out by the fact that very few men arrived with knowledge of the PIAT or elementary section and platoon tactics. Some reinforcements have never fired the Bren L.M.G. [Light Machine Gun] or handled grenades." His report echoed earlier complaints by the CSM of the Seaforths at Ortona, Conn Smythe in France, and Denis Whitaker in the Scheldt campaign—that Canada was sending untrained troops directly into battle where they were at best of little use, at worst killed. It was written about the time that Ralston was confronting King in the Cabinet War Committee, arguing that trained men—Zombies—were needed at once to keep the army up to strength.

Between October 1 and November 8, when at last Walcheren Island was taken, the Scheldt estuary cleared, and the water route to Antwerp opened, the polyglot Canadian army lost 703 officers and 12,170 other ranks, half of them Canadians. The loss of the officers was especially severe. Calls went out for trained reinforcements to move up to the forward reinforcement camps, especially infantry platoon commanders, whose life expectancy was one of the shortest in the army.

One of these was a thirty-seven-year-old Third Division subaltern, Donald Pearce, from Brantford, Ontario, who ended up with the North Nova Scotia Highlanders in Holland. Pearce, who had a Master's degree in English, was perhaps the only soldier in northwestern Europe to keep and maintain a personal journal during his entire tour of duty. It was not easy. First, it was against army regulations and might have led to a court martial had Pearce's notes been found. Second, there was the difficulty of finding writing materials. Pearce used the backs of cigarette packages, the labels from tin cans—anything that was available.

It was also a problem to transfer this "rat's nest of folded pieces and scraps of paper" secretly from his small pack to the larger one in the quartermaster's truck. "I'm definitely skirting trouble," he wrote. "If I were captured I'd be a mine of local colour." Fortunately, this tattered conglomeration of paper was preserved, for it gives us a unique close-up on the war, not from the observations of an army commander or a war correspondent but through the eyes of a footslogger writing directly from the front line. As Pearce himself noted, the daily sights, sounds, and experiences could not be invented or "recollected in tranquillity" but must be written down on the spot.

He was the ideal witness to war: observant, literate, sensitive. As the weary days dragged on and his comrades died, his journal began to reflect his own anger and frustration at the futility and unfairness of battle. In passages of introspection—unusual in so many war memoirs—he examined himself and his attitude to the bizarre circumstances into which he had been thrust. The knowledge that he was flouting army regulations "gave the subtle pleasure of secrecy to my daily deliberations." He lived two lives, "closely related, but at the same time separate." On the one hand was the life of action, "rough, pragmatic, fraternal"; on the other was the life on paper, "lived by another me, secretive and aloof." He thought it important to keep "the latter me . . . alive during the war, because, if by some fluke I should survive, that would be the me I would be taking back to Civvy Street." The soldier's role "always seemed a kind of trick life, almost a daily improvisation." Nineteen years later when he was putting together *Journal of a War*, he wasn't so sure. Re-reading those pages, he began to feel that "the literary me was the expedient, the invention, and that the soldier who was going through the war was the real me after all."

In fact, the soldier was also a powerful writer who described Caen as "a city that has lost the aspect of a city." Passing through on his way to the reinforcement camp, he wrote, "It is as though the place had been lifted bodily a mile high in the air, turned over at this point, and allowed to drop straight to earth again: an astonishing example of systematic destruction that has left little more than jagged mounds of lunar rubble . . . it seemed not a city but a mere conglomeration of bent and twisted pointed things, like ruined monoliths."

As he drove through rural France, it was "a more depressing sight to me than the poorest parts of England, even the London slums. The people have no soap. Their skin is chafed and sore. The children wear soldiers' cast-offs. . . . They are listless, pale, blank. Their hands are rough and chapped. Babies are often affected with severe acne, their faces paper-white, their lips drawn."

At his first posting in the holding area at Ambleteuse, in some recently evacuated German dugouts he heard stories of the notorious Dieppe raid from a man in his platoon who had been there. He told Pearce of a tough sergeant, shot in the chest as they hit the beach. "Did it come out the back?" the sergeant asked the man behind him, who told him that it had. "Christ, then I've been killed," the sergeant exclaimed, and fell over in a dead faint. Another of the Dieppe veteran's memories was that of a soldier suffering from "shell shock" who spotted a dead comrade lying in a heap by a shattered tree trunk, the top of his head torn off. The disoriented man "hurried over to the body, and engaged it in a one-sided conversation, asking repeatedly if he had seen the colonel, and if so, where could he find him." He also told Pearce of one assault company, badly shot up, most of its members killed. A corporal seeing the corpses of his friends shouted to the survivors, "They got all our best crap players." These second-hand experiences of battle, Pearce told his journal, "were considered immensely funny, at the time. They certainly don't seem so now."

He moved on through Belgium. In Ghent, he noted that the large shop windows carried posters: "SOLDIERS OF THE ALLIED NATIONS—THANK YOU FOR THE QUICK LIBERATION OF OUR DEAREST BELGIUM." The people "never speak of an 'invasion,' but always of 'the liberation,' pronouncing all the syllables slowly and emphatically."

His first experience of shellfire came early in November when a shell from a German anti-tank gun hit his Bren-gun carrier. He plunged out of the vehicle with the men, dived through a barbed-wire fence at the top of the dike, and dashed for a house fifty yards distant. Then the shells began to fall in earnest. "They kept it up all afternoon, all evening, all night, all next morning, right up to noon. . . . Every three minutes they sent a real big one over. It growled and groaned for several seconds before it struck."

During the barrage, his sergeant sat in the middle of the room, casually reading a newspaper. Pearce sat on the floor "and tried to discuss the war with a forced easiness." One man lay down and slept unconcernedly. Another played the gramophone as loudly as possible—Dutch dance music. ". . . I will never forget the tune as long as I live. . . . Most of the time my mouth was absolutely dry, my hands wet, my stomach in a tight lump. I was angry, too, angry at the whole situation, not at anybody." The shelling continued, and it was apparent that at any moment they could all be blown up. Each shell seemed directed at that room. Conversation ceased. "But my anger was much stronger than my fear. I felt with needle-keenness that my life was hanging by a thread, and depended on nothing more than the accuracy of some stupid grinning boy behind a field-gun; that my life made no more sense than the sewing-machine in the other corner . . . that I was completely reduced to impotence, or worse still, to insignificance. . . . I cursed and hated the complete idiocy of it all. . . . But it was less fear than disgust that really filled me. . . . I did not hate the Germans, but execrated the war as a whole."

Some of the men prayed silently. "I could not have forced myself, had I wanted to, to prayer. . . . The idea of God disgusted me as much as the war, and I felt that only a weak-minded person could drag theology into this stark and meaningless room . . . and to pray to God now was a nose-dive into an elementary mother-quest or father-quest. So, instead of taking God's name into my heart, I took it in vain again and again, silently, though others may have thought me praying."

The next day the shelling lifted, and the troops moved on to another area. "Why don't you stop fighting, now that you are so obviously beaten?" Pearce asked a captured German lieutenant. "I should have liked to," he replied, "and so would others. But there is a captain back of me with a pistol. There is a major back of him with another pistol.

490

And an officer of the General Staff in back of him with another. And the Gestapo is back of everybody. We cannot stop. Now you understand why you took us this morning without too much trouble. We have to have an occasion to surrender."

A few nights later Pearce, having been transferred to a rifle company, led a patrol to reconnoitre the next objective—the village of Knocke-sur-Mer. He fired his PIAT and his mortar into the town. "Not a stir from the German positions." Had they pulled out? The following morning the Canadians ripped through the defenders' barbed wire with bangalore torpedoes, poured through the gap into the main street, and witnessed a strange spectacle. "After about five minutes, German soldiers began worming out of the hill-sides from a dozen different holes and slits, and it gradually got through our heads that the place was now ours, and almost without asking." They captured two hundred prisoners, "all of them packed, polished, dressed, ready for capture, waiting to surrender." The Germans formed up in orderly squads, apparently prearranged, happy their war was over, "excepting the Jerry officers, who didn't like being herded into platoons and ordered about by Jordan, my Negro corporal. . . . One oddity. It appeared that nothing would wipe the fixed, arrogant expression off the German officers' faces—that tense, fathomless, famous Teutonic calm."

After a brief leave in Brussels, Pearce returned "to the frozen dykes, the ice-fields, sleepless nights, guarding and patrolling the front." The land here east of Nijmegen was badly wasted. "What is not flooded is blasted and torn by shelling. Walls of houses are full of ragged holes. Roofs dangle and sag; interiors ruined from being occupied by vagrant horses and goats. . . . The celebrated windmills no longer turn; most have their blades shot away or chewed up by shell-fire. . . ." All the talk was of the enemy's last gasp, the German offensive near the Ardennes to the south—the so-called Battle of the Bulge. As Pearce wrote: "Everybody happy the attack didn't come through here. It was certainly expected, and we are a 'thin red line' if there ever was one."

By the end of November they had crossed from the Netherlands into Germany southeast of Nijmegen, a land of ravines "very different from ours, sterner, harsher, more solemn, more beautiful even, more sharply beautiful, almost chiselled, without being simply singular or craggy. . . ." Pearce began to sing Wagner—*Parsifal* and *Tannhäuser*—and scribbled in his journal: "It is fascinating to me how perfectly Wagner's image of Siegfried or Parsifal goes with this landscape." As they moved through the wooded ravines and twisting valleys, one thought amused him: that the V-1 and V-2 flying bombs the Germans were launching at England were to them "black 'holy grails' . . . quest-objects, with miraculous virtues for the salvation of a whole people, sought through forests of tribulation (the difficulties of war-time production), pursued by beings of charmed significance (the Nazi scientists), hard to win, but, if won, able to compensate the sufferings involved in the search. . . ." To Pearce "the profoundly Teutonic, medieval qualities of the modern German mind are so evident . . . here that I can't see how people can argue that we are at war with a mere corps of Nazi officials. . . . We are fighting centuries of German culture. . . . We are at war with the German imagination, an unbroken river of force for how many generations?"

On Christmas Day everything was dead still, "not a single sound anywhere." Both sides seemed to have called off the war for the moment and gave each other "a Christmas present of silence. . . ." One of his riflemen, an oddball named Fraser, "somewhat given to fits of rashness," slipped unnoticed out of the company area and sauntered for half a mile "unarmed, head down, hands in pockets, making a deliberate target of himself for German snipers just across the river." He exchanged waves and greetings with the enemy on the far bank, who tossed their hats into the air and threw snowballs at him like schoolchildren. They showed no interest in shooting him as he returned for Christmas dinner.

Pearce's task now was to patrol the river and guard the bridge at Nijmegen, the last left intact for a hundred miles. In February, after being detached for a month as an instructor at divisional NCO school, he rejoined his unit, taking a route that led through the recently captured Reichswald, for two or three centuries a prized hunting resort of the German upper class, and more recently taken over for an exclusive political retreat by top echelon Nazis such as Hermann Goering. It had been a natural strongpoint for defenders of the famous Siegfried Line, and Pearce was curious to see what a thousand guns and a thousand rounds per gun over a period of eleven hours of continuous shelling had done. What he saw from the back of a 15-hundredweight truck was "only the incredible wake of destruction stretching away behind us like a film-strip of a forest run backward in slow motion. It was simply a tangled mass of chewed and broken forest trees, blasted trenches and smashed equipment; a jungle of logs tossed this way and that, through which our tortuous road threaded around and between shell-craters. The bent, branchless tree-trunks stood like old sodden celery-stalks. You would think some herd of animals out of pre-history had charged the forest in line and with tusks and feet rooted it up, as if it had been a mere vegetable garden."

They drove on toward Cleve, the ancestral home of Anne, Henry VIII's fourth wife, once a town "full of colourful buildings, rich villas, fine streets, and historical monuments," where ancient buildings had now become nothing more than "nightmare blueprints . . . with only a few girders and twisted walls left. . . ." All the land from the river to the city centre was under four feet of water, and here the troops shifted into Buffaloes—large, semi-armoured, amphibious tracked vehicles. As they roared down the flooded streets, "the wash . . . swept in through living-room windows, opening and closing front or side doors with its swell. . . . People stared expressionlessly at us out of attics. Cattle put their heads out of kitchens. The water licked at the knockers on the front doors. High up over the city, the fort of the 'Flanders Mare,' looking very jagged now with its battered walls and broken roof, squatted like a toad presiding over a city of death."

On March 3 Pearce and his platoon took part in the street fighting and house clearing in the heavily defended city of Udem. A handful of snipers, perched in the attic of a three-storey house, held them up for half an hour until their two company tanks silenced them and cut off their escape route. The Germans came out through the back garden, dangling white cloths on long poles. "It was vastly disconcerting," Pearce recorded. "Instead of a squad of Nazi supermen in shiny boots and packing Lügers, we were confronted by five of the most unkempt, stunted, scrubby specimens I have ever had the pleasure of capturing. Two of them couldn't have been more than fourteen on their next birthday."

In Lieutenant Pearce's journal his earlier descriptions, eloquent but relatively objective, even a little wide-eyed, had by now been replaced by a sour, despairing tone that hinted at an inner torment. "When will it all end?" he wrote the day after capturing the child-soldiers. "The idiocy and the tension, the dying of young men, the destruction of homes, of cities, starvation, exhaustion, disease, children parentless and lost, cages full of shivering, starving prisoners, long lines of hopeless civilians plodding through mud. . . . What keeps this war going, now that its end is so clear? What do the Germans think of us, and we of them? . . . I do not feel as if I were fighting against men, but against machines. . . . The prisoners that come over hills with their hands up . . . have no relation, almost, to anything for me. I can't connect them with the guns they have just laid down. . . . It is becoming hard for me not to feel sometimes that both sides are the common victims of a common terror, that everybody's guns are against everybody ultimately. . . .

"Once I could say you cannot be disgusted with the war, because it is too big for disgust, that disgust is too shallow an emotion for something involving millions of people. But I am disgusted now. . . . Once I used to get quite a thrill out of seeing a city destroyed. . . . But it is not that way any more. All I experience is revulsion every time a fresh city is taken on. . . ."

The impersonal aspect of the long-distance battles revolted him. "Dozens upon dozens of gun-crews . . . two or three miles away from the city simply place shell after shell into hundreds of guns and fire away for a few hours . . . and then . . . the firing stops, the city has been demolished, has become an ash heap, and great praise is bestowed on the army for the capture of a new city."

He realized that all this ruination was necessary to save lives, yet "it fills me with disgust because it is all so abysmally foolish, so lunatic.

494

It has not the dramatic elements of mere barbarism about it; it is straight scientific debauchery. . . . It is disgusting . . . that a towering cathedral, built by ages of care and effort, a sweet labour of centuries, should be shot down by laughing artillerymen, mere boys, because somebody with a machine-gun is hiding in a belfry tower." That this obscenity should be necessary, he wrote, "galls me to the bones." The matter of sides in the war "temporarily becomes irrelevant, especially if someone at my elbow says, like a conquering hero: 'Well, we sure did a job on the old church, eh?'"

On March 20 things cooled off. The troops were pulled out of the line, living in caves in the unmangled part of the Reichswald and sleeping on mattresses made from spruce boughs. The weather was growing warmer, and the shattered forest was full of rumours that the war was almost over. Few of the newcomers had heard such rumours before. Pearce found it odd that he was now one of the oldest fighting members of the battalion, the last of the platoon officers who were there when he first arrived eight months before. "The others have gone out on stretchers, or are in graves, and hundreds of men with them."

He asked himself the old questions that every veteran fighter has asked: why was he still alive and whole? What was he being preserved for? The battalion looked different to him now. He had thought of it as a fixed fighting unit. "Now it appears a highly fluid affair, the only fixed things being the hat-badge and the strangely persistent *esprit*."

On March 27 the long-awaited bridgehead across the Rhine was effected at last. The battalion headed for the river, singing as they drove along because they were to be the first Canadians to cross over to make bridging possible for the rest to follow. After a long wait they were shuttled across in Buffaloes with clouds of Spitfires and Typhoons roaring overhead. The sky, indeed, was alive with planes coming in waves as far as the binoculars could reach, "like schools of fish, swarm after swarm, formation on formation, they poured across the sky in endless hordes. . . . It was as if the overhead armada was sucking us in tow." But Pearce was too spent to marvel at the spectacle. Crossing the Rhine, he felt "as if I had merely crossed a muddy street. A sense of drama within me was disappointed."

On the east side of the river was the old German town of Bienen. Flanked on both sides by newly released flood waters and threaded by a single main dike-road, it constituted a serious bottleneck on the route to Berlin. British troops had attacked it twice without success. Kesselring, the German commander, had ordered this strong point held, and the North Nova Scotia Highlanders were ordered to capture it "at all costs."

A heavy artillery barrage preceded the assault. When it lifted, the Canadians dashed forward, with Pearce's platoon assaulting in a single extended wave over the top of the dike and down the other side. Ten of his men were hit at once and others were falling as the platoon tried to advance; to their dismay, the Germans, hidden in a series of pits directly to their front, had their range. In Pearce's words, the survivors were pinned down and "on the way to extinction."

At this point, Fraser, the oddball who had taken part in the Christmas Day snowball fight with the Germans, stood up, walked deliberately over to two of the enemy pits, and "as if he were an invisible man, deposited one hand grenade in each trench, turned about, and loped back to our ditch. On the way back he was shot in the back. But . . . he had left behind three wounded and four dead Germans. . . ."

Pearce called to his men to follow him to join the breakout. But only one man was left to follow Pearce—all the others were wounded or killed—and he too fell, shot in the knee. The company commander, trying to rally what was left of another platoon, was also wounded. Pearce called for stretcher-bearers, but none arrived.

At this point something happened to him, something that any man under fire for eight months would recognize. On "a plainly insane impulse" he tried to nip along the dike to company headquarters, located in a house a hundred yards away, in order to get aid. The top of the dike was under hot fire, but none of that mattered to him as he set out at a trot. He seemed to be living a charmed life. Twice he was sniped at; twice the snipers missed. Someone in a hole in the field to his right yelled at him to get under cover with him and, by doing so, saved his life. Although the trip was now pointless—the medical unit had finally arrived—Pearce still felt he should make a report to his CO.

His mind was a blank. All memory of the man who had saved him vanished. "I hadn't any idea, apparently, of how far gone I was emotionally. Instead of furnishing a coherent account, I simply stood in front of him weeping inarticulately, unable to construct a sentence, even to force a single word out of my mouth."

Finally, his request to be relieved of front line duty, which he had submitted some weeks before "when it had really begun to break me," was approved. In his journal he wrote: "So now, at the start of our breakthrough into the heart of Germany, I shall be heading the other way, toward Army Rear, and not toward Berlin. . . . I shall never know why I came out of that battle; it literally did not figure. But I know it was to be my last. This I will accept, and will not regret that it is the end."

In April, with VE-Day (Victory in Europe) less than a month away, he wrote this in his journal: "The other day we took a German prisoner who could not have been more than fourteen years old and who said he had been in the army only two months. As we sent him to the P.O.W. cage, he clung to his rifle and pleaded with us not to take it from him for he had signed for it and didn't know what would happen to him if he failed to turn it in."

Victory night, May 8, 1945, found Pearce back in England stationed at Aldershot. Germany had surrendered, unconditionally, but there was little evidence of celebration. "Nobody shows that he feels any special emotion. The prolongation of the expectancy of this hour has drained all special emotion out of it. How different from the last war. . . . Now they seem to need cheer-leaders. Everyone is that weary. . . . How exhausting this war has been, can be seen in this very evening's dispiritedness." The following day, London's ecstatic celebration provided a contrast to the matter-of-fact attitude of the old army camp.

Between that night of victory and the two atomic blasts three months later, which brought Japan unconditionally to her knees, Pearce continued to muse over the war and its effect on him. This is where the war ends, he told himself, as he lay in an Aldershot hospital that June, "right here, in these god-damned tan-coloured wooden shacks." To him "the whole war seems . . . a quite private experience; I mean, for everyone. Each man talks about a quite different war from mine, and ultimately everyone is separated from everyone by layers of privacy and egoism." He refused "to play the game of comparing experiences. . . . [The old soldiers] make noises . . . about what went on in their various battalion actions, and it all comes from some other time, some other place. . . . We sit there comparing memories, or fictions, or nightmares, made up of other men's deaths, with smiles. Take it away."

12

The offshoots of neglect Ten depression years had swung many Canadians to the left, and five years of wartime strictures had accustomed them to government intervention. When the war ended, they were eager for the kind of dramatic change that only peace could make possible. Hence the CCF rapidly zoomed to a position of influence, toppling a resurrected Arthur Meighen. John Bracken, who succeeded Meighen as Tory leader, sensed the political wind and renamed his party the *Progressive* Conservatives, but it was the slightly left-of-centre Liberals who were seen as the real progressives. What the voters wanted was socialism if necessary, but not necessarily socialism.

In the long run, the Liberal Party became the beneficiary of the divisive effects of the 1944 conscription crisis. In Quebec, the fires of revolt were banked; in the rest of the country, basking in the post-war boom, tempers had cooled. As in Alice in Wonderland's race, everybody had won. French Canada, thanks to months of protest, could rejoice that only a paltry few had had to be conscripted. In Ontario and the West, the pro-conscriptionists could boast that they had won the day.

Alone among the major Allies, Canada insisted during most of the conflict that the war effort be voluntary. It could be argued that had the government imposed conscription in the early days of the war, a united nation might have marched into battle unmarked by dissension.

498

That, of course, is nonsense. The shadow of 1917 still hung over the nation, and King was far too wise to plunge the country headlong into the kind of searing dispute that would hamper the war effort, tear Canada apart, and—equally important—shatter the Liberal Party.

In the Allied world, Canada's position was unique. Quebec was a state-within-a-state; so was the new empire of the West, while Ontario was as much a prisoner of its history as was French Canada.

The Québécois were isolationist. Beyond their own boundaries, political and economic power were denied them. Ottawa was virtually closed to them, not only because of the language strictures but also because of the prevailing attitudes of their Anglophone compatriots. Contrary to the belief of English-speaking Canadians, they had long ago rejected France. Why should they be forced to fight for a mother-land that had ignored them for two centuries?

Nor could they have any feeling of loyalty to their British conquerors. The ghost of Henri Bourassa haunted the cobblestones of Quebec City. To the Québécois, the vaunted Empire was the alien agency that had bested them on the Plains of Abraham. They would fight to the death to defend their country's shores. But the shores of a foreign land? *Non!*

The rest of Canada was hard put to understand that attitude, which they considered narrow and unenlightened. Surely the best way to defend Canadian shores was to meet the enemy on his own soil and prevent him from bringing the conflict to Canada! Quebec did not buy that argument, and, to be fair, the tens of thousands of young Anglophones who refused to join the active army didn't buy it either. At the outset of the war Mackenzie King faced a dilemma: on the matter of enforcing conscription he was damned if he did and equally damned if he didn't. His solution was characteristically and typically Canadian—caution and delay.

The inevitable was postponed, put off, avoided, and finally faced in the spring of 1945, by which time fewer than 2,500 NRMA recruits were taken on strength of the units in action overseas. That being so, what was all the fuss about? When the much abused Zombies began to trickle into his unit in late March, Donald Pearce noted in his journal:

"There is, of course, considerable prejudice against them. I received them with, I think, decency and kindness, though I had some inner misgivings. But for some reason they have made excellent soldiers, so far; very scrupulous in the care of their weapons and equipment, certainly, and quite well versed in various military skills. Of course, I only take them as I find them; but so far I find them to be good."

Yet the NRMA reinforcement figures are illusory. In addition to the 16,000 conscripts available for active service in the final months of the war, thousands of other so-called Zombies had not waited for conscription but had rushed to join up when they realized that overseas service would soon be made compulsory. Many of these went into action when the German army, apparently on the brink of defeat in the autumn of 1944, proved surprisingly resilient. Allied casualties were lower than expected in 1945, and hindsight suggests that the army, even if under-strength, could still have finished the war with honour. Yet it is inarguable that in November 1944, the First Canadian Army was short of trained fighting men, and the only way to bring it up to strength was by conscription.

But did we really need a First Canadian Army? Again, hindsight suggests that we did not. A fully operational army in the field requires a substantial administrative structure. Such an ambitious force, top-heavy with headquarters staff, was not anticipated by Mackenzie King in the early days of the war. During the Great War, the Canadian command had operated at corps level and won the respect of their allies. In the Global War, King was pushed hard, not so much for strategic reasons as for reasons of military ambition and national pride, to raise his sights. The generals used the crises following the fall of France and the bombing of Pearl Harbor to strengthen their political influence. McNaughton, Stuart, and Crerar were all culpable. In the autumn of 1940, Crerar, then chief of the general staff, lobbied hard for a budgetary increase and, after 1942, managed to have all financial restrictions on military spending removed.

King wanted to keep the army compact and to focus Canada's war effort on supplying air training and munitions. "Generals are invariably wrong," he told Bruce Hutchison and Grant Dexter during one of those cozy, off-the-record discussions he had from time to time with John Dafoe's top political reporters. "All our generals are concerned about was to be in at the kill."

The ambitious Crerar, pressing for promotion to lieutenant general, was convinced that Canada had the manpower to support no fewer than *six* divisions overseas as well as two for home defence. He had a two-corps overseas army in mind from the beginning, and to that end he managed to secure the support of both Ralston and the British war office. His later appointment as commander of the Second Division (when Major General Ken Stuart succeeded him as CGS) gave him the opportunity to lobby Alan Brooke, chief of the imperial general staff, and Bernard Paget, commander-in-chief of the home forces, for a new "force headquarters." Having two Canadian divisions in action overseas gave the British commanders an excuse to promote McNaughton from operational command of the Canadian Corps and, in effect, shunt him aside to the administrative post of "force commander" of the two corps.

Canada was still in the imperial orbit. With the top British leaders and his own minister of defence urging military expansion and with the Japanese war machine loose in the Pacific, King found himself out-manoeuvred. On January 26, 1942, the prime minister gave in and announced the formation of a two-corps Canadian army of five divisions overseas and three on the Pacific Coast (the idea of a sixth for overseas was dropped). In Grant Dexter's view, "The army is wrecking the country. Eight divisions cannot be sustained." But rejecting the army's demands would expose King to another divisive cry for conscription.

In the *Journal of Military History*, Paul D. Dickson put his finger on the problem: Crerar was threatening the most delicate of balances—the civil-military relationship. The generals pressed the politicians hard and the generals won. In June 1941, Victor Sifton had warned King that the top military leaders were involved in a plot to double the size of the army. Sifton was right. The army that Crerar proposed was too big for a country committed to voluntary enlistment. It had too large a proportion of non-fighting men in its ranks. Far too many volunteers chose to join the easier branches of the forces, such as the service corps, ordnance corps, or even the artillery, rather than the infantry with its exhausting route marches and high casualty rate.

The Canadian public was enthusiastic about the big army. It would give Canadians a place in the international sun. Yet the First Canadian Army for most of its service in northwestern Europe (until the two divisions arrived from Italy near war's end) was little more than half Canadian in its makeup. The polyglot force contained one Canadian corps, one British corps, a Polish division, and, from time to time, various smaller units—Czech, Dutch, Belgian. As far as international kudos went, Currie's lean Canadian Corps emerged from the Great War with far more lustre than Crerar's army did from the Second.

The dispiriting years between the wars, when the armed forces were virtually ignored by the politicians and the public, had a devastating effect that could not be expunged in those frantic months when the army expanded like a hot-air balloon. Crerar was the best available leader, but he was no Arthur Currie. Another veteran gunner, Andrew McNaughton, ingenious and invaluable, was promoted beyond his abilities. It was his stubborn nationalism, honed to a bright sheen by the memory of his counter-battery work at Vimy, that denied Canadian soldiers, especially officers, the battle experience that could have helped change the course of the war in Normandy during the battle for Falaise.

The army itself was run by men with little operational experience, since its headquarters staff and its direction were Canadian. From the point of view of military efficiency, it would have made more sense to proceed with a single Canadian corps, nurtured in the bosom of a seasoned British army commander as the First was in Italy—a blow, perhaps, to the national sense of esteem, but one that might also have dampened the military ambitions that provoked the crisis of 1944. The soldiers who splashed onto Juno Beach, who battered their way past Falaise, who cleared the channel ports, who endured the soggy hell of the Scheldt, who breached the barrier of the Rhine, and who fought their way into Germany and victory, deserved better than they got.

502

INTERBELLUM III
New Beginnings

1

The men who returned from the battlefields of the Global War were universally known as "veterans," in contrast to the survivors of the Great War, who were called "returned men." The difference is subtle but significant. The phrase "returned man" now has about it the whiff of a cast-off, like an Eaton's parcel found wanting. But *veteran* suggests a man of experience, a dyed-in-the-wool survivor, an adept, a kind of military elder statesman. We use it today to describe long-standing politicians, seasoned hockey stars, and familiar screen idols.

The word was used as an adjective in the immediate post-war years. It dominated the Yellow Pages as thousands used the new confidence gained from their years in service to branch out on their own. Baby-sitting services, taxi companies, landscape firms—all gained notice and prestige by making it clear that they were operated by men who had served their country.

Few wanted to stay on in the armed forces, which had dropped from an optimum strength of 669,000 in 1944 to less than 40,000 in the early post-war years.

Some of those who enlivened these pages became noteworthy after their return to Canada. Donald Pearce moved to the United States and took post-graduate work at the University of Michigan where he gained a Ph.D. degree. By the time he published his *Journal of a War* in 1965 he was a full professor of English at the University of California. John Harvie, who survived his prison days in Germany, became a civil engineer in Canada and published his memoir, *Missing in Action*, in 1995 after his retirement. Ray Silver was working on another book at the time of his death in 2001. Charles Martin published his story, *Battle Diary*, in 1994 and was the subject of a CBC documentary that same year. Hal Lawrence became a professional writer. In 1980, one of his books, *A Bloody War*, won first prize at the annual Authors' Awards sponsored by the Periodical Distributors of Canada. The Three Musketeers returned to Vancouver where both Maitland and Ladner became senior partners in two of the city's leading law firms while Burke

504

formed his own company, World Wide Travel. One man who did not come home was a former university classmate of mine, Robert Hampton "Hammy" Gray, who joined the navy's Fleet Air Arm. Hammy won the Victoria Cross posthumously when he sank a Japanese destroyer with a direct hit before plunging to his death. The date was August 9, 1945. Five days later, Japan ceased fighting.

The government did not want to repeat the indifference shown in 1919–20, when the returned men were left to fend for themselves. More than 140,000 ex-servicemen were given loans under the Veterans' Land Act to return to the soil and/or build their own homes. Every ex-soldier, sailor, or airman could apply for a bonus based on his years in service. Thousands took advantage of the offer for financial assistance while attending school or taking vocational training.

The campuses exploded with mature students who cared little about extracurricular activities, but were determined to use every possible moment to better themselves. As a result, a kind of schism opened between the striplings just out of high school and the older undergraduates, who took their future seriously and had learned to apply themselves. One of these was a friend of mine, Don Thompson, a sergeant-instructor at basic training, who had only a Grade Seven education when war was declared. After his discharge he breezed through Grade Eight and all four high school years in a single twelve-month period, then went on to university to become a civil engineer.

Though tens of thousands of workers were laid off when the war ended, the jobless days of the thirties did not return. By war's end, four and a half million had work. By the end of the decade, the figure was five million. The percentage of women in the work force, however, began to drop back to its 1939 level. By VE-Day, 80,000 women had been laid off from war industries. In 1946, all three women's military services were disbanded. The war had changed one demographic statistic: the proportion of married women in the workforce, which had tripled during the war, remained comparatively steady. But, as Ruth R. Pierson has made clear in her study of the period, this growing tendency for gainfully employed women to combine marriage and a job was not

505

in itself liberating. "Instead it heralded a pattern that would prove immensely oppressive to women, that of the double day of labour."

Women were marrying earlier as a result of the war, and as one Gallup poll suggested, a vast number wanted to continue working. The jobs available to them were the traditional ones that suggested the persistence of the pre-war, male-female hierarchy: teacher, secretary, waitress, nurse, and the like. Pierson reported that "the war intensified the traditional demands on women to be exceptionally supportive of men." After the war ended there was "an indisputable reaction against war's upheaval, including the unsettling extent to which women had crossed the sex/gender boundaries. The war's slight, but disquieting, reconstruction of womanhood in the direction of equality with men was scrapped for a full-skirted and re-domesticated post-war model, and for more than a decade feminism was once again sacrificed to femininity."

Canada did well by her soldiers, sailors, and airmen—the ones who wore uniforms. The scandal is that she almost totally ignored members of the fourth branch of the service, the merchant seamen who had risked their lives daily and suffered the greatest hazards. A man who went to sea with the merchant navy took one chance in ten of losing his life, facing the most extreme danger among all those in the services. In the RCAF the figure was one in sixteen, for the army, one in thirty-two, for the navy, one in forty-seven. Dr. Helen Creighton, the folksinger and writer from Dartmouth, Nova Scotia, wrote: "If there is one class of war service which commands the respect of everyone without reservation, it is that of the merchant navy. It is possible that people who live inland are not fully aware of the debt we owe them. We who live by the sea look at the merchant ships, the tankers, and cargo vessels that come in and out of the harbour. Sometimes they are laden with ice, sometimes they show signs of battle. The life rafts are plainly visible and when the weather is severe and one pictures the plight of men forced to leave their ship and float in one of these for hours or perhaps days, one marvels that men are brave enough to go to sea in such craft."

Because they wore no uniform, the merchant seamen were ignored and sometimes even reviled as slackers. During the war, Canada had the fourth-largest merchant fleet in the world; after hostilities ceased, it was abandoned, leaving more than 12,000 former seamen to walk the streets looking for work. For eighteen months after the war they had little chance of getting jobs ashore, for these went to the veterans.

The government services were virtually closed to them as Doug Fraser, one of the leading spokesmen for the wartime merchant mariners, has emphasized in his book *Postwar Casualty: Canada's Merchant Navy.* "Unfairness of opportunity was the rule rather than the exception. . . . Qualifications didn't matter much because we non-veterans couldn't get a foot in the door. That applied to the federal civil service and by implication to provincial government employment as well."

Little effort was made to rehabilitate non-uniformed seamen who had served in the North Atlantic or on the dreadful Murmansk run. The latter was, perhaps, the most dangerous in the history of sea warfare, with 104 ships destroyed and 1,200 lives lost. Merchant seamen were paid less than their opposite numbers in the navy, and they received none of the benefits that the government extended to uniformed service personnel. As Fraser wrote, "the Canadian government gave no indication, specific or implied, that it wished to hear from us again."

During the war, national security made it impossible to publish the losses of ships or men. When a tanker was torpedoed or blown up and all her crew killed, no details appeared in the press. The names of those who died in this way were never listed, although later coverage revealed the identity of Royal Navy casualties. Fraser charged that "the curtain of silence . . . continued for many years. Casualty lists for the merchant navy were decades late in gaining their deserved place on monuments to those who died or went missing through enemy action."

Almost half a century went by before the department of veterans' affairs at last recognized the civilian sailors as war veterans and made disability pensions and other benefits available to "qualified individuals." But what did "qualified individuals" mean? To an embittered Fraser, the "so-called benefits . . . represent only token recognition, based as they appear to be on the applicant's income being below the poverty line."

After half a century, many ex-seamen found it difficult to prove they were qualified. In those pre-computer days, many necessary documents were destroyed, perhaps because they took up too much space or because there was no directive to preserve them in the National Archives. Many seamen like Francis Martell of Cape Breton, Nova Scotia, had to search out their own proof of service. Martell had shipped out at age sixteen. He was one of the lucky ones, for he managed to locate his former captain in a Nova Scotia nursing home. The old skipper signed a statutory declaration that Martell had served with him on the *Champlain Park* beginning in 1943.

On January 9, 1995, Doug Fraser helped organize a Canada-wide series of demonstrations made up of former seamen who wanted the government to make retroactive cash payments to cover the long years when they had been ignored. It came too late. Only 3,050 were still alive—about a quarter of the original force. Their average age was seventy-eight years; the survivors were dying at the rate of one every three days, and that rate was increasing. Many of those who had helped keep the Atlantic lifeline open and who might have protested were too ill or incapacitated to. Fraser's demonstrations had some effect. The government dragged its feet for four more years and then, in 1999, announced that it was placing merchant navy veterans on the same footing as the other services for pensions and allowances. For the dwindling company of aging survivors, that was a victory of sorts, albeit a paper one.

2

Mr. Brown A month after the Global War ended, not with a whimper but with a bang in the nuclear rubble of Hiroshima and Nagasaki, the Cold War had its genesis. It began, though nobody was aware of it at the time, in Ottawa, Canada, not in one of the major capitals of the world. The date was September 5, 1945. On that hot and humid late summer night, a stocky, furtive little man in a pale grey suit walked into the offices of the Ottawa *Journal* and offered the editors the scoop of the century.

This was Igor Sergeievich Gouzenko, a cipher clerk in the act of defecting from the Russian Embassy. Squirrelled away on his person were 109 damning documents, stolen from the embassy and exposing the presence in Canada of a secret Soviet spy ring.

Gouzenko had no difficulty getting into the editorial offices of the *Journal*. In those days, long before security guards and gimlet-eyed receptionists, newspapers' doors were wide open. Anybody could walk in with a story or a complaint, or even (as I once reported in Vancouver) a bottle of rye ordered by phone from an accommodating bootlegger. They were a motley crew, these visitors. I can remember some of them when I worked on the desk of the Vancouver *Sun*: the crocodile of midgets being shepherded into the newsroom by a circus press agent; the brown and bearded little man who claimed to be roller skating around the world; the self-styled inventor who insisted he was going to soar off the Granville Street bridge on homemade wings if we'd send a reporter to watch him fly. (We did; he didn't.) As far as the *Journal*'s staff was concerned, this pale and nervous creature with the heavy Russian accent, the strong jaw line, and the bushy eyebrows was just part of the passing show. He was obviously in a state of panic, but no one would hear him out; and so they sent him on his way.

Gouzenko's subsequent peregrinations around official Ottawa desperately, but vainly, trying to tell his story have a bizarre quality that might be laughable had he not been serious. Here he was, trying to reveal one of the great secrets of the day: that the Russians had a clandestine spy ring of apparently sober citizens—one of them a Member of Parliament—operating under the very noses of the RCMP. This tale had all the qualities of a film noir, replete with dark corners, midnight knockings, breathless escapes, furtive characters, and endless frustrations. And, of course, Hollywood *did* make one three years after the fact, with Dana Andrews in the role of an un-Gouzenko-like defector.

In unravelling Gouzenko's forty-eight-hour mission, as John Sawatsky has done in two books, the old cliché from "pillar to post" springs to mind. He goes first to the *Journal*, climbs to the sixth floor, then in a panic leaves and returns to his apartment. His young wife urges him to go back with his sweat-dampened documents. There he buttonholes the night editor, but his heavy accent makes him almost incomprehensible. "It's war. It's war," he seems to be saying. "It's Russia."

Nobody understands what he means. War? With Russia? The war is over; Russia is our gallant ally. The propagandists have transformed that country's image during the years of hostilities, playing down the brutal aspects of the Communist regime and praising the valiant stand of the Russian armies at Stalingrad. Pro-Russian films and books, such as *Mission to Moscow*, diplomat Joseph Davies's paean to the warm-hearted Russian people, and the fulsome coverage of the Canadian-Soviet Friendship Council have helped convert Joseph Stalin into a genial, pipe-smoking uncle, turning black, if not into white, at least into an acceptable shade of grey.

At the *Journal,* the preoccupied night editor puts Gouzenko off, suggesting he either see the RCMP or wait until morning. Gouzenko goes to the justice building only to be stopped by a Mountie at the door who won't let him speak to the minister, Louis St. Laurent. It's past five o'clock and the offices are closed.

Back he goes to his apartment. Officially he is secretary to the military attaché at the Russian Embassy, Colonel Nicolai Zabotin, who is, in reality, the secret head of Soviet military intelligence for Canada. Gouzenko, Zabotin's cipher clerk, won't have to go to work until noon. Early next morning his wife, Svetlana, stuffs all the secret documents into her purse and the couple set off with their two-year-old son, Andrei, to try again.

Back at the justice building, they wait in growing panic for two hours, only to be told that St. Laurent will not see them; instead, they are urged to return to their embassy and give the documents back. They traipse back to the *Journal* again, where a young cub reporter, Marjorie Nichols, speaks to them, looks at the documents, shows them to her editor, and tells him, "quite frankly, I think they're nutty as nits." They are told to go either to the police or to the government. As Russians, they fear the police but jump at the suggestion that they go again to the justice department to apply for naturalization papers.

510

There they are shunted to the crown attorney's office, where they are asked to come back the next day to take out naturalization papers. When they learn that the process will take years, Svetlana Gouzenko bursts into tears.

Fernande Joubarne, the crown attorney's secretary, sympathizes with their plight. She parks them in the crown attorney's office, runs upstairs, collars a *Journal* court reporter, and shows him the documents. He says he can't touch the story; his boss has already turned it down. She calls another friend, Mackenzie King's private secretary, Sam Gobeil, and tells him the story. "They need help. Somebody has got to protect these people or else they will be killed by the Russians." He promises to call her back and does so: "Have nothing more to say or do with that man," he tells her. "Get rid of him as soon as you can."

Mlle Joubarne, who emerges as the heroine in this bungled chronicle, begins "phoning, phoning, phoning," in Svetlana Gouzenko's memory, "trying to find someone and explaining to everyone in English and in French—finally phoned her priest and couldn't get anywhere."

The Gouzenkos go home to their apartment, weary, frustrated, and growing more terrified every minute—with good reason, for somebody is soon banging on their door. It is Zabotin's contact man; when the couple do not answer, he leaves. In a panic, Gouzenko goes out onto the balcony, climbs over the railing, and blurts out his story to his neighbour, an RCAF non-commissioned officer, who bicycles off to the police station. The police can do nothing because the apartment is Russian property. But they promise some surveillance.

The Gouzenkos find refuge with another neighbour—a prudent move. Late in the evening, four more Russians from the embassy staff break in the door of Gouzenko's apartment and ransack it. Gouzenko, taking advantage of the promised surveillance, sends a pre-arranged signal to a constable on the street (he turns his bathroom light off). The police arrive and the Russians, protesting, depart.

Meanwhile, Norman Robertson, undersecretary of state for external affairs, is dining with William Stephenson, the Canadian-born British intelligence agent known as the Man Called Intrepid. When Robertson tells his dinner companion about the Gouzenkos' attempts to see the justice minister, Stephenson urges him to ignore the prime minister's orders (conveyed through his secretary) to turn Gouzenko over to the Russians. He advises Robertson to phone the RCMP and place the Gouzenkos first under surveillance and later under protective custody. The next day Gouzenko finds himself for the third time at the justice building being interrogated by the Mounties.

Thus ends the Gouzenko family's convoluted mission. Mackenzie King, on his part, is mainly concerned that the incident will lead to a break in diplomatic relations with the Soviets ("The man might be a crank trying to preserve his own life"). King continues to stall until the RCMP report that Gouzenko's revelations are genuine. Fred Rose was a spy; trusted civil servants were sneaking information to the Russians, who apparently had a mole working in Washington, D.C. (later identified as Alger Hiss), and, to cap it all, Alan Nunn May, a British scientist working on a secret atomic project in Canada, was part of the network. Now King is really disturbed. He has been seduced by his own pipe dream of a world in which the wartime allies can stroll together, hand in hand, like children gambolling in a diplomatic meadow. Now that fancy is in danger of being snuffed out by this obstreperous cipher clerk.

What to do? King, in a quandary, travels to Washington to see Harry Truman and then travels to London to see Clement Attlee, Churchill's successor. The Canadian ambassador in Washington is now Lester Pearson, who is pretty sure King wants to be told to bury the disclosures in the interests of international peace. But the Americans won't play; they say, in effect, "You handle it;" and when the days drag on and on for five months with no action in Ottawa, they leak the whole sordid story to Drew Pearson, the best-known Washington columnist of the time, who breaks the news in a radio broadcast on February 3, 1946. It is a bombshell; the Canadian cabinet, even Jack Pickersgill, who ran the prime minister's office, have been in the dark, and King, at last, is forced to act.

So ends chapter one of the great Canadian spy story.

512

The next chapter began on February 6, when a royal commission to investigate the Gouzenko affair was launched before two supreme court justices. Now, in a panic, Canada embarked on the worst invasion of civil liberties since the forced removal of the Japanese Canadians. As a result of Gouzenko's revelations under oath, close to two dozen people were eventually arrested, subjected to intense investigation, held incommunicado, and denied the right to counsel and also the right of habeas corpus. For the next six months these actions became a hot civil liberties issue. To King, who sympathized with the civil libertarians, it was "the worst fix I've been in in my career." He pushed for an interim report and, in the end, got three.

A series of show trials followed the final royal commission report. Of the twenty-one men and women arraigned, ten received prison sentences of up to six years (among them Fred Rose and Sam Carr, secretary of the Communist Party) and one was fined. In two cases charges were withdrawn; eight were acquitted and two others had their sentences turned on appeal. But, as the historian J.L. Granatstein has pointed out, the commission report itself showed a clear presumption of guilt before the court cases began, and so a fair trial was almost impossible.

Earlier, on March 5, one month after the Gouzenko revelations were made public, Winston Churchill, in a speech in Fulton, Missouri, put a new phrase into the language when he declared that an "iron curtain has descended" upon Eastern Europe. Those words echoed down the decades for most of the half-century that followed.

To Mackenzie King, Gouzenko's documents suggested a coming struggle for world domination. "Now," King declared, "the conflict is whether the U.S. or Russia shall control the world." In his view either a new world war was inevitable or the Russian people would "come to have their eyes opened" and refuse to be the victims of a new military power. He saw himself as God's instrument "in the play of world forces and other forces beyond" to achieve that end and bring about "a real brotherhood among the common people of the earth," a remarkably vain and naive fancy for a supposedly hard-headed politician and

513

one that paralleled the wide-eyed proposals for labour peace in his *Industry and Humanity*.

Gouzenko continued to remain in the headlines, wearing in public the now famous hood that concealed his identity and preserved the myth that Soviet assassins were seeking him out. In the early years it made sense to treat him as a witness needing police protection. Then the threat was real; but for the rest of his life? It is doubtful that Gouzenko himself believed that. Anybody who wanted to track him down could do so easily; many journalists, in fact, did exactly that. I remember well the night he appeared on *Front Page Challenge* wearing his trademark hood and speaking in a muffled voice. I also remember the day he walked into my office at *Maclean's*, sans hood, a stocky, brown-eyed man whom my secretary introduced, with a wink, as "Mr. Brown." He immediately identified himself as the notorious defector. He was an ordeal for the Mounted Police, who he insisted must continue to protect him forever, and also for anybody who took his name in vain, for he was the most litigious public figure in Canada. He told and re-told his story, always for a handsome fee, and produced two literary works, one of which was his ghost-written memoir, *This Was My Choice* and the other, a novel, *Fall of a Titan*, which surprisingly, won the Governor General's Award. Nobody dared say that he had the help of a ghost in producing that epic. It wasn't worth the long legal battle that the tenacious Russian would certainly have undertaken.

His place in history is secure. Because of his initial decision—an act of considerable courage—the sides were drawn up and the world divided into them and us. As Denis Smith has indicated in *The Diplomacy of War*, the illusions about the Soviet ally could not have been sustained after the uneasy certainties of the Global War. In the United States and Canada, politicians and public "seemed to require a new secular faith, and greeted its emergence with relief."

All the ugly paraphernalia of the Cold War lay ahead—a half century of witch hunts and blacklists, security clearances, charges of disloyalty and treason, careers wrecked by rumour, public servants toppled and in at least one case driven to suicide by whispers, nonconformity confused with perfidy, the spectre of suspicion stalking the nations, and, worst of all, young men dying by the thousands in foreign climes in the service of a flawed ideal that we now realize had little substance.

3

The big change

The period between the end of the Global War and the start of the Korean conflict is perhaps the most significant five years in the history of Canada's twentieth century. In those immediate post-war days, the nation was on the cusp of change. In spite of the huge cost of the war, the boom was on—the housing boom, the baby boom, the mining and drilling boom, the new immigration boom.

Exposure to Europe had helped change moral attitudes. Liquor was no longer a demon. Wartime strictures on dress were cast aside as women succumbed to the New Look with its emphasis on billowy, ankle-length hemlines, and youths adopted the zoot suit, with its big lapels, knee-length jacket, and baggy trousers. The brave and bountiful new world promised by the wartime ads became a reality as women stormed the stores for scarce nylon stockings, heralding a plastics revolution that would forever transform the old glass-and-metal economy.

Consumers were eager to cash in their enforced savings and spend, spend, spend. In the hospitals, penicillin was the new drug of choice, with other miracles to follow. American television began to leak into the border cities and would soon make Hopalong Cassidy a household name once again. Though nobody had yet heard of pizza, espresso, sushi, or Szechuan, a revolution in eating habits was on the way. People still travelled by rail, but funds to complete the Trans-Canada Highway were at last available. Supermarkets, shopping centres, and even sidewalk cafés were just around the corner. In those Elysian years the future seemed unlimited—nothing looked impossible.

Mackenzie King retired in November 1948, a month short of his seventy-fourth birthday, convinced that his handling of the manpower crisis in 1944 was the triumphal climax of his career. Revisionists transformed his memory. In a eulogistic article in *Maclean's* following his death two years later, Blair Fraser wrote that "to meet Mr. King at close range . . . to listen to him talk, was to realize the charm he had and to know why he was such a forceful personality at international gatherings. In public he was both cold and dull. . . . Privately he was just the opposite . . . his private talk was blunt, forthright and memorable."

When his body lay in state after his death in July 1950, a mother brought her little boy to see it and tried to explain who Mackenzie King was. "He was a great prime minister," she told him, "and he was prime minister longer than anyone was before. He did great things for Canada. The things he did will make Canada a better place for you to grow up in. He was . . ." but she could not continue. She stopped talking and began to cry. As Fraser wrote: "Of all the millions of words poured out in tribute to Mackenzie King none gave him surer promise of immortal memory."

The new prime minister, Louis St. Laurent, whom King had co-opted directly into the cabinet in the early war years, was the quintessential Canadian. His paternal forebears had been in Quebec since 1653; his mother, a schoolteacher, was Irish; he himself was perfectly bilingual. I remember listening to him with awe when he addressed the General Assembly of the United Nations at its first session at Lake Success, New York, in 1947. There, he performed the neat parlour trick of switching from unaccented English to French in the middle of a sentence without missing a beat.

He was sixty-six when he took office, a suave, avuncular figure, soon to be dubbed "Uncle Louis." His parents had wanted him to be a priest, but he preferred the law and swiftly rose to become a leading corporate and constitutional lawyer, much in demand. He had no interest in politics, but he took the job of minister of justice at King's urging in 1941 because he felt he must do his part in the war effort. When Grattan O'Leary, the editor of the Ottawa *Journal*, once asked him whether there was much difference speaking to the Supreme Court and to the House of Commons, St. Laurent replied, "Before the Supreme Court, anger would be fatal; in the House sometimes it is desirable to appear angry."

O'Leary, a spirited Tory, wrote in 1947: ". . . not since Laurier has any French-Canadian political leader done so much to soften asperities between the two races." As little as two years earlier O'Leary had written, "A French Canadian as leader of a party in Canada, much less as Prime Minister, would have been unthinkable." Now, he felt, the country would accept St. Laurent—a man without personal vanity or "cheap ambition . . . essentially a product of humility. No public man of our time has been so free of guile or of the posturings of the demagogue, or of the treachery and ruthlessness of the careerist." Without the war, St. Laurent would have been lost to Canada. "War emergencies produced him," O'Leary wrote, [and] "brought to politics a fresh figure of dignity. . . ."

With the advent of St. Laurent, the country entered a new political era, illuminated by a drastic change from the public performances of Mackenzie King. At a Thanksgiving dinner in Algoma East during the by-election that put Lester Pearson into Parliament, St. Laurent was invited to make a short speech, a prospect that troubled Jack Pickersgill. A French Canadian addressing an Anglo-Saxon audience in a Protestant church? That could cause problems. Pickersgill needn't have worried. St. Laurent began by speaking of his own hometown of Compton, in the heart of the English-speaking Eastern Townships, and comparing it with the community of Little Current, where the dinner was held. He recalled that his home had been next to the local Methodist Church and "when he said that the pumpkin pie he had just eaten tasted exactly like 'punkin pie his mother used to make,' I looked at the audience and realized it did not matter what he said after that!" In public, Pickersgill noted, St. Laurent seemed to respond naturally to an audience and "to lose entirely the appearance of stiffness he often showed when he was alone with one or two people." In that, he was the antithesis of King, stuffy and self-conscious at a public meeting, but warm and at his best with one or two listeners.

By the time St. Laurent became prime minister, Alberta had ceased to be a have-not province thanks to vast new oil discoveries at Leduc, just outside Edmonton, and at Redwater, farther north. The Leduc boom was touched off on February 13, 1947, on Mike Turta's farm, when Imperial Oil brought in Leduc #1, the most important oil well ever discovered in Canada outside of Alberta's Turner Valley. Within a day the rush was on as oilmen poured in from Calgary, Toronto, Vancouver, and the northern United States and began taking out leases on Leduc land, buying from farmers and selling to anyone who would pay the price. One man made $75,000 that way. The oil rights to one single quarter-section were sold eleven times, always at a profit. Within two months, oilmen large and small had six million acres under lease, paying as much as $400 an acre. Since in most cases, however, the government of Alberta and not the original farmers owned the mineral rights to the land, the province began to grow rich on oil royalties.

Alberta would never be the same again. Scott Young described the scene in the two-storey brick hotel at Leduc. "Citizens and farmers alike are almost lost in the dozens of men in plaid and khaki shirts, high boots, wide-brimmed hats and oil-stained overalls—wildcatters, the men who search for new oil fields. The pool room is full of oilmen off shift, drillers and cathead men and lead tong men and derrick men. Upstairs in the hotel, past the deserted desk with its 'No Rooms Vacant' sign, oilmen sit around a blanket-covered table and play quiet, dollar-limit poker. . . . And among oilmen and farmers alike the talk is not of crops but of the latest drill stem test at Number Five, or the $130,000 that Pete Hairysh got for his half section, or the $41,000 the widow Kate Malchak got for her quarter, or the $58,000 for which Bill Sucz sold the quarter he had worked for 30 years." The boom exploded fifty miles to the northeast in 1948, when a new oil-producing zone, four times as thick as Leduc's, was found at Redwater—a billion dollars' worth of high-quality petroleum, hidden beneath the rolling prairie. Alberta was on a roll.

By 1947, the year of Leduc, the temperance movement that had suffered a setback when the soldiers returned from the Great War was now in full retreat. Every province was preparing to move from dry to wet; even Prince Edward Island, the driest province of all, stopped insisting that people get a doctor's prescription before they could buy liquor and began to open government liquor stores. Halifax voted two to one to allow the sale of beer and wine by the glass. British Columbians were agitating for a loosening of liquor laws, especially after a Vancouver newspaper revealed that the town rejoiced in a half-dozen private clubs where a martini could be downed, no questions asked, without so much as a membership fee. Quebec, of course, had always been wet, but it was Ontario that led the attack on the temperance forces that dominated English-speaking Canada. In January 1947, George Drew's province passed the new Liquor Licence Act, and by April, cocktail bars began to open in major Ontario cities.

The public went mad. When my wife and I arrived in Toronto from the West that June, we found we had to struggle to make our way through the block-long crowds that waited outside the Silver Rail on Yonge Street—one of the first bars to open in the city. In just nine months, on an outlay of $100,000, this establishment made a profit of $90,000. In one month the customers walked off with 70,000 paper doilies especially ordered from England by the Rail's management. In the first six months they pocketed 28,000 plastic forks used to fish cherries from Manhattan cocktails. People drank as if they had just survived a trek across the Sahara—and without much sophistication: liqueurs before dinner, martinis with dessert.

As one bartender, Eddie Paltry, told me, "people here don't really know how to drink yet. They are learning slowly. At the beginning, they come in here, some of them, you know, and they try to start at the top of the menu and work right down. It is all so new, you see. One fellow, he'll come in and order whisky, then rye, then a gin drink, then maybe a bottle of beer, then he'll have a crème de menthe, then an eggnog, then another beer, then a Scotch, then he'll finish with a beer. What that does to the stomach I don't know, but it's not good."

Things quickly quieted down. One bar that lost 10,000 menus in the first three months to souvenir hunters lost only 3,000 in the next nine. Customers began to settle down to a few staple drinks. The food started to get better; entertainment was added, thanks to increased competition. In April, fourteen bars had been licensed in Toronto; by the end of the year there were thirty-five. The big change was underway, not only in staid old Toronto but all across Canada, as province after province went wet and the new sophistication took over.

In mid-February 1949, as most of the country was becoming used to the new attitude toward liquor consumption, five thousand workers in the asbestos mining area of Quebec's Eastern Townships launched a strike that stopped work for more than four months, galvanized the province, and heralded the slow deterioration of the Duplessis regime. One sympathetic priest, Jacques Cousineau, a Jesuit activist from Montreal, predicted it would live as "one of the most important events in the social history of Canada." Like an earlier post-war quasi-revolutionary work stoppage, the Winnipeg General Strike of 1919, which helped launch J.S. Woodsworth into the political arena, the strike at Asbestos gave Pierre Elliott Trudeau a rostrum that eventually led to Ottawa and the prime minister's office.

The strike was part of the process of change that affected post-war Canada in general and Quebec in particular. As Trudeau himself observed, five years after the fact, it wasn't the date or place or the particular industry: ". . . chance could well have dictated that the strike break out in another location than Asbestos." Ostensibly it was a strike for higher wages and greater work benefits, but it was more than that; its emotional impact on public opinion was such that it awakened many Québécois to the problems of their own society. As Gérard Filion wrote in *Le Devoir* after the strike was settled in June, it was a great misfortune, but it was far from useless. "The social climate of Quebec is no longer what it was six months ago. Today we are beginning to acquire a social conscience." To Trudeau, "the drama at Asbestos was a violent announcement that a new era had begun."

The strike was marked by riots, violence, mass marches, and the importation of strikebreakers by the asbestos companies, the largest of which was Canadian Johns-Manville. The Duplessis government was solidly on the side of the companies, declaring the strike illegal and sending in squadrons of provincial police who used brutal tactics against the strikers on more than one occasion. To Premier Maurice Duplessis,

520

the strikers were "saboteurs" and "subversive agents." Significantly, however, the Church was on the strikers' side. As Gérard Dion noted in the Trudeau-edited study of the affair, the Church "clearly saw that the very survival of the Catholic trade union movement was at stake in this conflict."

When a group of University of Montreal students poured into Asbestos, travelling in cars festooned with banners reading "Long Live the Asbestos Strikers," Father Cousineau took their part, urging that they become "a generation who value social justice higher than legality." When Johns-Manville threatened to evict strikers from their rental houses (owned by the company), another priest, Louis Philippe Camirand, chaplain of the Asbestos local, declared that company agents would not take a stick of furniture out of the houses "except over my dead body." The bishop of Sherbrooke, Philippe Desranleau, sent a letter to all his clergy declaring that "as bishop I whole-heartedly support the asbestos workers in their just demands." From his pulpit in Notre Dame Cathedral, Monsignor Charbonneau, archbishop of Montreal, declared, "There is a conspiracy to destroy the working class, and it is the church's duty to intervene."

The climax came early on May 5—"Bloody Thursday"—after Johns-Manville hired 234 strikebreakers from neighbouring towns as permanent employees. This frightened and enraged the strikers. Violence followed: clashes between strikers and "scabs," a dozen injured policemen imprisoned in the basement of a local church, the Riot Act read, some two hundred strikers arrested amid witnesses who gave accounts of police brutality. The strikers were taken to the Iroquois Club for "questioning." There they were kicked, beaten with truncheons, punched, shoved against the walls, and so badly marked that some had to be released rather than be seen by the public during a trial that followed.

Two months later the strike was settled—significantly, through the mediation of Archbishop Roy of Quebec, who had been the wartime chaplain of the Royal 22nd.

For the rest of Canada, the Asbestos strike drew the spotlight to three activists who would later help transform the politics of the nation. These were Jean Marchand, the young secretary general of the Canadian Confederation of Catholic Labour, Gérard Pelletier, the activist reporter for *Le Devoir*, and Trudeau, who, with Pelletier, was arrested by the provincial police and given half an hour to get out of town, an order they resolutely disobeyed. It was this same trio, dubbed the Three Wise Men, who would eventually be lured into federal Liberal politics in 1965. All were given cabinet posts, and Trudeau, three years later, would become the first Canadian prime minister born in the twentieth century, a prophet as well as a product of the big change of the post-war years.

On April 1, 1949, with tensions rising in Asbestos as Bloody Thursday approached, 348,000 Newfoundlanders became Canadians overnight after a hard-fought battle that required two referendums before confederation with Canada was achieved by the narrowest of margins. The newest Father of Confederation was a diminutive, bow-tied jack-of-all-trades, with beak-like features and a driving energy that seemed inexhaustible. Joseph Roberts Smallwood had been a printer, pig farmer, advance man for a movie producer, union organizer, thriller writer, sometime dweller in New York flophouses, and host of the wildly popular Barrelman series on radio, which made him the best-known man on the island. He was "Joey" to enemies and supporters alike, a one-man band who had managed, through the force of his personality and his peripatetic campaigning, to convince his suspicious Newfoundlanders that union with Canada was the island's salvation.

This was a remarkable feat; nothing quite like it had occurred in Canadian politics, nor would anything like it occur again. Canadian politicians have rarely been known for the kind of all-out, single-minded driving force that Smallwood exhibited in his crusade to bring about confederation. Here was a man who had no political experience, who was best known as a radio performer, and who had so little knowledge of Canada that he didn't even know the names of half the provincial premiers.

In Newfoundland, until Smallwood had his say, confederation was a dirty word. Smallwood himself was originally opposed to union with the mainland, but without him it is highly doubtful that the island would have become a Canadian province. In his long campaign to take Newfoundland out of the colonial doldrums, he managed to visit 1,100 of the island's 1,300 villages. It was even said that he could call at least 100,000 citizens by name—an impossible claim, but one that suggests his legendary stature.

Smallwood began his campaign to convince his reluctant fellow islanders to join Canada late in 1945 when the British government indicated that it was prepared to restore independence and self-government to the island, which had been governed by a commission of civil servants since 1933. A national convention was proposed to discuss the colony's future. Smallwood saw his opportunity, decided to be a delegate at the convention, and spent two months relentlessly swotting up on the subject of confederation. As a result, he became an ardent supporter of union and got himself elected as delegate for Bonavista by a vote of 2,129 to 222—the largest majority in an otherwise indifferent colony. The convention sounded out both London and Ottawa on the subject. The British were chilly, but the delegation to Ottawa got a warmer reception, partly because Mackenzie King had now begun to think of himself as a twentieth-century Father of Confederation.

In the words of his biographer, Richard Gwyn, Smallwood "by sheer persistence . . . had got everyone talking about Confederation, even those who passionately opposed it. . . . [He] was producer, director, stage-manager, stage-hand and star actor of the Confederation movement. . . ." He wrote speeches for his supporters, drafted strategy, and had the final say. Confederation, he declared, offered "a new hope for the common man." But when the convention ended its sittings on January 29, 1948, the delegates recommended only that responsible government and commission government should be placed as choices on the ballot paper for the coming referendum.

This was a setback. Responsible government could easily lead to union with the United States, which had its eye on the island. The Americans' aggressive presence on this coastal outpost was already a matter of concern to Ottawa. On three sites—Harmon Field at Stephenville, Argentia, sixty-five miles southwest of St. John's, and Fort Pepperell, just outside the capital—the United States had full control thanks to the 1941 leases by which Great Britain traded air bases for destroyers. Here the Americans had absolute right of jurisdiction over any offence committed by a non-British subject. If a GI murdered a local citizen, he would be subject to an American, not a British, court. Outside the leased area, anywhere in the province, the U.S. courts also retained jurisdiction over any offence "of a military nature" committed on a non-British subject.

When a Newfoundlander was shot and wounded by an American military policeman, his lawyer told him he had no recourse to his own courts. When two St. John's citizens got judgments after a collision with a U.S. military vehicle on the city's streets, they found they couldn't collect. When a Newfoundland customs officer trying to search cars on a public highway for smuggled goods was stopped at pistol point by an American, he found himself under arrest by the American, who threatened to shoot a fellow Newfoundlander who tried to release him. The Newfoundlander sued and was awarded damages, but he too found he couldn't collect. The American invasion of Newfoundland parallels that of the Canadian North during the building of the Alaska Highway. One Stephenville citizen described the early days when "they came in with their bulldozers, knocking people's houses down almost before they'd have time to get out. One barn was burnt with the horse still in it. . . ."

No matter how the referendum turned out, the occupation would continue because the leases extended for ninety-nine years. Canada would have considerably more clout with the United States on the island's behalf, but only if confederation became law—and confederation wasn't even an option on the ballot! Smallwood was determined that it would be. He launched a protest campaign against the twenty-nine members of the convention who had voted to thwart the confederation forces. "Twenty-nine dictators" he called them. Nearly fifty thousand telegrams and letters of protest poured in. On March 10, 1948, the Commonwealth relations secretary, Philip Noel-Baker, after discreetly checking with Ottawa, announced that it "would not be right to deprive the people of the opportunity of considering the issue." On June 3, the voters were given three choices: commission government, responsible government, or confederation with Canada. Responsible government won: 69,400 to 64,006 for confederation, and 22,311 for the status quo. Because the rules required a clear majority, a run-off vote had to be held. On the night of July 22, 1948, confederation squeaked through, 78,323 votes to 71,334.

The following April, Newfoundland became part of Canada, and Smallwood, as head of the majority Liberal Party, became premier, a post he held for two decades. Eventually the Americans, without giving up anything vital, moved to satisfy Canadian public opinion by modifying the arbitrary actions under the 1941 leased bases agreement with what had become a Canadian province.

Gouzenko, Smallwood, Trudeau—those names, once unfamiliar to the mass of Canadians, would enliven the front pages in the decades that followed. On July 24, two days after the Newfoundland vote, three of the asbestos companies reached agreement with the unions, and the men returned to work. It was, in effect, the beginning of the end of one of the longest and most significant work stoppages in Canada. Eleven months later, the army of North Korea crossed the 38th Parallel and plunged the world into a new war.

Big Jim Stone

1

Canada's century, to recall Laurier's optimistic and oft-quoted vision, can be divided roughly into two halves. All the wars and all the unnecessary battles in which our youth was squandered belong to the first—from the autumn of 1899 to the summer of 1953. From that point on, we have concerned ourselves not with war but with peace.

The first war of the century, which took our soldiers to South Africa, and the last, which took them to Korea, bracket the period neatly, confining these tumultuous years like bookends on the shelf of history. They have a good deal in common, these two minor conflicts whose chronicles pale when compared with the two great blood baths that mark our time. In retrospect, we should have stayed out of both.

Each caught us by surprise. Each found the government was reluctant to become involved, but was induced to give way to public opinion. In each instance, Canadians were told at the outset that this would be a short campaign against an enemy who could easily be bested and that the boys would be home from the battlefields by Christmas.

In both South Africa and Korea, we entered the fray out of a sense of commitment to an imperial concept—supplying a token force in the first to enlarge the vision of a united empire, in the second to support the fiction that this was a United Nations effort and not an American Cold War adventure.

In each war, the high command was flawed, and new leaders had to be found after the enemy turned out to be surprisingly resilient. In South Africa, Redvers Buller was shunted aside to make way for the much acclaimed General Roberts. In Korea, General Walton Walker, killed in an accident after the enemy all but drove the active units of his Eighth Army off the peninsula, was replaced by Matthew Ridgway, who changed the course of the war.

In South Africa, the British, faced with an unexpectedly stubborn resistance, found it necessary to call for additional Canadian forces for something more than a token effort. In Korea, a single battalion had to be increased to an entire brigade group after the Big Bug-Out.

In each war the generals found that tactics of the past did not fit the terrain. Massed armies clashing on open fields in the days of the thin red line made little sense on the veldt, nor were battalion tactics possible in the conical hills of Korea, where the conflict became a platoon commander's war.

In each war victory finally proved elusive. In South Africa, the capture of Pretoria seemed to end the struggle; instead it begat a guerrilla war that dragged on for another two years. In Korea, the recapture of Seoul and the return of United Nations troops to the 38th Parallel seemed to bring that "police action" to a close; instead, it settled into a static but equally bloody conflict on Great War lines that also dragged on for two more years.

In both wars, young Canadians had to do battle in a distant land where the culture was strange, the language incomprehensible, conditions forbidding, and the enemy evasive. Their opponents did not fight according to the so-called rules of war, nor were the troops trained for the kind of conditions that were thrust upon them. Endless, exhausting marches across the sere desert in the cauldron of South Africa, and decades later over the frigid hills of Korea's formidable spine, put almost as many men out of action as the enemy's bullets.

Casualties were low in both wars—low, that is, when compared with the dreadful bloodletting in the two world conflicts. In South Africa, 244 Canadians laid down their lives, half from disease. In Korea, where the Canadian forces were larger, 516 soldiers died, but of these, only 312 were killed in action. As in South Africa, the rest died of disease and other causes.

The Korean War began on June 25, 1950, when some 135,000 North Korean troops crossed the 38th Parallel, the demarcation line between the communist-controlled North and the so-called democratic South. As in South Africa, the opening move came as a complete surprise to politicians and military leaders alike. One wonders why. The border had for some time been in a state of turmoil. The United Nations Commission on Korea had warned that civil war could break out at any time. Major troop movements north of the Parallel suggested that something was up. Yet when Douglas MacArthur's headquarters in Tokyo received a report forecasting an invasion in June it was ignored. American Intelligence soft-pedalled suggestions that war was likely. The North Koreans, it was felt, might indulge in subversion and guerrilla attacks, but nobody expected an all-out war. By 1950 most U.S. troops, who had been occupying Korea since the Japanese surrendered, had left the country, leaving only a token force in place when the North Koreans struck. In effect, the United States had bypassed Korea as a potential hot spot, preferring to concentrate its defence strategy on the Philippines and Japan.

It was generally held that the Soviets and Chinese had instigated the attack and that this was part of what right-wing Republicans in the United States were calling the "international Communist conspiracy" to take over the globe. That attitude—that the communist world was a vast monolithic structure whose leaders danced to the same tune—continued through the Vietnam War. "If we don't stop them in Asia, they'll be in Seattle," one prominent American—Al Capp, creator of L'il Abner and a frequent guest on American talk shows—told me.

In fact, both the Chinese and the Russians were hesitant. Stalin, preoccupied with Eastern Europe, was unwilling to risk war with the West but changed his mind and prepared to supply the communist North with Russian weapons when it appeared that the United States, by withdrawing its troops, would not fight to defend the South. The Chinese were standoffish and would remain that way unless their own territory was threatened. The pervasive idea of a monolithic communist empire did not take into account the national aspirations of a formerly subject population.

The North Koreans wanted a united nation on their own terms, not UN terms. But to much of the world, Korea was no more than a counter in the widely held "domino theory"—that country after country would topple into the Red monolith unless these piecemeal attacks were stopped cold. As U.S. president Harry Truman put it, "If South Korea is allowed to fall, Communist leaders would be emboldened to override the nations closer to our own shores." Truman was prepared to intervene at once, whether or not the United Nations decided to take some form of direct action. As he told Dean Acheson, his secretary of state, "Dean, we've got to stop these sons of bitches no matter what." The Korean War quickly developed into an American war, run by Americans, with token forces from other Western countries supporting the fiction that this was a UN effort.

The invasion also caught Canada by surprise. When the news reached Ottawa, Minister for External Affairs Lester Pearson told reporters, off the record, that he "did not expect a U.S. military response to the invasion." On that he was dead wrong. The American reaction, he confessed, had surprised him as much as the invasion itself. On June 27, the UN Security Council, meeting at Lake Success (with the sulky Soviets not in attendance), put its official stamp on the American venture and asked other nations to join with the United States to repel the attack and "restore international peace and security to the area."

Canada remained hesitant. Challenged in the House, Pearson, a longtime advocate of collective security, declared that the government wanted to make sure that this really *was* a UN operation and "not merely an endorsement by the United Nations of unilateral action by the United States," which, of course, it was. In the words of Oliver Franks, British ambassador in Washington, who supported Truman's commitment, the UN involvement "was merely a fig leaf for executive action."

The memory of Hong Kong still hung over Parliament Hill. Canada was doing its best to wriggle out of any commitment in Korea. That same week, St. Laurent emphasized that Canada's part in carrying out the UN resolution would not involve participation in war "against any state," and used the words "police action" to describe the situation. At the same time he offered the bare minimum—three destroyers for service in Korean waters.

In truth, Canada did not have enough fighting men to support an international force in Asia. In the aftermath of V-J Day the bulk of her army had long since been demobilized. Any future war, it was held, would be fought in Europe where Canada's contribution would mainly involve the navy and air force (shades of 1938 and King's wistful hopes for a limited war). By 1950, Canada had no more than 20,000 men in khaki. Brooke Claxton, the minister of defence, was one who felt that, from a military point of view, Canada should avoid entanglement in Korea.

Meanwhile, the North Koreans, having captured Seoul, the South Korean capital, were sweeping down the peninsula. The lightly equipped ROK (Republic of Korea) Army was no match for the seasoned troops of the People's Army of North Korea, equipped with one hundred medium tanks as well as a formidable brigade of Soviet T-34 monsters. On July 14, the secretary general of the United Nations put on the pressure. Trygve Lie shot off a tough letter to the Canadian government (which, to St. Laurent's anger, he also released to the press), declaring "an urgent need for additional effective assistance." A token offer of three destroyers was clearly not enough. The United Nations wanted troops, and Canada didn't have them.

Lie waited four days for a reply. There appeared to be no urgency. Claxton was in Newfoundland; St. Laurent was off fishing and annoyed when the press tracked him down. "I wish reporters wouldn't bother me when I'm on my holidays," he complained. Following a hurried meeting of the Chief of Staff's Committee on July 18, he declared that "no dispatch of Canadian ground troops is recommended." At a cabinet meeting next day, Claxton concurred. The United States, in his view, was getting into "something to which there is really no end." But Pearson sensed trouble. He pointed out that the United States was putting pressure on other countries to send troops to Korea "mainly for psychological reasons." The fig leaf had to be kept in place.

There followed a long discussion in Washington between Pearson, Acheson, and Lie that persuaded Pearson to tell the cabinet Canada should take some further action—to support the United Nations, rather than the United States. It must never appear that the Canadian beaver was bending to the wishes of the American eagle. Canada should distance herself from their neighbour, Pearson explained, by making it clear to the international community that "we fight only as a result of UN decisions, and with other UN members." That, of course, was exactly the cover story that the Truman administration wanted.

The press, caught up in the long-standing Canadian hunger for international acclaim, was also pushing hard for Canada to jump into the conflict. As the *Globe and Mail* thundered, early in July, "Canada, to the dismay of her citizens, is once again fumbling an opportunity in . . . international affairs." At the end of the month, with rumours flying that Ottawa was contemplating a military presence in Korea, the *Globe and Mail*, with other major Canadian papers, gave the process an additional nudge: "It will be gratifying if the Cabinet at last acknowledges this country's duty to send ground forces. . . ."

Both Claxton and St. Laurent eventually acquiesced. On the night of August 7, the Prime Minister addressed the nation by radio, insisting that the confrontation in Korea, which at that moment resembled a rout, was not a war but merely a "police action intended to prevent war by discouraging aggression." St. Laurent invoked an earlier war. Anything less, he indicated, would be a form of the same kind of appeasement that had encouraged Hitler in the 1930s.

At last it was agreed that to stop the communists, Canada would supply a special force of brigade strength available for a year's service in Korea—but *only* in Korea. Canada wanted no part of any other dangerous Asian quarrel, notably the one brewing in Formosa, where Chiang Kai-shek's army was holed up, backed by the U.S. China lobby and straining to invade the mainland. The shadow of the earlier adventure hung over the House, where one member warned, "I do not want to see another Hong Kong, where ill-trained and ill-equipped men were sent into battle." Every assurance was given that this time the new Special Force would be properly trained and equipped. That, of course, would take time. Recruiting must start immediately.

The results were spectacular. Would-be soldiers jammed the recruiting depots that had been hurriedly set up across the country. By September, less than a month after the prime minister's announcement, 12,983 men had volunteered to join the Special Force for Korea in contrast to a mere 2,204 who signed up to join the regular army. Half who enlisted initially for eighteen months' service were veterans of the

Global War; 20 percent of these were former NCOs; another 20 percent had trades useful to the army.

Here was an apparent anomaly. The long, debilitating war in Europe had ended a scant five years before. The Canadian government shrank from getting involved in a new one. But a large proportion of the nation's youth were ready to risk their lives in a strange country thousands of miles away. Why?

There were several reasons. A good many veterans joined because, after the excitement of battle, life in post-war Canada seemed deadly dull. Others were fleeing from marriages that didn't work, from a heavy burden of debt, from jobs they loathed, from the law; some were moved by a sense of comradeship with their buddies who had also enlisted, and, most of all, because they were young and adventure beckoned—a free, all-expense-paid trip to an exotic land. Loyalty? Patriotism? The communist menace? These were ephemeral alibis. There was none of the flag waving that had marked the South African call to arms, none of the hatreds or the demonization of the enemy that had caused earlier generations to join the "fight for freedom." The recruits went off across the seas for the same reason their grandfathers had flocked to the Klondike—because they had an excuse (as the search for gold had been a perfectly acceptable alibi in the lean days of '98). In 1950, the Cold War provided a socially expedient cover for the chance to escape and the hope of glory.

The English-Canadian Sunday of those pre-television days—no movies, no entertainment, no booze, no sports—was like a cold douche to veterans who had been seduced by the cafés of Rome and the pubs of London. To Ken McCormand, who had served with the 18th Field Company building bridges in Belgium, "Civilian street seemed so bland. But as soon as you went back into uniform for Korea, things started getting exciting again."

Most of those who joined up knew nothing about Korea—its history, its culture, or its terrain of unclimbable hills. George Henderson was on a walking tour across Canada when he heard Lester Pearson speaking on the radio. He thought "walking around Korea would be the same

534

as walking in Canada," and so joined up immediately, only to discover that "walking in Korea was not so great."

Laurent Seguin, a twenty-three-year-old carpenter from Valleyfield, Quebec, joined up "for adventure and to see part of the world."

Don Hibbs was driving a taxi in Galt, Ontario, when he heard the prime minister on the radio. He didn't have a clue about Korea. "All I knew was, I'd missed out on the Second World War. And I wanted to be a soldier, you know, pulling pins out of grenades with my teeth like I'd seen in those John Wayne war movies. . . . I thought it'd be great to be a real soldier. I wanted to be a hero."

Lesley Pike of Carbonear in the new province of Newfoundland wanted to leave his hometown in search of a different life. "I'd always wanted to go to St. John's. I'd never been outside Newfoundland. And partly because I became a Canadian on April 1, 1949, I decided to volunteer for the Canadian army."

Jean Pleau, a seventeen-year-old French Canadian from a Montreal suburb, joined because he wanted to learn English in order to get a job. In Montreal, a knowledge of both languages was virtually mandatory. "Join the navy and you'll learn English," a relative told him. His mother had to sign for him, and he was soon aboard a destroyer heading for Korea.

Such was the sense of urgency that the military was not prepared for the response to the prime minister's announcement. The morning after St. Laurent's radio address the commanding officer of Toronto's personnel department found several hundred would-be soldiers on his doorstep. Recruiting officers, used to handling some dozen men a week, were swamped by an unexpected wave of volunteers who were signing up by the hundreds. Currie Barracks in Calgary was all but submerged; all training and other activities had to be cancelled to deal with recruitment. Across the country, military headquarters were besieged by volunteers pouring in on trains and buses, eager to join the Special Force for Korea, so named to distinguish it from the Permanent Force and soon to be known as the 25th Infantry Brigade.

The new unit would be recruited from the second battalions of three Permanent Force regiments—the PPCLI, the Royal Canadian Regiment, and the Royal 22nd—the famous Van Doos. Their commander would be John Meredith Rockingham, a six-foot-four-inch Australian-born Vancouver executive with a wartime reputation for fearlessness and toughness in Europe. Having risen from subaltern to brigadier, he had won two DSOs for gallantry and leadership under fire.

Rockingham, superintendent of Pacific Stage Lines, was dealing with officials of the transit union when the call came from Ottawa. "What are you going to do about our demands?" one of the union leaders asked.

"Nothing," Rockingham replied. "You can all go to hell as far as I am concerned." Then he phoned Ottawa and accepted the post.

Rocky, as he was universally called, chose his own senior officers for the new brigade. The three battalion commanders were seasoned veterans, each of whom wore the blue-and-red ribbon of the Distinguished Service Order and had commanded battalions in the Global War. Jacques Albert "Mad Jimmy" Dextraze, the wiry, cocksure commander of the 2nd Battalion, Royal 22nd, had been "woodlands manager" for the Singer Sewing Machine Company. Jim Stone, a big, balding ex-farmer with a bristling moustache who ran a summer resort, would command the 2nd PPCLI. To lead the 2nd RCR, Rockingham plucked Robert A. Keane from army headquarters. The broad-shouldered, cigar-smoking Keane had been commander of an armoured car regiment during the previous war.

These experienced commanders now found they had to pay for the near panic in which the new force was recruited. The turnover in manpower was phenomenal because of the hasty and haphazard system by which volunteers were enlisted. As Stone remarked, "they were recruiting anybody who could breathe or walk." The minister of defence, appalled at the long lines of prospective soldiers waiting to sign up at the various recruiting posts, had ordered a speed-up that only increased the problem. In Stone's view, Claxton had "pushed the enlistment along because he was a politician at heart and didn't give a damn about what else was happening. . . . We had to show some of the first guys how to put their shoes on." As one officer put it, "when

536

the political heat is on, you can't reject anyone who's able to walk."

Under this pressure the army signed up some misfits, including one man of seventy-five and another with an artificial leg. The heat was certainly on. John Beckwith, a young army intern who did medical examinations in Toronto, told historian John Melady "we were supposed to take veterans because we had all the medical records on these guys. No recruit was supposed to be accepted until his record was assessed. . . . But then we found that the whole thing was a bit of a political game." Because Toronto and Montreal were trying to see who got the most recruits, procedure was scrapped in the interests of winning the race.

Beckwith would always remember one man who showed up "with a big bloody scar from his neck to his belly." Asked what it was, he replied, with a straight face, "Appendectomy." En route to a brigade training at Fort Lewis, Washington, Beckwith shared a bus seat with a man who'd been captured at Hong Kong. "Aren't the mountains beautiful?" Beckwith asked as they passed Mount Rainier. When there was no answer, Beckwith shouted the question in his seat companion's ear. "What mountains?" the new recruit asked. It turned out he was not only half deaf but also half blind. Another who slipped through the hasty screening kept complaining that a friend was running around inside his hat. He actually made it to Korea but was soon shipped back as a schizophrenic.

"The enlisting procedures were atrocious," Don Fliegler at the Petawawa camp recalled. "I spent two months getting rid of the riffraff we had enlisted. The medically unfit, the deserters, the people who slipped through the cracks . . . and had to be discharged. What a pile of paper!" The 2nd Battalion RCRs alone had five hundred AWL in September and October of 1950. Some men even slipped through the navy's recruiting centres. The most notorious was Frederick Waldo Demara, an American who posed as a surgeon, Dr. Joseph Cyr. He got to Korea and actually performed operations on North Korean and American wounded before he was unmasked and went on to achieve a certain immortality when Tony Curtis portrayed him in the Hollywood movie *The Great Pretender.*

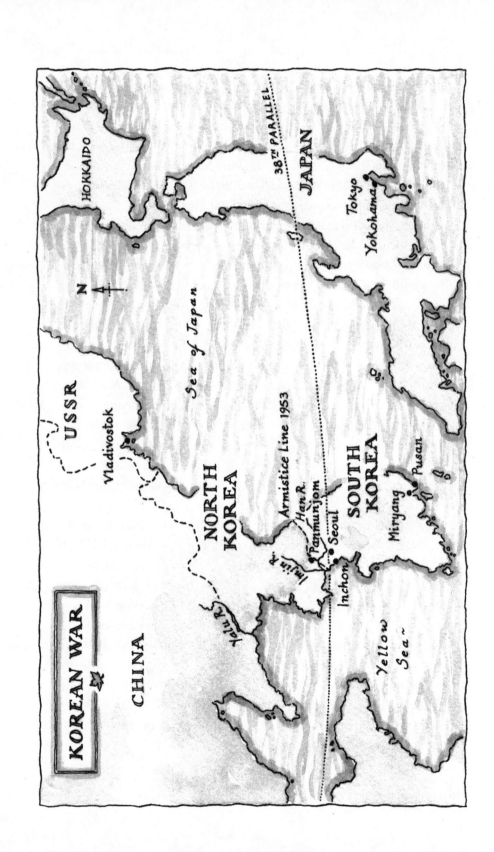

By the end of March 1951, the figure for discharged recruits and unapprehended deserters was 25 percent of the total number enlisted—a whopping statistic compared with the 7 percent for the first seven months of the Great War and 12 percent for the same period in the Global War.

The political panic to rush a Canadian force to Korea stemmed from a corresponding panic on the peninsula in the summer of 1950. The North Korean army swept south, crushing all opposition, until it left the defenders clinging to a tiny toehold in a perimeter surrounding the port of Pusan at Korea's southern tip. The ROK army had collapsed under the suicidal and reckless attacks of the better-trained, Soviet-equipped invaders. Some 45,000 ROK troops had simply melted away, leaving the Americans with a ragtag force scraped together in haste to defend the indefensible. Having abandoned Korea in their overall Asian defence plan, the Americans now dumped hundreds of untrained youths into the perimeter and pushed them north, often to certain death, to help slow the North Korean attacks that MacArthur had been convinced would never come.

The clerks, electricians, drivers, and other non-combatants of the 3rd Battalion of the U.S. 29th Infantry were rushed to Pusan from their occupation duties in Japan. All they'd had was basic training, but they went into battle immediately and were torn to pieces by the North Koreans. Of 757 men who were thrust into the fray, 311 were killed outright, 100 more were taken prisoner, and scores were mortally wounded. They were badly served by their high command with mortars that had never been test fired, machine guns still coated with packing grease, and radios without batteries. Philip Deane, a future Canadian senator who covered the war for an English newspaper until he was captured, reported how one American officer exploded in a blaze of anger over these deficiencies. "It's a goddamn shame. Not a tank yet, not a three-inch Bazooka, no mines. Sending those kids up the line like that's as good as issuing them a death sentence."

If you believed the Hollywood movies, "retreat" was not a word in the American lexicon. Now the folks back home were faced with reality.

Marguerite Higgins, who covered the early months of the war for the New York *Herald Tribune*, wrote, in a much quoted report: "I saw young Americans turn and bolt in battle, or throw down their arms cursing their government for what they thought was embroilment in a hopeless cause."

Philip Deane, wounded and taken prisoner on July 23 and forced to march for miles on bare feet, caught the sense of despair and betrayal in the words of a GI struggling along beside him: "This is unfair. Bloody unfair. They brought us over here without telling us what it was all about. They threw us into battles, platoon by platoon against whole divisions. They sacrificed us and now we're lost. . . ."

While the North Korean grip tightened around the shrinking Pusan perimeter and the Canadian government's hastily recruited brigade prepared for training, a daring plan was taking shape in the mind of Douglas MacArthur, who had been named commander-in-chief of the UN command in Korea. More and more MacArthur's thoughts had been fixed, "with almost mystical conviction," in Max Hastings's phrase, on a possible amphibious landing on the west coast at Inchon, twenty miles southwest of Seoul. In that way he could leapfrog past Pusan—a tactic he had so successfully used in the South Pacific—seize the Korean port, relieve Seoul, and drive the enemy back beyond the 38th Parallel.

In Washington the joint chiefs were cool. After a long, hard look at this intricate and precarious proposal, they declared against it. Yet in the end MacArthur won out. A grand gesture was needed. American morale was at a low ebb—the troops dispirited, the politicians, goaded by the General's early and purposely pessimistic reports, contemplating the possibility of imminent collapse. In fact, although few realized it, the communists, with their supply lines stretched too far, had worn themselves out in repeated attacks on Pusan. Again, army intelligence had got it wrong: the North Koreans no longer enjoyed numerical superiority; in fact, Lieutenant General Walton Walker of the U.S. Eighth Army had twice as many men on Korean soil as Kim Il Sung, the North Korean dictator.

The war of containment that Truman and his consultant, John Foster Dulles, had contemplated, was about to become a war of conquest because of MacArthur. He laid it out to his foremost commanders on August 23 at a meeting in the Dai Ichi building in Tokyo: "It is plainly apparent that here in Asia is where the Communist conspirators have elected to make their play for global conquest. The test is not in Berlin or Vienna, in London, Paris or Washington. It is here and now. . . ."

The enemy's intelligence was as flawed as that of the Americans. The landing at Inchon on September 15 by the 5th Marines caught the North Koreans by surprise—a stunning success with only twenty of the invaders killed. At the same time, the enemy, stretched to the limit, released their stranglehold on the Pusan perimeter in the face of renewed American attacks and fled north to the 38th Parallel.

In Washington euphoria reigned. The communists had been taught a lesson, the job had been done, the enemy was back behind the line of demarcation. "The end of the war loomed as plain as the mustache on Stalin's face," *Life* magazine assured its readers. MacArthur himself reported that organized resistance on a large scale was beyond the capabilities of the enemy and suggested that the troops would be home by Christmas. In the words of the UN mandate, the task of its members "to repel the armed attack and to restore international peace and security in the area" had been accomplished. But the United Nations reckoned without MacArthur and his mystic sense of destiny on the one hand and the half-million Chinese troops massed north of the Manchurian border on the other. For this rash imprudence, young Canadians would pay in blood.

2

The panic was over, and so, apparently, was the need for any sizable force from Canada. On October 4, Brigadier F.J. Fleury, commander of the newly formed Canadian Military Mission, Far East, had a lengthy conversation with MacArthur, who told him that operations in Korea would, for all practical purposes, be successfully completed in a month.

An entirely new war

That meant the Canadian brigade would not arrive in time to fight. A few days later the confident general indicated that Canada might prefer to send a "token force to show the flag," a suggestion appealing to Ottawa since it allowed a Canadian presence in Korea without the prospect of casualties and a chance to re-muster the brigade for service in Europe.

The battalion chosen to go was from the PPCLI because its headquarters were closer to the embarkation point at Seattle than the others, because it had received a bit more training, and because its commander, "Big Jim" Stone, had the most experience.

There is a sense of déjà vu in all this. In spite of South Africa, Hong Kong, and Dieppe, history was repeating itself like a series of scratchy images projected on a flickering screen. Once more, Canada, in the interests of international co-operation and hungering wistfully for international prestige, was preparing to send an expedition of untrained soldiers into a foreign war zone for "non-combat service." Once more, an ambitious commander failed to heed the warnings of his own Intelligence and was preparing to plunge recklessly into a new adventure. Once more the Western world was assured that the boys would be home for Christmas, the precise phrase used by MacArthur in a message to his troops as he launched an offensive designed to end the war.

There was no holding him back, for Inchon had given him the status of a military saint. The British, the Canadians, and, to a lesser extent, the Americans were convinced that the original UN policy was the right one. The North Koreans were again safely behind the 38th Parallel. The last thing the various member nations wanted was any move that might lead to war with China. As Dean Acheson wrote, "an attempt to establish a united Korea could easily lead into general hostilities. . . . Very definitely the policy of our government is to avoid a general war in Asia." Yet MacArthur asked and on September 29 was given permission to cross the Parallel and destroy—not contain—the North Korean army. The crossing must be kept quiet for fear of causing trouble at the United Nations and, although military operations north of the Parallel were permitted, the general was explicitly told that no non-Korean ground forces could be used in the northeastern provinces bordering on Chinese or Soviet territory, an order MacArthur managed to ignore. Nor could he authorize air strikes or naval action in Russian- or Chinese-controlled territory.

ROK troops crossed the Parallel on September 28; the Eighth Army followed in full force on October 9 and began a headlong pursuit of the fleeing North Koreans. In this so-called war of containment, it was MacArthur who had to be contained, but little effort was made to rein him in. He'd been right about Inchon, and his political masters had developed what Acheson called "an uneasy respect for the MacArthur mystique."

Now, with the McCarthyites seeing communists under every bed and the Cold War accelerating, especially in the United States, the war in Korea had taken on the character of a crusade—at least in the minds of MacArthur and his supporters.

At lunch in Tokyo with MacArthur, his wife, and a small group of officers, Captain Jeffry Brock, the "galloping ghost of the Korean coast," tackled the supreme commander on the subject of the United Nations' war aims. Brock was commander of the task force of Canadian destroyers and minesweepers that had supported the Americans during the Inchon landing. Now here he was, suggesting to a supreme commander who brooked little opposition that in his personal view Canada would consider the UN action accomplished, now that the invaders had been expelled from South Korea. Wouldn't it be better, he argued, to halt the advance in the narrow neck of the peninsula, i.e., at the 38th Parallel?

One can imagine MacArthur's minions shifting in their seats. One argued with the supreme commander at one's peril. But Brock was a Canadian—that allowed him some leeway—and MacArthur was luxuriating in the warmth of victory and the blind certitude of his sacred mission. He told the Canadian that there was nothing to worry about— not a chance of the Chinese interfering. Brock knew better, and said so. From the deck of his leading destroyer, *Cayuga*, at the mouth of the Yalu River, he had seen Chinese troops assembling. But MacArthur was certain that China would not intervene. The United Nations had complete air supremacy: why would the Chinese chance an intervention? If they did, they would achieve nothing. Brock was not convinced. The Chinese would arrive armed with sticks and brooms if necessary, he argued. The supreme commander didn't budge. "Brock," he said, gesturing with his fist, "I have them in the palm of my hand. The palm of my hand!" When Brock asked what would happen if the Russians offered to give Mao Zedong air support, MacArthur cast the suggestion aside. "They won't do it," he said, raising his fist again. "I have complete air and sea superiority. I have them in the palm of my hand!"

All that fall the Chinese themselves had tried to make it clear that the new object of the war—the conquest and political reorganization of Korea—was unacceptable. On September 25 their acting chief of staff told the Indian ambassador to Beijing that they "did not intend to sit back with folded hands and let the Americans come up to their border." These and similar comments were dismissed in the West as a form of communist propaganda. Cold War paranoia had blinded the Americans, who felt that the neutral Indians were far too cozy with the Chinese. Thus, on October 3, a warning by Chou En-lai, the Chinese premier, that his country would intervene if the Americans crossed the Parallel was not taken seriously. On October 10, the day after American troops entered North Korea, Chou, who was also minister of foreign affairs, declared unequivocally that his people could not "stand idly by" and that this new invasion represented "a dangerous trend toward extending the war." Thousands of Chinese soldiers, described as "volunteers" by their government, had already entered North Korea, in the hope of avoiding an all-out war. But the U.S. Central Intelligence Agency was still arguing on October 12 that there was no convincing evidence that the Chinese planned to resort to full-scale intervention.

By October 25, 130,000 Chinese soldiers and porters had crossed the Yalu River by night and established a bridgehead in North Korea. So carefully were they camouflaged, and so blind was MacArthur's intelligence staff to the possibility, that nobody twigged.

Once again in this yo-yo war, the situation was reversed because of MacArthur's overweening arrogance. The Inchon landing, instead of ending the war, had started it all over again. The plan to destroy the North Korean army and reunite the two countries was now consigned to the scrap heap. How could communism be contained if Chinese troops in their thousands thrust their way back down the peninsula? As Lester Pearson told a radio audience, there wasn't much use trying to establish a united and free Korea if that policy carried "the slightest menace to Korea's neighbours." The Canadians and the British saw the intervention as a nationalist move to prevent the Americans from crossing the border into Chinese territory. The Americans, immersed in Cold War philosophy, believed that Russia was behind the invasion as part of its push for world domination.

In the first few days the Chinese attacked and bested the ROK forces and badly mauled the American 8th Cavalry. MacArthur was not concerned, especially when the Chinese unaccountably broke off the engagement. Had they shot their bolt, as the general believed? Or were they returning to traditional tactics that went back to the days of Genghis Khan—to withdraw slowly, lull the enemy into complacency, then turn about and mount a savage counterattack?

After a nineteen-day pause that confirmed the general in his flawed conviction, MacArthur launched, on November 24, a final offensive to win the war. Now events began to accelerate. Two days later the Chinese responded by routing the Americans and the South Koreans, driving them back pell-mell to the 38th Parallel. Caught by surprise and unnerved by unfamiliar tactics and terrain, the American army broke in the face of the Chinese onslaught in what the GIs called "bug-out fever"—one of the most humiliating defeats in American history. On December 15, General Walton Walker's Eighth Army crossed back over the 38th Parallel, still moving south—a retreat of 120 miles in just ten days. In the bitter words of one infantry colonel, it was "a sight that hasn't been seen . . . the men of a whole United States Army fleeing from a battlefield, abandoning their wounded, running for their lives."

The debacle slowed down at the Han River, where Walker decided to make a stand defending the river. Now every piece of equipment and every man would be needed, including the half-trained PPCLI who were at sea en route to Korea and the remainder of the unwanted Canadian brigade still training at Fort Lewis, Washington. The Princess Pats had embarked from Seattle on November 25, expecting to take part in MacArthur's final offensive. After a twenty-three-day journey to Yokohama and on to Pusan, the Canadians were confronted with what MacArthur correctly called "an entirely new war." While they were in transit, the character of the Korean conflict had effectively been reversed. Rather than joining a gung-ho American assault on enemy territory, the PPCLI were expected to shore up an inglorious retreat.

By the time they reached Pusan, they were ill-prepared for battle. Like the Canadians sent to Hong Kong, they couldn't be trained aboard a tossing troopship. Many were not only out of shape but also hungry because the American troops on board had been messed first. Corporal George Cook was one who remembered an instance when a dinner of spaghetti and meatballs was reduced by the end of the line to little more than a few pots of plain pasta.

As the Canadians moved down the gangway of their vessel, the *Private Joe P. Martinez*, they were greeted by a covey of Korean girls waving tattered flags and by a band playing a popular song of the day, "If I Knew You Were Coming I'd Have Baked a Cake." The warmth of the welcome was soon dissipated when an Eighth Army officer showed up to inform Lieutenant-Colonel Stone that the token force, shipped to Korea to "show the flag" and perform occupation duties, would be in the front line in just three days.

Stone objected. He had no intention of throwing half-trained troops into action "before they knew what to do once they got there." But the more he objected the more insistent the American became. "I told him my men were not trained," Stone recalled, "and he replied that we had come to fight not to train."

Once again the memory of Hong Kong was invoked. According to his own account, Stone commandeered an airplane and flew to Seoul, where General Walker was already planning to put the Canadians into battle as part of the British 29th Brigade. Walker's chief of staff was not sympathetic. The Canadian training, he pointed out, compared favourably with that of many of the troops already in combat. But Stone had the final word in the form of a directive. "In the event that operations are in progress when you arrive in Korea, you are not to engage in such operations except in self-defence until you have completed the training of your command and are satisfied that your unit is fit for operations. This restriction in your employment has been communicated to the Commander, United Nations Forces, Korea."

Walker had not seen the directive, but when he was shown it, he backed off, saying he didn't want to cause any political trouble. Stone returned to Pusan with the promise that arrangements would be made for the battalion to complete its training out of the battle zone. Walker gave Stone eight weeks to whip his men into shape.

On New Year's Day, 1951, the Chinese launched a new offensive, recapturing both Seoul and Inchon and driving south down the peninsula at a cost to the 29th Brigade of 230 casualties. But this time history did not repeat itself. Thanks to Big Jim Stone's dogged initiative, an untrained and poorly equipped contingent of Canadian troops had not been led to the slaughter. Ottawa, in framing its instructions to prevent another Hong Kong, had chosen the right man to carry them out.

With the American Eighth on the verge of collapse, morale was at a new low and defeatism was in the air. A secret report to his chiefs of staff by the British general, Leslie Mansergh, described the GIs' training as "quite unsuited to that type of country or war and, in spite of lessons learnt, they will not get clear of their vehicles." The Americans, he pointed out, had never studied or been taught defence. Instead they relied on "mechanized and mechanical advances at great speed." Again, the military assistant to the British ambassador had reported in December that "the U.S. Army is still roadbound." The British and Canadians had absorbed the lessons of Exercise Spartan and Normandy: stay off the roads; keep to the high ground. Stone understood that and set about training his men to scale the toughest hills in the training area. Walker did not. He was primarily a tank man, not an infantry soldier.

Suddenly the whole complexion of the war changed. Two days after Stone left Seoul, Walker was tragically killed when his Jeep struck an ROK truck. He was replaced by Matthew Bunker Ridgway, a thirty-six-year-old veteran—ruthless, decisive, bold, intelligent, and considered one of the outstanding American soldiers of the Global War. Like Montgomery and Patton, Ridgway had flair; on his shoulder straps he habitually wore two live grenades that became as much a trademark as Patton's ivory-handled pistols, Montgomery's two-badged beret, and MacArthur's corncob pipe. To one American battalion commander, it was "magic" the way Ridgway took a defeated army and turned it around. He was a breath of fresh air, the sort of showman his army desperately needed. He not only raised its sagging morale but he also got the troops off the roads and taught them to seize the high ground—ridges so steep, hills so precipitous that the padre of the PPCLI had to omit from church service that fine old hymn "Unto the Hills Around Do I Lift Up My Longing Eyes."

The PPCLI's training took place at Miryang, fifty miles north of Pusan. On its first climb, half the battalion was forced to fall back exhausted. Stone was a hard taskmaster, cursed, feared, and eventually praised by his men. He instituted a tough program stressing hard physical exercise, the tactics required in this strange, mountainous land, where the key unit was not the battalion but the platoon and its three ten-man sections.

To instill discipline, Stone built a detention camp—"Stone's Stockade"—a large tent surrounded by sixteen strands of barbed wire, where malcontents could be taught to obey orders. It was, in Stone's estimation, "the toughest field punishment camp since Admiral Nelson." Stone made it so harsh "that if a man lasted two days in there he pleaded to get out." If the commander felt the soldier had learned his lesson in that time, however, he let him go. Prisoners in the stockade had their heads shaved and a yellow circle painted on their fatigues. There was no rest. They were forced to run obstacle courses up and down hills, through muddy water, and under barbed wire with a full pack on their backs. They were not allowed to sit down even to eat but munched their rations while running on the spot, nor were they given time to relieve themselves.

If a man committed a military crime, such as being Absent Without Leave, Stone refused to accept any excuse. In one remarkable instance, two soldiers in training managed to leave the camp and hitchhike to the front lines, where they joined a U.S. unit in action. One was actually awarded a Silver Star during his service. But when the pair returned to Miryang three days later, Stone, after congratulating them, sentenced them to the stockade.

Stone's tough regime separated the potentially fit from the permanently unfit. "Bad legs, wheezy lungs, and weak hearts were exposed." The battalion was a victim of the hasty recruiting the previous summer and fall. At Miryang, Stone weeded out sixty "non-battle casualties"— "scruff" as he called them, "sorry specimens of manhood"—suffering from complaints that ranged from broken eardrums to flat feet, from chronic bronchitis to hypertension. One man who had evaded the "unfit for battle" category was sent home when he was caught not firing his weapon. Only then was it revealed that he had a glass eye. He had made it through the medical in Canada by holding first his left hand over his eye and then his right hand in order to read the charts.

In March, after the battalion got into action, eighty-six more "non-battle" casualties were shipped out. The problem was not confined to the PPCLI. By February, more than a thousand men had been discharged from the Special Force as "unlikely to become efficient," a costly and embarrassing statistic that demonstrated Canada's unseemly panic to rush men into the Korean maelstrom. As Stone dryly put it in his report to the Canadian general staff, "Canada is the place to discover weaknesses in the individual, not a battle theatre."

But not all of Stone's "scruff" were weeded out before the battalion finally came into action on February 21, as the members of No. 1 Section, No. 4 Platoon, Baker Company, were to discover. Stone had been able to whip his battalion into shape in six weeks, a fortnight shorter than the eight he'd been allowed. The Canadians joined the 27th British Commonwealth Brigade at the front on February 19. There, after advancing on Hill 404, they were shaken by a grisly spectacle: sixty-five American corpses, slaughtered by bullet and bayonet the previous night as they slept in their sleeping bags. They hadn't dug in or even posted sentries, providing a stark lesson to Stone's unbloodied troops, who from that night on dispensed with their sleeping bags and slept in their boots.

With little delay the men of No. 4 Platoon became the first Canadians to come under attack. The shots came high—a burst of machine-gun fire from the apparently empty hills, shaking the needles from the squat pines and cracking over the heads of No. 1 Section. During training, a self-assured young reinforcement, Alex Fairfield,* had been boasting to his new comrades that they had nothing to worry about. "All you have to do is lie back and figure where the firing is coming from; then you fire back," he'd say confidently. Now, facing the real thing, white and nervous, he was shouting: "Where's our support? Where's our support?" The section leader, Kerry Dunphy, had, in the interests of section morale, promised $5 to the first man to kill a Chinese. Now, as the men began to inch forward, Fairfield won the award.

He moved up the trail, got down on one knee, carefully brought his rifle to his shoulder, practised breath control as he'd been taught, got three shots off, and knocked over an enemy sniper at one hundred yards. But then a weird thing happened. Fairfield stood up. His whole demeanour changed. Holding his rifle over his head, he began to run back through the trees, screaming and shouting, his pack and weapon catching on the branches. "I gotta see the major!" he cried out. "I'm in no shape for this! I gotta see somebody!" And that was the last the section saw of Fairfield, who was shipped back to Canada as unstable.

* The name but not the action is fictitious.

To a war correspondent like me, travelling comfortably by Jeep down *The* the broad Han Valley in the spring of 1951, with the soft mists rising *ravaged* from the river and the hillsides ablaze with azaleas and rhododendrons, *land* Korea was truly the "Land of the Morning Calm." But to the troops, toiling up those monotonous ridges—identical volcanic spines stretching off endlessly in every direction toward the horizon—this luckless nation was close to a living hell. No one can ever forget the stench that rose from the rice paddies, an all-pervading stink that assailed the nostrils day and night, wafting through city and village, plot and pasture, giving the impression that the country was one vast latrine. And so it was, for this assault on the senses rose from the piles of human ordure— night soil, to use the euphemism—dumped as fertilizer into the sinuous paddies that wound round the contours of the hillsides. Here were the breeding places of the venomous ants whose bites led to dangerous infections, and the round worms, some a foot long, that lived in the human intestine and were said to affect as much as 90 percent of the population.

And the rats!—so big, in one soldier's description, "that it would make you think they were wearing combat boots." They were everywhere: so many, one Canadian recalled, "that I used to think that all the rats in Asia came down to Korea because there was a war on. They were in our supplies, in our bunkers, in our beds, and in our dreams. But then you'd waken and the dream would be real. A half-dozen beady eyes would be staring at you." The mites that lived on the rats transferred to the soldiers, biting them on the wrists and neck and causing hemorrhagic (Song) fever. A disease for which there was no cure, it made the blood clot, eventually clogging the liver and causing victims to die from their own bodily poisons.

During the monsoon season, the humidity caused a number of skin conditions including ringworm, which could be treated by daubing the infected parts with fountain-pen ink, an old remedy that discoloured shirts and trousers. More than one unfortunate soldier suffered from blood poisoning brought on by cuts and scratches sustained when he went to ground during a bombardment and landed on bits of rusted barbed wire.

Rats, lice, mites, and barbed wire were no strangers to battlefields. Canadians had suffered from them in previous wars, but in previous wars the soldiers had a cause, or thought they had. What was the cause in South Korea? Democracy? Freedom? Ludicrous notions. Life under the newly propped-up president, Syngman Rhee, the unpopular dictator of a corrupt regime, could hardly be said to be democratic. The soldiers who observed first-hand the brutality of his army and his police force bullies could hardly be expected to swallow the propaganda that this was a fight for freedom or even that it was a battle against the Soviet menace. To the troops, it was a civil war between "the gooks," as they were called.

I spent some time with Corporal Dunphy and his section, ten men who were as cynical as their American counterparts about the war. Dunphy, the only man with a university education, thought he knew what he was fighting for when he joined up. "I thought it was a great thing that the UN was sticking its neck out." But after a few weeks in Korea, his attitude changed. All the talk about "the liberty-loving Korean people" sickened him. "Maybe the guys on top really believe that. I guess that Triggie Lie comes over and says, 'How're things going here?' and old Siggie Rhee says, 'Well, we desire freedom' and all that business. But what the hell have they got to gain from freedom as long as they've got their rice? It seems that you've got to take somebody's word for it that the Korean people are 'liberty loving.' I haven't met a gook yet who was."

To the UN troops, every Korean was a gook, whether he came from the North or the South. The soldiers from the North were despised; so were their South Korean counterparts, who were the first to flee when the Chinese arrived. There was no hatred for these new combatants, who were universally known as "chinks" and were rather admired because they suffered the same hardships even more resolutely than their UN opponents.

552

With the help of interpreters and U.S. Army Intelligence records at a prisoner-of-war camp in Pusan, I built up a picture of a typical Chinese soldier—a thirty-year-old peasant, married, with two children, who would rather be back in his native village than slogging through Korea's sticky clay. Unable to read or write, he was often confused by the lectures he received on politics. His main concerns were not with the coming world revolution or the imperialistic aggression of the bloody Wall Street bankers, or even the liberation of the Korean people, but with the simpler and more pressing business of getting two bowls of rice a day. He lived an austere and disciplined life, fraught with hardships that any Westerner would have found intolerable, but he did what he was told and, when ordered, would stay in his slit trench and fight to the end.

If they were prepared to fight to the death, it was partly because the Chinese propagandists told them that if they surrendered they would be beaten, questioned, and dismembered alive. But much of the political "indoctrination" failed to indoctrinate. Only about 10 percent were out-and-out Communists, though these were placed in key positions in their units. One Chinese prisoner, asked to explain the difference between communism and democracy, replied that "under communism you march all day and dig foxholes all night. Under democracy you ride in a Jeep and never dig at all."

Both the Chinese and the UN troops had one thing in common apart from the arduous marches and the vermin in the slit trenches: they knew nothing about the country in which they had been ordered to fight and very little about the people they were supposedly fighting for. I interviewed one Chinese prisoner, Wu, who was shipped off by train from Manchuria into an infantry division and had no idea he was in Korea until somebody finally told him. Later, when he got into action and saw the bodies, he was surprised to learn that he was fighting American soldiers. Nobody had told him about that, either.

Korea was truly a battlefield "where ignorant armies clash by night." In its headlong rush to follow the American lead and get into action as quickly as possible, the Canadian Army had made no effort to tell the

553

troops who signed up anything about the Koreans, their history, or their society. One Canadian on arriving at Pusan remarked with surprise that he thought he was going to a tropical country. "All the war films we had seen showed tropical country with guys walking through the jungle." He was speedily disabused of that fancy: the cold was so intense that the troops in training had to edge their way around a foot-high ridge of ice before they could reach the showers. Nor were the Canadians ever given a clear idea of why they were in Korea. Bob Perley, a Maloset Indian from New Brunswick, arrived with the PPCLI under the impression that he was fighting Chiang Kai-shek's army until somebody corrected him.

If the troops were confused, it was because their political and military leaders were themselves at odds about the war's aims. At first it had been a police action to roll the invaders back north of the 38th Parallel. Then it had been an all-out effort to drive all the way to the Manchurian border, destroy the North Korean army, and effectively unite the country—a fantasy exploded by the entry of the Chinese. By March, it dawned on the chief participants, who had never been in total agreement, that MacArthur was giving every indication of touching off a new world war.

With Ridgway's revitalized Eighth Army moving north to the Parallel again—Seoul was recaptured in mid-March—the supreme commander was ordering the bombing of bridges over the Yalu, urging "hot pursuit" of the Chinese beyond the Manchurian border, and pushing for the use of Chiang Kai-shek's forces to launch an attack on the Chinese mainland, a daydream that suggests the depths of MacArthur's fantasy world.

America's allies were horrified by the implications of this sabre rattling; so was the U.S. state department. On March 31, 1951, Canada spoke out through Lester Pearson. The United Nations, he told the Canadian Bar Association, "refuse to be stampeded into action, such as a massive attack toward the Manchurian border. That kind of talk," Pearson said, "only served to weaken the unity of action in Korea. The war ought to be contained and efforts made to negotiate an honourable peace."

What boggles the mind is how close the Americans came to using the atomic bomb in Korea. The current sentiment was that there was no nuclear threshold isolating atomic weapons from the more conventional armaments. The horrifying corollary of nuclear radiation was not really understood. From the outset of the war MacArthur and the joint chiefs had advocated the use of atomic weapons against enemy lines of communication. Following the devastating Chinese attacks in November 1950, Truman, at a press conference, had made it clear that the use of atomic weaponry was under "active consideration" and that the United States would take "whatever steps [are] necessary to meet the military situation," including the possible use of the Bomb.

Awash in Cold War propaganda, American public opinion began to demand that the atomic bomb be used if it would slow communist invasion. Four large veterans' organizations petitioned Truman to use "any means necessary" to halt the onslaught. MacArthur went further. On December 24 he prepared a list of "retaliation targets" requiring a total of *twenty-six* atomic bombs. What if Ridgway had not been able to hold back the Chinese tide and had faced the prospect of annihilation? At least one military analyst, Harry G. Summers, Jr., has suggested that in that case atomic weapons might well have been used.

Fortunately, Ridgway turned the war around. The police action was creaking along—but at what cost? I was in Seoul in 1951 after it was "liberated" for the fourth time. I described it that spring as "a carcass of a city," without electricity, without food, fuel, or running water— a city of 1.5 million reduced to one-tenth of its population. Most were crowded into the old market at the city's east gate, trying to sell everything they owned in return for the most valuable property of all: food. Seoul was a tragic symbol of MacArthur's foolhardy military ambitions. He had goaded the Chinese into war, and, by invitation, the Chinese had picked the country clean. They had looted Seoul of every grain of rice, every stick of fuel, every curtain and window blind, every piece of cloth, every blanket, all the silver, brass, and jewellery they could find, and left every automobile stripped and gutted.

What a bizarre sight it was to drive down those broad avenues and boulevards and encounter, at each intersection, an ROK policeman, immaculately uniformed, directing non-existent traffic, halting my Jeep, then waving me on as if we were both enmeshed in a rush-hour gridlock.

I was in the seaport of Pusan when Truman fired MacArthur after the general had once too often overstepped the bounds. The GIs who walked the streets that day, bewildered at what was for them an unexpected turn of events, were not angry at the general's dismissal—as a vocal section of the American public certainly was—only baffled. The politics of the Korean War was beyond them, and nobody in control had gone to the trouble of telling them what it was all about.

MacArthur was admired but not loved. The troops tended to refer to him as "Dugout Doug," an unfair reference to his abandonment of Bataan after Pearl Harbor in order to continue the fight from Australia. Yet, in a sense, the pejorative name applied; the Dai Ichi building in Tokyo was indeed his dugout, where, surrounded by sycophants who fed him flawed intelligence reports, he remained oblivious to events in a country he rarely visited.

Because of his insistence on winning an unwinnable war, Pusan had become a port bloated with refugees—300,000 of them to add to the normal population of 600,000. This was a city that had never had enough elbow room. It clung to its gummy red clay like a sailor to a mast, the roofs of its houses jostling each other, the narrow lanes cutting through them like ruts and often vanishing into a choppy sea of buildings. Now it had mushroomed into a vast refugee camp where one person in three had no home at all, save a cave in the hills or a paper shack on the ridges above.

One could not escape the tragic shacks of Pusan. They were clustered by the thousands along the water's edge and along the railway line. They hugged the craggy promontories in silent accusation. In one of these hovels, high above the city at the head of a broad tier of stone steps, I came upon a little widow of thirty-seven named Tak Sook Kyn. Her husband had vanished, and her two-year-old baby, whom she had carried on her back down the peninsula from North Korea, was dead of exposure and hunger. Now she and her family and relatives existed under conditions far worse than any suffered in the Canadian hobo jungles of the thirties. Their hovel was made entirely of cardboard squares cut from U.S. C-ration cartons, supported on a flimsy match-wood frame and covered with straw mats. Here, in a space seven feet long, five feet wide, and four and a half feet high, eight people lived, ate, and slept—Mrs. Tak, her two surviving daughters, her mother, her sister-in-law and her husband, and their two small boys.

When I first crouched through the opening and over the mud floor I was appalled. Here was a single shelf made from an old board, a string across a corner from which hung some tattered grey and mauve clothing, a pot embedded in baked clay that served as a stove, an old Canadian rye whisky bottle that did duty as a canteen, and at the door a neat row of little slippers.

How could people live like that, I asked myself. But when I heard Mrs. Tak's story, told in a soft, emotionless voice, the little shack took on a new and warmer dimension, and I came to understand why, after her long travail—balancing her meagre belongings on her head, goading her children on, shivering in the blizzards, scrabbling in the paddies for the remains of the rice crop to make a gruel—her spirits lifted when she first walked through that curtain door. Hungry, weary, she was close to the end of her tether. Yet, as she put it, her heart sang a little. For the first time in months she could pause in her weary peregrinations up and down that shattered peninsula. To a stranger from another world her situation might have seemed desperate. But to Mrs. Tak, her children, and her relatives, this was more than a refuge. At last she had found what she had longed for. It may not have been much, but to her it was everything. For now she had a place of her own, purchased for a few handfuls of hoarded rice. To her and her family, this impossible shelter was *home.*

4

"Be steady! For Canadians, the battle of Kap'yong was to the Korean War what
Kill, the battle of Paardeberg Drift was to the South African. Both were
and don't Canadian victories—two shining moments in otherwise murky con-
give way" flicts. It tells us a good deal about our change in attitude over half a
century that the first was greeted with scenes of wild enthusiasm in
Canada while in the spring of 1951, excitement was all but non-existent.
The battle was fought on April 24 and 25, and it is proper to recall that
the 2nd Battalion of the PPCLI, which held out against odds that were
at least three to one (some accounts put them far higher), became the
only Canadian battalion in history to be awarded the coveted U.S.
Presidential Citation.

As Jim Stone reported in his clipped, military style, "We were surrounded . . . our positions were infiltrated and subjected to heavy
attacks by a determined enemy at short range and in close country.
We stayed, fought, and withdrew on orders in soldierly fashion. This
in itself was unique in Korea, where 'bug out' was the accepted manner
of withdrawing." Stone didn't need to point out that most American
soldiers in Korea, except the Marines, were draftees; the Canadians
were all volunteers.

That April 23, the 27th British Commonwealth Brigade, of which
the PPCLI was a part, was in reserve, blocking the ancient invasion
route down the Kap'yong valley and into South Korea. Ridgway's
forces were stubbornly fighting their way back toward the 38th Parallel
when, on April 22, the Chinese launched their spring offensive—a
massive assault designed to punch a hole in the line, drive on to sur-
round and capture Seoul, and then advance through South Korea to
destroy the U.S. Eighth Army. They hit the weakest spot in the line,
striking with great force against the ROK units on the left and driving them south on the run. The British brigade, with the PPCLI and
the Royal Australian Regiment in the forefront supported by New
Zealand gunners, was moved up to fill the gap left by the fleeing
South Koreans.

The Kap'yong gateway was guarded by two irregular wooded hills. One, known as Hill 504 because it was 504 metres high, was held by the Australians on the east side of the river valley. Hill 677, on the west, was held by the Canadians. The enemy launched a set piece attack at 10 p.m. The Chinese crept through the underbrush of Hill 504 on padded feet, so cunningly camouflaged that it was difficult to detect their presence until they were almost on top of the defenders. Suddenly whistles blew, drums sounded, and the howling, yelling enemy descended in waves upon the Australians. So intense was the attack that a controlled withdrawal was impossible. The defenders were blown back by the tidal wave of the assault. Even battalion headquarters was overrun. The PPCLI were left in a critical position, all alone on their hill with no friendly troops on either flank.

Fortunately, Stone was a veteran of mountain warfare in Italy, and all his key officers were equally seasoned. From his vantage point he had been able to look down across the valley and witness the attack on the Australians. The enemy needed to take Hill 677, which still dominated the route to the south, and Stone with his practised eye could see that the next attack would be launched against his eastern slope. He ordered Baker Company to shift its position and to dig in to protect the back door of the battalion area, a move that probably saved his troops from disaster.

Once again the Chinese soldiers in their padded clothing launched their standard form of attack, blowing shrill whistles, sounding bugles, wailing like banshees to cow the enemy. The Canadians were not cowed: "Be steady! Kill, and don't give way," Stone had ordered. The Patricias were heavily outnumbered at this point—a division against a battalion—and once again the Chinese came in waves, fording the river, charging up the flanks of the eastern ridge again and again, as, again and again, the Canadians drove them off.

The situation was desperate, but there was worse to come. This savage battle was only a diversion for an even greater assault on the opposite side of Hill 677. It came at one in the morning of April 25. Trip wires laid by the Canadian pioneer platoon the previous day triggered a brilliant burst of light that exposed the attackers. So overwhelming was the Chinese onslaught that part of the defence perimeter began to fall into their hands. By three o'clock, No. 10 Platoon was cut off and No. 12 completely overrun. To the mind of Captain Wally Mills, the Dog Company commander, their only option was to pull out. Stone refused. "If we ever lose this hill, we lose it all," he said. Mills had one alternative—a dangerous one—to call down "friendly fire" on his own troops.

"Will you fire artillery right on top of my position?" he signalled Stone.

"Are your men dug in?" Stone asked.

Mills assured him they were, whereupon Stone told him to keep his head down and get ready. He got in touch with the New Zealand artillery and his own mortar company and told them to fire right into the wooded area where Dog Company's men crouched in their slit trenches. As Stone described Mills's ordeal, "We didn't have a single man wounded, but it certainly got rid of the Chinese around him."

But it did not stop them. They kept attacking in waves, clambering over the corpses of those who preceded them while the Pats held on. At last the attacks slowed, but now another problem faced the defenders: the regiment was completely surrounded. Its supply lines had been cut; the exhausted Canadians were running out of food, water, and ammunition, and they had no way of knowing how long the ordeal would continue.

At four o'clock Stone called Tokyo and asked for an air drop. To the battalion's relief, four big C-119s—Flying Boxcars—dropped everything he'd asked for, and so accurately that out of one hundred packages, only four landed outside the battalion-held position. Harley Welsh, helping to man an American .30 calibre machine gun and catching a brief nap while his partner kept watch, barely escaped being hit when one pallet of supplies bounced three feet from his post. "God," Welsh remembers, "if it had hit me I'd have been a pancake." For his comrades, it was, almost literally, manna from Heaven—"one of the most beautiful sights I can ever remember seeing," as one veteran of the battle remembered. "I was so hungry my stomach was in knots."

That was the one high note on which the battle finally ended. The Canadians' stubborn stand at Kap'yong may well have saved Seoul from another invasion. As it was, the centre of the UN line held, thanks not only to the Canadians but also to the Australians, who helped to blunt the original attack at fearful cost, and to the New Zealanders, who fired 14,500 artillery shells during the battle. At almost the same time, twenty-five miles farther west, the British 29th Infantry Brigade was fighting the bloody battle of the Imjin River, north of Seoul, against an equally determined Chinese advance. The British broke the attack but took a brutal beating. The Gloucestershire Regiment, cut off and isolated—most of the air drops fell outside their perimeter—was virtually wiped out. That tragedy dominated the world's front pages, overshadowing the Canadian victory, which had been won with far fewer casualties. But the PPCLI had their Presidential Citation and the first Chinese spring offensive had failed.

Meanwhile, the brigade force that had been training at Fort Lewis, Washington, had arrived in Korea. Hastily recruited in the summer of 1950 in the gloomy days of the Pusan perimeter, the brigade was a force whose presence after the Inchon landing seemed unnecessary until the Chinese entered the war. Then, once again, the pressure was on Canada. By February 1951, the Canadian government abandoned the wistful hope that the force might be switched to Europe as the country's contribution to NATO. Ottawa agreed that the remainder of Rockingham's 25th Infantry Brigade should "shortly proceed" to the Far East to join the 2nd PPCLIs. "Shortly" meant two months. The brigade left Seattle on April 19 and 21. By the time it reached Pusan during the first week in May, the situation again reversed itself.

The concept of winning and losing, as in a football game, was deeply embedded in the military consciousness, although, in truth, most wars have in the end been limited conflicts. This was true of Korea, where both sides had come to realize that they could not "win." The American public was turning against the war, and the Chinese were suffering appalling losses. They tried one last time in mid-May—the second

561

phase of their spring offensive. Again they cut a hole in the weakest section of the line; again the ROK army gave way. But even this preliminary success collapsed. On May 24 the Chinese were forced to pull back, having lost 17,000 men killed and 36,000 wounded. Three days later the untried soldiers of the 25th Canadian Infantry Brigade joined the UN forces making their second advance across the 38th Parallel since the Chinese had entered the war.

On May 28 the brigade fought its first battle when the Royal Canadian Regiment tried to take Kakhul-Bong—Hill 467—from whose dizzy pinnacle the Chinese defenders could look down on the main road and observe every movement of the attacking regiment. The RCRs took the neighbouring village of Chail-li and started to claw their way up the hill in the driving rain. Without an air strike or artillery cover to support them, they were forced to withdraw, having gained nothing at a cost of six dead and twenty-five wounded.

This was the first serious engagement involving the brigade and also the last of its kind. On June 5 the Chinese agreed to meet UN negotiators on the 38th Parallel. Three days later the opposing teams discussed terms for a ceasefire. The war seemed to be over, but of course it wasn't. As in South Africa, the fighting did not end; it was the tactics that changed.

5

The static war Peace at last! An unpopular war was about to end. The negotiations, it was expected, would take no more than six weeks. How starry-eyed it all seems in retrospect. In fact, the peace talks stretched out over two years and seventeen days and required 575 stony-faced meetings before a solution was finally reached. By that time the long-drawn-out arguments had gobbled up eighteen million words. And all during this weary process, men continued to fight and die in the forbidding hills of Korea. Far more soldiers—and far more Canadians—were killed after the armistice talks began at Kaesong than were killed in the mobile war of 1950–51.

562

For this was no longer a mobile war but a static one that harked back to the Great War, complete with barbed-wire entanglements, trenches, dugouts, a profusion of mines and heavy guns, and a no man's land through which, in the dark of the night, men with blackened faces moved stealthily on patrol in search of a kill. It was a war in which the opposing sides faced each other, a mile or so apart, each attempting, month after month, to gain some advantage—a hill, a ridge, a piece of muddy ground, a prisoner or two, a momentary edge that might make a difference as the talks droned on. This was not the kind of war that young Canadians, drilled in the tactics of fire and movement, had expected or been trained for. There would be no long marches now, no massive troop build-ups, no attempt to punch through enemy lines. And no victory.

The negotiations for an armistice broke down in August after each side accused the other of violating the ceasefire agreement. They resumed on October 25 and moved from the rubble of Kaesong to Panmunjom, eight miles to the west in neutral territory between the opposing armies and protected from attack at night by a giant searchlight.

To the Chinese, the truce negotiations meant very little. It is doubtful whether their troops were told the fight might end at any time. But a young Canadian trying to stay alive in what the Patricia's war diarist called a "twilight war" could not help but be haunted by the possibility that he might be the last man killed in Korea. The war was not going to end by military action but by political decisions. "I cannot avoid a tightening of the heart," wrote Captain Charly Forbes, commander of the mortar platoon of the Royal 22nd battalion, "at the thought that this night I could be killed and that tomorrow the war would end with a sudden armistice."

Captain Forbes made that comment as his battalion faced its toughest test on the nights of November 23 through 25, 1951. The Chinese leadership knew that their original plan to seize and unite the peninsula under Communist control had been frustrated, just as MacArthur's plan to unite it under Syngman Rhee had failed. Now their purpose was to gain as much advantage (that is, as much ground) as possible before the armistice was signed. The talks had no sooner begun than they launched a series of probing attacks across the neutral zone. Their main objective was a towering crag that overlooked the entire area, known to the Canadians as Hill 355 and to the Americans, more colourfully, as Little Gibraltar.

The American infantry had held the heights, but the force of the Chinese attack on November 23 threw them back. The Chinese now held Hill 355 and a second hill to the west, leaving the Canadians, who had moved into the saddle between, facing entrapment. This was the 2nd Battalion of the Royal 22nd, whose stubborn commander, Lieutenant-Colonel Jacques Dextraze, had no intention of retiring. "We're being attacked by a major Chinese force," he had told his battalion over the wireless. "We will hold our positions. We will fight to the end."

Hold it they did, at a cost of sixty-three casualties. In four days the mortar platoon fired 15,000 bombs, burning out the barrels of the 81-mm guns, which were glowing red hot until they became transparent. One infantry platoon hurled forty cases of grenades at the waves of attackers because rifle fire would have given away their position.

The battalion counted 742 Chinese corpses in the area but estimated enemy casualties as at least twice that number. The odds had seemed insurmountable. At one point a single platoon—No. 11—found itself under attack from three hundred Chinese who enjoyed a ten-to-one advantage. A "friendly" barrage of tank shells on its position saved it from annihilation. And one unit—Dog Company—endured a forty-eight-hour travail without sleep, exposed to the snow, to the freezing cold of the day until it was relieved by Baker Company. Charly Forbes thought the Van Doos should also have received a presidential citation, but none was forthcoming. Still, in the words of David Bercuson, the most recent military historian, it was "one of the finest defensive actions in the history of the Canadian army."

To most Canadians, names like Ortona and Dieppe, Vimy and Pretoria have a certain resonance. But there was little to differentiate one Korean hill from another and no way in that sea of craggy ridges to give it any personality. Every hill on the map had a number as an

564

indication of its height in metres, but with certain exceptions—Pork Chop Hill or Little Gibraltar, both named by the Americans—there was little to stir the emotions or raise the pulse in this numerical nomenclature. Who, today, save for a few veterans and a gaggle of military historians, remembers 355? The troops knew it well, for it was the scene of some of the heaviest fighting in the static war. Eleven months after the Van Doos clung to it—with Dextraze's words "no withdrawal, no platoons overrun, no panic" ringing in their ears—it was the turn of their sister unit, the 2nd Battalion of the Royal Canadian Regiment, on October 23, 1952. Again they held Hill 355 against some fifteen hundred Chinese at a cost of sixty-seven casualties, four more than the French Canadians had suffered.

The Chinese tried to demoralize their opponents by using words as well as guns, broadcasting propaganda over loudspeakers, always accurately identifying the units opposite them, and often using seductive feminine voices to suggest that the war was not really a Canadian concern. On December 14, 1951, three weeks after the Van Doos' stubborn stand at Hill 355, they tried a different tack, placing piles of Christmas stockings at the Pats' Baker Company outposts. These were stuffed with handkerchiefs with communist slogans, peace dove pins, cigarette holders, and plastic finger rings. That same night a Korean boy appeared at Charley Company, laden with similar gifts and carrying a "Signature Book for Demanding Peace and Stopping War." All this effort proved as futile as the UN's attempts to subvert the enemy with showers of leaflets.

As the negotiations continued at Panmunjom, the so-called police action began to resemble Paul Fussell's "troglodyte war." Because the Americans had overwhelming air power, the Chinese lived like moles in a maze of tunnels and dugouts held up with wooden pillars, as in mine shafts. The Canadians lived and slept in bunkers dug into the walls of their trenches. These had begun as slit trenches but as the static war dragged on became more sophisticated. The larger command post bunkers were solidly built with a log framework, layers of sandbags, corrugated metal, waterproofing, and at least five feet of rock and dirt on top to provide protection from the constant enemy shellfire. The smaller bunkers for three or four men were simply covered holes, constantly rebuilt and repaired, especially during the typhoon season when a single storm raging far out in the China Sea could send 100 m.p.h. winds and driving rain, enough to wipe out all the platoon bunkers and bury the inmates in a load of sandbags and debris when the roofs caved in.

Serving in such conditions was so hazardous to morale that troops had to be relieved after a year of service. The Americans rotated their troops individually, but Guy Simonds, chief of the general staff, succeeded in having the Canadian forces rotated by units so that, for example, the 2nd PPCLIs were replaced by 1st Battalion, and a year later 1st Battalion was sent home and replaced by 3rd. This was a welcome change from the two world wars in which some men had remained overseas for years.

In the Korean War there were many echoes of past conflicts. Lord Alexander, governor general of Canada and former field marshal, visited Korea during these months and was immediately reminded of the Great War battlefield at Ypres. Jim Stone's memory harked back to the mountains of Italy in the Global War. Comparisons with the South African battles were also invoked. But in other respects, the Korean War was unlike any other war of modern times. The stalemate in Korea, as Bercuson has pointed out, was not the result of a balance of forces or an Allied inability to manoeuvre in the face of a wall of defensive fire, as in the Great War. It was, instead, the result of a political decision.

It was a war in which platoons fought in isolation. To Robert Peacock, a platoon commander with the PPCLI, it was "very personal and localized." He saw little of his fellow officers and encountered the regimental sergeant major only once in his entire time with the battalion. His platoon operated on its own, assigned, as were the others, to one area of the forward line remote from the rest of the battalion and even its headquarters. As such "there was an awful temptation to develop an insularity, which could be damaging to unit morale."

566

It was also a war in which the aggressive spirit was downplayed during the static period. No brigade commander could launch an offensive that involved more than one platoon. Thus, it was not possible to test men in battle or to estimate the toughness of the enemy. One Canadian observer, Captain J.R. Madden, made that clear in his report on the front line positions. "Company after company occupied the same hills, lived in the same bunkers and fought from the same trenches. A company commander was called upon to display little initiative. As long as he insisted upon the observance of certain fundamental principles he was safe."

All wars have their long, boring hours between brief, violent bouts of action. Most of the period at the front is spent digging and waiting. There comes a time, especially in a static war, when men grow stale from too much inactivity. Civilians have always wondered, as they did during and after the Great War, how, when the orders were given, soldiers could climb so eagerly up and over the parapet in the face of a devastating enemy barrage. In fact, as many have explained, after a long period of confinement in the trenches, thousands actually experienced a sense of relief when they went over the top. But in Korea there was no change of scenery, or of personnel, or even of conversation or banter. The only breaks in the monotony were the endless patrols into no man's land.

This had become a war of constant patrols, a technique that went back to the days of 1914–18 and one in which the Canadians of the early fifties had received no training. Patrolling required unfamiliar skills involving stealth, hand-to-hand combat, night vision, camouflage. The new arrivals had to learn these tactics on the spot and at considerable cost. As the official history of the PPCLI explains, "there was no such thing as an all-purpose patrol; patrolling had become a special craft." There were standing patrols that guarded specific areas of defence, fighting patrols that were raiding parties, reconnaissance patrols to collect information and identify prisoners, roving patrols that were sent looking for trouble in designated areas, and, finally, nuisance patrols consisting of a handful of scouts and snipers whose job was to make noise and seduce the enemy into a chase.

That the cost could be high was soon clear to the fresh 1st Battalion of the Patricias after the 2nd Battalion was rotated home. On one freezing, dark night in January 1952, a patrol from A Company had completed its mission and was working its way home when it strayed on to a protective minefield. One man was injured and a stretcher party was sent out to bring him back. In trying to remove him, the stretcher party tripped a second mine, killing both the injured man and one of the rescuers and seriously wounding four others. That same night, a vehicle at the rear of the Canadian position was ambushed. Another patrol hurried to the spot, only to discover too late that the Chinese had booby-trapped the vehicle, causing four more casualties. As the PPCLI history remarks, "There were few tricks of the trade that the Communists overlooked."

Did all this patrolling activity, which contributed to the mounting casualty rate in Korea, really make sense? The Americans certainly thought so; the 1st Corps, to which the Commonwealth Brigade reported, insisted that each forward unit must dispatch a strong fighting patrol against known enemy positions and that at least one enemy prisoner should be taken every three days. Major General A.J.H. Cassels, the Commonwealth Division's commander, challenged the wisdom of this rigid policy. The American high command might want to keep their own men on their toes in this way—that was up to them—but for Commonwealth troops he felt obliged to balance the value of such operations against their cost. As Cassels pointed out, "The Chinese knew what was going on and simply laid back, waiting for their enemies, and took toll of them." One American division had lost between 2,000 and 3,000 men in such futile encounters. Nor did Cassels feel that prisoners were worth the price of capturing them. Chinese manpower was inexhaustible and the prisoners' value to intelligence "was almost nil."

Cassells therefore reduced the frequency of such raids. In May, the Canadians carried out 484 patrols, but of these only 48 were ambush patrols, 20 fighting patrols, and 2 reconnaissance patrols. The Great

War had taught the British some lessons. Perhaps they remembered that Arthur Currie, who opposed the Canadian habit of sending out large fighting patrols, was vindicated when the 4th Division was weakened just before Vimy as a result of a patrol that failed.

But the patrolling did not end. More than a year later, on May 2, 1953, the newly arrived 3rd Battalion of the RCRs, which had been in the line for less than a fortnight, suffered devastating losses when a company fighting patrol ran up against a battalion-sized Chinese force in the neutral zone. Able Company was badly mauled, and when Charley Company dispatched its standing patrol to aid the survivors, it too was shattered. The Chinese had reached the RCR's forward trenches before they were driven back again by friendly fire called down upon the survivors. This was one of the bloodiest encounters of the static war, with two officers and twenty-three men killed, twenty-seven more wounded, and one officer and seven men missing.

For the Canadians, it was also the last. Patrols could not win the static war. The bitter truth was that peace would come only when the Chinese decided that it made sense. The Americans tried everything, from their aggressive and costly program of fighting patrols to an operation code-named Snare. This goofy plan, which seems to have been designed by a lunatic at Eighth Army headquarters, was intended to fool the Chinese into thinking "the UN had folded its tents and silently stolen away" (in the sarcastic words of the RCR's official historian). For six days not a shot was to be fired along the lines, no movement in daytime, no odd noises at night. Would the Chinese be fooled by such tactics? Cassels, who considered it a "hare-brained scheme," thought not. It would only encourage the enemy to take liberties.

He was quite right. The Chinese began to appear on the skyline immediately, digging into the forward slopes and conducting themselves with "exasperating freedom," as the Patricias' diary put it. "On the seventh day our guns suddenly blasted out with the air of a man in a terrible temper who could contain himself no longer." The Chinese troops who had been cavorting on the slopes dived for shelter and stayed there "five hundred yards closer to us."

As the months dragged on into years, an atmosphere of compla-cency, sloth, and sloppiness was apparent on some patrols: men going out in trousers that, through regular scrubbing, had been bleached almost white and loomed out of the darkness like neon signs; men lighting cigarettes during an ambush; men shouting and joking while recon-noitring an enemy position. This slackness stemmed from the political decision to soft-pedal the war because of the fear of starting it up all over again.

As always in war, the elders made the decisions and the young men died. The peace talks moved in fits and starts. Begun in June 1951, sus-pended in August, resumed in October at Panmunjom, they were again abandoned a year later. When the two sides first met, 111 Canadians had died in Korea. In the static war that followed, 200 more would be sacrificed. Ridgway's pressure had originally forced the Chinese to the table. Would an additional thrust north, as some argued, lead them to an earlier agreement? Perhaps, but at what cost to the nation's youth?

This was very much a young man's war. Bob Peacock, the PPCLI platoon leader, described himself as "an old man of twenty-three." His men averaged between nineteen and twenty. One was seventeen; the "grandfather of the platoon" was twenty-eight. What were they sacri-ficing their lives for? "No one I can remember talked about the ideals of the United Nations or other lofty reasons for serving in the war," Peacock wrote. "To some, it was just a job, but in most cases it was the 'great adventure' with the individual out to prove himself before getting on with other things in life."

A great adventure in which nobody expected to be killed—a "sit tight and stay safe" war fought by men who had enlisted for a year and knew that if they stayed alive for that time they would be sent home. No gallant advances here, no heroic last stands, no unnecessary sacrifice, and very little propaganda about saving the free world. The free world, indeed, was so weary of the war that the troops in Korea began to fear people back home had forgotten them. On October 5, 1951, a Gallup poll in the United States reported that 67 percent of its respondents agreed that this was "an utterly useless war." At one point, Hal Straight, the unorthodox managing editor of the Vancouver *Sun*, decided to test reader interest in the war. He ran the same Canadian Press report from Korea on the front page for three days in succession. Only three readers spotted and commented on the repetition.

The early enthusiasm had vanished. At the beginning of 1952 Rockingham's brigade was under strength by a total of four hundred men, and the flood of volunteers had slowed to a trickle. Korea had drained the Canadian army of both leaders and equipment. The 3rd PPCLI Battalion, detailed to train reinforcements for its sister battalion in Korea, didn't have enough qualified platoon leaders to do the job. As Chris Snider, newly graduated from officers' school, discovered, "almost all those individuals were in Korea, thus, almost without exception, each of us a novice was assigned to a platoon as its commander and left to sink or swim."

The battalion was plagued by a shortage of vehicles, ammunition, even uniforms. Snider found that the best the new arrivals could get was mechanics' overalls with whatever web equipment was available. "It was not uncommon to see twenty shades of colour and style on the weekly battalion parade." Departing draftees often had to remove equipment from soldiers under training. "At times one would see recruits . . . wearing a mixture of civilian clothing with whatever military kit was available."

When the new battalions of the three regiments—PPCLI, RCR, and Royal 22nd—reached Korea, they had to be outfitted with a mixture of British and American equipment, boots, and parkas, some of which turned out to be more suitable than the Canadian. The new arrivals replaced the old combatants between late fall 1952 and spring 1953. Coincidentally, the interminable Panmunjom talks had broken down during the same period from October 8 to April 26. The negotiators stopped negotiating, but the guns kept firing.

By this time the soldiers of the second battalions were back in civilian life, having served their original eighteen months, while the veterans of the first battalions—the original Permanent Force units—had already bidden Korea goodbye and also good riddance after a year. It was a period marked by two significant events: the election of General Dwight Eisenhower to the U.S. presidency and the death of Joseph Stalin. "I shall go to Korea," Eisenhower had declared during the 1952 campaign. The war-weary Americans, all agog, propelled him into office, and off he went for a three-day visit that did little to end the war but boosted civilian morale. After the election, the aging MacArthur came out of the shadows with his own solution. If the Russians wouldn't go for the unification of Korea, he told his colleague Ike, the Americans should clear the country of enemy forces by atomic bombing of their military concentrations and installations in North Korea. That, MacArthur advised, plunging deeper into his dream world, should be accompanied by the sowing of radioactive materials to close enemy supply lines north of the Yalu. The chiefs of staff followed up by recommending that dramatic surprise attacks on China and Manchuria, using nuclear weapons, be considered—another "day of infamy." Even Ike himself and his belligerent secretary of state, John Foster Dulles, seemed to go along with this chilling proposal, agreeing that the taboo surrounding the use of nuclear weapons would have to be destroyed.

Was this mere bluff to frighten the Chinese into returning to the table? Would the popular general have risked worldwide opprobrium had the enemy turned savage and tried to thrust their way back down the peninsula? We will never know. Certainly, with Stalin's death in March 1953 making the enemy less rigid, with the Americans rattling the nuclear sabre, and with the Chinese having squeezed the last drop of propaganda advantage out of the long and tedious impasse, both sides had every reason to bring the war to an end. Suddenly the wearying squabble about what to do with the thousands of prisoners in UN detention was solved. A Neutral Nations Repatriation Commission would decide who would stay in South Korea and who would be allowed to return home. In April, Operation Little Switch had seen an exchange of wounded and ill prisoners. On August 5, in Operation Big Switch, some 75,000 Communist prisoners (of whom fewer than 6,000 were Chinese) were sent north, while nearly 13,000 Chinese and North Koreans opposed to Communism, and Americans (and 32 Canadians) were sent south. The repatriation commission was left to decide the fate of more than 22,000 Communist soldiers, of whom all but 137 agreed to repatriation; the remainder opted for resettlement in South Korea and Formosa.

Peace was at hand, but the guns roared on until the last moment. In the final two months of the static war, the UN gunners flung 4.5 million shells at the Chinese, who answered back with 1.5 million. Small wonder that Robert Peacock of the PPCLI felt edgy. Like so many others, he did not want to be the last casualty of the war. When the armistice was at last signed on July 27, Peacock found himself back on Hill 355, approximately where the regiment had started out two years, two weeks, and three days before when the peace talks began at Panmunjom.

There were still a few air strikes that morning and some limited shelling, but at ten o'clock, the appointed hour, an uneasy quiet fell over the front lines. Peacock and the others emerged from their trenches and looked out over the former no man's land to find the hills and ridges covered by a human sea of Chinese soldiers, all waving flags and banners and calling out messages of brotherly love over loudspeakers, asking the UN troops to cross over to meet them. "The psychological effect of seeing the masses of Chinese coming out of their trenches and dugouts into the open is one which no one who was there will ever forget," Peacock wrote.

The Canadian troops were dumbfounded by the extraordinary numbers, which exceeded the UN forces by a ratio of four or five to one. Chris Snider, the platoon commander with the 3rd PPCLI, explained to his men that these masses were a propaganda ploy, since there wasn't enough room for them all in the tunnels in the Chinese defence works known to exist. The Chinese had brought forward their reserves for the display and lit huge bonfires in celebration.

Peacock, who through various circumstances had served longer than his year in Korea, managed to get shipped back to Canada the next day. His fellow soldiers in the PPCLI had to wait until October; the other two battalions left the following spring.

The welcome was, to put it mildly, subdued. More than one historian of the Korean affair has called it Canada's forgotten war. Ted Barris, in *Deadlock in Korea*, refers to it as "The War That Wasn't," and tells the story of Don Leier, a Saskatchewan farm boy who served with the 37th Field Ambulance, Royal Canadian Army Medical Corps, north of the 38th Parallel. In the early 1960s, back home in Saskatoon, Leier went to a veterans' loan office to get a down payment for his first house, which many Global War veterans were receiving at the time. He was flatly refused. "Korea was no war, just a police action," he was told. "

Canadians like Leier had taken part in the first and, one hopes, last of the serious post-nuclear wars. By its end the nation had sent 21,940 fighting men and women to the war zone. Of these, 312 died or were killed in action—a comparatively small price to pay for the nation's plunge into the maelstrom, but more than enough.

The United States paid a staggering bill in blood; but then, it was their war. They sent 1,319,000 troops to the Korean theatre of whom 33,629 were killed and another 105,768 wounded. Their allies suffered 3,063 killed.

The Asians took the worst beating; 844,000 South Korean soldiers were casualties, and half these were fatal. The Chinese and the North Koreans lost an estimated 1.5 million. We have no idea how many Korean civilians on both sides of the famous Parallel were killed, mutilated, or starved or uprooted and driven from their villages and homes, but the number must be astronomical. These were the real victims of an unwanted civil war that went on too long and solved very little.

It was the treatment of the "gooks" that bothered me during my days of witness in that sad and wasted land. What the hell are we doing here, I asked myself. It was the same question the soldiers asked that no one in authority bothered to answer. When I returned to Canada in the early summer of 1951, I tried to put some of these vagrant thoughts into words:

What have we done in Korea that is positive? Sure, we're winning the old-fashioned war of brawn. But how about the newfangled war for men's minds? Have our actions in Korea

574

made more friends for the Western world? Have we been able to convince the Koreans themselves that the phrase "our way of life" is something more than a slogan? Have we succeeded in selling our brand of democracy to this proud but unhappy race?

. . . If we had gone to Korea as an invading army of conquerors with the express purpose of humiliating the citizenry we could have done no worse than we have done in the name of the United Nations, the Western world, and the democratic way of life.

I gave some examples from my own experiences:

The memory of an aging Korean who stumbled when unloading a crate from a plane and the little pip-squeak of a GI private who seized him by his faded coat lapels and shouted in his face: "You sonofabitch—if you do that again I'll punch you in the nose!"

The spectacle of a young man, his feet half eaten away, dying of gangrene, but refused medical attention by a number of army medical officers because he was a Korean and didn't count.

The Canadian private who emptied his Bren gun into a Korean grave and the GI who shouted loudly to a crony in a bus in Pusan about how much he hated the gooks. I will not forget the look on the face of the Korean bus driver who overheard him.

Nor could I forget the khaki river of soldiers flowing through the narrow streets, many drunk, not a few arrogant, most with too much money to spend: a shifting montage of jeeps driving lickety-split down lanes built for oxcarts, of voices cursing the men who didn't move out of the way quickly enough, of faces leering and winking at the women, of hands dispensing the largesse of democracy—a piece of gum here, a bit of chocolate there—to the ragged, hungry children begging on the curb.

"You Americans are so stupid," a serious young Korean university graduate told me. "You have made prostitutes of our women and beggars of our children. Surely you are not going to make the mistake of thinking the Koreans love you?"

He was an accredited war correspondent, who wore the United Nations patch and uniform, as I did; but, unlike me, he was not allowed into the officers' mess as the Japanese correspondents were. He was a "gook."

In Korea, we have given very little thought to anything but the military expediency of the moment, whether it encompasses the breaking of dikes in a paddy field, or the tacit support of a government that is about as democratic as Franco's. . . . You can't burn away an idea with gasoline jelly, but can only destroy it with a better idea. But this lesson hasn't been put into practice. Our soldiers are sometimes referred to as "the ambassadors of democracy," but the painful fact is that they lack both training and talent for ambassadorship. They have been taught how to fight and they fight well. They have not been taught how to act and they act badly.

The bitter irony is that similar words might easily have been written (and indeed *were* written) a generation later during the American war in Vietnam—one that didn't benefit from any restraining influence of the United Nations. The Americans learned nothing from the Korean war, as their experience in Indo-China shows, and this time they had no international fig leaf to use as a fragile camouflage. The Americans continue to fight imperialistic wars.

Happily, we have stayed out. If the Korean action had a lasting benefit, it served as a significant if flawed guide to the future. For the next half century, Canada concentrated on peace and international peacekeeping.

The Education of Lester Pearson

On Saturday, October 7, 1950, the Canadian secretary of state for external affairs, an ardent baseball fan, sat in his New York hotel room with Lord Alexander, the governor general, trying to watch the World Series on television. The New York Yankees were sweeping the series from the Philadelphia Phillies, but Mike Pearson's mind was elsewhere. He was still smouldering with embarrassment and anger at what seemed to be a blatant double-cross by the United States at the United Nations General Assembly that morning.

Hostilities in Korea were apparently coming to a close with the North Koreans on the run following MacArthur's landing at Inchon. The Canadians took the cautious view that once the 38th Parallel was crossed and the status quo restored, the United Nations would have discharged its obligations. But the Americans, flushed with the Inchon victory, wanted to continue the pursuit across the Parallel to punish the North Koreans and destroy their army. When Pearson suggested that the United Nations should be very cautious about extending its mandate to include an invasion of North Korea, the Americans demurred, saying, in effect, "This would be to throw away our victory." That attitude, suggesting that modern wars can be won like baseball games, belonged to the past. It had no meaning in the twentieth century, as the Americans themselves would learn in their next colonial struggle in Vietnam. As Pearson recalled, the American attitude to the enemy was, "We have him now at our mercy; we must go beyond the 38th Parallel and destroy him."

Faced with this intransigence, Pearson had then proposed "the inevitable Canadian compromise." If the Americans insisted on the UN troops crossing the border, why not first give the North Koreans three or four days of grace to see whether they were prepared to negotiate an armistice? And if the border *was* crossed, Pearson suggested, it would be reasonable to stop at the northern neck of Korea between the

39th and 40th parallels, a point far enough from the Chinese border to calm Chinese fears that their territory might be threatened.

"The Americans agreed that this was not an unreasonable—indeed that was a wise—course," Pearson remembered, ". . . and proposals to this end would be put forward at a meeting of the Assembly the following morning." To Pearson, all the elements seemed then in place for ceasefire negotiations and maybe an armistice.

To his "amazement and disgust," next day the chief of the American delegation, Senator W.R. Austin, did an about-face. He asked the Assembly for support for an immediate pursuit of the North Koreans beyond the Parallel and for their destruction. He went further and asked for a continuation to the Chinese border to destroy the aggressor. That resolution, adopted by the Assembly, spoiled Pearson's enjoyment of the World Series game and lengthened the war by two years.

This disheartening episode, as Pearson later called it, marked a change in his attitude toward the United States and the United Nations. At the outset, it will be remembered, he had urged a reluctant St. Laurent and an equally reluctant defence minister to send an expeditionary force to Korea, over the reservations of several cabinet colleagues, who asked at the time, "What would Mr. King do?" and supplied the answer, "He wouldn't be getting involved."

Pearson, a firm advocate of collective security, took a broader view. An amiable son of the manse, he had been engagingly starry-eyed at the prospect of the United Nations stepping in to enforce its moral authority over the invading North Koreans. At that time he did not quarrel with his American counterpart, Dean Acheson, who insisted that the North Korean attack had been "mounted, supplied, and instigated by the Soviet Union." That was flummery. The new war was part of the continuing struggle between the United States and the Soviet Union for mastery of the Far East. What was, in reality, a vicious war between two Korean dictatorships was blown up to monstrous proportions in an atmosphere of Cold War politics. But to Mike Pearson, this "act of high courage," as he publicly called the police action, was the first step to some form of world order.

Pearson was haunted by the distasteful memory of the Riddell incident in the mid-1930s, when Canada had repudiated its own man at the League of Nations. He himself, as a young diplomat, had supported Riddell's attempt to impose sanctions against Italy during Mussolini's Ethiopian invasion. Now for the first time, in Pearson's words, "an assembly of the nations had formally condemned and voted against an aggressor and, unlike the League of Nations in 1935 and 1936, had followed through." Privately he had some reservations. To be effective, he knew, everything must be done to emphasize the collective character of the operation; every effort must be made to keep the action of the United States within the framework of the United Nations.

The Korean War gave Pearson the opportunity to advance his personal dream: the establishment by the United Nations of a military force to resist aggression. The proposal to recruit a brigade of volunteers to serve under the United Nations in Korea was his. He wanted other countries also to make a portion of their own forces available for collective defence in the future whenever an emergency arose. That idea was considered impractical at the time, but Pearson never abandoned it in the years that followed.

After the Inchon landing and MacArthur's hot pursuit of the North Koreans past the 38th Parallel, his enthusiasm and his idealism began to flag. What hope was there for an international peacekeeping force when the United States was clearly going its own way in Korea? The alarming prospect that the police action might be inflated into a major Asian war could not be dismissed. In Taiwan (Formosa), the Nationalist Chinese generalissimo, Chiang Kai-shek, was holed up with the remains of his army, eager with American help to plunge into the Korean conflict, especially after a visit from General MacArthur. Pearson tried to make it clear to Parliament that the UN action involved only the defence of South Korea, not of Taiwan.

The time was ripe for a negotiated peace. But the Americans rejected such a proposal made by the Indian representative to the United Nations, just as the Allies had rejected a similar proposal by Lord Lansdowne at the height of the Great War. The wheel of history was turning full circle. Canada, having once sent volunteers to South Africa to shore up the New Imperialism, was preparing to send volunteers to Asia to shore up a newer imperialism.

The Americans were still seduced by the concept of a winnable war. The original plan to return to the status quo after North Korea had been forced to abandon its attempts to annex the South was tossed aside. With the willing agreement of the United Nations, that goal was transformed by American determination to unite the peninsula, impose democracy on the North, and draw the nation into the American sphere of influence.

These objectives, couched in the highly moral tones characteristic of all wars of conquest, melted away when the Chinese entered the conflict as a result of MacArthur's impetuous drive to their border. Clement Attlee, the British prime minister, disturbed by this new escalation, by veiled threats to use the atomic bomb, and by MacArthur's dangerous hubris, made a hurried trip to Washington to explore a negotiated peace, only to find himself stonewalled by Acheson, who declared that "to cut, run, and abandon the whole enterprise was not acceptable."

Pearson's disillusionment was growing. Quiet diplomacy was brushed aside in December when he made it publicly clear that Canada opposed the Americans' insistence that they had sole authority to use the atomic bomb, and further that "we should try to begin negotiations with the Chinese Communists by every means possible." By the United States, this heresy was treated as little more than a pinprick. At the end of January, a vainglorious MacArthur declared that "the stake we fight for now is more than Korea. It is a free Asia." One day later, February 1, 1951, the Americans pushed through a resolution at the General Assembly branding the People's Republic of China an "aggressor" in the war. Pearson voted for the proposal reluctantly, succumbing to American pressure as he later admitted.

By now his original enthusiasm for the United States' "act of high courage" was clearly extinguished. The Americans didn't want to negotiate, nor did the Chinese, who wanted all foreign troops out of Korea and also Taiwan and were demanding a seat at the United Nations.

Pearson had lost all hope for a ceasefire. He walked a difficult path, bowing to American pressure while at the same time trying to maintain an almost religious faith in the United Nations. By the time peace talks finally began in June it was clear that Canada's vaunted quiet diplomacy had not worked. The talks stuttered on for another two years before an armistice was signed. Korea had been laid waste geographically, but politically nothing had changed.

The original UN pledge of "a unified independent and democratic Korea under a representative form of government" had long been forgotten. The United Nations' reputation was badly bruised by its new image as a lackey for the United States. Pearson's eyes were still focused on the international scene; he remained committed to the principles of collective security, world peace and stability, and Western forms of democracy. A chapter in his memoirs was titled "Sovereignty is not enough." He saw the growing control of the United States over the Canadian North, especially the Distant Early Warning Line against Soviet attack (started in 1954), less as a threat to Canadian sovereignty than as a co-operative effort by two North American partners.

Pearson learned from the Korean experience. Any future co-operative effort could not be used as camouflage to support the ambitions of one country, whether it be the United States or the Soviet Union. What was needed was an independent force under the United Nations, free to enforce a ceasefire during an international crisis while a political settlement was being worked out.

Such a crisis arose on July 26, 1956, when the Egyptian prime minister, Gamal Abdel Nasser, nationalized the Suez Canal following the withdrawal of financial support by the United States and Great Britain for his pet project, the construction of the Aswan High Dam on the Nile. Americans thought that the Egyptians, who had irritated them by recognizing Communist China, were getting far too cozy with the Soviet Union.

The Israelis touched off hostilities with a lightning thrust toward Suez on October 29; the French and British followed two days later after Nasser rejected their ultimatum that he withdraw from the canal. Their stated purpose was to stop the fighting and keep the canal open. Their real purpose, Pearson suspected, was to overthrow the difficult dictator, who had resisted all attempts to impose any kind of colonial control over the one-time protectorate. Those days were long gone, a reality that escaped Attlee's rash successor, Anthony Eden, who still thought in terms of gunboat diplomacy, "a hang-over from the great Imperial days," in Pearson's assessment. Pearson saw the English-French attack as an "ill-conceived and ill-judged enterprise . . . an amazing miscalculation of forces and circumstances."

The Suez crisis marked a turning point in Canada's relations with the mother country. Automatic Canadian response to imperial pleas, which Henri Bourassa had scorned half a century before, belonged to another age. When Britain had called for token aid in South Africa, Canada had replied, not with the single battalion asked for, but with two. In the Great War and the Global War, it would have been unthinkable for her to stand aloof. In Korea she had welcomed the concept of a united British Commonwealth division in which all the imperial offspring would battle side by side. But with Suez, the Commonwealth was split, with Australia and New Zealand standing with Britain and the Asian members opposed to the intervention—"a flagrant violation of the UN Charter," in the official Indian government statement.

The breach between Canada and Great Britain was widened when St. Laurent learned, to his fury, that Eden had planned the invasion secretly without informing the Canadian government. "I had never before seen him in such a state of controlled anger," Pearson recalled; it took all his diplomatic skills to calm the prime minister, who wanted to send Eden "a pretty vigorous answer" to his message instead of the "calm and courteous reply" that was finally dispatched. It was necessary, however, to make it clear that Eden could not count on Canada's automatic support. As Pearson put it, no doubt with Arthur Meighen's ill-timed phrase in mind, "This was no situation for 'Ready, Aye, Ready.'"

For Mike Pearson, jockeying between Ottawa and New York, these were stressful days. He flew to Manhattan on November 1, spent the day lobbying the delegates, and the long night (until 4 a.m.) at a marathon session of the General Assembly. The sides were drawn up when the United States sponsored a resolution demanding an immediate ceasefire. If Canada voted for it she would certainly antagonize Britain and France. On the other hand, Pearson considered the ceasefire resolution an ineffective approach because no provision had been made to supervise or enforce a cessation of hostilities. Pearson abstained from the vote and asked for the floor to explain his abstention. It was a tactical move giving him time to express his own point of view, one that he had been turning over in his mind and had already discussed with St. Laurent.

In the hurly-burly that accompanied the debate—the sound of strident voices, the frequent interruptions and consultations, his colleagues lobbying the delegates—he scribbled out his speech at his desk in the Assembly. As one delegate remarked, "few public servants I have known, even seasoned United Nations pros, had the power to work so effectively in that kind of turmoil."

This was Mike Pearson's finest hour. A ceasefire, he told the Assembly, was not enough. "In six months we'll go through all this again if we do not take advantage of this crisis to pluck something out—how was it Hotspur put it: 'out of this nettle, danger, we pluck this flower, safety'—if we do not take advantage of this crisis to do something about a political settlement, we will regret it. The time has now come for the UN not only to bring about a ceasefire, but to move in and police the ceasefire and make arrangements for a political settlement." Pearson went on to say that he would like to see a provision in the resolution authorizing the secretary general to make arrangements for a United Nations emergency force.

The following day a weary Pearson lunched with Dag Hammarskjöld, the UN secretary general, talked with the United Kingdom representative, Sir Pierson Dixon, who seemed "uncertain and dispirited," then flew to Ottawa to meet the cabinet and to gain approval for a resolution to create a United Nations force. He met with the acting British high commissioner, spent some time with his own department, and was back in New York by dinner. It was a rough flight, but Pearson was so preoccupied with what was to face him "that I forgot to be air sick."

Another all-night session followed, with Pearson's leg-men, as he called them, lobbying the senior advisers of the various delegations. Finally, Canada was able to put forward its own draft resolution asking the secretary general to submit, within forty-eight hours, a plan to set up an emergency United Nations force to secure and supervise a cease-fire. The resolution passed, 57 to 0, with 19 abstentions. At that moment, in the early hours of November 4, 1956, history was made and a United Nations Emergency Force was created. As Pearson wrote later: "We did not put it exactly in those terms but that is what we meant." Even Britain and France did not vote against it.

The lobbying had paid dividends. Pearson's personal popularity was a major factor. He had been president of the Assembly in 1952–53, and the fact that he was on a first-name basis with half the foreign ministers helped. The peacekeeping force, the first in history, was formed under a Canadian general, E.L.M. Burns, but without the use of British or French soldiers. Canadians, because they wore British battledress and because the name of the regiment available for peacekeeping (the Queen's Own Rifles) had an unfortunate connection with the imperial past, would not be involved directly.

The UN initiative did not end war. Small, bloody wars would continue. From Africa to the Balkans, men and women would fight and die and civilians would suffer as they always had. But big wars— world wars fought in the air and on sea and land—were far less likely to occur. The terrifying presence of a nuclear deterrent together with the UN peacekeeping initiative would help ensure that.

Canada was now embarked on a new course, markedly different from those wartime years in which she gained her maturity. *Wartime*. That much-used label, which covered everything that was goofy and everything that was heart-rending in those turbulent times, has had little meaning for the new generations who have grown up after the 1950s. For them, the word is a relic of "the olden days," a phrase suggestive of noble paladins and banners unfurled—the kind of romantic vision that doomed so many of their fathers.

Those olden days are long gone. The scars of war have healed. Vimy has been manicured clean of mud, its pockmarked slopes softened by a green mantle of Canadian pines. The drowned island of Walcheren has risen again from the waters of the gloomy Scheldt, its loam more fertile than before, thanks to that very silt in which Canadian soldiers once floundered. Two rusting artillery pieces wrested from the enemy in the gumbo of Flanders still guard the faded monument in Dawson City's Minto Park. Minto? Save for a handful of scholars, few Canadians remember him—our governor general in the Boer War days, when a British peer could conspire secretly with a militia chief to send Canadians off to die for the Empire in a strange and distant land.

Unlike other nations, we have enjoyed a fifth freedom since the peace was signed at Panmunjom: Freedom from war! *Freedom from heartbreak*: no more sombre telegrams, no more casualty lists, no more weeping mothers, no more absent husbands. *Freedom from frenzy*: no more white feathers, no more patriotic twaddle, no more conscription squabbles, no more white lies. *Freedom from regimentation.* No more censorship, no more meatless Tuesdays, no more ration cards, no more marching in step.

For his delicate negotiations at the time of the Suez crisis, Mike Pearson was awarded the Nobel Peace Prize, underlining the truth that in spite of all those fourteen-odd years of bitter conflict—on almost every continent except our own—we are not a belligerent people, nor is Canada a warlike nation. We save our aggressive emotions for ice hockey and rejoice in the new title of peacekeepers, a proud and honourable name that has given us a modicum of the international acclaim we have always craved, with precious little blood wasted in the process. The Peaceable Kingdom? Truly.

AUTHOR'S NOTE

This book has had a long gestation period. My original plan was to write a lively history of the twentieth century designed for the millennium year. That proved to be unworkable. Not only did I lose six months to a major illness but it soon dawned on me that much of the evidence I would need for the later decades was not yet available. A work of this kind depends on the spadework of others—on personal memoirs, autobiographies, scholarly studies and reassessments, political diaries, historical investigations, and other material that may not yet be accessible. Equally important, it requires the sober second thought that comes only when the author can stand back from the wall of history and look at it from afar. Only in recent years, for instance, have we been able to view the Great War from a new perspective.

For these reasons I chose to concentrate on the first half of the century, with which I had more than a nodding acquaintance through my researches for *The Promised Land, Vimy,* and *The Great Depression.* I was well into the new work, which I had tentatively titled *The Uncertain Country*, when I began to realize that these remarkable and unusual fifty-odd years had a unique and unifying theme—war. I scrapped my manuscript and began again, leaning, as every narrative historian must, on the labour of those who had gone before.

The available material is voluminous, thanks to the high-quality output of Canada's scholarly historians and also, more recently, to the narrative abilities of the growing number who write for a broader audience. In the past, the two groups have tended to disparage one another, the professionals claiming that the popular narrators were too journalistic and too intent on being "interesting," the narrators insisting that the professionals were too academic and consequently boring. Neither understood that there have long been two separate audiences for works of history: one that thrives on minuscule detail and expert analysis, the other that simply wants to read a good yarn. In recent years each has learned from the other. The journalists have adopted some of the rigours of academe; the professional historians have begun to use anecdotes and human character to enliven their work. It is now difficult, sometimes, to distinguish one from the other.

I would be hard put to categorize many of the books in my bibliography, which includes the works of novelists and playwrights as well as history professors, war correspondents, social commentators, political philosophers, and journalistic gadflies. I am indebted to them all.

Many of the books listed here are not specifically about war, but about war's effects. Every prime minister from Laurier to St. Laurent has had at least one biographer. Mackenzie King occupies an entire shelf. We must be grateful that his diary, which he allegedly wanted posthumously edited and partially destroyed, has been preserved so that we have him as he was, warts and all. The liveliest biography, however, Bruce Hutchison's *The Incredible Canadian*, appeared before the famous diary was available to researchers, and is still the most readable.

Memoirs abound. Borden's run to two volumes to match a two-volume biography. Pearson has three, if we count the one that was cobbled together after his death. James Gray's prairie histories also qualify as memoirs and can be read for both enjoyment and insight. Of the Massey memoirs, Raymond's is livelier than Vincent's but less useful, perhaps, for the historical researcher. I greatly enjoyed Hugh Keenleyside's look backward, which helped me to illuminate the Age of Faith.

For the lay reader, most regimental histories tend to be pretty dry (with Farley Mowat's the outstanding exception), but soldiers and war buffs like myself will find them useful. I found most of the Great War novels pretty awful, but one or two, such as Harrison's brutal *Generals Die in Bed*, were eye-openers. It has taken the best part of the century for a work such as Timothy Findley's brilliant novel *The Wars* to emerge from the detritus of that ghastly ordeal.

The literature of the four Canadian wars is very large, and I have been forced to pick and choose carefully though not entirely from Canadian sources. Any reader wishing a full history of the Boer War must turn to Thomas Pakenham's definitive study. For Canada's role, however, T.G. Marquis's contemporary account is useful. I have also used the personal stories of Hubly, Hart-McHarg, Morrison, and Maud Graham to provide some of the spice.

The best overall history of the Great War in my view is that of John Keegan, the British military analyst. Three brilliant social analysts— one British, two Canadian—have examined the significance of that war in relation to the times and, indeed, to the century. Paul Fussell's *The Great War and Modern Memory*, Modris Eksteins's *Rites of Spring*, and Jonathan Vance's *Death So Noble* make wonderful reading.

Much of the Canadian emphasis has been on the battle of Vimy Ridge; some readers may find the extensive bibliography in my own history of that victory useful. The second and third battles of Ypres are also well documented from a Canadian point of view. The most compelling and critical study is by the English writer Leon Wolff, but I can also recommend the several works of Daniel Dancocks. Both John Toland (1980) and J.F.B. Livesay (1919) have dealt with the Great War's last year, notably the famous Last Hundred Days in which the Canadians again distinguished themselves.

The several Great War studies by Desmond Morton (one of them in partnership with Jack Granatstein) were very useful, as was John Swettenham's study of the Canadian Corps, *To Seize the Victory*. For sheer pleasure, I would recommend Sandra Gwyn's remarkable *Tapestry of War*, a sequel to *The Private Capital*. I also leaned heavily on Peter Buitenhuis's study of wartime propaganda and fiction and Jeffrey Keshen's analysis of propaganda and censorship in the war period.

John Keegan has also written the best overall study of the Global War. The several works of the official Canadian historian, Charles Stacey, are equally invaluable. That war resulted in a formidable library of volumes, many of them critical. Canadians cannot seem to read enough about Dieppe, a tragic adventure that has brought an outpouring of controversial arguments, as I have indicated in the text.

In addition to the standard works on the Canadian role in the war by such military historians as Granatstein, Bercuson, and Goodspeed, I have selected a number of "I Was There" accounts from literate survivors—Scislowski, Pearce, Harvie, Martin, Kipp—that give a personal dimension to a complicated tale. In addition to Dieppe, every Canadian battle has had its biographer—John A. English on Normandy, R.W. Thompson on the Scheldt, Mark Zuehlke on Ortona, to name three. Denis Whitaker, with the assistance of his wife, Shelagh, produced three histories on the major Northwest Europe campaigns. He was personally involved in them all. I liked Martin Blumenson's *The Battle of the Generals* and must also record my admiration for James Eayrs's two volumes on Canada's defence policies (or the lack of them) in the mid-war years, for Elizabeth Armstrong's examination of the wartime conscription crisis in Quebec, published fifty years after the event, and for Richard Malone's two revealing memoirs of his days as a Canadian on Montgomery's staff.

The best general book on the Korean War comes from the British journalist and historian Max Hastings. He has not been able to give much space to the Canadian effort, but two recent works, David Bercuson's *Blood on the Hills* and Ted Barris's popular narrative *Deadlock in Korea* make up for that deficiency. Bercuson is an academic and Barris a journalist but these labels no longer have significant meaning since each uses the other's techniques, and both must be considered professionals.

Two periodicals proved essential in preparing this book. The *Canadian Historical Review*'s contributors have, in dozens of articles, provided well-documented insights into our wartime past and shone a light into undiscovered corners of our history. *Maclean's* magazine, in its various guises since 1905, has continued to introduce its readers to the Canadian story and enlighten them on that part of the past that lurks just beyond the hill of memory. In the 1950s, when I was a member of the editorial staff, the magazine instituted a series of popular historical articles known as "Flashbacks," each designed to tell a compelling tale and also to give a sense of the period. There must have been more than fifty, and I have made use of several in this book, together with George Drew's investigative reporting for the magazine in the thirties and Blair Fraser's later Ottawa commentary.

None of this would have been possible without the meticulous work of a trio of dedicated women, whom I have dubbed the "three Jans." Jan Tyrwhitt, who has acted as editor on so many of my books, forced me on more than one occasion to re-examine my prose style and fill in glaring gaps in my narrative. Janet Craig, who has been my long-time copy editor, has gone over my text with the finest of combs and rescued me from my own grammatical and illogical imbecilities. Last, but not least, Janet Berton had been my backstop, catching me out when I have proven too obscure, checking the awkwardness of my expression, forcing me to defend each of my assumptions and to adapt some of the military lingo for the lay reader.

I am also indebted to George Dick and his predecessor, Joan Forsey, for digging out the scores of books, periodicals, unpublished manuscripts, and other materials on which this work is based, thus allowing me to work at home, thanks to the photocopier and its electronic cousin, the fax. My gratitude also goes to my agent, Elsa Franklin, for her advice and also her insistence that I persevere with the book after my illness tempted me to scrap it, and to Barbara Sears for her incisive comments, which I took to heart and acted upon. My manuscript in its various forms has again been typed with incredible speed by my secretary, Emily Bradshaw, who has, in addition, helped organize my notes and bibliography. Finally, my thanks to the staff of my publisher, Doubleday, especially John Pearce and Meg Taylor. If there are errors in this long and complicated history, blame me.

INFANTRY UNITS AND RANKS IN THE BRITISH AND COMMONWEALTH FORCES DURING THE GLOBAL WAR

UNITS

Army Group, commanded by a **field marshal**

Army, composed of two or more corps and commanded by a **lieutenant general**

Corps, composed of two or more divisions and commanded by a **lieutenant general** or a **major general**

Division, composed of two or more brigades and commanded by a **major general**

Brigade, composed of three battalions and commanded by a **brigadier** (called brigadier general in the Great War)

Battalion, composed of four companies and commanded by a **lieutenant-colonel**

Company, composed of four platoons and commanded by a **major** or a **captain**

Platoon, composed of three sections (four in the Great War) and commanded by a **lieutenant** or a **second lieutenant**

Section, under command of a **corporal** or a lance corporal

Regiment, commanded by a full colonel, and made up of one or more battalions, though the term is often used synonymously with battalion. The battalions rarely served together in action and were often assigned to different areas of war. Thus each of the three battalions of the Princess Patricia's Canadian Light Infantry served in the Korean War but at different periods.

RANKS

Non-commissioned officers (NCOs):

Regimental sergeant major, assisting the adjutant of a battalion

Company sergeant major, assisting the commander of a company

Sergeant, assisting the commander of a platoon

BIBLIOGRAPHY

Anon. *A Brief History of the Student Christian Movement in Canada, 1921–1974.*
Toronto: SCM Press, 1975.

Abella, Irving, ed. *On Strike: Six Key Labour Struggles in Canada 1919–1949.*
Toronto: Lorimer, 1975.

Acland, Peregrine. *All Else Is Folly.* Toronto: McClelland & Stewart, 1929.

Adachi, Ken. *The Enemy That Never Was: A History of the Japanese Canadians.*
Toronto: McClelland & Stewart, 1976.

Adams, Ian. "For King and Country," *Maclean's*, July, 1968.

Adams, John Coldwell. *Sir Charles God Damn: The Life of Sir Charles G.D.
Roberts.* Toronto: University of Toronto Press, 1986.

Allen, Ralph. *Home Made Banners.* Toronto: Longmans, Green, 1946.

——— *Ordeal by Fire: Canada, 1910–1945.* Toronto: Doubleday Canada, 1961.

Allen, Richard. *The Social Passion: Religion and Social Reform in Canada,
1914–28.* Canadian University Paperbacks, no. 132. Toronto: University of
Toronto Press, 1971.

Alonso, Harriet Hyman. *The Women's Peace Union and the Outlawry of War,
1921–1942.* Knoxville: University of Tennessee Press, 1989.

Anahareo. *Devil in Deerskins: My Life with Grey Owl.* Toronto: New Press, 1972.

Anderson, Frank W. *The Rum Runners.* Frontier Books, no. 11. Calgary, Frontiers
Unlimited, 1966.

Anglin, Gerald. "The Smallwood Saga," *Maclean's*, August 15, 1949.

——— "What Union's Done to Newfoundland," *Maclean's*, August 15, 1950.

Armitage, May L. "The First Woman Magistrate in Canada: A Character Sketch of
Janey Canuck," *Maclean's*, October 1, 1916.

Armstrong, Elizabeth H. *The Crisis of Quebec, 1914–18.* New York: Columbia
University Press, 1937.

Bacchi, Carol Lee. *Liberation Deferred? The Ideas of the English-Canadian Suffragists, 1877–1918.* Toronto: University of Toronto Press, 1983.

Bailey, Thomas A. "Theodore Roosevelt and the Alaska Boundary Settlement,"
Canadian Historical Review, June 1937.

Baird, Irene. *Waste Heritage.* Toronto: Macmillan Canada, 1939.

Baker, W.M. "A Case Study of Anti-Americanism in English-speaking Canada: The
Election Campaign of 1911," *Canadian Historical Review,* December 1970.

Bannerman, James. "The Year We Went Wild for the Prince of Wales," *Maclean's,*
April 26, 1958.

Barris, Ted. *Deadlock in Korea: Canadians at War 1950–1953.* Toronto: Macmillan
Canada, 1999.

Beattie, Margaret. "A Brief History of the Student Christian Movement in
Canada." Ph.D. thesis, 1972.

Belfield, Eversley. *The Boer War.* London: Leo Cooper, 1975.

———— and H. Essame. *The Battle for Normandy.* Philadelphia: Dufour Editions, 1965.

Bell, McElvey. *First Canadians in France.* Toronto: McClelland Goodchild Stewart, 1917.

Bendiner, Robert. *Just Around the Corner: A Highly Selective History of the Thirties.* New York and London: Harper & Row, 1967.

Bercuson, David J. *Maple Leaf Against the Axis: Canada's Second World War.* Toronto: Stoddart, 1995.

———— *Blood on the Hills: The Canadian Army in the Korean War.* Toronto: University of Toronto Press, 1999.

Berger, Carl. *The Sense of Power: Studies in the Ideas of Canadian Imperialism, 1867–1914.* Toronto: University of Toronto Press, 1970.

Berton, Pierre. *The Royal Family.* Toronto: McClelland & Stewart, 1953.

———— *The Mysterious North.* Toronto: McClelland & Stewart, 1956.

———— *The Promised Land.* Toronto: McClelland & Stewart, 1984.

———— *Vimy.* Toronto: McClelland & Stewart, 1986.

———— *The Great Depression, 1929–1939.* Toronto: McClelland & Stewart, 1990.

———— "They're Only Japs," *Maclean's,* February 1, 1948.

———— [Bert Franklin, pseud.] "Ontario at the Bar," *Maclean's,* September 1, 1948.

———— "George Drew," *Maclean's,* March 1, 1949.

———— "Corporal Dunphy's War," *Maclean's,* June 1, 1951.

———— "Seoul's the Saddest City," *Maclean's,* June 1, 1951.

———— "The Long Ordeal of Mrs. Tak," *Maclean's,* June 15, 1951.

———— "This Is the Enemy," *Maclean's,* July 1, 1951.

———— "The Real War in Korea," *Maclean's,* August 1, 1951.

———— "There'll Always Be a Massey," *Maclean's,* October 15, 1951.

Betcherman, Lita-Rose. *The Little Band: The Clashes Between the Communists and the Political and Legal Establishment in Canada, 1928–1932.* Ottawa: Deneau Publishers, 1983.

Biggar, E.B. *The Boer War: Its Causes and Its Interest to Canadians.* Toronto: Samuel Biggar, 1899.

Bird, Michael J. *The Town That Died: The True Story of the Greatest Man-made Explosion before Hiroshima.* Toronto: Ryerson Press, 1967.

Bird, Will R. *And We Go On.* Toronto: Hunter-Rose, 1930.

———— "What Price Vimy?" *Maclean's,* April 1, 1936.

Blake, Raymond B. *Canadians at Last: Canada Integrates Newfoundland as a Province.* Toronto: University of Toronto Press, 1994.

Bland, M. Susan. "'Henrietta the Shoemaker and Rosie the Riveter': Images of Women in Advertising in *Maclean's* Magazine, 1939–50," *Atlantis,* Spring, 1983.

Bliss, Michael. "The Methodist Church and World War I," *Canadian Historical Review,* September 1968.

—— *Right Honourable Men: The Descent of Canadian Politics from Macdonald to Mulroney.* Toronto: HarperCollins, 1994.

Bloch, I.S. *Is War Now Impossible?* London: Department of War Studies, King's College, 1899; reprinted, 1991.

Blumenson, Martin. *The Battle of the Generals: The Untold Story of the Falaise Pocket: The Campaign That Should Have Won World War II.* New York: William Morrow, 1993.

Bobak, E.L. "Seeking 'Direct, Honest Realism': The Canadian Novel of the Twenties," *Canadian Literature,* Summer 1981.

Borden, Robert Laird. *Robert Laird Borden: His Memoirs.* Toronto: Macmillan Canada, 1938, 2 vols.

Bothwell, Robert, and William Kilbourn. *C.D. Howe: A Biography.* Toronto: McClelland & Stewart, 1979.

Bourassa, Henri. *The Duty of Canada at the Present Hour.* Montreal: Le Devoir, 1915.

Bowman, Charles A. *Ottawa Editor: The Memoirs of Charles A. Bowman.* Sidney, B.C.: Gray's Publishing, 1966.

Braithwaite, Max. "The Year of the Killer Flu," *Maclean's,* February 1, 1953.

Bray, R. Matthew. "Fighting as an Ally: The English Patriotic Response to the Great War," *Canadian Historical Review,* 1980.

Brogan, Denis W. *The Era of Franklin D. Roosevelt: A Chronicle of the New Deal and Global War.* New Haven, Conn.: Yale University Press, 1950.

Brown, Col. J.S. *Report of Reconnaissance into the Peninsula of Northern Michigan and Part of Wisconsin Undertaken October 27th to November 8th, 1926.* Ottawa: Directorate of History, National Defence Headquarters, n.d.

Brown, Robert Craig. *Canada's National Policy 1883–1900: A Study in Canadian-American Relations.* Princeton: Princeton University Press, 1964.

—— *Robert Laird Borden: A Biography.* Toronto: Macmillan Canada, vol. 1: 1854–1914, 1975; vol. 2: 1914–1937, 1980.

Brown, Stanley McKeown. *With the Royal Canadians.* Toronto: Publishers' Syndicate, 1900.

Bruce, Hon. Herbert A. *Varied Operations: An Autobiography.* Toronto: Longmans, Green, 1958.

Buitenhuis, Peter. "Writers at War: Propaganda and Fiction in the Great War," *University of Toronto Quarterly,* Summer 1976.

—— *The Great War of Words: British, American, and Canadian Propaganda and Fiction, 1914–1923.* Vancouver: University of British Columbia Press, 1987.

Buller, A.H. Reginald. *Essays on Wheat.* New York: Macmillan, 1919.

Burns, E.L.M. *General Mud: Memoirs of Two World Wars.* Toronto: Clarke, Irwin, 1970.

Bussey, Gertrude, and Margaret Tims. *Women's International League for Peace and Freedom 1915–1965: A Record of Fifty Years' Work.* London: George Allen & Unwin, 1965.

Callaghan, Morley. *That Summer in Paris: Memories of Tangled Friendships with Hemingway, Fitzgerald, and Some Others.* Toronto: Macmillan Canada, 1963.

Campbell, John P. *Dieppe Revisited: A Documentary Investigation.* London: Frank Cass & Company, 1993.

Careless, J.M.S. *Frontier and Metropolis: Regions, Cities, and Identities in Canada before 1914.* Toronto: University of Toronto Press, 1989.

Charlesworth, Hector. *I'm Telling You: Being the Further Candid Chronicles of Hector Charlesworth.* Toronto: Macmillan Canada, 1937.

Cherry, P.C. "Sir William Mackenzie," *Maclean's,* June 1911.

Child, Philip. *God's Sparrows.* London: Thornton Butterworth, 1937.

Christie, N.M., ed. *Letters of Agar Adamson, 1914 to 1919: Lieutenant Colonel, Princess Patricia's Canadian Light Infantry.* Nepean, Ont.: CEF Books, 1997.

Cleverdon, Catherine Lyle. *The Woman Suffrage Movement in Canada.* Toronto: University of Toronto Press, 1974.

Coates, Kenneth, ed. *The Alaska Highway: Papers of the 40th Anniversary Symposium.* Vancouver: University of British Columbia Press, 1985.

——— and W.R. Morrison. *The Alaska Highway in World War II: The U.S. Army of Occupation in Canada's Northwest.* Toronto: University of Toronto Press, 1992.

Connor, Ralph [pseud. of Charles W. Gordon]. *The Sky Pilot in No Man's Land.* New York: George H. Doran, 1919.

Cook, Ramsay. "Dafoe, Laurier and the Formation of Union Government," *Canadian Historical Review,* September 1961.

———; Brown, Craig; and Carl Berger, eds. *Conscription 1917.* Toronto: University of Toronto Press, 1967.

Copp, Terry. *The Anatomy of Poverty: The Condition of the Working Class in Montreal 1897–1929.* Toronto: McClelland & Stewart, 1974.

——— "Ontario 1939: The Decision for War," *Ontario History* 86, no. 3 (September 1994).

——— and Robert Vogel. "'No Lack of Rational Speed': 1st Canadian Army Operations, September 1944," *Journal of Canadian Studies* 16, nos. 3–4 (1981).

Creighton, Donald. *The Forked Road: Canada 1939–1957.* Canadian Centenary Series. Toronto: McClelland & Stewart, 1976.

Croft, Frank. "When Show Business Was All Talk," *Maclean's,* May 21, 1960.

——— "Phrenology Had All the Answers," *Maclean's,* September 24, 1960.

Cronin, Fergus. "The Rumour That Killed a General," *Maclean's,* May 12, 1956.

Crosbie, John C. *No Holds Barred: My Life in Politics.* Toronto: McClelland & Stewart, 1997.

Cunniffe, R. *The Story of a Regiment.* Lord Strathcona's Horse (Royal Canadians) Regimental Society, 1995.

Dafoe, John W. *Canada: An American Nation.* New York: Columbia University Press, 1935.

Dale, Ernest A. *Twenty-One Years A-Building: A Short Account of the Student Christian Movement of Canada, 1920–1941.* Toronto: Student Christian Movement, 1942.

Dancocks, Daniel G. *Sir Arthur Currie: A Biography.* Toronto: Methuen, 1985.

———— *Legacy of Valour: The Canadians at Passchendaele.* Edmonton: Hurtig, 1986.

———— *Spearhead to Victory: Canada and the Great War.* Edmonton: Hurtig, 1987.

———— *Welcome to Flanders Fields: The First Canadian Battle of the Great War: Ypres, 1915.* Toronto: McClelland & Stewart, 1988.

Davidson, Margaret F.R. "A New Approach to the Group of Seven," *Journal of Canadian Studies,* November 1969.

Dawson, Corningsby. *The Glory of the Trenches.* Toronto: Gundy, 1918.

Dawson, R. MacGregor. *The Conscription Crisis of 1944.* Toronto: University of Toronto Press, 1961.

Deacon, William Arthur, and Wilfred Reeves, eds. *Open House.* Ottawa: Graphic Publishers, 1931.

Deane, Philip. *I Was a Captive in Korea.* New York: Norton, 1953.

Dewey, A. Gordon. "Canada's Part in the Britannic Question," *Canadian Historical Review.* December 1927.

Dickson, Lovat. *Wilderness Man: The Strange Story of Grey Owl.* Toronto: Macmillan Canada, 1973.

Dickson, Paul D. "The Hand That Wields the Dagger: Harry Crerar, First Canadian Army Command and National Autonomy," *War & Society*, October 1995 (University of New South Wales).

———— "The Politics of Army Expansion: General H.D.G. Crerar and the Creation of First Canadian Army, 1940–41," *Journal of Military History,* April 1996.

Diefenbaker, John G. *One Canada: Memoirs of the Right Honourable John G. Diefenbaker.* Toronto: Macmillan Canada, 1975.

Diubaldo, Richard J. "The Canol Project in Canadian-American Relations," *Canadian Historical Papers*, 1977.

Doran, George H. *Chronicles of Barrabas 1884–1934.* New York: Rinehart, 1935, 1952.

Drew, George A. *Salesmen of Death: The Truth about the Warmakers.* Toronto: Women's League of Nations Association, 1933.

———— "The Truth about the War," *Maclean's*, July 1, 1928.

———— "The Reply and the Rebuttal," *Maclean's*, November 1, 1928.

———— "Canada's Armament Mystery," *Maclean's*, September 1, 1938.

597

Duncan, Sara Jeannette. *The Imperialist: A Critical Edition*. Ottawa: Tecumseh Press, 1996.

Dunmore, Spencer. *Above and Beyond: The Canadians' War in the Air, 1939–45*. Toronto: McClelland & Stewart, 1996.

Eayrs, James. *In Defence of Canada*. Toronto: University of Toronto Press, vol. 1, *From the Great War to the Great Depression*, 1964; vol. 2, *Appeasement and Rearmament*, 1965.

Eggleston, Wilfrid. *Literary Friends*. Ottawa: Borealis Press, 1980.

Ekirch, Arthur A. *Ideologies and Utopias*. Chicago: Quadrangle Books, 1969.

Eksteins, Modris. *Rites of Spring: The Great War and the Birth of the Modern Age*. Toronto: Lester & Orpen Dennys, 1989.

Ellul, Jacques. *Propaganda: The Formation of Men's Attitudes*. New York: Knopf, 1965.

Endacott, G.B. *Hong Kong Eclipse*. Hong Kong: Oxford University Press, 1978.

English, John A. *The Canadian Army in the Normandy Campaign: A Study of Failure in High Command*. New York: Praeger, 1991.

Evans, W. Sanford. *The Canadian Contingents and Canadian Imperialism: A Story and a Study*. Toronto: Publishers' Syndicate, 1901.

Ferguson, G.V. *John W. Dafoe*. Toronto: Ryerson Press, 1948.

Ferguson, Ted. *Kit Coleman: Queen of Hearts*. Toronto: Doubleday Canada, 1978.

Ferns, Henry, and Bernard Ostry. *The Age of Mackenzie King*. Toronto: Lorimer, 1976.

Fetherstonhaugh, R.C. *The Royal Canadian Regiment, 1883–1933*. Montreal: Gazette Printing, vol. 1, 1936.

Fleming, Rae Bruce. *Railway King of Canada: Sir William Mackenzie, 1849–1923*. Vancouver: University of British Columbia Press, 1991.

Ford, Arthur R. "Some Notes on the Formation of Union Government in 1917," *Canadian Historical Review*, December 1938.

Forster, Donald, and Colin Read. "The Politics of Opportunism: The New Deal Broadcasts," *Canadian Historical Review*, September 1979.

Francis, R. Douglas; Jones, Richard; and Donald B. Smith. *Destinies: Canadian History Since Confederation*. Third edition. Toronto: Harcourt Brace Canada, 1996.

Franklin, Stephen. *The Heroes: A Saga of Canadian Inspiration*. Canadian Illustrated Library. Toronto: McClelland & Stewart, 1967.

Fraser, Blair. "Why Did They Spy?" *Maclean's*, September 1, 1946.

——— "The Taming of No. 3." *Maclean's*, November 1, 1948.

——— "It's a Great Day for Alberta," *Maclean's*, November 15, 1948.

——— "Priests, Pickets and Politics." *Maclean's*, July 1, 1949.

——— "Mackenzie King, As I Knew Him." *Maclean's*, September 1, 1950.

Fraser, Doug. *Postwar Casualty: Canada's Merchant Navy*. Lawrencetown Beach, N.S.: Pottersfield Press, 1997.

Frayne, Trent. "Grey Owl, The Magnificent Fraud," *Maclean's*, August 1, 1951.

Friar, Ralph and Natasha. *The Only Good Indian: The Hollywood Gospel.* New York: Drama Book Specialists, 1972.

Fussell, Paul. *The Great War and Modern Memory.* New York: Oxford University Press, 1975.

Gaffen, Fred. *Ortono: Christmas 1943.* Canadian War Museum, Canadian Battle Series no. 5. Ottawa: Balmuir Book Publishing, 1988.

Gardham, John. *Korea Volunteer: An Oral History from Those Who Were There.* Burnstown, Ont.: General Store Publishing, 1994.

Garrod, Stan. *Sam Steele, Soldier.* Don Mills, Ont.: Fitzhenry & Whiteside, 1979.

Gibson, Frederick W., and Barbara Robertson, eds. *Ottawa at War: The Grant Dexter Memoranda, 1939–1945.* Winnipeg: Manitoba Record Society, 1984.

Gilbert, Martin. *Winston S. Churchill.* Boston: Houghton Mifflin, vol. 7, *Road to Victory 1942–1945,* 1986.

Godwin, George Stanley. *Why Stay We Here?* London: Philip Allan & Company, 1930.

Goodspeed, D.J. *The Road Past Vimy: The Canadian Corps 1914–1918.* Toronto: Macmillan Canada, 1969.

Gordon, Charles W. *Postscript to Adventure: The Autobiography of Ralph Connor.* New York: Farrar and Rinehart, 1938.

Graham, E. Maud. *A Canadian Girl in South Africa.* Toronto: William Briggs, 1905.

Graham, Roger. *Arthur Meighen: A Biography.* Toronto: Clarke, Irwin, vol. 1, *The Door of Opportunity*, 1960; vol. 2, *And Fortune Fled,* 1963.

——, ed. *The King-Byng Affair, 1926: A Question of Responsible Government.* Toronto: Copp Clark, 1967.

Granatstein, J.L. *The Generals: The Canadian Army's Senior Commanders in the Second World War.* Toronto: Stoddart, 1993.

——— and R.D. Cuff, eds. *War and Society in North America.* Toronto: Thomas Nelson, 1971.

——— and J.M. Hitsman. *Broken Promises: A History of Conscription in Canada.* Toronto: Oxford University Press, 1985.

——— and Desmond Morton. *A Nation Forged in Fire: Canadians and the Second World War, 1939–1945.* Toronto: Lester & Orpen Dennys, 1989.

——— and Peter Neary, eds. *The Good Fight: Canadians and World War II.* Toronto: Copp Clark, 1995.

Grant, S. "The Northern Nationalist," *Canadian Historical Association*, Annual General Meeting, 1982.

Graves, Robert. *Goodbye to All That.* London: Cassell, 1929.

Gray, Archie W. *The Towers of Mont St. Eloi.* Rodney, Ont.: Gray Printing, 1933.

Gray, James H. *The Boy from Winnipeg.* Toronto: Macmillan Canada, 1970.

———— *Booze: The Impact of Whisky on the Prairie West.* Toronto: Macmillan Canada, 1972.

———— *The Roar of the Twenties.* Toronto: Macmillan Canada, 1975.

———— *Bacchanalia Revisited: Western Canada's Boozy Skid to Social Disaster.* Saskatoon: Western Producer Prairie Books, 1982.

Griffin, Frederick. *Variety Show: Twenty Years of Watching the News Parade.* Toronto: Macmillan Canada, 1936.

Groulx, Lionel. *The Iron Wedge* [*L'Appel de la Race,* translated by S.J. Wood]. Ottawa: Carleton University Press, 1986.

Grove, Frederick Philip. *In Search of Myself.* Toronto: Macmillan Canada, 1946.

Gwyn, Richard. *Smallwood, the Unlikely Revolutionary.* Toronto: McClelland & Stewart, 1968.

Gwyn, Sandra. *The Private Capital: Ambition and Love in the Age of Macdonald and Laurier.* Toronto: McClelland & Stewart, 1984.

———— *Tapestry of War: A Private View of Canadians in the Great War.* Toronto: HarperCollins, 1992.

Hallett, Mary, and Marilyn Davis, eds. *Firing the Heather: The Life and Times of Nellie McClung.* Saskatoon: Fifth House, 1993.

Hallowell, Gerald A. "Prohibition in Ontario, 1919–1923," *Ontario Historical Society Research Publication*, no. 2, Ottawa, 1972.

Harris, Lawren. "The Group of Seven in Canadian History," *Canadian Historical Review,* June 1948.

———— *The Story of the Group of Seven.* Toronto: Rous & Mann, 1964.

Harrison, Charles Yale. *Generals Die in Bed.* Hamilton, Ont.: Potlatch Publications, 1930.

Hart-Davies, Rupert, ed. *Siegfried Sassoon Diaries, 1915–1918.* London: Faber and Faber, 1983.

Hart-McHarg, W.F.R. *From Quebec to Pretoria, with the Royal Canadian Regiment.* Toronto: William Briggs, 1902.

Harvie, John D. *Missing in Action: An RCAF Navigator's Story.* Montreal: McGill-Queen's University Press, 1995.

Hastings, Max. *The Korean War.* New York: Simon and Schuster, 1987.

Hawkes, Arthur. "Mr. Bourassa's Views on the Participation of Canada in the War." [Pamphlet.] 1916.

Heeney, Arnold. *The Things That Are Caesar's: Memoirs of a Canadian Public Servant.* Toronto: University of Toronto Press, 1972.

Hitsman, J. Mackay. *Military Inspection Services in Canada, 1855–1950.* Ottawa: Department of National Defence Inspection Services, 1962.

Housser, F.B. *A Canadian Art Movement: The Story of the Group of Seven.* Toronto: Macmillan Canada, 1926.

Howard, H.C. "Canada's Costly Mistakes in the Great War," *Saturday Night*, September 10, 1938.

Howe, Douglas. "Gouzenko," *Maclean's*, December 15, 1946.

Hubly, Russell C. *"G" Company, or Everyday Life of the R.C.R.* St. John, N.B.: J & A McMillan, 1901.

Hughes, Sam H.S. "Sir Sam Hughes and the Problem of Imperialism," Canadian Historical Association *Report*, 1950.

Hunter, H.T. "The Truth About the Bren Gun," *Maclean's*, July 1, 1939.

Hutchison, Bruce. *The Incredible Canadian*. Toronto: Longmans, Green, 1952.

Hutton, Eric. "The Day Canada Went to War," *Maclean's*, September 12, 1959.

Hyatt, A.M.J. "Sir Arthur Currie and Conscription: A Soldier's View," *Canadian Historical Review*, September 1969.

———— *General Sir Arthur Currie: A Military Biography*. Toronto: University of Toronto Press in collaboration with the Canadian War Museum, 1987.

Jackson, A.Y. *A Painter's Country: Autobiography of A.Y. Jackson*. Toronto: Clarke, Irwin, 1958.

Jaques, Edna. "End of Steel," *Maclean's*, August 1, 1943.

———— "They Ride with Death," *Maclean's*, September 15, 1943.

Karsh, Yousuf. *In Search of Greatness: Reflections of Yousuf Karsh*. Canadian University Paperbooks. Toronto: University of Toronto Press, 1963.

Kealey, Gregory S., and Peter Warrian. *Essays in Canadian Working Class History*. Toronto: McClelland & Stewart, 1976.

Kealey, Linda, ed. *A Not Unreasonable Claim: Women and Reform in Canada, 1880s–1920s*. Toronto: Women's Press, 1972.

Keegan, John. *The Second World War*. New York: Viking, 1989.

———— *Six Armies in Normandy: From D-Day to the Liberation of Paris*. London: Penguin, 1994.

———— *The First World War*. London: Hutchinson, 1998.

Keenleyside, Hugh L. *The Growth of Canadian Policies in External Affairs*. Durham, N.C.: Duke University Press, 1960.

———— *Memoirs of Hugh Keenleyside*. Toronto: McClelland & Stewart, vol. 1, *Hammer the Golden Day*, 1981.

Kerr, W.B. *Shrieks and Crashes*. Toronto: Hunter-Rose, 1929.

———— "Historical Literature of Canada's Participation in the Great War," *Canadian Historical Review*, December 1933.

Keshen, Jeffrey A. "All the News That's Fit to Print: Ernest J. Chambers and Information Control in Canada, 1914–19," *Canadian Historical Review*, September 1992.

———— *Propaganda and Censorship during Canada's Great War*. Edmonton: University of Alberta Press, 1996.

Kipp, Charles D. "Because We Are Canadians: Memoirs of World War II." Unpublished manuscript.

Kitz, Janet F. *Shattered City: The Halifax Explosion and the Road to Recovery.* Halifax: Nimbus Publishing, 1989.

Klinck, Carl F., ed. *Literary History of Canada: Canadian Literature in English.* Second edition. Toronto: University of Toronto Press, vol. 2, 1976.

Knightley, Phillip. *The First Casualty.* New York: Harcourt Brace Jovanovich, 1975.

Knox, Gilbert. *The Land of Afternoon: A Satire.* Ottawa: Graphic Publishers, 1924.

LaPierre, Laurier L. *Sir Wilfrid Laurier and the Romance of Canada.* Toronto: Stoddart, 1996.

Laporte, Pierre. *The True Face of Duplessis.* Montreal: Harvest House, 1960.

Lawrence, Hal. *Victory at Sea: Tales of His Majesty's Coastal Forces.* Toronto: McClelland & Stewart, 1989.

Leacy, F.H., ed. *Historical Statistics of Canada.* Second edition. Ottawa: Statistics Canada, 1983.

Leed, Eric J. *No Man's Land: Combat and Identity in World War I.* Cambridge: Cambridge University Press, 1979.

Leuchtenburg, William E. *Franklin D. Roosevelt and the New Deal, 1932–1940.* New York: Harper & Row, 1963.

———— *The FDR Years: On Roosevelt and His Legacy.* New York: Columbia University Press, 1995.

Levitt, Joseph, ed. *Henri Bourassa on Imperialism and Bi-culturalism, 1900–1918.* Toronto: Copp Clark, 1970.

Light, Beth, and Joy Parr, eds. *Canadian Women on the Move 1867–1920.* Toronto: New Hogtown Press and the Ontario Institute for Studies in Education, 1983.

———— and Ruth Roach Pierson, eds. *No Easy Road: Women in Canada, 1920s to 1960s.* Toronto: New Hogtown Press, 1990.

Lindsay, Oliver. *The Lasting Honour: The Fall of Hong Kong, 1941.* London: Hamish Hamilton, 1978.

Livesay, J.F.B. *Canada's Hundred Days: With the Canadian Corps from Amiens to Mons, Aug. 8–Nov 11, 1918.* Toronto: Thomas Allen, 1919.

Long Lance, Chief Buffalo Child. *The Autobiography of a Blackfoot Indian Chief.* London: Faber and Faber, 1929.

———— "Before the Redcoats Came," *Maclean's*, February 15, 1923.

Lower, Arthur R.M. *Colony to Nation: A History of Canada.* Toronto: Longmans, Green, 1946.

———— *Canada: Nation and Neighbour.* Toronto: Ryerson Press, 1952.

———— *Canadians in the Making: A Social History of Canada.* Toronto: Longmans, Green, 1958.

———— "Canada at the Turn of the Century, 1900" *Canadian Geographical Journal,* July 1965.

McCaffery, Dan. *Air Aces: The Lives and Times of Canadian Fighter Pilots.* Toronto: Lorimer, 1990.

McClung, Nellie L. *The Next of Kin: Those Who Wait and Wonder.* Toronto: Thomas Allen, 1917.

——— *The Stream Runs Fast: My Own Story.* Toronto: Thomas Allen, 1945.

——— *In Times Like These.* Toronto: University of Toronto Press, 1972.

McDougall, Robert L, ed. *Our Living Tradition.* Fourth series. Toronto: University of Toronto Press, 1962.

——— *A Narrative of War: From the Beaches of Sicily to the Hitler Line with the Seaforth Highlanders of Canada 10 July 1943 – 8 June 1944.* Ottawa: Golden Dog Press, 1996.

MacDonnell, Tom. *Daylight Upon Magic: The Royal Tour of Canada, 1939.* Toronto: Macmillan Canada, 1989.

MacGibbon, Duncan Alexander. *The Canadian Grain Trade.* Toronto: Macmillan Canada, 1932.

MacGillivray, Kenneth. "The Day Halifax Blew Up," *Maclean's,* May 1, 1951.

McIntosh, Dave. *Hell on Earth: Aging Faster, Dying Sooner: Canadian Prisoners of the Japanese during World War II.* Toronto: McGraw-Hill Ryerson, 1997.

McKenty, Neil. *Mitch Hepburn.* Toronto: McClelland & Stewart, 1967.

McKeown, Michael G. *Kapyong Remembered: Anecdotes from Korea.* 25th anniversary paper. Winnipeg, 1976.

MacLeod, Elizabeth S. *For the Flag, or Lays and Incidents of the South African War.* Charlottetown: Archibald Irwin, 1901.

MacMechan, Archibald. "Canada as a Vassal State," *Canadian Historical Review,* December 1920.

MacMurchy, Dr. Helen. *Infant Mortality.* Toronto: Legislative Assembly of Ontario, 1910.

MacTavish, Newton. "Our National Crisis," *Canadian Magazine,* July 1968.

Maher, James, and Rowena Maher. *Too Many to Mourn: One Family's Tragedy in the Halifax Explosion.* Halifax: Nimbus Publishing, 1998.

Malone, Richard S. *Missing from the Record.* Toronto: William Collins Sons, 1946.

——— *A Portrait of War 1939–1943.* Toronto: Collins, 1983.

Mander, Christine. *Emily Murphy, Rebel: First Female Magistrate in the British Empire.* Toronto: Simon & Pierre, 1985.

Marquis, T.G. *Canada's Sons on Kopje and Veldt: A Historical Account of the Canadian Contingents.* Toronto: Canada's Sons Publishing, 1900.

Maroney, Paul. "The Great Adventure: The Context and Ideology of Recruiting in Ontario, 1914–17," *Canadian Historical Review,* March 1936.

Marriott, Anne. *The Wind Our Enemy.* Toronto: Ryerson Press, 1939.

Marsh, D'Arcy. *The Tragedy of Henry Thornton.* Toronto: Macmillan Canada, 1935.

Martel, Gordon. "Generals Die in Bed: Modern Warfare and the Origins of Modern Culture," *Journal of Canadian Studies,* Fall/Winter, 1981.

Martin, Charles Cromwell. *Battle Diary: From D-Day and Normandy to the Zuider Zee and VE.* Toronto: Dundurn Press, 1994.

Massey, Raymond. *When I Was Young.* Toronto: McClelland & Stewart, 1976.

Massey, Vincent. *What's Past Is Prologue: The Memoirs of the Right Honourable Vincent Massey.* Toronto: Macmillan Canada, 1963.

Masters, D.C. *Reciprocity 1846–1911.* Booklet no. 12. Ottawa: Canadian Historical Association, 1961.

────── *The Winnipeg General Strike.* Toronto: University of Toronto Press, 1950.

Melady, John. *Korea: Canada's Forgotten War.* Toronto: Macmillan Canada, 1983.

Mellen, Peter. *The Group of Seven.* Toronto: McClelland & Stewart, 1970.

Mellish, Annie Elizabeth. *Our Boys Under Fire, or New Brunswick and Prince Edward Island Volunteers in South Africa.* Charlottetown: Examiner Office, 1900.

Miller, Carman. *Painting the Map Red: Canada and the South African War, 1899–1902.* Kingston: Canadian War Museum, University of Natal Press, and McGill-Queen's University Press, 1998.

Moir, John S. *Character and Circumstance: Essays in Honour of Donald Grant Creighton.* Toronto: Macmillan Canada, 1970.

Montgomery, L.M. *Rilla of Ingleside.* Toronto: McClelland & Stewart, 1920.

Morris, E.W.B. *With the Guns in South Africa.* Hamilton: Spectator Printing, 1901.

Morton, Desmond. "Sir Wilfrid Laurier and the Use of Canadian Troops for Overseas Service," *Canadian Geographical Journal,* July 1965.

────── *Ministers and Generals: Politics and the Canadian Militia, 1868–1904.* Toronto: University of Toronto Press, 1970.

────── *A Military History of Canada.* Toronto: McClelland & Stewart, 1985.

────── *When Your Number's Up: The Canadian Soldier in the First World War.* Toronto: Random House of Canada, 1993.

────── and J.L. Granatstein. *Marching to Armageddon: Canadians and the Great War 1914–1919.* Toronto: Lester & Orpen Dennys, 1989.

────── and Cheryl Smith. "Fuel for the Home Fires," *The Beaver,* August/September, 1995.

Mowat, Farley. *The Regiment.* Toronto: McClelland & Stewart, 1955.

Munro, John A., ed. *The Alaska Boundary Dispute.* Issues in Canadian History. Toronto: Copp Clark, 1970.

Munro, Ross. *Gauntlet to Overlord: The Story of the Canadian Army.* Toronto: Macmillan Canada, 1945.

Murphy, Emily Ferguson. *Janey Canuck in the West.* Second edition. London: Cassell, 1920; reprinted, Toronto: McClelland & Stewart, 1975.

Murrow, Casey. *Henri Bourassa and French-Canadian Nationalism.* Montreal: Harvest House, 1968.

Nakano, Takeo Ujo. *Within the Barbed Wire Fence: A Japanese Man's Account of Internment in Canada.* Toronto: University of Toronto Press, 1980.

Neary, Peter. *Newfoundland in the North Atlantic World, 1929–1949.* Montreal: McGill-Queen's University Press, 1988.

Neatby, Herbert Blair. "Laurier and a Liberal Quebec: A Study in Political Management." Ph.D. thesis, University of Toronto, 1956.

Nesbitt, Leonard D. *The Story of Wheat.* Calgary: Alberta Wheat Pool, 1953.

Newton, Thomas Woodhouse Legh. *Lord Lansdowne: A Biography.* London: Macmillan, 1929.

Nolan, Brian. *Hero: The Buzz Beurling Story.* Toronto: Lester & Orpen Dennys, 1981.

——— and Jeffrey Brian Street. *Champagne Navy: Canada's Small Boat Raiders of the Second World War.* Toronto: Random House of Canada, 1991.

Norris, Armine. *Mainly for Mother.* Toronto: Ryerson Press, 1920.

Novak, Dagmar. "The Canadian Novel and the Two World Wars: The English-Canadian Literary Sensibility." Ph.D. thesis, University of Toronto, 1985.

Obe, George Roy Stevens. *Princess Patricia's Canadian Light Infantry 1919–1957.* Published for the Historical Committee of the Regiment, Hamilton Gault Barracks, Griesbach, Alberta.

O'Connor, Edward. *The Corvette Years: The Lower Deck Story.* Vancouver: Cordillera Publishing, 1995.

Orchard, David. *The Fight for Canada: Four Centuries of Resistance to American Expansionism.* Toronto: Stoddart, 1993.

Ormsby, Margaret A. *British Columbia: A History.* Vancouver: Macmillan, 1958.

Pacey, Desond. *Creative Writing in Canada.* Toronto: Ryerson Press, 1964.

Page, Robert J.D. "Canada and the Imperial Idea in the Boer War Years," *Journal of Canadian Studies*, February 1970.

——— *The Boer War and Canadian Imperialism.* Booklet no. 44. Ottawa: Canadian Historical Association, 1987.

Pakenham, Thomas. *The Boer War.* London: Weidenfeld and Nicolson, 1979.

Pearce, Donald. *Journal of War: North-West Europe 1944–1945.* Toronto: Macmillan Canada, 1965.

Pearson, Lester B. *Mike: The Memoirs of the Right Honourable Lester B. Pearson.* Toronto: University of Toronto Press, vol. 1, *1897–1948,* 1971; vol. 2, *1948–1957,* 1973.

Peat, Harold R. *Private Peat.* Indianapolis: Bobbs-Merrill, 1917.

——— "You Will Yet Be Glad," *Maclean's*, August 1918.

——— *The Inexcusable Lie.* New York: Barse & Hopkins, 1923.

Pedley, James H. *Only This: A War Retrospect.* Ottawa: Graphic Publishers, 1927.

Peers, Frank Wayne. "The Politics of Canadian Broadcasting, 1920–1939." Ph.D. thesis, University of Toronto, 1966.

Penlington, Norman. *The Alaska Boundary Dispute: A Critical Reappraisal.* Toronto: McGraw-Hill Ryerson, 1972.

Pettigrew, Eileen. *The Silent Enemy: Canada and the Deadly Flu of 1918*. Saskatoon: Western Producer Prairie Books, 1983.

Pickersgill, J.W. *The Mackenzie King Record*. Toronto: University of Toronto Press, vol. 1, *1939–1944*, 1960.

———— *My Years with Louis St. Laurent: A Political Memoir*. Toronto: University of Toronto Press, 1975.

Pierson, Ruth Roach. "The Double Bind of the Double Standard: VD Control and the CWAC in World War II," *Canadian Historical Review*, March 1981.

———— *"They're Still Women After All": The Second World War and Canadian Womanhood*. Toronto: McClelland & Stewart, 1986.

Piva, Michael J. *The Condition of the Working Class in Toronto, 1900–1921*. Ottawa: University of Ottawa Press, 1979.

Porter, McKenzie. "Varley," *Maclean's*, November 7, 1959.

Potrebenko, Helen. *No Streets of Gold: A Social History of Ukrainians in Alberta*. Vancouver: New Star, 1977.

Preston, Richard A. *Canada and "Imperial Defense."* Durham, N.C.: Duke University Press, 1967.

Purcell, Gillis. "Wartime Press Censorship in Canada." April 12, 1946. Unpublished manuscript.

Quinn, Herbert F. *The Union Nationale: A Study in Quebec Nationalism*. Toronto: University of Toronto Press, 1963.

Raddall, Thomas H. *Footsteps on Old Floors: True Tales of Mystery*. New York: Doubleday, 1968.

———— *In My Time: A Memoir*. Toronto: McClelland & Stewart, 1976.

Read, Daphne, ed. *The Great War and Canadian Society: An Oral History*. Toronto: New Hogtown Press, 1978.

Reader's Digest Association (Canada). *The Canadians at War 1939–45*. Westmount, Que.: Reader's Digest, 1969; second edition, 1986.

Regehr, T.D. *The Canadian Northern Railway: Pioneer Road of the Northern Prairies, 1895–1918*. Toronto: Macmillan Canada, 1976.

Reid, Brian A. *Our Little Army in the Field: The Canadians in South Africa, 1899–1902*. St. Catharines, Ont.: Vanwell Publishing, 1996.

Reid, Gordon. *Poor Bloody Murder*. Oakville, Ont.: Mosaic Press, 1980.

Reyburn, Wallace. *Glorious Chapter: The Canadians at Dieppe*. Toronto: Oxford University Press, 1943.

———— "What We Learned at Dieppe," *Maclean's*, October 1, 1942.

Reynolds, L.C. *Dog Boats of War: A History of the Operations of the Royal Navy D Class Fairmile Motor Torpedo Boats and Motor Gunboats 1939–1945*. Somerset, U.K.: Sutton Publishing, in association with the Imperial War Museum, 1998.

Riddell, Walter Alexander. *World Security by Conference*. Toronto: Ryerson Press, 1947.

Roberts, Charles G.D. *Canada in Flanders*. London: Hodder and Stoughton, 1914–18.

Robertson, Heather. *More Than a Rose: Prime Ministers, Wives and Other Women*. Toronto: Seal, 1991.

Robinson, Geoff, and Dorothy Robinson. *It Came by the Boat Load: Essays on Rum-running*. Summerside, P.E.I.: Alfa-Graphics, 1972.

Rose, Clifford. *Four Years with the Demon Rum 1925–1929*. Saint John, N.B.: Acadiensis Press, 1980.

Roy, Gabrielle. *The Tin Flute*. Toronto: McClelland & Stewart, 1959.

Roy, Patricia E.; Granatstein, J.L.; Iino, Masako; and Hiroko Takamura. *Mutual Hostages: Canadians and Japanese during the Second World War*. Toronto: University of Toronto Press, 1990.

Ruffman, Alan, and Colin D. Howell, eds. *Ground Zero: A Reassessment of the 1917 Explosion in Halifax Harbour*. Halifax: Nimbus Publishing in association with the Gorsebrook Research Institute, 1994.

Russell, Peter, ed. *Nationalism in Canada*. Toronto: McGraw-Hill, 1966.

Rutherdale, Robert. "Canada's August Festival Communitas, Liminality, and Social Memory," *Canadian Historical Review,* June 1996.

Rutherford, Paul. *A Victorian Authority: The Daily Press in Late Nineteenth-century Canada*. Toronto: University of Toronto Press, 1982.

Salmond, John A. *The Civilian Conservation Corps, 1933–42: A New Deal Case Study*. Durham, N.C.: Duke University Press, 1967.

Sanford, John. "Queen of the Sob Sisters," *Maclean's*, January 15, 1953.

Sassoon, Siegfried. *Memoirs of an Infantry Officer*. London: Faber and Faber, 1930.

Sawatsky, John. *Men in the Shadows: The RCMP Security Service*. Toronto: Doubleday Canada, 1980.

——— *Gouzenko: The Untold Story*. Toronto: Macmillan Canada, 1984.

Saywell, John T. *"Just Call Me Mitch": The Life of Mitchell F. Hepburn*. Toronto: University of Toronto Press, 1991.

Schull, Joseph. *Laurier: The First Canadian*. Toronto: Macmillan Canada, 1965.

Scislowski, Stanley. *Not All of Us Were Brave*. Toronto: Dundurn Press, 1997.

Scott, Jack [John Forbes]. "Why B.C. Draws the Colour Line," *Maclean's*, February 1, 1948.

——— "The Passionate Princess," *Maclean's*, April 1, 1952.

Shapiro, Lionel S.D. "Dieppe as the Germans Saw It," *Maclean's*, March 1, 1946.

Sharp, Paul F. *The Agrarian Revolt in Western Canada: A Survey Showing American Parallels*. New York: Octagon Books, 1971 [originally published in 1948].

Sher, Julian. *White Hoods: Canada's Ku Klux Klan*. Vancouver: New Star, 1983.

Shipley, Robert. *To Mark Our Place: A History of Canadian War Memorials*. Toronto: NC Press, 1987.

607

Siegfried, André. *The Race Question in Canada*. New York: Appleton, 1907.

Simon, Paul. "Heroine in a Black Hat: Emily Murphy," *Edmonton Journal*, June 7, 1998.

Simonds, Peter. *Maple Leaf Up, Maple Leaf Down: The Story of the Canadians in the Second World War*. New York: Island Press, 1946.

Sitkoff, Harvard, ed. *Fifty Years Later: The New Deal Evaluated*. Philadelphia: Temple University Press, 1985.

Smith, Allan. *Canadian-American Public Policy*. No. 3. Orono, Me.: Canadian-American Center, 1990.

Smith, Denis. *Diplomacy of Fear: Canada and the Cold War, 1941–1948*. Toronto: University of Toronto Press, 1988.

Smith, Donald B. *Long Lance: The True Story of an Impostor*. Toronto: Macmillan Canada, 1982.

———— *From the Land of Shadows: The Making of Grey Owl*. Saskatoon: Western Producer Prairie Books, 1990.

Smith, Goldwin. *Canada and the Canadian Question*. Toronto: University of Toronto Press, 1971 [originally published in 1891].

———— *In the Court of History: An Apology for Canadians Who Were Opposed to the South African War*. Toronto: William Tyrrell, 1902.

Socknat, Thomas P. *Witness Against War: Pacifism in Canada, 1900–1945*. Toronto: University of Toronto Press, 1987.

Spence, Ruth Elizabeth. *Prohibition in Canada*. Toronto: Ontario Branch, Dominion Alliance, 1919.

Spettigue, Douglas O. *Frederick Philip Grove*. Toronto: Copp Clark, 1969.

———— *FPG: The European Years*. Ottawa: Oberon Press, 1973.

Stacey, C.P. *The Military Problems of Canada: A Survey of Defence Policies and Strategic Conditions Past and Present*. Toronto: Ryerson Press, 1940.

———— *The Victory Campaign: The Operations in North-West Europe, 1944–45*. Ottawa: Queen's Printer, vol. 3, *Official History of the Canadian Army in the Second World War*, 1960.

———— *Six Years of War: The Army in Canada, Britain and the Pacific*. Ottawa: Queen's Printer, 1967.

———— *Arms, Men and Governments: The War Policies of Canada 1939–1945*. Ottawa: Queen's Printer, 1970.

———— *A Very Double Life: The Private World of Mackenzie King*. Toronto: Macmillan Canada, 1976.

Stairs, Denis. *The Diplomacy of Constraint: Canada, the Korean War, and the United States*. Toronto: University of Toronto Press, 1974.

Stanley, George F. *Canada's Soldiers: The Military History of an Unmilitary People*. Third edition. Toronto: Macmillan Canada, 1974.

Stead, Robert J.C. *The Cow Puncher*. Toronto: Musson, 1918.

608

Stevens, George R. *Canadian National Railways*. Toronto: Clarke, Irwin, vol. 2, *Towards the Inevitable, 1896–1922,* 1962.

——— *The Royal Canadian Regiment,* vol. 2. London, Ontario, 1967.

Stevenson, J.A. *Before the Bar: Prohibition Pro and Con*. Toronto: J.M. Dent, 1919.

Stewart, Robert. *Sam Steele: Lion of the Frontier*. New York: Doubleday, 1979.

Stirling, John. *The Colonials in South Africa 1899–1902: Their Record, Based on the Despatches*. Edinburgh and London: Blackwood, 1907.

Stone, James R., and Jacques Castonquay. *Korea 1951: Two Canadian Battles.* Canadian War Museum, Canadian Battle Series, no. 6. Ottawa: Canadian Museum of Civilization, 1988.

Stratford, Philip. *André Laurendeau: Witness for Quebec*. Toronto: Macmillan Canada, 1973.

Summers, Harry G., Jr. *Korean War Almanac*. New York: Facts on File, 1990.

Swettenham, John. *To Seize the Victory: The Canadian Corps in World War I.* Toronto: Ryerson Press, 1965.

Taylor, Charles. *Six Journeys: A Canadian Pattern*. Toronto: Anansi, 1977.

Thomas, Clara, and John Lennox. *William Arthur Deacon: A Canadian Literary Life*. Toronto: University of Toronto Press, 1982.

Thompson, Eric. "Canadian Fiction in the Great War," *Canadian Literature,* Winter 1981.

Thompson, John Herd. "The Beginnings of Our Generation: The Great War and Western Canada." Canadian Historical Association *Papers,* 1972.

——— *The Harvests of War: The Prairie West, 1914–1918*. Toronto: McClelland & Stewart, 1978.

——— with Allen Seager. *Canada, 1922–1939: Decades of Discord*. Toronto: McClelland & Stewart, 1985.

Thompson, R.W. *The Eighty-Five Days: The Story of the Battle of the Scheldt*. London: Hutchinson, 1957.

Toland, John. *No Man's Land: 1918, The Last Year of the Great War*. New York: Doubleday, 1980.

Trudeau, Pierre Elliott, ed. *The Asbestos Strike*. Toronto: James Lewis & Samuel, 1974.

Tucker, Gilbert Norman. "The Naval Policy of Sir Robert Borden, 1912–14," *Canadian Historical Review,* March 1947.

Twichell, Heath. *Northwest Epic: The Building of the Alaska Highway*. New York: St. Martin's Press, 1992.

Unwin, Peter. "The Mohawk Princess," *The Beaver*, October/November, 1999.

Vance, Jonathan F. *Death So Noble: Memory, Meaning, and the First World War*. Vancouver: University of British Columbia Press, 1997.

van Paassen, Pierre. *Days of Our Years*. New York: Dial, 1946.

Villa, Brian Loring. *Mountbatten and the Dieppe Raid*. Second edition. Toronto: Oxford University Press, 1994.

Vining, Charles. [R.T.L., pseud.] *Bigwigs, Canadians and Otherwise.* Toronto: Macmillan Canada, 1935.

—— "Mr. Dafor," *Maclean's*, October 1933.

—— "Mr. House," *Maclean's*, June 1934.

Vipond, Mary. "Best Sellers in English Canada, 1899–1918: An Overview," *Journal of Canadian Fiction*, November 24, 1979.

Vokes, Maj. Gen. Chris, with John P. Maclean. *Vokes: My Story.* Ottawa: Gallery Books, 1985.

Wade, Mason. *The French Canadians.* Toronto: Macmillan Canada, 1955.

Warner, Philip. *Field Marshal Earl Haig.* London: Bodley Head, 1991.

Warren, Arnold. *Wait for the Wagon: The Story of the Royal Canadian Army Service Corps.* Toronto: McClelland & Stewart, 1961.

Watson, Brent Bryon. "From Calgary to Kap'yong: The Second Battalion, Princess Patricia's Canadian Light Infantry's Preparation for Battle in Korea, August 1950 to April 1951." Ph.D. thesis, University of British Columbia, 1995.

Weir, E. Austin. *The Struggle for National Broadcasting in Canada.* Toronto: McClelland & Stewart, 1965.

West, Bruce. *Toronto.* Toronto: Doubleday Canada, 1979.

Whitaker, Denis, and Shelagh Whitaker. *Tug of War: The Canadian Victory That Opened Antwerp.* Toronto: Stoddart, 1984.

—— *Dieppe: Tragedy to Triumph.* Toronto: McGraw-Hill Ryerson, 1992.

—— *Victory at Falaise: The Soldiers' Story.* Toronto: HarperCollins, 2000.

Wilkes, Fred. *They Rose from the Dust.* Saskatoon: Modern Press, 1958.

Williams, David Ricardo. *Duff: A Life in the Law.* Vancouver: University of British Columbia Press, 1984.

Williams, Jeffrey. *Princess Patricia's Light Infantry.* London: Leo Cooper, 1972.

Willison, Sir John. *Reminiscences, Political and Personal.* Toronto: McClelland & Stewart, 1919.

Windsor, Edward, Duke of. *A King's Story: The Memoirs of the Duke of Windsor.* New York: Putnam, 1951.

Wodson, Harry M. *Private Warwick: Musings of a Canuck in Khaki.* Toronto: Sovereign Press, 1915.

Wolff, Leon. *In Flanders Fields: The 1917 Campaign.* New York: Viking, 1958.

Wood, Herbert Fairlie. *Strange Battleground: The Operations in Korea and Their Effects on the Defence Policy of Canada.* Ottawa: Queen's Printer, 1962.

Young, Scott. "Pay-off in Oil," *Maclean's*, June 15, 1947.

Ziegler, Philip. *King Edward VIII: The Official Biography.* London: Collins, 1990.

Zinn, Howard, ed. *New Deal Thought.* Indianapolis: Bobbs-Merrill, 1966.

Zuehlke, Mark. *Ortona: Canada's Epic World War II Battle.* Toronto: Stoddart, 1999.

INDEX

Brown, Brig. Gen. James Sutherland "Buster," 249-53, 309

Brown, Stanley McKeown, *quoted*, 36

Bryce, Lord, and investigation of atrocities, 168

Buchan, John, 1st Baron Tweedsmuir, 167, 316-17, 318, 427

Buchenwald, 411, 412-16

Buck, Tim, 297

Buitenhuis, Peter, *quoted*, 167

Buller, Gen. Sir Redvers, 42, 44, 45; *quoted*, 66-67

Bulletin (Edmonton), *quoted*, 92, 108

Bureau, Jacques, 258, 259

Burke, Cornelius, 421, 423, 424, 425, 504-5

Burke, Rosa, 97

Burlington, Vt., 250

Burns, Gen. E.L.M., 428, 465, 584; *quoted*, 203

Burstall, Maj. Gen. Sir Henry, 236, 237

Byng, Lt. Gen. Julian, Viscount Byng of Vimy, 155, 174-75, 176-77, 180, 211, 255; and King-Byng Affair, 261-65; *quoted*, 180

Cabinet War Committee, 362, 376, 381, 384, 396, 400

Caen, France, 457, 488-89

Caillaux, Joseph, 191

Calgary, 100, 238

Callaghan, Morley, 271-72

Cambrai, France, 162, 211

Camirand, Louis Philippe, 521

Campbell, John S., *quoted*, 387

Canada in Flanders, quoted, 168

Canada's Fighting Airmen, 346

Canadian armed forces: in South Africa, 40-44, 45, 49-52, 54-67; in First World War, at Armentières, 141-42, at Ypres, 142-47, at Somme, 152, at Vimy, 177-80, in Last Hundred Days, 208-13; in Second World War, 192, 327-28, 446, 457, 500, 502, at Hong Kong, 336-45, in England, 362-65, move to expand, 366, 447, 500, at Dieppe, 371-73, 379, 382-85, in Sicily, 433, in Italy, 435-46, in Northwest Europe, 453-62, 479-97, reinforcement problems in, 464-65; in Korean War, 529, 533-37, 546-47, 548-50, 553-54, 558-62, 564-65, 568

Canadian Authors Association, 268

Canadian Bookman magazine, 269, 270, 271

Canadian Broadcasting Corp. (CBC), 296, 323, 348

Canadian Clubs, Association of, 221, 282

Canadian Corps: in First World War, 138, 147, 154, 174, 178, 180, 203, 207-8, 209-13, 244; in Second World War, 377

Canadian Forum magazine, 269

Canadian Johns-Manville, 520, 521

Canadian Legion, 331

Canadian literature, 10-11, 265, 268-72, 299-305

Canadian Machine Gun Corps, 173

Canadian magazine, 269; *quoted*, 26

Canadian Military Gazette, 31

Canadian Military Mission, Far East, 541

Canadian Mounted Rifles, 152-53; 2nd Battalion, 56, 64; 4th, 179, 186, 256; 5th, 186

Canadian National Exhibition, 236-37, 324

Canadian National League, 117

Canadian National Railways, 96, 258

616

617

620

Seoul, South Korea, 532, 540, 547, 554, 555

separatism, 192

Service, Robert, 15-16, 126, 163; *quoted*, 162

Sévigny, Albert, *quoted*, 130-31

Shafter, Gen. William Rufus, 12

Shand, David, *quoted*, 146

Shaughnessy, Lord, 194

Shepherd, Bert, 455

Shepherd, Pte. George, *quoted*, 35

Sherbrooke, Que., 219

Shipley, Robert, 126; *quoted*, 129

Sicily, 424, 432, 433, 437

Siegfried, André, 31-32

Siegfried Line, 492

Sifton, Clifford, 88, 91-94, 117, 263; *quoted*, 86

Sifton, Victor, 501

Silent Enemy, The (film), 281

Silliker, Gordon, *quoted*, 152

Silver, Ray, 409-12, 504

Silver Rail, 519

Sime, Jessie G., 271

Simonds, Gen. Guy Granville, 428, 431, 433, 437, 448-51, 452, 460, 470, 485; characterized, 484; *quoted*, 381, 566

Simonds, Peter, *quoted*, 428

Simpson, Wallis, 238, 317

Skagway, Alaska, 84

Skelton, O.D., 313, 316, 392

Smallwood, Joseph Roberts "Joey," 522-25

Smart, James Allan, 263

Smith, A.J.M., *quoted*, 270

Smith, Donald B., 279, 280

Smith, Pte. Ernest "Smoky," 439

Smith, Goldwin, 75-77

Smith-Dorrien, Brig. Gen. Horace, 44, 52, 56, 147

Smythe, Maj. Conn, *quoted*, 463-64

Snider, Chris, *quoted*, 571, 573

snipers, 438

Social Credit theory, 295

Social Departure, 98

Social Gospel, 102

social reforms, 244

Soldier Settlement Board, 353

Somme offensives, 149-54, 167, 177, 179

South Africa, 34, 42-80 *passim*, 176

South Africa Association, 30

South African Constabulary, 67

South African League, 29

South African Light Horse, 176

South African War, 20, 23, 41-80 *passim*, 137; compared with Korean War, 528-29

South Beveland, Netherlands, 486

South Korea, 530; armed forces of (ROK), 532, 539, 543, 545, 558

South Saskatchewan Regiment, 383

Soviet Union, 389, 392, 509, 510. *See also* Russia; USSR

Sowing Seeds in Danny, 11

Spanish-American War, 11-13

Sparks, R.P., 258-59

Special Force for Korea, 533, 535, 549

Spectator (Hamilton), 29, 130

Spettigue, Douglas O., 284-85

Spion Kop, battle of, 28

Spitsbergen, Norway, 376

Stacey, Col Charles P., *quoted*, 365, 428, 429, 459, 480, 482

Stalag Luft III, 411, 416

Stalin, Joseph, 274, 372, 375, 510, 530, 572

Star (Montreal), 29, 30, 77, 164, 302, 354; *quoted*, 31, 87, 119

Star (Toronto), 164, 278, 346, 356; *quoted*, 75, 152

629

Arthur Meighen

Henri Bourassa

Sir Wilfred Laurier

Pauline Johnson